DRIVEN PATRIOT

★ ★ ★

THE LIFE AND TIMES OF JAMES FORRESTAL

BY

Townsend Hoopes

AND

Douglas Brinkley

BLUEJACKET BOOKS

NAVAL INSTITUTE PRESS
Annapolis, Maryland

Naval Institute Press
291 Wood Road
Annapolis, MD 21402

First Bluejacket Books printing, 2000

Library of Congress Cataloging-in-Publication Data
Hoopes, Townsend, 1922–
    Driven patriot : the life and times of James Forrestal / by Townsend Hoopes and Douglas Brinkley.
        p. cm.
    Originally published: New York : Knopf, 1992.
    Includes bibliographical references (p.) and index.
    ISBN 1-55750-334-6 (alk. paper)
    1. Forrestal, James, 1892–1949. 2. Cabinet officers—United States—Biography. 3. United States—History, Naval—20th century. 4. United States—Military policy. I. Brinkley, Douglas.
E748.F68 H66 2000
973.917′092—dc21
[B]   00-40188

Printed in the United States of America on acid-free paper ∞
07 06 05 04 03 02 01 00   8 7 6 5 4 3 2 1

DRIVEN PATRIOT

TO

MICHAEL V. FORRESTAL
H. STRUVE HENSEL
JOHN H. OHLY
CHARLES J. V. MURPHY

who were eager to see the publication of this book,
who made valuable contributions to its development,
but who died before it was completed

CONTENTS

LIST OF ILLUSTRATIONS

ACKNOWLEDGMENTS

WE ARE GRATEFUL to a number of people and institutions for their individual and collective assistance during the preparation of this manuscript, between the summer of 1988 and the spring of 1991; especially to Michael Forrestal for granting us special access and reproduction rights to his father's papers in the Seeley G. Mudd Library at Princeton University, and for giving generously of his own time for long interviews about family life. The staff at the Seeley G. Mudd Library extended every courtesy and consideration. The directors of the Franklin D. Roosevelt, Harry S. Truman, and Lyndon B. Johnson libraries, and their archival staffs, were generous guides to relevant papers in their collections relating not only to James Forrestal but also to other leading government figures of the era. The Office of the Defense Historian (in the Office of the Secretary of Defense) and the U.S. Naval Institute led us to oral histories by major defense officials and senior military commanders of the World War II and early Cold War periods. Senior staff members of the military and diplomatic branches of The National Archives were important sources for documents of both periods.

The journalist and author Charles J. V. Murphy conducted research for a biography of James Forrestal for several years, but died in 1987, before he could begin the actual writing. Through the courtesy of his daughter and research collaborator, Edythe M. Holbrook, we obtained all of their working papers, including interviews with Michael Forrestal and a number of Forrestal's friends and associates who were no longer alive when we started our project in 1988. Several of these interviews were conducted by Mrs. Holbrook. H. Struve Hensel, a moving force in the original effort to persuade Mr. Murphy to undertake a book on Forrestal, was equally a source of encouragement for our efforts. His personal counsel, supplemented by his private papers, provided authoritative assistance to our development of the chapters on naval procurement.

John H. Ohly provided detailed expertise with respect to the organization and operation of the Office of the Secretary of Defense (OSD) during Forrestal's tenure, and the Ohly private papers, to which we had access, proved to be rich in historical detail. Steven L. Rearden, whose book on the formative years of OSD was a basic reference in our work, led us to important additional materials and contributed valuable insights. Marx Leva provided useful personal papers and offered valuable suggestions to improve the manuscript, as did Najeeb Halaby and Professor Robert W. Love of the United States Naval Academy. Peter Walker, who had contemplated writing his own book on Forrestal, generously turned over to us his several interesting interview notes. Alfred Goldberg, the Defense Historian, and his associate, Ronald D. Landa, read the entire manuscript with scholarly discernment, and saved us from a number of embarrassing factual errors. Professor Robert Sobel of Hofstra University, an authority on business history and the author (among other books) of *The Life and Times of Dillon Read* (1991) provided expert advice and counsel on our Wall Street chapters.

We are grateful to the Paul H. Nitze School for Advanced International Studies of The Johns Hopkins University, which administered for our benefit a fund for research and travel expenses established by several friends of Forrestal, originally to support Mr. Murphy's endeavor.

Through the generosity of the Rockefeller Foundation, Townsend Hoopes spent a month as a Scholar-in-Residence at the Villa Serbelloni in Bellagio, Italy.

A small grant-in-aid from the Harry S. Truman Library Institute helped finance last minute research.

Martha Runner (in Westport, Connecticut) typed endless chapter drafts over a period of nearly three years, with fidelity and zeal; Deborah Waring (in Bethesda, Maryland) provided expert supplemental secretarial support.

Our editor, Ashbel Green, was a source of valued professional counsel, as was his assistant, Jenny McPhee. We are also indebted to our copy editor, Jeffrey Smith, and our production editor, Melvin Rosenthal, for technically perfecting the manuscript.

We note with sadness that, in addition to Charles J. V. Murphy, three other men who made valuable contributions to our work, and who looked forward with keen anticipation to the publication of this book, died during the course of its development—namely, Michael Forrestal, John H. Ohly, and H. Struve Hensel. We dedicate this book to these four men.

T.H. D.B.

PREFACE

I MET James Forrestal for the first time in Washington, in early 1947, during the fight for military "unification." He was Secretary of the Navy and I was the young assistant to Walter Gresham ("Ham") Andrews, a senior Republican congressman from Buffalo, New York, who was Chairman of the House Armed Services Committee and had been a near-contemporary of Forrestal's at Princeton. The two men were friends and professional colleagues. On a broad range of postwar military issues, Andrews was eager for the support of the new crop of congressmen—among them John F. Kennedy and Lyndon B. Johnson—most of whom had only recently shed their World War II uniforms. One very effective way to cultivate these comers was to invite them to small buffet suppers in the ornate committee room, with its elegant crystal chandeliers and polished mahogany dais, there to rub elbows with the leading military figures of the day and listen to their informal after-dinner remarks. Along with Secretary Forrestal came many of the great men of World War II, including General Dwight Eisenhower, Admiral Chester Nimitz, General Omar Bradley, Secretary of War Robert Patterson, and Assistant Secretary of War John J. McCloy. They were larger than life, authentic war heroes, architects of the momentous democratic victory over tyranny in every quarter of the globe. They were heard with respect and not a little awe.

On these occasions, and even more in his frequent testimony before the Armed Services Committee, on subjects ranging from the navy budget to the grave disorder in devastated Europe, Forrestal was as impressive a figure as I have ever met. Projecting a charged but perfectly contained intensity, superbly well informed and articulate, physically fit and custom-tailored, he made his points with a forcefulness and candor that were always tempered by an innate grace. I, a recent Marine lieutenant who aspired to meaningful public service, found in him the model hero. A year later he invited me to join his staff in the newly formed Office of the Secretary of Defense, where I served as a young-man-of-all-work through his resignation in early 1949 and for several years thereafter. I experienced his suicide as a towering loss to the country and a profound personal tragedy.

Over a long span of following years, I was increasingly surprised and disappointed at the continued absence of a Forrestal biography, and I gradually reached the conclusion that potential candidates for the task found it difficult to come to grips with the subject owing to the manner in which Forrestal had ended his life. Then, in 1963, Arnold Rogow's book *Forrestal: A Study of Personality, Politics and Policy* appeared. This was, on its own terms, a competent and not unfair assessment, but it suffered from the fact that Rogow had never met his subject and had never experienced the Washington milieu at firsthand. Moreover, he approached the matter as a psychobiographer who was primarily interested in Forrestal as a case history of neurosis at the highest levels of government. The result was a rather clinical, narrowly focused account, emphasizing the ultimate breakdown of a life which in its entirety had been rich in ebullience, variety, and accomplishment. It seemed to me and others that a major gap in the biographical history of World War II and the postwar period remained to be filled.

I thought intermittently of undertaking the task, but the feasibility of a new scholarly effort seemed to recede as time passed and more and more of Forrestal's contemporaries departed the scene. Then, in 1987, I was offered the research papers of the journalist-author Charles J. V. Murphy, who had begun work on a Forrestal book several years before, but had recently died, at age eighty-three, without having started the actual writing. He had, however, interviewed a number of figures in the Forrestal story who were no longer alive, and the existence of these candid interviews greatly enhanced the prospects for producing a biography that would possess a personal dimension beyond the public record. I decided the project was feasible.

A major factor in this decision was the availability of Douglas Brinkley, a young visiting research fellow at Princeton's Woodrow Wilson School, who had taken on the extra task of helping Murphy six months before Murphy's death. Brinkley was fascinated by what he had learned about Forrestal, and was eager to participate in a new biographical effort. We talked about how we might work together, and I came to the conclusion that his natural gift for historical research, his intelligence, and his energy would be invaluable to the project. As we discussed how the book might be organized and developed, the decision that he should become coauthor, as well as research assistant, was a natural evolution.

In the course of the past four years, we have both learned a great deal more about James Forrestal than I knew during the long-ago days of my privileged apprenticeship at the Pentagon. We hope this book will help to fill the considerable gap in the record regarding Forrestal's life and career. We hope as well that it will serve to deepen the general understanding of American life and American policy-making during the crucible years before, during, and just after World War II.

TOWNSEND HOOPES
Bethesda, Maryland
October 1991

I

★ ★ ★

MAKING READY

★ ★ ★

CHAPTER 1

Forebears, Parents,
and Siblings

JOURNEYING sixty miles north of New York City along the eastern shore of the Hudson River, one enters Dutchess County, for the most part a parkland of well-kept stone fences and spacious country residences, including the hereditary estate of Franklin Delano Roosevelt at Hyde Park. But there is also a more plebeian southern tip, and it was there that James Vincent Forrestal, who was to be FDR's Under Secretary and then Secretary of the Navy during World War II, and subsequently America's first Secretary of Defense, was born on February 15, 1892.

It was the same year that Grover Cleveland reclaimed the White House from the Republican incumbent, Benjamin Harrison, aided by the presence of a third candidate, James B. Weaver, who was running on the People's Party ticket. The main issue was "sound money" and Cleveland, running as a "Union Democrat," was able to make decisive inroads into the ranks of normally Republican middle-class businessmen who endorsed his promise to retain the gold standard. Both Harrison and Weaver favored the adoption of free silver.

A generation after the Civil War, Americans were rapidly evolving out of subsistence farming and rail-splitting into manufacturing, commerce, and international trade. It was the age of dynamic, unfettered free enterprise, which brought forth transcontinental railroad empires, nationwide monopolies in steel and other manufactured goods, and the consolidation of vast financial power in Wall Street.

Forrestal's birthplace, Matteawan, New York, nestled between the Fishkill Mountains and the Hudson River, was a typical plank-sidewalk river town, evolving as the nation evolved, moving as the nation moved toward its rendezvous with the twentieth century. Matteawan and the adjoining village of Fishkill Landing formed the Township of Fishkill. The two com-

munities were of comparable size* and virtually indistinguishable even to
the observant eye, yet they remained politically separate.¹ Sporadic efforts
were made to merge, but negotiations always broke down over the question
of what to call the new entity. Finally, on July 1, 1913—when Forrestal
was twenty-one years old and away at Princeton—the issue was resolved.
Both communities being located at the foot of Mount Beacon, a county
landmark, the combined town would be called Beacon.

By the end of the nineteenth century Fishkill Township had become an
important railroad center in the Hudson River Valley. From there freight
cars were shipped by steam ferry across the Hudson to Newburgh, where
they were transferred to the rails of the Lake Erie and the Western railroads, then moved farther westward into the expanding American continent. One line, the Hudson River Railroad (later the New York Central),
carried passengers south along the river from Fishkill Landing to Grand
Central Depot in Manhattan and north to Albany. A passenger steam ferry
crossed the river to Newburgh and provided service to various points on
both sides of the river.²

The commercial and civic heart of the township was Main Street, running eastward from the ferry landing through the village of Matteawan to
the foot of Mount Beacon. The ferry building was a small white saltbox
over whose door hung a large billboard on which weather forecasts, ferry
delays, and local news items were posted, alongside an advertisement
("Fishkill Landing: Oysters in Every Style") for the company restaurant,
run by Willie Hawkins, a black man from Newburgh.³ Power for the town's
economy was furnished by the swift-flowing Fishkill Creek, which generated plenteous energy for the small mills that turned out hats (wool, straw,
silk), carpets, and woodworking machinery. In the 1890s, Matteawan
ranked just below Danbury, Connecticut, in the manufacture of hats, and
there were eight millinery shops on Main Street run by the wives of the
town's most esteemed and fashionable citizens. The creek also powered a
large factory owned by the New York Rubber Company, which emitted
strong, unpleasant odors throughout the town whenever a stiff wind blew
from the north (and to which Forrestal awarded a navy "E" in 1943 for
the "excellence" of its contribution to the war effort). There was a plant
for making bricks and one that turned out air brakes for railway cars, and
a laboratory run by Benjamin Hammond, who had come from Mount Kisco
to develop insecticides. Along the wharf beside the Hudson River sat heaps
of coal and stacks of lumber, brought in by ships to sustain the town's
growing commerce and construction.⁴

Almost every European nationality was represented in the township, but
Italians were by far the most conspicuous, comprising a sixth of the pop-

*According to the 1890 census, Matteawan's population was 5,961; Fishkill Landing's, 4,296.

ulation, followed numerically by Irish, Germans, Dutch, and Scandinavians. In northern Dutchess County, where the English and Dutch gentry were firmly established, Old World customs and aristocratic airs continued to prevail, but in Fishkill Landing and Matteawan the large infusion of Italians and Irish in the second half of the century had overwhelmed the original Dutch and Huguenot influence, accelerated the melting-pot process, and created a population of predominantly middle-class strivers determined to shed their bleak European heritage and become Americanized.[5] "Beacon and Dutchess County are as good an example as there is of what constitutes American life," Forrestal told workers at the New York Rubber Company plant when he returned in 1943. He was speaking as a high government official in the middle of a global war, when patriotism and ethnic unity were deemed essential ingredients of the war effort, but the words also reflected his own Irish-Catholic heritage and his boyhood experience, with its emphasis on hard work and self-reliance. "This city and county are representative of the amalgam of peoples which has given this nation extraordinary growth and world power within a century . . . I am proud of the fact that in this town the sons and daughters of these immigrants went to school together, played games together with children of other origins without thought of bigotry, bias or prejudice. There were and probably still are the jealousies and animosities which are part of the normal complexity of human relationships. But broadly speaking, the individual in this community, whether a descendant of the Dutch patroons, of the English colonials or the recently arrived immigrants, stood on his own feet and was judged as an individual on his own merits and character."[6]

If Forrestal was here reflecting on his own experience, he must have had even more in mind his father, an immigrant Irish Catholic in an America dominated by Protestants who feared that this new infusion would depress wages and create a voting bloc controlled by Rome. In 1947 he wrote to Ernest Havemann of *Life:* "My father raised a family of three on an income which ranged from $600 a year to $2,500. There were no luxuries. A 25-cent ticket to the circus once a year was difficult to come by, but he planted the fundamental ideas of work, of independence, and the idea that the privileges of citizenship carried definite responsibilities, and, above all, that whatever you got for nothing should be regarded with deep suspicion, because somewhere along the line one lost either independence, self-respect or honor."[7]

Forrestal's father, also James, was born in County Cork in 1848, in the midst of Ireland's worst potato famine. At age nine he boarded one of the first steamboats (which sank on the return trip) and headed for America to join his mother, Anastasia, then in the domestic service of an affluent Irish-American family in Matteawan. His father had died in Ireland, and his mother had taken a second husband—a man named Patrick Kennedy, also

Major James Forrestal

Mary Ann Toohey Forrestal

employed by the same family. There was no one to meet James when he arrived in America, so the boy made his way alone across Manhattan to Grand Central Depot and there boarded a northbound train for Fishkill Landing. He had left behind in Ireland his only sibling, a sister, Mary Forrestal. A few years later she too made the bold voyage to America, where, after a brief stay with her mother and brother in Matteawan, she joined the Order of the Holy Cross, taking the name Sister Mary Leonard. In 1879, with a group of pioneering nuns, she moved west to found the first Catholic convent in the Mormon outpost of Salt Lake City, and remained there until her death at the age of eighty-six.[8]

The young immigrant from Cork was educated in the Fishkill and Matteawan schools, then chose the trade of carpentry, at first working throughout Dutchess County as an itinerant apprentice, learning his craft, making friends, and saving money. By 1875, when he was twenty-seven, he had acquired enough skill and savings to start his own firm, the James Forrestal Construction Company, which built homes, but also manufactured sashes, doors, blinds, moldings, window frames, and flooring.[9] The business grew, and three years later he married Mary Ann Toohey, a young high school teacher, born and raised in Matteawan, the daughter of Mathias Toohey, who had come from Ireland in 1840.[10] The Tooheys were also in the construction business and owned respectable tracts of land in southern Dutchess County. More devout than the Forrestals, they built the first Catholic church in the area, St. Joachim's, on land they owned; they occupied the pew nearest the altar and boarded the priest, Father Terrence F. Kelly, for several years until separate quarters could be provided for him.[11] Both of Mary Toohey's parents had died when she was five, leaving her to be brought up by relatives. A bright, disciplined, strong-minded girl, she grew into a handsome, though not a beautiful, woman and a Catholic who practiced her religion with formidable rigor. Physically large, with dark, heavy features and high cheekbones, she was typical of the hardy Irish peasantry.[12]

In 1880, two years after his marriage, James Forrestal was appointed a major in the 21st Regiment of the New York National Guard and was thereafter known as ''the Major'' to friends and colleagues everywhere. A genial extrovert, amiable drinking companion at all six Main Street saloons, regular participant at Bob Van Tine's stationery store, which served as the local forum for debates on town, county, and national affairs, he deferred in domestic matters almost totally to his domineering wife. A believer in the character-building virtues of competitive sports, he seems to have been an idolatrous fan of John L. Sullivan, the Irish-American bare-knuckle heavyweight champion, and to have memorized every punch he threw until James J. Corbett knocked him out after twenty-one historic rounds in 1892. Along with thousands of other Irish-Americans, the Ma-

The Forrestal house in Matteawan, ca. 1897

jor's love for the pugilist was unconditional despite Sullivan's well-publicized and -documented private life as a drunkard, adulterer, wife-beater, and bully.[13]

He also took great pleasure in military parades and patriotic celebrations and fervently supported America's entry into both the Spanish-American War and World War I, although he fought in neither and was in any event too old for active service in the latter. At the same time, as Ernest Havemann wrote in *Life* in 1948, "like so many of his transplanted countrymen, he kept a fierce patriotism for his homeland [Ireland]."[14] This paternal trait troubled the future Secretary of Defense during his boyhood days, for he felt strongly that American patriotism should not be diluted. More broadly, the young Forrestal seems to have been somewhat embarrassed by the whole ambience of his lower-middle-class Catholic Irishness, with its unbreakable links to the old country and its rigid subservience to the Church. He evinced a natural affinity for the wealthier, more socially accepted Protestant families of Matteawan, and this spurred a determined ambition to escape the manifest limits of his heritage, to get beyond the town and out into the greater world. Yet he was never able to erase completely the indelible imprint of his origins, and during his last months in

public office he seemed to be groping desperately for a reconnection
with his roots. On March 17, 1949,
Secretary of Defense Forrestal made
a speech to the Friendly Sons of St.
Patrick in New York in which he ex-
tolled the Irish virtues and, by implication, his own association with
them. "The fighting spirit of America would hardly be half the fine
thing it is, if it were not for the
Irish," he told his fellow descen-
dants from the Emerald Isle. For
the Irish were "not merely fighters"
but "fighters for just causes . . .
for political freedom, for liberty of
conscience, for equality of opportunity."[15]

Henry, James, and William, ca. 1895

In 1881, three years after marrying, the Major built a rambling
Victorian house at 62 Fishkill Avenue in Matteawan, a house that still
stands, relatively unchanged. He also
purchased enough adjacent land for an office and a carpentry shop and
continued to buy property in and around the township. By the early 1900s
his firm had built fifty-eight homes and a reputation as perhaps the most
fastidious residential construction company in southern Dutchess County.[16]

IN 1883, the first of three sons, William, was born. Six years later, after
two miscarriages, Mary gave birth to Henry, and three years after that, in
1892, to James Vincent Forrestal. Family and friends immediately dubbed
the youngest boy "Vince" to distinguish him from his father, and he was
known by that name right through his college years and World War I—until
he began his career in Wall Street. Assuming full charge of her sons'
upbringing, Mary Toohey Forrestal soon decided that William should have
a career in music; Henry could go into business (which did not interest
her); James, the cleverest of the three and the object of her greatest expec-
tations, must enter the priesthood.

The first-born, called "Will," was a frail, introspective boy who rejected his father's example of extroverted manliness and yielded easily to
his mother's plan for his life. By his teens, he had become a reasonably
accomplished pianist and a devotee of Mozart and Brahms. After gradu-

ating from the local high school, he took some business courses in New Rochelle, then briefly joined the family firm, but found that it demanded a more aggressive personality than he possessed. Unhappy in the world of commerce and emotionally dependent on his mother, he returned to his music and spent the rest of his life giving piano recitals around the county to small but appreciative audiences, living with his mother in Matteawan, developing no close friends, and never marrying. He died of a heart attack in 1939 at the age of fifty-six.[17]

Henry, the "handsome one" of the Forrestal boys, was in every sense his father's son: warm and outgoing, gregarious to a degree some thought bumptious, and a natural politico. He made numerous lifelong friends and was eagerly sought after as a speaker at Beacon civic and social gatherings. After graduating from high school, he turned down a scholarship from Syracuse University to enter the family business, which he ran with modest success after his father's death, until he himself retired in 1940. His daughter remembered him as a compassionate, even-tempered man of quite conservative political views who was fond of quoting a German proverb which translates as "Let your head save your heels."[18]

Mary, whose teaching experience had left her with a low opinion of the local schools, insisted on instructing her sons at home during their formative years, enriching the three R's with a dash of Latin and placing considerable emphasis on literature and classical music. Under her tutelage, all three became voracious readers and, although Will was the only musician, all developed a genuine enthusiasm for classical music, especially opera. Daily life in the household consisted mainly of rules and routine: chores and classes in the morning and more classes after lunch; then a tea break in the late afternoon, followed by long hours of study straight through to bedtime. Mary Toohey Forrestal was a stern, rather dour matriarch and an unreluctant disciplinarian, ever ready to take a hickory switch to young male rumps for mental or moral lapses. Regular attendance at Mass was mandatory, a bedtime curfew was rigidly enforced, and swearing and the telling of jokes were forbidden. Herself a slave to routine, Mary's sole indulgence was an occasional afternoon outing with a friend or one of her boys in a horse-drawn carriage—or, as technology advanced, in the company's Model T Ford.[19]

She gave strict orders for quiet in the house during study hours, a rule she rigorously enforced and which all male Forrestals, including the Major, dutifully obeyed. According to Ernest Havemann, the Forrestal boys were raised in "an atmosphere where getting things done was not only socially desirable," but was also understood as the key to their future.[20] "I know from my own experience," Forrestal wrote in 1947, "inasmuch as she handled most of my instruction up to about the age of ten—that she was an uncompromising disciplinarian."[21]

* * *

WITH AN INBORN affinity for the give-and-take of politics, the Major was throughout his life an activist in the Democratic Party in New York State. Grover Cleveland appointed him postmaster of Matteawan in 1894 (a patronage position he held for four years), and he was a delegate to two Democratic national conventions. James Farley, who began his career as a party organizer and later managed Franklin D. Roosevelt's major campaigns and served in the Cabinet as Postmaster General, remembered Major Forrestal as "one of the most striving people" in New York State politics and well known to the pros in Albany.[22]

In October 1910, the Major and Morgan H. Hoyt, publisher and co-owner of the *Matteawan Journal,* an important Democratic newspaper in Dutchess County, were en route to Poughkeepsie as delegates to the Democratic State Convention. As they rode on in a buggy behind the Major's little bay mare, their talk turned to the choice of a Democratic candidate for the state senate. Hoyt had heard about a "young chap from up Hyde Park way named Roosevelt," and they agreed such a name "would be popular," inasmuch as the Oyster Bay Roosevelt—Theodore—was then at the peak of his fame.[23] Franklin D. Roosevelt, who received his party's nomination at the Poughkeepsie convention, made a decidedly favorable impression on both Hoyt and Major Forrestal. "Of perfect physique," Hoyt later wrote, "with ruddy cheeks and that invariable smile which was to be such a big asset to him later in life; with that look of determination and assurance which won for him so many bitter political battles, he promised he would put all the energy he possessed into a winning fight."[24]

After gaining the nomination for state senate, Roosevelt made the first "official" campaign speech of his career in Fishkill Landing, where he was introduced to the small gathering by Hoyt. Later they became lifelong friends, and whenever Roosevelt was a candidate for whatever office he came to Beacon the day before election, always speaking on the same spot where he had made that first campaign speech and always insisting that Morgan Hoyt introduce him. The day before the 1944 election, when he sought an unprecedented fourth term in the White House so he could consolidate the great victory of arms then discernibly in the making, the President of the United States joked that "Morgan Hoyt has been introducing me for 100 years."[25]

To the surprise of many in 1910, the young Democratic candidate for the state senate beat his favored Republican opponent, an old pro named John F. Schlosser, who headed the State Volunteer Fireman's Association. Morgan Hoyt and Major Forrestal worked hard for his election; Roosevelt stayed in the Forrestal house when he was campaigning in the township and gave the Major an inscribed photograph as a token of his appreciation. Two years later, when Roosevelt ran for reelection, Major Forrestal campaigned even harder for him.[26] Neither man could foresee that the senator-elect would one day become President of the United States and would appoint the Major's youngest son to his Cabinet.[27]

Growing Up Irish

BY ALL ACCOUNTS, James Vincent Forrestal was one of the smartest kids in town—perhaps the smartest—and by most accounts, he knew it. It was not merely that he was quick and accomplished in his studies; it was also that he was unusually discerning from an early age, mature beyond his years, keenly aware of subtle social and economic distinctions and possibilities. One part of him was merely serious and practical—Morgan Hoyt, for whom he worked at the *Matteawan Journal* during and immediately following his graduation from high school, thought him "one of the most level heads I have ever seen for a boy his age."[1] But beneath these surface manifestations of the Horatio Alger syndrome lay qualities of jesuitical complexity and secretiveness wedded to extraordinary discipline and placed in the service of a driving ambition, early determined upon but slow to find focus or definition beyond a perceptible gravitation to the effective exercise of power. His mother was not the only one who discerned qualities of mind that might recommend him for a life in the Church hierarchy. Some years later in New York, the playwright Philip Barry, a fellow Irishman and by then a close friend, dubbed him "Jimmy the Priest."[2]

MANLINESS AND THE PRIESTHOOD

FORRESTAL, however, seems to have resisted his mother's plans for him from the moment he became aware of them. He was not interested in religion and felt repressed by her strict tutelage, which he associated directly with the severe doctrines of the Catholic Church. There began a contest of wills between mother and son in which the son progressively triumphed through successive acts of defiance, but at the cost of creating a permanent gulf between them.[3]

The Matteawan High School basketball team, James Forrestal
(first row, center), captain

A frail child who almost died of pneumonia during infancy, Forrestal worked hard to become strong and physically fit, almost as though to arm himself against his mother's overpowering personality. Absorbing his father's belief in the virtues of competitive sports, he played first base on the high school baseball team and captained the basketball team, no doubt making up in agility for what he lacked in height (he was five-foot-eight at maturity) and no doubt achieving a more prominent athletic record at Matteawan High than he would have done in a larger school. He also played tennis, a favorite sport and one at which he became quite proficient, preferring late afternoon matches on the court behind the Matteawan Episcopal Church.[4] At Princeton, his small size combined with his striking organizational ability cast him most frequently in the role of team manager.

The manly art of fisticuffs was flourishing in turn-of-the-century America and was probably the most popular sport in Matteawan, especially after an 1896 state law declared it legal, provided the fights were conducted under the auspices of established athletic clubs. In Matteawan, athletic clubs meant Irish saloons. Matches were held on Friday and Saturday after drinking hours, in a field behind Ed Dillon's Main Street saloon. They pitted regional pugilists or village boys against each other in bloody, vicious trials of brutality and stamina egged on by an assemblage of besotted male enthusiasts who placed bets on their favorites. The Major loved them, but Mary Forrestal forbade her sons to witness, much less participate in, such vulgar and violent activity.[5] Forrestal obeyed his mother and refrained from fighting, but at Princeton and later during the early Wall Street years, he defied her ban and became an enthusiastic boxer who would sometimes spend two hours a day sparring in a gym at the corner of 42nd Street and Broadway, and later at the New York Athletic Club.

The resort to this particularly intense form of recreation was characteristically Irish, as well as a belated acknowledgment of his father's influence and a further rejection of his mother's Victorian strictures. It was another measure of his determination to be strong and tough and independent. He relished the physical contact and moved with the grace of a fencing master, and when he suffered a broken nose (not once, but twice, during too vigorous exchanges with his professional coach), he chose not to have it repaired. The broad, flattened nose markedly changed his appearance, adding a slight touch of menace, emphasizing the tough features that were framed by close-cropped hair, and further concealing the brooding Jesuit who lurked within. In his early thirties, he looked not unlike the actor Jimmy Cagney playing the role of a champion welterweight or a well-groomed, almost respectable gangster. There was an attractive incongruity between his battered face and his well-cut, double-breasted suits and English shoes. Two of Forrestal's favorite possessions during the Wall Street years were boxing lithographs, signed by George Bellows, which he had purchased on impulse at a Manhattan gallery. His son, Michael, who inherited them, said his father had no idea who George Bellows was—he bought the lithographs because he liked boxing.[6]

JOURNALISM AND COLLEGE

AFTER TUTORING with his mother, Forrestal attended the church school at St. Joachim's and then the Matteawan High School on Spring Street, from which he was graduated at the age of sixteen. There were only six in his class: three boys and three girls. His grades were consistently superior—100 in American History, 95 in English, 93 in Physiology and Hygiene, 90 in Latin, 81 in Algebra.[7] Passionate about American history and English, he later claimed to have been especially influenced by Miss Eunice Sherwood, a plump, reddish-haired English teacher with "pinch-nose glasses."[8] In terms of "character, intelligence and . . . the ability to inspire curiosity and provocative discussion," he wrote to her in 1947, "teaching at Matteawan High did not suffer by comparison with what I found at Dartmouth and Princeton."[9]

This letter deftly finessed the truth that Forrestal failed to enter Princeton in 1911, though the failure was not due to any deficiency on his part. The problem was that Princeton seriously doubted the academic standards and the quality of instruction at Matteawan High. Also, the letter was written at a time when he was flirting with the idea of running for public office— New York governor or senator—a circumstance loaded with temptation to gild the truth. Yet Forrestal did remember his schooling at Matteawan as the foundation of his education and opportunity, and felt a sense of kinship with other young men from that place who had the brains and the longing to escape its narrow limits and seek distinction in the wider world, but who lacked the money for an Ivy League education. After he became established in Wall Street, working confidentially with the principal of Beacon High School, he secretly financed the college educations of at least three students and subsequently placed at least one of them in a Wall Street banking firm.[10]

Midway through high school, Forrestal briefly considered a career in carpentry and worked one summer as an apprentice to his father, but later wrote of the experience in a manner suggesting he had never been serious. Carrying shingles up a ladder one day, "I got bitten on the behind by a wasp when I was in no position to defend myself, and that ended all ambition to become a carpenter."[11] More genuine was a literary, journalistic bent. In high school he edited the yearbook (called *The Orange and Black*) and ran the school library with a girl who later married his brother Henry. He devoured books, especially the works of Dickens and Shakespeare, and was not above capitalizing on his reputation as the brightest kid on the block by carrying serious books under his arm to impress the girls with his intellectual qualities. He continued to tote books under his arm throughout his life, to read extensively, and to impress women.[12]

The definitive break with his mother occurred just after he was graduated from high school, when he flatly rejected the seminary and went to work for his father's friend Morgan Hoyt, at the *Matteawan Journal*. This was a six-column, four-page daily, originally set entirely by hand and printed on a press in the nearby town of Pine Plains. In Forrestal's day, however, the job was done by a linotype machine.[13] Hoyt, a man of disciplined intelligence, moderately liberal views, and much goodwill, seems to have been a central influence on the lives of several young men who came to work for the *Journal*. Forrestal admired him and may have considered him a role model. Hoyt in turn was impressed by Forrestal's boundless energy, discipline, and "very strong and sound ideas—far beyond the range of his age level. . . . He was one of the keenest, hardest-working and personable boys we had ever known on the *Journal*," with a faculty for "scenting news" and turning out "good news stories."[14] Hoyt's son Philip also worked on the paper for a year, and the two boys became close friends. Two years older, Philip went on to Princeton, returning for the holidays with tales of fashionable eating clubs, drinking binges, and sophisticated behavior in the wider world, all of which kindled the younger boy's expanding imagination, hopes, and ambitions and pointed him directly toward Princeton.[15]

During his last year in high school, Forrestal fell in love with Margaret MacNamara, a strawberry blonde who was two years younger and equally Irish. She hoped they would marry and settle down in Matteawan as soon as he was graduated, but it became evident that Forrestal was determined upon a college education, that indeed a primary purpose of his newspaper work was to earn the money he would need beyond the amount his family could or would provide.[16] Forrestal told Ernest Havemann in 1947 that his father's income never exceeded $2,500 a year. While that figure, in the early 1900s, gave the family a respectable middle-class standing, the full cost of a Princeton education (then about $600 a year) would have been a formidable burden. Beyond money, however, it is a plausible inference that a college education for his sons was not a high priority in Major Forrestal's scale of values, nor perhaps even in Mary's. Both believed in the benefits of education, but in the early 1900s a high school diploma represented a very respectable level of learning and prestige—more than enough of a start, by contemporary community standards, for any enterprising young man. College was for the precious few; it was not a mainstream aspiration. There were more important goals for investment, like using what assets one had to expand one's business or to buy more land. Their son Henry had turned down a scholarship to Syracuse to enter the family business, and the Major almost certainly regarded that as a sensible decision. He would not object if his youngest son insisted on college, but he would provide only so much help; the boy would have to work for the rest. Forrestal understood this and was determined.

By the time he was seventeen or eighteen, then, Forrestal had developed an undeflectable ambition to get beyond the town, outdo his father and brothers, escape his mother and the priesthood, and realize a potential he sensed himself to possess without as yet being able to give it tangible shape or content. The immediate objective was to get to Princeton, that embodiment of everything high and splendid and sophisticated, so utterly different from life and prospects in Matteawan. In the circumstances Margaret MacNamara's dream of domestic bliss with her high school sweetheart never had a chance. Forrestal urged her to finish high school (she was prepared to drop out so they could marry) and indeed to go on to college, and she did both of these things. Their relationship lasted for several years, until shortly after he left Princeton, but it must have been increasingly evident that their goals in life were steadily diverging. Forrestal steadfastly avoided the question of marriage, and in 1916 Margaret married a young doctor at the Matteawan State Hospital.[17]

In search of broader experience and more money to finance his college education, Forrestal left the *Journal* after two years to join the Mount Vernon *Argus* in a Westchester County town thirty miles from Matteawan. It was on both counts a disappointing experience. The *Argus* office was located on the third floor of a dingy building above a soda fountain and a bank, and his job consisted of soliciting "personal ads" at a salary of eighteen dollars a week. He boarded with the widow of an Episcopalian minister, and his fondest memory of Mount Vernon was that she was a passingly good cook; otherwise, it was an unpromising episode. "There was no Newspaper Guild then," he wrote a friend in 1947, "but even had there been, I doubt I would have won a case for more pay." Working hard to develop a writing style he could call his own, he recalled that "although I was rather pleased with my own copy, I was apt to put more emphasis on style than facts—which led to some difficulty on the first night that I covered the City Council, when I confused the person of the Garbage Collector with that of Mayor and pursued the error in the story of the next day."[18]

Having no visible future at the *Argus,* he sought new opportunities and, probably with major help from Morgan Hoyt, secured the far better job of city editor on the Poughkeepsie *News Press*. This was a big step up for an eighteen-year-old, for Poughkeepsie was the county seat and the *News Press* its leading Democratic newspaper. Forrestal's first assignment was to cover the same election campaign that brought Franklin D. Roosevelt to public office, and it was during that 1910 contest that he first met the future President.[19] Years later, when Forrestal was appointed Under Secretary of the Navy, Morgan Hoyt wrote a story suggesting that the appointment had its roots in that long-ago meeting. "There have been many reasons advanced as to why Roosevelt chose a former Wall Street man to become a member of his official family," Hoyt wrote. "My guess is that . . . Forrestal so impressed him in 1910 that . . . he remembered him, although he had not seen him for 25 years."[20] In truth, these were the wishful sentiments of an old man. Forrestal's appointment in 1940 reflected FDR's generic need to recruit able men from the business community to help with the urgent effort to prepare the country for war and his equal need to give the administration a bipartisan character, thus to strengthen national unity. Forrestal was recommended to the President by Supreme Court Justice William O. Douglas, with whom he had worked on Wall Street reform when Douglas headed the Securities and Exchange Commission. Roosevelt did not recall the Beacon connection until Forrestal later had occasion to mention the name of Morgan Hoyt.

During his years at Princeton, Forrestal became a reporter for the *Daily Princetonian* and was elected its editor at the end of his junior year. Meanwhile he returned to work for the *Matteawan Journal* during summer vacations, and so gave every indication that journalism, for which he had both strong aptitude and liking, would be his chosen career. In the summer of 1914, he scored a journalistic coup that seemed to point the compass firmly in that direction. An inmate named Harry K. Thaw escaped from the Matteawan State Mental Hospital on a Sunday morning about 6:00 a.m. The *Journal* was informed an hour later and quickly recognized the sensational nature of the story. Thaw was no run-of-the-mill mental patient but a wealthy eccentric who had been convicted of murdering the famous architect Stanford White for allegedly seducing Thaw's wife. The trial had been played out in newspaper headlines. Morgan Hoyt was determined to give the story front-page coverage, and Forrestal made the inspired suggestion that they get out an extra edition that day (no Sunday papers were printed in Dutchess County or Manhattan). Hoyt agreed, and the *Journal* went into high gear. Forrestal wrote a melodramatic story of Thaw's escape and the progress of his flight, vividly describing the escape car racing through neighboring Stormville with guns blazing. His fellow reporter Roy Gilland portrayed the three men who had helped engineer the escape, while Hoyt wrote a psychobiographical background piece on Thaw and his wife's affair with Stanford White. By two in the afternoon they were ready to go, and the press was soon churning out 1,200 copies an hour.[21]

Several thousand copies of the extra edition were sent to Poughkeepsie and Newburgh and, at Forrestal's suggestion, a group of newsboys was dispatched to Manhattan, where they sold one hundred copies at twenty-five cents each. By the next day, reporters were streaming out of New York City into Matteawan on the scent of further dramatic leads and Hoyt arranged a press conference with Forrestal as spokesman. The Associated Press praised him for a ''great story'' and hired him to write an additional piece for its wire service.[22] This further evidence that he possessed a natural affinity for newspaper work seemed, in combination with his success on the *Daily Princetonian,* to reinforce the general impression that he would make it his career. But when the time came to choose, circumstances found him determined to make his mark on a broader, higher stage.

★ ★ ★

CHAPTER 3

The Princeton Years

IN THE AUTUMN of 1911, disappointed by his failure of admission to Princeton but determined to escape Matteawan, Forrestal entered Dartmouth College in Hanover, New Hampshire, an institution which then ranked measurably lower than the top-drawer Ivy League schools and was, according to Forrestal's later friend Eliot Janeway, "a natural gathering place for poor, ambitious Irish boys."[1] He stayed only one year. Little is known about the brief Dartmouth period except that he developed an intense dislike for the fraternity system, took up skiing on weekends, and turned in a respectable academic performance. In any event, he did well enough to be accepted at Princeton as a transfer student in the sophomore class: "Mr. Forrestal . . . was a good student, somewhat above the average in standing, gave us no trouble, and we were very sorry to have him withdraw," Dean Charles Emerson of Dartmouth wrote to Princeton professor C. W. McAlpin.[2] On his application to Princeton, Forrestal described his father's occupation as "contractor" and in the blank marked "occupation in view" he wrote "newspaper work."[3]

According to the *Fifty Year Record* of the class of 1915, published in 1965, Forrestal came to Princeton "unheralded, unknown and unfinanced."[4] A shortage of money was always a major concern during his college days. Although his 1963 biographer, Arnold Rogow, claimed that his family gave him at least $6,000 over the three years he was at Princeton, this seems unlikely.[5] Probably the Major paid his son's tuition of $150 and perhaps another $150 toward room and board, leaving Forrestal to scrape up the other half of his basic costs and all his spending money. This he seems to have done out of precollege savings, by working each summer for Morgan Hoyt's newspaper, and by carrying several odd jobs at Princeton during the college year. To save on room and board, he lived off campus with the family of Columbus A. Titus, a janitor in Whig Hall, in a small clapboard house at 58 Wiggins Street in one of the dingier sections of town.[6] During his senior year, however, his slender financial margins were significantly improved when he earned $1,200 as editor of the *Daily Princetonian,* a new affluence that permitted him to indulge a developing penchant for the stylish clothing shops on Nassau Street and after-dinner drinks at the Nassau Inn. But on the whole he was a poor boy in a rich man's school, and this fact shaped his outlook, then and in the years ahead.[7] F. Scott Fitzgerald, also shaped by Princeton, later wrote that only 20 percent of an average class came from public high schools, yet it furnished "a large proportion of the eventual leaders." Compared to their counterparts from prep schools like Groton, St. Paul's, Andover, Exeter, and Lawrenceville, "the business of getting to Princeton has been more arduous, financially as well as scholastically. They are trained and eager for the fray."[8]

Princeton's prestige was then at an all-time high, although the class of 1915 was later described by its own historian as "mediocre" both academically and athletically. Woodrow Wilson had served as university president from 1902 to 1910, leaving to become governor of New Jersey two years before Forrestal arrived, and his legacy permeated Princeton life. He had tried to make the university "something more than a country club with an intellectual atmosphere" and had vigorously preached the credo of "Princeton in the nation's service."[9] Nothing could have more powerfully reinforced this rhetoric than his own election as President of the United States in 1912. He received the news at 10:00 p.m. at his home in Cleveland Lane, surrounded by a tumultuous, cheering crowd of Princeton students (including Forrestal) and the entire college band, all of them assembled on the front lawn. "Gentlemen," Wilson told them, "this is not a moment for a feeling of congratulations, but one of dedication to high responsibility."[10]

An infectious spirit of reform ran through the campus in those years. Princeton students pressed for an end to "horsing" (the time-honored humiliation of freshmen) and compulsory chapel, and for changes in the rules governing the elite eating clubs.[11] This progressive spirit extended beyond campus life when the new university president, philosopher John Grier Hibben, called on Princeton graduates everywhere to understand the moral duties associated with being a part of America's social-intellectual elite, especially the duty to acknowledge their noblesse oblige. In speeches to the alumni Hibben held up the current undergraduates as bearers of the new standard. They "are not, as in times past, so exclusively concerned with the problems of campus life. Their interests have gone out into the fields of the moral, social, industrial, and political problems of the day."[12]

Forrestal's keen mind and sensitive political antennae absorbed the majestic currents of new thought sweeping through hallowed academic halls and was excited by them, for they spoke of a broad, reasoned, uplifted approach to life that was a world removed from the mundane calculations of daily existence in Beacon. Inspired by new possibilities in everything he saw and heard, from the Gothic beauty of the campus to the high-minded brilliance of his professors, he plunged into Princeton life with the fervor of a religious convert, bursting with enthusiasm, eager to master the rules of the new order, and determined to succeed.[13] He did remarkably well his first year, achieving a 4.3 average (on a scale of 1 to 5), then slipped to 3.8 in his junior year, reflecting lower grades in English and politics. In the first term of his senior year, the average dropped again, to 3.1, once more a consequence of problems with English, but he always stood in the upper half of his class.[14] It was, however, in extracurricular activities that Forrestal established himself as a leader at Princeton, for these were natural outlets for his energy, ambition, and political instincts.

As a senior at Princeton

An inherent shyness brought him a transitory reputation as an aloof, rather antisocial fellow, "but it didn't take him long to get underway," as a fellow member of the Cottage Club, William Long, later recalled. "Forrestal would often stand at the gate of Nassau Hall. If he didn't know your first name when you passed by the first time, he would look it up. The next time it would be 'Hello' and first name." According to Long, by the time Forrestal left Princeton he knew not only every undergraduate by name, but also the names of their fathers and grandfathers, what they did in the world, whether they had "social standing," and how much money the family was worth.[15] Another classmate acknowledged Forrestal's intelligence, but thought him a blatant "young man on the make" who spent an unattractive amount of time and effort cultivating "the people who counted."[16] His classmates later voted him "Most Likely to Succeed," but apparently perceived something more complex beneath the drive of the ambitious striver and political operator, for they also voted him "Biggest Bluffer" and "The Man Nobody Knows."

He cut a wide swath on campus, drawing on his practical journalistic experience in Beacon and elsewhere to win election to the editorial board of the *Daily Princetonian* in his sophomore year, and to its chairmanship two years later. He was also chairman of the *Nassau Herald,* the senior yearbook; a member of the Senior Council (described in his day as that "august figurehead" of Princeton's political democracy); chairman of the Princeton Chapter of the Red Cross; founding member of the International Polity Club; and member of the Law Club. He did not play any team sports, but would often box at the gym or play informal but intense tennis and squash.[17]

The Cottage Club, which ranked as one of the more prestigious among Princeton's eating clubs, attracted (as F. Scott Fitzgerald described its traditional membership in *This Side of Paradise*) "an impressive melange of brilliant adventurers and well-dressed philanderers."[18] Forrestal was duly invited to join, and did, and there met a number of men who would become important business connections and lifelong friends, including George Rentschler (later a successful industrialist and prominent social figure in New York and Long Island), George Riegel (who directed advertising for Brooks Brothers and contributed poetry to *The New Yorker),* and Robert Christie, Jr. (who became a fellow partner of Forrestal in Wall Street). To most of his Cottage Club buddies, "Runt" Forrestal was an ingrained opponent of the social-economic status quo—"always anti-this and anti-that"—who, after downing two martinis, would launch into "the Forrestal spiel," which included the basic theme that the eating club system was too elitist, too undemocratic, and too shallow in its purposes. Significantly, however, he did not resign from Cottage. In truth, he had fallen in love with Princeton and the system; they had become for him synonymous with everything successful and strong and graceful and charming.[19]

EDITOR OF "THE PRINCE"

WHILE FORRESTAL wrote for the *Daily Princetonian* primarily because he had previous newspapering experience and was good at it, his choice of this vehicle for gaining prestige and exercising influence on campus also reflected political acumen. Writing for the *Nassau Literary Magazine* might bring modest and transitory notoriety (as F. Scott Fitzgerald's main character in *This Side of Paradise* sagely noted), but making the editorial board of "The Prince" virtually guaranteed "lifelong benefits" as well as immediate "campus acclaim."[20] Forrestal "heeled" (competed for a staff position on) the paper with such other aspirants as Hamilton Fish Armstrong (later the editor of *Foreign Affairs*) and Robert McLean (later president of the Associated Press) and quickly impressed the lordly chairman, Ferdinand Eberstadt, known on campus as "King Eber" for his dominating personality, incisive brilliance, and athletic ability. Eberstadt

Forrestal as chairman of
The Daily Princetonian

Ferdinand Eberstadt at
Princeton, 1912

found Forrestal "a serious, quiet—one might say obscure—person" who went about his work in "a quiet, determined fashion" and soon outclassed the other heelers by superior advance planning and diligence. Before long his associates discovered that Forrestal had beaten them to the sources of important stories, for he was perceptive in sizing up a situation and thorough in exploiting it: "He had studied the old files to discover what stories regularly popped up at certain times during the academic year, and had gone out and signed them up in advance."[21]

Eberstadt became the younger man's mentor, almost certainly playing a major role in securing Forrestal's invitation to the Cottage Club and also positioning him for election as his successor as chairman of the newspaper. Eberstadt always called him "James," and they became lifelong friends and professional associates on Wall Street and later in government. They shared, among other things, a consuming interest in the larger questions of political and economic power.[22] Eberstadt was the more direct and willful man, basically tougher-fibered, readier to run higher risks, yet also possessed of a keener ability to perceive and protect his own interests in a given situation. At Princeton he established a reputation as a prankster par excellence, and was briefly suspended for pouring cold water over a security guard early in his freshman year, but he returned to achieve an enviable record: in addition to editing the newspaper, he made Phi Beta Kappa, ran on the track team, and managed the football team.[23]

The *Daily Princetonian* first appeared in 1876 and was soon acclaimed by a New York weekly magazine as "varied, racy, and thoughtful"—one of the best college newspapers. In the years following, it regularly indulged in "pungent criticism" of the college administration and developed a reputation for fearless disregard for authority in general. In 1890, the college authorities decided to end the impudence, advising the undergraduate editors that "ungentlemanly" remarks about any person, or stories "injurious to the reputation or interests of the college," were no longer acceptable. In the Eberstadt-Forrestal period, a pugnacious editorial spirit resurfaced, but now the college authorities declined to censor or even protest, which permitted Forrestal to proclaim with impunity that "we have offended any number of people and we are proud of it."[24]

In his senior year, he coauthored a book with James Bruce, president of the Association of Eastern College Newspapers, entitled *College Journalism,* published by Princeton University Press in 1914. Essentially a "how to write" tract, it contained a section on the technical aspects of good newspaper writing, illustrated by model editorials taken from college papers across the country. In the preface, Forrestal and Bruce instructed aspiring college journalists to be bold and incorruptible: "Put old institutions to the test of reason; question mildewed conventions; suggest revisions in the curriculum and in the official regulations; avoid pessimism, while showing that the best can be retained and attained. You will be thoroughly damned for your trouble, but you will render a great service to your university."[25]

A recurring theme of Forrestal's editorials was the shallow purpose, the pretension, the excessive elitism of prevailing undergraduate attitudes at Princeton, which he found especially entrenched among those who came from rich and privileged families. "The scions of these families have always been destined for a college education. Their fathers, realizing the value of a smattering of polite culture, feel that the son should have the opportunity of parading a degree before his little world. It will give him more assurance in his social experiences and, as a logical consequence to that, a certain prestige in business. . . . A young man is sent to college nine times out of ten for social preferment to be converted into business preferment four years later by some marvelous process. . . . College education in itself is useless. Only when it is melded to life, and when the theoretical has been focused upon the practical, does a college education begin to yield its return at the legitimate rate of interest."[26]

Some thought, then and later, that these assaults on class privilege and snobbery reflected Forrestal's undergraduate reading of Karl Marx and Friedrich Engels, in addition to the almost universal response of the young to their first confrontation with an unfair, unequal world. There is no reason to doubt the role played by these factors, but one cannot fail to hear primarily the voice of the very smart poor boy from Beacon, where a college education was rare and hard to come by—a voice mingling resentment with wistfulness, a rejection of wealth and social preferment with a yearning to possess them.[27] Like the slightly younger Scott Fitzgerald, Forrestal was the poor boy with his nose pressed against the window of the candy store. Unlike Fitzgerald, however, he would not be content with merely chronicling the rich. The final sentence of the editorial may be read as a road map for his own later path to financial success: "Only when it is melded to life, and when the theoretical has been focused upon the practical, does a college education begin to yield its return at the legitimate rate of interest."[28] Though he may have understood it only subconsciously at the time, he was, in response to the influences at work all around him, developing a firm determination to become one of the rich.

Significantly, he ceased to be a practicing Catholic while a student at predominantly Protestant Princeton; at the same time he began increasingly to neglect family ties in Beacon, moved chiefly by his mother's unforgiving disapproval of the course on which he was now embarked. Although he later made several (unsuccessful) attempts to appease her—the gift of a fur coat, the offer of a New York apartment—it was at Princeton that he decided to put his early life resolutely behind him, to the point almost of rejecting the idea that it had ever been a part of him, or had any relevant claims on his future. After World War I, he never spoke of his origins, never visited his family, and never told his children anything whatsoever of their Forrestal relatives. From Princeton onward, until he became a famous public figure, and thus the subject of press interviews in which the acknowledgment of humble beginnings enhanced his reputation or served his political ambitions, he presented himself as if sprung full-blown into Wall Street out of nowhere—a man without a past.

The catastrophic war in Europe, destined to decimate a whole generation of leaders and destroy the Victorian order, began in August 1914. Despite Woodrow Wilson's prompt declaration of American neutrality, the developing barbarism at the center of the civilization from which American culture and values were mainly derived set off alarm bells throughout the country, and rapidly became the focus of heated debate on every college campus. It was in this charged climate of opinion that the economist Norman Angell gave a guest lecture at Princeton. While his immediate purpose was to criticize President Wilson's hostility toward Mexico, as evidenced by the sending of American troops to the Mexican border in 1913, Angell placed great emphasis on the general principle of settling international disputes through diplomacy rather than military force; specifically, he urged Princeton students to form a group for the serious discussion of global issues, especially for the development of peaceful solutions to international conflict. Forrestal, Hamilton Fish Armstrong, and a few others were subsequently instrumental in establishing a forum called the International Polity Club and in persuading leading Americans to come to Princeton to address the great questions of the day.

The automobile tycoon Henry Ford spoke on the importance of military preparedness: "A nation whose purpose is pacific," he declared, "may exert a strong influence in behalf of peace by armament strong enough to command respect." Former President Theodore Roosevelt lectured on public service: "We have a right to expect college men of the type turned out by Princeton to take their part in national politics. They must not feel they have special privileges or should be set apart from their fellows or they will be of no service."[29]

In a follow-up editorial, Forrestal urged the university administration to institute a continuing lecture series on the European war, for this would be, he wrote in fuzzy prose, "the interlinear translation of a college education—where the theory of scholasticism might be translated into terms of the practice of life on earth." He also urged the Polity Club to broaden its base by taking in "associate members" beyond the founding "inner circle," but argued that only the latter group should be allowed to lead the discussion at club meetings.[30]

ABRUPT DEPARTURE

AT THE PEAK of his undergraduate influence and prestige in the early spring of 1915, his senior year, Forrestal was visited by Dean Mathey, a young associate in the Wall Street banking house of William A. Read and Company. The two young men had much in common, for Mathey had graduated from Princeton three years before, had been an editor of the *Princetonian,* and a member of the Cottage Club. He was in town to recruit bright, articulate men to become bond salesmen on Wall Street, and it was a tested rule of thumb that anyone who had risen to the eminence of chairman of the newspaper was automatically a worthy candidate for investment banking. This was a time when Wall Street still claimed the chosen youth of the nation, when "the bright boys from the best colleges" went there "because that was the way one got rich and carved out a career—whether in law, finance, government service or even politics." The "dull boys from the same colleges, the well-born athletes and playboys . . . socially at ease, intellectually incurious and indolent, drifted there because . . . it was the easiest place for them to make a living."[31]

Forrestal was flattered by the attention and impressed by Mathey's assurance of excitement and big money in the bond business, but his mind

was apparently set on a career in journalism; he may also have considered
the offer too obvious a temptation to join the very forces of privilege and
pretension against which he was inveighing editorially, with vigor and passion. In any event, he declined. But Mathey kept the door open, letting
Forrestal know that if he ever wanted a job, it would be waiting for him.
If Mathey was unavailable, Forrestal was to make an appointment to see
William A. Phillips, the sales manager, and tell him that Mathey said
to put him to work. This is exactly what Forrestal did eighteen months
later, in the fall of 1916.[32]

Thus, riding high as the days moved swiftly toward graduation exercises,
toward that ritual celebration of individual and collective efforts, triumphs,
and excitements that would bond the class of 1915 forever after, Forrestal's
sudden decision to withdraw from Princeton just a few weeks before the
culminating event must have come as a considerable shock to his friends
and a bitter disappointment to himself. Why he took this drastic step, and
took it so abruptly, remains unclear. According to the most reliable account, he was lacking one needed course credit when he transferred from
Dartmouth and never made up the deficiency, although the Princeton administration called the matter to his attention on several occasions.[33] According to another account, he had a serious disagreement with an English
teacher, which led unexpectedly to a failing grade in the final term of his
senior year. Whatever the cause, the effect was a sudden, probably shattering sense of humiliation—an abrupt descent from the exalted role of
class leader (the man voted ''Most Likely to Succeed'') to the status of a
pariah who would be excluded from the happy line of classmates, in white
flannels and Princeton blazers, moving to the podium to receive their di-
plomas and a congratulatory handshake from President Hibben.

It must have been a black moment dominated by sudden awareness that
he had failed himself and also his family. An intense pride—or perhaps
what Ferdinand Eberstadt later assessed as his friend's innate ''fear of
disgrace''[34]—required that he leave Princeton forthwith. But it also made
going home to Beacon an equal impossibility. If he could have returned
there in triumph, a manifest success, it is reasonable to believe that later
relations with his mother and father and brothers would have been more
normal and cordial, even on the assumption that ambition and ability would
in any event have carried him far beyond Beacon. But at that dark moment
in the early summer of 1915, Beacon must have represented everything in
his Irish-Catholic, lower-middle-class background he had thought to have
transcended, but which now seemed a fate he could not escape. Yet escape
and transcendence were the categorical imperatives. There was no going
back. There was only the primal need to undo the failure, to prove himself
again by thinking and working longer and harder than anyone else, by
applying the fruits of his education to the practical (as he had instructed

others editorially) so that life would yield a return "at the legitimate rate of interest." One lasting consequence of this moment was the perhaps subconscious but categorical decision to sever his links with Beacon.[35]

He found immediate employment in Newark as a clerk/handyman with the New Jersey Zinc Company, but the pay was humble and the physical labor arduous. After two frustrating months, Robert Christie, Jr., arranged to get him a job with the American Tobacco Company, where his father was a senior executive. This involved selling cigarettes and cigars to retail outlets on the East Side of Manhattan, an occupation Forrestal found only a little more congenial than manhandling heavy boxes in the squalor of industrial New Jersey. Both jobs must have caused him to wonder at the harsh discrepancy between the Olympian prestige of a college newspaper editor and the impoverished obscurity of the same young man confronting the necessity to make a living in the real world. Still nurturing the idea of a career in journalism, he got himself hired a few months later as a financial reporter for the New York *World*. Here too the pay was meager, but the job brought him into contact with stockbrokers, bond salesmen, bankers, and entrepreneurs in Wall Street, and he discovered that not a few of them were Princetonians. He was impressed by their well-dressed affluence and the exciting nature of their work, and quickly concluded that participating in the fascinating Wall Street game of money-making promised far greater rewards and satisfactions than merely writing about it.[36]

Fifteen months and three jobs after leaving Princeton, Forrestal presented his raincheck to the sales manager at William A. Read and Company. William Phillips had heard about him through Dean Mathey and, after a remarkably brief interview, Forrestal found himself hired and on the overnight train to Albany, where he would be the firm's bond salesman for upper New York State, an area that included not only Albany, Utica, and Schenectady, but also the western cities of Buffalo and Rochester. Phillips, who was renowned as a supersalesman, had put Forrestal at the starting gate and told him to run. Mathey later wrote that this expression of confidence had a "lasting influence" on Forrestal and on the way in which he subsequently developed his own administrative practices. Like Phillips, Forrestal came to believe in finding good men and letting them run.[37]

Forrestal discovered his niche in selling bonds; it was for him a challenging enterprise that brought to bear his analytical powers, his ability to master complex detail, his orderliness and precision, his willingness to work long hours, and his persuasive political skills. He energetically cultivated his Princeton connections all over northern and western New York State and used this network to become known to major bankers and investors in the region. He sold a lot of bonds and was exuberantly climbing the ladder to financial success after less than a year on the job. Then on

April 6, 1917, Woodrow Wilson, unable any longer to reconcile American neutrality with German submarine attacks against American shipping in the Atlantic, declared war on Germany, throwing the great potential weight of American power onto the scales of the bloodiest war in history in an impassioned effort ''to make the world safe for democracy.'' Caught up in the emotional excitement of this dramatic new development, Forrestal, like most of his contemporaries, felt it was his duty to enlist.

II

★ ★ ★

A SWIFT ASCENT

★ ★ ★

CHAPTER 4

Love and Marriage
in the Jazz Age

IERCE, chauvinist patriotism rose like a sudden swamp fog in the wake of President Wilson's declaration of war on the Kaiser's Germany and quickly became the dominant emotion on the American scene—stirred by the ubiquitous recruiting poster showing a stern Uncle Sam pointing an imperious finger above the caption ''I Want You,'' amplified by rousing war songs like ''Over There,'' and sustained by Liberty Bond rallies on every street corner. Like his contemporaries in the college-bred elite, Forrestal was ready to play the role of responsible citizen, to serve his country in time of war and national peril. But with a Princeton education and a short but successful stint as bond salesman behind him, he assumed the army would not, in its eagerness to obtain his services as an officer, insist on the usual dreary, bureaucratic formalities. To his surprise, the army insisted. ''I went off with Bunny Warren, Ken Reynolds, and Johnny Gilette to Madison Barracks'' (near Albany), he wrote in 1947, but the group was turned away ''for failing to go through channels. I assumed my selling experience would enable me to talk my way into the Army, but the Army had different ideas.''[1]

Another close friend from Princeton, Ed Shea, then convinced him they should together enlist in the Marine Corps to be certain of getting their full measure of glory. But standing in line at the Marine recruiting office in Albany, they were transfixed by a scene unfolding just ahead of them. A young, well-dressed college man (very much like themselves) was filling out his papers when he made the mistake of asking the sergeant when he could expect to receive his commission. The taut, leather-faced marine, wearing a campaign hat with chin strap drawn tight, looked at the young man with ice-water eyes: ''If you pass your physical, which I doubt, you'll go to boot camp at Parris Island. After a year, if you're *very* exceptional, you may be a corporal.'' At hearing this bleak forecast, the young man lost all interest in the Marines and walked out. With hands on his hips, the sergeant turned to the long line of potential recruits standing along two walls of the room. "There goes another one of those goddamn born leaders," he said with heavy sarcasm. Forrestal and Shea looked at each other, nodded silently, and quietly departed.[2] As Secretary of the Navy in World War II, Forrestal developed a glowing admiration for the bravery and tenacity of the Marines, but in 1917 he and his fellow Princetonians expected to fight a gentleman's war.[3]

After debating enlistment strategy for a few more days, they signed up in the Naval Reserve at the Brooklyn Navy Yard. This did not entail an immediate call to active duty, and over the next several days they managed to join another group of Princetonians who had decided to take private flying lessons in order to qualify for naval flight training. With funding provided by the rich parents of one member of the group, twelve young men, including Shea and Forrestal, went off to learn their aviation basics on the rolling pastures of East Greenwich, Rhode Island.[4]

Among these would-be gentlemen aviators, Forrestal was certainly not the best, and was possibly the worst, remembered by his peers as a "generally inept pilot" who was "downright dangerous when attempting to land."[5] Although a well-coordinated athlete, he was not a natural aviator, but tense and stiff at the stick of the Curtiss Jenny trainers. He damaged two aircraft in landing attempts and had not earned his pilot's license when the group was called to active duty on July 5, 1917. Nevertheless, he was sent with the others to flight school in Canada for training with the Royal Canadian Flying Corps, while sufficient training facilities in the United States were being created as rapidly as possible. Forrestal's flying improved in Canada, and he earned his commission as ensign and his wings as Naval Pilot Number 154.[6] The American officer in charge of the detachment, Ensign F. S. Allen, wrote the following report at the end of the training period: "J. V. Forrestal. Good flyer. Not a technical mind. Used to write for magazines. Has helped me with official paper work. Dependable worker, but lacks practical push. With a little experience will make a good officer. Needs toning down from a radical socialistic attitude with the men, and worrying about whether it is right to be a soldier."[7] Allen must have seen qualities of leadership in Forrestal that offset his "radical socialistic attitude with the men," for he ranked him second in a class of twenty-one cadets.

But Forrestal was sent to desk jobs in Massachusetts and Texas, where the commanding officers recognized his superior talents for clear thinking, clear writing, and administration. There was also, apparently, a brief stint in Norfolk, Virginia, where he did some flying ("You chewed me out for stunting a plane that shouldn't have been stunted," he told Rear Admiral Patrick N. L. Bellinger in 1943. Bellinger, who was commander at Norfolk in World War I, didn't remember. "I've chewed out a lot of ensigns in my

*Naval flight training in Canada, 1918; Forrestal is third
from right in the back row*

time,'' he told the navy Under Secretary).[8] In January 1918, Forrestal went
to Washington and was assigned to the Aviation Division in the Office of
the Chief of Naval Operations, where he remained until January 1920,
nearly fourteen months after the armistice. Eager to go overseas to the war
zone, he lobbied his navy superior, Commander Kenneth Whiting, at every
opportunity, but his entreaties fell on deaf ears. On one occasion, he sent
a civilian colleague in the department, a man named Charles Eidlitz, to
plead his case, but Commander Whiting told him: ''Forrestal's never going
over, because I will need him to take charge of this office when I go over.''[9]
So Forrestal sat out the war in Washington, was promoted to lieutenant
junior grade, but never saw combat and never flew a plane again.

Very little is known of those two years spent as an obscure junior officer
in the Department of the Navy—where he lived, who his companions were,
how he spent his free time. There is no indication that he formed any
lasting friendships or regarded the experience as significant to his personal
development, although it did teach him certain habits of administration.
He was disappointed, and in retrospect slightly embarrassed, by not having
served overseas, and he never mentioned his war record in later years. There
is, however, some indication that the undergraduate editor's approach to

public issues—liberal, egalitarian, idealistic—still dominated his private philosophy, although his stance was not entirely clear. In the only letter preserved from that period, he wrote to his former teacher, Professor Collins at Princeton, to express concern at the rising chauvinism and jingoistic spirit in the country as the fighting in Europe grew more merciless and the human losses mounted appallingly in the meat grinder of trench warfare: "In these abnormal times, there is temptation for people to drop all thought of everything but the main business of war. It seems to me there will be a particularly keen need for Princeton, for there is going to be a very real danger of this nation being taken over by Prussianism, even though we beat the Prussians. And the light of liberal education, as you and your colleagues have interpreted it at college, is one of the strongest weapons with which to contest the ideas of Mr. Dewey, Dr. Flexner and the Rockefeller Foundation et al."[10]*

THE SPIRIT OF THE AGE

B Y JANUARY 1920, Forrestal was back at his job as bond salesman for William A. Read, where the heady atmosphere of Wall Street—at the onset of a decade soon to be known as the Roaring Twenties—seemed to submerge his "socialistic" instincts in the universal race to get rich. Like most men back from the war, he felt an urgent need to make up for lost time. He was young and ambitious, filled with energy and expectation, and the future beckoned.

To understand Forrestal in the 1920s and 1930s, it is important to appreciate the tenor of the times. Nineteen-twenty was the dawn of the Jazz Age, which ushered in a riotous new spirit of unfettered social behavior and money madness, a spirit of sophisticated irresponsibility which was in some large part a psychological reaction to, and subconsciously designed to mask, the terrible legacy of carnage left by the European war and of disillusion left by the failed peace process at Versailles. There are in the Forrestal story distinct echoes of F. Scott Fitzgerald, especially of *The Great Gatsby*. In a notable essay on Fitzgerald, the critic Malcolm Cowley described the central ethos of the time, when all the ambitious young men "were bitterly determined to be successful and . . . they had been taught to measure success, failure and even virtue in monetary terms." Behind their desire for the "glittering things" was the dream of "a new status and a new

---

*John Dewey and Abraham Flexner were teacher-philosophers who held that an idea is valid only if it is useful to practical life. Forrestal seems here to be arguing against his earlier view that theory must be melded to practical life. The meaning of his reference to the Rockefeller Foundation is cloudy.

essence, of rising to a loftier place in the mysterious hierarchy of human worth.''[11] No one believed seriously in equality, but in gaining a life of comfort and distinction that wealth could buy. All were guided or driven by the Horatio Alger conviction that one could surpass his fellows by dint of exceptional enterprise and hard work. Being or getting rich was not an absolute prerequisite to the exciting and inviting life that was opening up in New York after World War I—some of its most attractive practitioners were people in the arts, professional idlers, or poorly paid journalists—but the rich were essential to the structure. Their New York houses and apartments, their estates and clubs on Long Island or across the Hudson River in New Jersey, provided the essential setting for the development of luxury, leisure, and privileged license.[12]

Another central aspect of this period, and especially of the milieu into which Forrestal now entered, was a pervasive and powerful sexuality. The novelist John O'Hara, who became one of Forrestal's friends and later one of Josephine Forrestal's lovers,[13] frequently captured in his stories this facet of life among the rich in New York and Long Island. One of O'Hara's male characters, respectably married, remarks that he was astounded and a little shocked when he had occasion to count up the number of his incidental affairs.[14] Another character, an actress, holds forth at a Long Island house party to her Wall Street lover on the sheer sexual drive engendered by her fame and his money.[15] Joseph Wood Krutch, a leading literary critic of the period, wrote in his autobiography that marital fidelity was not unknown, but was generally concealed and, when exposed, called for apology.[16] Youth, fame, and money were especially combustible materials in the 1920s, and much zest, care, and energy were devoted to the sexual chase and to overcoming inherited sexual inhibitions. As Cowley wrote, "Wives deceived their husbands joylessly, out of a sense of duty."[17] Fitzgerald wrote of Long Island as "that slender riotous island."[18]

Forrestal had glimpsed the rich life, in all its possibilities, at Princeton. Young men born to it had been his companions there and later in naval pilot training. Now, on his return from the war to New York and Wall Street, it loomed suddenly within reach—not a remote dream, but a realistic goal. He had tried newspapering, but its fringe satisfactions could hardly compete with the excitement and material rewards of investment banking and the boundless expansion of experience that money could provide. At age twenty-eight and benefiting from his base of operations at William A. Read, he set out to become one of the rich, and did so with a speed that was remarkable even on Wall Street and in a decade of general and rapid enrichment. The fifteen to twenty years that followed were years when Forrestal acquired the feel and habit of success, useful connections by the hundreds, a number of devoted friends, a family of his own, and a strong notion that the orthodox rules of human intercourse did not bind him. In a certain sense, he both grew up during this period and managed to evade the ordinary obligations of maturity. [19]

DURING the immediate postwar years, Forrestal became known among his banking associates for a "terrific drive," a sardonic charm, and a social shyness, particularly in the company of women. There was also a sense that he was "different"—a word that frequently recurs in the recollections of him in the 1920s. His emphasis on personal efficiency was widely remarked. With a group of fellow strivers, he signed up for an evening course in cost accounting at New York University to hone his ability to interpret balance sheets and income statements. Soon his fellow students noticed that Forrestal always arrived ten minutes late and left ten minutes early. Asked to explain, he told them, "Nothing useful happens at the beginning of the class. Students are taking off their coats and the instructor is arranging his papers. And toward the end, the instructor is merely reviewing material already covered and no one is listening. I have better things to do with my time." [20]

Dean Mathey, who had originally recruited him for the firm, thought him "a mixed-up guy," by which he meant "cynical about wealth" and "at times very much a socialist . . . cynical about society and his social obligations," yet eager "to be included in the parties of New York's exclusive social set, such as the Davisons, the Jock Whitneys and the Bob Lovetts." Mathey acknowledged that Forrestal set a work pace—rarely leaving the office before 9 p.m.—that he and others could not, or would not, match, and he accepted it with good grace when Forrestal was made a partner in the firm in 1923, well ahead of Mathey, who was three years older. At times, however, he found the younger man "hard to take," for Forrestal seemed both to embrace and to disdain the whole Wall Street process and the values by which its practitioners lived. Striving for wealth with unambiguous zeal, he was at the same time slightly contemptuous of it. Desiring the best things and the glamour of possessing them, he was nevertheless more socially detached than socially competitive. He could be "surprisingly rude" to people who mattered and at the same time "extremely kind" to underlings and casual acquaintances. [21]

Possessed of a first-rate mind and keen social-political antennae, Forrestal was at this stage a young man feeling his way through strange new territory. Brashly determined to be rich, to overcome his social limitations, to "fit in," he was equally determined to do so on his own terms. The dichotomy produced a complex and rather split personality, and the split continued throughout his life, although it was camouflaged by successive layers of experience.

With Edward Shea, Artemus Gates, and John H. Vincent, Forrestal shared apartments first at 660 Madison Avenue and later at 32 Washington Square West, and the group became known in social circles as the Four Horsemen. Shea, the affable younger colleague from Princeton (class of 1916) who had been with Forrestal in naval flight training, was reestablishing himself at the Tide Water Oil Company, of which he would become president in 1931. "Di" Gates was a darkly handsome man from Cedar Rapids, Iowa, who had captained the Yale football team in 1917 and flown in the war as a naval aviator. He worked for the Liberty National Bank, which in 1921 was merged with New York Trust. He would soon marry the boss's daughter, Alice Davison, whose father, Henry P. Davison, was president of New York Trust, a partner of J. P. Morgan, and a fixture in New York and Long Island society. Johnnie Vincent was a charming product of Hotchkiss, Yale, and Harvard Law School who was settling into law practice with the firm of Lord, Day and Lord, also after service in the war. Both Gates and Vincent would later be associated with Forrestal in the navy during World War II.[22]

Despite his killing pace at the office, Forrestal's boundless energy and resilience enabled him to keep up with the intense social life which the Four Horsemen generated or abetted, and through his roommates he met a number of beautiful, socially prominent young women, including Priscilla and Phyllis Baldwin, the twin daughters of Joseph Clark Baldwin, a rich Coolidge Republican who ran the United Dyewood Corporation. Weekend parties at the Baldwin homes in Oyster Bay and Bedford included debutantes, diplomats, and even royalty.[23] Vincent was regarded as the "real" intellectual among the Four Horsemen, but Forrestal was generally considered the most attractive—"He always seemed to know a little bit about everything."[24] A large part of his charm lay in the perception that he was "different" and in his spirited wearing of the difference like a defiant banner which at once proclaimed his lack of pretension and his demand to be accepted for what he was. Initially perhaps he came to this posture out of an innate honesty and shyness, but he quickly realized it was also an effective social gambit.

Confronting the mores of the high and the rich, he adopted an air of amused, slightly sardonic detachment, as though he were a social scientist from afar clinically observing an esoteric subspecies of Man, but he carried it off with such confidence and goodwill that most were charmed rather than offended. Meanwhile, he was rapidly adopting as his own their manner of dress and speech, their way of handling headwaiters, their clubs, their cultural preferences, their recreations, and their aura of superior privilege conferred by nature. He began having his suits made at Anderson and Sheppard in London, bought his shoes from Peale and his shirts from Beal and Inman. He affected a dark green double-breasted smoking jacket. There was no doubting his instinct for elegance and the well-born. "Jim liked to be seen,'' Robert Lovett remembered, ''at the opera, at the right parties, and especially in the company of good-looking girls.''[25]

The posture of debonair detachment subtly armored him against intrusion and made him a person of a certain mystery, beyond easy reach. And combined with the fact that he was recognized as a rising star on Wall Street—the ferocious worker, the serious student of finance, the acute judge of markets, the rich young man who was getting richer—these attributes made him intrinsically attractive to many, who were impelled to ponder and pursue him, to know him better, even when he consistently stretched or evaded the rules of ordinary social protocol.

He developed, or discovered, during this period one of his distinctive characteristics: an abhorrence to committing his person, definitely, absolutely—to a dinner date, a theater date, a peripheral business meeting, or anything which risked his ''getting stuck'' in a situation that might prove uncongenial to his preferences of the moment. He became notorious for failing to appear at dinner parties to which he had formally accepted invitations, yet his bad manners seemed only to enhance his standing with injured hostesses, who were grateful if he actually showed up for their *next* party. In this there was some calculation, but elusiveness was an intrinsic trait. He was aware of it and said quite frankly to patient, forbearing friends that he had to be free to do whatever seemed desirable or necessary at the moment.[26]

LOVE AND MONEY

IF THESE "exceptional" and "different" qualities often brought him admiration from men, they made him especially attractive to women. He was handsome, charming when he chose to be, and imbued with a lean and vibrant animality. Aware of his effect and something of an actor, while remaining outwardly reserved and shy, he worked in discreet and fastidious ways to fashion for himself a private life of disciplined indiscipline, which soon included brief or extended affairs with a number of bright and attractive women. They longed to break through his armor, to find and confront the inner man who so beguiled them; none, it appears, ever did, for while seeming to promise much, he gave far less of himself than they had expected. He was instinctively resistant to any genuine surrendering of self, as though he understood that his essential strength lay in a tight singleness he must always protect. This inability to commit himself deeply to any person—man, woman, or child—reflected a fundamental need to be independent and self-reliant, to build for himself a sort of majestic singularity that would enable him to escape the entangling compromises and humbling fetters that bind ordinary men and ordinary lives. Perhaps it was also part of a continuing effort to escape his dominating mother. In the context of modern society, it was a quest doomed to fall short in the best of circumstances, but Forrestal, as it turned out, also lacked the necessary psychological resources—the inner toughness and supreme self-confidence—to sustain the kind of splendid, impervious aloneness he unendingly sought.

In the 1920s, however, and in the context of a young man's transitory love affairs, this truth was not yet apparent, which left his women, not with a sense of future tragedy, but with recollections mingling fondness with frustration and admiration with disappointment. Encounters with attractive women on his own terms became a habit which continued after he was married and throughout his life. In 1933, when he was forty-one, a woman who had known him for several years put the question bluntly: "Don't you love any of these women? Don't you *care* for them at all?" He replied that he was "always fond of people he knew well, and hoped they would remember him with some affection." He spoke, the woman recalled, "with the emotional detachment of an old man counting his trophies."[27]

In 1923, the year Forrestal became a partner in William A. Read, the four Washington Square bachelors decided to get out of town for the summer, in part to stay in touch with a number of their young banking and business friends who had married and moved to Long Island. Notable among these was Robert A. Lovett, Yale class of 1918 and a naval aviator with many combat hours in the war. As Naval Pilot Number 66, he had been one of the first sent overseas, where, attached to the British Royal Air Service, he flew Handley-Page bombers against German targets at Zeebrugge, Bruges, and Ostend and later became a serious student and advocate of air power.[28] In 1940 his private analysis of Hitler's Luftwaffe and of the American industrial effort required to meet the threat so impressed Secretary of War Stimson (to whom the report was given by navy Under Secretary Forrestal) that he summoned Lovett to become his Assistant Secretary of War for Air. A man of clear, civilized intelligence with "a great feeling for human situations in which the mind is put to work,"[29] Lovett was sure in action, wise in counsel; at the same time he was one of the funniest men of his generation, "full of brief sophisticated witticisms, rueful humors, and a perception of incongruity that expanded in bureaucratic circumstances where such perceptions ordinarily wither away."[30] After World War II, he served with distinction as Under Secretary of State and Secretary of Defense, in the Truman administration, although he was a Republican, and later became a valued adviser to Presidents Kennedy and Johnson. In 1923, he was making a start in the banking business and had just married Adele Brown, youngest daughter of James Brown, the senior partner of Brown Brothers and Company (which later became Brown Brothers, Harriman).[31]

The small house the Four Horsemen rented in Locust Valley became their weekend base for golf, tennis, swimming, watching polo matches that featured players like Tommy Hitchcock and Averell Harriman, drinking cocktails, and pursuing women. Their regular Sunday luncheon, preceded by drinks on the veranda, became a social centerpiece for the younger set. Although their tastes in women varied widely, the roommates adopted during part of that first summer the curious tactic of focusing on one girl at a time and courting her in sequence. As Adele Lovett remembered it, this meant that if the lady in question was dancing with one of the Four Horsemen, she knew the other three would soon cut in in a predetermined pattern.[32] Vincent and Forrestal were regarded as especially elegant and graceful dancers who often took their young women for tea dancing at the Plaza during the week. One of them recalled of Forrestal: "You knew when he took the first step with you that it was going to be just fine—he was rhythmic and graceful and in control."[33]

While he was without question one of the more eligible bachelors about town, Forrestal gave his friends the strongest impression that marriage was an institution he was determined to avoid, for he was convinced that most men ruined their business careers by marrying too young. The typical wife, he opined, was a demanding yet utterly dependent creature who could only be a burden to an ambitious man. Children were another form of impediment he was not prepared to accommodate. If he ever did consider marriage, he said, the woman would have to be a truly independent spirit and there would have to be an understanding about a family.[34]

JOSEPHINE OGDEN

H IS FRIENDS were thus genuinely surprised and mystified when he married Josephine Ogden on October 13, 1926, at the Municipal Building in Manhattan in the presence of no family on either side and no friends.[35] He was thirty-four and a conspicuous success on Wall Street. She was a bold and creamy beauty of twenty-six. The previous afternoon he had left a cryptic note in the office for Dean Mathey which read: "Dean—I am committing the mistake called matrimony. Name of unfortunate victim, Ogden. Will be back Monday. Tried to see you to advise, but you were out. J.V.F."[36]

It took a while for friends and colleagues to unravel the mystery of Josephine Ogden. Her family had come from Fairmont, West Virginia, and was part of a large clan, originally of yeoman farmers, who had arrived in America from Bradley Plains in England in the 1640s. Her father, Howard Newton Ogden, had been a scholar and teacher and later a public official. One uncle, Herschel, garnered a comfortable fortune by building and managing a chain of newspapers throughout the state; another uncle, William, became a notorious town drunk. Howard Ogden left his faculty post as head of the English Department at West Virginia University to start a night law school in Chicago. It was there that he married Olive Margery Mayers and that his four children (three daughters and one son) were born. Josephine (called "Jo"), born in 1900, was the youngest. Shortly thereafter the family returned to Fairmont, where Howard became chairman of the State Public Service Commission. Jo grew up there in relative rural affluence, gaining a flair for color and clothes from her mother, who was an expert seamstress, and a love for horses and dogs from her father, who was devoted to the outdoor life of riding and hunting. She rode ponies from childhood, became an expert horsewoman at an early age, and was later (as Mrs. James Forrestal) a flamboyant figure in the Meadowbrook Hunt on Long Island and the Rombout Hunt in Dutchess County. When she was thirteen, her father was struck down by a fatal heart attack at the age of fifty.[37]

Facing financial stringency, Mrs. Ogden moved back to Chicago and put Jo and Dana, the two younger children still at home, in public school. A naturally dramatic and rebellious spirit who had been pampered by her father and did not get on well with her mother, especially in the new circumstances, Jo was soon conspiring with the maid to organize parties that featured kissing games like "spin the bottle." Immediately after graduating from high school, and in open defiance of her mother, she eloped with a young man from Louisiana named Adam Tonquin Stovall, who promised to take her around the world on their honeymoon. Things started off well, but in Singapore they ran out of money and she discovered that Stovall's only resources were those he acquired by playing poker and rolling dice. With considerable fortitude and resolution, she abandoned the ne'er-do-well bridegroom and made her way home to get a divorce and enter the University of Chicago.[38]

Johnnie Vincent, whose father was a dean at that university, met Jo Ogden there in 1919 (seven years before she married Forrestal) on a visit home from Harvard Law School and shortly before he entered law practice in New York. She was a bright and beautiful nineteen-year-old coed with the added dimension of a divorced woman, and Vincent was immediately taken by her striking good looks and vitality. As Jo's mother had by then arranged for her to finish college at Smith, Vincent invited her to pay a visit to New York on her way to Massachusetts. She never made it to Smith. A few evenings of theater and nightclubs with the charming, erudite Vincent, and she abandoned the idea of college in favor of a handsome new man and a career in the big city.[39]

With Vincent's help she became a chorus girl in the Ziegfeld Follies— for about two years. Then she met Frank Crowninshield, the editor of *Vogue,* at a Ziegfeld Halloween party, and he hired her for a position on the magazine's staff. By that time, Josephine Ogden was a tall, slender, stylish woman with lustrous dark hair. Diana Vreeland, later the editor of *Vogue,* noted her "magnetic dark eyes,"[40] and Adele Lovett described her "distinctively chiseled" features.[41] John Dos Passos, in his novel *The Great Days,* in which both Forrestal and Josephine emerge only slightly disguised, described her as "stunning" and possessing "the tall Gainsborough look of a titled Englishwoman."[42] She possessed also a distinctly Southern manner, but not the one associated with magnolia blossoms and gentle deference. She was irreverent, witty, given to inelegant speech, a stimulating but also an abrasive person. It was well known that several young women on the *Vogue* staff were there because they had met Crowninshield at parties, but beyond her physical beauty Jo Ogden impressed the publisher with her sharp, practical intelligence and her flair for fashion. The *Vogue* staff in New York was quite small—rarely more than six editors and subeditors during the 1920s—and it was a talented group.[43]

The Condé Nast magazines—especially *Vogue, Vanity Fair,* and *House & Garden*—were setting the standards of taste and fashion for an American upper class which had emerged from the war in a frivolous mood and in a period of reckless prosperity. *Vogue* became synonymous with extravagant elegance and the sophisticated insouciance of the times.[44] After only a brief apprenticeship, Jo had her own monthly column, "Seen in the Shops," which kept readers abreast of the latest styles and trends as they emerged in New York, Paris, and London. The women who subscribed to *Vogue* also wanted to know how to wear the new flapper clothes, and her column offered fashion advice for every conceivable occasion: dining out, gala balls, a trip to the American South, the Army-Navy game, golf outings, the Easter Parade, or watching a polo match. She instructed the younger set on the wearing of proper riding attire, pajamas, and evening clothes. She also wrote the captions for the magazine's photographs and illustrations. Her chic, metallic prose soon earned her a certain recognition in the New York fashion world.[45] Meanwhile, she moved in those fast-paced circles of transient celebrity where the fashion world intersected with the emergent café society, frequented speakeasies like Jack and Charlie's "21," the Stork Club, and El Morocco, or went to the Dover Club to see a new comedian named Jimmy Durante. She was a beautiful, flamboyant, somewhat strident young woman, and always a fashion plate. At elaborate parties thrown at Condé Nast's apartment at 1040 Park Avenue, she met and became an acquaintance of people like George Gershwin, Edward Steichen, P. G. Wodehouse, Robert Benchley, and John O'Hara.[46]

Forrestal undoubtedly met Jo Ogden through John Vincent shortly after she arrived in New York, but it was not until 1925—about five years later— that they seem to have met again, or to have become aware of each other, when both were in Paris on business. Their affair—by reliable reports a passionate one—began after a cocktail party on the Left Bank and continued clandestinely over the next year in Paris, New York, and London or on shipboard en route to one or another of those places. Vincent became aware of it and gracefully bowed out to marry another woman; no doubt Shea and Gates also knew, but no one guessed that marriage was in the offing. Only Edward Fiske, who ran the Dillon, Read* office in Paris and had seen the lovers together there, thought the relationship looked serious, an opinion he expressed to Adele Lovett on a trip home in early

Josephine Forrestal, photographed by Cecil Beaton, ca. 1925

1926. When she asked Forrestal if there was any truth to this, he grinned and said "Might be," but refused to provide further enlightenment.[47]

There was endless speculation on what had brought them together, and why they married. The combustible elements of youth, beauty, brains, money, and budding fame were all there in abundance and are more than sufficient to explain the initial attraction. But what was it that made this a consequential relationship for both of them? As with most complex relationships, the full truth of this one is encased in interwoven strands of emotion, will, and accidents of chance that can never be satisfactorily unwrapped; at the time, even close friends could make only intelligent guesses. The lady's willful determination, combined with evidence that she was passionately in love, was probably the decisive factor, but in 1925 Jo's determination to marry may have been reinforced by a growing awareness that her career at *Vogue* was on a slippery slope. She was annoying her editor with an increasingly haughty "do-as-I-please" attitude, which suggested she now fancied herself one of the celebrities she was paid to write about. She was missing deadlines with unacceptable frequency.[48] Such behavior was an early manifestation of a basic trait: she didn't wear well. But there was no doubting that she was very much in love. "Jim Forrestal was the man I wanted," she told a journalist long afterward, and what she wanted she went after, without concealment or indirection.[49] She saw in him in 1925 and ever afterward "the exceptional man" and tried with her varied talents, and according to her own lights, to do those

*William A. Read and Company became Dillon, Read and Company in 1923. See Chapter 5.

things that would reinforce what she perceived to be his rightful claim to distinction. That she often failed in this endeavor, indeed became as the years passed an ever more visible embarrassment to his public position, was almost certainly the supreme tragedy of her life.

And what did Forrestal see in her, in 1925, beyond her youth and beauty? What qualities produced in him that rare combination of excitement, respect, and affinity that made her different from all the others? Or was it, as some surmised, that he had reached a stage in life where his position on Wall Street required that he settle down with an attractive, cultivated wife who would be the chatelaine of an elegant house, a charming hostess to his business colleagues and his friends? There is some weight to this rationale, but standing alone it does not suffice, for had that kind of marriage been Forrestal's objective, it seems more likely he would have settled on one of the several rich and socially prominent young women whom he had squired, pursued, or conquered over a number of years. Jo was well bred, but she had neither social standing in New York nor any money. It seems closer to the probable truth that the qualities which most attracted Forrestal were her fierce independence, her rebellious spirit, her unvarnished candor, and her intriguing combination of cynicism and ambition. In her he recognized a good deal of himself—a fellow outsider, a fellow rebel, a fellow climber. He also envied her extroverted exuberance—she was a creature of the Jazz Age who followed her own whims, did wild things—for while he shared some of the same impulses, he could only rarely break through the layers of his own intense reserve to give them expression.

AN OPEN MARRIAGE

SO THEY WERE MARRIED, but did Forrestal really want this kind of permanent commitment? His cynical note to Mathey—"Dean— I am committing the mistake called matrimony"—suggests he harbored doubts about the wisdom of the step, even as he was about to take it. And it strengthens the view that Jo's determined ardor and his own youthful passion overcame his more sober judgment of the matter. By agreement theirs was to be an "open marriage," with each free to move through society together or separately, as they chose—an escape clause that may have been the key point in the bargain. A friend, aware of Forrestal's instinctive need to be unfettered, said some years later, "I think he honestly felt that marriage would not change his life very much. Later, I think he was surprised to find himself married."[50]

At the beginning they even talked of retaining their separate apartments, but in fact Jo moved immediately into Forrestal's quarters at 32 Washington Square.[51] This experiment in open marital living (bold though not unique in the Roaring Twenties) reflected the fierce independence of both parties and a shared youthful ignorance of the emotional and psychological dangers that lay hidden in it. Forrestal did not conceal this peculiar condition of his marriage or his reputation for continued, unimpeded success with other women. Adele Lovett said of him during this period and later: "He was just plain promiscuous."[52] Whether Jo also had affairs in the early years of the marriage is not known, but she had always lived her life as a free spirit. Their friends were variously dubious, amused, and envious; very few were shocked—it would have been "stuffy" to be shocked, and other couples were entering into similar arrangements. In the main, it was the married men who were envious and their wives who were dubious, the wives believing that the Forrestals' arrangement set a dangerous example for their own husbands. A typical female recollection was that "the men envied Jim—they thought he had it made."[53] He did in a sense, but there is no evidence that his affairs, in this period or later, brought him any sustaining comfort or emotional growth. They seemed separate and apart from his "real" life on Wall Street and later in government.

Relaxed and confident in the late 1920s

At the same time, what was superficially workable for him was much less so for Jo. Although she kept to the bargain she had presumably entered upon with enthusiasm, it became for her a progressively impossible situation. Always taut and rather strident, she grew more so as the years of youth fell away and her taste for café society, the theater, fabrics, decor, and flower arrangements proved unfulfilling. Moreover, because Forrestal's life was more and more consumed by the demands and excitements of his ascending career on Wall Street, Jo was, like most other wives of ambitious businessmen, then and now, on her own for long stretches of time. Unfortunately, she found little satisfaction in the traditional roles of wife and mother. Having given up her career at *Vogue,* she became, as her niece later put it, "unfocused"; her creative energies flowed into a series of relatively trivial ventures, like jewelry design and the fabrication and sale of silk flowers. Most were abortive, some mildly disastrous; none satisfied her soul.[54] She began to drink.

On the testimony of close friends, however, the Forrestals were very much in love during the first year or so of their marriage. Diana Vreeland,

for one, who dined with them frequently, remarked to her husband that
"Jo is the secret side of Jim's life. He is crazy about her."[55] She was a
lovely young woman, a charming, witty companion, quick in riposte, and
with a special flair for entertaining. And she brought her own friends and
acquaintances into Forrestal's life—an eclectic group of actors, writers,
fashion people, and other assorted bohemians, including Roland Young,
John O'Hara, and Eddie Cantor. They represented a striking contrast to
the run of generally staid bankers, lawyers, and stockbrokers with whom
Forrestal spent his working days.

Michael Forrestal later said, "Ma was the more interesting of the two.
Compared to her, Dad was just a boring, successful banker. He called her
his window on the world. He knew she could connect with people, ideas,
and experiences which, left on his own, he would have missed."[56] It seems
closer to the truth that Forrestal enjoyed the novelty of these often flamboyant people, but in rather small doses, and the novelty soon wore off,
just as the novelty and charm of being married wore off. As time passed,
and far more from preference than necessity, he would stay home with
Dillon, Read work in the evening, while Jo went off to "21" with the
journalist John McLain or various other ornaments of café society. In general, however, their first year or so together seemed happy and richly varied
with no hint of the tragedies to come.

The decidedly unstaid banker Robert Lovett and his beautiful wife,
Adele, became important people in their lives about this time. The two
men had met in 1922, worked on banking deals together, admired each
other's breadth and incisiveness, and soon become fast friends. Lovett
cleared the way for Forrestal at the Racquet & Tennis Club in town and at
Piping Rock on Long Island. Adele became his friend as well, and when
he married Jo the Lovetts took her also under their confident wing.[57] Ellen
Barry thought "Bob Lovett was something of a Beau Ideal" for Forrestal.
There is no doubt that the Lovetts became the Forrestals' principal spon-
sors and mentors in New York society. After Michael Forrestal was born
on November 26, 1927, it was the Lovetts who persuaded them to move
to Long Island.[58]

★ ★ ★

CHAPTER 5

Getting Rich
on Wall Street

A N INVESTMENT BANKER, Forrestal wrote to Ernest Havemann in
1947, is "essentially a merchant" who offers the credit of nations,
states, municipalities, or private companies to "the possessor of
savings." Investment banks provide "a channel" through which savings—
whether held in banks, insurance companies, or private hands—are provided to "those enterprises, public or private, needing capital."[1] Success
in this profession, Forrestal told Havemann, demanded a composite of
imagination, ability to persuade, attention to detail, rigorous follow-up,
and the capacity to work with other people. In the same letter, he observed
that, while Calvin Coolidge was ridiculed for asserting that the "chief
business of the United States is business," the former President's remark was merely "a self-evident fact" about life in capitalist America.[2]
In political philosophy, he had come a long way from the "radical socialist" tendencies noted at Princeton and in the navy during World
War I.

As NOTED in Chapter 4, it was not until January 1920, more than a year
after the Armistice, that Forrestal gained release from active duty in the
navy and returned to his old job as bond salesman. His return in the first
year of the Roaring Twenties coincided with dramatic, far-reaching changes
in nearly every aspect of American life. These were, in the main, changes
that offered extraordinary economic opportunities for those who were favorably positioned.

As a consequence of the war, the United States now held the preeminent
economic position in the world, and American business thus stood on the
threshold of greater growth and larger profits than ever before—through a
combination of (1) expanded markets, both domestic and foreign, (2) a

great increase in electric power generation and its use in new mass-production manufacturing, (3) the reorganization and consolidation of major industries on a national scale, and (4) the introduction of innovative management and selling techniques. The decade of the 1920s also ushered in the beginning of mass consumer marketing, made possible by the revolutionary concept of buying on the installment plan and sustained by more extensive, more aggressive, more sophisticated advertising.[3]

There were equally dramatic changes in the nation's financial markets. Before the war, common stocks were generally considered speculative risks because stock prices fluctuated widely and dividend payments were inherently uncertain. Serious investors preferred to deal in high-grade bonds which yielded a regular 4 percent return and rarely lost any of their intrinsic value. But a new philosophy of corporate financing emerged during the war, borrowed in part from the experience and practice of the utility companies. In essence, this involved retaining the lion's share of corporate "earned surplus" for reinvestment in new equipment and future expansion while at the same time paying out a small but reliable dividend to the common stockholders. This new approach enhanced the attractiveness of common stocks for both large and small investors and soon led to a growing fascination with "playing the market," a pastime which during this go-go decade became as much a part of the crazed social tapestry of America as saxophones, flapperism, bootleg whiskey, and Babe Ruth. It was a pastime that fueled an acceleration of corporate expansion and profits for nine exhilarating years, until the money markets unraveled in an orgy of speculation and ended in the Great Crash of October 29, 1929, just two months before the end of the decade.[4]

Passive administrations in Washington, under Warren Harding, Calvin Coolidge, and Herbert Hoover, friendly to business, hostile to the earlier progressivism of Theodore Roosevelt and Woodrow Wilson, were determined to return the country to an imagined Victorian utopia and give business easy money and a free rein, unfettered by government regulation or intervention. Supported by what appeared to be a popular mandate, successive Republican administrations also rejected the idea that America's new power and influence required it to shoulder international responsibilities—in its own interest—to assure the recovery and stability of the precarious postwar world. Continuity of this hands-off policy was assured by the extended presence of Andrew Mellon, who served as Treasury Secretary under all three Republican Presidents (it was later said that "three presidents served under him").[5] The head of a powerful Pittsburgh clan and one of the richest men in the world, Mellon proclaimed that "government is just a business" and proceeded to run it on that basis. Throughout the decade, he fought off all efforts to increase public works or public services, starved the Interior and Agriculture departments, held down appropriations for the army, and cut naval shipbuilding programs. At the same time, he increased the budget of the Commerce Department, under its Secretary, Herbert Hoover, and arranged tax rebates for the very rich, whose continued well-being he considered vital to the national prosperity. At the end of the decade the 60,000 richest families in America had a net worth equal to that of 25 million families at the bottom of the pyramid.[6]

The Roaring Twenties were thus a time of turning inward and backward, and of withdrawal from government action at home and abroad. They were also a time of new and lofty status for American business and of extraordinary opportunity for ambitious men on Wall Street.

CLARENCE DILLON

FORRESTAL'S RETURN to Wall Street also coincided with dramatic changes at William A. Read, all centering around the remarkable figure of Clarence Dillon.

The only son of a comfortably affluent Jewish clothing merchant named Samuel Lapowski, Clarence Dillon was born in San Antonio, Texas, in 1882. When he was fifteen, his parents sent him to Worcester Academy in Massachusetts and thence to Harvard. He was tall, with a long oval face and dark complexion, a quick, bright young man with easy manners, but self-possessed and reserved. He knew his own mind and kept his own counsel. At Harvard he never worked very hard or stood very high academically, but became known for "his positive genius" as a poker player, and it was there he acquired the nickname "Baron" because "Clarence" didn't seem to fit a fellow "who would sit up most of the night in a no-limit poker game, without benefit of tobacco or beer," winning more than his share of "the stiffest stakes in the Yard."[7] Clearly he had a flair for calculating the odds. The name Lapowski kept him out of the more prestigious social clubs, and he smarted from the snub, but while he was still an undergraduate his father changed the family name to Dillon (which was his wife's maiden name). The Baron took pride in his Harvard education and stayed active in university affairs throughout his life. When the field house burned

Clarence Dillon

down during the winter of 1930, Dillon—in a show of support for both his alma mater and his son Douglas, who was varsity football manager—donated a new gymnasium, which was called Dillon Field House.[8]

After college, his classmate Armin Schlesinger persuaded him to work for the Milwaukee Coke and Gas Company, which was controlled by the Schlesinger family, and it was there, two years later, that he met with a bizarre accident which led to romance, marriage, and access to the capital which later established him on Wall Street. In the summer of 1907, he was a weekend guest at the country place of a prominent family named Douglass, whose daughter he was courting. Early Monday morning, as Dillon stood on the platform of the suburban station waiting for the local train to take him back to Milwaukee, a large Newfoundland dog walked out on the tracks. An express train thundered through, struck the dog, and hurled the animal's heavy, lifeless body against Dillon, who fell to the ground unconscious. He was taken back to the Douglass home, where his life hung in the balance for several days, but Anne McEldin Douglass nursed him lovingly back to health. They were married within a few months and went abroad on a honeymoon that lasted two years. Living the dilettante life in Paris, Dillon studied architecture and dabbled in painting, but apparently never considered either as a possible career.[9]

Returning to Milwaukee, he joined his brother-in-law, George Douglass, in founding the Milwaukee Machine Tool Company. By 1912, they had a prosperous business and sold it for a handsome capital gain. About the same time, one of his wife's rich relatives died and Dillon went to New York to handle the settlement of the estate with a prominent attorney there named George W. Wickersham. The New Yorker, much impressed by Dillon's personality, promptly introduced him to William A. Read as "the brightest young man I have met in a long time." Read also took a fancy to Dillon, and it developed that Dillon's Harvard roommate, William A. Phillips, was one of Read's promising younger partners. The result was that Dillon was persuaded to try his hand at investment banking. He in turn persuaded Read that Chicago was a large, untapped market for securities, and when Read sent him there to test his acumen, he quickly proved his point. Called back to New York, he was made a partner of the firm on April 1, 1916, at the age of thirty-four. By a strange coincidence, William Read was stricken the same day with a fatal illness and carried to his home, where he died within a week.[10]

Dillon had financial genius in his fingertips, and his unusual ability and maturity made him a natural leader as the firm struggled to compensate for the loss of its principal partner. He was informed, incisive, and possessed of a manner that suggested the absolute self-assurance of a superbly agile mind and that half concealed the inherently cold, ruthless core of the man. Major financiers on Wall Street like Jacob H. Schiff (Kuhn, Loeb) and Henry P. Davison (J. P. Morgan and Company) found him "capable and level-headed."[11] The famous speculator Bernard Baruch thought him "one of the keenest minds on Wall Street," and the seniors in his own firm began to lean on him for advice and guidance. When Baruch became chairman of the War Industries Board in 1917, he invited Dillon to go with him as personal assistant and troubleshooter.[12]

Two years in wartime Washington gave him a worldwide perspective on economic and political conditions and greatly enriched his contacts. Prominent financiers and businessmen calling on Baruch were initially received by his assistant, whom they found impressive—a courteous, self-contained young man who seemed to know a great deal without saying much. A seasoned financier when he returned to the firm in early 1919, Dillon was asked by his partners to become their chief executive officer. Three years later, after he had successfully organized a $100 million syndicate to underwrite a steel venture which became the Youngstown Steel and Tube Company, he executed a bold coup, forcing his partners to give him a controlling interest in the firm and to change its name to Dillon, Read and Company.[13] From that point on, the firm became the creature and projection of one man. Cool and confident, daring but thorough, Clarence Dillon never allowed a social or philosophical bias to affect his pragmatic business judgments. His desk was a clean table with a single telephone, in an office whose bareness was relieved only by a globe of the world standing in a window recess. "There is no pomp about the man," *The New Yorker* said in its 1928 profile, but there was an unmistakable aura of authority.[14] Paul Nitze, a young Dillon, Read employee who later carved out his own distinguished career in government, remembered him as "elegant in dress, distinguished in appearance and manner," but domineering and something of a martinet.[15] "Hell on people," columnist Eliot Janeway remembered, a man who treated his partners like glorified employees, to be rewarded or dispensed with at his sole discretion.[16] He alone determined their individual percentage interest in the profits from year to year and compensated them with relative parsimony. After he gained control of the firm, and until he retired from active management in the early 1930s, he pocketed from 60 to 70 percent of the annual profits. No other partner received more than 10 percent, and most lived in much lower brackets.[17] Despite these facts, Dillon was, after his retirement, committed to the myth that in his active years the firm had been a chummy family of equals.

FORRESTAL'S INTELLIGENCE, thoroughness, and single-minded competitive drive brought him quickly to Dillon's attention, for these traits meshed well with the older man's style of management. Bond salesmen were paid eight dollars a week plus a $350 drawing account (which represented an advance against earnings), and they earned commissions up to one point—or ten dollars—on the sale of each $1,000 bond.[18] Forrestal's persuasive salesmanship was soon selling so many bond issues that he was chosen to succeed William A. Phillips as sales manager and was made a partner of the firm in January 1923, shortly after Dillon engineered his takeover.[19] Arthur Krock claimed in 1947 that the Baron had promoted the thirty-one-year-old Forrestal "because it was cheaper to make him a partner than to pay his commissions."[20] But Ferdinand Eberstadt's son, Frederick, remembered his father's remark that, of all his young salesmen, Forrestal was regarded by Dillon as "the one with the dedication and the chutzpa to make it big."[21] There is also some indication that Dillon's regard for Forrestal included genuine affection, some evidence that the cold and brilliant banker perceived in the hungry young boy from Beacon a kindred, or at least a complementary, spirit.

Understandably, Dillon became a role model for Forrestal, who, as sales manager, sought to emulate a number of his mentor's traits, especially Dillon's posture of clear, hard, rational mastery of each situation based on total information. Like Dillon, he spoke with precision, in well-crafted sentences, drank sparingly, took regular exercise to stay in physical shape, and began to read serious biography and history. Like Dillon, he affected a pipe, puffing quietly away at the morning meeting of his sales staff while he gave them their instructions and exhorted them with a no-nonsense pep talk. He was "all business; laconic speech; no light touch," Paul Nitze remembered, but even in his directness, "he cultivated an air of mysteriousness."[22] Although Forrestal developed a style of rather intimidating brusqueness, he was less naturally tough and autocratic than Dillon—far more willing, for example, to delegate responsibility and more generous in sharing credit with his subordinates for a job well done.[23] At the end of each long day, usually after everyone else had left the office, he would dictate a memorandum summing up the debits and credits of the day's performance and laying out the schedule for the next day. During the 1920s, Forrestal was instrumental in building a competent "syndicate operation" which put at his disposal 752 salesmen employed by affiliated brokerage firms throughout the country. This placed Dillon, Read in a position to compete successfully with J. P. Morgan; Kuhn, Loeb; Goldman Sachs; and other major investment banking houses on the largest underwritings.[24]

The House of Morgan and the Kuhn, Loeb firm were the twin pillars of Wall Street eminence at the end of World War I. The first, led by "Jack" Morgan, son of the founder, was a distinguished collection of Yankee traders gone highbrow: "like a rare breed of dog or horse, they shared a certain aura . . . [and] were trying to invent an American aristocracy—themselves."[25] The second, dominated by the elegant Otto Kahn (who was Ferdinand Eberstadt's first cousin), was an equally distinguished group of German Jews, almost all of them related to each other by blood or marriage and noted for their "high-toned and exclusive character" and their enthusiastic patronage of the opera and the ballet.[26] By comparison, Dillon, Read was a collection of new men, ambitious arrivistes led by a buccaneer of exceptional ability who was determined to push his firm into the very front ranks of Wall Street. Forrestal's organization and management of a large, well-trained sales staff was a major instrument of the Baron's strategy, enabling him to carry off several spectacular deals that soon presented themselves.

THE GOODYEAR DEAL

IN NOVEMBER 1920, the Goodyear Tire and Rubber Company, the largest manufacturer of tires in America, based in Akron, Ohio, and supplying 50 percent of all original tire equipment for automobiles, was on the edge of bankruptcy. In the immediate postwar boom, the automobile industry had experienced unprecedented expansion, and this had stimulated comparable growth in the steel, rubber, glass, and leather industries, which supplied the major automobile components. Goodyear sales had grown to $200 million in 1919, and orders on hand suggested to its confident management that $300 million was a not unreasonable goal for 1920. Then, suddenly, the country was in a severe recession, automobile sales ground to a halt, and the tire business collapsed. Inadequately capitalized from its inception in 1898, Goodyear was suddenly besieged by rubber brokers, fabric mills, machinery manufacturers, and other creditors demanding their money. But there was not enough money. To make matters worse, the company had never developed solid connections with sources of large capital in New York, a fact reflecting the founders' Midwestern suspicion of Wall Street. When negotiations were finally undertaken with the Guaranty Trust Company to work out a $30 million refinancing plan, Goodyear's president, Frank Seiberling, refused the proposed terms as too onerous.[27]

With bankruptcy and receivership impending, a New York lawyer, Paul D. Cravath, acting for Goodyear, called together a conference of creditors and bank representatives to underline the gravity of the situation. Several banks agreed to help if someone would take a clear lead, but the cost of a rescue operation had now risen to $90 million. At that point, Cravath turned to Clarence Dillon. After reflecting on the problem overnight, Dillon agreed to underwrite $30 million in twenty-year Goodyear bonds to provide needed working capital, provided that others would be responsible for selling $27.5 million in convertible debenture bonds to pay off existing bank loans, and provided further that Goodyear would issue another $33 million in "prior preferred" stock to pay off the merchandise creditors, with an 8 percent dividend payable until each creditor received 125 percent of his claim. In a bleak financial climate that precluded direct bank borrowing on the needed scale, Dillon's strategy was to raise the money by selling to the public a range of Goodyear securities, but the terms for the buyers had to be exceptionally attractive to ensure success.[28]

In addition, Dillon required that 10,000 shares of "management stock" be issued to three trustees representing the bondholders, the debenture bondholders, and the merchandise creditors. The trustees (of whom Dillon was one) would effectively control the company through their power to vote the "management stock." They would name a majority to the board of directors and select executives for the two top management positions. Control would continue until the twenty-year bonds were paid off.[29]

At the time, the Goodyear financing was the largest and perhaps the most complicated corporate rescue operation ever undertaken. Forrestal and his efficient sales staff quickly sold the $30 million bond issue, mainly to wealthy individuals and a few institutions who were persuaded to "get in on a good thing." Dillon installed a young Milwaukee lawyer, Edward G. Wilmer, as president of Goodyear, and Wilmer wisely chose to retain the men responsible for the company's excellent performance in manufacturing and sales. Within eighteen months, operations were profitable, and by 1925 the sales volume was back to $200 million and profits approached $20 million. Investors in the new bonds and preferred stock thus prospered. The deal established Dillon, Read as a banking house of the first rank and the Baron, who was approaching his fortieth birthday, as the new wizard of Wall Street.[30]

There was, of course, an underside to the affair. The onerous obligations of the refinancing, which had to be met before any dividends could be paid to regular shareholders, kept Goodyear poor despite good earnings. This in turn produced intense resentment among the original shareholders in Akron and throughout Ohio. By 1926, Goodyear had paid out some $28 million in scheduled retirements of bonds, debentures, and prior preferred stock and $26 million in interest charges. Several stockholder suits were in the courts attacking the refinancing plan as exorbitant and unfair. In the same year, Frank Seiberling, Goodyear's former president, filed suit against Dillon, Read for loan charges of a "usurious nature." The most serious claim was that Dillon, Read, in undertaking to hire the two top managers, had charged Goodyear a fee of $500,000, but had then paid the two executives salaries of only $30,000 apiece. The banking firm, it was charged, had skimmed off the rest. The real issue, however, was control of the company. Seiberling and the Ohio stockholders wanted to break the power of the trustees and restore control of Goodyear's destiny to its original owners. The suit was filed in Cleveland, where Forrestal had established an office to facilitate the sale of Goodyear bonds. Dillon, Read's first response was to frustrate the suit by closing the Cleveland office and withdrawing from business in Ohio. The matter was pursued in New York. Ferdinand Eberstadt, then a partner in the law firm of Cotton and Franklin, handled the litigation for Dillon, Read.[31]

During the trial in New York, Forrestal, called as a witness for the defense, argued that the tough conditions attached to the Goodyear reorganization plan in 1921 had been required by the company's precarious financial situation and the general economic recession in the country; both conditions, he said, made the effort to sell new Goodyear securities a highly hazardous undertaking. "It was necessary to attach some unusual features, like high call rates and high interest rates, if the issues were to attract the investment public."[32] He expressed the opinion that Dillon, Read had made money on the deal primarily because it had been willing to take major risks when no other financial house was prepared to do so. Now that Goodyear was restored to profitability, he said, Seiberling preferred to believe he had been taken advantage of.[33] Forrestal's arguments were cogent, but the need for a public defense of the deal's morality made him uncomfortable. The *New York Times* reported that he "seemed nervous in his answers and squirmed uneasily during the questioning, sipping cup after cup of water."[34] This was perhaps the first evidence of what was to become a pattern of intensely emotional reaction to any criticism that seemed an adverse reflection on his standards of right and wrong or on his personal integrity. He was thin-skinned about criticism of this kind. More than that, an ability to see both sides of the issue, wedded to some want of inner certainty, seemed to grant at least partial credence to the opposing arguments, even when the facts fully supported his own position. This trait was to become a source of both rare strength and grave weakness in later years.

Finally on May 12, 1927, a settlement was reached, involving the substitution of longer-term bonds and debentures for the 1921 securities together with the issuance of additional "prior preferred" stock in place of a cash payout. In exchange for these concessions, the creditors terminated the trustee arrangement and Goodyear regained control of its operations.[35]

THE DODGE BROTHERS DEAL

THE DARING and profitable operation to rescue Goodyear had startled and impressed Wall Street in 1921, but an even more spectacular triumph was in the making. In the spring of 1925, by purchasing, apparently with frictionless ease, the fabled Dodge Brothers Automobile Company for $146 million in cash, the firm established itself as the equal of any investment house on Wall Street. The new success revealed once more Clarence Dillon's fertile imagination and cold, calculated daring—and the remarkable efficiency of the sales force headed by Forrestal. But consolidation of the triumph was in fact a near thing, saved from embarrassing failure only by a clever eleventh-hour ploy carried off by Forrestal and Eberstadt.

The Dodge Brothers, Horace and John, had conducted a manufacturing business in Detroit since the turn of the century. Their first major contracts were to make automobile parts for Henry Ford, in payment for which they took stock in the Ford Motor Company (and sold it back to Ford for $25 million in 1919). By 1914 they began manufacturing their own Dodge automobiles and soon built an extensive network of profitable franchise dealerships. Then, on a trip to New York City to attend an automobile show, they stayed at the Ritz-Carlton and sent a bellboy out for a bottle of bootleg whiskey, Prohibition being then in force. Within a year they were both dead of wood alcohol poisoning. This was 1920. Their two widows inherited control of the business and continued to monitor its operations over the next five years, all of which were profitable. But the automobile industry was undergoing rapid change, becoming more competitive and more volatile, and the widows began to feel that the burdens of running the giant enterprise were too great to bear.[36]

When Charles Schwartz, a partner in the Wall Street firm of Bache and Company, heard they might be interested in selling the company, he chartered a locomotive and private railroad car and made the fastest trip then recorded from New York to Detroit; there he persuaded the widows to give him an option to purchase their business. Back in New York, Schwartz went to Bernard Baruch for advice, and Baruch told him without hesitation to "go to my friend Clarence Dillon." So Schwartz took his option to Dillon, who agreed to pay him a 10 percent finder's fee on the eventual purchase price if Dillon, Read was chosen as the firm to handle the Dodge sale.[37] When it became known that Dillon, Read was negotiating with the widows, the firm of J. P. Morgan bluntly told the Baron he should step aside, as it wished to buy the Dodge Company for its own client, General Motors. Such an intervention today would be a clear violation of antitrust regulations, but in 1925 it was the normal butting practice of Wall Street billy goats, as well as an expression of Morgan's intimidating preeminence. The Morgan intervention presented Dillon with a serious problem: He was not going to yield; at the same time, he understood that some accommodation would be greatly preferable to a hostile confrontation. Moreover, he could not hope to consummate the deal if the Morgan firm offered the widows a higher price than that at which Dillon, Read could be sure of selling new Dodge securities (determining the optimum price for public offerings is the critical factor in every investment banking deal). Dillon resolved the problem by obtaining the Morgan firm's agreement to a competitive bidding procedure.[38]

The Dodge Company valued itself at $90 million, and the Morgans were confident that a bid somewhat above that figure would win the day. Meanwhile, however, Clarence Dillon was organizing a buying syndicate ready to pledge $150 to $200 million to buy "a company" (the Baron would not identify Dodge) and then to participate in offering its new securities to the public. When the final bids were opened, Dillon, Read had offered $146 million—or $56 million above the company's tangible asset value. It has been suggested that Schwartz, who had won the confidence of the widows, was privy to inside information and thus maneuvered to be sure Dillon, Read got the deal. But the Dillon, Read offer was substantially above the Morgan bid because it was based on a wholly new theory of corporate valuation. Dillon, Read counted the extra $56 million as corporate "goodwill," and for the first time in Wall Street history a new issue of securities was priced on the basis of the company's "future earning power" rather than on its assets. Forrestal, now recognized in the firm as the resident expert on pricing an issue, played a major role.[39]

Accomplished in the gestures of self-promotion (possibly learned from Baruch), Dillon met with the press to tell them he had signed a single check to the widows for $146 million and to announce cheerfully that Edward G. Wilmer, whom he had in 1921 installed as president of troubled Goodyear, would become the new president of Dodge. His desk was clean, he was relaxed and polite, and he appeared to be spending his morning browsing in a small volume of classical Greek plays. The ease with which he seemed to direct such great undertakings deeply impressed the financial press, and they soon surrounded him with a "sacerdotal aura" which was never dissipated during his lifetime.[40] Many of his rivals had considered the Goodyear rescue a lucky accident; few of them were prepared after the Dodge deal to deny that he was a financial genius.

The deal was announced on April 1, 1925. Within ten days, the "syndicate operation," under Forrestal's direction, was finding eager buyers for the Dodge bonds, preferred stock, and the Class A common. Total sales of the new securities came to $160 million, which meant that Dillon, Read not only recovered its cost, but also turned a profit of $14 million. In addition, the firm maintained full control of the Dodge Company by retaining ownership of all of the Class B common, the only shares that carried voting rights; this was the equivalent of the "management stock" device employed in the Goodyear deal.[41]

The Dodge deal was the largest cash transaction in American industrial experience, and it deeply stirred Wall Street. Many applauded Dillon, Read's unprecedented success, but the old-line houses resented the Baron and his colleagues as unbecomingly aggressive and flamboyant. The House of Morgan was vocally annoyed at having been outfoxed, and the belittling extended to Forrestal, who seemed to embody precisely the same upstart qualities they deplored in the Baron. Forrestal was a particular target because it was known that he was fast becoming Dillon's closest and most valued associate. For a brief moment after the Dodge deal consummation, rumors on Wall Street suggested that the old-line firms, led by Morgan, were conspiring to give Dillon, Read its comeuppance, but the dramatic size and nature of the deal itself and Clarence Dillon's astute handling of the public relations put both him and his firm beyond the reach of even their most powerful detractors.[42]

A footnote to this success reflects Clarence Dillon's approach to negotiations. After the deal was done, he met with Charles Schwartz, who had brought him the opportunity and was entitled to a finder's fee of 10 percent, or nearly $15 million. Dillon opened the conversation by saying he thought 10 percent on "such a very large transaction" was more than Schwartz really deserved. When Schwartz replied, "Clarence, you and I have a written agreement on that," Dillon looked at him: "I know we had a memorandum agreement, but I'm talking reality and this is real money." Whereupon Schwartz took the memorandum out of his pocket, tore it up, threw it at Dillon's feet, and said, "Clarence, if that is what your word means, then this is what I think of your written contract." Whereupon Dillon said, "You'll get your money."[43]

Another footnote to the Dodge deal: A few days after its consummation, a young man arrived at Henry Forrestal's house in Beacon, New York, where he presented the keys to a shiny new Dodge sedan that was parked on the street. It was a brotherly gift from Forrestal, complete with Henry's initials painted in gold letters on the front doors.[44]

OVER THE NEXT three years, Dillon, Read discovered that responsibility for corporate operations is generally less glamorous and more difficult than the execution of a financial coup. The automobile industry experienced a downturn in 1926, which persisted for more than two years. Dodge common stock dropped in value, as did the bonds and the preferred, and there was general pessimism about the future of the company. But the Baron and his partners then had a stroke of good luck. Eberstadt, who had by now moved from his law firm to become a partner in Dillon, Read in 1926, vividly recalled the day of redemption: "One day in 1928, God appeared to us in the guise of Walter P. Chrysler, and he offered to buy the Dodge Company."[45]

Chrysler had been operating head of the Buick division of General Motors. When the Maxwell Motor Car Company failed and went into receivership in 1925, the company's investment banker, Kuhn, Loeb, recruited him to take over the operation, but with expanded production facilities and a new name. Chrysler needed the respected and popular Dodge cars, their dealer organization, and their assembly plants to give his new company the strength to compete with Ford and General Motors. Dillon, Read was eager to negotiate the sale of Dodge, but Walter Chrysler wanted to acquire more than the Class B voting shares, although they would have given him unquestioned control. He insisted that at least 90 percent of all outstanding issues—preferred, Class A, and Class B common—be exchanged for equal shares of stock in the new Chrysler Corporation. Although he never explained his reason for imposing this condition, it was apparent that he wanted to avoid a replay of the costly, protracted lawsuits against Dillon, Read by disgruntled Goodyear shareholders which had muddied the waters for several years. Chrysler wanted a decisive vote of confidence in his new corporation by Dodge stockholders before he would make the purchase.[46]

The Class B common stock presented no problem—Dillon, Read owned all of it—but persuading the preferred and Class A shareholders to exchange 90 percent of their Dodge shares for equal Chrysler shares proved to be a major challenge. The stock was widely held, with many shares in the names of children whose fathers or grandfathers had purchased it for long-term retention. Chrysler's original offer to buy Dodge was good only for thirty days—the month of June 1928—and despite herculean efforts, Forrestal and his sales force had arranged for deposits of only 86 percent of the preferred and 76 percent of the Class A common by June 23. The deadline was extended three times by mutual consent, but Walter Chrysler finally insisted that his condition be met by July 30 or the deal was off. Two days before the final deadline, the firm had 88.5 percent of the preferred stock (short by 10,000 shares) and 86 percent of the Class A common (short by 80,000 shares).[47]

With time running out and the Baron's reputation on the line, Forrestal and Eberstadt devised a daring plan to save the deal. They proposed that Dillon, Read go into the open market with an offer to buy the required remainder of Dodge stock at an attractive premium above the current market price. This would cost the firm about $5 million. Then, to hedge their position, they proposed simultaneously to sell the same number of Dodge shares, which they would obtain by secretly borrowing the needed shares that were held in "street name" accounts by firms friendly to Dillon, Read. They executed this cunning double maneuver with efficiency and dash and met Walter Chrysler's condition within the July 30 deadline. Wall Street was astounded and impressed. Dillon, Read's total profits over three years on the purchase, management, and resale of the Dodge Company were reckoned at $40 million, and Forrestal and Eberstadt became the new "Golden Boys" of Wall Street.[48] But the Baron, who did not enjoy sharing either glory or profits with subordinates, was predictably restrained in thanking and rewarding his two brilliant young men. "They saved Dillon's ass," Eliot Janeway said many years later, "but got little thanks for it."[49]

FORRESTAL AND EBERSTADT

AFTER PRINCETON, Ferdinand Eberstadt had gone on to Columbia Law School and then to military service on the Mexican border with the fashionable New York cavalry unit called Squadron A, while Forrestal was finishing Princeton and learning to fly for the navy. Their paths crossed again, in the early 1920s, and their mutual respect and warm friendship grew steadily from that point onward. Eberstadt became without question Forrestal's closest associate, adviser, and confidant during the Wall Street years, during World War II when both men were in government, and in the stormy postwar period when Forrestal remained a high official and Eberstadt had returned to private life. Their friendship was an attraction of opposites. Eberstadt was brilliant and powerfully assertive, with an impulse to act quickly and accept large risks. Forrestal was equally brilliant but more intuitive, as well as more cautious and reserved, slower to decide and hesitant to risk his basic position. Together they shared a passion for confronting large issues, public and private, and a superior gift for synthesis.[50]

Eberstadt's father, like Forrestal's, was a European immigrant, but from Germany, a man who developed a prosperous import-export business in New York City. His mother, who had studied to be a concert pianist and had left the Catholic Church, was Venezuelan, but with some German blood. "My grandfather was a Jew," Eberstadt's son, Frederick, told an interviewer in 1987.[51] But Eberstadt himself made the ecclesiastical migration into the "WASP Ascendancy," which Joseph Alsop defined as that inner group of White Anglo-Saxon Protestants who "enjoyed substantially more leverage than other Americans," and until quite recently "supplied the role-models followed by other Americans, whether WASP or non-WASP, who were on their way up in the world."[52] Eberstadt became a solid Episcopalian and married Mary Van Arsdale Tongue, a proper Baltimore girl of the same religious persuasion.

In business, he was the embodiment of dynamic force and ambition. An exceedingly agile mind combined superb logic with a persuasive intensity that often swept away all counterarguments, but he was temperamental and frequently explosive. Edward F. Willett, who at different times worked for both Forrestal and Eberstadt, recalled that Eberstadt "was always firing people and then hiring them back the next day."[53] Totally convinced of his own superior abilities, he was determined to make sure the world recognized their worth and paid for them in worldly coin. Most people found him fascinating, but many found him impossible to work with, for he was undeniably arrogant and disdainful. Eliot Janeway did not mince words: "A real nut-cutter," he called him.[54]

He made his first mark on Wall Street in the underwriting of foreign bonds, an opportunity created by the bitter, intertwined problems of British-French-Italian war debts and German reparations. During the war the United States lent $7 billion to its allies and added $4 billion in further loans and credits after the Armistice. This constituted a just debt, but the question of repayment was inextricably entangled in the British, French, and Italian demands for reparations from Germany—in the amount of $33 billion—which they had imposed under the terms of the Treaty of Versailles. While there was no legal link between the two obligations, the Allies took the position that they could not repay the United States unless they received a concurrent stream of German payments. But the Germans could not conceivably pay such a huge indemnity in cash (at the time, there was not that much money in the world), and it soon became apparent that a combination of French hatred and British–Italian–U.S. high tariffs would also prevent them from paying out the reparations by selling goods and services.[55]

The Coolidge administration was unwilling to cancel or reduce the Allied debt ("They hired the money, didn't they?" was the laconic President's stated position), but it was equally unwilling to use governmental influence to effect a rational compromise among the several parties. As a result, a myopic arrangement known as the Dawes Plan passed the problem to a consortium of private American banks headed by J. P. Morgan and Company, which was confident that a solution could be found in the sale of German bonds to American investors. From this notion evolved a strange triangular movement in which the American people provided money for the Germans to pay reparations to the British, French, and Italians so they in turn could repay their war debts to the United States government. The scheme rested entirely on the continued willingness of private American investors to buy German securities, and remarkably enough it worked for nearly five years. When, however, the stock market began to fall apart in early 1929, Americans quickly lost their taste for foreign securities. When the flow of American money was halted, all German reparations payments ceased, and so also did Allied payments on the war debt. The "supreme folly" of the Dawes Plan, in the view of one historian, was that "it kept Germany alive by artificial respiration" when it could have "breathed naturally" if the United States had used its great influence to insist upon a program of cooperative and reciprocal tariff reductions. In the end the Dawes Plan left American investors with bales of defaulted German bonds. The refusal to allow German goods to trade freely in international markets left the world with "the fury of economic panic breaking over Germany," followed by Adolf Hitler and a German policy of murderous revenge.[56]

Eberstadt could not be blamed for the folly of governments nor for exploiting the opportunity the situation presented to Wall Street bankers.

While still working as a lawyer, he was instrumental in lining up millions of dollars in such foreign business for Dillon, Read, and his particular success with the Germans so impressed the Baron that he offered him a partnership in 1926. As this meant an immediate tripling of Eberstadt's income, he promptly accepted, for, as his son said later, "He realized he was doing banker's work at lawyer's pay."[57] Dillon sent him back to Europe, where his forcefulness and brilliance soon dominated the firm's offices in Paris and Berlin. By early 1927 Dillon, Read had marketed German bonds in the amount of $160 million—exceeding the performances of both J. P. Morgan and National City Bank by a comfortable margin.[58]

In Germany, Eberstadt developed close connections with leading financiers and government figures, including Hjalmar Schacht, president of the central Reichsbank, and Gustav Stresemann, the ill-fated chancellor and later foreign minister, who was also the most gifted and genuinely democratic German politician of the period. According to Eberstadt's biographers, his close ties also extended to Stresemann's charming and elegant wife and to at least one leading actress of the Berlin stage. A kind of desperate gaiety dominated the cabaret nightlife in the "sin capital of Europe" during the 1920s, and the young, energetic Eberstadt was there for weeks at a time.[59]

After he made his first real money, Eberstadt's private life was increasingly devoted to Target Rock Farm, his thirty-acre estate on Long Island near Lloyd's Neck at the eastern edge of the "Gold Coast." After successive infusions of money, this eventually featured a twenty-five-room mansion, two guest cottages, tennis courts, swimming pools, horses, cows, chickens, and a dog for each of the four children. There in this "Wagnerian Valhalla," he played out the stereotypical role of German father, stern but loving, adoring his children, but ruling them with an iron hand.[60] He and his wife became professional gardeners who raised prize-winning roses and rhododendrons and took deep pleasure in the beauty of their woods and fields and lovely sea vistas. They exhorted their four children to love the outdoors and to work at being healthy and strong, and later insisted on gathering the grandchildren for Sunday dinners and long summer holidays. To Eberstadt, who personally drew a sharp distinction between his professional and private lives, this was all very *gemütlich,* and Target Rock Farm was a bastion of idyllic family warmth and solidarity. In fact, he carried the same personality traits into both realms, with the result that his children ended up with an overwhelming sense of patriarchal oppression. "He never wanted us to be individuals—just puppets, his creations and his to dominate," his oldest daughter said bitterly after his death. And one grandchild remarked that, despite Eberstadt's endless lectures on the family as a unified and loyal force, it "blew apart like a hand grenade" as soon as he was gone.[61]

* * *

EBERSTADT WAS BACK in New York in late 1927 in time to handle the Goodyear lawsuits and to play a decisive role, with Forrestal, in the dramatic resale of the Dodge Company to the new Chrysler Corporation. The admiration, trust, and affection between the two men continued to grow— "They were like brothers," Frederick Eberstadt recalled—and they saw each other constantly in New York, accepting the fact that social gatherings with their families were precluded because their wives heartily disliked each other. Frederick Eberstadt, who was frequently taken along to lunch and given carte blanche with the menu to keep him occupied while the two men talked business, saw in Forrestal a number of the same qualities which others remarked in his father: "a sort of modern day Zeus . . . an awesome presence . . . highly sophisticated, tense . . . capable of silent scorn."[62]

In the wake of the spectacular Dodge-Chrysler success, the Golden Boys of Wall Street began to talk privately about starting their own firm. Things were going very well, but they clearly understood the limits to their potential at Dillon, Read. The Baron held all the reins in a tight grip, and his imperious presence dominated the scene (Forrestal learned to handle his intimidating habit of asking a second question, and then a third before the first could be answered, by puffing slowly on his pipe and saying, "I'm thinking").[63] The Baron arbitrarily decided the allocation of profits and kept the lion's share for himself. If they were honest with themselves, the Golden Boys had to acknowledge that they were permanent lieutenants to a patron who demanded discreet subservience and rewarded them with money, but would never permit them to share in responsibility for the policies of the firm. As masters in their own house, they would throw off the habit of submission and set the policies; moreover, there would be vastly more millions to make. Together they had the prestige and the skill to make a great success of it. The economy had never been more buoyant.

Almost certainly, Eberstadt was the initiator and intense promoter of the breakaway scheme, while Forrestal listened closely, puffed on his pipe, and contributed his own thoughtful embellishments of the basic plan. The firm would be called Eberstadt and Forrestal and would include Robert Christie, Jr., the able treasurer of Dillon, Read, who was also Forrestal's Princeton classmate. Eberstadt would apply his conceptual imagination and assertiveness to get the deals; Forrestal would apply his mastery of financing techniques, his thoroughness, and his convincing salesmanship to merchandise them to the public. By early December 1928, there was agreement to move ahead; Eberstadt confidently leased office space for the new firm and declared to Forrestal, "The die is cast."[64] At the moment of decision, however, Forrestal developed second thoughts. He wondered whether they shouldn't "wait another year to see how things work out"[65] and gradually exposed a deep-seated reluctance to proceed. The idea of giving up his solid position at Dillon, Read for an uncertain venture on his own suddenly seemed an excessive risk; furthermore, he appeared uneasy at the prospect of a confrontation and break with Clarence Dillon. He was now worth $5 or $6 million; on reflection that seemed enough.

It was a revealing moment for both men. The aggressive, totally confident Eberstadt wanted independence and wealth on a far larger scale, and had no qualms about a sharp, even hostile break with the Baron. The more reserved, more cautious, more inwardly doubtful Forrestal showed that, contrary to his carefully cultivated image of tough loner, he was in fact a man more comfortable with—and dependent upon—the framework of a sheltering institution and the good opinion of his boss.

Eberstadt was undoubtedly disappointed and frustrated by Forrestal's eleventh-hour development of cold feet, but the incident did nothing to attenuate the friendship; indeed, it seemed to strengthen their sense of mutual respect and mutual need. During the later years in Washington, Forrestal acted upon the instinct that Eberstadt's incisive boldness was a compensating force he needed close at hand. Eberstadt recognized, in 1928, that without Forrestal his immediate hope for a successful new firm was beyond realization. And with the passing years he seemed to appreciate that Forrestal's natural caution and diplomacy, and his great thoroughness, were important counterweights to his own impetuous tendencies.[66]

However, Eberstadt's powerful impulse for more money and greater recognition was not diminished but only rechanneled by Forrestal's rejection. In what appears in retrospect a reckless gamble doomed to failure, he decided to demand that the Baron substantially increase his percentage interest in the firm and also change its name to Dillon, Read and Eberstadt. Shortly before Christmas, he began arriving at the office with conspicuous punctuality, attending to a range of business, but primarily hoping Clarence Dillon would call him in to discuss some matter that would give him an opening. But the Baron was otherwise occupied. Finally, after two weeks, Eberstadt hung up his hat and coat one morning, walked directly into Dillon's corner office, said good morning, and then began to recount all the deals he had done for the firm, the millions of dollars in German bond issues he had negotiated and brought to the firm for marketing in the United States and the millions of dollars in American bond issues he had successfully placed in Europe, especially with Jewish banks.[67] As Dean Mathey recalled, "He had it right down to the penny. He knew exactly how much money Dillon, Read had earned on every one of those deals."[68] At the end of the recital, he told Dillon he thought the record justified an increase in his share of the firm from 3 to 10 percent. Without blinking an eye, Dillon said simply, "You're fired."[69]

The Baron was probably sorry to lose a man of Eberstadt's ability, but to grant his demand would have required equal upward adjustments for two or three others, including Forrestal. An equity share of 3 percent was about standard for a small handful of "senior partners," excepting only William A. Phillips, who had been the Baron's Harvard roommate and was his close friend and second in command. Phillips, a bland, bespectacled personality who "had a way with bonds," owned 10 percent.[70] To raise Eberstadt, Forrestal, and Mathey to that level would have required a totally unacceptable reduction of Dillon's commanding equity position, and there was never the slightest possibility he would agree to it. Years later, Frederick Eberstadt reflected on the breakup: "My old man felt he wasn't getting his share of the gravy . . . he never underestimated his due . . . so he had a bust-up with Dillon . . . but I don't think he intended to quit."[71] The Baron's son, Douglas Dillon, later commented that because both men possessed "overpowering personalities," it was "inevitable that they would break up sooner or later."[72] Many years after the breakup, they did reestablish cordial though never intimate relations. A year after Pearl Harbor, when Eberstadt was laboring for the War Production Board, a letter from Dillon said, "If anyone deserves a good Christmas, it is you . . . I want you to know how deeply grateful we all are for the job you are doing."[73] And years later, in 1968, Eberstadt wrote, "Dear Baron: It is a long time since I have seen you, and I miss you and I hope you will give me a ring sometime when you are in town so that we can get together . . . I have nothing in mind except to 'confess and seek absolution.' As ever, Sincerely, Ferdinand Eberstadt."[74]

At the end of 1928, Eberstadt's share of the Dillon, Read partnership came to about $3 million, and he withdrew it about one-third in cash and two-thirds in securities held by the partnership. After a brief stint with Owen D. Young at the Second Reparations Conference in Paris, he joined the Otis Corporation, an investment banking operation formed by Cyrus Eaton of Cleveland. There he got his 10 percent ownership, but the company collapsed in the 1929 crash and he lost most of his money, though not his determined drive or sense of humor. Paul Nitze, then a Dillon, Read employee, went to see him on some business matter in 1930 and found himself walking through rows and rows of empty desks at the Otis Corporation, grim testimonials to a failed company. When Nitze finally located him at the far end of the deserted suite, Eberstadt said to him with gallows humor, "I have no problem that money won't cure."[75]

Ever self-assured in crisis, Eberstadt offered to stay on and reorganize Otis if he were given a 50 percent interest, but Cyrus Eaton declined the offer. In 1931, he established his own firm, F. Eberstadt and Company, "because no one would give me a job," as he was later fond of telling his friends.[76] It was started on a modest capital base of about $100,000 borrowed from Roland and Averell Harriman and included $5,000 borrowed from his wife, but in a few years Eberstadt's brilliance and determination had established a niche in the financing of smaller growth companies that were generally ignored by the largest banking houses. "I couldn't wait for Myron Taylor to bring me [an opportunity to handle an underwriting for] U.S. Steel," he told *Fortune* magazine in 1939, so he had no choice but to work "further down the corporate scale" with companies that earned "from $250,000 and up."[77] This cultivation of "little blue chips" proved successful and earned both the money and the reputation on which Eberstadt built a far larger success in the period after World War II. In the Fabulous Fifties, his Chemical Fund realized a profit of $112 million on an investment of $600 in the fledgling Xerox Corporation.[78] During this same period he developed a close working relationship with André Meyer of Lazard Frères, and together they pioneered many investment techniques, including the leveraged buyout, which for good or ill became conventional practices in Wall Street. When Eberstadt died in 1969, near the age of eighty, he left a personal estate of about $50 million.[79]

★ ★ ★

CHAPTER 6

Surviving the Crash of 1929

IN THE PERSPECTIVE of history the epic crash of 1929 is seen to have been caused less by a runaway stock market than by critical weaknesses in the institutional structure of finance capitalism.[1] By itself the Great Bull Market of the 1920s was not an unreasonable reflection of America's dramatic postwar economic growth, but the mechanisms for stability which had seemed adequate in 1914 proved unable to cope with the tremendous expansion in the volume and variety of financial transactions after the war. Especially were they unable to control the speculative frenzy fueled by the increasing availability of brokers' call loans, which permitted investors to purchase stocks on very small "margins"—i.e., largely with borrowed money. Using this kind of leverage (a term not widely used in the 1920s), investors could make fortunes with very little capital in a steadily rising market.

Brokers' loans, which were repayable on demand, became so popular and so profitable for lenders that by the mid-1920s they had attracted large amounts of money from corporations and even from conservative Wall Street investment banks. At the beginning of the decade, outstanding brokers' loans amounted to about $1 billion; by 1926 they stood at $2.5 billion, and by January 1929 they were over $6 billion.[2] Surrounded by an aura of seemingly endless prosperity, business leaders considered brokers' loans an easy, almost riskless way to increase their profits—certainly easier than actually manufacturing automobiles or radios. The loans earned high interest rates and could be liquidated on demand; moreover, as the borrowers used the loans to buy more stocks, the process served to enhance the value of the corporations making the loans. "Like royalty in a constitutional monarchy," as John Brooks wrote of this period, bankers and businessmen were paid handsomely for simply existing: "A plum tree had been grown, tended, and brought to fruit just for their shaking."[3] But what seemed the perfect investment was in fact illusory and dangerous. "Each market was feeding the other, with no new goods or services produced," creating only a fictitious "aura of wealth."[4]

By 1928 responsible people felt that stock prices were dangerously inflated and that the operation of the market was getting out of hand. In March of that year, the fledgling Federal Reserve Bank of New York, led by the dedicated Benjamin Strong, moved to dampen speculation by raising the discount rate from 3½ to 5 percent and also to dry up the money supply by selling $300 million in bonds to member banks. This maneuver failed, however, to stem the tide, for the major sources of brokers' loans had now moved beyond the control of the Federal Reserve.[5] In addition, the authority of the Federal Reserve System was frontally challenged by several powers in the private banking community, who resented it as an irksome, intrusive holdover from the Wilson presidency. Charles E. Mitchell, head of the National City Bank, an incurable optimist who had put his bank deeply into brokers' loans and into speculative stock purchases for his own account, promptly picked up the gauntlet thrown down by the young and untried Federal Reserve. If and when the Federal Reserve attempted to curb lending, Mitchell declared, he would advance $25 million to brokers and traders.[6] A Princeton economist applauded Mitchell's riposte and attacked the Federal Reserve for having "undertaken a punitive excursion against the stock market"; furthermore, he proposed open revolt: It was time, he said, for the New York banks to declare their independence of "an outmoded institution forced upon the business community by antique reformers."[7] By this time even J. P. Morgan and Company, the vaunted cornerstone of Wall Street responsibility, was in the business of making brokers' loans. So the speculative frenzy continued to gather momentum.

The final failure was governmental. In his State of the Union message of December 4, 1928, President Coolidge assured his listeners that "no Congress ever assembled . . . has met with a more pleasing prospect than that which appears at the present time. . . . Regard the present with satisfaction and anticipate the future with optimism."[8]

DILLON'S FORESIGHT

PAUL NITZE, the son of an English professor at Amherst College, graduated from Harvard in 1927 and took a job as an accountant in a box factory in Bridgeport, Connecticut. After a year or so, he moved on to a position with Bacon, Whipple, a small Chicago investment firm eager to obtain a share of the market for German securities which had been so profitable for Wall Street in the mid-twenties. In fact, the bloom was already off the German rose, but lacking current information, the Chicago firm proposed to send Nitze, then twenty-three years old, to explore the situation and render a report. Nitze, who knew no one in Germany, turned to his Harvard classmate Frederick Ames for help, and Ames's mother gave him a letter of introduction to Clarence Dillon. The Baron met with Nitze, gave him letters to several German bankers and industrialists, and asked to receive a copy of Nitze's report after his return.[9]

Although Wall Street in early 1929 was still moderately bullish on the German economy, Nitze found German stock and bond prices seriously inflated and prospects for industrial earnings and profits quite poor. He was made uneasy by the speculative fever in Berlin and by a growing political turmoil which threatened extreme solutions to festering social and economic problems that were rooted in Germany's enforced exclusion from normal international trade. This was three years before Hitler came to power. Returning to Chicago through New York, the young Nitze called on Dillon, who invited him to spend the weekend at Dunwalke, his 1,000-acre estate near Far Hills, New Jersey (on whose grounds he had erected statues of his two heroes, David and Napoleon).[10] This was September 1929, and uncertainty about the American economy was in the air. There had been a small break in the stock market in March, and prices had oscillated throughout the summer without recovering the stability that stockbrokers and analysts had come to expect from a decade of "permanent prosperity." Still, only a few people seemed seriously worried. Paul Warburg of Kuhn, Loeb warned that unless "the orgy of unrestrained speculation" was halted, a crash was inevitable and would be followed by "a general depression involving the entire country." But optimists accused him of "sandbagging American prosperity," and the man in the street gave his primary attention to the new "talking pictures" and the forthcoming World Series, in which the Philadelphia Athletics were pitted against the Chicago Cubs. But September was the month in which the stock market began to show signs of serious trouble.[11]

Riding through the New Jersey countryside in Dillon's chauffeur-driven Rolls-Royce, Nitze asked what importance the older man attached to the market break in March and the more recent evidence of weakness. Did it presage a recession? The Baron said no, he did not foresee a recession, but "something far more significant—the end of an era." With clarity and detachment he then proceeded to discourse on the character and life cycle of "eras" in history. Some periods were dominated by military leaders, others by fervent religious figures, still others by charismatic political personalities or men of business. "I have observed," he said, "that when the men of money, the bankers and merchants, dominate affairs, the eras tend to be relatively short. Since the Civil War the men of Wall Street have had more influence in shaping our national affairs than any other group. I myself have more influence, when I choose to exercise it, than do all but the most powerful politicians. But I have a profound feeling that a dramatic change is now in the making. When it comes, it will end Wall Street's domination."[12]

Gravely impressed, Nitze asked how Dillon planned to meet the new circumstances. Dillon told him, "I have already acted." Just two days before, he had ordered wholesale reductions in the Dillon, Read staff, from a total of nearly seven hundred down to fewer than one hundred, including termination of the entire retail sales operation. "Because I acted now, they can all find other jobs," Dillon said. "If I had waited six months, they would face unemployment."[13] By such foresight and cold action, the Baron braced his firm to meet the definitive stock market crash that would come six weeks later and to weather the long debilitating years of the Great Depression that followed.

ANATOMY OF THE CRASH

THE STOCK MARKET declined sharply from October 14 through October 19, but the drop did not cause a panic. Some thought it was precisely the adjustment needed to "shake out the lunatic fringe." Thousands of eager investors, it was said, had been waiting for just such a break in the market so they could buy in at more reasonable prices. Stock prices firmed up on the twenty-first and twenty-second, but plunged severely on the twenty-third, causing paper losses of more than $4 billion.[14] Wall Street was now extremely nervous, but no leaders stepped forward to rally the market. The Federal Reserve had been neutralized by Charles Mitchell and his ilk, and President Herbert Hoover in Washington and Governor Franklin Roosevelt in Albany disavowed the legal right to intervene. Prices opened lower on October 24 and fell further as an avalanche of selling orders overwhelmed the machinery of the stock market. "Quaking fear knocked the props from under the dizzying structure of credit," and by the end of the day $9 billion in paper values had been wiped out.[15]

At this point a worried group of leading bankers—including Mitchell of National City, Albert Wiggin of Chase, Seward Prosser of Bankers Trust, William Potter of Guaranty Trust, George Baker of First National—convened at the Morgan office at 23 Wall Street, under the de facto leadership of Thomas Lamont, the leading Morgan partner. Some, like Mitchell, now feared their institutions might go under if the decline were not halted. A pool of some $20 to $30 million was raised to bolster the price of key stocks, and Richard Whitney, vice president of the Stock Exchange and closely linked to Morgan (his brother George was a Morgan partner), was designated as agent for the group. He rushed to the floor of the Exchange and went to the U.S. Steel trading post, where, in a loud, clear voice, he bid for ten thousand shares of U.S Steel at two points above the last sale. He moved on to other posts, shouting similar orders as he went, and it became apparent to all those around him that a ''bull pool'' organized by Morgan was operating in a determined effort to stop the panic. Thunderous cheers rose from the floor, and the market once more rallied. President Hoover and the *Wall Street Journal* each made reassuring statements, and one major investment trust ran large ads in many newspapers bearing the single word ''S-T-E-A-D-Y.''[16]

This was a Thursday. Stocks rose on Friday, but declined slightly on Saturday morning. The opening hours of trading on Monday, October 28, destroyed most of the remaining surface optimism. Prices fell steadily, and thousands of margin calls—demands for immediate repayment of brokers' loans—were scheduled for the next morning. The end came on Black Tuesday, October 29, in a flood of sell orders, margin calls, and dumping. Sixteen million shares were traded, and $30 billion of paper value vanished. ''Haggard men stood dazed before clogged tickers and watched their golden dreams dissolve in the sizzling acid of panic. Great sections of the market fell like turrets of an iceberg into an engulfing sea.''[17] There was no further effort by the Wall Street Establishment to cushion the fall or arrest the panic—in all probability the situation had passed beyond even their power to save. According to one cynical account, however, its members had no further interest in a salvage operation. On October 24 they had intervened to rally the market, primarily to buy time for a double operation: With one hand they held up stock prices with fair bids for key securities; with the other they slowly sold off large blocks of stock in their possession. Having stabilized their own positions after four days of trading, ''they stepped aside on October 29 and let the market plunge to perdition.''[18]

OWING to Clarence Dillon's foresight and decisive action, and to the collective sagacity of the partners, Forrestal and his colleagues survived with their capital essentially intact. Indeed, Forrestal paid $300,000 in taxes in 1929 and would have paid an additional $95,000 if he had not arranged, by creating a private Canadian company, to shelter income of $896,000 on a tax-free basis.[19]

There was a cumulative slowdown in financial activity after the crash, brought on by a traumatic loss of confidence in the stock market and its practitioners, but the leaders of the Stock Exchange remained blind to the need for reform measures to curb glaring abuses, and no pressure for it came from Washington. Still, few expected a severe depression, and indeed the worst might have been avoided had not President Hoover been gripped by a dismal political paralysis, especially between November 1929 and April 1930.[20] Insisting that the stock market crash had been a passing phenomenon unrelated to the basic strength of American business, Hoover pursued a strictly hands-off policy toward both the economy and the financial markets while managing to ignore the steady shrinkage of confidence, credit, and employment. His public statements, designed to be reassuring—"there is nothing in the situation to be disturbed about"; "the crisis will be over in 60 days"; "the business of the country is back to normal"— were greeted at first with derisive laughter, then later with bitter rage by millions who were suffering the torment of joblessness, homelessness, and hunger.[21]

It was permissible within Hoover's economic philosophy to "prime the pump" with certain types of government expenditures, and he initiated several large-scale public works projects like the Hoover Dam, confident that their trickle-down effect would restore vitality to the economy. But his actions came too late, and he underestimated the depth of the malaise. Moreover, his administration did nothing to compensate for the swift evaporation of private American bank loans to Europe or of the American market for German securities.[22] As a result of this, the largest Austrian bank, Kredit-Anstalt, failed in 1930 and triggered a chain of bank failures throughout Europe which soon made it impossible for Germany to continue reparations payments. The Depression thus deepened and spread, in Europe and America, making way for the dictators Hitler and Mussolini, in Germany and Italy, and creating volatile social unrest everywhere.

By the middle of 1930, Dillon, Read, having made a judgment that both government and corporate bonds would be very difficult to sell, was turning down deals. A year later, anticipating political upheaval in Germany, the firm closed its office in Berlin. Nevertheless, despite the Baron's prediction that an era had ended, most of the partners expected an early upturn, for they saw the 1929 crash as an analogue to the recession of 1921. That economic shock had been severe, but the rebound had been strong and sustained.

★ ★ ★

CHAPTER 7

Family Life

ON FEBRUARY 2, 1929, the Forrestals bought a thirty-acre estate in Old Westbury which featured a comfortable manor house built in 1820 and known as The Old Brick.[1] It was a move that brought them onto the Gold Coast along the North Shore of Long Island, an exclusive colony of great wealth and privilege gracefully distributed through the loosely adjoining communities of Great Neck, Sands Point, Sea Cliff, Glen Cove, Locust Valley, Old Westbury, Huntington, Oyster Bay, Cold Spring Harbor, and Lloyd's Neck. Mansions of regal dignity were set upon expansive, meticulously maintained green acreage dotted with stables and enclosed swimming pools, enclosed tennis courts, polo fields, and yacht basins, all framed by magnificent trees and protected by stone walls and closed iron gates. Some of the inhabitants were the heirs of America's legendary rich—J. P. Morgan, Andrew Mellon, Cornelius Vanderbilt Whitney, F. W. Woolworth. More were successful, socially prominent Wall Street bankers, lawyers, and businessmen who counted their millions in single digits.[2]

THE LONG ISLAND SET, as it came to be known, lived generally by graceful codes of protocol and maintained an air of decency and dignity even when its behavior fell from grace, as happened with increasing frequency during Prohibition and the Roaring Twenties. Liquor stills were set up in the basements of estates, and the lavish parties got wilder with each passing year. The North Shore was the setting for F. Scott Fitzgerald's novel *The Great Gatsby*, "that slender riotous island . . . where gay young women were surrounded by men in tuxedos, and there were eddies of conversation and splashes of laughter, and corks popped and liquor flowed, and you knew it was a time that would never come again."[3]

On nearby Peacock Point the Henry P. Davisons lived in a splendid Georgian mansion and also provided handsome, well-staffed houses on the estate for their son, Trubee, and for their daughters and sons-in-law, Alice and Di Gates and Frances and Ward Cheney. The Robert Lovetts kept an apartment in town, but spent the summer months in a comfortable gardener's cottage on a large estate in Locust Valley.[4] Another summer couple on the North Shore in the 1930s were Stuart and Evie Symington. She was the daughter of a United States senator from upstate New York, James W. Wadsworth, who in 1941 (as a Republican member of the House of Representatives) would cast the decisive vote to extend the compulsory military draft act and thus avoid dismantlement of the United States Army, just three months before Pearl Harbor. The Wadsworth family was noted for its musical talent, and Evie was its star, good enough for regular bookings as a "society chanteuse" at elegant Manhattan night spots like the Sert Room of the Waldorf-Astoria. Stuart Symington was an aggressive, not-quite-successful young businessman from Baltimore and a graduate of Yale (class of 1923). He and Forrestal became golfing companions and social friends, and in 1938 Forrestal used his broad contacts to help the younger man become president of Emerson Electric Company in St. Louis, where he made his fortune manufacturing power-driven gun turrets for bombers during the war. Later, when Forrestal was Secretary of Defense and Symington was Secretary of the Air Force, the latter's all-out advocacy of air power supremacy would clash directly with Forrestal's efforts to achieve a military establishment of "balanced forces." The relationship would turn bitterly antagonistic.[5]

Although initially reluctant to leave New York, Jo Forrestal found her new house a "Victorian delight", and plunged into its renovation with her distinctive enthusiasm and flair. She bought marble mantelpieces, removed wraparound porches, and decorated the house in warm colors. Michael remembered extensive use of blue, "deeper than the blue of the sky." Blue silk draperies with gold trim and black tassels were a feature of the living room, the largest space in the house, and "wherever possible" there was wallpaper.[6] The house was a personal challenge, an opportunity to express her own sense of style. "Jo was creative," Diana Vreeland said. "She knew how to make a house interesting."[7]

There was, of course, a necessary domestic staff, and Jo did most of the hiring. A Mr. and Mrs. Duffy served as cook and gardener; Stanley Campbell, a retired actor/dancer from the London vaudeville with a rich cockney accent, was the butler and Forrestal's valet; slender and distinguished in appearance, he would often perform a few dance steps in the kitchen. The chauffeur, Patrick O'Toole, whisked his master from Old Westbury to Wall Street in the morning and back again at the end of the day in a Rolls-Royce. There was a nanny for Michael and later for Peter. Jo also kept a lady's maid, which was rare even on the North Shore, but she was very particular about her clothes, anxious that they be pressed, stitched, and handled with utmost care.[8]

Mainly through the Lovetts, the Forrestals were soon in the social swim, invited to elaborate lawn parties built around polo matches and tennis tournaments, to intimate dinners, debutante parties under pink tents, and endless cocktail parties. Forrestal treated the new social situation with characteristic detachment, while relishing its high style and pace, its comforts and its privileges. He arrived late for dinner parties or not at all, traveled extensively, and arranged regular weekend golf with Lovett, Gates, Symington, and others at Piping Rock or the Creek Club.[9] He found the scene agreeable and, because he refused it a full commitment, did not feel bound by it. Jo, who was left alone to establish the family roots in the community, was made aware of assured social graces she had only partially assimilated, and discovered that her personality did not always sit well with the local gentry. Bob and Adele Lovett were warm, supportive friends, as were Di and Alice Gates, but even with them Jo had a sense of imitating and competing—a realization that made her defensive and acerbic, but more determined than ever to be accepted on an equal footing. Adele was a special friend who laughed away Jo's sardonic verbal jabs and occasionally eccentric behavior. "She used to criticize my shoes," Adele remembered with a smile years later, "called them cloddish. But money wasn't a consideration for Jo, while in those days my allowance was limited. I told her I supposed she was right. She was an attractively natural woman who said and did exactly as she pleased."[10]

A reaction more typical of the community came from Mrs. William Lord, whose sister Marie was Mrs. Cornelius Vanderbilt Whitney (and later Mrs. Averell Harriman) and whose house was "just around the corner" from the Forrestal estate. Frances Lord found Jo "smart as a whip," but "pushy and rather brazen." In Forrestal's frequent absences, Jo would often invite herself over to the Lords' for a drink or dinner "or just show up."[11] She was adept at getting herself to a great many parties alone, invited or uninvited; Bob Lovett said, "You never knew when she was going to turn up."[12] She worked her way into the Meadowbrook Hunt and rode regularly through the expansive acreage of the North Shore in pursuit of the fox—a striking figure in black habit and long skirt, with a black veil drawn tightly across her face, riding sidesaddle. She was an expert rider of dash and courage, but Mrs. Lord remembered that the group nevertheless "continued more or less to snub her."[13]

The Ferdinand Eberstadts lived in nearby Lloyd's Neck, but the families rarely saw each other socially, for there was no common ground between the wives. Mary Eberstadt, a graduate of Bryn Mawr devoted to home and garden, disdained Jo's penchant for café society, her furs, jewelry, and designer clothes. Jo thought Mary a bore and a prude. Their husbands accepted a fact they could not alter.[14]

Forrestal was the more readily accepted by his new neighbors, though they found him, beneath a controlled cordiality, unremittingly serious and hard to know. At weekend picnics or cocktail parties, where he frequently carried a book under his arm, he might display a detached and sardonic humor, as though commenting on the scene from outside it, but he was rarely light-hearted or casual. His views were heard with respect, but they were mainly on heavy subjects, like the state of the economy or the political situation in Germany.[15] His friend Dan Caulkins thought him "good-natured and amusing, but not a natural conversationalist. He probed relentlessly, always wanting the facts, and rarely asked for opinions. When he did, he wasn't really interested in the answer. His standard response was a terse 'You're goddamned right,' which he used so often that it became a sort of joke among his close friends."[16] It was Eliot Janeway's observation that Forrestal never gained a sense of belonging anyplace and that he was on the North Shore of Long Island "in his own no-man's-land . . . the non-Jewish equivalent of the wandering Jew."[17]

Josephine Forrestal as a member of the Meadowbrook Hunt

Lovett was responsible for introducing Forrestal to his Yale classmate, the playwright Philip Barry, with whom he had renewed a friendship in Boston after the war, when Lovett was a student at the Harvard Business School and Barry's first play, *A Punch for Judy*, was being performed at the 47 Workshop. Later in New York and Long Island, the Barrys brought Robert Sherwood, Robert Benchley, Dorothy Parker, and John O'Hara into the Lovetts' interesting and eclectic circle, which now also included the Forrestals. Forrestal and Barry became close friends—"They shared the Irish thing," Ellen Barry said,[18] by which she seemed to mean their common roots in lace-curtain Irish-Catholic gentility, though the Forrestals were, in fact, less "lace-curtain" than the Barrys.

Barry came from a middle-class family in Rochester, New York, but, unlike Forrestal, he married wealth. Ellen Semple grew up in a New York town house and an eighty-acre farm in Mount Kisco, the daughter of Lorenzo Semple, a partner in the international law firm of Coudert Brothers.

Her father's wedding presents to the young couple included a cottage on the farm and a house in Cannes, which they christened Villa Lorenzo. The playwright quickly discerned in Forrestal's complex intensity the same jesuitical qualities that had caused Forrestal's mother to mark him for the Church, called him "Jimmy the Priest," and thought him possessed of "a tortured Irish nature." In the 1929 crash, Forrestal showed his friendship by covering Barry's margin accounts with his own money until the market stabilized, a generous act which saved the Barrys from being wiped out.[19]

In top form on Wall Street, ca. 1930

Another who "shared the Irish thing" was the novelist John O'Hara, who became a Forrestal friend and frequent house guest and with whom the investment banker spent many weekend hours discussing Catholicism and its impact on the Irish in America. O'Hara's biographer, Matthew Bruccoli, wrote that "O'Hara delighted Forrestal," and the main character of O'Hara's searing novel *From the Terrace*—an ambitious young man of humble origins who is determined to be a major success on Wall Street whatever the cost—bears a striking resemblance to Forrestal.[20] Not all of the North Shore residents were "delighted" with O'Hara, and Mrs. Lord probably reflected the local consensus when she described him as "rude and drunk most of the time," and said that after several unpleasant encounters, she went out of her way to avoid sitting next to him at dinner.[21]

O'Hara stayed in touch with both Forrestals over the years, but developed a copious correspondence with Jo. Writing after the war from Hollywood where he was working on movie scripts "in the lair of the Metro lion," he observed "no startling metabolic changes" in himself as a result of his recent marriage and fatherhood. "The black Irish volatility of which you spoke is on call. . . . You must realize that my father, when he was 55, broke a man's jaw with a punch . . . [and] my paternal grandfather [a major in the Union cavalry] pinked his best friend with a saber in a drunken brawl . . . my brother was shot at in a crap game a few years ago. So you see, quality tells." In the same letter he took a swipe at certain members of the Long Island Set whom he perceived as having slighted him. "You know that one of my great disadvantages is that my pleasant side, less startling, less spectacular, is ignored by such press agents as [John] McClain, that arch friend who didn't even bother to send Belle a telegram when the baby was born. . . . [But] if a lead-pony of Joan Payson's dropped a colt, old McC would be at Cartier's buying a 14 kt. crupper. If I seem bitter, it's only because I'm bitter."[22]

A MARITAL CRISIS

THE FORRESTALS' MARRIAGE thus proceeded on rather separate tracks, converging in certain ways and at certain times that provided some mutual support. Forrestal was in the main the impressively successful Wall Street deal-maker—a self-centered, ambitious, tireless striver—but also the serious reader of history and philosophy, driven by a powerful urge to expand his knowledge and experience, to realize the full potential of a questing mind, though for ultimate purposes which neither he nor his business colleagues and Long Island neighbors perceived with any specificity in the early 1930s. And while wrapped in the privileged trappings of a conventional upper-class life-style, he discreetly evaded convention whenever it pleased him. Jo, on the other hand, was an unfocused bundle of energy and willfulness, seeking and not finding a sufficient purpose for her life. Both a lack of interest in motherhood and the particular circumstances of her marriage denied her a needed emotional security. Plenty of money and constant social activity could not conceal a gnawing loneliness, an indefinable unhappiness, a growing anxiety just beneath the surface. And indeed in 1929 there was a severe crisis in the marriage. Forrestal was involved in an affair with Phyllis Baldwin, a woman "possessed of a haunting English beauty," with whom, according to Ellen Barry, he had "been in love for years."[23] This time it appeared to be serious, with indications that the lovers were intent upon marriage. Angry and distraught, Jo fought like a cornered tigress to prevent a divorce, first by getting herself pregnant, then by displaying at ladies' luncheons pieces of intimate female apparel found in her husband's closet.[24] She became tense and suspicious of everyone, even her few good friends. One afternoon at Adele Lovett's, when Jo complained of a stomachache, Adele suggested the traditional remedy of castor oil, not knowing her friend was pregnant. Reacting with hot anger, Jo accused Adele of trying to bring on a miscarriage that would put an end to her marriage.[25]

The combination of her pregnancy and raw willingness to create a public scandal over Phyllis Baldwin carried the day, for with the birth of their second child, Peter, on August 2, 1930, Forrestal apparently gave up any further thought of divorce, accepting that event as one which effectively locked him in. A part of this resigned response was generalized Catholic guilt; another was an acute sensitivity to any controversy which appeared to impugn his own actions, combined with a deep need for the outward appearance of propriety. (Ellen Barry recalled an incident a few years later when she and Jo were photographed in Palm Beach in French lounging pajamas, which were becoming the fashionable costume for cocktail parties. Forrestal saw the picture in a New York newspaper and immediately sent Jo a telegram which said in effect, "Don't ever display yourself like that again." It was another example, Ellen Barry said, of his curious duality: "On the one hand, he wanted to live—or give the appearance of living—a quite conventional life; at the same time, he insisted on being free to do as he pleased."[26])

It is also reasonable to conclude that he abandoned the idea of divorce out of a genuine affection and respect for Jo. Despite the emergent truth that their purposes and interests diverged at every important point, he continued to see in her a woman of striking vitality, a fighter, a climber like himself, and he could hardly have failed to be impressed by the tenacity with which she fought to keep the marriage. For her part, she saw him always as a man destined for ever higher achievement and so accepted the painful truth that he was a congenitally unfaithful husband and a workaholic for whom career was categorically the first priority and she and their life together a distant second. This major crisis in the marriage brought them to a sober understanding of what was possible between them and what was not, which elements of their marriage could be safeguarded and nurtured and which were irrevocably lost. The crisis qualitatively changed and, in a sense, strengthened the relationship: "Their friendship became important," Adele Lovett said, "their marriage less so."[27]

The new understanding, painfully arrived at, seemed to give them both a greater freedom to pursue their strong separate drives. According to Michael, his father's goal in the early 1930s was "not complicated." It was "simply to be a tremendous success on Wall Street, to accumulate money, which also meant power . . . The old man cared a lot about power," but to him it meant primarily "power to keep the country going, to make it better, to keep the system open for opportunity so that other people like himself could make it on their own,"[28] as America slowly and painfully pulled itself out of the Great Depression. As it turned out, Forrestal was not primarily interested in money. A fierce patriotism and a developing sense of personal responsibility for the security and economic stability of the country underlay his conception of power, as his later career in government would demonstrate.

Josephine's goals lay elsewhere. She wanted "to project her personality onto something," more specifically, to be recognized as an influence, a power, in what she perceived as the challenging task of elevating American taste in fashion and interior design; she wanted to change the way Americans furnished their houses, the way they dressed, the way they entertained. Her sphere of operations was confined to upper-class, monied taste, primarily in New York and Europe. "New York is a wonderful place," she told Michael, "but most of it is done in such gross taste. They have to want better, prettier things." It was clear to the son that his mother had "no interest much in bringing up children or leading a normal middle-class American life," but she was "deadly serious" about fashion; in such matters "the old lady was a worker."[29]

Having given up her career at *Vogue,* however, she lacked a public audience for her views, a circumstance which some friends thought left her "all dressed up with no place to go" and contributed to her tragic unraveling in later years.[30] But in the early 1930s, she was eager to pursue her goal through self-expression—to become in her own dress, her own house, her own parties the embodiment of what taste and style should be. She gave her house in Old Westbury an "exciting decor," and, by tacit agreement with her husband, initiated and managed nearly every aspect of their life on the North Shore. Forrestal paid no attention to whether the lawns got cut or the gardens trimmed, whether the servants performed efficiently and were paid on time, or whether the roof leaked. Jo managed all of these things. She also arranged all of their dinner parties, including the guest lists, which meant there was always a generous sprinkling of writers, movie people, and fashion people to leaven the loaf of the banking and business families who constituted the mainstream local gentry.

O'Hara, Benchley, and the Barrys were regulars at the Forrestal dinner table; on rarer occasions the guests included exotics like Greta Garbo and folk heroes like Gary Cooper. When Michael was introduced to Gary Cooper, the little boy admitted his intense admiration for the movie star's latest picture, *The Lives of a Bengal Lancer.* Cooper said he would send him the film, and "sure enough six days later, four huge thirty-five-millimeter metal cans arrived," Michael recalled years later, "impossible to do anything with, of course, but they arrived." The local gentry began saying that if you wanted a taste of bohemian life, you should get yourself invited to Jo Forrestal's dinner parties because "it was all there." Did Forrestal enjoy these parties at which he was perhaps more guest than host? Michael thought "they were a welcome distraction" from the unending labors in Wall Street, where he was "an absolute grunt grind." But they were not more than that. Forrestal played tennis once or twice with Gary Cooper and some of the others, but "was not particularly taken with the Hollywood crowd."[31]

BEEKMAN PLACE

SOMETIME IN early 1932 the Forrestals made a decision to have a place in town—and not an apartment but a house, and not an existing house but one built to their specifications. In the trough of the Great Depression this was a singular decision, but Forrestal had now emerged as Clarence Dillon's most valued partner, his net worth was more than $5 million, and the acquisition of a distinguished residence in the city was a logical next step, one that would announce his professional eminence and serve to elevate the Forrestals socially to a place not much below the Whitneys, the Harrimans, and the Loebs. "Ma always chose where we lived or where she thought Dad should live," Michael said many years later,[32] but in this case Forrestal appears to have been the initiator. Just past his fortieth birthday, confident, brainy, and rich, he wanted a place in the inner circles of New York society for reasons directly connected to his conception of power and influence; an elegant town house was a necessary vehicle. To make it beautiful and to entertain with distinction were responsibilities he laid on his wife. "Jim expected this of her," Ellen Barry said, "to see to it that they were solidly established in the upper crust."[33] Jo accepted the idea with enthusiasm, for she longed to be back in Manhattan with café society and the beautiful people, and a new town house provided a special opportunity to make a striking aesthetic statement. They would keep the Long Island place for weekends, and their sons would go to school on the North Shore.

A site was chosen on the corner of 49th Street and Beekman Place on the East River, arguably the most elegant neighborhood in town. The existing structure was demolished, and Harold Sterner, a young architect who had turned to painting to support himself through the Depression, was set to work.[34] The result was a splendid Georgian house of clean lines and classical proportions, in marble and brick. Large bay windows faced the East River, while arched Palladian windows graced the sides fronting on Beekman and 49th. The front door opened onto a small enclosed square at the foot of 49th Street. The house had five levels, including a basement apartment with its own entrance which the Forrestals made available to transient bachelors and other friends. The central feature was a large open space, oval in shape and extending upward from the marble foyer to the roof, in which a graceful circular staircase connected the floors. On the first floor was Forrestal's favorite room, the library, where he liked to repair with male guests after dinner, with brandy and cigars and serious talk; the living and dining rooms and the kitchen were on the second level. On the third floor was Jo's bedroom suite, dominated by a king-size bed with a headboard shaped like a sea scallop, suggesting a setting romantic enough for a painting by Botticelli. The children and the servants had bedrooms on the fourth floor. The living and dining rooms were sophisticated and graceful in their simplicity, designed for entertaining, with comfortable furniture covered in soft silks, often pinstriped with blues and pinks predominating. Forrestal had his own bedroom-study near the master bedroom, but it was furnished like a smoking room on the *Queen Mary*—rather art deco with walls of cork, a desk and a leather chair, a few lamps, and a bed built into the wall. One of his favorite Bellows lithographs on boxing hung over the desk.[35]

The Forrestal townhouse on Beekman Place

The house was a great success, and Jo entertained with distinction and flair. Forrestal took great pride in what his wife had done and praised her to their friends for her style and "theatrical eye," a phrase which in one sense was code for a family joke. Her overriding aim in decor was to achieve a dramatic effect, and she approached the task in the manner of a stage designer, being far less concerned about authenticity. In furnishing the Beekman house, she shopped mainly in secondhand places on Third Avenue, picking up paintings, couches, lamps, and statues which Forrestal and their sons began describing as "eighteenth-century Irish fake." The Renaissance painting in the dining room was a fake, as was an impressive statue of the Venus de Milo rising out of shrubbery in the marbled foyer. "Everything is easily replaceable," Jo told them with a laugh."[36]

The roughly seven years at 17 Beekman Place (1933 to 1940) were happy and productive ones given the inherent limitations of the marriage, now acknowledged by both parties. They led quite separate lives most of the time, yet safeguarded the areas of mutual admiration and respect. It was difficult to discern much emotional warmth in the relationship, and both parents neglected the children, but the marriage was synergistic in the sense that each contributed something which strengthened the total situation—and their friendship endured. Jo had her own friends, male and female; Forrestal pursued his business career, his voracious reading in history and politics, and his friendships with other women. One of these was Louise Macy, a striking young woman from California who worked as a fashion editor on *Harper's Bazaar*. She and Forrestal were often seen to-

Forrestal's upstairs study at Beekman Place

gether at "21" with Robert Benchley, who regarded "Louie" Macy as something of a protégé—"she was beauty and magic all in one—she was an event."[37] But it is likely that Benchley was there largely for protective coloration, for "Louie" was eighteen years younger and called him "Gramps." Some years later, when she married President Roosevelt's principal adviser, Harry Hopkins, Benchley said smugly to a friend, "I place my women well."[38]

Jo continued to express herself in lavish entertainment. After a dinner dance which the Forrestals hosted in the Persian Room of the Plaza, the gossip columnist Cholly Knickerbocker wrote, "There's no doubt about it, when Jo Forrestal decides to give a dinner she corrals an interesting and entertaining group of guests. No stuffed shirts and highly upholstered dowagers for Jo."[39] She went to fashion shows in the daytime and nightclubs in the evening, in company with a range of fashionable, rather shallow people. On one of these excursions, in 1937, she was fingered by a hatcheck girl as she left the Plaza with her friend Richard Hall. When their car reached the front door at Beekman Place they were confronted by two gangsters with guns, who relieved Jo of jewelry worth $50,000. Forrestal was asleep upstairs in the house and never heard a thing. Whether deliberately or inadvertently, Jo recounted the incident to enough people to ensure several stories in the *New York Times,* a spate of publicity that greatly displeased her husband.[40]

But the worst was yet to come. Eleven years later columnists Drew Pear-

son and Walter Winchell mounted an ugly attack on Forrestal as a sinister
agent of Wall Street and the major oil companies, in the context of the
heated emotional debate over the partition of Palestine and the creation of
a Jewish state. Someone tipped them to the old robbery story in the *Times*,
and they replayed it in their radio broadcasts and newspaper columns, but
with malicious distortion designed to show up Forrestal as a physical coward. As Pearson described it, Forrestal witnessed the stickup from an upstairs window and immediately fled out the back door of the house in fear
and trembling.[41] What was more significant than a deliberate fabrication
by a pair of nasty journalists was its devastating effect on Forrestal in 1948.
He was deeply shaken by the intensely personal and unfair nature of the
attack. It was an assault on his manhood.

THE FORRESTALS traveled extensively in the 1930s. Dillon, Read had
offices in London and Paris, and when Forrestal went abroad on business
Jo often accompanied him, splitting off to visit friends on the Riviera or
elsewhere while he attended to his business, then rejoined her and their
hosts for the weekend. In 1936 they were photographed by *Town & Country*
attending the Salzburg Festival with well-known members of European
high society. On another occasion, when they were guests at the Philip
Barrys' small villa near Cannes, the two couples drove to St. Tropez in the
Barrys' Mercedes, which had, for some reason, an uncomfortable backseat. There was much joking about this during the picnic lunch on the
beach, and when Forrestal found a friend whose yacht was sitting in St.
Tropez harbor, he nonchalantly abandoned the others and returned to
Cannes by boat. Was this because he wanted to avoid another ride in the
uncomfortable backseat? "Perhaps," Ellen Barry recalled, "but mainly
because he insisted on being completely independent—free to go and do
as he pleased at every moment."[42]

Jo occasionally went to Europe without her husband, but seemed reluctant to leave him on his own. During one absence in 1936 (on a trip with
Marie Harriman), *Town & Country* gossip columnist Alice-Leone Moats
included Forrestal, along with Condé Nast and others, in a list of "married
men in season . . . worthy of attention, while their wives are away, by
hostesses who know a filet mignon from a sole meunière."[43]

Springtime usually meant a trip to visit friends in Hobe Sound, a resort
which stretched along Jupiter Island north of Palm Beach and emerged
during the 1930s as perhaps the most exclusive Florida gathering place for
the rich or famous of New York. By 1941 its social epicenter was the Island
Club, run with panache and strict attention to the habits and manners of
its upper-class clientele by Mrs. Joseph Verner Reed, who qualified as one
of them.[44] Within the Long Island crowd, the Lovetts were among the first
to discover the sophisticated simplicity of the place, and soon built a tran-

quil beach cottage called Sea Change on the ocean side. "We bypassed Palm Beach and settled in Hobe Sound because it was a very primitive, quiet place," Adele Lovett said some years later, "but I ruined it by going back to New York and telling my friends about it." Soon thereafter, "they started coming down in hordes."[45] Before long Philip Barry had built a house, and he was followed by, among others, John P. Marquand, Jock Whitney, Averell Harriman, William Lord, Paul Shields, Gary Cooper, and the boxer Gene Tunney, who had married into New York society. From Grosse Pointe came Dan Caulkins and Edsel Ford. With a few notable exceptions, Mrs. Reed refused to accept Jews at Hobe Sound. Adele Lovett "kept resigning" from the club when such "dear friends" as the Arthur Sulzbergers, who owned the *New York Times,* and the Harold Guinzburgs, who owned Viking Press, were excluded.[46]

The Forrestals stayed with the Lovetts or took rooms at the club. Forrestal was a trim athletic figure who worked at keeping himself in top physical shape by playing strenuous tennis and golf, swimming in the ocean, and sunning on the beach. Jo took special pleasure in the daily lunches out of doors, often on the Lovetts' patio, which usually included ten or twelve good friends. On such occasions, she was in her element, dressed in chic, becoming beach clothes, displaying her long beautiful legs and crisp, sardonic wit ("a professional cynic," an admiring Arthur Krock called her in the 1940s).[47]

MICHAEL AND PETER

I F THERE ARE reasons to conclude that Forrestal was a man who should never have married, there are equal reasons for doubting he should ever have been a father. Like marriage, children represented limitations he could not really accept—on his own intellectual, social, and physical development, on his compelling work in Wall Street and later in Washington, on his freedom to come and go as and when he pleased. For her part, Jo considered marriage a necessary socioeconomic vehicle, but found little emotional or psychic satisfaction in the role of mother. Yet by the end of 1930 the Forrestals, perhaps to their surprise, had two sons. Michael was born thirteen months after they married, probably before either fully understood the intensity of their separate, selfish drives or the slippery implications of their commitment to an "open marriage." Peter's birth three years later seems to have been a weapon deliberately forged by Jo to prevent a divorce. This combination of attitudes and circumstances was destined to result in neglected children and tragic endings.[48]

According to the doctor who delivered Michael, Forrestal "barely registered" when informed over the phone that he now had a son. His only question concerned the child's weight; he added that he would try to drop around to see Jo and the baby the next morning, if his schedule permitted. It was Jo's mother who, having come to New York by train from Chicago, had taken her to the hospital.[49] When at length he accepted the family situation as permanent, Forrestal attempted in various ways to be a father to his sons, but his sporadic efforts were at best awkward and at worst destructive. There was considerable emotional and physical distance between father and sons for a number of years. He seldom asked about their studies and never helped with their homework. To the extent he gave them any attention, it was usually to push their development as athletes and social beings, for he wanted them to be good at sports and to have friends; above all, he wanted them to be self-reliant, able to take care of themselves "without crutches." This was "the one fierce feeling he had about his children," Michael remembered many years later.[50] "Never coddle a growing boy," Forrestal once told Ellen Barry. "Let the little bastards learn to stand on their own feet."[51]

This insistence that his sons not grow up overprotected or too rich reflected several related factors, but primarily the ingrained perspective of the poor Irish kid from Beacon who had made it entirely on his own. According to Michael, Forrestal was privately contemptuous of those of his neighbors who lived on inherited wealth, and came to believe as time passed that "the whole Wall Street apparatus" was in major respects a discreet conspiracy to protect the already rich, rather than an engine to encourage new risk-taking and thus increase the country's total wealth. This belief made him a convinced Wall Street reformer in the late 1930s, but his efforts were always made behind the scenes, never in declared or open rebellion against the system. He was also aware that the North Shore in the 1930s was an island of extravagant indulgence in a sea of general economic misery, when a third of the nation was unemployed and several million Americans lived on the edge of starvation.[52] He wanted to put his sons into public school in the town of Roslyn, adjoining Old Westbury, and was dissuaded only when Jo and his friends told him bluntly what he would be letting them in for: They would be "hated by the townies" because they were "rich kids." Reluctantly accepting this truth, Forrestal enrolled them in Greenvale Academy, a private day school in Old Westbury. To complicate matters, Michael developed a nervous stutter when he was six or seven, a condition which it is reasonable to infer was brought on by unresolved tensions in the family relationships. He recalled that it was "a terrible speech problem, which embarrassed my mother enormously. You know, she could almost not take me anywhere." As a consequence, he was sent off for a year to a special school in Bristol, Rhode Island, an experience which he remembered as "absolutely horrible—like something out of *Oliver Twist.*"[53]

In the early years, Jo was the more attentive parent, but only relatively so. She "received" her sons in the morning as she breakfasted in bed and they prepared to leave for school, long after Forrestal had departed for Wall Street. She saw to their proper clothes and proper manners, but the true focus of her interests lay elsewhere. As a consequence, there was not much home life for the boys, no family gatherings to play card games or read books together, indeed, not much time together at all, and little visible warmth or affection. Forrestal worked long hours all week on Wall Street and spent his weekends on the golf course. Jo went to fashion shows and luncheons, planned dinner parties, and went riding. Most of the time the boys ate with the servants.

Michael came to realize early on that he was emotionally and intellectually on his own; his response was to grow up fast and to achieve a posture of rugged, wary self-reliance which ironically caused his mother to brand him a "square" and to criticize him for being "born forty years old."[54] Peter, on the other hand, became very dependent on his mother, whom he adored and from whom he inherited a kind of dark, brooding handsomeness and a moody, stubborn personality.

After several years at Greenvale, when Mike was ten and Peter seven, they were sent to school in Switzerland. One senses, again, it was their mother's initiative—she wanted them to "see Europe" and "learn a foreign language"—and Forrestal acquiesced because he thought the experience might strengthen their self-reliance. Or there may have been a less exalted parental purpose. "I don't know," Michael said years later, "it may have been just to sort of get us out of the way."[55] Jo chose Le Rosey, a reputable cosmopolitan school on Lake Geneva attended by the scions of great wealth and social standing, including royal princes. But Forrestal predictably objected, insisting instead on a school he had heard about—a small school in Coppet, called La Châtaigneraie, where learning was taken seriously and student life was disciplined and spartan. So the two tender-aged, involuntary candidates for cultural enrichment and self-reliance were put aboard a French liner, the *Champlain,* and sailed for Europe at the end of summer in 1937.[56]

It turned out to be a nightmare experience. What Forrestal, the thorough researcher of markets, had failed to find out was that La Châtaigneraie was one of a chain of schools run by the disciples of Frank Buchman, the evangelical founder of the Oxford Group movement, which was dedicated to the "Moral Rearmament" of society through the nurturing of "God-controlled" leaders. Who were his shining exemplars? On his return to England from the 1936 Olympic Games in Berlin, Buchman had declared: "I thank heaven for a man like Adolf Hitler who has built a frontline of defense against the Anti-Christ of Communism."[57]

La Châtaigneraie was not only strict, it was rough, repressive, and "weird." Michael remembered that the school discouraged students from writing home and in fact censored all outgoing mail: "We got beaten a good deal by the masters, and it was very cold." There were about sixty students in all, but they were a mixture of many ages and nationalities and included men in their twenties and even early thirties. Michael and Peter were by far the youngest. Several students represented opposing factions in the bitter civil war then raging in Spain between the democratic loyalists and General Franco's Fascist rebels. This led to some vicious encounters: "People were being killed in the woods—kids with knives, killing each other. The whole thing was like something out of a grotesque prewar movie." After somehow enduring this scene for nearly nine months, Michael managed to send his father an uncensored school brochure. As soon as he saw it, Forrestal recognized his terrible mistake and immediately sailed for Europe. "He himself came over, unbelievably, like a deus ex machina, and pulled us right out."[58]

The whole family then went down to Biarritz to stay with friends, but the Buchmanite horror had apparently not softened Forrestal's determination to require self-reliance of his young sons. At some point—this was the summer of 1938, when Europe hovered on the brink of war—the boys were shipped off to England for a country weekend with family friends on the Isle of Wight. Their parents were to follow a few days later. But Jo forgot to give the boys their passports, and they were detained at Le Havre and put in jail for three days under suspicion as German couriers. "With the war about to start, the French were very antsy about espionage," Michael remembered, "and the jail was very unpleasant."[59] The U.S. consul at Le Havre finally got in touch with the Dillon, Read office in Paris, and located Forrestal at the Ritz Bar there. The French authorities allowed the boys one phone call, so Michael called his father. As Michael remembered it, Forrestal said, " 'Mike, I gather you're in jail in Le Havre.' I said, 'Yes, we are.' He said, 'Well, I guess you have the situation under control.' I said, 'I don't think we do.' But he said, 'Oh yes you do, because I've talked to the French and they're going to let you out. So you should proceed to England as planned, and when you get to Sir John Hussey's, give me a ring here at the Ritz Bar.' And I thought: This is the end. He's sitting in the Ritz Bar in Paris, and he's not going to come down and take us out of this dreadful hole. I had no assurance that the French were going to let us out."[60]

The missing passports arrived by special messenger, and the boys were released from jail. They then got themselves by ship to Southampton, but found they didn't have a dime left to pay for their ferry passage to the Isle of Wight; Mike manfully resolved this problem by selling his watch to the captain of the ferry boat. When they at last reached their destination, they were welcomed by the Husseys, who had been alerted to meet all arriving boats for two days. It appeared that Forrestal had been in close touch with the situation from the time he heard about their detention and was pleased with the sturdy fortitude with which they handled the situation. But fifty years later, Michael was not appeased: "It was absurd, I mean absurd, some kind of fantasy he had about self-reliance. You can't do that with kids."[61]

Back in New York in the fall, the family decided they would spend the whole year in the city, and the boys were enrolled in St. Bernard's, a private day school. As between Long Island and New York, they definitely preferred the open spaces of the North Shore, in part because going to St. Bernard's meant walking a long six blocks from Beekman Place to catch the school bus at Park Avenue. This involved running a gauntlet of jibes and occasional physical assaults from sneering neighborhood kids who found "our absurd school uniform"—blue blazers and matching Eton caps—"a natural target for scorn."[62] When they complained to their parents and pleaded to be chauffeured to school, Forrestal refused, but arranged instead for them to take boxing lessons. Neither Michael nor Peter was enthusiastic about this, but they went through the motions. Stuart Symington's son, Jim, who was later a three-term congressman from Missouri, was pitted against Michael on several occasions. "We stood toe to toe and exchanged fake, featherweight punches," he remembered. "Not a blow was struck in anger."[63]

Finally, the boys' bitter complaints about New York sank in, and they were sent off to the Aiken School in South Carolina. The initiative was Jo's—she had learned of it through her fox-hunting friends on Long Island and had ridden with the Aiken Hunt. Forrestal initially objected, arguing that Aiken was just a resort town for the horsey set, but Jo prevailed and at long last Michael and Peter found a happy, comfortable refuge, thanks largely to the qualities of the headmaster, Harold Fletcher. Aiken was a small school whose students and faculty comprised a kind of extended family and exuded a good deal of warmth and compassion. The headmaster's house was the center for dinners and parlor games every Sunday, and he and his wife gave their students an abundance of affection and moral support. Michael and Peter thrived in this atmosphere and indeed became so attached to the Fletchers that they often spent their vacations with them in later years—after they had gone on to Exeter and Andover—sometimes at Aiken and sometimes at the Fletchers' summer place in Christmas Cove, Maine.[64] On the eve of his departure from the small school he loved, Peter summed up his feelings in a letter to his mother: "Dear Mom . . . I had a simply grand time in Aiken. I guess there wasn't a second when I wasn't having fun, what with riding, dragging, golfing, tennis, baseball, swimming and of course parties. There was hardly a lunch or dinner when I wasn't out with the whole gang."[65] Forrestal came to have a warm admiration for Fletcher and his school, writing several years later to Thomas Lamont that the headmaster had made it into a "first-rate school . . . thoroughly soaked in the democratic tradition . . . [It] has a fine facility for catching the interest and stirring the imagination of young boys."[66]

Michael's development at Exeter into an unusually intelligent, sturdily self-reliant young man began to impress Forrestal, especially when he found that his older son possessed a passion and a talent for political thought. "It was the beginning of communication between us because we now had a subject for conversation," Michael said years later.[67] During his senior year (1944), Michael was in charge of a mock political convention which involved campaigning on campus for leading presidential candidates. Michael wrote to his father that Senator Joseph Ball, a liberal Minnesota Republican, was emerging as the Exeter favorite for President, notwith-standing Franklin Roosevelt's announced intention to run for a fourth term. Without telling his son, Forrestal (by now Secretary of the Navy) arranged to fly to Exeter on the opening day of the mock convention, bringing Senator Ball with him as the principal speaker. Forrestal and Ball both spoke to the convention, and Ball ran away with the student vote.[68] Michael was warmed and elated by his father's support, "the first time he had shown more than a passing interest . . . It was a great coup."[69] Both parents were on hand at graduation the following June to hear him speak as class valedictorian. Forrestal had also arranged for a navy plane to pick up Harold Fletcher in South Carolina and bring him to Washington, from which point they all flew on together to New Hampshire. It was a happy occasion, and Forrestal was unabashedly proud of his son and his accomplishments.[70]

Michael went on to Princeton and from there to the navy's Russian Language School, which led to postwar assignments in Berlin and Moscow. Later, he worked for the Marshall Plan in Paris under his father's friend Averell Harriman and was graduated from Harvard Law School in 1953.

Peter Forrestal, three years younger, never really established a relationship with his father and did not appear to win his admiration. More charming, more insouciant than his older brother, he was also more stubborn and rebellious. Trying to evaluate Peter in response to an inquiry from the

Michael (left) and Peter Forrestal at a horse show in Aiken, 1941

Michael and Peter, ca. 1946

headmaster of Andover, Forrestal mentioned that his son was "somewhat immature with respect to responsibility; somewhat undisciplined as to the control of his whims; apt to get mad in games." In an odd further comment, he thought Peter was "inclined to read too much—the rather normal escapism of adolescence."[71] Peter was his mother's child, which is to say spontaneous, aesthetic, willful—characteristics instinctively resistant to routine, discipline, or strict logic—but Forrestal, who was determined that parentally prescribed fundamentals should prevail, kept pushing him toward his own model of responsible behavior. The summer before Peter entered Andover, Forrestal sent him to Culver Military Academy in Indiana to undergo eight weeks of training as a cavalry trooper, and warned him in a letter that Andover would be "a great deal different" from Aiken. "More freedom" would require "more discipline on your part if you are to get the results."[72]

Peter's response was to become increasingly rebellious. He openly disagreed with his father's views on just about everything, adopted a capricious attitude toward schoolwork, cut classes, and ran up bills at the River Club in New York. On broad intellectual questions, Forrestal (now the embattled Secretary of Defense) tried to adopt a gently disarming tactic. He once told a friend he always tried to "precede what I have to say to Peter by telling him that I fully appreciate that he will disagree, think it is stupid, and pay no attention to it. That always makes him a little mad, and he listens in spite of himself.''[73] With regard to club bills, he wrote sternly: "I don't want bills coming in to your mother that she doesn't know about . . . She has plenty of annoyances in dealing with the current problem of running a house under difficult conditions, and I don't want her burdened more than is necessary." As an afterthought, he added, "When you write her, keep your correspondence as cheerful as possible. Save your squawks for me."[74]

His reaction to Peter's erratic performance at Princeton was also gentle— and humble in the sense that it hinted at his own failure to graduate: "I know in my own case that failures in attendance resulted in getting much less out of courses than I otherwise would have. I used to make the excuse that I was engaged in making my own way, but as a matter of fact it was my own shortcomings and failure to plan my time."[75] When Peter's delinquencies persisted and he seemed on the verge of getting kicked out of Princeton, Forrestal called on Harold Fletcher to be his emissary to the college administration. Fletcher had a long talk with the dean, which settled matters favorably, and Peter went on to graduate in 1951. But he was only nineteen at the time of his father's death in 1949, and they had never really known or understood each other.[76]

Behind his simplistic, no-nonsense demands that his sons be self-reliant and mature, Forrestal seemed at least intermittently aware of his shortcomings as a father, yet powerless to alter the circumstances or change course. He kept a black notebook in which he was wont to copy quotations, jokes, or snatches of poetry that struck his sense of relevance. At one point during his Washington years, he entered a poignant passage from a longer work by a Siamese poet, Kamut Chandruang, *My Boyhood in Siam,* which he read as applying especially to American life. The passage read:

> It is sad, I think, that [Americans] have so little time for love. Their men have no time for their wives and children. The father goes to work, the children go to school, and they reunite only in those hours when exhaustion forces them to sleep. The vacations are for rest not for love. . . . [77]

CHAPTER 8

★ ★ ★

The Struggle for
Wall Street Reform

WITH Franklin D. Roosevelt's inauguration in 1933 came determined efforts by the new administration to impose reforms on
Wall Street. These were aimed at requiring "full disclosure"
of the facts underlying the offer and sale of securities and thus at putting
an end to the widespread misrepresentation (careless or fraudulent) which
had bilked millions of unsophisticated investors and destroyed public confidence in the whole American financial system. Government statistics
showed that 7 million individuals owned common stock in the two hundred
largest industrial corporations, but 88 percent of them owned less than a
hundred shares; at the same time 1 percent of the stockholders owned 50
percent of the shares, a fact which, as one official put it, "accentuated the
need for investor protection."[1]

Operating under laws of mounting toughness and scope passed by Congress in 1933, 1934, and 1935, the newly created Securities and Exchange
Commission, led successively by Joseph P. Kennedy, James Landis, and
William O. Douglas, established detailed controls over the stock exchange
and the practices of brokers and dealers, and also forced the dissolution of
public utility holding companies.[2] These vigorous governmental intrusions
into the hitherto quasi-private club outraged a large segment of the financial
and business communities and produced for a time "a strike of capital,"
which added to the continuing stagnation in Wall Street. Forrestal, along
with several other enlightened bankers, was aware of the need for structural
changes in Wall Street practices and played an important role in the reforms
achieved by the SEC, especially under Douglas, toward the end of the
decade. But he operated behind the scenes.

Ferdinand Pecora was counsel to the Senate Committee on Banking and
Currency and to its Subcommittee on the Stock Exchange Investigation,
which became the spearpoint of congressional efforts to develop informa-

tion on which to base far-reaching Wall Street reforms. Pecora got the job on the strong recommendation of Bainbridge Colby, Woodrow Wilson's last Secretary of State. The Sicilian-born Pecora had come to America with his family in 1886 at the age of four and by 1918 had become assistant district attorney of New York County. An aggressive liberal who admired the social and legal philosophy of Oliver Wendell Holmes, Louis Brandeis, and Benjamin Cardozo, he headed effective probes into abuses in the bail-bond business and the milk-graft scandals in the city health department in the 1920s and sent the perpetrators to jail.[3] He carried a black briefcase, which contained what *Newsweek* called his "sensational findings."[4] Initially, Congress had in mind a limited inquiry, into "short selling" and other relatively minor abuses, but heavy pressures from the new Democratic majority, which had been swept into office with Franklin Roosevelt in 1932, led to a broadening of the investigation. It was now to include all the basic practices of private banking firms "whose personalities and affairs were . . . shrouded in deep aristocratic mystery."[5]

As the subcommittee's principal prosecutor, Pecora was seeking headlines that would make clear to the public the practices which had led to the stock market crash, and to the ensuing Depression, which by early 1933 had fastened unprecedented economic and social misery on the whole country. He and the majority of the subcommittee were determined to expose Wall Street as a den of pirates and cheats. "Three-quarters righteous tribune of the people," he was also "one-quarter demagogic inquisitor."[6]

In May and early June of 1933, the J. P. Morgan and Kuhn, Loeb firms were called to testify. At the opening session a bizarre incident was created when a press agent from Ringling Brothers Circus popped a female midget onto the lap of the astonished Jack Morgan, while alerted photographers snapped pictures. Whatever the intent of the prank, it had the odd effect of rather "humanizing" the august Morgan and transforming his public image from greedy plutocrat to something more doddering and benign. The astute Morgan team promptly took advantage of this change in public perception by making "candor under inquisition into a kind of arrogance, a form of noblesse oblige."[7] Disdaining any effort to be defensive or secretive, they answered even the most sensitive questions with unembarrassed forthrightness and provided all documentation requested by the subcommittee. The hearings disclosed that the House of Morgan selected its own clients and never submitted a statement of the firm's financial condition to depositors. ("Why not?" Pecora asked. "They never asked for it," Jack Morgan replied.) It was further disclosed that profits were divided on a fifty-fifty basis—that is, half to Morgan himself and half to his partners. The Kuhn, Loeb witnesses adopted the same kind of lofty stance and general tactic.[8]

During the Morgan and Kuhn, Loeb testimony, press coverage was extensive. Stories appeared daily on the front page of the *New York Times,* and *Time, Newsweek,* and *Business Week* ran feature articles. J. P. Morgan's appearance before the committee and the disclosure of his firm's practices aroused intense public interest, for they seemed to expose "the whole anatomy of Wall Street chicanery and corruption," as William O. Douglas expressed it.[9] But Congress then closed shop for its summer recess, scheduling testimony from Dillon, Read in October. By that time, public attention had dwindled and coverage of the hearings rarely made the front pages; the Dillon, Read testimony was carried in the financial sections, and few magazines ran any further stories. As reported by *Newsweek,* these autumnal sessions "were wanting in the fireworks and histrionics that marked the Morgan and Kuhn, Loeb testimony. Only a handful of spectators sat in the ornate Senate Caucus Room . . . all that emerged was a mass of dreary details."[10] The press tended to blame Pecora for the drop in public interest, feeling that his grasp of "high finance" was rather elementary and his questions often "trivial." They concluded that he was hunting only for "small game," in the process of promoting his own ambitions for elective office. Several senators appeared to share this view as the proceedings droned on. Senator Carter Glass, a Democrat from Virginia, stalked out of the room in exasperation one day, remarking as he left that "I am tired of trying to make these hearings interesting."[11] From Dillon, Read's point of view, waning press and public interest in the investigation was an unexpected piece of good luck, and its spokesmen worked at keeping the hearings dry as dust.

DILLON AND THE INVESTMENT TRUSTS

THE FALL HEARINGS ran from October 3 through October 13. The focal point of the subcommittee's interest in Dillon, Read was its organization and management of two "investment trusts" and the use of "earned surplus" from the first to finance the second.

The investment trust of the 1920s (whose present-day analogue is the mutual fund) was a financial vehicle designed, as the *Harvard Business Review* explained in a 1925 article, to give the investor "a high degree of safety" owing to the fact that the securities of the trust were backed by a wide range of other securities, i.e., stocks and bonds of other corporations. Whereas holding companies sought to acquire control of the corporations in which they invested, investment trusts merely held such securities as collateral for their own issues. Shortly after World War I, the investment trust became a favorite instrument of those American bankers who wanted to deal in foreign securities (both private and governmental), for it was a means of reducing the risk for the small investor and thereby of overcoming the ingrained American distrust of foreign securities. Paul Warburg of Kuhn, Loeb advocated the creation of "powerful investment trusts" as a means of enabling "the little fellow" to hold foreign securities "in a modest and safe manner." By 1921, Wall Street had formed forty such trusts, some specializing in a single industry (domestic or foreign) and some concentrating on the governmental or private securities of a single nation, e.g., Germany. By 1926, the rising stock market, easy money, and the American public's growing interest in owning common stocks had tripled the number of investment trusts, and the expansion continued unabated. By the end of 1929, Wall Street had organized 770 such trusts, 265 of them launched in that year alone. Whereas total trust assets were perhaps $1 billion in 1926, they exceeded $7 billion by the end of 1929.[12]

Clarence Dillon's testimony on October 3, 1933, made clear that while investment trusts may have provided safe investment for "the little fellow," they were clearly designed to assure that the lion's share of the profits went to the organizing bankers. The tone of the hearing was, on the whole, cordial. Indeed, Pecora began by advising the senators that Dillon, Read had provided "the fullest possible measure of cooperation and assistance" to the investigation: "At no time has there been the slightest hindrance or obstacle placed in our path by their office."[13] In all probability, the firm gained favor with the subcommittee by the tactic of flooding it with more papers than its small staff could assimilate, but most of the Dillon, Read partners did feel a genuine need for reasonable reform and sought to cooperate with the investigation. Nevertheless, in the opening skirmish, Clarence Dillon deftly stonewalled persistent attempts to disclose either his own percentage ownership in the firm or the percentage ownership of his partners. (Legally speaking, they were not partners; rather, they were shareholders in a privately held corporation.)

SENATOR COUZENS: "Mr. Pecora, ask him the percentage that they own."

MR. PECORA: "Senator Couzens suggests that you also state the percentage of proportions of stock of this joint stock corporation owned by each of the stockholders."

MR. DILLON: "The stockholders are Clarence Dillon, Abbott Trading Corporation, The Beekman Co., Ltd., E. J. Bermingham, Isabelle Bollard, R. H. Bollard, W. M. S. Charnley, W. M. L. Fiske, W. M. A. Phillips, Roland L. Taylor. What was your question, Senator Couzens?"

SENATOR COUZENS: "The percentage of stock which each holds in that corporation."

MR. DILLON: "Of stock?"

SENATOR COUZENS: "Yes."

MR. DILLON: "I have no objection to giving any information to this committee that you feel will be helpful to you. But I am wondering if a statement of the interests of the various members is something you want me to tell publicly. If you feel it is going to help you in your deliberations, that it be given publicly, I have no objection to doing so; but I would appreciate it if you would consider whether that is pertinent."

SENATOR COUZENS: "So far as I am concerned, if I know who controls the corporation I am satisfied, speaking personally."

MR. PECORA: "I think similar consideration was requested by members of the firm of J. P. Morgan & Co. and that the committee at that time accorded them that consideration."

SENATOR COUZENS: "But we did get who controlled the firm of J. P. Morgan & Co."

MR. PECORA: "Mr. Dillon, who is the principal stockholder of Dillon, Read & Co.?"

MR. DILLON: "Mr. Pecora, if Senator Couzens and his associates feel that information is going to be helpful if given publicly, I have no objection to giving it. But, naturally, I prefer not to do so."

THE CHAIRMAN (SENATOR FLETCHER): "If you have no objection to giving it I see no reason why it should not go in our record."

MR. DILLON: "I have no objection, Mr. Chairman, to answering any questions whatsoever, and I have no objection at all to answering that question if you gentlemen decide it will help you in your deliberations. But, naturally, there are some things I prefer not to have in the public record. But I am prepared to answer anything you want."

MR. PECORA: "I think, perhaps, if you would give the information Senator Couzens has indicated that he is especially desirous of having as going to the control of this joint-stock association, that would satisfy our immediate purpose."

SENATOR COUZENS: "That would satisfy me, Mr. Pecora. I am not attempting to speak for the other members of the subcommittee, but if he will give that information that will be sufficient for our purposes at this time."

MR. DILLON: "I own the majority of the stock."

SENATOR COUZENS: "How much stock is out?"

MR. DILLON: "How many shares?"

SENATOR COUZENS: "Yes."

MR. DILLON: "I haven't the exact figure here. But there are between 73,000 and 74,000 shares. I haven't just the exact figures, but can furnish them later."

SENATOR COUZENS: "That is sufficient."

THE CHAIRMAN: "What is the par value of the stock?"

MR. DILLON: "$1 par value."

SENATOR COUZENS: "How many shares do you own, Mr. Dillon?"

MR. DILLON: "We haven't that figure here, but we can get it for you."

SENATOR COUZENS: "All right."[14]

Pecora then zeroed in on the matter of the firm's two investment trusts—"The United States and Foreign Securities Corporation" (Trust #1), formed in 1924, and "The United States and International Securities Corporation" (Trust #2), formed in 1928.

Trust #1, capitalized at $30 million, was formed to handle a wide range of stock and bond flotations to finance industrial, transportation, and mining undertakings mainly in foreign countries. It was organized as follows: The "first" preferred stock (250,000 shares @ $100 and paying a cumulative 6 percent dividend) was sold to the public for $25 million. Dillon, Read purchased all of the "second" preferred stock (50,000 shares @ $100) for $5 million and created 1 million shares of common stock. The firm itself took 25 percent of the common stock at zero cost, and individual partners in the firm purchased 50 percent of the common stock for $100,000 (20 cents per share). Dillon, Read and its partners thus held 75 percent of the common shares. The balance of the common was offered to holders of the "first" preferred @ $25.[15]

Trust #2, capitalized at $60 million, was organized by Trust #1, and followed the same pattern. All of the "first" preferred stock was sold to the public for $50 million (500,000 shares @ $100 and paying a 5 percent cumulative dividend). Trust #1 purchased all of the "second" preferred for $10 million (100,000 shares @ $100) and also took 2 million shares (80 percent) of the common stock at zero cost. The remaining 500,000 common shares were offered to holders of the "first" preferred stock @ $25.

On the second day of the hearings, Pecora summed up the effect of these transactions. For an outlay of $5.1 million, Dillon, Read had acquired effective control of two investment trusts with assets of $90 million. Challenged to refute that statement, Dillon quibbled about one or two minor points, but then said, "That is correct." The subcommittee was severely critical of the decision to use $10 million of "earned surplus" from Trust #1 to set up Trust #2, for, as the senators saw it, that money should have gone to the public holders of the common stock of Trust #1 in the form of dividends.[16] The testimony continued.

SENATOR COUZENS: "So you sacrificed the common stockholders of the first trust to create a second trust . . . ."

MR. DILLON: "We could have taken that $10 million and invested it in something else . . . in Steel common or anything else."

SENATOR COUZENS: "I know, but you did not buy Steel common. You bought something which you yourself controlled. So I do not think it is quite comparable."

THE CHAIRMAN (SENATOR FLETCHER): "It enabled them to get control of $60 million more."

SENATOR COUZENS: "Certainly."[17]

The hearings also revealed that Dillon, Read charged substantial fees to organize the two trusts and to distribute their securities—for example, Trust #1 paid the firm $3.3 million to market its "first" preferred issue and $1 million for organizing Trust #2. Moreover, the 250,000 common shares in Trust #1, acquired by Dillon, Read at zero cost, were worth $14,500,000 by late 1928. In addition, individual partners in the firm held 500,000 common shares in Trust #1 @ 20 cents, representing an aggregate cost of $100,000; in 1928, these shares were worth $29 million.[18]

Pecora also demonstrated that the two trusts had purchased large blocks of securities issued by corporations whose chairmen or presidents sat on the board of Trust #1 and who recommended that both trusts buy the stocks and bonds of their companies. Asked whether the public had been fairly treated in receiving only 25 percent of the common shares in Trust #1 and 20 percent in Trust #2, Dillon replied: "We could have taken all that profit. We could have bought all the common stock." Senator Alva B. Adams, a Colorado Democrat, told Dillon that his answer brought to mind the famous quotation from Lord Clive when he first arrived in India: "When I consider my opportunities, I marvel at my moderation."[19]

FORRESTAL'S EMBARRASSMENT

WHILE DILLON, READ was lucky in that the testimony of its spokesmen came at the end of the hearings, when press and public interest were in decline, Forrestal was unlucky in being the only member of the firm singled out for investigation of his personal finances. He testified on October 13, the last day of the hearings, and Pecora led him relentlessly through a maze of maneuvers that Forrestal and his personal bookkeeper-assistant, Paul Strieffler, had taken to minimize or to escape personal income taxes in 1929 and subsequently.

The focal point of the interrogation was the disposition of Forrestal's portion of the 500,000 common shares of Trust #1. In 1924, he had received 7,500 shares at the original price of 20 cents per share; then as the stock appreciated and he rose in the firm, he was given 1,700 additional shares @ 75 cents and later 12,800 shares @ $10. He thus owned 37,000 shares at a total cost to him of about $28,500. By late 1928, these were worth approximately $2.2 million.[20]

In that year, Forrestal simultaneously organized two companies—the Beekman Corporation of Delaware and the Beekman Company Ltd. of Canada. He (and subsequently his wife) were the sole owners of Beekman-Delaware, and that entity in turn owned all of the stock of Beekman-Canada. In July and August of 1929, 20,000 of his 37,000 shares in Trust #1 were transferred to Beekman-Canada and valued on its books at about $1.2 million. Within a few weeks, about 17,000 of the transferred shares were sold in the open market for $896,410.65, on which no Canadian taxes were owed (because these were capital gains, on which Canada imposed no tax). Later in the same year, Forrestal "borrowed" another $770,000 from Beekman-Canada and "paid back" these "loans" by transferring to Beekman-Canada some of his Dillon, Read partnership shares which were nontransferable and had no public market value. Because this money was taken from Beekman-Canada in the form of loans rather than capital gains, it avoided taxation in the United States.[21]

Transactions such as these were legal and not uncommon in the unregulated Wall Street environment of the 1920s. Nevertheless, their disclosure in the somber aftermath of the market crash, which had wiped out thousands of investors and plunged the country into the Great Depression, produced a public attitude of moral censure and frequently of outrage. Furthermore, it was the political purpose of the subcommittee to expose the exceeding deviousness of traditional Wall Street practices as a means of clearing the way for public support of drastic legislative reforms. Puffing on his pipe, Forrestal responded to Pecora's relentless grilling with cool poise, but the disclosures were embarrassing, and many of his answers left an impression of deliberate evasion. He disclaimed all knowledge of tax matters, telling the senators that the two companies had been "caused to be organized" by his bookkeeper, Paul Strieffler, who served as president and treasurer of both, and by his personal attorney, John Vincent.

MR. PECORA: "Who is Mr. Strieffler?"

MR. FORRESTAL: "He is my assistant, and has handled, in addition to other duties, all of my financial transactions, all tax matters for me."

MR. PECORA: "Did you ask Mr. Strieffler to become president and treasurer of the Beekman Company Ltd.?"

MR. FORRESTAL: "No, I cannot recall that I did. Mr. Strieffler came to me, after he had consulted with my counsel as to the formation of the company, and asked me for permission to proceed with it . . . And he was elected president, and I do not recall, speaking quite frankly, that I asked him to take the position."

MR. PECORA: "Does Mr. Strieffler receive any salary for his services as president and treasurer of the Beekman Company Ltd.?"

MR. FORRESTAL: "Yes."

MR. PECORA: "What salary does he receive?"

MR. FORRESTAL: "$100 a month."

MR. PECORA: "What was the purpose you had in mind when you caused the Beekman Company Ltd. and the Beekman Corporation of Delaware to be incorporated, either in December 1928 or the early part of 1929, whenever it was?"

MR. FORRESTAL: "As I recall it, either I myself had heard of the incorporation of companies in Canada with some advantages in the handling of taxes, or Mr. Strieffler had mentioned it to me. Which of those two is correct I do not recall, but in any event that was the basis for the inception of it, and from that there flowed the conversation with Mr. Vincent, and subsequently, through him and Mr. Knollenberg, who was his associate on taxation."

MR. PECORA: "What had you heard about the advantages of organizing a company in Canada with respect to tax matters?"

MR. FORRESTAL: "I had heard, very frankly, nothing specific, Mr. Pecora. I had never followed taxation myself in any detail."

MR. PECORA: "What were the advantages in tax matters that you had heard about in connection with Canadian companies?"

MR. FORRESTAL: "I had heard nothing."

MR. PECORA: "You said that the thing that prompted you, or one of the things that prompted you, to cause the Beekman Company Ltd. and the Beekman Corporation of Delaware to be incorporated was because you had heard something about the advantages accruing therefrom in tax matters. Don't you recall what those advantages were?"

MR. FORRESTAL: "I am sorry I cannot be more specific than that because that is all that I recall. I may add to that, that I had never—in previous years, or in that year—I never had myself known anything on taxes except the total amount of taxes that I paid which, naturally, I was interested in knowing."

MR. PECORA: "When you caused these two companies to be organized after someone said something to you about advantages in tax matters to be derived therefrom, did you cause them to be organized with the hope of obtaining some advantage with regard to your income tax?"

MR. FORRESTAL: "I frankly only—I knew nothing about the details of taxes. I knew that my counsel, Mr. Vincent, who acted not only as counsel, but with whom I had a personal relationship—I had complete confidence in him, and when this suggestion was made to me, whether it was made by my assistant or by somebody else, I instructed him to go to Mr. Vincent, lay the whole matter before him, and to follow exactly and specifically whatever suggestions or whatever advice of any kind my counsel gave."

MR. PECORA: "Who made that suggestion to you that caused you to do what you said you did?"

MR. FORRESTAL: "I have already said, Mr. Pecora, I am not sure where it came from. Mr. Strieffler, I think, made the suggestion, but I am not certain that he did."

MR. PECORA: "What was the specific suggestion he made to you that prompted you to act upon it?"

MR. FORRESTAL: "I cannot recall anything more in detail than that—that it was desirable."

MR. PECORA: "What was it, in substance?"

MR. FORRESTAL: "I will say this: It was desirable to look into the matter."

MR. PECORA: "To what end?"

MR. FORRESTAL: "Undoubtedly there must have been a consideration of taxes involved in it."

MR. PECORA: "Just what consideration of taxes? Did you hope to be able in some fashion within the law to minimize your income payments?"

MR. FORRESTAL: "My natural desire was to pay the minimum taxes that were legally proper for me to pay."[22]

As Forrestal was the sole owner or beneficiary of both companies, Pecora asked whether it was clear that they had been, since their inception, "your alter ego"? Senator Couzens, pursuing the same point, summed up: "In other words, leaving out all legal technicalities and entities, the fact was that you were just switching money back and forth from one pocket to another." Forrestal replied, "Well, I had not thought of it in that fashion."[23]

Because the Dillon, Read hearings did not receive much press attention, and the public had begun to exhibit a general indifference or perhaps a sullen resignation to disclosures of this kind, Forrestal might well have shrugged off his own testimony as a transitory embarrassment. As Douglas Dillon later said, "Everyone was doing it at the time."[24] In fact, however, Forrestal came away from the hearing with a deep sense of moral discomfort. His fundamental drive for success, combined with a natural secretiveness, had permitted him to condone such manipulations so long as they were private. But when they were exposed to public view, some inner guilt or residue of earlier "socialistic attitudes" deprived him of his usually sturdy composure for several weeks. "He seemed very strong," Douglas Dillon remembered, but found it hard to "push aside" any public criticism. "Whenever he was criticized publicly, not privately, he sort of fell apart." After the interrogation by Pecora, "he thought what he had done was godawful, which it certainly wasn't," but "it upset him terribly, and he just sort of vanished from the scene for several days. He left. He wasn't around. You couldn't find him."[25] Eliot Janeway felt he had suffered "a sort of temporary breakdown."[26] In Douglas Dillon's view, the same thing happened later in Washington when Forrestal was attacked in the press by Drew Pearson and Walter Winchell: He ended up accepting, in some part, the judgment that his tormentors were right, "that he had done all those things which of course he hadn't. . . . He was very uncertain about himself in some ways."[27]

END OF AN ERA

FORRESTAL RECOVERED his composure after the Senate hearings and continued to demonstrate a characteristic firmness and discipline in business affairs. The Pecora ordeal, however, and especially the ensuing stagnation in Wall Street, drained the Baron of his enthusiasm for a continuing active role in investment banking, and soon thereafter he moved out of the Dillon, Read offices at 28 Nassau Street and relocated himself at 40 Wall Street, leaving the day-to-day running of the firm to Forrestal (who was now president), William A. Phillips, and Dean Mathey. "After the crash there wasn't any business for a period of years," Douglas Dillon remembered, and in the absence of exciting major deals, "my father just got bored with the business, so he turned it over to Forrestal and the partners who were left"[28] and devoted most of his time to his private interests and hobbies, which included stained-glass windows, thoroughbred cattle, and the wines of France. Immensely rich, the Dillons lived from autumn through spring at 635 Park Avenue amidst their collection of Whistlers and Rembrandts, then moved in summer to the estate in New Jersey to enjoy their fine herd of Guernseys, or traveled to France to inspect their spacious and reputable vineyards at Château Haut-Brion. As to Dillon, Read business, the Baron "followed what they were doing, but only for a couple of hours a day"; at the same time there was never any doubt that he remained in control of major decisions. Forrestal met with him or conferred by telephone several times a week, and Douglas Dillon, then in his middle twenties, was assigned as the informal liaison between his father and Forrestal and sat at a desk just outside Forrestal's office.[29]

With the Baron's departure there was a reallocation of equity shares and profits. He kept one-third and left two-thirds to the remaining partners. By the late 1930s, Forrestal's share had risen to 24 percent, but it amounted to a larger share of a progressively smaller pie.[30] The exciting large-scale deals of the 1920s were gone and the whole money market was paralyzed; Wall Street was a ghost town of shattered dreams and empty boardrooms; the prestige of the entire banking community was in steady decline, eroded by scandal and public disillusion, though only one indictment came out of the Pecora Hearings (involving the aggressive speculator Charles E. Mitchell for perjury and fraud—he was acquitted of criminal charges, but required to pay $1.1 million in back taxes and damages).[31]

Later in the decade, Richard Whitney, by then president of the New York Stock Exchange, was convicted of criminal embezzlement and sent to Sing Sing prison for misappropriating bonds owned by the New York Yacht Club (of which he was treasurer) and bonds and cash belonging to the Gratuity Fund of the Stock Exchange itself. Because Whitney was the broker for the House of Morgan and his brother George a Morgan partner, his disgrace delivered a shattering blow to the heart of the Wall Street Establishment. (Whitney and Franklin Roosevelt had been schoolmates at Groton. When the SEC chairman informed him that Whitney had been arrested for embezzlement, the President exclaimed in astonishment, ''Not Dick Whitney!'')[32] These and other exposures battered the morale of the banking community and also drained away talent as a number of first-rate men left to pursue other careers, and the brightest young college graduates, animated by the growing spirit of reform, shunned Wall Street and headed for Washington and jobs with the New Deal.

The middle 1930s were not, however, entirely devoid of business opportunities, and Forrestal, as active head of the firm, organized and carried out several significant deals. One involved the financing of the Triborough Bridge, which Robert Moses, New York City's aggressive Commissioner of Public Works, proposed as a substitute for an antiquated ferry service linking Manhattan with Brooklyn and Queens. In the course of devising the financial arrangements, Dillon, Read invented the concept of ''induced revenues,'' which reflected the calculation that a bridge, because it could carry a much larger volume of traffic per hour or per day, would be more than a substitute for the ferry service; it could be expected to generate far larger revenues. This proved to be the case.[33]

Forrestal also put the firm into several oil deals which expanded his contacts with leaders in that industry and gave him insights into the growing importance of Middle East oil for the economies of the United States and Western Europe. This knowledge shaped his later position on the issues of the Palestine partition and the creation of Israel in 1947–1948. One of these deals involved Texaco, which had a strong domestic marketing and distributing organization, but needed a large reliable source of crude oil. About this time, Standard Oil of California obtained a concession in Bahrain and sent a noted geologist, E. L. DeGolyer, to analyze the possibility of major oil fields beneath the barren desert sands of adjacent Saudi Arabia. No wells were drilled at the time, but DeGolyer called the geology "promising," an assessment which proved to be a classic understatement, for it was soon apparent that Saudi Arabia had the largest oil reserves in the world. Forrestal, who was following the situation, then developed the idea that Standard Oil's reserves in Saudi Arabia could be married to Texaco's domestic marketing organization. The result was the creation of a new company, CALTEX, which gave Texaco a half interest in Standard Oil's Middle East production and Standard Oil a half interest in Texaco's domestic distribution system. As Saudi Arabian reserves were further developed, CALTEX was reorganized as a multicompany consortium known as the Arabian-American Oil Company (ARAMCO).[34]

THE HIDDEN-HAND REFORMER

FRUSTRATION in the financial community during this same period found a convenient scapegoat in Franklin Delano Roosevelt and all his works, and produced in many places of business an outpouring of bitterness and hatred for "That Man in the White House" combined with a growing sense of despair for the future of capitalism. Breadlines and intractable economic stagnation opened the door to political polarization, to a fear of "the clash of classes and eventual crash of all we care about in America," as diplomat William Bullitt wrote.[35] Demagogues, crackpots, and visionaries rose up on every side—Governor Huey Long of Louisiana promised $6,000 a year to every American family under the slogan "Every Man a King"; Charles E. Coughlin, a Catholic priest in Detroit, drew millions of rabid followers to radio sermons that poured inflammatory abuse on bankers, Jews, J. P. Morgan, Russia, gold, and eventually the New Deal; the Townsend Plan, developed by a retired California physician (and containing the embryo of the subsequent Social Security System), promised to end the Depression by giving everyone over sixty a government pension of $200 a month.[36]

There was deep concern about the rise of "socialism" in Western Europe and especially the infection of "international communism"; at the same time, however, American business viewed Russia as a vast untapped market for manufactured goods, a market so large that enthusiasts were convinced it could absorb American surplus production and end the Depression. Business leaders lobbied Washington for diplomatic recognition of the Bolshevik government and for the extension of economic credits to finance Russian purchases. Senator Walter F. George of Georgia, "who had visions of clothing Russian peasants in American cotton," urged Roosevelt to make a serious bid for that market; without it, he argued, the cotton-growing states were facing economic ruin.[37] The whole capitalist system seemed under siege, and many businessmen put the blame primarily on Roosevelt and the New Deal.

Nevertheless, as the decade unfolded, and especially after FDR's reelection in 1936, the more rational leaders in Wall Street began to acknowledge that the Democrats were in Washington to stay and that regulation of the securities business was inevitable and stabilizing. A handful of the wiser heads indeed came to realize that the New Deal reforms, far from aiming at the destruction of American business enterprise, were designed in fact to preserve it—by requiring it to become more responsible, more accountable, and more equitable so that American society would not fall prey to the extreme left-right, Communist-Fascist polarization that was wracking all of Europe. They perceived that the New Deal was far less revolutionary than it was reformist. One of these wiser heads was E. A. Pierce, a prominent stockbroker and later a founding partner of Merrill, Lynch, Pierce, Fenner and Beane. A son of Maine and a lumberjack in his youth, he had no pretensions to blue blood or high standing in New York society, but he was a man of mature judgment and a voice of reason in the struggle between the reformers and the Bourbons who ran the still unreformed Stock Exchange.[38]

Another wise head was Paul Shields, a tough, cold Wall Street operator (known to his close friends as "Old Warmheart") originally from Montana, whose small brokerage firm was a lesser satellite in Dillon, Read's orbit. Whenever Forrestal organized a selling syndicate, Shields and Company was a reliable participant in the distribution. Shields and Forrestal liked and trusted each other, discovered they shared an addiction to total immersion in their work, and became close friends and social companions. Shields became an open Roosevelt supporter and a useful communications link between Wall Street and the New Deal; later he was instrumental in obtaining Forrestal's first appointment in government, and served him as an intermittent personal adviser during the war and afterward. Both men recognized the need for intelligent regulation of the securities business, but Shields was willing, as Forrestal was not, to accept the financial and social risks of aligning himself publicly with the reformers and against the encrusted but powerful defenders of the status quo.[39]

After passage of the landmark Securities Exchange Act of 1934, FDR appointed Joseph P. Kennedy as the first SEC chairman, a move that looked to New Deal reformers like a cynical and inexplicable sellout to the Bourbons, for Kennedy was not just a Wall Streeter but a notorious speculator and stock manipulator. In the event, however, he proved absolutely determined to carry out the provisions of the act, especially to require that issuers of new securities tell the truth about them to the public. Using his inside knowledge of Wall Street's shadier practices, he set up "Trojan Horse listening posts" and was soon gathering the information needed to take legal action against numerous unreformed operators.[40]

Richard Whitney, who had welcomed the Kennedy appointment as a "sane and sound" approach to regulatory measures he wished to be ineffectual, soon linked Kennedy with FDR as "traitors to their class," and organized within the Stock Exchange a strategy of surly obstruction to every SEC move. James Landis, who succeeded Kennedy in 1935, was more legalistic, but also more conciliatory toward the Wall Street Establishment. It remained for William O. Douglas, who succeeded Landis in 1937, to break the power of the Old Guard and transform the Stock Exchange from a cozy private club to a responsible public organization.

Soon after his appointment, Douglas received a telephone call from Forrestal, who said he was speaking for Shields. Shields, who sat on the board of directors of the Stock Exchange, would like to work with Douglas to reform that institution.[41] That call proved the beginning of a triangular friendship which continued during the war years in Washington and thereafter. Shields and Douglas, both Westerners, were direct and open advocates for the causes they believed in, while Forrestal operated effectively behind the scenes, but with an indirectness that made him vulnerable to the charge of lacking the courage of his convictions. Shields never accepted a government job. Douglas was appointed to the U.S. Supreme Court in 1939 and was one of three men, the others being Harry S. Truman and James F. Byrnes, whom FDR seriously considered for his running mate in the 1944 presidential election.[42]

In late 1937, Douglas asked Forrestal's advice on the drafting of an SEC rule for "short selling." Forrestal told him he would arrange for an expert to meet with him, provided the meeting itself was secret and provided further that when the rule was announced no one would divulge the name of the adviser. Douglas accepted these conditions. Forrestal then told him, "Your man is my partner, Clarence Dillon. He will meet you next Sunday at his Park Avenue apartment. Be there promptly at nine in the evening."[43] Douglas was made a bit nervous by the discovery that his contact was to be none other than the "Wolf of Wall Street," for although Dillon had recently made several "New Deal speeches" that made him sound like a convinced reformer, his autocratic qualities were well known. Some years before, Douglas had been a young associate in the New York law firm of Cravath, Swaine and Moore, where he had heard the story that Dillon had kept the senior partner, Robert T. Swaine, cooling his heels in an outer office for two hours—at which point Swaine had stormed out in anger and frustration. On the appointed evening, Dillon kept Douglas waiting only thirty minutes. The "liveried butler offered me a scotch and soda at nine o'clock, another at nine-fifteen, and a third at nine-thirty. Then Clarence Dillon swept into the room with the dignity and grace of a Barrymore." Fully briefed and alert, Dillon studied a sheet on which Douglas had written three possible short-selling rules. He was lost in thought for perhaps five minutes; then he stood up, handed the paper back to Douglas, and, swearing him once more to secrecy, said, "If you want to do an effective job, take the first one of those three rules." It was, in substance: No one may sell short at less than one-eighth above the last sale price. Announced and promulgated soon thereafter, this regulation, known as the "uptick rule," remains unchanged to this day.[44]

Forrestal played a larger, though still behind-the-scenes role in the Roosevelt administration's major effort to break up the public utility holding companies. Wendell Willkie, then counsel to one of them (the Commonwealth and Southern Corporation) argued that holding companies represented the essence of capitalistic enterprise and denounced FDR's attempt to break them up as "socialistic." Forrestal strongly supported FDR's purpose, though not primarily on philosophical grounds; to his practical mind, the holding companies were so blatantly monopolistic that an attempt by the banking community to defend them would only further tarnish Wall Street's reputation for unfairness. Working closely with leaders at the SEC, Thomas G. Corcoran at the White House, and Congressman Sam Rayburn, Forrestal served as the "inside man," covertly raising a good deal of money to fund the campaigns of congressmen who were prepared to vote for the breakup. Paul Shields was the "bagman" who "fetched" for Forrestal in this enterprise, physically collecting the money from anonymous business supporters of reform and delivering it to Rayburn. The Public Utility Holding Company Act was signed into law in 1935.[45]

Following Richard Whitney's exposure and arrest in March 1938, resistance to Stock Exchange reform quickly collapsed. All of the SEC demands were met (including a rule that required every member firm to make available the firm's financial condition to any customer who asked for it), and William McChesney Martin, Jr., a thirty-one-year-old broker from St. Louis, became the new full-time chairman of the Stock Exchange.[46]

Forrestal had the greatest respect for Douglas's strength of character and for the reforms he carried through with unflinching courage. They became close friends, yet Forrestal would not risk his own standing with the Wall Street Establishment by expressing open support for the reforms or by acknowledging that Douglas was anything more than a casual acquaintance. Douglas perceived the ambivalence, accepted it with good grace, and did not allow it either to affect his feeling of affection and admiration for his friend or to place limits on his availability to Forrestal whenever private advice or help was needed in later years. Nevertheless, there is in Douglas's summary of the relationship a sense of disappointment and even of implicit scorn: "The River Club and Wall Street in New York City were Jim's spiritual headquarters, and I was not a favorite in either place. Jim never embraced me publicly; indeed, he sought to dissociate himself from me in the public eye. Since his own closest ties were with the Establishment, his psyche demanded that *It* think well of him. Yet he rebelled against it, and I was an expression of his rebellion."[47] Like much else in the life of this secretive, sensitive man, Forrestal's true feelings about the Wall Street Establishment would remain shrouded in ambivalence to the very end.

By the late 1930s events at home and abroad were creating new conditions that pointed to dramatic change. The somber, disappointing early years of the decade gave way to gathering crisis in Europe, and the world began careening toward the measureless explosion of another great war. The new circumstances imparted a strange frenetic quality to life, and they found Forrestal eager for new challenges and a change of scene. Much of the zest was gone from the investment game, and the titular presidency of Dillon, Read was proving to be a sort of triumph of form over substance, for the Baron had only partially retired, leaving a situation of divided authority rather than a concentration of the firm's affairs in Forrestal's hands. He felt a renewed impulse to get out from under the dominating presence of his mentor and to declare his independence in a new setting. Moreover, always sensitive to the locus of real power, he saw that power was now moving inexorably to Washington and government. At forty-eight, he was at the top of his form, a prominent figure in Wall Street with wide connections in the upper reaches of national and international business, endowed with enormous intellectual and physical energy, a lean and athletic multimillionaire made confident to the point of cockiness by twenty years of unbroken professional and financial success.

He expressed to Paul Shields a desire to get out of Wall Street and into the Washington maelstrom, and Shields, who thought this a "terrific idea," went to Douglas, now a Supreme Court justice, to ask his view. "Sure," Douglas said, "Washington is a great place for seminars in the area of adult education."[48]

III

★ ★ ★

THE MIGHTIEST FLEET

★ ★ ★

CHAPTER 9

Washington 1940

WILLIAM O. DOUGLAS spoke directly to the President about Forrestal and gave him a strong recommendation. Liking what he heard, FDR turned the matter over to his White House assistant Thomas G. Corcoran for a further check on Forrestal's abilities and reputation. Corcoran, a New York lawyer during the 1920s and early 1930s before he joined the New Deal, had represented Dillon, Read during the Pecora investigation. As a White House assistant, he had worked with Forrestal to secure passage of the Public Utility Holding Company Act.[1]

Although he may not have been fully aware of it, Forrestal was one of many bankers, industrialists, businessmen, and lawyers whom the administration was now earnestly recruiting for prominent roles in the developing preparedness effort. Paul Shields was a central figure in the effort to identify the best men in Wall Street, and had taken Forrestal to a brief meeting with FDR at the White House in 1938.[2] The eerily quiescent "phony war" phase of hostilities in Europe, following the Nazi destruction of Poland in 1939, ended abruptly in the spring of 1940. Hitler's legions suddenly lunged westward in a series of swift, ruthless attacks that came to be known as "blitzkrieg." Norway and Denmark were invaded in April; then France, Holland, Belgium, and Luxembourg were attacked in May, and all of Western Europe was quickly brought under Nazi control. The world was especially shocked that France, thought to be impregnable behind her Maginot Line, was forced to surrender within a few weeks. By midsummer Britain stood alone, saved from immediate invasion only by thirty-five miles of English Channel and the supreme courage of the Royal Air Force. Much of the world was stunned, then transfixed in a paralyzing sense of terror, by the spectacle of this new and apparently invincible mechanized savagery.

In the deepening crisis of civilization, President Roosevelt recognized the urgent need to call upon reputable talent in the business community to help mobilize and convert the American economy to defense production. But to obtain a positive response it was first necessary that he call a truce in the ideological war between business and the New Deal to assure business leaders there would be no more castigation of "malefactors of great wealth," a phrase of FDR's which had polarized the situation in 1936. This assurance was an ingredient of the message brought by Paul Shields indicating that FDR wanted Forrestal as one of his administrative assistants in the White House. At some point in the process, the President telephoned Clarence Dillon to ask him to release Forrestal for service in Washington.[3]

FDR used the sudden debacle in Europe to declare a U.S. production goal of fifty thousand military aircraft (a figure that seemed totally unrealistic at the time) and simultaneously to push through a shaken Congress a relaxation of the neutrality laws and the enactment of a compulsory military draft. By executive order, he also transferred fifty overage American destroyers to the desperate Royal Navy in exchange for American base rights in Bermuda, Newfoundland, and other British possessions in the western Atlantic.[4] In beleaguered Britain, Churchill was called to be the King's First Minister in what many feared was merely the prelude to the nation's final defeat. But the new Prime Minister rallied the British people—and most of the civilized world—with electrifying words that clothed an iron resolve none could misunderstand: "We shall defend our island, whatever the cost may be, we shall fight on the beaches, we shall fight on the landing grounds, we shall fight in the fields and in the streets, we shall fight in the hills; we shall never surrender."[5]

Forrestal was not entirely surprised by the swift collapse of the European democracies, and he understood its grave implications. He had reached the private conclusion that France and Britain, sapped by years of pacifism and complacent refusal to see the danger of Hitler, would be defeated without all-out American support; yet America remained deeply divided on the issue of intervention and was lagging seriously in its own military preparedness. These perceptions strengthened Forrestal's developing conviction that governmental power, not money power, had become the decisive factor for influence in the world. If one desired to exercise major influence, one needed to operate the levers of government. Still, he was not certain that an undefined position in the White House was a good fit for his talents, and he displayed characteristic ambivalence during the preliminary negotiations. In a handwritten note to Corcoran, he said: "Just to clarify our talk of yesterday: I have some misgiving whether I can be effective in the role you outlined and I think there are better men available. Bob Lovett is one who comes to my mind. But this is no time for prima donna tactics and I don't want to be in that light. The whole picture is too serious for that. So I am giving you my proxy—and I shall be happy either way it works out. I want neither publicity nor glory—the price of both is too high. As ever, J.V.F.''[6]

A few days later, he nonetheless went through a curious minuet with Paul Nitze. He asked, "Do you think I should take it?" Nitze replied with other questions: "Do you expect to find it interesting? Do you have any feel for this kind of work?"

"I don't know," Forrestal said, "I know New York, but I don't know much about Washington. From what I've heard, bureaucratic politics is a slippery business."

"If it doesn't work out, what will you do?"

"I'll come back here."

"Well, I guess the main question," Nitze said, "is whether you will regret having missed a large opportunity, if you end up declining the offer." Forrestal looked at him. "I've made up my mind," he said, "I'm going."[7]

CONGRESS had given statutory basis in 1939 for FDR's practice of employing a small group of administrative assistants (initially four, but later increased to six) to serve as informal extensions of his eyes, ears, and legs, to perform an indefinable range of tasks too complicated or sensitive to be handled by the regular bureaucracy. In the main, their function was to get information and condense and synthesize it for the President's use, to remove bureaucratic roadblocks to forward movement on particular programs, to find palatable solutions to often heated policy disputes between Cabinet members. The assistants had no authority over anyone in any department or agency and were expressly prohibited from interposing themselves between the President and any other officer of the government. They were moreover sworn, in FDR's phrase, to a "passion for anonymity." Broadly speaking, they operated with considerable effectiveness, helping to keep affairs tolerably coherent in the inherently loose and frequently chaotic organizational structures and administrative methods that characterized the New Deal. This was so because they were brilliant men dedicated to serving their chief, and because it was understood throughout the government that they did in fact represent the President's wishes.[8]

At various times from 1936 to 1945, this shifting group included Thomas Corcoran, James Rowe, Benjamin Cohen, Jonathan Daniels, David K. Niles, and Lauchlin Currie, in addition to Forrestal. Corcoran, perhaps the most famous and least anonymous, was a product of Harvard Law School who had clerked for Justice Oliver Wendell Holmes. By the late 1930s, his influence was at its peak, but beginning to wane as the President and the nation shifted emphasis from ending the Depression to preparing for global war. Corcoran's memorandum on Forrestal for the President said: "Following up your suggestion that you might want to take Forrestal as one of your administrative assistants to help find the men with 'big names' and organizing ability to handle the problem of industrial production of war materials . . . He has been the acknowledged leader of your crowd in Wall Street . . . His specialty is industrial personnel—he has been rounding up management material for Dillon's companies for a long time . . . He has enormous courage to do things that have never been done. He has pioneered financing jobs that everyone else in the Street was afraid to touch. He has followed the German situation closely for many years because of Dillon's post-war German financing . . . He understands the situation thoroughly and bitterly, and he has followed you eagerly in your perception of the need to get the nation ready.''[9]

The memorandum overstated the case on the points of political allegiance and initiative. Forrestal was not "the acknowledged leader of your crowd in Wall Street''; he was a Democrat by heritage who voted for the party's candidates, but he was not a New Dealer, either intellectually or philosophically, nor had he been an open advocate of reforms in the investment banking business. Nevertheless, the Corcoran memorandum provided an accurate assessment of his great strengths—he was a competent organizer of large business enterprises; he had drive and imagination; as a member of the administration he would attract other "big men" with the requisite organizing abilities. FDR was duly impressed by these credentials. On a more personal level, he may also have been favorably disposed by the fact that the Forrestals had recently become his neighbors near Hyde Park.

THE FARM IN DUTCHESS COUNTY

IN THE EARLY SPRING of 1940, Jo Forrestal had made another impulsive decision and had made it, according to Michael, "mostly without consulting Dad." She decided abruptly to leave their estate in Old Westbury and buy a farm in Salt Point, New York, a part of Dutchess County. There appear to have been several considerations: Forrestal had just decided to go into government, and the indications were he would become an assistant in the White House; Jo was keenly aware that the drop in his earned income would be precipitous—from $190,000 to $10,000—and Long Island living was expensive. She felt war was definitely coming, and with it the rationing of food and other basics that would make it advantageous to live on a farm. According to Michael, her instinct also told her it would be "politically smart" to live closer to President Roosevelt and his beloved retreat at Hyde Park.[10]

On a more personal level, she was aware that she had more or less worn out her welcome on the North Shore. She had successfully pushed her way into numerous social situations there, but in the process had alienated a goodly number of people and earned the real friendship of very few. More recently, she had quarreled seriously with Adele Lovett, perhaps her only real friend, over the operation of a business partnership they had formed to design, manufacture, and sell wax-dipped fabric flowers under the name "Constance Spry." Jo designed the flowers, and Adele was the business manager. Whatever the cause of the dispute, Adele had found Jo's behavior so irrational and outrageous that she broke off the partnership and told her erstwhile friend to "go see a psychiatrist."[11] The inference is that, reluctantly accepting the truth that she did not wear well, Jo decided—as she had decided in similar circumstances at *Vogue*—it was time for a change of scene.

In any event, she moved the family "very suddenly, practically overnight."[12] She put the Old Westbury estate on the market, and the family never lived there again, although the house did not sell for several years. According to one account, Forrestal subsequently failed to keep up the mortgage payments and the bank foreclosed.[13]

The farm she bought featured a comfortable white frame house on Netherwood Road, with Mount Vernon–like colonial pillars across the front, together with a large barn and other outbuildings, which she quickly filled with several good horses, countless dogs, and various other animals. It became her new enthusiasm, her new mode of self-expression, her own special place. With greater ease than on Long Island, she was accepted into the local Rombout Hunt, became a good friend of the Master of Hounds, Homer Grey, and happily papered the walls of her dining room with a photographic collage of herself sitting astride her hunters, jumping over hedges, galloping down wooded trails and across open fields. She named the place Animal Farm, and it must have been a warm reminder of her childhood days in West Virginia. Harold Fletcher came to stay for a few weeks and organized a work program for Michael and Peter and some visiting friends from the Aiken School. They worked long hours cutting and baling hay, and Michael and the headmaster attended local grange meetings to talk planting, harvesting, and politics with the local farmers.[14]

Jo's purchase alerted FDR, who was famous for the proprietary care with which he checked on every newcomer to his part of Dutchess County, and either granted or withheld the overlord's welcome. In this case, the Squire of Hyde Park gave his warm assent in a letter to Forrestal of April 11, 1940, at least a month or two before the newcomer's name was brought to his official attention in Washington.

April 11, 1940

My dear Mr. Forrestal:

When I was at home on Sunday I heard to my great pleasure that Mrs. Forrestal has bought the old Marshall farm just over the Pleasant Valley line from the Town of Hyde Park. I hope that this Spring that you and she will come over and see us at Hyde Park—and I think I may be of some help in telling her of the history of the place.

For instance, across the road from the house is a small building which was used for town meetings of what was then the Town of Clinton, prior to 1821. It is a delightful farm and I am very glad that we shall be neighbors.

Very sincerely yours,
Franklin D. Roosevelt[15]

Forrestal replied in a handwritten note.

My dear Mr. President:

It was a friendly and gracious thought that your letter of last week reflected—about my wife's purchase of the Marshall farm. I appreciate it deeply and I shall look forward to a visit with you some time in the summer, with great pleasure. Maybe we can reminisce a bit on the days when you and Dick Cornell toured the hustings of Dutchess and Columbia back in 1910!

Thanks again for your neighborly interest.

Respectfully yours,
James Forrestal[16]

It is likely that the reference to the campaign for state senator in 1910 revived FDR's memory of Morgan Hoyt and Major Forrestal and so gained standing for the Wall Street banker as a man from a family with roots in Dutchess County and a record of support for FDR. This bonding ingredient placed the budding FDR-Forrestal relationship on a more personal, more neighborly basis than Forrestal was ever able to achieve with Harry Truman. FDR and Forrestal exchanged gifts at Christmas during the war, and FDR wrote occasional notes asking that Forrestal drop by the White House to fill him in on his most recent inspection trip to the battlefronts.[17]

Forrestal accepted the new living arrangements in Dutchess County without demur, no doubt relieved that Jo had found a new outlet for her restless energies, and pleased that Animal Farm was proving an agreeable place for her and their sons to spend the summers. It meant he could concentrate totally and without distraction on his demanding new job in Washington.

WASHINGTON ON THE EVE OF GLOBAL WAR

FORRESTAL'S APPOINTMENT to the White House and, a few months later, to the navy was seen by the press as part of the administration's increasing shift to reliance on Wall Streeters and other businessmen, and this rekindled the ideological conflict between business and the New Deal which had flamed or simmered since FDR's first election, in 1932. The press was very alert to this situation. The liberal magazine *Newsweek* (then owned by Averell Harriman), acknowledging that "of all the first rate investment banking houses, Dillon, Read has come closest to showing a New Deal leaning," nevertheless concluded that Forrestal's appointment "casts a shadow over the whole future of the New Deal in the war-economy phase into which we are entering." The magazine expressed specific concern that control of the emerging rearmament program would pass into the hands of private industry, despite FDR's assurances to New Dealers that it would remain with them. "On its face, Mr. Forrestal's appointment is the most marked step toward freezing the New Dealers out. Able as Mr. Forrestal is, it is unbelievable to think it was his brains alone that recommended him to FDR . . . what Mr. Forrestal had that those SEC employees would have lacked is long-standing personal friendships with top flight bankers."[18]

Time, a more centrist publication, took a more sanguine view. Acknowledging that the "civil war" still raged, it lumped the Forrestal appointment with others from business—notably the more important appointments of Henry L. Stimson as Secretary of War and of Frank Knox as Secretary of the Navy on June 19. It argued that, the need for rearmament being a reality, the need for talented administrators from business and the professions was self-evident. Moreover, there was, *Time* discerned, an urgent need for a bipartisan approach to the mobilization effort so that a united America could face the mortal dangers gathering on the horizon. It therefore praised the President for reaching out to his erstwhile adversaries and applauded "businessmen" for responding to the call, despite a feeling that the New Deal had "fleeced them, sabotaged them, investigated and ridiculed them" since 1932.[19]

This was a perceptive news story. Roosevelt, though he disliked the necessity of bringing businessmen into government, fearing they would trample the social and political achievements of the New Deal, was aware that the old-line government departments and agencies lacked the imagination and the capacity for the swift, intelligent improvisation which the mobilization effort demanded and would demand in even greater measure if the United States should be plunged into actual war. They were too heavily encrusted with habit and routine, too slow moving, too resistant to change. Beyond these major deficiencies, the federal bureaucracy in 1940 was simply not large enough or possessed of sufficiently broad or varied talent to manage the herculean task of organizing the national economy to support a global war. For their part, most leading American businessmen were fully alive to the supreme threat to democracy and capitalism posed by Hitler, Mussolini, and the military clique in Japan. They were patriots and pragmatists far more than they were anti-Roosevelt ideologues.

WHEN FORRESTAL reported for duty at the White House on June 29, 1940, Washington was still a provincial Southern town, dominated architecturally by the Greek temples of the federal government, but notable also for imposing foreign embassies, elegant private houses, lovely green parks—and teeming Negro slums; a town of racial segregation and terrible summer heat unrelieved by air conditioning; a town with an impotent local government run with Southern efficiency by three commissioners appointed by the President; a town with hardly one restaurant above the level of blue-plate special, no serious theater or other artistic creativity, and no nightlife; a town of dilapidated taxicabs which stopped, by law and custom, to pick up additional passengers whenever the driver spotted an opportunity.

The native upper class, called Cave Dwellers, owned the banks, department stores, and real estate firms, or lived on wealth accumulated elsewhere; they entertained elegantly in their own houses, departed in June for Maine or Cape Cod and in January for Palm Beach and Hobe Sound, and generally shrank from publicity and public affairs. In particular did they distance themselves from the gray mass of government employees who toiled in the Greek temples along Pennsylvania and Constitution avenues at an average salary of less than $3,000 a year and who lived in garden apartments and modest bungalows, mainly in the District but also across the Potomac River in Arlington. In earlier days, the links between town and government had been stronger and more cordial, characterized by a certain proprietary attitude on the part of the local elite. But with the coming of the New Deal in 1933, the Cave Dwellers had ceased to accept personal responsibility for the shaggy new governmental animal in their midst; they refused any longer to watch over it like some collective surrogate for the Founding Fathers, but treated it warily as an alien presence.[20]

As David Brinkley, then a newly arrived young newspaperman from North Carolina, remembered their reaction: "The city of Washington—*their city* . . . had been taken over by a lot of pompous, ill-dressed, argumentative New Dealers, some of whom didn't even shave every day. Maybe they knew about egg marketing and consumer economics, but what else did they know?"[21] With FDR's arrival, the Cave Dwellers conspicuously pulled up the drawbridges and took refuge within the confines of their native bastions—the Metropolitan and Sulgrave clubs in town, the Chevy Chase Club in suburban Maryland. For their part, the New Dealers —social workers, farm economists, liberal lawyers, union organizers—met disdain with counterdisdain. Who gave a damn about rich socialites? They were obsolete. It was now the people's turn on center stage, and the New Dealers were surrogates for the common man, brigade leaders in the militant crusade to end the Depression and bring into being a more bountiful, a more just, a more equitable America. In Brinkley's engaging metaphor, they were "political chiropractors eager to get their thumbs on the national spine, to snap it and crack it until the blood again flowed outward to all the extremities of American life, returning it to health and prosperity."[22]

Unfortunately, although the New Deal programs established the foundations for profound ameliorative social change in the longer run, the short-term economic results were inconclusive. After Roosevelt's landslide reelection in 1936, very little had gone right for the administration. The President's attempt in 1937 to give the Supreme Court a liberal majority by enlarging its membership—thereby to gain judicial support for New Deal programs that the "old" court was regularly declaring unconstitutional—ended in bitterness and defeat. In the same year, the economy fell back once more, after a hopeful but fragile recovery, into a severe recession; the already high level of unemployment rose further, the stock market plunged, and the 1938 congressional elections brought to office a large crop of virulent conservatives—men fiercely opposed both to the socioeconomic experiments of the New Deal and to a Rooseveltian foreign policy that was groping for adequate measures, including military buildup, to deter or avert the oncoming war in Europe.[23] As a practical matter, the New Deal domestic program was a dead letter after 1938. At the same time, the focus of national attention and concern was shifting to the ominous threats posed by Nazi Germany, Fascist Italy, and Imperial Japan.

All of this had a pronounced effect on the atmosphere and the demographic-social mix in Washington. Change was coming swiftly. Hundreds of businessmen were arriving to man the new, loosely defined mobilization agencies (each known by an unpronounceable acronym and collectively called "alphabet soup" by critics), and thousands of young women were converging on the city from all over the nation to serve as secretaries and filing clerks in the swelling clerical army, induced by salaries in the range of $1,600 to $2,400 per year, which seemed a fortune to small-town America in the constricted 1930s. Suddenly, as Jonathan Daniels recorded it, Washington "was crowded from the slums around the Capitol to the mansions over Rock Creek. There were all sorts of people in the crowding . . . millionaires in their new Navy uniforms in the big houses on Kalorama Road, and down below them the old converted mansions turned into boarding houses bulging with country girls. People moved in and out of Washington like a procession . . . unwashed, unfed people disgorged from the early Pullmans to the shortage of taxicabs; senators with their vests unbuttoned in the evening; congressmen dancing at the Shoreham; the dipsomaniac wife of a tough official; Georgetown gardens in May.''[24]

Yet despite the urban congestion, the city remained a place of natural beauty, closely fringed by fields and remnant forests, making room for nature in its very midst. In his evocative essay ''Spring in Washington,'' Louis Halle wrote: ''The city passes over Rock Creek Valley on bridges 120 feet above . . . The muskrat swims and raises its young in the woodland stream beneath Connecticut Avenue, never knowing of the crowded buses and taxis that swarm overhead.''[25]

As America drifted closer to the cataract of global war, Washington became once again the dominant focal point of the nation's attention. The American people rediscovered that their capital city was located ''not merely between Maryland and Virginia, but also somewhere between American awe and American derision, between the statistics and the bewilderment, between the political scientists and the political people. It rises like a monument and a mirage on the shores of the Potomac.''[26]

ASSISTANT TO THE PRESIDENT

F ORRESTAL'S tour of duty in the White House lasted only two months— from June 23 to August 22, 1940. Some accounts have described it as a generally restless, unsatisfying period of service, but this characterization was disputed by James Rowe, another FDR assistant, and by Paul Nitze, whom Forrestal summoned from New York within two weeks of his arrival.

Ostensibly, his first assignment was to look into the adequacy of U.S. diplomatic efforts to neutralize growing German influence in Latin America and to swing Latin American governments to the support of the European democracies. The German opportunity in Latin America resided not only in the prestige and fear generated by Hitler's military conquests, but in the historically unfavorable trade balance between North and South America. Despite FDR's Good Neighbor Policy, U.S. restrictions on agricultural imports prevented South Americans from earning sufficient foreign exchange to purchase the quantities of U.S. manufactured goods they wanted. Now Germany was offering to take their raw materials and agricultural commodities and promising to deliver an abundance of high-quality German manufactured products in return. Because the German economy was government-controlled, Washington feared that Hitler could manipulate both purchase and sale prices and thus secure economic domination in South American markets, followed by a steady growth of political influence. Already there were scores of Nazi agents in South America negotiating deals, gathering political and military intelligence, and spreading the word that Hitler's Germany was the wave of the future.[27] The problem was a serious one, and there were sharp differences within the administration over how to attack it. Cordell Hull's State Department, with strong backing from the British and French, urged that the Latins be brought into line by means of tough economic sanctions.[28] Henry Wallace, the Secretary of Agriculture, fearing such a tactic would backfire, wanted to work patiently with local socialists and the radical left to obtain broad Latin American support for the democratic cause.[29]

Yet this somewhat abstruse political assignment was in large part a cover for another task for which Forrestal's talent and experience were better suited—the secret development of what later became the vital air-supply line through northern Latin America to Africa. Here it was necessary to build a series of military airfields, including several in the Caribbean to reinforce the defense of the Panama Canal.[30] But given U.S. nonbelligerency in the European war and the fact that FDR was boxed in by strict neutrality laws and strident isolationist opinion, the matter had to be handled covertly. Forrestal's solution was to enlist in the enterprise his friend Juan Trippe, president of Pan American Airways, and to use normal Pan Am operations as the cover for building the needed airfields. To pay for the work, discretionary government funds had to be secretly passed to Pan Am from the Bureau of the Budget. The audacity of the maneuver disquieted several of Forrestal's White House colleagues, especially Rowe, who was acutely aware that FDR's efforts to awaken the country to the Hitler threat were being heavily attacked by powerful isolationists, like Senator Gerald Nye, Republican from North Dakota, who stood ready to expose and excoriate even legitimate and legal defense preparations. Rowe told Forrestal, "You're doing a dangerous thing. Nye will find out what you have done. And if war doesn't come, and they find those expensive empty airfields and all that equipment scattered around Latin America. You'll be run down, horsewhipped, and hung."

"I'll risk it," Forrestal said with a tight smile. "We're going to war."[31]

Despite his initial skepticism, after watching Forrestal for a while, Rowe remembered saying to himself, "This fellow is going to make it." What impressed him was Forrestal's quiet, wary, but thorough survey of the new terrain and the way in which he identified and rapidly made himself known at the critical points of action and decision—in the White House, the relevant executive agencies, and the Congress. In contrast to the usual business tyro who scorned the mechanics of bureaucracy, Forrestal showed an instinctive feel for the sometimes labyrinthine, Machiavellian processes and seemed to enjoy working his way through them. As Rowe observed him, he was a natural and skillful political operator.[32]

Forrestal had sent a peremptory telegram to Nitze at Dillon, Read: "I expect you in my office Monday morning." Nitze, then thirty-three, took the Sunday night train, The Owl, down to Washington and presented himself in Forrestal's large office on the first floor of the old State-War-Navy Building (now known as the Executive Office Building), next door to the White House. Forrestal's room was grouped with the offices of other FDR assistants, an area they sometimes referred to as Death Row to emphasize their vows of public silence and anonymity. Forrestal greeted Nitze by pointing to the far corner of the office. "There's a desk over there. It's yours."

"What do you expect me to do?"

"Help me."

"Who will pay me?"

"Congress provides no salary for assistants to administrative assistants to the President. Dillon, Read will pay you."

"Where will I live?"

"You can stay with me."[33]

The proposed salary arrangement would today be castigated as a blatant "conflict of interest," but in 1940 the situation was urgent and the press less inclined to investigative reporting.

Without further argument, Nitze moved into the large house Forrestal had rented on Woodland Drive, behind the Shoreham Hotel overlooking Rock Creek Park. The owner, Ambassador Joseph Grew, was posted to Japan and would be interned there for several months following the attack on Pearl Harbor. With help from Nitze and Rowe, Forrestal designed an Office of the Coordinator for Inter-Latin American Affairs and recommended Will Clayton, Ferdinand Eberstadt, and Nelson Rockefeller for the top job. FDR rejected Clayton on political grounds and Eberstadt because of his "too prickly" personality, but agreed to appoint Rockefeller (and later accepted Clayton for the deputy position).[34]

Forrestal had come to Washington with his butler-valet, Stanley Campbell, leaving Jo and their sons to join him after the summer heat had abated. The house on Woodland Drive quickly became a lively haven for temporary bachelors, serious men engaged in serious work in a capital city gradually awakening to the high probability of wrenching war. In addition to Nitze, Nelson Rockefeller was a frequent boarder, and Forrestal's personal counsel, Charles Detmar, was another. Dinner guests included New Deal Brain Trusters like Tom Corcoran and Benjamin V. Cohen. The efficient, temperamental Campbell (who remained in Forrestal's household until 1946) ran the house, dispensing drinks and meals and rooms to transients whom he knew or judged to be friends of Forrestal. Resident officials, congressmen, and other Washington figures began to learn they were welcome at Forrestal's table, provided they could contribute something to his knowledge and understanding of Washington and government and the unfolding drama in Europe and the Pacific. It was understood, then and later, that you worked for your supper at Forrestal's house.[35]

This was an exhilarating period for a gifted man in his prime, discovering challenges larger and more consequential than he had encountered in Wall Street, but challenges for which he had a natural aptitude. There were, of course, immense difficulties and frustrations, but Forrestal was armed with rare intelligence, energy, and resilience. The patriot and secular Jesuit was ready to commit all of his latent passion to the supreme task of preparing America for a war that had become unavoidable—and in which victory was absolutely necessary if the failed system of Western democratic states was to gain another chance. He had discovered his true métier.

CHAPTER 10

★ ★ ★

New Burdens

FORRESTAL'S SELECTION as Under Secretary of the Navy demonstrated the classic mix of politics, personality, timing, and chance that determines almost all such appointments in the American system. The House Naval Affairs Committee had just completed a major study of navy organization—a time-honored and generally futile occupation. Then FDR, who was the navy's reigning godfather, put his foot down. He would approve only two changes: (1) the merger of two technical bureaus (the Bureau of Construction and Repair with the Bureau of Engineering, the new entity to be called the Bureau of Ships) and (2) the creation of the new post of Under Secretary.[1] On June 20, he signed this reorganization bill and simultaneously appointed two distinguished Republican internationalists to the Cabinet—Henry L. Stimson as Secretary of War and Frank Knox as Secretary of the Navy—an act that measurably strengthened the bipartisan approach to war preparedness and simultaneously angered those Republicans at the GOP Convention in Philadelphia who were locked into a fierce internecine struggle between the isolationist Robert Taft of Ohio and the internationalist Wendell Willkie, a lawyer whom Harold Ickes later dubbed "the barefoot boy from Wall Street." Two days later Marshal Pétain surrendered to Hitler in the forest at Compiègne and the German army entered Paris.

On July 18, the Democratic Convention meeting in Chicago nominated FDR for a third term, and the next day he signed the "two-ocean Navy bill," which provided a 70 percent increase in naval construction. This translated to 250 warships displacing 1,325,000 tons, including 7 battleships, 6 battle cruisers, 19 aircraft carriers, 60 light cruisers, 150 destroyers, and 140 submarines.[2]

Frank Knox in 1940 was publisher of the Chicago *Daily News* and had run as the 1936 Republican vice-presidential candidate in tandem with Kansas governor Alfred M. Landon, when the GOP was buried under the Roosevelt landslide. He was a bluff extrovert of rugged physique and big-hearted impulses, not a great intellect, but a successful entrepreneur who had spent most of his life in newspapering and politics. As a young man he had been with Theodore Roosevelt's Rough Riders in the Spanish-American War, and he later commanded an ammunition train in France during World War I. Beginning as a ten-dollar-a-week reporter, he and a partner were soon able to buy a Michigan newspaper, to which they later added the Manchester (New Hampshire) *Union Leader* and the Chicago *Daily News*. Knox had consciously patterned his own life and career on the precepts of Theodore Roosevelt; he believed in the Strenuous Life, Manifest Destiny, the Big Stick, Progressivism, and much else that characterized the vigor and directness of that earlier President.[3]

In 1940, FDR found Knox attractive because he was a vocal supporter of U.S. rearmament and responsible internationalism and also because his coming into the Cabinet would simultaneously mute his criticism of domestic New Deal programs. Knox at first declined FDR's offer, but in the week following Hitler's invasion of the Low Countries, while lunching at the White House, he told the President he was at his service, on one condition: that he have a "Republican companion" in the Cabinet. It was this conversation that led FDR to appoint, as Knox's "opposite number" at the War Department, Henry L. Stimson, a man of far greater relevant experience and intellectual distinction. Stimson was an outstanding international lawyer who had once before served as Secretary of War (in the Taft Cabinet), as governor general of the Philippines, and then as Secretary of State in the Hoover administration. At seventy-two, he was still lucid, vigorous, "possessed of a formidable concentrating power," and totally convinced of the need to confront the totalitarian menace.[4]

FDR had in mind that Thomas Corcoran would become Under Secretary of the Navy, but Knox asked Corcoran "as a personal favor" to forgo this and to stand instead as a candidate for the new post of Assistant Secretary of the Navy for Air. Corcoran agreed, but Knox did not fill that job for a full year, and then it went to someone else. He first offered the Under Secretaryship to William J. Donovan (World War I hero, prominent New York lawyer, and soon to become famous as the organizer and head of the wartime intelligence organization, the Office of Strategic Services), but Donovan declined. Knox then offered it to Ralph Bard, a Chicago banker and personal friend. Bard also declined, then changed his mind, but too late. Forrestal, who was Knox's third choice, had already accepted.[5]

Forrestal had many supporters for the post, including Justice Douglas, Secretary of the Interior Harold L. Ickes, Bernard Baruch, Corcoran, and probably Harry Hopkins. As Ickes recorded in his diary: "I think it was Tom who was largely influential in bringing Forrestal here . . . and then, at Tom's suggestion, I told Frank Knox that I thought he would make a good Under Secretary of the Navy."[6] Immediately following his own swearing in, Knox had begun the search for his principal civilian assistants. "All offices close at noon Saturday," he wrote to his wife in New Hampshire on July 14, "so when I got back from the White House Bill Donovan, John Sullivan, Jack Bergen of New York, Jim Forrestal of the White House staff and I went aboard the *Sequoia*, the Secretary of Navy's yacht, had lunch aboard and cruised down the Potomac until about six o'clock. Then Bill and I got into dinner clothes and went to dine with the British ambassador, Lord Lothian, at 8 pm. This morning I played golf at Burning Tree Club with Forrestal, Captain Deyo (my aide) and a friend of Deyo's just arrived from Shanghai. Then at two o'clock we boarded the *Sequoia* where John Sullivan and wife and Jim Forrestal's wife were awaiting us, and had dinner aboard and cruised the afternoon and evening, getting back around nine o'clock."[7]

Sullivan, a New Hampshire lawyer and politician who became Secretary of the Navy after the war, was also a candidate, but Forrestal clearly made the stronger impression, and on August 22 he began his seven-year tour of duty in the Navy Department. Barely a week later, Knox again wrote to his wife: "Jim Forrestal is going to be a great relief to me and will make my job much easier."[8]

After his own appointment, Forrestal favored Corcoran for the Assistant Secretaryship, but Corcoran then confided that he really couldn't get along with Knox, so Bard, whose hesitation had cost him the Under Secretary's job, became Assistant Secretary. A year later Artemus Gates, Forrestal's banking and golfing friend from New York and Long Island who had also flown for the navy in World War I, was appointed to the new post of Assistant Secretary of the Navy for Air. At the end of the war, Forrestal assessed him as an able subordinate—"no genius . . . [but] completely honest, loyal and very tenacious."[9]

That same autumn of 1940, Forrestal was instrumental in bringing his good friend Robert Lovett into government, although not into the Navy Department. The navy post that later went to Gates would have been a natural for Lovett, but Secretary Knox seemed in no hurry to fill it. During September and October, Lovett had conducted his own private study of the American aircraft industry (where he had wide contacts with leading executives) and had reached the somber conclusion that it was not equal to the demands all-out war would present. "This will be a quantitative war," he argued, but the industry's traditional approach was qualitative. "The gestation period for a human is nine months. For an aircraft it is at least two years from design to factory door. For advanced designs . . . three or four years."[10] It was essential, he argued, that the automobile companies be "brought into the game" as subcontractors so that their assembly-line techniques could be applied to the mass production of major components like tail assemblies and aircraft engines. The aircraft industry leaders agreed with his assessment and urged him to carry the message to the Roosevelt administration.[11]

Lovett went to Forrestal, who agreed with his friend's analysis and arranged a luncheon with Robert Patterson, the new Under Secretary of War. Also impressed, Patterson asked for a written report. At the time, Lovett had only summary notes, which he sent off to Patterson a few days later with the plea that they "be read with the same sympathy which would be extended to a hen if she were asked to produce, on short notice, an ostrich egg."[12] Within a week, Stimson appointed Lovett as his Assistant Secretary of War for Air. Early in the following year, after he had settled into his job, Lovett told Forrestal, "There is so much deadwood in the War Department that it constitutes a positive fire hazard."[13]

THE TROUBLE WITH JOSEPHINE

ANOTHER MAJOR CRISIS in the Forrestals' marriage occurred in late 1940, just a few months after Forrestal began to confront the towering problem of rebuilding the fleet as the peril of war moved closer. He had arrived in Washington in June. Jo had joined him at the end of the summer heat in mid-September. The precise cause of what happened next will never be known, but there seems to have been a complex of factors, including her advancing addiction to alcohol. There was in the atmosphere of late 1940 a generalized fear and anxiety brought on by the war in Europe, as people everywhere were compelled to confront the consequences of Hitler's mechanized barbarism which that spring and summer had swept away the democratic armies and governments of Norway, Denmark, Holland, Belgium, Luxembourg, and France. For Jo Forrestal there was also the specific strain of moving from the familiar milieu of New York, Long Island, and Dutchess County to the quite different social culture of governmental Washington, with its relentless focus on public issues and its endless political discussion at dinner parties. She quickly discovered an instinctive dislike for the whole process; Washington seemed to her a boring, one-company town devoid of "beautiful people" in Diana Vreeland's meaning of the term. But it was more than boredom. Reflecting many years later, Michael Forrestal thought his father and mother had been "a good team" in New York, moving on different tracks yet playing compatible, mutually reinforcing roles. In Washington, however, where there was no theater, fashion, art, or café society, Jo had nothing to stimulate her bright, aggressive, unintellectual personality. She came to detest what she considered the pomposity and hypocrisy of politicians and public officials, and began to punctuate her disenchantment with startlingly crude or abrasive remarks at dinner parties and by drinking without restraint. At a deeper level of discontent were the cumulative strains of her marriage and the impossible emotional bargain these had created for her.[14]

Whatever the mix, Josephine Forrestal suffered a mental breakdown near the end of the year. She went through a period of hallucination, screaming that the "Reds" were after her, her family, and her friends and declaring that her sons, then away at Aiken School, would be kidnapped. She suspected everybody— the household staff, Forrestal's assistants in the Navy Department, even

Josephine Forrestal, 1940

recently acquired Washington acquaintances—of conspiring to bring harm to her and those dear to her.[15] The breakdown appears to have come as a stunning surprise to Forrestal, but the way he chose to handle it imposed heavy new emotional burdens, from which he was never thereafter released and which progressively aggravated the many unresolved strains and inner tensions in his own life.

When Jo's symptoms did not abate after nearly a month, Adele Lovett persuaded Forrestal to take Jo to New York to see Dr. A. L. Barach, who was Marie Harriman's psychiatrist. She entered Doctors Hospital and remained for about two weeks, at which point she refused to stay any longer and returned to Washington. Thereafter she never acknowledged the fact of her breakdown, and Forrestal made no effort to insist that she undergo further medical treatment of any kind. He concluded it was better to let her go on leading a "normal life" under no apprehension that she had suffered anything more than simple exhaustion. It was a touching decision, but one which added grievously to the already heavy emotional burdens on the marriage, for the facts were otherwise.[16]

Philip and Ellen Barry were waiting for Forrestal at the Lowell Hotel in New York the night he came from the hospital after talking to Dr. Barach about his wife's condition. He was somber and subdued as he told them the doctor's diagnosis: clinical schizophrenia.[17] They had given her one electric shock treatment, which had produced a violently unpleasant reaction in her body and mind, and she had adamantly refused to permit anything more to be done to her. Out of compassion for her, perhaps out of a kind of helpless ignorance or a fear of uncovering the truth that his own

behavior was a contributory cause, Forrestal decided to live with Jo's illness without disclosing it to anyone. He told his sons their mother was
"like a fine Swiss watch whose mainspring had been too tightly wound,"
but he never told them anything else.[18] As late as October 1988, twelve
years after his mother's death, Michael Forrestal claimed never to have
heard of Barach's diagnosis. He was skeptical and defensive. Barach, he
said, was known as "a kind of fraud" who "hurt" a lot of people, but he
admitted that his mother "was never quite the same again" after 1940.[19]
It is now an accepted medical view that schizophrenia results from an
imbalance in the blood that is frequently caused by alcoholism in a previous
generation. There is no evidence that either Jo's father or mother was an
alcoholic, but one of her West Virginia uncles was known as the town
drunk. The Forrestals' younger son, Peter, was an alcoholic. Ellen Barry,
who knew him as a child, thought him not only unusually sensitive but
also schizophrenic.[20]

From the end of 1940, Forrestal understood he was living and dealing
with a sick and vulnerable wife. He had several options: insist that she be
placed under the care of a psychiatrist, place her in a sanatorium, or divorce
her. He chose instead to accept her refusal of further treatment and indeed
to accept her denial of any defect, to keep the secret of her illness and to
carry on as though nothing had happened. But something had happened,
and there followed a progressive deterioration of her self-control and thus
of her life. Although its most obvious manifestation was her inability to
manage drink (combined with an ever greater compulsion to drink), it
became apparent to a number of close observers that the trouble went much
deeper. Adele Lovett thought she had gone "plumb crazy,"[21] and numerous
Washingtonians sensed a bitter pent-up frustration behind her increasingly
coarse language and bizarre behavior. "She was vulgar beyond belief,"
one close friend of Forrestal's remembered. "Wives would literally flee
when they heard she was in town."[22] A Washington socialite, Oatsie
Lighter, sensed that "something far more fundamental than an inability to
handle alcohol was wrong with Jo Forrestal."[23]

She tried, intermittently, to find a role in Washington, and Forrestal tried
to help her. As an unpaid consultant to the navy, she enlisted the well-
known dress designer Mainbocher to design the WAVE uniform, and it was
a success—far more distinctive and stylish than its army and Marine Corps
counterparts. There was a brief speaking tour in Maine in 1943, under the
auspices of Congresswoman Margaret Chase Smith, several trips to London
"on government business" to study the "practical experience" of the British WRENS, and after the war a trip to Brazil. But these activities gave
her no sustained sense of purpose, and the press was indifferent or unkind—its initial reaction to the WAVE uniform was that engaging Mainbocher was a bit of undemocratic snobbery.[24]

Her attitude toward Washington and the war effort remained basically derisive, and she was not above dashing off handwritten letters to FDR that seemed to reflect both special pleading and a skewed insouciance. Whether she meant to be taken seriously or simply to exercise a brittle wit was not easy to discern. Writing in July 1943, she told the President, "I like the last speech even better than the one before Congress. And not solely because of the promise of more coffee and sugar either." Then, shifting gears, she noted "an important governmental reform I'd like to call to your attention. If the Executive wishes to keep its deserving bureaucrats (meaning the Forrestals) housed and working, it had better provide duration quarters of a congenial nature. There is far too much misplaced sympathy for the poor—they at least have the opportunity to improve themselves." In an accompanying note to FDR's secretary, Grace Tully, she entered a veiled complaint that the Under Secretary of the Navy did not have his own yacht. "If we could only get a boat, we could have another nice boating dinner on the river. My mind is certainly remaining on recreation these hot days." [25] FDR, who saw both letters, answered her briefly in obvious amusement and good cheer: "Dear Jo, when I was in Jim's place, I used to steal the President's yacht. It helped to solve the rent problem, and the Navy provided the food. I see no reason why Jim and you should not steal the *Sequoia* whenever Frank is away. If a German plane comes along, hide in the bushes and if you catch lots of fish you can have them for they are not rationed." [26]

For company and amusement while her husband worked sixteen-hour days in the Navy Department, Jo Forrestal latched on to a group of young Washington socialites, including Ceci Carusi, Dorcas Hardin, Oatsie Lighter, and Bootsie Hearst, who included her in their parties, but were put off by her stridency and cynicism and her fragile mental balance. As Lighter recalled, "One moment she would be talking with perfect calm and good sense, and the next moment she would be dissolving in hysterical laughter." [27] According to Gertrude Legendre, a New Yorker who worked for the OSS and played tennis with Forrestal, friends took turns surreptitiously "pouring Jo's drinks into flower pots, but she always got another one." Legendre recalled one evening at the British Embassy when Jo passed out with her head on the dinner table, [28] and Lighter remembered a dinner in a private home when "Jo's behavior was off the wall and Jim spent the entire evening with his head in his hands." [29] Journalist Joseph Alsop once said, "Jo was like a wild bird. You never knew whether she would fly into the curtains or out the window." [30] A White House aide, noting her jet-black hair, almond-shaped face, and pale white skin, was reminded of Charles Addams's Morticia; he also observed that she was "conspicuously absent" from the social functions arranged for Cabinet and sub-Cabinet wives. [31]

There was other evidence of a mental illness that went beyond alcoholism, that indeed made the drinking a relatively minor surface manifestation. One of Forrestal's secretaries recalled several occasions when his office received a sudden call about some eccentric action of Jo's that required immediate "damage control" to avoid publicity. A particular incident involved her kicking a child as she was walking along Connecticut Avenue. Forrestal immediately dispatched his aide to pick her up before the police arrived.[32] His working day was subject to interruption at any time by this kind of emergency.

The war and postwar years were thus witness to sad social scenes of provocative stridency, coarseness, indiscipline, and drunkenness, which led to cumulative embarrassment and humiliation, a tragicomic situation, a deadly farce, somehow made worse by the fact that Forrestal grimly ignored everything—he said nothing and he made no effort to change his wife's behavior. He did, however, charge Stanley Campbell, his butler, to keep a close watch on her daytime activities and "to reel her in when she went bonkers."[33] "It was a touching relationship," after 1940, Ellen Barry recalled, "and never an unkind word."[34] But the Forrestals were public figures in Washington, visible and discussed as they had not been in New York, and Jo's difficulties were accordingly the subject of much talk, some pity, but miraculously little notice in the press. Among Forrestal's friends and admirers, there was growing wonder that he persisted in the marriage. No one seemed at the time to have calculated the nature, weight, or consequence of this new burden when added to the official burdens of his office and the war.[35]

But wars are won and great public issues resolved by men who are not overwhelmed by circumstance, and at this time Forrestal was at the top of his form—tough-minded and resilient, a seasoned executive and also an instinctive political operator who swam well in the swift-moving currents of Congress and the bureaucracy. He was, moreover, driven by a fierce patriotism naturally reinforced by the pressures of the war. Thus, for several years he was able to cope with this private darkness, to take it mainly in his energetic stride, and to deflect its impact on his own performance. As the years passed, however, it took an increasing toll.

★ ★ ★

CHAPTER 11

Encountering the Navy

ALTHOUGH GENERALLY rated the second-best fleet in the world—after Great Britain—the United States Navy in 1940 was in certain respects an antique joke, an organizational anomaly, unprepared for the supreme crisis that lay ahead. As one inside expert observed, no one starting fresh would ever have designed anything like the Navy Department, and its organization reflected a century and a half of push, pull, and adjustment to a variety of financial, technical, and political pressures.[1] What was most evident was that it lacked the organizational symmetry which had been imposed on the War Department by an exceptionally able Secretary of War, Elihu Root, in 1903, during the presidency of Theodore Roosevelt. Root had broken the independent, divisive power of the several army branches—artillery, infantry, cavalry—and consolidated full administrative control in a single Chief of Staff, who was, however, bound by law "to use all his professional skill and knowledge in giving effect to the purposes and general directions of his civilian superior or make way for another expert to do so."[2] Thus, clear-cut deference to civilian authority was a condition of service for the Army Chief of Staff. Over time, this philosophy permeated the training and thinking of the army officer corps so that by World War II it was accepted and assimilated as a basic tenet of army service in the American democracy. In the navy, which had never undergone reorganization by an Elihu Root, civilian-military relationships were still brittle in 1940, and authority was widely diffused.

The navy consisted of three major elements: the fleet, the technical bureaus and shore establishment, and the civilian administration.

The Chief of Naval Operations (CNO) was superior to the separate fleet and squadron commanders and was responsible for the fighting readiness of all U.S. naval forces. In theory, he also exercised authority over the bureaus, but he was in fact dependent on them for technical support of the operating forces; indeed, he had to negotiate with each bureau chief on all major matters, for the segment of his own staff responsible for procurement and technical support was traditionally weak, perhaps owing to the concentration of finite expertise in the bureaus.[3] Moreover, in 1940, neither the CNO, Admiral Harold Stark, nor his staff seemed able to grasp the real dimensions of mobilization requirements or the urgency of the world situation. Stark was a competent naval officer, decent and honest though not conspicuously aggressive—"a man who could call a spade a spade, but who was generally regarded more as planner than fighter."[4] Endowed with a thick shock of white hair and burdened with the nickname of "Betty," he and his immediate staff were affectionately known throughout navy headquarters as Snow White and the Seven Dwarfs.[5] His detractors thought him "listless and ineffective, a bureaucrat by instinct."[6]

The several bureaus (Ordnance, Ships, Aeronautics, Yards and Docks, Supplies and Accounts, Personnel) were a cat's cradle of uncoordinated baronies, each of which asserted near-absolute sovereignty in its own field and each of which had direct links, well nurtured and of long standing, with the Naval Affairs Committees in the Senate and the House. In organizational theory, the bureaus and shore establishment existed solely to support the fleet at sea, to provide it with the ships, guns, aircraft, and trained personnel that would enable it to fight; in fact, the CNO, the fleet commanders, and even the Navy Secretary exercised only nominal control over the bureaus. In 1798 the U.S. Navy had copied the British navy's shipboard organization in minute detail, but had never taken the important next step of establishing a precise hierarchy of authority between and among the CNO, the fleet commands, the technical bureaus, and the civilian Secretary.

Each bureau had its own special characteristics and traditions. "Bu-Ord," known as the Gun Club, was considered the most conservative and powerful, staffed by regular officers who served rotating tours of duty in the bureau and at sea. They boasted that "our ships are designed by men who do not go to sea; and our planes by men who do not fly; but, by godfrey, our guns are made by the men who will fire them."[7] Admiral Stark; the CNO; Admiral William D. Leahy, who became FDR's White House Chief of Staff in 1942; and Admiral J. O. Richardson, Commander of the Pacific Fleet, were all graduates of the Gun Club. During World War II, Bu-Ord's sixteen-inch guns performed well, but its torpedoes were frequently and dangerously ineffective, many of them passing under their targets. Bu-Ord also produced quite ineffective antiaircraft guns until late in the war, when civilian scientists invented the proximity fuse.

"Bu-Ships" (created in 1940 from a merger of the Bureau of Engineering and the Bureau of Construction and Repair) was largely the bastion of the "battleship admirals," who were engaged in a struggle for strategic primacy with the "carrier admirals," the naval aviators from "Bu-Aer." "Bu-Yards and Docks" controlled the sprawling shore establishment of shipyards and dry docks. "Bu-Pers," in charge of all manpower matters, was a powerful unit because it was responsible for training officers and men and because it played a large role in determining officer assignments to the fleet. Admiral Chester Nimitz, who commanded the Pacific Fleet during most of World War II, was Bu-Pers chief in 1940. The Bureau of Supplies and Accounts was the navy's quartermaster, bookkeeper, and paymaster, endowed with all of the tangible and intangible power and influence that gravitate to the holder of the key to the warehouse and the purse.

Civilian authority and control in the navy were vested in a civilian Secretary supported by an Under Secretary and two Assistant Secretaries, all appointed by the President and confirmed by the Senate. But genuine civilian control of the navy was a fragile, ephemeral condition, for naval officers, though they paid it lip service, generally lacked the intellectual and philosophical commitment to the concept which animated their army counterparts. Historically, navy secretaries fell into three categories: (1) those who were mere figureheads, furnishing a façade of civilian authority, but exercising no effective control or influence, (2) those who performed well as ambassadors from the naval command to Congress and other civilian agencies, but lacked controlling power within the navy, and (3) the rare and great Secretary, who, while representing the navy to the government at large, also gave it strong leadership and exercised effective control over both its policy and its organization. Most incumbents of the office had been weak and ineffective. Theodore Roosevelt appointed five navy secretaries in seven years, and one of them, Victor Metcalf, acknowledged that his duties consisted of "waiting for the Chief of the Bureau of Navigation [forerunner to the Chief of the Bureau of Personnel] to come in with a piece of paper, put it down before me with his finger on a dotted line, and say to me 'Sign your name here.' "[8]

Rarely challenging the principle of civilian supremacy frontally, the uniformed navy worked assiduously to wrap its Secretaries in flattery and perquisites, to give them plenty of nineteen-gun salutes, side boys, and a yacht for cruising the Potomac River, while yielding little information, authority, or control. In 1940, this general condition was complicated by the fact that President Roosevelt had spent eight years as Assistant Secretary and continued to assert a proprietary claim over the navy's functions and personnel. He kept a well-thumbed copy of the *Navy Register* (the official list of all officers on active duty), insisted on a major role in promotions to flag rank, and played favorites. And while he expressed a firm belief in civilian control of the navy, he preferred to exercise it himself as President, which did not necessarily strengthen the hand of the Navy Secretary. In 1940, he sent the Pacific Fleet to Pearl Harbor on maneuvers, an

assignment that its Commander expected to last a month or two. But
FDR ordered Admiral Richardson
and the fleet to remain there until
further notice because, as he explained, this would serve as a
"deterrent" to the Japanese. Richardson, who knew that more men
and munitions were required to put
his ships in fighting condition and
that these increments were not
available in Hawaii, went twice to
Washington to urge the fleet's return
to the West Coast. Instead of returning the fleet, Roosevelt removed
Richardson and appointed Admiral
Husband Kimmel, whose name
would become indelibly, though not
entirely fairly, associated with the
disaster at Pearl Harbor on December 7, 1941.[9]

*As Under Secretary of the Navy,
ca. 1944*

In 1940, the office of the Secretary of the Navy was a mongrel catchall
of sixteen agencies (which grew to sixty by 1946), mainly minor functions
that did not fit easily into one of the bureaus or the operations staff under
the CNO. The most important was the Office of Judge Advocate General
(JAG), the navy's legal staff charged with providing competent advice on
all matters of naval law. But the JAG was staffed mainly by line officers on
temporary duty (so-called sea lawyers—a derogatory term—who had perhaps gone to night law school in Washington) and was, as a practical
matter, competent only to deal with court-martial proceedings.[10]

Such were the complexities and confusions of existing organizational
relationships when Forrestal arrived at the Navy Department.

FORRESTAL AS ADMINISTRATOR

T HE DUTIES of the Under Secretary were not spelled out in the new
law creating the position, but were left for definition by the Secretary
of the Navy; the basic division of labor had, however, been agreed upon
during Forrestal's preliminary talks with Knox. The Secretary would concentrate on questions of high policy and public relations, would be responsible for liaison with the White House, and would in general manifest the
patriotic, nonpartisan character of the national preparedness effort. To For-

restal would fall the formidable administrative task of organizing, directing, and coordinating the entire navy procurement effort—a task whose
ultimate dimensions and complexities were only dimly perceived in 1940
and were grossly underestimated, especially within the uniformed navy. In
addition, the position of Under Secretary, being without precedent or
standing in a highly structured, traditional environment, was certain to be
tested to determine the limits of its authority. Indeed, because civilian
control over the navy was historically tenuous, even the authority of Secretary Knox was by no means assured.

A few days before his appointment, Forrestal telephoned Charles Detmar, a puckish, brilliant younger partner in the law firm* retained by Dillon, Read, and asked him what he was doing the following weekend.

"Nothing of consequence," Detmar replied.

"Could you come down to Washington for a few days?"

"How many shirts should I bring?"

"Two or three should be enough."[11]

The suggested number of shirts (in the pre-drip-dry era) turned out to
be a serious underestimation of the need, for Detmar did not get back to
New York for several months.

Forrestal wanted the lawyer's advice on how to define his own new responsibilities, how to organize the office, how to determine what expertise
and personal qualities were needed in the Under Secretary's immediate
staff. Like Nitze before him, Detmar moved into Forrestal's rented house,
began immediately to function as his principal assistant, and remained
a trusted counselor and adviser long after he had returned to his law
practice.[12]

In addition to Detmar, Forrestal's initial staff consisted only of his naval
aide, Commander John E. Gingrich, and his secretary, Katherine Starr
Foley. Unlike the usual military/naval aide to civilian secretaries who han-
dles minor personal, social, and logistical chores, Gingrich quickly became
a substantive assistant on a wide range of organizational and policy matters. When he reported to Forrestal, who had just been sworn in, he asked
what the new Under Secretary would like him to do. "Take off your coat
and get to work," Forrestal replied. "Don't you want to check on my
qualifications?" Forrestal replied with a single word, "No."[13] At the end
of the war, Forrestal wrote to President Truman citing Gingrich as "invaluable to me . . . far above the ordinary officer in his understanding of
the Navy's relations with the public."[14]

The first task was to wangle suitable quarters for the Under Secretary
(there having never been a previous need to provide these); this was accomplished by ousting a segment of the Op-Nav staff from the suite adja-

*Wright, Gordon, Zachary, Parlin and Cahill (later known as Cahill, Gordon).

cent to Secretary Knox's office on the "second deck" of the Main Navy Building, one in a long row of "temporary" structures left over from World War I which ran along Constitution Avenue near the Lincoln Memorial. Gingrich's second, far more important task was to serve as Forrestal's road map to the navy, his indispensable guide through the labyrinths of naval organization, custom, tradition, and special vocabulary, for Forrestal was a stranger in a new country with an urgent need to learn fast and well. During the early months of this shakedown cruise, Gingrich and Detmar sat side by side in an outer office, screening every paper that came to the Under Secretary's attention and every person who wanted an appointment. To the extent possible, they divided the work between military and legal/business matters, but the heavy inward flow soon made this impractical, so they became interchangeable "young men of all work," relying on continuous consultation with each other to avoid serious mistakes.[15]

In early 1941, Ferol Overfelt, who had graduated first in his class at Annapolis but then gone into banking, was brought in to share the increasing staff work load, and he in turn was responsible for recruiting Eugene Duffield, a journalist who headed the Washington bureau of the *Wall Street Journal*. Duffield's assignment was public relations in the broadest sense, preparing press releases, writing or editing Forrestal's speeches, and serving as the main channel and coordinator for gathering and presenting the wide range of facts which Forrestal ceaselessly demanded. Kate Foley, a tall, brisk, smartly tailored woman, handled Forrestal's official and personal schedules and supervised a small pool of typists. This was the original inner staff, but it became the established staff pattern for most of Forrestal's government service—a triumvirate of legal counsel, administrative aide, and public and press relations man, plus secretarial and stenographic support.

Detmar remained for eight months and was followed by a succession of lawyers, all from the Cahill, Gordon firm—James D. Wise, William M. Dulles, Mathias F. Correa, John Sonnet, and John T. Connor. The only wartime exception to this legal monopoly was Frank C. Nash, a native Washingtonian. Gingrich remained with Forrestal until late in the war, when he left to command the new cruiser *Pittsburgh;* he eventually rose to four-star rank. Duffield remained until the conclusion of the war and later became, with Walter Millis, coeditor of the posthumous *Forrestal Diaries.* Kate Foley stayed to the bitter end in 1949.[16]

Struve Hensel, another lawyer who became one of Forrestal's most valued associates, remembered the first time he entered the new Under Secretary's office: Forrestal was grimly signing hundreds of contracts that had come to him, helter-skelter, from the bureaus. With navy mobilization moving at a quickening pace in the late summer and fall of 1940, some $4 billion worth of "letters of intent" were being translated into full-scale contracts, to be signed by the Secretary of the Navy or his designee—and Knox had given Forrestal full authority in the area of procurement. Three-foot stacks of contracts sat on Forrestal's desk, and more were piled beside it, rising to desk level.[17]

They were a hodgepodge of everything—for facilities, ships, equipment, uniforms, ordinary supplies—yet they were by no means *all* of the contracts being made by the navy. Others, in many cases more important ones, were being signed by bureau chiefs without even the formality of Secretarial approval; for instance, a contract to build a single ship authorized the "cognizant bureau" to approve "amendments," which was interpreted by the bureau to include an increase in the number of ships in the contract—e.g., from one to fifty. All contracts were written on a simple standard form issued government-wide by the Treasury Department, a form used for everything from ships and airplanes to screwdrivers. The only variant—the only point to be negotiated—was price. But since most contracts were based on competitive bidding, the navy contracting officer needed only to understand "that three was less than four," as Hensel scornfully put it.[18]

This archaic contracting procedure was unavoidably wasteful, for it provided no coordinating point in the process, not even to identify situations where several bureaus were competing against each other for the same materials or equipment. The only review point in the system was the Office of Judge Advocate General, but the JAG was concerned merely with assuring itself that the contract had been developed by "authorized" bureau personnel and that it conformed to law. The process provided for no substantive review to determine whether the contract made any sense, e.g., whether a contract to build an aircraft carrier was being given to a company that made rowboats, whether the navy was getting its money's worth, whether the future position of the navy was adequately protected. In short, the navy system of procurement was "absolutely impossible in time of major war," as Hensel assessed it. "Maybe if you had all the time in the world, and didn't care when you got delivery or how your order impacted on other contracts or items imbued with equal or greater national priority, the Navy system might work. It would have been expensive and foolish, but it might have worked."[19] In a sense it did "work" in the period of drift and stringent budgets between world wars, but it could not meet the urgent situation in 1940.

Forrestal was frustrated and surprised at finding these archaic precepts and procedures in the navy's contracting system, for he recognized procurement as the area of absolutely decisive consequence for naval expansion and the whole national defense effort. Confronting the full monarchy of the bureaus, he quickly established himself as a tough, impatient executive—a man imbued with an absolute sense of urgency, determined to end the irrational procedures he had uncovered in his new domain. He was not an organization man in the conventional corporate sense or a chief executive who depended on his staff to do his thinking. The staff gathered the facts; he sifted, weighed, and synthesized them into his own conclusions and judgments. Reflecting his experience on Wall Street, his mind and administrative habits were those of an investment banker accustomed to negotiating deals and wrestling personally with complicated situations. At Dillon, Read, if something went wrong with a company in which he had an interest, his practice was to bring in an expert manager to straighten things out. He was trained to recognize or anticipate problems and to find the talent capable of fixing them. James Rowe, who worked with Forrestal in the White House, came to believe that bankers made better executives than lawyers: "They are accustomed to taking risks. They have to move fast and decide quickly, in situations where crucial factors cannot be measured precisely. They act and accept the consequences. Lawyers have a tendency to dawdle, to nitpick, to be insensitive to the consequences of their own procrastination."[20]

Aware of the gigantic unsolved problems besetting the mobilization effort, Forrestal was jealous of his time and impatient with those who lacked a thorough grasp of the subject at hand. He admired minds that worked swiftly and were capable of succinct encapsulation, and many people annoyed him by bogging down in excessive detail. He demanded that people speak their piece as concisely as possible, be ready to answer his questions with brevity, and then depart. He handled large meetings masterfully, but would lose patience and could be very curt with anyone, no matter what his status, who seemed vague, elusive, or unprepared. He developed a blacklist of problem characters who were not to be admitted to his office under any circumstances.

At the same time he sought to use the whole Navy Department to satisfy his hunger for information, and in this sense he could not be called an orderly administrator. His brisk impatience to learn, to resolve, was unceasing, and feeling the need for certain information in a hurry, he would send two or three assistants, unbeknownst to each other, to obtain it. Yet there was at times not only confusion, but also a strange anomaly in all the haste. The facts, background considerations, and interrelationships of some complicated issue would be assembled at top speed on Forrestal's order and rushed to him. Then that would be the end of it for a long time. With all the factors assembled, he was slow to decide, an attribute which reflected an ingrained habit of studying both sides of a question, combined with an anxiety to be sure he understood the point of view of the person or group who opposed his own. Among those who knew him well, there was disagreement as to whether he was exceptionally careful and methodical, or indecisive. No one doubted his inherent caution. Persuasion, based on appeal to logic and reason, was his principal tool for dealing with men and problems, for it was his enduring assumption that he would have to continue to work with those with whom he disagreed. It was not in his makeup to blow away the opposition by a simple assertion of superior authority. At the same time, no one could deny that navy procurement was moving briskly forward under his direction.[21]

As he plumbed the Navy Department for relevant internal information, so did he use the prerogatives of office to extend his knowledge of broader issues. Industrialists, senators, congressmen, newspaper editors, educators, labor leaders, and ambassadors were his constant guests—at breakfast, lunch, or dinner—in his private dining room at the Navy Department, at home, or on board the *Sequoia*. His preference was for small groups where he could exert his considerable powers of persuasion or pump knowledgeable people for their own views. His energy seemed limitless, and he was constantly on the go. Frequently he held more than one breakfast meeting and on at least one occasion managed four business conferences during lunch—soup with Secretary Knox, the main course with his own guests, dessert at the White House, and coffee at the Metropolitan Club. Grudgingly, he acknowledged the obligatory cocktail party, which loomed large in wartime Washington life, but when attendance was unavoidable he worked the room like a seasoned pol—a cordial hello here, a deft word of congratulation or reassurance there, but always moving. Frequently he was clocked in and out in eight minutes flat.[22]

An integral part of each galvanized, high-speed week was physical exercise, usually taken on Sundays or in the early afternoon of a working day before returning to the office for late conferences or to sign the outgoing correspondence. This took the form of tennis at various courts around town—the Chevy Chase Club, the Army-Navy Country Club, St. Albans School—or golf at Burning Tree or Chevy Chase. In winter or when it rained, he turned to badminton. Regrettably for his partners, these athletic interludes seemed not a respite from, but merely a continuation of, the high-pressure urgency with which he conducted his official business. Hensel endured one grim, unsmiling round of golf and concluded that Forrestal had managed to convert that graceful game into "a cult of violence"; he declined all further invitations.[23] Nor did the end of the war change this approach. In the Truman period, Clark Clifford conceded that tennis with Forrestal was "not much fun," for he showed no lightness or congeniality, "just raced through the game with a clenched jaw," indifferent to winning or losing. Clifford later concluded that Forrestal not only lacked a sense of humor (which Clifford regarded as indispensable to survival in high-stress jobs), but was also irritated by levity in others.[24] In fact, Forrestal was noted for a sardonic wit most of his life, but Clifford's observation was generally accurate with regard to the period from 1946 on. Always and everywhere, Forrestal seemed to be testing himself against some formidable, impossible standard of persistence and stamina, pressing against ordinary physical and intellectual limits, implicitly insisting that the challenge never be relaxed. Playing tennis with John J. McCloy, the Assistant Secretary of War, who was a seasoned tournament competitor, he continually sought reassurance that McCloy was not easing up on him to make the match more even.[25]

COMMUNICATING WITH THE PUBLIC

FORRESTAL HAD a keen sense of public relations and went out of his way to cultivate leaders in the Congress, as well as his superiors and colleagues in the Executive Branch. He maintained a "tickler file" to remember birthdays and anniversaries and heaped effusive praise on congressional leaders who were important to the destinies of the navy. Thus, when Georgia senator Walter F. George became chairman of the Finance Committee, Forrestal buttered him up with appropriate flattery: "In these critical times it is important that such posts be held by somebody in whose fundamental patriotism the country believes, and I can assure you that this is the case with yourself."[26] He supplied Kate Foley with a notebook indicating the form he wanted to use in addressing key people in the government: "Jimmy" Byrnes, "Ed" Stettinius, "Bernie" Baruch, "Don" Nelson. He experimented with abbreviating his own name, James Vincent Forrestal, quickly discarded "Vincent" and then the initial (remarking jokingly that he was giving up the "V" for victory). Within a few months he resolved to use the single word "Forrestal."[27]

IN HIS ROLE as number two to Knox, and out of a sense of both protocol and personal modesty, Forrestal initially made little effort to publicize himself or appeal directly to public opinion. At the same time, he was aware that public understanding and support were essential ingredients for the success of government programs in a democracy, especially for a war mobilization effort whose effects permeated the entire society. As he later wrote to his friend Arthur Krock: "When I came down here, I remarked, and I think it may have been to you, that anyone serving in government had really two functions: (1) he had to do a good job, and (2) he had to convince the public that a good job was being done. In business there is the same need, but not to the same degree because, after all, the income account is the criterion of the corporation executive's success or failure."[28] His own efforts at public persuasion were directed primarily at opinion makers, essentially a select group of Washington commentators and journalists that included Hanson Baldwin, Walter Millis, Arthur Krock, Walter Lippmann, and their publishers.

Some public speeches were nevertheless obligatory, but at first he was not a good speaker. This defect owed something to his innate public shy-ness (he was aware, as he told one audience, that "even self-conscious modesty is boring")[29] but even more to the gray bureaucratic material written for him by the navy staff. After he had droned through a few such dreary speeches, he found their effect so dispiriting, for both himself and his audience, that he concluded he would have to write his own stuff if he expected to have any impact. As he explained later, this placed him in a dilemma, for he was loath to allocate the time required to fashion distinc-tive public statements: "It was not modesty that prevented me from ac-cepting speaking invitations, but my strong feeling that I couldn't be thinking about the happy bromide and felicitous cliché at the same time that I was trying to learn a new and complex business."[30] Nevertheless, his public appearances steadily improved as he mastered the intricacies of his job and became more accustomed to the techniques of public speaking.

It was literally true that he himself wrote the first draft of a speech, but his staff, and especially Eugene Duffield, had plenty to do with the finished product. One difficult chore for Duffield was running down the quotations Forrestal often inserted from memory; his recollections were about 90 percent accurate, but verification of the elusive, doubtful 10 percent was apt to entail arduous, and not infrequently fruitless, research. Between October 1941 and June 1946, Forrestal delivered 110 speeches, in addition to a radio address from Guam following the battle for Iwo Jima, as well as a hundred uncounted, extemporaneous talks to business groups, journal-ists, and clusters of naval officers and sailors on the battlefronts of Europe and the Pacific.[31]

At times the multiplicity of his interests generated confusion for all con-cerned, not excluding himself. To some, it seemed he was attempting to master too much too quickly in areas where mastery required comprehen-sive background knowledge, seasoned by time and deep reflection. Given the urgencies of both war and his own driving personality, there were inevitably a few bizarre incidents. One officer from Op-Nav[32] who was working closely with him on several procurement programs told this story:

Those of us who worked with Forrestal on a day-in and day-out basis were at the end of a squawk box, and I used to get sent for anywhere from one to six times a day, as did the others. As is well known, Mr. Forrestal didn't pay much attention to the clock when he was working, and that made things pretty tough on those who were working with him, particularly his staff.

One day I went bird shooting in Virginia, and while I was gone he wanted me for something. Frantic efforts were made to get me on the telephone, but of course I was where I couldn't be reached, and the next morning everybody jumped on me, more or less breathlessly, because I had gone to a place where he couldn't get me the day before. When I went in to find out what he wanted, he said, "Oh, yes, now I remember. You told a story a couple of days ago and I wanted to be sure I got the punch line correct!"

To strangers he projected an air of grim, hard-bitten determination in a desperate situation, yet among old friends he was sometimes unable to conceal his sheer exhilaration at finding himself in this new job with its limitless challenge in this particular world crisis, a job that fitted his natural talents like a glove. To a young New York lawyer whom he was interviewing for a job over dinner in late 1940, he indicated that "America was on the edge of a precipice," in grave danger of disaster, including the serious threat of foreign invasion unless preparations for war were greatly and swiftly accelerated. Furthermore, Forrestal told the young man, he held these views so strongly that he "probably wouldn't last more than a few months in Washington." He would either find the job unbearably frustrating or make such insistent demands that it would be politically inexpedient for Roosevelt to keep him. For these reasons, he could give the young lawyer no assurance of employment for "more than a few weeks or months." The young man did not take the job.[33]

There was a good deal to be grim about in late 1940. A month after FDR's election to a third term, a 4,000-word message arrived from Churchill. The heart of it was a warning that Britain's liquid financial assets were being rapidly drained away by the total effort to fend off Hitler's air assaults and to defeat what appeared an impending attempt to invade England by sea: "The moment approaches when we shall no longer be able to pay cash for our shipping and other supplies. . . ."[34] The problem posed was how the United States could go on sending war materials to Britain in the face of the "cash and carry" requirement of the U.S. Neutrality Laws. FDR's ingenious solution, after a period of creative cerebration while cruising the Caribbean in the U.S.S. *Tuscaloosa,* was the formula that came to be known as Lend-Lease, a means of providing munitions to allies without immediate charge and to be repaid not in dollars, but in kind, after the war was over. As FDR unveiled it to the press, "Suppose my neighbor's home catches on fire, and I have a length of hose. . . . If he can take my garden hose and connect it up to his hydrant, I may help him put out his fire."[35] That winning homespun analogy was followed on December 29 by a speech in which he declared that the United States "must be the great arsenal of democracy"*—a speech that sent a thrill of hope across the whole anti-Nazi world, shifted American opinion toward greater support for pre-

---

*This phrase was supplied by the French political planner Jean Monnet in a talk with FDR at Hyde Park.

paredness (though not for war), and assured passage of the Lend-Lease legislation by the Congress. After passage of Lend-Lease, Churchill declared in the House of Commons that this was "the most unsordid act in the history of any nation."[36]

Lend-Lease for Britain, and subsequently for Russia and China, raised the critical problem of balancing the needs of viable foreign allies against the needs of America's own armed forces. In general, both the army and navy were opposed to releasing supplies to foreign governments when they were needed for America's own embryonic defense program. After the Nazi invasion of Russia in 1941, Knox and Forrestal fought hard against granting military equipment to the Soviets for purposes which the Soviets refused to specify, especially products that were critically short for U.S. Navy requirements, like machine tools and aluminum for aircraft production. Forrestal was particularly disturbed by the Soviets' inability or unwillingness to explain how the machine tools would be used, and this was the birth of his deepening suspicion of the closed, secretive Soviet system.[37] The Army-Navy Munitions Board, headed jointly by Patterson and Forrestal, asked the President to give it the right to determine relative priorities between allies and the U.S. military forces, but FDR assigned this authority to Treasury Secretary Henry Morgenthau, who reflected FDR's strategic view that support for the fighting forces of Britain, the Soviet Union, and China must have first priority. This necessity for choice was painful, reflecting the hard fact that the whole civilized world was up against what Eric Larrabee later called "the iron laws of material insufficiency."[38] Before Pearl Harbor there was not enough war production anywhere to meet the needs of desperate Allied efforts to stem totalitarian onslaughts on widely separated battlefronts and simultaneously to bring American armed forces to a state of readiness. Victory for the Allied cause did not seem historically ordained; defeat seemed the more likely outcome.

Despite such disagreements with the White House over the allocation of war resources, and despite the grave perils facing democracy in the darkling winter of 1940–1941, Forrestal was exhilarated by his job and the attendant excitements and creative tensions of life in Washington; he was charged with energy, physically and mentally resilient, even mordantly witty—all signs of that special happiness that comes when one's talents and powers are fully called upon. In February 1941, when British Air Chief Marshal Sir Hugh Dowding arrived in Washington to provide a further list of Great Britain's urgent needs—bombers, ships, field guns—under Lend-Lease, Forrestal was called to the White House to represent the navy in the talks. Emerging from the conference, the two men were surrounded by reporters, and the Air Chief Marshal expressed irritation at their insistent questions. He told them curtly: "I don't talk to the President and then come out and tell you what was discussed." Rebuffed, the reporters turned to Forrestal, who merely smiled archly and said, ''I speak only Chinese.''[39]

And when Duncan Read, a former Dillon, Read partner and now a reserve naval officer on active duty, paid a call on the Under Secretary that same winter, he found his former Wall Street colleague highly pleased with his situation and full of bounce. ''I've got a wonderful job,'' Forrestal told Read. ''Knox loves to deal with public relations, but he lets me run the Navy.''[40]

CHAPTER 12

★ ★ ★

Asserting Civilian Control

UNTIL THE FATEFUL, liberating blow was struck by the Japanese at Pearl Harbor, Americans remained fiercely divided on the issue of isolation versus intervention and even on the question of greater military preparedness to defend the nation. Some isolationists were pacifists, but others were extremely belligerent—they were prepared to fight, provided all battles were staged on U.S. territory and were fought without allies. Believing the United States had made a terrible mistake in 1917–1918 by fighting in France in company with allies who turned out to be cynical, selfish ingrates, they were utterly opposed to all "foreign" wars, but ready to mount a "100 percent American" defense of North America.[1] The interventionists, on the other hand, were convinced that America's fate was bound up with the fate of Western civilization, embodied not only in America, but also vitally in the European democracies. Were these, together with their great industrial capacity and scientific skill, to fall permanently under the modern barbarism of Hitler's Germany, America would be progressively isolated, an island in a totalitarian sea, thereafter forced to take defensive measures that would ultimately destroy its democratic character. FDR's view was that if war proved unavoidable, the United States should fight it as far from its shores as possible, with the greatest number of allies that could be enlisted in the common cause, regardless of ideology and without undue concern about potential allied ingratitude until after the common enemies had been defeated.[2]

Through 1940 and 1941, this obsessive, unresolved issue shaped the policy of national mobilization; it was a tight knot severely constricting possibilities for a coherent foreign policy. Every democracy in continental Europe was writhing under Nazi oppression, and England was enduring savage air attacks which seemed the precursors of invasion, but the density of the isolationists was impenetrable. After the fall of France, Senator

Robert Taft said, "No one knows what they [the Germans] may do until they are freed from the present war, but when their purposes become apparent we can take the steps that may be necessary to meet the particular kind of German 'blitzkrieg,' if there is such a blitzkrieg, at the time we find out what it is."[3]

Having very little political room for maneuver, Roosevelt developed no clear blueprint for the future, but worked at sinuously threading his way between opposite perils, one step at a time. Meanwhile, the mobilization effort lacked coherence and momentum because the government lacked the unified public support necessary to impose on American industry a mandatory conversion to war production. In 1938, as Europe trembled on the brink of war, FDR had asked to see the available war plans. Because these were formally updated every four years, he was given the 1936 plan, but this did not suit him, as it provided for no preliminary or preparatory actions prior to an actual declaration of war. The next update was rushed to completion in 1939, but by that time Europe was already at war. As a consequence, the American mobilization effort operated from the beginning as a series of ad hoc, makeshift arrangements buffeted by conflicting political pressures.[4]

The first mobilization agency, established that same year, was a civilian advisory committee called the War Resources Board, whose duties were to assist in mobilizing the nation's economic resources and to perfect plans for placing the industrial economy on a war footing. But public announcement of the group ran into a hornet's nest of opposition from both New Dealers and isolationists. The name War Resources Board and its references to "war planning" and "mobilization" raised the hackles and deepest fears of the isolationists. New Dealers were angered by the predominance of businessmen and the absence of labor representatives on the board. Henry Wallace, though in full support of the President's purposes, spoke out against the board's domination by Wall Street bankers and corporate executives.[5] Hugh S. Johnson, formerly head of the National Recovery Administration, warned that New Dealers did not "intend to let Morgan and Dupont men run the war."[6] Ironically, the outbreak of war in Europe in September 1939 had the effect of strengthening the average American's determination to stay out of it; he disliked even thinking about defense preparations, on the theory that thinking might lead to action. Thus did those who saw urgent defense preparation and national mobilization as the keys to democratic survival find themselves fighting simultaneously on two political fronts—against the isolationists and against those liberals whose primary concern was to consolidate the social gains of the New Deal.

Thrown on the tactical defensive, FDR let the War Resources Board die quietly six weeks after its formation, while he maneuvered to find a less controversial vehicle for advancing the mobilization effort. To meet the need, he resurrected (from a 1916 statute) the Council of National Defense (consisting entirely of Cabinet members) and a supporting Advisory Commission.[7] As it turned out, the Cabinet group never met and all work devolved upon the Advisory Commission. To assure political balance, and quiet his critics from within the New Deal, he appointed his favorite labor leader, Sidney Hillman of the Amalgamated Clothing Workers of America, as an offset to William Knudsen of General Motors and Edward Stettinius of U.S. Steel.[8] Unfortunately, once appointed, the Advisory Commission received no further guidance from FDR and so began to function with no rules of operation, no definition of its relationship to the army and the navy, and no agreement as to whether it might act on its own or only with FDR's specific approval. A deliberate omission was a chairman with any authority. When the press asked "Who is the boss?" Roosevelt replied "I am."[9]

The mobilization effort thus limped along and might well have collapsed had it not been for the bracing infusion of orders for 6,000 aircraft and hundreds of extra aircraft engines from Britain and France (before the French military collapse in June 1940). These early orders from Europe brought into being new assembly lines in American aircraft factories and probably advanced American defense preparations by eighteen months.

In June 1940, Donald Nelson, a vice president of Sears, Roebuck, was brought in with the title of Coordinator of National Defense Purchases—to work with the Advisory Commission. Unfortunately, FDR never decided where Nelson's authority began and the commission's authority ended. As a practical matter, therefore, all military contracts had to be cleared by both Nelson and the commission, but the criteria for clearance soon became another bone of contention in the ideological warfare between the businessmen and the New Dealers. One group wanted "good business deals," while the other was primarily concerned with maintaining "labor's rights and social gains." This was the general situation when Forrestal arrived at the Navy Department in late summer.[10]

On December 18, 1940, Stimson and Knox, together with their Under Secretaries Patterson and Forrestal, called upon FDR to say that the headless, seven-man Advisory Commission was a hopeless vehicle—it had "six men too many" in Stimson's phrase—and had to be reorganized or scrapped.[11] They urged the President to appoint a single chairman, preferably Knudsen or Bernard Baruch. What the President gave them (on January 7) was a new agency, the Office of Production Management (OPM), but with two "copilots." At a press conference, a reporter asked him why he refused to have a single responsible head for OPM. He replied, "I have a single, responsible head. His name is Knudsen and Hillman." He would tolerate no "czar" or "poobah" in Washington, for under the Constitution, "You cannot set up a second President of the United States." He insisted on holding all the reins in his own hands. The newspapers began referring to the leaders of OPM as Mr. Knudsenhillman.[12]

Later in 1940, when the War and Navy departments complained once more of the "toothless" OPM and the need for a mobilization "czar," FDR created yet another organization called the Supply, Priorities and Allocation Board (SPAB) to coexist with OPM and to be headed by Nelson. Fortunately, this illogical excrescence disappeared into the War Production Board (the successor to OPM) right after Pearl Harbor. With America at last at war, FDR was finally willing to endow the mobilization effort with the power to bring about mandatory conversion of the economy to war production, and Nelson was named chairman of the WPB. The man from Sears, Roebuck was a pleasant, patient, and conciliatory fellow who ruffled no feathers and presented no political threat to FDR. But he was also procrastinating and reluctant to exercise the vast new powers now granted to the War Production Board. Years later, a journalist who read the history of this period "with disbelief" arrived at the judgment that "the nation had never been led with greater genius nor governed with greater ineptitude."[13]

NAVY OPTIONS

WITHIN THE NAVY there were three plausible options for controlling and coordinating the swift expansion of naval procurement: One was to give the job to the Chief of Naval Operations; a second was to give it to the Bureau of Supplies and Accounts; the third was to place full responsibility in the Under Secretary.

The CNO had a strong claim, on the theory that a military commander ought to control his own supply train. But historically his Op-Nav staff had shown no serious interest in procurement and had developed no expertise. Moreover, like most ranking naval officers at the time, Admiral Stark seemed not to appreciate the scale of industrial effort required to assure naval superiority in the event of war. The navy's role in World War I had been comparatively small, confined essentially to shepherding convoys between the American East Coast and Europe. Naval expenditures from 1916 through 1919 were $3.5 billion, compared to $100 billion for the army, and it was the army requirements that generated the need for large-scale conversion of the economy to military production. These facts, plus the self-perception of the navy as an entity apart, strongly influenced the thinking of senior naval officers as World War II approached.[14]

The Bureau of Supplies and Accounts had managed naval procurement in World War I, thereby establishing a certain claim to similar responsibility in 1940. But Admiral Raymond Spear, the bureau chief, also underestimated the size of the task ahead, arguing that naval expansion would require only increased orders from normal sources of supply, which ignored, among other things, the high probability that those "normal sources" would already be committed to manufacturing materials for the army, the Coast Guard, the British, and the French. In addition, Spear was firmly wedded to old-line navy practices like competitive bidding and standard form contracts, which proved time-consuming and useless as mobilization proceeded.[15]

The third option was to place direction, coordination, and final authority for all naval procurement in the Under Secretary. This idea was supported by the strongest logic, for the task required both a broad and a sophisticated understanding of American industry—a truth not widely appreciated inside the uniformed navy in 1940. Knox and Forrestal, with FDR's approval, had chosen this course after assessing the problem. It thus became Forrestal's challenge to build a powerful two-ocean fleet—the largest, most powerful navy in history—at a time of rampant confusion and in the face of opposition and resistance from within the navy itself.

THE "CERTIFICATE" CONFUSION

As THE DEFENSE buildup gathered momentum, the first critical shortage to emerge was facilities. New manufacturing and assembly plants were required for everything from tanks and turbines to aircraft, but private industry was reluctant to make such new investments, for businessmen reasoned either that war might not come or that it would be over in a few years, leaving them with large amounts of surplus capacity. To meet this problem, Harry Hopkins persuaded the Reconstruction Finance Corporation to build plants at government expense ($300 million worth in 1940–1941), then lease them to companies which had obtained government contracts. At the same time, the Advisory Commission sagely calculated that a good deal of corporate money could be raised for the defense effort if private contractors were allowed to amortize the new facilities in five years instead of twenty. This required a change in the tax laws, but both FDR and the Congress were persuaded, and the change was made. The new law stipulated that the War and Navy departments must "certify" which plants (to be constructed with private money) were necessary for the defense effort and thus eligible for the quick write-off.[16]

The navy's handling of the ensuing flood of applications for these certificates vividly revealed to Forrestal the mare's nest of irrational and conflicting organizational and procedural arrangements in the Navy Department and the extent to which it was unprepared to cope with the developing scale and pace of the mobilization. Pursuant to instructions from the Advisory Commission, the navy had created a certification unit in the Judge Advocate General's office and had developed procedures under which three types of certificate could be granted. These were (1) a certificate of "necessity," indicating that the new facility was essential to the defense effort, (2) a certificate of "non-reimbursement," indicating that the navy was not separately compensating the contractor for the new facility (beyond the five-year write-off provision), and (3) a certificate of "government protection," giving assurances that the facility could not be disposed of or used for purposes other than to fulfill the stipulated contract without government approval.[17]

These JAG procedures, when turned over to the navy bureaus for processing, produced total confusion. Many officers simply did not understand the purposes of the new tax law underlying the certificates, and the JAG made no effort to educate them, since it operated on the Olympian theory that it would give advice if asked but would not initiate guidance.[18] Moreover, the Advisory Commission had put the whole process in motion without establishing any clear standards or criteria for certificate clearance. Which plants were necessary? And what level of contract price and profit constituted non-reimbursement for a facility? In addition, the JAG and the bureaus failed to appreciate that the Advisory Commission intended to exercise its statutory authority to review decisions made by the army and navy, not merely to rubber-stamp them.

The Advisory Commission was willing to accept a military judgment that a particular new plant facility was "necessary." But Leon Henderson, the commission member in charge of price controls, was suspicious that "reimbursement" for a new facility was being hidden in the price/profit terms of the contract so that the contractor was in reality getting a double benefit, i.e., a quick tax write-off plus a larger-than-warranted profit. Through his influence, the Advisory Commission established a case-by-case review procedure which threatened to derail the whole enterprise, for neither the army nor the navy would accept Henderson as the arbiter of military prices, and their reasoning stood on solid practical ground: If they established procedures to meet his requirements, the applications from contractors would simply dry up, the tax law providing for five-year amortization would be a dead letter, and this would force the government to pay in full for all defense-plant expansion.[19]

Faced with this immediate mess, Forrestal turned to a ycungish lawyer, Struve Hensel, from the firm of Millbank, Tweed in New York, who was recommended by Charles Detmar. Hensel accepted the assignment because, as he recalled, "my marriage was not going well at the time" and on the understanding that he would be in Washington for no more than sixty days. The task was to analyze the whole certification procedure in the navy and make recommendations for sensible rules and regulations, including an authoritative point of final decision. Hensel, who had never met Forrestal, found him "terse, quite direct, and no-nonsense. All of that appealed to me." He was provided with an assistant, a lawyer from California named W. John Kenney, who had served on the Securities and Exchange Commission. "He was a New Deal Democrat and I was a conservative," Hensel recalled, "but we agreed on everything—especially on what was needed for more efficiency in government. He became one of my closest friends."[20]

The heart of Hensel's penetrating analysis of the non-reimbursement problem was a recommendation that the contractor and the navy should provide the Advisory Commission with a price/profit analysis and certify that no reimbursement beyond accelerated depreciation was hidden in it. Hensel argued that this should suffice, unless Henderson could point out a substantive error in the price/profit analysis. He also recommended that Forrestal move the certification supervisory unit out of the JAG and into his own office in order to control the flow of all navy submissions to the Advisory Commission.[21]

This sensible solution was challenged inside the navy by John Vincent, Forrestal's old friend and now a special assistant to the Under Secretary. For reasons unknown, Vincent became the front man for the view of the bureaus that the Advisory Commission should be required to accept a flat navy assertion that the contract contained no hidden reimbursement—no questions asked, no ifs, ands, or buts. In this view, Hensel's proposed price/profit analysis was an affront to the navy's honor and integrity. Vincent's position was the polar opposite of the Leon Henderson position and Hensel thought them both politically impossible. What he sought was a sensible compromise, but Vincent was supported by many high-ranking naval officers. "The boys in blue loved his idea, and Vincent, who had easier access to Forrestal than I did, was trying to make me out as a traitor to the Navy cause."[22]

Never one to run from a fight, Hensel showed in this episode the innate toughness and clarity of mind that were to make him invaluable as one of Forrestal's principal enforcers of civilian authority throughout the war. "Sharp memos were exchanged and personalities became involved. The Vincent-Hensel confrontation was bloody and notorious," Hensel recalled, but when the issue was clearly explained Forrestal came down firmly on Hensel's side, thereby sending a clear signal to the bureaus that civilian authority would prevail. With the help of his army counterpart, Robert Patterson, Forrestal then persuaded Leon Henderson to accept the compromise solution.[23]

Vincent was "told to stay quietly in his corner," and soon departed for a job with the Maritime Commission. Hensel returned to New York at the end of 1940, after persuading Forrestal to take on Richard Kyle, another Wall Street lawyer, to head the new certificate supervisory unit in the Under Secretary's office. Kyle seemed another of those thousands of people who descended on Washington in the strange, uneasy period of incipient war before the lightning flash of Pearl Harbor, impelled by a restless desire for change in their lives that owed as much to personal disquiet as to patriotism, and perhaps more. "Kyle's marriage was really on the rocks and he wanted to get out of town,"[24] Hensel remembered.

THE CONTRACTS MESS

H AVING FOUND and imposed a rational solution to the dispute over certificates of necessity and non-reimbursement, Forrestal next addressed himself to the larger mess of navy contracting which the earlier row had revealed. Again, he was made aware that the mobilization authorities were extremely dissatisfied with the imprecise, overlapping, uncoordinated "requirements" for materials and items being submitted by the navy, and it was evident to him that a system of integrated submissions was imperative: The navy could not blithely go its own slipshod way, for naval procurement plans now affected the whole national economy. But the uniformed navy was slow to comprehend this truth and naturally disposed to resist it. Meanwhile, the quickening pace of mobilization was generating a Niagara of uncoordinated, unexplained, unjustified contracts for signature by the Under Secretary.

In March 1941, Forrestal recalled Hensel from New York to analyze the whole problem of navy contracts and to submit recommendations. Hensel, in turn, called once again on Kenney, and together they found that the navy system of making contracts, partly centralized and partly decentralized, was largely the result of historical evolution—which is to say, accidental. To guide their analysis, Forrestal had stated his own view of the proper division of labor between the civilian secretariat and the uniformed fleet: "The fighting men tell us what they want, what they must have to fight the war. We undertake to get it all for them, at the best possible price for the nation and in the time the navy has to have it. Where the conduct of the war at sea is concerned we stay out of the navy's way."[25] In keeping with Forrestal's precept, Hensel reasoned it was for the uniformed navy to say what it needed, but for legal and business experts to draft the contracts, taking into account broader factors like available facilities and resources, national priorities, and cost. He also concluded there must be a shift to tailor-made, negotiated contracts in order to create performance incentives for the contractor, to protect the navy, and to save money.[26]

The Hensel-Kenney report (submitted to Forrestal on March 25, 1941) provided a lucid description of existing navy contract procedures and their weaknesses, as well as a terse list of recommendations. The most important of these urged the establishment of a Procurement Legal Division in the Under Secretary's office, to be headed by a civilian lawyer of "substantial experience and reputation" whose own subordinate lawyers would serve as special counsels in each bureau. It was of the utmost importance, Hensel argued, that the new office be staffed entirely by civilians and operate with complete independence of uniformed naval channels. Under the proposed arrangement, each special counsel assigned to a bureau would be responsible exclusively to the chief attorney of the Procurement Legal Division, but would review all bureau contracts in their formative stage and would be present as legal adviser to the bureau chief during the negotiation of all important contracts. Contracts above $500 million would be submitted for direct review and approval by the Under Secretary. The bureau chiefs would sign all the contracts and be responsible for their successful execution.[27]

Forrestal passed these recommendations to the Judge Advocate General for comment. The JAG, Rear Admiral Walter B. Woodson, wore immaculate uniforms, affected a pince-nez which dangled from a silk cord around his neck, and bore himself with the overweening self-confidence of an officer who had once served as naval aide to Assistant Secretary Franklin D. Roosevelt. His comments on the Hensel-Kenney report were resoundingly negative. In his considered view, "The Secretary of the Navy is not empowered, without further legislation," to establish any new entity charged with "handling important legal business of the Navy independently of the Judge Advocate General."[28] According to Woodson, the JAG was the only permitted legal authority in the navy; it had exclusive jurisdiction.

This kind of narrow, *ex cathedra* pronouncement confirmed Hensel's view that Woodson was a "total disaster as a lawyer" and a "pompous ass" in the bargain,[29] a view Forrestal shared, and with Forrestal's approval and encouragement, Hensel disputed the JAG's opinion as a matter of law. In a forceful memorandum of April 28, 1941, he argued that there was no statutory restriction on the Secretary of the Navy's authority to organize the contracting process in any way he chose; current naval regulations might be inhibiting, but the Secretary had full authority to change these.[30]

At the same time, Hensel was advising Forrestal that the proposed Procurement Legal Division "will never accomplish the desired purpose" if forced to function under JAG control: "Unfortunately, neither the JAG nor any of the officers or civilians in his department with whom I have come in contact have had the necessary commercial experience. Just as a civilian attorney cannot be easily turned into a naval officer, so a naval officer needs more than a license to practice to become a real lawyer."[31] Opposition to the idea of a Procurement Legal Division, especially one that was independent of the JAG, grew more intense within the uniformed navy. The bureau chiefs complained that civilian lawyers in their midst would seriously disrupt their operations, and the CNO responded to their distress by insisting to Forrestal that any "contracting lawyer" in the bureaus should be put in uniform.[32]

Forrestal endorsed the Hensel-Kenney report, but before throwing down the gauntlet he decided to seek a change in the law that would conclusively refute the JAG claim to sole jurisdiction over legal business in the navy. He also sought authority to hire fifteen additional lawyers at salaries in excess of $5,000 a year (the prospects for salaries above this level were narrow, as the pay of Cabinet officers was $10,000). Opposition quickly developed in the House Naval Affairs Committee, headed by "Uncle Carl" Vinson (the "swamp fox" from Milledgeville, Georgia), much of it stimulated by Admiral Woodson, whose JAG office was the only authorized channel for navy liaison with Congress. A month after President Roosevelt had declared an "unlimited national emergency," in the same month that Hitler's legions were rolling eastward across Russia, and five months before Pearl Harbor, the atmosphere in Vinson's committee was still myopic and penny-pinching. Why were more lawyers needed? it was asked. And why do they require such exorbitant salaries—$6,000 to $7,500? Finally, after great struggle, the congressional mountain brought forth a legislative mouse—authorization for one additional full-time attorney—on July 25, 1941.[33]

Undaunted by this tepid encouragement, Forrestal quickly moved to de facto establishment of the new organization for centralized contract control. He asked Hensel to become chief attorney in the new unit, and when Hensel demurred—protesting that he was "too young and unknown, without sufficient reputation"—Forrestal told him, "Stay and I will give you the reputation."[34] The second step was to hire a cadre of lawyers on "temporary employment contracts" at a per diem rate of twenty-five dollars. Even here the redoubtable Woodson presented a memorandum asserting that per diem arrangements had been declared illegal by the Comptroller General; more broadly, he argued that establishment of a Procurement Legal Division would be "fundamentally unsound" and would "disrupt the present organization" of legal affairs in the Navy Department, which were "running smoothly."[35]

Forrestal was not deterred by this opposition, but characteristically decided to avoid a head-on collision, while at the same time moving ahead. Instead of issuing a formal directive, he brought the new unit into being through a series of conversations with the bureau chiefs, supplemented by memoranda that laid down the conditions essential for his own control of the contract process: All lawyers in the new unit would be civilian and remain so; lawyers assigned to each bureau would be given adequate office space near the bureau chief; they would participate in the physical preparation of contracts and, wherever possible, in the preliminary negotiations with the contractor; they would be responsible only to Hensel and through him to the Under Secretary.

The new legal division thus operated without benefit of a formal directive during the last six months of 1941 and all of 1942, but continued to meet with hostility and suspicion throughout the uniformed navy. Vinson blew hot and cold in his feelings about it and even introduced a bill to abolish it. As Hensel recalled, "The atmosphere was rancorous" and sometimes brought to the surface the underlying attitudes of naval officers toward civilians, particularly toward young civilian lawyers without established place in the hierarchy, who were nevertheless presuming to exert considerable authority. On at least one occasion, Hensel's deputy, Kenney, "was admonished to rise whenever a senior naval officer entered his office."[36] But Forrestal gave his young lawyers unremitting support, and gradually the organizational logic and coherence of the scheme became apparent to a clear majority in the uniformed establishment, and cooperation became less grudging.

On December 13, 1942, a full year after Pearl Harbor, Forrestal signed a directive formalizing the Procurement Legal Division and all attendant procedures. Hensel became General Counsel of the Navy Department, and his lawyers in the several bureaus were given appropriate status. The precipitating factor in this case was a meeting on December 9 initiated by Vice Admiral Frederick Horne, the Vice Chief of Naval Operations. He called on Forrestal in company with all the bureau chiefs, some of whom claimed still to be unclear as to the purposes and authority of the Under Secretary's legal unit. Horne told Forrestal the navy now "felt it best to have the matter discussed frankly, and settled."[37]

Going around the room, Forrestal asked each bureau chief for his views on the legal division and whether its work was satisfactory to the bureau. The Chiefs of Yards and Docks, Ships, Aeronautics, and Ordnance all testified that the system was working well in their jurisdictions and had in fact made a considerable contribution to efficient contracting. Only the Chief of Supplies and Accounts sounded a negative note. He was "not aware" as to "just what role" was being played by "Mr. Richard Kyle," who was Hensel's man in that bureau. "Have you ever asked Mr. Kyle?" Forrestal asked him. The admiral replied in the negative. "Well, then why are you bringing the matter up here?" Forrestal's tone was now sharp and impatient. Thrown on the defensive, the admiral stammered that it was "most unusual" to have an outside representative in the bureau "whose authority and position were not clearly defined." But Forrestal evaded the exchange with a curt, dismissive reply. "If you have not asked Mr. Kyle what services he performs, there is no purpose to airing your complaints at this meeting."[38]

The redoubtable Admiral Woodson spoke up to say he had always tried to cooperate with Hensel's group, but had found that this was unfortunately "a one-sided affair." Noting that "Mr. Hensel had a representative in all of the bureaus," he asked plaintively, "Why doesn't he have a representative in my office?" As the JAG procured nothing for the navy, this silly statement might have been expected to evoke amusement, but the bureau chiefs sat stolid and unsmiling while Hensel and Detmar exclaimed in unison, "What would he do?" To that sensible question, Woodson had no answer.[39]

Woodson's insistent assertions of outmoded JAG prerogatives finally became an annoyance that Forrestal decided he could do without, so he arranged for his reassignment elsewhere. Woodson was replaced by another sea lawyer, Rear Admiral Thomas Gatch, whom Hensel found little improvement over his predecessor. A year later, when Gatch was given command of the battleship *South Dakota,* Hensel went to Forrestal arguing that "an expensive ship like that" should be kept in competent hands. Forrestal laughed and said to him, "You're judging Gatch as a lawyer. You will find that he knows how to command a battleship." And he did. "Forrestal knew better than I did about that."[40]

Forrestal's handling of the complicated and politically explosive contracting problem is a representative example of his administrative method. By patient persuasion, by pushing an idea informally, by implementing it on a trial basis, he gradually built a favorable consensus which he then formalized. Although brusque in manner and outwardly impatient, he was in fact both patient and persistent in pursuing consultations and negotiations with those who disagreed with him. He was confident that demonstrated workability plus frequent, well-timed restatement of the facts in face-to-face discussion, as one reasonable person to another, could usually produce a decision acceptable to all parties.

★ ★ ★

CHAPTER 13

Gathering Momentum

CREATION OF the "certificate" and "contract" units in Forrestal's office were moves in the right direction, but they covered only relatively small parts of the overall procurement problem. In mid-1941 the navy still had no centralized means of controlling this sprawling, gargantuan enterprise, now growing at a fantastic pace. Responsibility continued to be distributed among the CNO, the bureau chiefs, and the Under Secretary. Well into 1941, data on navy "requirements" were still going to the Office of Production Management directly from the individual bureaus, and OPM still found them to be grossly deficient—imprecise, unreliable, overlapping, and sometimes bearing no relation to appropriations approved by Congress.[1] OPM expressed its dissatisfaction in increasingly blunt terms, urging Knox and Forrestal to establish a central control point that would integrate the navy submissions and assure their accuracy. At the time, the War Department was far better organized to deal with the civilian mobilization agencies. A chief statistical officer, located in the office of the Under Secretary of War, directed a staff of forty people responsible for coordinating the paper flow.[2]

A closely related, galling frustration for Forrestal was the casualness with which Admiral Stark and the Op-Nav staff were providing guidance to the bureaus on the future composition of the fleet. As one perceptive officer, Rear Admiral C. W. Fisher, wrote to the Under Secretary in 1941, "Hand to mouth methods must give way to annual programs. What is the Navy going to procure or order in 1942? Who knows?"[3] Forrestal expressed his impatience at this dithering and equally at the lack of concern for "balance" in the procurement of closely related end-items—"Are ammunition needs keeping pace with gun production?"—and he asserted the obvious need to plan production further ahead: "We must think in terms of eight months from now. It will be painful to do it, but it must be done; otherwise the Office of Production Management cannot properly operate.''[4] Even as he wrote this, OPM was beginning to insist that the army and navy express their requirements at least eighteen months in advance, but the navy was not, in mid-1941, organized to meet even the Under Secretary's less exacting standard.

One egregious incident finally provoked Forrestal to decisive action. On August 15, 1941, FDR approved a British escort vessel program providing for the construction of fifty ships in American shipyards. He directed the navy to determine its own requirements for such a vessel, to add these to the British order, and then to expedite the actual shipbuilding. Four months later, Stark and his planners were still debating the number of U.S. escort vessels and their particular specifications. Not until February 1942, three months after the shock of Pearl Harbor, was agreement finally reached on the design of what came to be called the Destroyer Escort and on the quantitative total (250 ships). Only then did production begin.

Donald Nelson, watching this painful process from his anomalous position of "priorities coordinator," just before his appointment as head of the War Production Board, confided to his diary that "1941 will go down in history, I believe, as the year we almost lost the war before we got into it."[5]

BREAKTHROUGH TO CENTRALIZED CONTROL

FINDING THE situation intolerable, Forrestal called together, in the waning months of 1941, Detmar, Hensel, Edwin Booz (a management consultant who was working for Secretary Knox), and Ferdinand Eberstadt, his close friend from Wall Street. The problem was how to jolt the mulish, hidebound navy into a realization that it must, henceforth and forthwith, conduct its procurement with a sense of urgency and on an entirely integrated basis. The supply situation had radically changed. Gone were the days when the bureaus could meet their requirements without rigorous planning and scheduling—because facilities and materials had previously been in plentiful supply. Money had been the limiting factor; now money was available in astonishing amounts, but materials, facilities, and labor were stretched thin because the aggregate demands of the army, navy, Lend-Lease, and the civilian economy were reaching unprecedented levels.

Out of this concentrated analytical effort, lasting several weeks and involving broad consultation within the navy and outside it, came the main features of the Office of Procurement and Material (OP&M).* This was

---

*OP&M in the navy should not be confused with the Office of Production Management (OPM), which was under the direction of the White House. At the time, the confusion, if any, was short-lived, for OP&M came into existence at about the same time OPM was reorganized and renamed the War Production Board (WPB).

established under Forrestal's supervision by a general order from the Secretary on January 30, 1942, seven weeks after the attack on Pearl Harbor.[6] Forrestal regarded it as his "principal contribution to the acceleration of the Naval building program."

Under OP&M, each bureau was ordered to state its "requirements" for the next two calendar years, by major end-items expressed in not less than million-dollar units. For example, the Bureau of Ships would be required to say how many battleships, aircraft carriers, destroyers, cruisers, and patrol vessels it intended to build in that time period. In addition, the major end-items would be broken down into their principal components, e.g., turbines, aircraft engines, armor plate. Then a schedule would be established for the purchase and delivery of each category. Such detailed planning would reveal shortages and bottlenecks in the procurement process and thus the need for a shift in priorities or additional industrial capacity. The staff elements needed to support OP&M were transferred from various parts of the navy and brought together under Rear Admiral Samuel M. Robinson (a former chief of the Bureau of Ships). They provided central statistical reporting and control, coordination of machine tool production, allocation of machine tools to navy contractors, and a centralized corps of inspectors to monitor the performance of all industrial plants under contract to the navy.[7]

The establishment of OP&M was the critical breakthrough. It made possible, for the first time, the truly integrated planning and execution, under skilled and sophisticated civilian leadership, of all navy procurement needed to meet the supreme test of battle in the far-flung war. Without it, or something like it, the building of the fleet would have continued to flounder, with incalculable consequences for the course of the war and the security of the United States. Forrestal's vital contributions were his comprehending intelligence, his determination to direct, supervise, and inspire—"all with the sole object of supporting the fleet," as Hensel stated it. Forrestal became "the center of the management web . . . and his desk became the focal point, the command center, for Navy Department management."[8] From this point forward, he operated virtually as "Co-Secretary" and had complete authority over the vast naval procurement program and all its attendant functions. He lunched weekly with Knox and kept him fully informed, and their relationship was a warm and cordial one endowed with a great deal of mutual respect. Knox encouraged his younger colleague to do his utmost for the common cause and never showed the slightest resentment at Forrestal's gathering reputation and prestige.

GEARING UP THE MUNITIONS BOARD

THE ARMY-NAVY Munitions Board was the coordinating mechanism created in 1922 to develop plans for national mobilization in the event of another war. But in 1940, with World War II already unleashed in Europe and threatening to engulf Asia, primary responsibility for actual mobilization of the American economy had passed to civilian agencies. Nevertheless, the Munitions Board was destined to play a powerful role in the process, for with the creation of an Under Secretary of War and an Under Secretary of the Navy, leadership of that body became, for the first time, synonymous with high-level responsibility for military procurement.

Forrestal and Robert Patterson, the Under Secretary of War, worked well together, and indeed became the synchronized driving force in the swift and historically unprecedented military buildup. Patterson was an upstate New Yorker from Schenectady who was graduated from Union College and later from Harvard Law School. He had enlisted as a private in World War I, fought in France, risen to the rank of captain, and been decorated for bravery. President Hoover appointed him to a district judgeship in New York, and in 1939 FDR elevated him to the Federal Circuit Court of Appeals. Henry L. Stimson made Patterson's appointment as his deputy in the War Department a condition of his own acceptance of the Cabinet post.[9] An erect man of medium height, he bore himself austerely yet without pretension, and one journalist thought the impression of sternness evaporated "when he smiled, which he did often."[10] He held burning convictions about the war effort, especially about the need for compulsory military service and sacrifice on the home front, and he showed a disposition to fight for his policy positions without conceding a need to compromise. His adversaries on the War Production Board argued that if Patterson had his way, "the homefront would be as weak as a hookworm victim," to which Patterson retorted that such opinions reflected a preference for "coddling the people and fighting a soft war."[11] Where Forrestal was inherently cautious, less disposed to confrontation, and open-minded to reasonable compromise, the frugal, dogmatic Patterson preferred frontal assault. "His relentless prodding and lashing, and his moral fervor, drove the industrial mobilization," wrote Ernest K. Lindley in *Newsweek*.[12]

After the attack on Pearl Harbor, Patterson succeeded in pressing the War Production Board to restrict severely the production of civilian aircraft, but could not eliminate the allocation of newsprint for comic strips or the manufacture of soft drinks. The second issue became something of an obsession with him and a source of much amusement among his colleagues. At every meeting of the Munitions Board he would thunder against the horrifying waste of sugar, rubber tires, and the manpower used in their production and delivery. On one occasion Forrestal found him staring intently out the window onto Constitution Avenue. "That's what I mean," Patterson exclaimed, "look at those Coca-Cola trucks out there—thousands of tons of sugar going to civilians when they should be going to the war effort." Forrestal grinned at him and said, "I'm sorry to disappoint you, but I'm informed that those trucks are on their way to the Naval Air Station from which the Coca-Cola will be shipped to our forces in the Pacific." Patterson scowled fiercely for a moment, then smiled and said, "OK, Clausewitz, you always have the answer."[13] Forrestal later wrote to Herbert Bayard Swope that "the Cromwellian-Roman austerity of standard which he [Patterson] sets . . . is difficult for the less virtuous to follow."[14]

SOMETIME IN MID-1941, the gathering momentum of war production was threatened by a sudden shortage of machine tools—an element essential to the mass production of aircraft engines, guns, ammunition, and numerous other major war items. Because the OPM efforts to resolve the problem were floundering, Forrestal and Patterson called Ferdinand Eberstadt from New York to analyze the problem. Eberstadt found that many prospective military contractors were understandably slow to place orders for machine tools until they had actually signed defense contracts, but that machine tool manufacturers lacked the financial strength or incentive to expand production except against firm orders. He also found that some contractors were hoping to use their "priority" authority under certain contracts to seize existing machine tools from users with lower priorities and thus obviate the need for their own purchase. The result was that few new machines were being made. With characteristic acuity, Eberstadt quickly cut through to the heart of the problem. He recommended that the army and navy themselves (1) place orders for a large pool of standard machine tools, (2) allocate them to contractors on a basis consistent with mobilization priorities, and (3) penalize defense contractors who failed to order their own machine tools in advance.[15]

Forrestal and Patterson then asked Eberstadt to analyze the operation of the Munitions Board as a whole and to make recommendations for its effective operation in the event of actual war, which they believed was coming inevitably and soon. He proposed that the board establish joint army-navy requirements for all raw materials, productive capacity, and equipment so that the overall mobilization agency (OPM, soon to become the War Production Board) could analyze the effect of total military requirements on the total economy. He added that the Munitions Board must anticipate and identify bottlenecks and shortages in all areas affecting the procurement and transportation of military items.[16] Finally, he recommended a full-time chairman. Forrestal and Patterson immediately asked him to take the job. He declined, then changed his mind immediately after the attack on Pearl Harbor. An admiring Struve Hensel called Eberstadt "a pure intellect, a thinking machine, operating beautifully."[17]

Equipped with a full-time chairman, the Munitions Board became, after America was in the war, an intelligent and relentless prod, forcing a reluctant War Production Board and its chairman, Donald Nelson, to an ever more rapid, more comprehensive conversion of the national economy to war production. In January 1942, the Munitions Board pushed to restrict civilian production of radios, refrigeration machinery, and metal office equipment. Nelson, who was consumer-oriented and awed by the vast extent of his new authority, still hesitated to order mandatory conversion of such items, but Forrestal, Patterson, and Eberstadt kept pushing.[18]

By April 1, they had achieved not only the above restrictions, but also an end to the manufacture of civilian automobiles for the duration of the war. They next turned their attention to the need for gasoline rationing as a means of extending the life of existing automobiles and trucks, especially of their tires. Rubber was in acute short supply because the chief source, the Dutch East Indies, had been captured by the Japanese. American farm interests and the oil industry fought hard against gas and rubber rationing, but the undeniable logic and force of the arguments made by Forrestal, Patterson, and Eberstadt made it much easier for Nelson to decide. Their insistence helped him over other tough hurdles as well—like the curtailment of railroad passenger travel, where they pointed out that the allocation of 328 passenger cars to carry spectators to the Kentucky Derby was a "somewhat remote" contribution to the war effort. They took the same position with regard to rail transportation to large football games. They protested the wartime expansion of rural electrification and even the continued manufacture of steel bottlecaps. The Munitions Board became, in short, a goad and a conscience manifesting a stern clarity of what was required to win the war—namely, a determined whittling down of the accustomed frills and indulgences of the peacetime economy.[19]

This was not the approach favored by Donald Nelson and other consumer-oriented officials at the War Production Board, and they fought several dogged rearguard actions against what they often resented as the military steamroller. Later in the war, when Eberstadt was serving as vice chairman of WPB, a New Deal cabal succeeded in persuading FDR to fire him, but the closely knit Munitions Board triumvirate, impelled by a degree of urgency that seemed to be shared by few others, succeeded in putting military programs well out in front of civilian programs, especially in the desperate year of 1942.[20]

Despite the steadily rising allocations to the war effort, aggregate home-front consumption in fact increased all during this period—from $67.4

billion in 1939 to $110.4 billion in 1944 and $122 billion in 1945—astonishing testimony to the underlying productive capacity of the American economy.[21] The war effort indeed ended the Great Depression. In Alabama, a black worker counted his fattened pay envelope after a week on the assembly line of a defense plant and exclaimed without the slightest intention to be unpatriotic: "Thank God for Hitler."[22]

With understandable pride, Forrestal summarized the direct impact of the mobilization effort on the course of the war in a speech to the Princeton graduating class of 1944: "The economy of the United States, even that sometimes abused sphere of activity known as business, produced an industrial organization and productive machine which have been able to pour out the torrent of weapons which today is swamping our enemies, and I mean that literally . . . Will this economy and government, so successful in war, fail in peace? No," provided there is a "bold and imaginative use of government credit" and "an atmosphere of confidence in which businessmen can take those ventures upon which a sound economy must rest."[23]

Forrestal made many tough, far-reaching decisions as Under Secretary and made them stick, but he made them carefully and, wherever possible, with the full support of his own organization. Believing that any major decision leaves scars, he tried to lead people toward what he felt was the right thing to do by presenting the facts and discussing alternatives. He preferred to leave open a path of dignified retreat for those who took a hard position in opposition to his own.[24] In a speech to the Harvard Business School alumni in the middle of the war, he reaffirmed this basic philosophy of management, and indeed of his personal life: "I have always said that business administration consists 90 percent of an ability to resolve and remove human frictions. I can assure you that this percentage, in government, could easily be raised to 98 percent."[25]

CHAPTER 14

★ ★ ★

Troubles with
Admiral King

ERNEST J. KING held the twin titles of Commander in Chief of the U.S. Fleet and Chief of Naval Operations during most of the war. A domineering personality, he vigilantly tended the fires of his own high ambition and kept a considerable distance between himself and most others. The son of a Scotch immigrant, he grew up in Lorain, Ohio, and was graduated fourth in the Naval Academy class of 1901.[1] Behind a bleak Scottish exterior, as Henry Stimson's biographer Elting Morrison wrote, "some intense spirit burned away, a spirit fed by incalculable devotions to self and service. Above and beyond all these was resolution—grim, harsh, ruthless . . . but above all, resolution."[2] He had a well-deserved reputation for toughness (a future CNO said, "he shaved with a blowtorch") and also for sudden bursts of terrible temper, although one of his daughters (he had five) called him "the most even tempered man in the navy—he is always in a rage."[3]

In 1944, during the confused and critical naval Battle of Leyte Gulf in the Philippines, King was sitting with the Combined Chiefs of Staff (the British and American military leaders), trying to get a fix on precisely what was happening. The briefing officer, Captain William Smedberg, a much-decorated destroyer commander who had been fighting in the Pacific for two years, explained that the Japanese force moving through the San Bernardino Strait included "two old battleships, the *Ise* and *Hyuga*." King interrupted him, saying, "Captain Smedberg is new here and has made a mistake. *Ise* and *Hyuga* are two of the newest Japanese battleships." Smedberg, who knew his facts, had the temerity to contradict his superior and set the record straight. Two hours later he was summoned to King's office: "Smedberg, I found out that you were right in this instance. But if you ever correct me again in the presence of my peers, I'll crucify you. That's all."[4]

He aroused strong feelings. Dwight D. Eisenhower, when he was a brigadier general in charge of War Department planning in 1942, thought King "an arbitrary, stubborn type with too much brain and a tendency toward bullying his juniors. But I think he wants to fight, which is vastly encouraging." At a later moment of exasperation with the Admiral's stiff-necked refusal of cooperation on some matter, Eisenhower confided to his diary that one way to speed the war effort would be "to get someone to shoot King."[5]

King was a naval strategist, and naval strategy—to be successful—must be ever aggressive. At an early stage in his career he absorbed Alfred Thayer Mahan's insight that sea power—control of the seas—can be maintained only by crippling all other contending naval forces; unlike an army, a fleet cannot seize only a portion of the sea and hold it defensively. Thus, the idea of a "strategic defensive" in the Pacific while the main Allied effort was concentrated against Hitler meant quite different things to Army Chief of Staff General George Marshall and to Admiral King. To King it meant, of necessity, an unrelenting effort to seek out, attack, and destroy the Japanese fleet. Some thought the Admiral's ceaseless urging of a greater effort against the Japanese may have been the crucial factor in persuading the British finally to accept the risks of direct assault on Hitler's Fortress Europa in 1944. Had they continued to balk, so runs this argument, they were fearful that the power of King's advocacy could have persuaded FDR to shift the full weight of the American war effort to the Pacific.[6]

There were differences between King and Marshall beyond strategy. One was the Admiral's visceral antipathy to the very concept of civilian control. He resented it, chafed under it, and sought by every means to minimize or avoid it. He hated to defer. He wanted to control everything and saw civilian authority basically as interference with his own prerogatives as supreme naval commander. On this point, King's view was a concentrated distillate—almost to the point of caricature—of the traditional attitude within the uniformed navy. Secretary of War Stimson referred, with both scorn and sorrow, to "The Admirals," whom he described as a collection of gentlemen "both anonymous and continuous . . . and still uncontrolled by either the Secretary or the President."[7]

Marshall, on the other hand, was military chief of a War Department that bore the marks of Elihu Root's reorganization in 1903, which had established unity of command under a single all-powerful chief of staff who was at the same time subordinate, by law, to the Secretary of War. In the process, Root and his successors had gradually inculcated throughout the officer corps a genuine intellectual and philosophical acceptance of civilian control. The result, on the eve of World War II, was that Stimson and Marshall were able to establish a close and cooperative relationship characterized by complete mutual trust and respect. Their offices were immediately adjacent, their doors open, and Marshall withheld no information from the Secretary of War. No doubt their solid characters and personalities also played a major role in the success of their relationship, but the army was much better organized on the threshold of World War II—for both strategic policy-making and mobilization—than was the navy, where civilian-military relationships remained loosely defined and therefore contentious.

Another important difference was that Marshall was a superb administrator, while King was a superb strategic thinker, but essentially indifferent to those aspects of his responsibilities not directly related to naval operations and fighting. He was impatient with and remarkably innocent of the daunting complexities of meshing navy material requirements with American industry for the greatest naval buildup in history. At the same time, he was not above administrative caprice that suggested he was, in part, a Scottish Huckleberry Finn with a boyish determination to thumb his nose at the world.[8] FDR, who was aware of King's shortcomings, nevertheless valued him as the keenest strategic mind on the Joint Chiefs of Staff and a man who loved to fight.[9]

Marshall's great talents as organizer, leader, and strategist were sustained by a private life of moderation and marital propriety, whereas the counterpoise to King's stern professional competence was "a private life of notable gaudiness," in Eric Larrabee's phrase. He liked alcohol and other men's wives and arranged to have plentiful portions of both. In the slow-moving years between the world wars, the navy had no more persistent partygoer or determined and notoriously successful pursuer of attractive ladies. He made no secret of this penchant and was said not to trust any man who did not drink or enjoy the company of women. Throughout the war he regularly left his office at four o'clock and disappeared until dinnertime. Occasionally, he was gone for two or three days at a time.[10]

A CAREER REVIVED

KING'S CAREER had seemed at an end when President Roosevelt appointed Admiral Stark as CNO in 1939. King was then sixty years old, and mandatory retirement came at sixty-four. Fortunately, Stark had great respect for King's ability, and even liked him. In July 1940, when FDR declared the United States would henceforward assume responsibility for the defense of the Western Hemisphere (which involved primarily guarding the ocean approaches), Stark persuaded him to offer King command of the Atlantic Squadron, a smallish flotilla of ships whose age and general condition reflected the decision made during the 1930s to allocate most of the navy's limited resources to the Pacific Fleet and the threat from

Japan. King accepted, despite the demotion from Vice Admiral to Rear Admiral. Seven months later, in February 1941, a substantially enlarged Squadron was redesignated the Atlantic Fleet and four-star rank was conferred on King. From the outset, he organized, trained, and drove his old ships and new men with accustomed toughness and resolution, determined to prove that extra zeal and unwavering devotion to duty by all hands would overcome the shortages of modern equipment, supplies, technology, and personnel. He braced his officers and sailors to accept the physical discomforts and dangers of escorting transatlantic convoys on the cold cruel sea and to cope with the psychological strains of fighting an undeclared war against German U-boats.[11]

In September 1941, when FDR ordered the fleet to escort the convoys two-thirds of the way to England, clashes with the U-boats became inevitable. A few days later the destroyer *Greer* had an inconclusive engagement with a German submarine—the German fired two torpedoes which missed, and *Greer* counterattacked with depth charges, but the submarine got away. FDR, however, promptly used the incident to define the attack on *Greer* as "piracy" and to declare that henceforth any "German or Italian vessels of war" entering waters within the American defense zone would do so at their own risk. In mid-October, the destroyer *Kearny* was heavily damaged by a torpedo while trying to protect a convoy against savage simultaneous attacks by a submarine wolf pack. And on October 31, the destroyer *Reuben James* was blown in half and sunk with a loss of 125 men, including all its officers. These violent clashes, in what Churchill called the "war of groping and drowning" in the cold North Atlantic, especially the loss of American lives in bloody combat, served to deepen the American people's understanding of the harsh realities of the world situation. To the surprise of some, it strengthened FDR's hand against the isolationists. After the sinking of the *Reuben James,* King strengthened his own hand by giving up hard drink for the duration.[12]

At this delicate stage of the crablike U.S. movement away from isolationism toward full, official involvement in the European war, King thus became a central instrument of FDR's policy of graduated boldness. In fact, the Battle of the Atlantic went very badly all through 1942, and the German submarine menace was not fully conquered until mid-1943. At the end, 4,786 merchant ships, together with 29 American and 158 British Commonwealth warships, had been sunk. About 40,000 Allied seamen, plus several hundred women and children, lost their lives. But 781 U-boats were sent to the bottom along with 32,000 German submariners. In the unnerving process, FDR gained a lasting respect for King as a resolute fighting man.[13]

Following the debacle at Pearl Harbor, the President turned to King to retrieve the physical and spiritual disaster that had befallen the navy on the morning of December 7. Both the Atlantic and Pacific Fleet commanders reported to Admiral Stark as CNO. FDR now proposed to revive the title of Commander in Chief of the U.S. Fleet (CINCUS) and to appoint King to command all naval forces in the war. Stark would remain as CNO, but would be relegated to long-range planning.

Pearl Harbor had put Stark under a dark cloud. Early on the morning of the attack, Naval Intelligence had decoded the message from the Japanese government to its envoys in Washington. This message instructed them to present their final note to the Secretary of State at precisely 1:00 p.m. Washington time. Their suspicions aroused, the intelligence officers calculated that 1:00 p.m. in Washington coincided with 8:00 a.m. in Hawaii. The director of Intelligence urged Admiral Stark to send an immediate message to Admiral Kimmel at Pearl Harbor warning him of the suspicious implications of the latest Japanese maneuver and stressing the need for a high state of alert. The navy's excellent communications could have delivered the message to Kimmel two hours before the attack. But Stark demurred on grounds of interservice protocol: The army was responsible for the air defense of Hawaii. The proposal was passed to the army, which tried to send the message to General Walter Short, the Army Commander in Hawaii, but its channels were clogged, so it turned to Western Union! The message arrived several hours after the Japanese attack.[14] In his 1944 review of the disaster, Forrestal blamed Stark for "submersion in details . . . to the extent that he became insensitive to the significance of events," and the general assessment was that Stark's record as an administrator left much to be desired.[15] In May 1945, in a letter arguing the need for constant vigilance, Forrestal reaffirmed his conviction that "the lessons of Pearl Harbor must not be forgotten."[16]

King, who was sympathetic to Stark, expressed doubts about the proposed new command arrangements; after careful consideration, however, he accepted, but set three conditions: (1) he wanted the title COMINCH instead of CINCUS, because the latter acronym sounded balefully defeatist ("sink us"), (2) he wanted assurances that he would not be called upon the meet the press or testify before Congress except under extraordinary circumstances, and (3) he wanted command authority over all of the naval bureaus. FDR readily acceded to the first two, but said the third one required a change in federal law (an arguable but dubious proposition).[17]

The resulting directive gave King "supreme command" of all naval "operating forces" and a direct reporting relationship to the President, while making him subject only to "general direction" by the Secretary of the Navy. This gave him more power than had ever been granted before to a U.S. admiral. Nevertheless, with Stark remaining as CNO, ambiguities concerning their responsibilities proved troublesome: the directive had not dealt, for example, with such questions as who would advise the President on overall strategy or who would represent the navy in strategic talks with the British. Within two months, it was apparent that, despite the good intentions of both admirals, their overlapping authority and responsibility was a source of major confusion. King insisted on a clarification, and FDR promised one.[18]

On March 12, 1942, FDR signed an executive order making King both COMINCH and CNO. Concurrently, Stark was sent to London to an expediently created post with the grand but rather empty title of Commander, U.S. Naval Forces, Europe. The new directive, drafted by King's staff, was too casually accepted by FDR, for it contained the words "and direction" over the bureaus. Moreover, when he signed it in the presence of Knox and King, the President made an offhand remark to the effect that he hoped this would help "streamline" navy organization. These heady ingredients of unprecedented new power stimulated King to precipitate one of the more bizarre incidents of the war.[19]

Returning to the Navy Department, King promptly initiated a plan to reorganize the navy into "four grand divisions"—personnel, readiness, operations, and material. Since the first three were already under his authority, his obvious target was the whole procurement responsibility— "material"—which had been established, after much blood and sweat, in the Office of Procurement and Material under Forrestal. King's basic conviction was that if civilians controlled procurement and production scheduling, they would obstruct his war plan by telling him what he could and could not have and when.[20] By early May, he had his plan in writing and had sent it to Knox and the President. FDR was appalled at what he quickly perceived to be the proposed emasculation of civilian authority in the Navy Department. This was no "streamlining," he wrote Knox, but a basic reorganization of the whole department in the middle of a war. He urged Knox to issue a counterplan that would neutralize King's ominous proposal, and he sent King a copy of his disapproving memo to Knox.[21]

Forrestal weighed in with his own views, to Knox. He felt King's plan would be a "major regression," an enormous setback to his own efforts over the past twenty months to organize and rationalize the burgeoning complexity of naval procurement. Under King's plan, all of this would be left to "a very inadequate section of the Office of the Chief of Naval Operations," which "has obviously all it can do in its own field."[22]

Viewed with Olympian detachment, King's plan could be called essentially an effort to organize the navy along the same lines as the War Department, with all uniformed components responsible to the senior military figure. Why then was it not welcomed? The answer lay in the sharp differences in the institutional cultures of the army and the navy and in the absence of either a tradition or a law subordinating COMINCH-CNO to the Secretary of the Navy. In addition, there was the special Roosevelt factor. FDR was essentially indifferent to the inner workings of the War Department, but took a strong paternal interest in the navy, assumed he knew it like the back of his hand, and resisted any development that might dilute his own ultimate control.

The real excitement began when King decided to ignore the President's clearly expressed reservations, and to forge ahead on his own over the even more explicit objections of Knox and Forrestal. On May 28, he issued an order to all bureaus and offices of the Navy Department putting his plan into effect, but in so doing chose not to inform anyone outside the uniformed navy. An officer from Forrestal's staff, visiting another office, happened to see a copy; so first Forrestal, then Knox, and finally FDR "got the word." A now quite agitated Roosevelt summoned Knox and King on June 9 and bluntly told King to cancel his order. He also made plain that any reorganizing would be done by himself and Knox. On June 12, to take out extra insurance, he wrote to Knox instructing him to rescind every paper dealing with navy organization issued by King over the previous thirty days, adding, "There may be more of them which neither you nor I have seen." The more he thought about it, he wrote, "the more outrageous I think it is that [King] went ahead to do, without your approval or mine, what I had already disapproved. . . . [King] is old enough to know better—and old enough to know that you are Secretary of the Navy and that I am Commander in Chief of the Navy."[23]

Forced to withdraw his sweeping plan, King sulked in his tent but without repentance. "The need for it was so obvious," he wrote later, "that I simply directed that it be put into effect. But I stumbled on one little pebble—I neglected to consult the President and the Secretary first."[24] As one of his senior subordinates put it, the game of reorganizing the navy was for King "a kind of disease," and propelled by the virus he continued to press his schemes on his resistant civilian superiors throughout the war. At the first Quebec Conference between FDR and Winston Churchill in August 1943, FDR sent still another note to Knox: "F.K., tell Ernie *once more*: No reorganizing of the Navy Department's set-up during the war. Let's win it first. FDR."[25]*

KING AND KNOX

WHILE CONTINUING to view King with "bemused affection,"[26] the President consistently backed Knox and Forrestal on navy organization. Nevertheless, Knox began to feel threatened by King's persistent

---

*The second Quebec Conference was held in September 1944. FDR and Churchill discussed postwar plans for Germany and military plans for the Pacific War.

grabs for power, and this moved him to an abortive attempt to get King out of town. Returning from the Quebec Conference, he suggested that King replace Nimitz as Commander of the Pacific Fleet, arguing that the top man should be in the theater of war where the navy's strategic influence was decisive. King privately thought this "the craziest idea," and, given his great influence as a member of the Joint Chiefs of Staff and the Combined Chiefs of Staff, it was.[27] In his official reply to Knox, he found the proposal "entirely unnecessary," for Nimitz was "carrying out his duties admirably" (presumably he intended no pun). At the same time, he blamed Forrestal as the real inspiration for the Knox proposal, and this was the beginning of an active, even bitter dislike for the Under Secretary which carried right on through to King's retirement at the end of the war.[28]

Having been a journalist and publisher for forty-two years, Knox was determined not only to handle the navy's public relations, but also to speak out frequently and forthrightly. On Armistice Day 1940, following FDR's reelection to a third term, he had declared that America was seeking to avoid war, "but not at the price of cowardice and dishonor." He had called Hitler "a greedy fanatic" and the war in Europe "an irreconcilable conflict" between democracy and totalitarianism. In June 1941, six months before Pearl Harbor, he told the Governors Conference at Mackinac Island that "the time to use our Navy to clear the Atlantic of the German menace is at hand."[29] Isolationists were enraged—Senator Burton K. Wheeler demanded that he be "thrown out of office"—but Stimson, Ickes, Walter Lippmann, Felix Frankfurter, and many others were delighted with such "astonishingly frank" talk, as was FDR.[30]

It was Knox's instinct to release all possible information, consistent with the safeguarding of military secrets, in the belief that an informed citizenry was the only reliable basis of public support for the war effort. Not surprisingly, this freewheeling approach brought him into conflict with King, and more generally with the conservative naval establishment as a whole. Although King was persuaded, later in the war, to talk privately to a select group of reporters on a more or less regular basis (with satisfactory results—there were no leaks), it was known that his conception of ideal press relations was to issue one communiqué at the end of the war saying "We won." He was always nervous that Knox, in his press conferences, would say too much, especially that he would reveal some fact that would tip the Japanese to the most critical, most sensitive, most secret secret of the war— that we had broken their operational codes. For his part, Knox felt that naval officers cloaked too many subjects in undue secrecy, and he operated with total self-confidence in his own ability to discern and maintain the fine line between important news and a breach of security. In October 1943, King forcefully recommended to him that "no book or article dealing with our submarine combat operations be published" until Japan had capitulated.[31] Disagreeing with even greater vehemence, Knox asserted the supremacy of navy "publicity" over navy "intelligence" and went on to say: "To put the matter bluntly, I know I have the experience to handle, without assistance, the question of Public Relations of the Navy."[32]

In late 1943, King put forward yet another of his reorganization schemes—this time to bring the naval shipyards under his command, on the grounds that ship repairs were taking far too long for fleet operations. In response, Knox and Forrestal counterattacked by proposing to separate King from his CNO job and to turn that over to Admiral Frederick Horne, one of King's two deputies. Horne would become Chief of Naval Logistics and Material, and the ambiguous title of CNO would be abolished. Knox and Forrestal reasoned it was his authority as CNO that King was using to launch his relentless forays into navy reorganization; at the same time, they noticed he was not paying much attention to the CNO's logistical duties, but had delegated most of them to Horne.[33] Under their proposal, King would get the title of Fleet Admiral and a fifth star (along with Marshall, Eisenhower, Nimitz, and the commanding general of the Army Air Forces, Henry "Hap" Arnold) and would be free to concentrate his talents and energies on commanding the far-flung operating naval forces.

Knox developed some White House support for the separation. Admiral Leahy learned, to his surprise, from Harry Hopkins that the President seemed favorable to the idea, and he later recorded his own view that the two jobs should indeed be split.[34] By January 1944, Forrestal had prepared a draft directive giving effect to the separation, and it was circulated for comment to the interested parties. As expected, King categorically opposed the idea, arguing vehemently that it was "necessary to have one man, and one man only, responsible for the military part of the Navy."[35] As he was, in fact, not exercising much guidance or authority over procurement, his argument was not entirely logical, but what mattered to him was prestige.

Drafts and counterdrafts went back and forth with no evidence of progress toward a solution acceptable to both sides. Finally, Knox voiced his exasperation in a memorandum to King: After reading all the drafts, he wrote, "I am oppressed by the fact that evidently I cannot get across to anyone what I want and what the President and I have agreed should be done."[36] But he never issued Forrestal's directive, apparently because he was not certain of full backing from FDR. Leahy later wrote in his memoirs that "the question could have been settled quickly by a strong Secretary of the Navy," but was regrettably allowed to become "a festering controversy."[37] When Knox died of heart failure on April 28, 1944, the matter was still unresolved.

KING'S ECCENTRICITY and administrative clumsiness created another bizarre episode, which became known as the Notorious Affair of the Gray Uniform. King liked the dark double-breasted blue uniform for officers,

but felt it was too severe and formal for many working conditions. At the
same time, he was irritated by the general wartime preference for khakis,
for these, in King's view, made army and navy officers virtually indistinguishable. He wanted a distinctive yet utilitarian work uniform for naval
officers, and this led him to design a single-breasted model in blue-gray
with black insignia and buttons.

Forrestal's procurement office was profoundly distressed, as was the War
Production Board, when it got wind of the scheme, for it would involve
millions of yards of newly woven cloth, a complicated dyeing process, the
design and manufacture of new insignia, and the allocation of several factories to carry out the manufacture of all these components. Plainly, it was
a highly dubious enterprise in a period when facilities and productive manpower were stretched thin. King's response to these objections was an
angry retort that outsiders were trying to disrupt his control of naval operations. What was remarkable was that he prevailed. He wore the first
blue-gray uniform to the Trident Conference in Washington in May 1943,
but it was an acknowledged disaster from the beginning. "Everyone loathed
it," according to Thomas Buell, King's biographer, and outside of Washington officers refused to wear it. Only in his own headquarters was he
able to enforce its use. In the Pacific, Nimitz virtually banned it. When
King retired, the gray uniform was retired with him.[38]

KING AND FORRESTAL

T HE TESTY RELATIONSHIP between the Navy Secretary and the principal naval commander continued after Forrestal succeeded Knox, in
large part because King's ingrained suspiciousness focused on Forrestal as
the chief plotter against him: "Forrestal believed, but never said to me,
that I had too much power myself . . . he hated like hell that I had both
jobs. But I was too strong for him to make any change."[39] King calculated,
shrewdly, that FDR would not in the last analysis countenance a change in
his 1942 directive, for that "would seem to the country that he had made
a mistake." His bitterness led him also to the belief that FDR shared his
own distrust of Forrestal's motives: "I think FDR knew what Forrestal
really was, and thought it was better for me to carry on with both jobs"
because Forrestal wanted "to manage the whole thing."[40] There was no
basis in fact for the notion that FDR distrusted Forrestal; on the contrary,
he held him in very high regard. King's twisted animosity concealed an
acknowledgment that Forrestal was a harder man to run over than
Knox.

Contrary to King's forebodings, when Forrestal succeeded Knox he decided to drop the struggle to separate King's functions, reasoning that the

civilian side of the navy already possessed de facto control of procurement, which made King's role in that function more titular than real. Moreover, he had no personal wish to denigrate King. Almost certainly he gave greater weight to the broader matter of the war effort, which at that moment was poised on the edge of great and fateful undertakings: In Europe the Normandy invasion (Operation Overlord) was only a month away, and in the Pacific the navy was preparing for a major showdown with the Japanese fleet in the planned army–navy–Marine Corps assault on Saipan, Tinian, and Guam in the Marianas Islands of the central Pacific. He was therefore con-

Forrestal and King share a light moment at a second-anniversary celebration for the WAVES, July 1944

cerned to avoid friction with King and to maximize civilian-military cooperation at a critical juncture of the war. As a result, not only did King retain his dual status for the duration, but the functions remained combined in the postwar navy.[41]

Forrestal thought King a brilliant strategist and a poor administrator, but always spoke of him with great respect and gave no hint, either publicly or privately, of any personal animus. King, on the other hand, nursed a set of grievances against Forrestal which appeared to be more personal and deeper-seated than the generic professional resentment he harbored against all civilian authority. Even the fact of being summoned to Forrestal's office agitated him inordinately; red-faced, he would pace up and down the outer office while the Secretary was finishing some long-distance phone call. One day, a nervous marine orderly slipped into Forrestal's office to murmur anxiously, "Sir, the Admiral is behaving something terrible out there."[42]

A large part of the friction between the two men stemmed from the interaction of their very different personalities and diametrically opposite approaches to problems, but Forrestal's temperament and mannerisms were more annoying to King than the other way around. Forrestal was more intellectual and less direct. Because he was both a careful administrator and a man interested in ideas for their own sake, he liked to experiment with various possibilities, to formulate several options or alternative solutions, turn them from one side to the other, and speculate on their pros and cons. One of his favorite ploys was to say, ''That sounds like a promising approach; what do you think of it?'' King's basic reaction to this was irritation, bordering on contained fury. He had already made up his own mind. What he wanted was a prompt decision leading to prompt action. Incisive, blunt to the point of rudeness, he accepted or rejected a proposition quickly, and moved on. He had no time to waste in idle talk or intellectual speculation. Another point of frustration for King was no doubt the fact that Forrestal was a more skilled bureaucratic operator than Knox, equally insistent but more effective in maintaining what he felt to be the proper balance of civilian-military authority and in asserting decisive civilian control in matters of major navy policy.

King may also have disdained Forrestal's innate social shyness, a trait that sometimes showed itself, especially during his early period in the Navy Department, in an almost embarrassing modesty and unease at social gatherings with senior naval officers. This was sometimes aggravated by a strained effort at camaraderie, accompanied by a self-conscious use of naval jargon—all of which seemed, and was, in sharp contrast to the stern, altogether formidable executive who sat behind the Navy Secretary's desk. Forrestal was indeed a curious mix of self-depreciation and self-advancement, of modesty and ambition. King's wary, skeptical soul chose to see only a devouring ambition. The Admiral's dour summing up a year after Forrestal's death was ''I didn't like him and he didn't like me.''[43]

RACE RELATIONS AND THE NAVY

B UT IF Forrestal and King were in disagreement on many issues, they were able to concur on the moral and practical need to broaden opportunities for blacks (then always and everywhere called Negroes) in the navy. In 1940, such opportunities were virtually nonexistent. The aristocratic culture of the navy officer corps accepted blacks as mess stewards to serve dinner in the wardroom and bring hot coffee to the bridge, but otherwise thought it necessary to exclude them from naval service. To protests from civil rights leaders, their answer was that segregation within the general crew being impractical in the confined living and eating spaces on shipboard, a policy of exclusion was the only practical solution; furthermore, experience had shown that even intelligent and able black petty officers were unable to maintain discipline among white subordinates, which created unacceptable risks to a ship's teamwork and morale, especially in wartime. Knox readily accepted this line of argument and warmly defended it: ''It is no kindness to Negroes to thrust them upon men of the White race.''[44]

But the navy position was an increasing embarrassment to the White House, especially after the 1941 promulgation of the Atlantic Charter embodying the Four Freedoms and after the nation was fully launched upon a war to destroy Fascist dictatorships and promote democracy. At the same time, the army was drafting large numbers of blacks for general duty, albeit in segregated units and under white officers. Aware of the depth and difficulty of the problem, FDR agreed that no swift or large-scale solution was at hand for the navy, but he pressed Knox to explore marginal opportunities, such as training blacks for service in musical bands, on small harbor craft, or at naval shore stations in the Caribbean. He recommended that the navy develop an initial plan to bring 5,000 blacks into such service categories. Knox, however, continued to resist, stiffened in his resolve by an officer corps that was dead set against any change in policy. A naval board formed to consider the President's proposals concluded that if restriction of blacks to the mess-stewards branch was discrimination, ''it was but part and parcel of a discrimination throughout the United States.'' The Commandant of the Marine Corps added that the desire of blacks to enter the naval service was largely an effort ''to break into a club that doesn't want them.''[45]

Further White House pressure finally brought forth, in April 1942, a navy program to accept 14,000 black enlistments in all general categories, but on a segregated basis. Elements of the black press called this ''progress toward a more enlightened point of view,'' but only 1,200 volunteers responded and 58 percent of these were rejected for physical or other deficiencies. Still further pressure, plus the use of black recruiters, raised the number of blacks in the navy to 30,000 by February 1943, but they were heavily concentrated at shore stations in repair depots and supply warehouses. In June 1943, several hundred blacks at an ammunition storage facility at St. Julien's Creek, Virginia, rioted against segregated seating at a musical show, and other, more serious racial disorders followed in the ensuing months. It was apparent that the navy's halfhearted concessions to wider opportunities for blacks was a failing policy.[46]

When Forrestal succeeded Knox in late April 1944, matters took a dramatic turn for the better. He had been for many years a member of the National Urban League, whose purpose was, and is, to broaden black opportunity, and he saw the problem of equal treatment essentially as one of efficiency and fair play. Indeed, he pressed this view on FDR within two weeks of becoming Secretary of the Navy. Recognizing, however, that little progress was possible without the active support of all senior naval officers, he sought Admiral King's cooperation. He was ''not satisfied with the situation here,'' he told King, and ''wanted to do something about it,'' but nothing was possible unless the senior officers were on board. ''I want your help. What do you say?'' Uncharacteristically, King, who had generally accepted the prevailing naval prejudice, did not answer immediately, but gazed reflectively out the window for several minutes. Then he said, "Mr. Secretary, we say we are a democracy and a democracy ought to have a democratic Navy. I don't think you can do it, but if you want to try, I'm behind you all the way."[47]

With King firmly committed to the effort, the rest of the navy brass "got the word" and there followed a predictably cautious, but steady, movement toward equality of treatment and opportunity for blacks. Forrestal started by assigning them to large auxiliary vessels—supply ships, tankers, and the largest landing craft—where they comprised up to 10 percent of the ship's complement. King insisted on equal treatment in matters of training, promotion, and duty assignments, but left the question of berthing to individual commanding officers; where the ratio of blacks to whites was small, the two groups were usually mingled in the same compartments. King insisted also on close attention to the selection of officers for ships with mixed crews—"certain officers will be temperamentally better suited for such commands than others"—and on a thorough indoctrination of the white sailors to minimize the danger of racial friction.[48] To the surprise of many, the experiment worked well and was gradually extended to small auxiliary vessels where integrated working, eating, and sleeping were unavoidable. This too worked with efficiency and only negligible racial friction. Also in 1944, 196 black enlisted men and 44 white officers and petty officers were assigned to a newly commissioned destroyer escort to test black seamanship. Similar assignments were made to a patrol craft, and both ships gradually replaced their white petty officers and some of their white officers with blacks. Among them was Ensign Samuel Gravely, who later became the navy's first black admiral.[49]

Forrestal continued to press for more black officers through direct commissioning from the ranks, by transfer to the college V-12 program, and by admission to the Naval Academy at Annapolis. While Knox was still Navy Secretary, King had authorized the promotion of twenty-two black officers from the ranks after a special segregated training program at the Great Lakes Training Center. By the end of the war sixty blacks had earned commissions, some as line officers but most as staff specialists in the medical, dental, engineer, and supply corps.[50]

Admission of black women to the WAVES (Women Accepted for Voluntary Emergency Service) was another matter pressed by the new Navy Secretary. Earlier in the war, the WAVE director, Captain Mildred McAfee (formerly president of Wellesley College), had urged this, but Bu-Pers opposed the move on the grounds that the WAVES had been created for the sole purpose of releasing male sailors for duty in the war zones. With sufficient black male sailors now on board, Bu-Pers saw no reason to recruit black women. This argument also had the support of Knox, who felt

Fleet Admiral King, Secretary Forrestal, Fleet Admiral Nimitz, 1945

the problem of integrating any women into the navy was difficult enough without the extra complicating factor of race. FDR was equally skittish, but when Thomas E. Dewey charged him with discriminating against black women during the 1944 presidential campaign, he quickly gave Forrestal the go-ahead. Bu-Pers made a final effort to quash the idea when it was discovered that only twenty-five black women volunteers could be found, far below the 250 considered the minimum number for an efficient segregated unit. In a meeting with Forrestal and Rear Admiral Randall Jacobs (the head of Bu-Pers), Captain McAfee, a determined liberal and feminist, argued that the twenty-five black volunteers, all college graduates, should be placed in an integrated training program with white WAVES. She felt, however, that a direct order from Forrestal was necessary to effect this. Forrestal agreed. Turning to the Admiral (who was a Southerner), he said, "Jacobs, you can take care of that, can't you?" The Admiral replied, "Oh yes, Mr. Secretary." The first two black WAVE officers were commissioned on December 21. By July 1945, seventy-two black WAVES had been graduated from the training center at Hunter College.[51]

THE KING-FORRESTAL SYNERGISM

OUT OF THE fractious, tense relationship between these two strong, quite different men, King and Forrestal, was fashioned the extraordinary naval victory in World War II. King was the brilliant naval strategist who won the battle of the Atlantic against the German U-boats and engineered the defeat of the Japanese fleet. Forrestal was the brilliant, tireless administrator without whose masterly contribution the navy mobilization program could not have been completed. From 1940 to June 1945 the fleet inventory grew from 1,099 vessels to 50,759 vessels; its ranks of officers and sailors increased from 160,997 to 3,383,196. There were 8 new battleships, 92 new aircraft carriers, 35 new cruisers, 148 new destroyers, 365 new destroyer escorts, 140 new submarines, and 43,255 new landing craft. Their design, construction, and delivery to the fighting forces was Forrestal's responsibility, although he was assisted, of course, by a great many dedicated and outstanding men, both civilians and uniformed professionals. But it was Forrestal primarily who analyzed, organized, rationalized, energized, and accelerated the whole vast, intricate process, and the procurement of that modern, powerful fleet was a precondition of victory. As Eric Larrabee has written, "The presence of King insured that this would be a fighting fleet, but the presence of Forrestal insured that it would be there in the first place for King to command."[52]

Forrestal's service as Under Secretary, from August 1940 to May 1944, his longest in one office, was a time of extraordinary accomplishment, and his role in building the World War II navy was the most tangible and unambiguous achievement of his public career. It was also a time of preparation for larger things to come. As Under Secretary, he met every challenge presented to him with professional competence, but more than that—with a kind of combative joy born of the heroic scale and complexity of the task, an innate patriotism intensified by the war, and a keen awareness of his own growth. It was a glowing time for him and also the time of his development as a public man. In this phase of his government experience he acquired the insights that would mature in the next, into what could be called his broad sense of what a democratic government requires—in terms of both commitment and means—to develop intelligent national policies and to carry them out with competence and consistency.[53]

CHAPTER 15

★ ★ ★

Secretary of the Navy

FOLLOWING THE unexpected death of the Navy Secretary on April 28, 1944, the *New York Times* headlined its story "Forrestal Looms to Succeed Knox," and everyone in Washington appeared to agree with Congressman Carl Vinson's influential view that Forrestal was "the logical man."[1] Although confirmation of the appointment was a matter for the Senate, Vinson's House Naval Affairs Committee passed a formal resolution: "No one has a more thorough knowledge of the Navy and no one is more eminently qualified to lead it through the remainder of this greatest of all wars to final victory."[2] *Time* described him as "a noted example of an able businessman turned public servant." Arthur Krock wrote of "his distinguished record" and the "high respect" in which he was held throughout the government. *Business Week* put him on its May 6 cover and waxed effusive: "Subordinates often describe him as 'a tough little cookie.' They mean it as a compliment and, while putting the accent on toughness, they don't underestimate the urbanity and persuasiveness in which it is packaged."[3]

Faced once again with exciting change, Forrestal suffered a characteristic bout of ambivalence. Eberstadt wrote to Paul Shields on April 28: "Just learned of Frank Knox's death, within a few minutes of which I got a call from Tom Corcoran. He is in the business of making a new Secretary of the Navy, and wants our friend to quit saying he does not want the job."[4] And a few days after his appointment, Forrestal said in a letter to a personal friend, Edward Bermingham, "I honestly would have been delighted to let somebody else carry this, although I had a hard time persuading my friends that was the case. I suppose the things you don't seek too hard are the things you get."[5]

There was little doubt, however, that FDR would elevate him, nor much that he would accept the appointment to a high place in the Cabinet in the middle of a great and consequential war. There was fleeting speculation that the President would make a further gesture to bipartisanship by choosing Wendell Willkie, his Republican opponent in 1940, or Lieutenant Commander Harold Stassen, the youngish former governor of Minnesota who was serving on Admiral William Halsey's staff in the Pacific. But Forrestal's credentials were much too impressive to overlook, and FDR wisely decided to carry on with the team that was winning the war. The appointment came on May 9 and was widely applauded. Said *Time,* "Not since 1941, when he elevated Harlan Fiske Stone to Chief Justice of the Supreme Court, has there been such unanimous approval of a presidential appointment. The press, the public, and the navy cheered."[6] That same afternoon, Kate Foley answered her telephone. It was Leslie Biffle, Secretary of the Senate, with news that FDR's message nominating Forrestal had arrived on Capitol Hill. He wanted to inform her that unanimous confirmation was a foregone conclusion. "Kate, tell him he's in." She stepped into Forrestal's large adjacent office: "You're the Secretary of the Navy." For several minutes he sat and grinned at her like a small boy, very pleased with himself. It was the only time, she said later, that anything broke through the mask that habitually hid his emotions.[7]

Appointment to the Cabinet marked the psychological end of his apprenticeship in government, reinforced his strong sense of patriotism, and consolidated his commitment to the cause of the United States Navy. After nearly four years of fighting with and for the admirals, exerting his utmost energies and abilities to give them the ships and guns and planes they needed to destroy the Japanese fleet—to transform the navy from the faded relic he found in 1940 to the mightiest naval armada in history—he discovered that he had absorbed a large part of its tradition and its mystique, its pride and its concerns for the future. The self-styled loner had become a brother-in-arms, a fully indoctrinated member of the tribe. "He looks Navy and is Navy," one journalist remarked. And another thought him "like the Navy, tough and elegant together . . . There is a quiet, animal quality about his apparent physical perfection . . . swift and easy, with the suggestion of possible violence and the surface of perfectly contained restraint."[8]

It was the beginning of his coming to full realization and assertion of his powers of leadership, the time when he began his "diaries" and the application of a restless intelligence to the larger issues of the war, the postwar settlement, and the question of how the U.S. government must be reshaped to meet its heavy new international burdens. He continued to monitor the momentum of the vast procurement process he had designed and driven, but now left more of its operation to others, notably Hensel, who was appointed Assistant Secretary, while he took up the role of principal spokesman for the fighting navy.

His immediate goal was to maximize public support for the navy's achievements in battle, but this was in marked contrast to an innate reticence about personal publicity. On May 11, 1944, he wrote to Henry Luce, the publisher of *Time* and *Life*: "To the extent that you can, I would appreciate it greatly if you would minimize the extent of my publicity, especially pictorial publicity. My reason is simple, even though it may sound a little specious: I think the degree to which anyone can work effectively here is almost in inverse ratio to the amount of time consumed in public appearances, speaking or social commotion . . . The best

On the cover of Time, *October 29, 1945*

publicity is success in battle—my motto unless for some reason I get fatheaded."[9] Luce replied a few days later, agreeing to Forrestal's request. He added, "Very likely the world would be better off with less journalism, but it is somewhat late in the day for me to come to that conclusion." This agreement notwithstanding, Forrestal was featured on the cover of *Time* seventeen months later.[10]

After returning from the landings in southern France in the late summer of 1944, he wrote in similar vein to Vinson: "The news out of the Mediterranean area, so far as the Navy is concerned, has been rather slight, but I think there will now be some improvement. My mission, I think, was fairly successful on this score, with the qualification that I got a little too much publicity myself . . ."[11] To Quentin Reynolds, who interviewed him at the same time for a story in *Collier's,* he said, "Look, you can't make a hero out of a man in a blue serge suit. So don't try. I'm a businessman trying to do a job down here and that's the whole story."[12] It was not the whole story, of course, even in 1944, and it became even less so with the passage of time and Forrestal's growing role in high policy. Jonathan Daniels, writing eighteen months later, was closer to the mark when he said, "From a background of business he had emerged, I felt, as a politician, but not as a politician merely. He talked as if he were a student of administration and bureaucracy."[13]

If he shied away from personal publicity, however, Forrestal was unshy and feisty about asserting his new Cabinet-level responsibilities and prerogatives. The first order of business was to arrive at a clear understanding with Admiral King on the question of ultimate civilian authority. He established a twice-weekly staff meeting with the ranking civilians and admirals at navy headquarters, but King conspicuously failed to show up for the first two meetings, claiming more pressing business. The following week, as the next meeting got under way, there was still no sign of the COMINCH, so Forrestal picked up the phone and called King. "Admiral," he said, in the presence of the entire navy hierarchy, "I thought you might be interested in attending my staff meeting this morning, as I am about to issue operational orders to the fleet." An irate but outmaneuvered King was there in five minutes, and thereafter attended the Secretary's staff meetings unless he was out of town.[14]

King remained unyielding, however, on the issue of informing the Secretary on the military deliberations in the Joint Chiefs of Staff, jealously preserving his strategic views and recommendations for FDR alone. Things were very different in the War Department, where Marshall kept Stimson fully informed and Assistant Secretary John J. McCloy had a standing invitation to sit with the JCS as Stimson's observer. Forrestal chose not to press the issue with King, but kept abreast of the military situation by lunching frequently with McCloy.

Testing his new influence at the White House, in July 1944 he submitted the names of Walter Dunnington, John Cahill, and John Kenney as candidates for the Assistant Secretaryship left vacant when Ralph Bard succeeded him as Under Secretary. When FDR, acting through one of his assistants, suggested John L. Sullivan for the post, Forrestal replied that he didn't have time to break in a new man; to underline his resistance he said to the White House intermediary: "There is one way to have power in Washington and that is always to be ready to leave at any time. I am ready to leave at any time."[15] After further discussion, he agreed to make Sullivan a Special Assistant, but this inadequate concession brought a personal intervention from FDR, who told him it would be "quite a comedown" for Sullivan, a prominent New Hampshire Democrat already serving as Assistant Secretary of the Treasury, to accept any lesser position in the Navy Department.[16] In the end, Forrestal bowed to the inevitable, but urged FDR, with jesuitical guile, to defer the appointment until after the November election so that his own three candidates would "keep working hard" in the belief that they still had a chance for promotion.[17]

Also on the political front, Forrestal worked to promote his good friend William O. Douglas for the Democratic vice-presidential nomination in 1944. When this effort failed, he told a reluctant Senator Harry S. Truman it was "his duty" to accept, "in view of the fact that the alternative would

In the presidential campaign, 1944.
Left to right: *Roosevelt, Stimson, Forrestal, and New York Governor
Herbert Lehman*

be Henry Wallace.''[18] Although he had been a self-described ''fractional Democrat'' in 1940, Forrestal now seemed a committed member of the party's moderate-to-conservative wing. Later that year he entered in his diary a bemused account of a day spent campaigning with FDR, the last day of the President's quest for a fourth term. Forrestal's comments reflected the fact that some prominent Democratic officeholders were less than enthusiastic in their support for FDR, and suggested that Forrestal was both attracted to the political process and slightly repelled by its more sordid realities:

November 4, 1944

I flew up to Boston today to join the President's train before the final speech of the campaign at Fenway Park . . . the railroad yard was full of political characters from Boston, policemen, Secret Service agents, photographers and reporters. All the political characters were in soft gray hats and turned-up overcoat collars . . . enveloped in conversation and cigar smoke, and there was a general confidential atmosphere about all hands. The scene carried me back to the torchlight parades and political meetings in the village of Matteawan.

Most of the conversation was centered around whether or not Bob Hannegan, the Democratic National Chairman, and Majority Leader of the House John McCormack were going to be able to persuade that leader of the Massachusetts Celts, the Honorable David I. Walsh, to introduce the President from the platform in Fenway Park. The Senator said he would go as far as Framingham but no farther—in other words, that he would smoke his cigar but wouldn't go upstairs. The intransigence was dealt with by the simple device of not stopping the train at Framingham. Even so, the Senator sat tight and did not appear on the platform that evening.[19]

FDR defeated Thomas E. Dewey to win an unprecedented fourth term in the White House, but his margin of popular support was the smallest since Woodrow Wilson's election in 1916. The South carried him in. It was evident to many voters that his physical powers were almost gone.

THE PUBLIC RELATIONS WAR

ONE OF Secretary Forrestal's high priorities was to publicize the navy's contributions to the war, and this led to his first active, systematic effort at public relations. At his first press conference on May 17, 1944, he declared that American naval forces could now "operate at will" within 1,500 miles of Japan and that this fact reduced the Japanese "outer defense bastions" to no more than "a nominal perimeter."[20] On May 24, he announced that navy aircraft had flown "2,005 sorties" against Japanese positions in the north, central, and south Pacific areas in the previous week.[21] A week later he introduced Admiral Edward Cochran, Chief of the Bureau of Ships, and Charles E. ("Electric Charlie") Wilson, Vice Chairman of the War Production Board, and praised them for the "astounding" achievement of exceeding production goals for new landing craft by 70 percent.[22] On July 5 he asserted that successful completion of the army-Marine assault on Saipan, begun a few days before, could "be expected with confidence" because Japanese morale "seems to be disintegrating." But looking ahead, he predicted that future battles along the island chain leading to Japan would become ever more "bitter and costly" as the enemy realized he was "cornered."[23]

His policy, he announced at that first press conference, would be "to tell what the Navy was doing and let the facts speak for themselves without embroidery." Underlining his adherence to Knox's practice of bringing in commanders from the fighting fronts to make firsthand reports to the press, he then introduced Major General William A. Rupertus, who had just led the First Marine Division in the successful amphibious invasion of Cape

Gloucester (on New Britain Island). Rupertus told the assembled reporters that his "smashing assault" had killed 4,000 Japanese and routed the famed 141st Japanese Infantry Brigade at a cost of 300 Americans dead and 1,022 wounded.[24]

Far more than Knox, however, Forrestal saw the need to organize a comprehensive public relations effort to bring home to the American people the magnitude, complexity, and significance of naval battles, amphibious landings, victories, setbacks, acts of heroism, and other milestones along the hard road to victory against a fanatical Japanese foe. Especially after the D-Day landings in Normandy, when public attention was riveted on the European Theater, he sensed that Eisenhower's advance across the familiar continental landmass was more readily understandable to the American public than were the brief, vicious Marine encounters on flyspeck islands—bearing strange names like Tarawa, Kwajalein, Eniwetok, Saipan—or confused air-sea battles that ranged over hundreds of square miles in the vast empty reaches of the Pacific Ocean. He noted that the army and the army air forces (which was already calling itself simply the Air Force) were skillfully publicizing their own daring exploits, and he understood—more quickly and more astutely than Admiral King and other senior naval officers—that public relations was an ineluctable, and vital, weapon in the already emerging rivalry among the military services for postwar dominance of organization, strategy, political influence, and money. In this struggle he was emotionally and intellectually a navy partisan, but far from satisfied with the navy's performance.

Shortly after taking over, Forrestal told King he wanted Captain William Smedberg, the principal Op-Nav intelligence officer, to brief the press "at least once a week and before every impending operation" to be sure they had "the necessary background to understand what the Navy was doing or planning to do."[25] King objected in general terms, but vehemently resisted the idea of having Smedberg carry out the briefings, for the captain was privy to all of the operational information deriving from the breaking of the Japanese code; an inadvertent slip of his tongue could give away the game. Smedberg recalled being summoned to Forrestal's office, where the angry Fleet Admiral confronted the Secretary of the Navy.

"Smedberg," King barked, "Mr. Forrestal wants you to brief the press and radio media at least once a week on our operations."

"Admiral," Smedberg replied, "I'm the last person in this headquarters who should do that." King nodded grimly and said, "That's exactly what I told the Secretary."

But Forrestal was adamant. As the younger officer remembered it, he said, "Admiral King, I've told you I want Captain Smedberg to brief the press. The Japs haven't been able to sink our fleet, but if you had your way it would get sunk—it would disappear because you refused to allow anything to be written about what the Navy is doing. The Air Force is telling the American people what they're doing, but no one is adequately telling the story of Navy achievements in this war. We are going to start telling that story, now." King once more demurred, saying, "What the Navy does will speak for itself, Mr. Secretary. We don't have to blow our own horn." But Forrestal disagreed, and Smedberg was soon providing a wide range of background and operational information to an eager press corps on a weekly basis, despite a stern private warning from King: "God help you if you ever tell them a damned thing about what we're going to do."[26]

Forrestal was certain that the navy did have to blow its own horn, but it was his style to work over and around recognized resistance within the service and to avoid confrontation and the issuance of direct orders wherever possible. In this enterprise he was incurably secretive and not above Machiavellian maneuver. A classic example was his action to energize navy public relations in the Pacific Theater, which he considered to be seriously lagging. The cause, as Forrestal perceived it, was Nimitz's indifference, reflected in his retention of a timid public information officer, Commander Waldo Drake, who consistently yielded to senior officers of Admiral King's persuasion on the question of security versus publicity. On a trip to London shortly after the D-Day landings in Normandy, Forrestal was escorted by Captain Harold "Min" Miller, whose handling of the British journalists impressed him. Back in Washington, he issued a direct order reassigning Miller to Nimitz's headquarters at CINC-PAC.* Passing through Washington en route to Hawaii in early August, Miller asked Rear Admiral Arthur Radford for an explanation, but Radford told him with a knowing smile that he would "have to see the Secretary." Forrestal came right to the point: "The American people have the impression that MacArthur is winning the Pacific War. So does the Congress. It isn't true, of course, but the public relations people at CINC-PAC don't seem to know how to make a strong case for the Navy. I want you to go out there and show Nimitz how the job should be done." Sensing a delicate situation, Miller suggested that Forrestal should first issue an order reassigning Commander Drake, but the Secretary demurred: "Nimitz likes and trusts him. I want you to ease him out. If you put that P.R. operation on a proper basis, I'll give you command of a big carrier." Delighted, Miller said, "Aye, aye, Sir."[27]

Miller duly reported to Nimitz and began working with Drake. At a Nimitz press conference shortly thereafter, several of the assembled correspondents openly expressed their wish that Miller take over Drake's job. Miller, who was present and unsuspecting, was embarrassed by the incident, which made clear to him the presence of Forrestal's hidden hand. Ten

*Commander in Chief, Pacific.

days later, Drake received orders to report to Elmer Davis's Office of War Information in Washington. Nimitz took the intrusion calmly and assured Miller that no blame would attach to him, but he was annoyed with the Navy Secretary, saying privately that "the publicity side of the war is getting so large, it almost overshadows the fighting side." A few months later, when Forrestal proposed that CINC-PAC publish its own daily newspaper, Nimitz dug in his heels and refused to comply. Forrestal finally gave up, but drew the conclusion that, with the possible exception of King, Nimitz was the stubbornest admiral in the navy.[28] When King retired at the end of the war, Forrestal opposed Nimitz as his successor, but President Truman nevertheless made the appointment.[29]

Succeeding Drake, Miller went on to organize a much wider, more vivid press coverage of naval operations at Saipan, Tinian, Guam, Iwo Jima, and Okinawa. He brought in fourteen airborne cameras to film the decisive air battle called the Marianas Turkey Shoot and lured notable magazine writers and photographers, like Quentin Reynolds of *Collier's* and Shelley Mydans of *Time-Life,* from the European Theater. Forrestal and Nimitz were highly pleased with the results, but in the end Forrestal reneged on his promise to give Miller command of a carrier or of any ship. "Min, I can find any number of captains fit to command a carrier, but in the whole Navy there is no one who can run CINC-PAC public relations as well as you do. Go back to the Pacific and finish the job. Then we'll talk about a new assignment." A deeply disappointed Miller realized the war would end "without my firing a pistol." In the late spring of 1945, he was recalled to Washington to become head of Navy Public Relations, but his career had topped out, and he retired a few months after V-J Day.[30]

In an effort to cast a wider net for navy support, Forrestal developed plans to send newspaper and magazine publishers (not merely reporters) and distinguished novelists and other writers to the Pacific battlefronts. Publishers made editorial policy, and editorial policy shaped public opinion. Novelists could convey the poignant human drama of quiet courage and selfless acceptance of harsh circumstance that never came through in the terse official communiqués. In the autumn of 1944, he arranged for the publisher of the *New York Times* to make an extended trip, but first had to overcome objections from FDR. In a memorandum to the President of September 27, he argued that the trip would "pay dividends" in press coverage and public understanding "because I am confident no one can have any idea of the size and scope of operations in that ocean until he has been there."[31] FDR gave his approval, but on the quixotic condition that Arthur Hays Sulzberger go as a representative of the Red Cross to inspect Red Cross operations in the area; presumably he was concerned about being criticized for giving preference to the *New York Times.*

Sensitive to the drama that was being acted out every day in deeds of sacrifice and heroism, devotion and endurance, physical pain and violent death, Forrestal was equally anxious to persuade writers of reputation to cover the war in whatever ways best suited their talents, but this endeavor bore meager fruit. Typical was the case of his friend John O'Hara. Forrestal tried to get him a navy commission—and Lovett tried to get him one in the army air forces—but O'Hara's ulcers and bad teeth could not pass the physical examination. Forrestal then suggested the "cloak and dagger" operations at Bill Donovan's OSS, but O'Hara showed little interest beyond an offer to donate his Duesenberg as a VIP vehicle.[32] Late in 1943 and suffering a sense of "guilt and futility" about his civilian status, O'Hara did join the OSS and was sent to a training camp in Quantico, Virginia, where he grew a beard and took the code name "Doc." But he resigned a month later, explaining he wasn't strong enough physically to take responsibility for other men's lives. He was thirty-eight years old.[33]

Forrestal expressed his regret about O'Hara in a letter to another friend and journalist, John McLain, saying, "It would have been good for him to have some sense of participation in the war . . . He certainly should be as good as a [John] Hersey or a [Robert] Sherwood. If I had my way, I would have a man of his writing ability on every task force in the Pacific." In the same letter, he described the kind of story he hoped would get written: "In the battle of the Coral Sea one of our pilots got lost and asked permission to land on a carrier other than his own. That carrier at the moment was making knots, just preparing to send her planes aloft. The Japs were close. The Captain, regretfully, had to deny permission. All he could do was give the course to the nearest landing and the distance, which was something on the order of 350 miles, well beyond the capability of the plane. The Captain finished his message with 'I am sorry and the best of luck to you.' The answer from the wandering pilot, who undoubtedly knew his number was up, was 'Thank you, and good luck to you.' "[34]

TOURING THE BATTLEFRONTS

FORRESTAL TOURED the far-flung battlefronts, becoming a familiar figure in khaki trousers and open-necked shirt without insignia and looking ten years younger than fifty-two; on at least one occasion he was mistaken for a junior officer and bawled out for getting in the way. On another day, in Pearl Harbor, he sat down at a typewriter in a small empty office and began pecking out notes for a short speech, his back to the door. A young ensign entered and a colloquy followed.

"If you're the jerk they sent to service the typewriter, you're working on the wrong one."

"Sorry. I'm not the repairman."

The Navy Under Secretary inspecting the seizure of Roi, Namur, and Kwajalein with Major General Harry Schmidt, USMC, and Vice Admiral Raymond A. Spruance, February 1944

"Then who the hell are you?"

"Forrestal."

The ensign nearly fainted against the wall, and was persuaded only with great difficulty that he was not about to be court-martialed.[35]

In early 1944, Forrestal was present offshore at the seizure of Roi, Namur, and Kwajalein, three treacherous, heavily defended coral atolls in the Marshall Islands. In July, he emerged from a conference with Dwight D. Eisenhower at the general's headquarters "somewhere in France" to say he was "tremendously impressed with the spirit of cooperation which the Supreme Commander has fostered among the British, the Americans and their Allies" and went on to draw a parallel with Admiral Nimitz's cooperation with General MacArthur in the Pacific: "These men just don't think destructively—except in terms of Germans and Japs."[36] He went on to Italy to witness Fifth Army troops fighting under the command of Lieutenant General Mark Clark and thence to Naples to board Admiral H. Kent Hewitt's flagship for the Allied landings in southern France on August 15.[37]

The landing force for Operation Anvil comprised a mix of three American and French divisions, plus a British airborne unit, and the supporting

Eisenhower and Forrestal "somewhere in France,"
six weeks after the Normandy landing, July 1944

naval force consisted of six battleships and ten destroyers, including most
of the Free French Navy. Paratroopers were dropped into the hills behind
the French Riviera, and amphibious troops stormed ashore, but there was
only light resistance, for the German army was already moving northward
to assist in efforts to contain the main Allied thrust, which had carried
beyond Paris and was approaching the German border. On the beach in
front of a famed resort hotel, a waiter met the troops with a tray of glasses
filled with champagne, and the press immediately dubbed the whole operation "The Champagne Campaign." Forrestal went ashore at Fréjus on
the afternoon of D-Day to observe the situation and talk with several
wounded soldiers at a temporary field hospital. He returned the next day
for an emotional reception in honor of the French commander, Admiral
Lemonnier, in the public square of St. Raphael, which culminated in the
mass singing of the "Marseillaise."[38] He also found time to ascertain
whether the small villa near Cannes owned by his friend Philip Barry had
been damaged by naval gunfire. Returning to the flagship, he cabled Barry:
"Villa Lorenzo intact."[39]

Forrestal's most dramatic and visible visit to a battlefront—his trip to the far northwestern Pacific in February 1945 to witness the Marine assault on Iwo Jima—developed out of a mix of motives. He was, first of all, caught up in the swiftly gathering momentum of the war against Japan, which seemed now to approach a climax as powerful American forces pressed against the empire's inner citadel. He was worried about the operation, for Iwo Jima was a formidable fortress—an island formed entirely of black volcanic ash, six miles long, shaped like a pork chop, and heavily fortified by hidden concrete bunkers and a labyrinth of underground trenches and tunnels; its terrain offered no cover or maneuvering room for the attackers, and its 20,000 defenders were expected to fight to the last man. Advance estimates of Marine casualties were 40 to 50 percent.

Iwo had been identified as a necessary target of the American advance because its capture would provide airfields for ''short-legged'' fighter planes needed to escort the B-29 bombers over the Japanese home islands, seven hundred miles away. The bombers were already raiding Tokyo and other major cities from bases in Guam and Saipan, but were suffering substantial losses because they lacked fighter escort. To increase the effectiveness of the bomber attacks and thus shorten the war was the rationale and justification for the terrible cost inherent in the plan to capture this island fortress. Forrestal understood that the appearance of the Navy Secretary on this particular battle line would be a boost to morale, but beyond that he wanted to see at firsthand the problems and dangers facing what had now become ''his'' navy and Marine Corps,* to observe the performance of equipment he had been instrumental in procuring, to get a smell and a feel for the continuum that links high strategy to the low bloody business of carrying it out in ''the roaring flux of forces that are aroused by war.''[40] In the process, as war correspondent Robert Sherrod wrote, he ''exposed himself to the dangers of warfare as no other United States official of his rank did in World War II.''[41]

Never far from his mind was the cause for which he had made himself—or the fact of his promotion had made him—principal spokesman: to tell the story of the navy's war to the American people. But the experience at Iwo Jima proved to be more profound and personally sobering than he had anticipated—it forced him to confront the terrible carnage of modern war and in so doing it permanently changed his thinking about war and peace.

Three days before the February 19 assault, the armada of amphibious forces was assembled at Saipan under command of Admiral Kelly Turner, the master of amphibious operations. At a morning press conference aboard Turner's flagship *Eldorado,* Forrestal told the seventy-odd reporters, ''You news correspondents have a responsibility somewhat like my own—to the public. The tremendous scale and scope of this war can best be conveyed

---

*The Marine Corps was and is an integral part of the navy.

to the people by the press . . . Back home there is a tendency to count the victory as already won, but in fact we are fighting a fanatical enemy who can be beaten only by death . . . This next target, Iwo Jima, like Tarawa, leaves little choice except to take it [in frontal assault] . . . by character and courage.'' He then summarized his own view of the broader strategic requirements for American security: ''First . . . seapower is vital to our country; seapower enables us to land on the enemy shore instead of his landing on ours; second, airpower alone would not win a war; third, no one in his right mind would undertake the mission of winning without airpower; fourth, the guy with the rifle and machine gun is the man who wins the war in the last analysis—and pays the penalty to preserve our liberty.'' He added a typical grace note of personal modesty: ''It has been said here this morning that you are honored to have me present. Quite the reverse is true. It is a high privilege for me to see in action the quality of leadership America has produced.''[42]

The overall commander of the landing forces, Lieutenant General Holland (''Howling Mad'') Smith, a gruff old man, was choked up when he briefed the reporters on the details: ''The stage is set. Everything has been done that can be done . . . The Japs have no barracks above ground on Iwo. We have got to dig them out. There is no maneuver ground. This is a frontal attack . . . We may have to take high casualties on the beaches— maybe 40 percent of the assault troops. We have taken such losses before, and if we have to we can do it again . . . We have never failed and I don't believe we shall fail here. It's a tough proposition. That's the reason we're here.''[43]

General Smith's grim assessment of the task ahead underestimated the actual difficulties and human costs of the Iwo operation. Even after an intense, systematic bombardment of all known Japanese targets for three days by massive naval gunfire, including the sixteen-inch guns of eight battleships, the Japanese garrison conducted a defense of unprecedented skill and tenacity. They made no attempt to defend the beaches or to expend their troops in classic, screaming banzai counterattacks, but hoarded their forces and made the marines pay heavily for every yard of advance. During the first critical days they were aided by the weather—strong winds and heavy rain created a choppy, sharp-breaking surf on the steep beaches, causing numerous landing craft to swamp or broach and soon turning the landing areas into a confused and tangled snarl of wrecked equipment. The congestion severely impeded vital resupply and the evacuation of wounded; American tanks bogged down in the soft volcanic ash, as murderous Japanese artillery fire poured down on the marines from higher ground. On D-Day+2 there were rumors that the assault force would have to be withdrawn, but the weather improved and the marines lived up to their reputation for tenacity. The original estimate to ''secure'' the island had been seven days. At the end of thirty-five days, Japanese defenders were still holding out at the island's northern tip and eight Marine regiments (two-and-two-thirds divisions) had suffered total casualties of 23,000, of which 5,931 were killed in action. There were an additional 2,548 casualties among army and navy personnel in the "beach control" units, including doctors and medical corpsmen. Of the original Japanese force of 22,000, 95 percent (or 20,917) died in the fighting, 216 were captured, and 867 emerged from caves several months after the fighting ceased and surrendered to the army garrison troops that had replaced the marines.[44]

After nearly getting his leg crushed between a small boat and Admiral Raymond Spruance's flagship, while transferring from the one to the other in the enormous ocean swells on D-Day + 2, Forrestal went ashore on Red Beach two days later guided by General Smith and accompanied by Admiral Earle W. Mills, Admiral Louis Denfeld, and Colonel Cornelius Vanderbilt Whitney of the air corps. Admiral Turner and General Smith had tried to dissuade him, arguing that a "hot" beach under artillery fire was no place for the Secretary of the Navy. "I don't think it's wise," Turner had said. But Forrestal, looking through his field glasses, had replied laconically, "Aren't those men I see on the beach?" The fighting had now been pushed a mile or so inland and, though the beach had been shelled that morning, Smith reluctantly accepted the risk that there would be a sufficient lull before the next bombardment to give the Secretary a look. As the party dashed from the landing craft into the nearest trench, they saw marines of the 28th Regiment, off to their left, raise the American flag atop Mount Suribachi, the sullen, forbidding mountain of volcanic ash that anchors the southern tip of Iwo.[45]

Spontaneous cheers and the cry "There goes the flag!" went up from American foxholes all across the island. According to Nimitz's biographer, Forrestal turned to Smith and said, "Holland, raising that flag means a Marine Corps for the next five hundred years,"[46] but the story may well be apocryphal. Forrestal's party moved a few yards inland to a blasted pillbox whose defenders had only recently been killed. A short distance away a stack of "some one hundred Jap bodies scented the morning air."[47] After thirty minutes, Smith, who was "getting extremely nervous" about Forrestal's safety, ordered a prompt departure. Later that day, standing on the deck of Turner's flagship, his face reddened by the chill wind and pelting rain, Forrestal removed his steel helmet and told reporters of his "tremendous admiration and reverence for the guy who walks up the beaches and takes enemy positions with a rifle and grenades or his bare hands."[48]

In a radio broadcast from Guam the next day he made probably the most emotional speech of his career: "Up the precipitous side of a 600-foot extinct volcano, so precipitous that it seemed almost vertical, went a platoon of American Marines. Even through a glass they seemed tiny figures scrambling skyward against a background of blue. And then a few minutes later, from the thousands of throats, upon ships, on land and on the sea came the sudden cry, 'There goes the flag' . . . We will be digging dead Japs, and even some live ones, out of Iwo for weeks to come . . . [but] in spite of all the skill of the Japanese defense, the Marines went ashore, and they have exacted a 4-to-1 toll. America is on the march in the Pacific—a march back to civilization, order and decency. . . . The way back is now being cleared by fighting men from every state of our union . . . You can be confident of them and you can be confident of their lead-

On the beach at Iwo Jima,
D-Day plus 4, February 1945

ers.''[49] Arthur Krock's column the next day called it a speech which ''thrilled the capital.''[50]

WE CANNOT GO FROM IWO TO IWO

DEPARTING GUAM on February 26, Forrestal flew to the Philippines for a conference with General Douglas MacArthur, who was engaged in the battle for Luzon. At luncheon with several ranking staff officers, he and the magisterial MacArthur discussed the course of the war. They agreed that the absence of the Japanese navy and air force at Iwo Jima reflected both heavy losses and an acute shortage of fuel. In fact, the Japanese air force was by now decimated and the navy largely sunk or immobilized. A combination of B-29 and submarine attacks was destroying factories and repair facilities and sinking the merchant ships that carried vital imports like diesel fuel and aviation gasoline. Nevertheless, MacArthur felt it was essential to secure a Russian commitment to enter the war—with at least sixty divisions—to prevent the very large Japanese army in Manchuria (estimated at 2 million men) from joining the final battle for the home islands. If the Russians entered in strength, he predicted the Pacific War would end in 1945, despite the daunting prospects for a direct American invasion of

Japan. The general's view rested heavily on his belief that "Orientals," when faced with a fundamental frustration of their strategy, "could be expected to dissolve in panic."[51]

Forrestal was impressed but not convinced by this assessment. At this time, neither Forrestal nor MacArthur knew anything about the development of the atomic bomb. After the war ended, MacArthur sought to deny he had ever argued the need for prompt and large-scale Russian forces to help bring the Pacific War to a successful close.[52] On his return to Washington a week or so later, Forrestal found a breezy note from FDR, who was himself just returned from the far more fateful Big Three Conference at Yalta. Its jaunty tone is astonishing given the circumstances and the known fact of the President's exhaustion: "Dear Jim: Just back—and I am greatly interested that you are now a member of the Amphibious Forces, and I am going to suggest that you wear Navy clothes above the waist and Marine Corps clothes below the waist. As soon as you get back let me know and do run in to see me and tell me all about it. As ever yours, F.D.R."[53]

Forrestal's reaction to the bloody trial at Iwo Jima was anything but jaunty. In the view of several close observers, the experience of seeing young Americans die by the hundreds, despite the most painstaking material preparations to hold down human losses, developed a hard new core in Forrestal's soul. To the extent he had previously reflected on it, war had seemed "man's corruption and disgrace," but the shock of Iwo Jima "turned his dislike of war into hatred of war,"[54] and the experience left physical marks on him—a new brassy petulance, deeper furrows in his brow, a grimmer and grittier look to his face. Several senior naval officers said later that no photographs taken of him from then until the end of his life ever showed him "truly smiling." Iwo Jima drove him to an intellectual search for a worktable philosophy of power that would sustain world peace after the victory had been won. "We cannot go from Iwo to Iwo," he told Rear Admiral Ellis Zacharias. "We must find a formula to sustain peace without this endless, frightful bloodshed."[55] His basic conclusion was that "those who hate war must maintain the power to prevent it," but he recognized the great political difficulties of realizing that condition. He was determined to come to grips intellectually with what he now perceived as the supreme postwar challenge for the United States: how to accept the need to hold great power and to use it commensurate with the nation's large and unavoidable new responsibilities in a shattered world; yet to use it without breaking faith with the American heritage of democratic freedom.[56] In the broadest sense, this became the quest that dominated, and obsessed, the remaining years of his life.

Deeply moved by the courage of the young men who were fighting and dying for the cause, Forrestal was shocked and outraged by a request that came at this time from his brother Henry. It was an unabashed plea that the Navy Secretary find a safe noncombatant billet for a nephew who was about to be drafted into the army. So great was Forrestal's anger that he broke off all further relations with his brother and brooded long afterward in disbelief on the question of how his own flesh and blood could have stooped to so shameful a proposal.[57]

For a brief moment in early 1945, his reflections on the American dilemma of power seemed to include a new awareness of his own potential for political leadership—at the highest level. On his return to Washington, he entered into his diary these cryptic and unexplained ''Specifications for a Presidential Candidate: (1) Looks, (2) Height, (3) Legal or political background, (4) Desire for the job, (5) Political experience.''[58]

* * *

CHAPTER 16

Ending the War

IN THE EARLY SPRING of 1945, the momentum of the Allied offensives against Germany, advancing from both East and West, made clear that the end of the European war was in sight. In the Pacific, American air, sea, and land forces had pushed to the threshold of Japan's inner citadel. The Big Three had just concluded, at a momentous conference in the Crimea, what appeared to be an agreement on a blueprint for a stable and peaceful postwar world.

The early returns from Yalta seemed euphoric to Forrestal, McCloy, and others attending the State-War-Navy Coordinating Committee meeting on March 13. Secretary of State Stettinius (who had succeeded Cordell Hull in November 1944) spoke glowingly of prospects for Russian-American relations: "Every evidence, he said, of the Russian desire to cooperate along all lines with U.S. . . .''[1] But by April 2 the bubble had burst. Now Stettinius was reporting "serious deterioration in our relations with Russia," brought to focus by Stalin's announced intention to send the Lublin Poles (the Communist government hand-picked by him) to the United Nations Conference at San Francisco instead of the London Poles (the democratic émigré government which had fled the Nazi invasion in 1939 and was supported by the Western Allies).[2] Concurrently, Ambassador Averell Harriman in Moscow was warning Washington of the broader Soviet threat to all of Europe: "The Communist Party or its associates everywhere are using economic difficulties in areas under our responsibilities to promote Soviet concepts and policies and to undermine the influence of the Western Allies. . . . We must clearly realize that the Soviet program is the establishment of totalitarianism, ending personal liberty and democracy as we know and respect it."[3] Behind these reports of Stalin's brutal assertion of Russian self-interest in Eastern Europe and his pursuit of Soviet Communist purposes in wider areas beyond lay the debris of FDR's failed strategy of postponement—meaning his determined effort to postpone all definitive peace treaties, regional arrangements, and territorial claims until the enemies of democracy were crushed and the foundations of the United Nations organization set in place. The consequences of this failure were bequeathed to Forrestal and the other American planners in the postwar period.

THE NEW PRESIDENT

S HORTLY AFTER LUNCH on April 12, in Warm Springs, Georgia, where he was resting after the rigors of his long trip to the Crimea and the exhausting Yalta negotiations, the man who had totally dominated American political life for twelve years, and its grand strategy since America's entry into the war, suffered a fatal cerebral hemorrhage. Vice President Truman, who had been almost entirely excluded from FDR's conduct of the war, who was not privy to his thinking or to the views of the military chiefs and the White House advisers on whom the President relied for counsel, thus came to power at what was politically the most critical point in the global conflict—the point where imminent victory in both Europe and the Pacific was forcing decisions of the gravest consequence, which FDR had deliberately worked to defer. As President, Truman would soon learn that the major foreign-military policies of his predecessor were riddled with ambiguities and could not in any event be long sustained in the swiftly changing circumstances of 1945. In a number of areas—like the future of Germany, the future of the Japanese Emperor, the question of a postwar economic program to rebuild the productive capacity of ravished nations—FDR had bequeathed no useful policies.

Forrestal and the rest of the Cabinet were called to the White House at 6:10 p.m. for Truman's swearing-in, and the Navy Secretary noted the event in his diary: ''Mr. Truman responded to the oath firmly and clearly. His only active omission was a failure to raise his right hand when he was repeating the oath with his left hand on the Bible.'' At the urging of the Chief Justice he did so, ''and the raised hand gave his performance dignity and firmness.''[4] As Forrestal left the sobering ceremony, he murmured to the Secretary of the Interior, Harold Ickes, ''Poor little fellow, poor little fellow.''[5] It was a comment that reflected, then and afterward, his difficulty in convincing himself that Truman was really qualified to be President. In the end he admired the straightforward man from Missouri, but he also underestimated his inner strength and tenacity.

To underestimate Harry S. Truman was an easy thing to do, for he had spent much of his life among hack politicians and had acquired many of their habits and mannerisms, although he had successfully transcended the stigma of the Pendergast machine of Kansas City. This background led him to appoint to high positions a number of friends and cronies who gave his administration a generally deserved reputation for mediocrity. Forrestal was disturbed by what he discerned as the new President's lack of reflectiveness and a pronounced tendency to oversimplify. This assessment was not inaccurate, was indeed shared by many observers, especially during the first frantic weeks of the Truman presidency. Staggered by the immensity of his new burdens and by the suddenness and simultaneity of their arrival ("I felt like the moon, the stars and all the planets had fallen on me"),[6] the new President sought to compensate by appearing decisive. But because his grasp of the fluid intricacies of war strategy and relations among the Allies was unsure, his tendency to shoot from the hip drove him into blunders. Yet Truman's great strength lay precisely in his being able to see complex problems in simple terms—terms that lent themselves to practical decisions. With the passage of time, that central strength emerged and was reinforced by his detailed knowledge and understanding of American history.

"Truman will not make a great, flashy President like Roosevelt," his friend Sam Rayburn, the Speaker of the House, declared, "but by God he'll make a good President, a sound President." John Nance Garner, who had been Vice President in FDR's first term, credited Truman with "a head full of good horse sense . . . [and] guts."[7] And the new President's biographer, Robert Donovan, later wrote, "There was a core of dignity in Truman that could withstand any man."[8]

THE POLITICS OF VICTORY

ON APRIL 25, Forrestal got word through Admiral King that Himmler, head of the Gestapo, had offered to surrender all German armies on the Western Front. The President was talking to Churchill on the telephone. With victory in Europe suddenly at hand, it was borne in upon Washington that very little had been decided with regard to Germany and a postwar settlement. The breakdown of the Yalta agreements over the question of "democratic" governments in Eastern Europe and the Red Army's surge into Central Europe were forcing a sudden reassessment of all previous assumptions.

Just three days before, Stalin had signed a twenty-year mutual security assistance pact with the Lublin Poles (by now called the Polish Provisional Government), a move that created a shock wave in an administration which believed the Yalta agreements prohibited such arbitrary and unilateral acts. A confused Truman convened an emergency Cabinet meeting the next day (April 23) at which Stettinius called Stalin's action a clear violation of the

Yalta accords. Admiral Leahy, a crusty conservative and no admirer of the U.S.S.R., but a man who had been close to FDR at Yalta, said that the vagueness of the language in those accords made it very difficult to assert a clear violation. Stimson argued for caution and prudence on broader, nonlegal grounds, advising the new President that it was necessary to try to understand why Poland—as the avenue of German invasion—loomed so large in Soviet security considerations.[9]

Forrestal sided with Stettinius. "I give it as my view," he told Truman and the Cabinet, that "this was not an isolated incident," but part of "a pattern of unilateral action" already extending to Bulgaria, Romania, Turkey, and Greece. His conclusion was that "we might as well meet the issue now as later on."[10] General Marshall reminded the President of the vital need for Soviet entry into the war against Japan. This restatement of "military necessity" sobered all concerned by bringing back to mind the recent slaughters at Iwo Jima and Okinawa and the expectation of even higher American casualties in the invasion of Japan—250,000 by the current reckoning of the Joint Chiefs of Staff and later revised upward to 400,000 (the atomic bomb was still an unproven possibility, though the state of its development was better known to Marshall than to Forrestal).[11] As his understanding of the situation improved, Truman was exasperated by the tangled web in which he was caught: Nothing, it appeared, had been settled on FDR's watch; everything was contingent and interdependent. It was in this mood of irritation that he met later the same day with Soviet Foreign Minister Vyacheslav Molotov (who was en route to the U.N. organizing conference in San Francisco) and told him "in plain American language" that the Russian treaty with the Lublin Poles was unacceptable behavior, that the Soviets had better adhere to the Yalta accords—or else. Relations could no longer be on the basis of "a one-way street."[12]

Earlier manifestations of arbitrary Soviet assertiveness had spurred Churchill to urge Roosevelt, after their meeting in the Crimea, that American and British forces must make the race for Berlin in open disregard of the Yalta understandings. But FDR and the Joint Chiefs of Staff had deferred to Eisenhower's decision—taken on the basis of purely military considerations—to stop at the Elbe River south of the German capital.[13] Churchill renewed his plea with Truman, but the State Department advised that an attempt to use occupation zones for political bargaining purposes would only invite further Soviet intransigence. Lacking an independent feel for the situation, the untested President accepted the views of his advisers and informed the Prime Minister that the United States intended "to adhere to our interpretation of the Yalta agreements."[14] This meant that the whole of Berlin became a part of the Russian zone.

On May 8 the Cabinet assembled at eight-fifteen in the morning to hear the President broadcast his V-E Day Proclamation: "Our victory is but

*Forrestal with General Eisenhower at Frankfurt Airport in late 1945
(the civilian in dark glasses at left rear is John F. Kennedy,
then a journalist)*

half-won. The West is free, but the East is still in bondage to the treacherous tyranny of the Japanese. When the last Japanese division has surrendered unconditionally, then only will our fighting job be done.''[15] At the
urging of Stimson, Forrestal, and Under Secretary of State Joseph Grew,
Truman also issued a separate statement which sought to put rational limits
on FDR's sweeping doctrine of ''unconditional surrender.''[16] As intelligence reports showed, this doctrine had discouraged incipient dissenters
within Hitler's command and now loomed as an even greater obstacle to
ending the war against Japan.

THE PACIFIC WAR was the navy's principal theater of operation, and
Forrestal's mind was now focused on the developing probability that the
Japanese defeat might occur with unexpected suddenness. Submarine attacks on shipping were rapidly strangling the economy, cutting off every
kind of vital import, including food, and relentless air bombardment by
carrier aircraft and long-range heavy bombers was decimating Japan's war
plants and ''paper cities.'' By June, mass firebomb raids by several hun-

dred B-29s at a time had destroyed one fourth of all buildings in Tokyo and left more than 3 million city residents homeless. The end of the European war would soon free up thousands of tanks, ships, aircraft, and trained units for transfer to the Pacific Theater. The Russians stood poised to attack in Manchuria. Plans were moving forward for a large-scale invasion of Japan in November, but in the midsummer of 1945 there was a developing sense that the end might come sooner.

Concerned that planning for the peace was "far below the quality of planning that went into the conduct of the war,"[17] Forrestal was intent upon defining a structure of postwar relationships that would be consistent with American interests. "How far and how thoroughly do we want to beat Japan?" he asked, "do we want to morgenthau [sic] those islands—do we want to destroy the whole industrial potential?"[18] His conclusion was the same one he had reached with regard to postwar Germany and had urged upon FDR (in company with Stimson, McCloy, the Joint Chiefs of Staff, and the State Department): to avoid the vengeful and myopic Morgenthau Plan, which sought to limit the German future to subsistence agriculture, and to identify long-term American interests in the broad context of an economic and political revival of Europe. The German nation, in Forrestal's view, must "be denied the means of making war . . . by supervision over a sufficiently long period . . . But to ignore the existence of 75 or 80 millions of vigorous and industrious people, or to assume they will not join with Russia if no other outlet is afforded them, I think is closing our eyes to reality."[19] He applied the same line of reasoning to Japan.

He was increasingly concerned about the menace of Russian Communism and its attraction for decimated, destabilized societies in Europe and Asia. Did the United States want and need a "counterweight" to Russian influence in the Far East? If so, "should it be China or Japan?"[20] Moreover, given the devastating impact of current American attacks on Japan, was there still need for a massive land invasion or for "quick Russian participation" in the war against Japan? Indeed, should Russia even participate in the occupation of Japan?[21]

To Forrestal, with his personal experience at Iwo Jima vividly in mind, the compelling problem was how to end the war with the least amount of additional bloodshed. In company with Stimson, McCloy, and Grew, he struggled through May and June to find a formula that would, without wholly retreating from the straitjacket policy of "unconditional surrender" inherited from FDR, induce the Japanese to lay down their arms. The group agreed that Japan should be allowed to retain its "own form of government and religious institutions" while being forced to eradicate "all traces of Japanese militarism."[22] The problem was to find the precise words and shade of meaning needed to persuade the Japanese. Their proposed solution was to offer surrender terms permitting Japan to retain the Emperor, but this idea was vehemently opposed in several quarters. In the State Department, Assistant Secretaries Dean Acheson and Archibald Mac-Leish (both representative of the intellectual left-center of the Democratic Party) argued that Japanese militarists had manipulated the throne in the past and might do so again.[23] James Byrnes, who had replaced Stettinius as Secretary of State just a few weeks after Truman's swearing-in, felt strongly that Congress would be angered, and he was reinforced by a predecessor, Cordell Hull, who thought the idea sounded "too much like appeasement."[24] Several senators had proposed that Emperor Hirohito be tried as a war criminal and appeared to be satisfied with the doctrine of "unconditional surrender" in its most literal sense, even if this led to a final bloodbath in the home islands that might cost 400,000 American lives.

According to Eric Larrabee, one proof of FDR's political genius was to make World War II seem to the American people like a logical extension of the domestic New Deal crusade—that is, opposition to the power of entrenched interests at home and opposition to vicious tyrannies abroad "were made to appear as but two articles of the same democratic, humanitarian faith."[25] There is much truth in the statement, but FDR's success in this endeavor had the curious effect in 1945 of making hard-line ideologues out of liberal New Dealers when it came to issues like compromise with evil dictators for the purpose of saving American lives or guarding against the destruction of all hope in the defeated enemy countries. It was notable that Forrestal and the other advocates of flexibility were not New Dealers, but pragmatic bankers, lawyers, and diplomats. They were thinking beyond the war to the need for structure and stability in the postwar world. The New Dealers, by and large, considered it immoral and politically dangerous to tamper with FDR's legacy of "unconditional surrender" and found it difficult to think beyond the winning of a total military victory for the forces of decency. As Forrestal put it in 1946: "We regarded the war, broadly speaking, as a ball game" to be finished "as quickly as possible," but with "little thought as to the relationships between nations which would exist after Germany and Japan were destroyed."[26]

FORRESTAL AND THE BOMB

MEANWHILE, the secret development of the atomic bomb was gathering its fateful momentum. On April 25, Henry Stimson, the Secretary of War, whose department had been solely and secretly charged with the project from the outset (under the code name of Manhattan Engineer District), went to the White House to inform the new President that "the most terrible weapon ever known in human history" would probably be ready for use in four months. This was also about the time that Forrestal and the navy were first officially informed of the bomb project although there is some evidence that certain persons in the navy had previous knowledge. General Leslie Groves, the officer in charge of the development, recounted the history of the undertaking and described the weapon. The matter-of-fact Truman "appeared impressed but not overwhelmed" by this information.[27] Stimson went on to tell the President there was as yet no settled policy regarding the "use or non-use" of such a weapon, but that the United States could not expect to maintain a permanent monopoly on bomb know-how and manufacturing capability; at the same time, he said, effective international control would involve more intrusive rights of inspection than sovereign nations had ever permitted.[28]

The upshot of the meeting was the appointment of an Interim Committee to advise the President on future nuclear policy. Stimson was named chairman, and another prominent member was Secretary of State Byrnes. Forrestal named his Under Secretary, Ralph Bard, to represent the navy.* From the beginning there was a presumption that the atomic bomb was a part of the war effort, and although several members felt that a warning should precede actual use of such a "horrible weapon," the overwhelming weight of opinion among policy-makers was in favor of using the bomb in an effort to win the war.[29] As the debate continued, the bomb began to be seen as a preferred alternative to an invasion with ground forces, primarily because it would, if it worked, save hundreds of thousands of American lives. Stimson argued that being "pounded" by atomic bombs would also be the lesser evil for the Japanese. Byrnes, the professional politician, was quick to sense the possibility that a stockpile of atomic bombs could give the United States decisive diplomatic leverage to dictate the peace and thus to shape the postwar world.[30]

As of June 18, however, when Truman gathered his principal advisers for a review of strategy before his departure for the Big Three Conference at Potsdam (which ran from July 17 to August 2), there was no certainty that the atomic device would work. The Joint Chiefs of Staff, although they now had before them the dreadful ordeal of the American assault on Okinawa, were unanimous in the view that a massive invasion of Japan was still necessary to end the war. Even King, whose conviction was now that the defeat of Japan could be accomplished by air attack and sea blockade alone, raised no objection to Marshall's assertion that the invasion of Kyushu (the southernmost home island) scheduled for November 1 was "essential to a strategy of strangulation."[31] Forrestal echoed King, pointing

---

*The other members were scientists Vannevar Bush, James Bryant Conant, and Karl T. Compton; Will Clayton, Assistant Secretary of State for Economic Affairs; and George Harrison, a special assistant to the Secretary of War.

out that "even if we wished to besiege Japan for a year or a year and a half, the capture of Kyushu would still be essential."[32]

The President did not take issue with this military advice, even as he was convinced that the assault on Kyushu—and the later, larger invasion to be aimed at the Tokyo Plain—would almost certainly meet with the same fanatical resistance encountered on Okinawa. There, in an island bastion 350 miles from the Japanese homeland, the defenders had fought from caves and cliffs and the stoneworks of old Chinese tombs. Despite the heaviest naval gunfire concentrations of the entire war—from six battleships, six cruisers, and eight destroyers—and equal bombardment from carrier aircraft and land-based artillery, the Japanese soldiers had emerged from their caves to fight with desperate ferocity, counterattacking again and again long after their prospects were hopeless. In the end they lost 100,000 men, but inflicted 45,000 casualties on the American ground forces. Meanwhile, offshore, the kamikaze squadrons (representing Japan's desperate adjustment to the decimation of its regular air force) pressed home their suicidal air attacks on the vast assemblage of American warships and amphibious vessels, sinking or damaging them by the score. Okinawa was only sixty miles long and two miles wide, and it was not the heartland of the Japanese Empire.[33] There loomed the nightmare that invasion of the home islands might provoke guerrilla resistance by the entire Japanese population.

On July 13, while the President was en route to the Potsdam Conference, intercepted messages from the Japanese Foreign Minister to his ambassador in Moscow brought the first evidence that Japan was seeking a way to end the war. The messages sought Russian mediation with the United States and some way of moderating the unconditional surrender terms. In his response on July 15, the Japanese ambassador bluntly told his government that it suffered from "a lack of reality"[34] if it believed Russia could be separated from its allies on this question. On July 24, he said Japan was now "entirely alone and friendless" and should surrender on any terms it could get. The Japanese Cabinet informed him that, because unconditional surrender was anathema, the nation had no choice but to fight on.[35]

On July 16, the day Truman arrived in Potsdam, the atomic bomb was successfully tested in the desert near Alamogordo, New Mexico. The ultimate weapon was now a reality. Suddenly there was a serious alternative to the invasion of Japan. Six weeks earlier the Interim Committee had recommended that the bomb (1) should be used against Japan as soon as possible, (2) should be used against a dual target—a military installation near civilian facilities, and (3) should be used without prior warning as to the nature of the weapon.[36] The recommendation had been extensively debated. Forrestal's representative, Ralph Bard, several times expressed his uneasiness about using the bomb against Japan, believing this would cause severe damage to the reputation of the United States as "a great humanitarian nation."[37] On June 27, he wrote a letter to Stimson which argued that the United States should arrange a meeting with Japanese emissaries "somewhere on the China coast" immediately following the Potsdam Conference. There the Japanese could be informed about the horrifying power of the bomb and also about the imminence of Russian entry into the Pacific War. Bard thought there was nothing to be lost by such an effort, and it might prove to be "the opportunity which the Japanese are looking for" as a justification for surrender. Stimson, however, did not reply to the letter, and Bard resigned from the navy three days later.[38]

Bard's misgivings were broadly shared by the group of nuclear scientists who had perfected the bomb, many of whom were Jewish refugees from Germany and Hungary. They approached the question with a kind of selective morality, having no compunctions about using the bomb against the perpetrators of the Holocaust, but feeling that dropping it on Japan would be "an international crime." They did not share the intense American anger against Japan brought on by the sneak attack on Pearl Harbor. They pressed hard, as did Bard, at least for a warning shot, a "demonstration bomb" to convince the Japanese that further resistance would lead to their total decimation. In the end, however, the Interim Committee concluded that such a course involved too high a risk of failure. What if the "demonstration bomb" failed to detonate? Or if it did go off, would the Japanese perceive anything more than "a lot of pyrotechnics"? Suppose the Tokyo government did not respond promptly, but found itself locked in extended debate over the meaning of the explosion. Would the United States be honor-bound to wait indefinitely for an answer? Finally, there was the fact that there would be only two bombs in the stockpile by early August.[39]

The strong inference is that Forrestal agreed with Bard, though not for the same reasons. He does not appear to have been troubled by the moral issue arising from use of the atomic bomb, but believed a continuation of massive air strikes with non-atomic weapons (including firebombs), the capture of Kyushu, and the tightening naval blockade could bring about surrender. This was also the general navy view, held by Admirals King, Leahy, and Nimitz.[40]

Even General Curtis LeMay, the apostle of massive air bombardment, said years later that use of the atomic bomb against Japan was "not necessary," but "we went ahead and dropped the bombs [on Hiroshima and Nagasaki] because President Truman told me to do it."[41] Forrestal, whose overriding concern at this juncture was to develop strategic counterweights to what he foresaw as burgeoning Russian/Communist power in Asia, may have feared that using the atomic bomb would aggravate the problems of Japan's economic recovery and produce hatred of America for years to come.

Whether he believed it possible to prevail against the gathering momentum to use the bomb is not clear, but he decided to attend the Potsdam Conference—uninvited—in the context of a trip to inspect U.S. Navy forces in Europe. There is a sense that he and the navy admirals were put out at being excluded from the President's delegation, in which Stimson and the War Department played so prominent a role. But there is nothing in the record to indicate that he actually pressed Truman to forgo use of the bomb; at most he seems to have argued for a formula that would induce Japanese surrender without need for either the bomb or invasion. For his part, the new President was apparently surprised and not entirely pleased at Forrestal's intrusion, and their two talks, over lunch and dinner, were not especially substantive. Moreover, Forrestal did not arrive in Potsdam until two days after Truman's announcement of the surrender terms. On July 26, Truman issued the Potsdam Proclamation, calling for the surrender of Japan (signed also by Great Britain and China, but not Russia, which was not at war with Japan). Secretary Byrnes, the chief custodian of FDR's "unconditional surrender" legacy, succeeded in excluding any reference to a future role for the Emperor, but the statement nevertheless reflected much of the proportioned pragmatism previously urged by Forrestal, Stimson, Grew, and McCloy. The proclamation said in essence: Japan's militarism must be eliminated and her war-making capacity destroyed; her home territory must be occupied and her conquered territories stripped away. But the term "unconditional surrender" was used only once—with reference to "all Japanese armed forces." The final sentence of the ultimatum said: "The alternative for Japan is prompt and utter destruction."[42]

As Forrestal and the other American pragmatists had feared, the Japanese hard-liners officially rejected the ultimatum on July 30. Truman, saying "There is no alternative now," gave orders for the atomic bomb to be used "when ready," but not before his departure from Potsdam on August 2. He had mentioned to Stalin on July 24, with deliberate casualness, that the United States had "perfected a very powerful explosive" which it was going to employ against Japan with the expectation that it "will end the war." Stalin's reply had been equally casual: He was glad to hear such news. But Truman did not want to be in conference with Stalin when the bomb was dropped.[43]

Doomsday at Hiroshima was August 6, while Forrestal was flying back to Washington from London. Seventy thousand persons were killed outright and at least as many were afflicted by the lingering death of poisonous radiation. Despite this stark new evidence of what lay ahead, the Japanese warlords still resisted capitulation, but Emperor Hirohito now intervened to insist they press the Soviets to mediate. Stalin's answer to that overture was coldness itself: The Soviet Union would consider itself at war with Japan the next day—August 8. The second atomic bomb obliterated Nagasaki on August 9 without specific authorization from Truman and appeared to reflect a lapse of civilian control, for the President had told Forrestal at Potsdam that no more than one would be dropped. But Truman's remark to Forrestal reflected the President's misunderstanding. The July 24 order to the senior air commander, General Carl Spaatz, instructed him to use additional bombs on agreed targets as they became available.[44]

On August 10, a broadcast from Tokyo expressed Japan's readiness to accept the terms of the Potsdam Proclamation, provided they did not contain ''any demand which prejudices the prerogatives of His Majesty as a Sovereign Ruler.'' In Washington, Truman summoned his senior advisers to consider whether the broadcast should be considered an acceptance of the ultimatum. Stimson, Forrestal, and Admiral Leahy said yes, but Byrnes, the New Deal politician, was adamantly opposed. The American people expected ''unconditional surrender,'' he argued, and would surely ''crucify'' the President if he accepted anything less. In a flash of perspicacity, Forrestal suggested that the President accept the Japanese condition, but call it unconditional surrender. Both Truman and Byrnes found this agreeable. The language of the final reply accepted a role for the Emperor, but made his authority subject to that of the U.S. Supreme Commander.[45] The Japanese war thus came to an end without the terrible trauma of a large-scale invasion, and Forrestal's agile mind, seeking a practical solution that would avert further bloodshed and destruction, made an invaluable contribution at a critical juncture. On the lower level of interservice politics, he persuaded the President to hold the surrender ceremonies aboard the U.S.S. Missouri in Tokyo Bay to assure the navy of a visible, if secondary, role, given the fact that the proceedings would be conducted by General Douglas MacArthur.[46]

Truman never betrayed any remorse over his decision to use the atomic bomb in the circumstances that confronted him. On the arguable assumption that, in the absence of the bomb, a massive ground invasion was required to end the war, he was almost certainly correct in believing that the atomic bomb had saved ''a quarter of a million of the flower of our young manhood'' and perhaps a million or more Japanese lives.[47]

★ ★ ★

CHAPTER 17

Private Life in the Nation's Capital

P RIVATE LIFE in Washington during the war matched the frenetic pace of official life and was in a real sense an integral part of it. Cocktail gatherings, dinner parties, and Sunday lunches often proved indispensable meeting places for busy men who had been unable to talk to each other during their crowded workday schedules. Ranking military officers—American, British, French, Australian—flew in from far-flung battlefronts with firsthand accounts of combat operations or political intrigues which enriched dinner party conversations and were counted a social coup for the hostess who could bring such men and such accounts to her table. Everyone in Washington was unremittingly focused on the tensions, uncertainties, and consequences of the encompassing war. The air was filled with an unrelieved electric excitement.

John McLain, the New York journalist who had played a lot of backgammon with Forrestal at the Racquet & Tennis Club, recounted several wartime incidents when he, as a navy lieutenant, was briefly passing through Washington en route to somewhere else: "Forrestal was kind enough to give me bed and board in his house . . . I would return shortly before dinner to find the table set for a dozen people and would suggest timidly that perhaps I should give my business to the cafeteria down the street, but Forrestal would hear none of it. 'Forget it,' he would say, 'these fellows might like to meet you.' These 'fellows' would turn out to be two admirals, a Marine Corps general, and probably Harry Hopkins. Forrestal would say, 'Admiral, this is McLain. He is just back from Algiers.' After that, even the most fearsome brass would regard me with a mixture of curiosity and respect. Secretary Forrestal was amused."[1]

The Forrestals were very much in the swim of Washington society, and when Jo was in control and on her good behavior, friends felt "they made a lively kinetic couple."[2] Unfortunately, such occasions were infrequent, for her condition did not improve, but grew worse with the passage of time. And though Forrestal was forbearing, he was also increasingly, and helplessly, exasperated. It was his habit to confer with his close friends, Lovett and McCloy, usually late at night when he was pondering or worrying over some current problem of the war. He would call one of them to see if a visit was convenient and then drop over for a highball or a glass of milk. McCloy noted that Forrestal's marital problem was never far below the surface of his mind. Often staring broodingly into space, he would ask, half to himself, "What do I do about Jo?"[3]

One instinctive reaction, necessary for the retention of his own balance, was to withdraw emotionally from his wife and her unsolvable predicament, insofar as possible. This he did, but it served only to widen the already great distance between them. The result was to deepen her loneliness and his own emotional isolation and to fray further the remaining strands of home and family life. Jo's response was to get out of Washington as often as possible, to move restlessly from New York to Long Island to Hobe Sound to the Virginia horse country (and, after the war, to Paris) with a sort of desperate aimlessness, adding to an already unenviable reputation for pushing herself into situations, uninvited and unexpected. As Ellen Barry recalled, "She would just call from the station and say 'I'm here.' "[4]

Finding release in riding horses, she would drive out into Virginia to borrow a mount from one or more of her casual acquaintances who kept stables there. As she rarely called in advance, however, the head groom would put her off until he could telephone the owner back in Washington for permission to give her a horse. Usually the answer was yes, but as time passed it was more frequently no. During one period she boarded her own horse at Merrywood, the Auchincloss estate in McLean where Jacqueline Bouvier Kennedy Onassis grew up. Jackie and her half sister, Nina Auchincloss, frequently exercised Jo's horse and regarded Jo as a daring and absolutely first-class equestrienne.[5]

Other incidents seemed to reflect either an unbearable loneliness or the compulsions of an illness she could not control. On a hot summer day in 1945, the wife of Captain Jerauld Wright (later a four-star admiral) got a sudden invitation for dinner that evening aboard the *Sequoia*. It was a command performance from the Secretary of the Navy. They were to meet at his residence for a drink before driving down to board the yacht. Phyllis Wright scrambled to get a sitter for their young children, and she and her husband presented themselves at Forrestal's house at the appointed hour. Soon Assistant Secretary John Kenney and his wife also arrived, and they all sat in the living room waiting for Forrestal. After an hour, Jo came downstairs alone and casually announced that Forrestal was out of town. It became apparent she had organized the party, knowingly exploiting her husband's command authority, simply because she did not want to spend the evening alone.[6]

Shortly after the Yalta Conference, on March 13, 1945, FDR's Appointments Secretary recorded in his diary: "All appointments slow in getting under way, and at 12:50 Mrs. Forrestal got in by the back door and upset everything by staying thirty-five minutes, talking about nothing in particular. Couldn't shoo her out, so had to ask Leon Henderson to come back after lunch to report on economic conditions in Europe."[7]

On another occasion after the war, Dean Acheson, then Under Secretary of State, dropped by for a predinner drink to confer with Forrestal on a particular matter. The Secretary of the Navy was in black tie preparing to go on to some official function. Jo was not going, nor did it appear that Acheson had dinner plans. When Forrestal rose to leave, he urged Acheson to stay and have dinner with "Josie," who greeted the suggestion with enthusiasm. Acheson stayed through one more round of martinis, at which point the condition of his hostess prompted him to the conclusion, as he later told his assistant, that he "had better get the hell out of there."[8]

In Paris in 1946, Forrestal's old friend Dolly Hoffman found Jo walking along the rue de Rivoli beside the Tuileries, alone in a driving rain. She stopped the chauffeured car to pick her up, but Jo insisted on going on alone, meanwhile cursing the "goddamned Paris weather" and asking half to herself "what in Christ's name" she was doing there. She did, however, accept Dolly's invitation to a small dinner that evening, and Dolly arranged for a gentleman friend to pick her up at her hotel, warning him not to give her a drink before they arrived at Dolly's apartment. Jo got predictably drunk during dinner, but what angered Dolly to the point of breaking the relationship was that near the end of the evening she "ground out her cigarette in my prettiest tablecloth."[9]

SEPARATE LIVES

BY THE MIDDLE of the war the Forrestals were leading completely separate lives, no longer looking to each other for any measure of emotional support.[10] Forrestal immersed himself almost totally in the rigors of his job, worked twelve-hour days seven days a week, and, in brief intervals of respite from official duties, sought out the company of attractive, intelligent women—for diverting talk, emotional comfort, and love. A number of Washington's beauties and leading hostesses were thoroughly taken by his combination of brilliance, taut charm, vibrant animality, and official power, and the evidence is that they gave him all he would take of their company and affection and love; in the event, however, this was not a great deal. For though he might expose to them some of his official concerns—how to end the war with Japan, how to reorganize the post-war government in Washington, how to confront the Communist threat—he rarely exposed his personal thoughts or anxieties; their attempts to give him comfort and reassurance seem in every case to have been deflected by the armor of his essential impenetrability. He could give himself to the United States Navy, to the war effort, and to his country, but apparently not to any woman. Hensel observed that Forrestal "liked the company of good-looking women, women of style and manners, brainy women; but if he found real joy in this, those of us who were close to him never observed it."[11] Paul Nitze added, "He enjoyed his successes with the ladies, but he did not really love anyone."[12]

Mr. and Mrs. Forrestal at the White House, late 1945

Because he was in the main discreet and secretive, it is not easy to identify the various women in his life during the Washington period, or to classify them as lovers or merely sharers of a cocktail or afternoon tea. He would drop by in the late afternoon or following some official reception or dinner. Or he would draw close friends into a delicate conspiracy: "Dear Dan," he wrote to his friend Dan Caulkins, "I will be stopping by your house this evening after work, about nine o'clock. Mrs. So-and-so [the current lady] will be there. Thank you for having her. Jim."[13]

He had a long affair with a Philadelphia divorcee, Eleanor Cuyler Walker, which began several years before he arrived in Washington and continued through the war years, notwithstanding her marriage in 1938.[14] Margaret Griggs, young wife of a British diplomat, who felt "he had such wonderful thoughts," and Kay Halle, a Cleveland department store heiress, are other names vaguely but persistently linked with his. Belle Donaldson, a young woman who worked for the Red Cross during the war (and later married President Eisenhower's first Secretary of the Air Force) was said to have been "a great love" during the last three years of Forrestal's life and to have been "desolated" by his suicide.[15]

If he ever came close to a serious relationship with a woman in Washington it may have been with Pauline Davis. Robert Lovett is authority for the statement that "Jim loved Pauline Davis,"[16] but the remark is not without ambiguity, for the lady in question possessed attributes which caused numerous people to "love" her. A petite, stylish beauty who was also very rich and very smart ("entirely feminine, but with a man's mind" was the prevailing view), she was renowned for her good taste and for giving the most splendid parties in wartime Washington. "Everyone loved her," her good friend Marian Christie recalled, "and everyone wanted a house and parties like hers."[17]

She had arrived from New York in 1934, already a divorcée and a widow, to help form the Federal Alcohol Control Bureau in the wake of the successful campaign to repeal the Volstead Act. In that battle she had headed the Women's National Organization for Prohibition Repeal and, though a Republican, had then gone to Washington in the dawning days of the New Deal to help finish the job. Divorced from her first husband, Morton Smith, by whom she had two sons, she had married Charles Sabin, president of the Guaranty Trust, with whom she enjoyed a deeply satisfying life in New York and Long Island. Sabin was the reputed love of her life, and his death in 1933 left her sad but "enormously rich." It was at that juncture of her life that she decided to make a fresh start in Washington.

In 1936 she married Dwight Davis, a fixture in conservative Republican circles. He had been Secretary of War in the Coolidge administration and later Governor General of the Philippines, as well as an amateur tennis champion and donor of the international tennis trophy, the Davis Cup, and the marriage established Pauline at the center of Washington society. Joseph Alsop thought her "enormously life-loving and life-enriching," but also "unusually shrewd" and possessed of "remarkable talents as an organizer."[18] As World War II approached, she became a senior executive of the American Red Cross, serving as Director of Volunteer Special Services for nearly five years, during which she was responsible for recruiting and training nearly a million volunteer Red Cross women. A society columnist remarked in 1942 that "Mrs. Davis is one of those rare women who, in addition to being very useful, are decidedly ornamental. One of the best dressed women in Washington, she is also one of the gayest and most amusing. It is hard to realize, looking at this tiny slender person with her amused brown eyes, that her favorite activity is 'organizing.' "[19]

Dwight Davis died in November 1945 at the age of sixty-six, which left Pauline a widow for the second time, but she continued her active life of social and cultural involvement without breaking stride. It was in the postwar period that she became famous for her red-and-white New Year's Eve balls, at which the two-color decor was elaborated, with minute attention to detail, in everything from tablecloths and wineglasses to the gowns of the lady guests. To these galas came all of the currently prominent statesmen and politicians, including President and Mrs. Truman. Dwight Davis had three grown daughters, "stiffly formal girls," who disapproved of their stepmother's clothes and parties and expansive joie de vivre, but Pauline was much too confident and positive to pay them any heed.[20]

Forrestal was attracted not only by her beauty and style, but also by her

conspicuous intelligence and competence. She had a frank and gracious way of meeting and dealing
with people of every background
and persuasion. She was warm and
feminine, yet seriously interested
and informed about major political
issues. Her house was amply staffed,
and she managed it with precision
and flair. To Forrestal she must have
been the embodiment of everything
Josephine had once seemed to be,
or promised to become, before her
tragic descent. It is a fair inference
that he admired, and perhaps loved,
Pauline primarily for that reason—
for he loved elegance and competence and self-control. Little is
known about their private relation-

Pauline Davis, 1945

ship or whether it was ever a love affair, but they were close friends and
confidants after 1945. Whether Forrestal gave to Pauline Davis any more
of himself than he was able to give to others remains an unanswered question, but it seems clear that neither she nor any of the others ever got close
enough to save him in his final desolation. The one note she wrote to him
in the hospital lacked intimacy, but perhaps she was being deliberately
discreet: "I am so glad to hear that you are feeling better—take care of
yourself—with love, Pauline."[21]

In the mid-1950s, several years after Forrestal's suicide, when Pauline
herself was dying, she put the question to her friend Adele Lovett: "Do
you think Jim would have married me?" And her friend, knowing Forrestal
well and being a woman of candor, replied, "No, dear, I don't think so."[22]

POKER WITH THE PRESIDENT

PERHAPS NOTHING better illustrated Forrestal's ambivalence toward
the social, backslapping, clubhouse side of politics than his halfhearted
efforts to ingratiate himself with the Truman White House, which was
composed, by and large, of provincial mediocrities from Missouri. FDR's
entourage, more erudite, broad-gauged, and easy-mannered, had been easier
for him to relate to, as had been that President's own aristocratic savoir-
faire. In the Truman period, Forrestal's Wall Street background, his intellect, his clothes and general demeanor, aroused feelings of defensiveness

and resentment in people like Matthew Connelly (the Appointments Secretary), Harry Vaughan (the rumpled factotum from the Missouri National
Guard who was military aide), and other Midwestern insiders of limited
scope like John Snyder (Secretary of the Treasury). Aware of this condition
and concerned about its impact on his effectiveness as Navy Secretary and
his standing with the President, Forrestal sought Clark Clifford's help in
becoming a member of Truman's floating poker game.[23] Truman liked to
play poker with the boys, a pastime which served as a counterbalance to
the almost "uxorious" devotion he gave his wife and daughter,[24] and as
President he arranged games three or four evenings a week, usually at the
homes of Cabinet members, who took turns playing host. Such stag affairs
were off the record, and the Secret Service took special precautions to
prevent the press or anyone beyond the inner circle from seeing the President either playing cards or drinking bourbon.

Forrestal considered poker a great waste of time and was uncomfortable
with the accompanying boozy small talk, but the political operator in his
soul told him it was important to cultivate this President after hours and
also to convince the White House staff that he could be one of the boys.
He was embarrassingly miscast for the role, however, and a man more
inwardly confident would have recognized this and forsworn the effort.
George Marshall, Robert Lovett, John McCloy, Dean Acheson, and others
of their stripe never considered such social politicking a necessary means
of establishing their bona fides with the Presidents they served; they were
what they were. At some level, Forrestal lacked their inner self-confidence.
To his detriment, he had the instincts of a political operator, but lacked
the genuine gregariousness, the alligator hide, and the infinite capacity for
suffering fools that are the marks of the professional.

The day came (in the fall of 1946) when it was Forrestal's turn to host
the presidential poker party at Prospect House, and he dispatched his faithful naval aide, Captain Smedberg, in the early afternoon to deal with the
Secret Service, arrange for the streetside blinds to be drawn, and otherwise
to see that all would be ready for the President's arrival. The captain's most
urgent mission, however, was to get Josephine Forrestal out of the house
and onto a train for New York, but when he told her the car was waiting
to take her to the railroad station, she said she wasn't going. She knew
about the poker party, and "If Jim thinks I'm not going to be here to greet
the President in my own house, he's crazy." When Smedberg reported this
intransigence to Forrestal, he said with some heat, "If you can't get her
on the two o'clock, get her on the three o'clock, and if you can't get her
on the three o'clock, get her on the four o'clock. Get her out of that
house." But Josephine retired to her bedroom and proved immovable.[25]

The guests arrived about seven, a small group—several notches above
the level of the Missouri gang—that included Fred Vinson, the Chief Justice;

Senator Warren Magnuson of Washington; Leslie Biffle, the Secretary of the Senate; Averell Harriman, the U.S. Ambassador to Moscow; and Clark Clifford, now the President's counsel. As the President entered, Josephine Forrestal came downstairs to meet him in the foyer. "Jim wanted me to go to New York, but I wasn't going to let you come into my house without greeting you." Truman was affable and courtly for a few minutes, after which Forrestal took his wife gently by the elbow and marched her back upstairs, saying "Now, Josie, you know this is a stag party." She did not reappear.[26]

The poker game began in earnest following dinner, but after a few minutes Forrestal asked Truman if Smedberg could sit in for him momentarily while he made a few urgent phone calls, to which the President genially assented. Forrestal returned after twenty minutes, but soon excused himself a second time and signaled Smedberg to take his place. "He never showed up again until the President was ready to leave. I figured he was bored and took a nap," Smedberg said later. The game continued enthusiastically for several hours, with the players generally deferring to the President's preferences. As Smedberg recalled, "He loved wild games, like seven card high-low; he rarely threw in his hand and always lost, as far as I could tell. And he drank bourbon continuously, but never got tight. He just got exhilarated and told terrible stories." Clifford, who was in charge of supplying potato chips and keeping the bartender alert to the needs of the players, never took a drink. "I think he drank milk," Smedberg recalled. At the end of the evening, Smedberg was surprised and slightly shocked to discover that, as Forrestal's stand-in, he had won $300, while the President had lost about $700. Truman was about to write a check when Clifford intervened. "No checks, Mr. President. I'll take care of this and you can take care of me tomorrow."[27]

The next morning, when the captain put his stack of five-, ten-, and twenty-dollar bills on the Navy Secretary's desk, Forrestal said, "My God, what's that?" Informed that it was "our" winnings from the poker game, Forrestal said, "You must be pretty good." Then he put the entire wad of bills into his desk drawer, and Smedberg "never heard another word about it."[28]

CHRISTMAS LONELINESS

THERE WERE other incidents which led the loyal and admiring Smedberg to the conclusion that Forrestal was, in small ways, morally obtuse and devoid of compassion for the private concerns of his staff members. His explanation was that Forrestal, having no real private or family life of his own, was often insensitive to the importance others attached to their scarce time with beloved wives and children; and also that he used his authority over subordinates to guard against his own aloneness. As December 1946 moved to within a few days of Christmas, Jo Forrestal left for New York, having arranged for Michael and Peter to spend the holidays in the warm circle of the Fletcher family at the Aiken School. On the twenty-third Forrestal called Smedberg on the intercom, instructing him to arrange for his plane the following day. "You and I are going to fly down to Palm Beach for a week or ten days."

Golfing at Chevy Chase Club, 1946

"On Christmas Eve?"

"Yes, bring your golf clubs."

The disciplined, unquestioning aide now quietly rebelled. Walking into the Secretary's office, he said that if this wasn't official business, he would like to be excused. He had been away from his family for endless months during the war, and they were all counting on this Christmas together. Forrestal looked at him without expression, then said, "Okay, Smeddy, we'll go down the day *after* Christmas." And they did.[29]

Alone on Christmas morning in the big house on Prospect Street, Forrestal telephoned another member of his staff, John T. Connor, a young lawyer from the Cahill, Gordon firm who was serving for a year as personal counsel to the Navy Secretary (he would later become president of Allied Chemical and Secretary of Commerce under President Lyndon Johnson). Connor remembered becoming vaguely aware that the telephone was ringing as he slowly emerged from a sound sleep, but it was his five-year-old son who answered the phone. When he finally picked up the receiver he heard an alert voice saying "Merry Christmas, John. How about a golf game at Chevy Chase?" Connor realized he had mumbled an acceptance before weighing the implications, for he was immediately confronted by an incredulous, indignant young wife: "You're not going to leave us to play golf on Christmas Day?" But he was already committed. In retrospect he felt his quick affirmation reflected an incident the previous day when the staff had been dismissed at noon, so they could make ready for the Christmas celebration. Preparing to leave, Connor had come upon Forrestal all alone in his office staring moodily into space. Connor asked if there was anything more he needed from the staff. The Secretary shook his head, but seemed eager to talk and invited the young lawyer to sit down. They chatted "about this and that" for more than two hours, but Forrestal "showed no inclination to go home and was still there when I finally left at four o'clock."[30]

Christmas Day was bright and mild, and the golf course was deserted. Forrestal and Connor cruised around in record time, both hitting the ball well, with Forrestal as usual playing "strictly for exercise, not for fun or even companionship." After they finished, he told Connor he was going back to the office, but would be glad to drop him at home "unless I cared to join him at the Navy Department." Anxious to spend what remained of Christmas Day with his young bride and bright-eyed son, Connor asked to be dropped off. As they bade each other farewell, exchanging "Merry Christmases" and "Thanks for the game," Connor hovered on the edge of inviting his boss in to share the family Christmas dinner, knowing that otherwise Forrestal would be spending a bleak afternoon and evening alone in the deserted Navy Department. But "my reserve, and his, held me back," and the moment passed.[31]

IV

★ ★ ★

THE COMMUNIST
CHALLENGE

CHAPTER 18

★ ★ ★

The FDR Legacy

UNTIL HE succeeded Knox, Forrestal's professional concerns necessarily began and ended with the operational problems of the navy. "I frankly confess," he wrote to Joseph Ridder at the end of 1944, "that I have only just begun to think about" issues of grand strategy and the shape of the postwar world "because . . . it seemed more important to concentrate on my own job."[1] As its principal civilian administrator, his energy and attention were consumed by the task of building and sustaining a naval force of unprecedented size and power which, under King's command, was relentlessly destroying the Japanese fleet, grinding down the German submarine threat, and providing awesome firepower and massive amphibious support for every landing operation from North Africa to Sicily, Italy, and France on one side of the world and from Guadalcanal to New Guinea, Tarawa, Saipan, Iwo Jima, and Okinawa on the other. As a second-level official, Forrestal was not a participant in shaping the grand strategy of the war, but later as Secretary of the Navy and Secretary of Defense, he inherited, along with other policy-makers in the Truman administration, the consequences.

FDR developed grand strategy and ran the war directly through his military chiefs, a condition which demanded considerable forbearance on the part of his Secretaries of War and Navy. Henry Stimson, who possessed the far greater intellect and the more relevant experience, participated in strategy more fully than did Frank Knox, but neither man was treated as a major adviser on the conduct of the war nor regularly invited to the conferences with Churchill and Stalin. In general, this same derogation applied to the Secretary of State, Cordell Hull, and later to Edward Stettinius, for FDR never recognized the need to integrate military and foreign policy planning except in his own person, and his instinct from Pearl Harbor on was to separate winning the war from organizing the peace. He made himself the only nexus and quite unconsciously elevated fragmentation of policy advice to a first principle. This approach to managing the war was a natural extension of his approach to managing the domestic programs of the New Deal. Stimson urged the President to establish an inner War Cabinet comprising his principal civilian advisers, but FDR rejected the idea and "only reluctantly" yielded to British pressure for an analogous organization in the military field, i.e., the Joint Chiefs of Staff.[2]

By the time Forrestal had become a principal player in policy-making, the basic strategy of the war had long since been set and the military outcome was visible in broad outline. What remained entirely murky, however, was the shape of the peace for which so much blood and treasure had been, and was being, expended. Much of the uncertainty was the product of unresolved tension—indeed direct conflict—between Europe's instinctive preference for solutions based on regional "spheres of influence" and America's deep-seated distrust of these, combined with an idealistic faith in a universal system of collective security. Woodrow Wilson had perceived the League of Nations as "an arrangement which will disentangle all the alliances in the world"—by which he meant a single political mechanism representing all of mankind and capable of resolving all international disputes, an organization that would end the need for secret treaties and other exclusionary arrangements.[3]

The Wilsonian ideal was deeply imbedded in the American psyche. Despite disillusionment with the harsh European attitude toward defeated Germany after World War I, as expressed in the punitive terms of the Treaty of Versailles, and despite their own refusal to join the League of Nations, American leaders and followers alike held implicitly, through the interwar decades, to Wilson's vision of how the world ought to be—must be—organized to assure the preservation of democracy. FDR was a Wilsonian in his bones, therefore ever alert to oppose or condemn any proposal that threatened to carve up the world. There was an economic as well as a political aspect to this position, for it was another firm American conviction that the prosperity of the U.S. economy depended on free access to world markets without any restrictions.

In the face of strongly asserted claims by Churchill and Stalin for special arrangements in particular regions—e.g., for dominant Soviet influence in Eastern Europe to provide a buffer zone against future invasions, for dominant British influence in Greece and other points in southern and central Europe to protect the lifeline of empire through the Mediterranean—FDR adopted a supple strategy of postponement, a determined effort to resist all political and territorial claims until the war was over. By skill and Dutch stubbornness he succeeded in deflecting the most consequential of these during most of the war, but the quest was impossibly idealistic and ultimately overtaken by events. It was also vulnerable to the charge of hypocrisy, for American political reality required clear-cut American dominance in several places—like the Panama Canal, the whole of the Western Hemisphere, and later the Pacific islands bloodily wrested from the Japanese. Were these not U.S. ''spheres of influence''? When FDR died in April 1945, the strategy of postponement was visibly collapsing.

TO AVOID A SEPARATE PEACE

WHEN HITLER attacked Russia on June 22, 1941, Washington immediately feared that Britain, suffering defeats in the Middle East and beleaguered in its home island, would recognize Stalin's claim to the Baltic States and eastern Poland (as provided in the 1939 Nazi-Soviet Pact) in exchange for Soviet assurances of predominant British influence in Greece and Turkey. FDR's first response was to draw Churchill into a meeting at sea, in Placentia Bay off Newfoundland (on August 12), out of which came the Atlantic Charter. Probably the most compelling statement of the war, it enunciated ''certain common principles'' on which the Anglo-American democracies ''base their hopes for a better future for the world.'' The key passages were these: ''They [U.S. and British governments] desire to see no territorial changes that do not accord with the freely expressed wishes of the people concerned,'' and ''They respect the right of all peoples to choose the form of government under which they will live.''[4] The Atlantic Charter was intended, and it served, as a beacon of hope in a darkened world, but it was also intended by FDR to create obstacles to a British-Russian ''spheres of interest'' deal. Although Churchill assured the House of Commons that the document did not apply to ''internal imperial questions,'' the British followed FDR's lead until late in the war.[5]

A British-Soviet deal was not, however, FDR's only perceived obstacle to a postwar peace based on Wilsonian principles. More troubling was the possibility that the Soviets, who were bearing alone and unsuccessfully the terrible weight of Hitler's demonic assault, and who suspected the Anglo-Americans of a readiness to let Germany and Russia bleed each other to death, would seek a separate peace with Hitler. Lend-Lease, which was being rushed unconditionally to the Soviets, was a useful but insufficient weapon to prevent such an outcome. Only the opening of a powerful second front in Western Europe—a massive Anglo-American attack through France or the Low Countries—held out the hope of convincing Stalin that his allies were reliable and thus of forestalling Soviet negotiations with Germany. But the obstacles to an early assault on Hitler's formidable West Wall were daunting.

In the spring of 1942, and for the first and only time in the war, FDR edged toward a ''spheres-of-influence'' arrangement for managing the postwar world. In the context of desperate military situations in the Pacific and on the Russian front, and with Britain continuing to take punishment from heavy German bomber attacks, he disclosed his thinking to the Soviet Foreign Minister, Vyacheslav Molotov, at the White House. The League of Nations was defunct, he told Molotov. The need now was to bring the Soviet Union into full partnership with the Anglo-Americans and to add China. The Big Four must be jointly responsible for dealing with the defeated Axis powers, and each would also have a regional responsibility for postwar security in its area of primary interest. This formulation foreshadowed the "two-tier" structure of the United Nations—that is, a General Assembly representing all nations, but a Security Council dominated by the major powers who were charged with acting together to keep the peace. FDR recognized the practical necessity for such a plan, but his immediate aim in 1942 was to keep Russia from flirting with a separate peace by offering Stalin a prominent role in postwar arrangements. At the same time, however, he was not prepared to confront publicly the deep-seated American antipathy to "spheres of influence." Fighting and not losing the war were uppermost in his mind.[6]

Molotov was interested in hearing these ideas for the postwar world, but wanted an answer to the more immediate Soviet concern: What was the President's position on a second front? FDR was almost too ready with an answer. He told Molotov he could inform his government it could expect a second front "this year."[7] General Marshall, who was sitting near the President, was visibly disturbed by the specificity of this commitment. The General had recently proposed to the British a massive assault across the English Channel, but the planning date was April 1943. He had also discussed the possibility of a much smaller, contingent operation in 1942, but this was to be seriously considered only if the Soviets were facing imminent collapse or, conversely, if the German defenses in Western Europe were dramatically weakened by a major shift of Hitler's divisions to the Russian front.[8] Informed of FDR's consequential pledge to Molotov, Churchill immediately sent Lord Louis Mountbatten, the adventurous chief of the British Commandos, to Washington to explain the dire problems of a cross-channel attack in 1942. When Mountbatten reported that FDR was nevertheless considering a "sacrificial landing" in 1942 if Russia was nearing collapse, the Prime Minister himself enplaned for Washington to reiterate Britain's implacable opposition.[9]

British reluctance to undertake a direct assault on Hitler's West Wall was decisively shaped by harrowing memories of losses in World War I, when bloodbaths in France and on the fields of Flanders had carried off the flower of an entire generation. But England's opposition to a cross-channel attack in 1942 was also based on military realities and was far sounder than the American impetuousness. More than the insufficient time remaining to assemble the forces and mount the operation, the danger lay in the acute shortage of war production to accommodate all the fighting fronts and in the undeniable fact that the American army was wholly untried in battle (except for those units, now destroyed or captured, which had been overrun by the Japanese in the Philippines and elsewhere). The subsequent performance of American forces in the North African fighting (characterized by courage and determination, but also by the mistakes and confusion typical of green troops) confirmed the rightness of British caution. Almost certainly, an attempt at large-scale invasion of Western Europe in 1942 would have been a military disaster, with profound consequences for the course and outcome of the war.[10]

With a second front foreclosed in 1942, FDR and Churchill agreed to an invasion of North Africa in November. Both leaders felt the need to regain the strategic initiative in the war, and this led logically to consideration of military operations that would damage Hitler without the risks of an unprepared assault on his central citadel. FDR was thus won over to Churchill's strong preference for a "peripheral" strategy, to the frustration of U.S. military leaders and the Soviet dictator.

Stalin was not mollified by the North African alternative, saying to Churchill in July, "I state most emphatically that the Soviet Government cannot tolerate the Second Front in Europe being postponed until 1943."[11] Invited to the next conference, at Casablanca in January 1943, he decided to stay home to make the most of his position as injured party. Once again Churchill deflected Marshall's insistence that the leaders must now agree to a major assault on the central citadel. The British leader was eager to exploit the success in North Africa by attacking Sicily, perhaps Italy, and elsewhere along what he liked to call the "soft underbelly of the Hitler crocodile." And the British were formidable in debate and united in their positions, as the Americans were not. Marshall stood firmly for a "Germany First" strategy, while King argued for more resources for offensives against the Japanese, and General Henry "Hap" Arnold was primarily interested in mounting a massive bombing offensive against Germany from England. FDR was intrigued by Churchill's proposals, for they seemed to offer the prospect of quick, moderately cheap victories in the Mediterranean, including the possibility of knocking Italy out of the war. So once again, the British view prevailed. Marshall had to be content with a firm commitment to build up the Allied base in England for a cross-channel invasion by May 1944.[12]

Realizing, however, that this further postponement of the second front would deepen Stalin's suspicions of Anglo-American intentions, FDR cast about for some gesture of reassurance and hit upon a fateful formula. At the final press conference in Casablanca (January 24) and speaking extemporaneously, he suddenly announced the doctrine of "unconditional surrender,'' saying peace could come to the world only through the total elimination of German and Japanese war power. Churchill was taken by surprise and later persuaded FDR that the idea should not apply to Italy, but the complicating doctrine was now embedded as an integral element of Allied strategy. There is little doubt that FDR's purpose was essentially tactical and that he did not think through the long-term implications. He wanted to reassure Stalin and at the same time bind Churchill with a single message: Despite further delay in the formation of a second front, the Anglo-Americans would fight until Germany was crushed; there would be no separate peace in the West.[13]

TIME RUNS OUT

B UT TIME had run out on the strategy of postponement. What rendered it henceforward without basis in reality was the Russian victory at Stalingrad in February of 1943, just a month after the Casablanca Conference. This was a basic turning point not only in the war, but also for the whole history of the postwar period. The exceedingly bitter fighting, begun in November, ended in the decimation of twenty-two German divisions and the taking of 80,000 German prisoners. Thereafter the Red Army was on the offensive and would not be contained within its own borders while waiting for the Anglo-Americans to reestablish their forces in Western Europe. It would occupy Eastern Europe. But how much farther west would Soviet power be extended? Where would the Anglo-American and Russian armies meet? What would be the political conditions in Germany and elsewhere in Europe when they met? What would be the state of Big Three relations? These now became the urgent questions.[14]

According to the British Foreign Secretary, Anthony Eden, FDR now realized the implications of the new situation and in private talks with Eden came to the same position Churchill had reached in 1942: Russia could no longer be denied the Baltic States, or a readjustment of the Soviet-Polish border westward to the so-called Curzon Line, or the whole of East Prussia. The still prospective Anglo-American cross-channel assault at Normandy had become part of a race for Berlin and the postwar control of Germany.[15]

Yet after grasping these hard new realities, FDR did nothing to adjust U.S. policy either privately or publicly. Meeting Stalin for the first time at the Teheran Conference in November 1943, he did not raise the question of U.S. economic assistance as a diplomatic lever with which to bargain for Soviet adherence to democratic concepts in Eastern Europe. He agreed, he said, that Russia was entitled to security on her southern border, but added quixotically that, owing to the fact of 7 million Americans of Polish extraction, he could not participate in any decision on the subject of Polish boundary changes. Nor did he make any effort to prepare American public opinion to face the new realities. The Atlantic Charter and the proposed United Nations remained the dominant public elements of his Wilsonian approach.[16]

Meanwhile, Stalin's position on Eastern Europe was hardening. He strongly supported the Lublin Poles against the London Poles, and obdurately insisted that the latter group come to terms with the former if it expected to have any role in a future Polish government.[17] In the summer of 1944, tensions between Russia and the Anglo-Americans were further aggravated when the Warsaw underground partisans, mainly loyal to the London Poles, saw an opportunity to rise up and destroy their Nazi occupiers. Soon the city was engulfed in a bitter street-to-street, house-to-house battle, but the Germans sent in reinforcements, and the situation of the underground grew desperate. American and British cargo aircraft flew numerous missions from bases in Italy to airdrop food and ammunition to the insurgents, but much of this material was captured by the Germans. FDR and Churchill appealed to Stalin for urgent help, but the dictator refused to allow American or British use of air bases in the Ukraine or to send in a Russian army that was poised on the Polish frontier. As James MacGregor Burns later described Stalin's purpose, "He did not propose to liberate Warsaw from the Nazis only to leave it in the hands of bourgeois Poles who were pawns of London and Washington."[18] By the end of September the uprising was crushed and a quarter of a million Poles were dead. Bitter exchanges between FDR and Stalin followed, but they altered nothing. They did underline the reality that politics—the quest for security and advantage—would not wait until the war was over.

The matter was further complicated by the American presidential election. Roosevelt, now campaigning for a fourth term in the White House, was promising the Polish-American Congress that the principles of the Atlantic Charter would prevail and that the integrity of Poland in particular would be protected.[19]

But the political-military landscape was being transformed with every passing day. On October 1, 1944, Finland and Bulgaria quit the Axis and Russian forces occupied both countries. Meanwhile, the Red Army was overrunning Estonia, Latvia, and Lithuania and advancing through Hungary and Yugoslavia to the borders of Greece and Turkey. British forces had landed in Greece. Churchill was suddenly so concerned about the control of southeastern Europe that he insisted on another Big Three conference immediately, but for FDR, in the middle of a presidential campaign, this was a practical impossibility. The result was that Churchill met Stalin in Moscow alone, with Ambassador Harriman sitting in as the U.S. observer. Churchill was playing a close game of realpolitik, aimed at avoiding a British-Soviet collision in the Balkans. Meeting with Stalin, he pushed across the table a single half sheet of paper with a stark, handwritten list giving Russia 90 percent predominance in Romania and 75 percent in Bulgaria, Britain 90 percent in Greece, and dividing Yugoslavia and Hungary fifty-fifty between Russia and the West.[20] Stalin paused only for a moment, then made a large tick on the paper with a blue pencil and passed it back to Churchill. The paper lay on the table between them during a long silence. Then Churchill said: "Might it not be thought rather cynical if it seemed we had disposed of these issues, so fateful to millions of people, in such an offhand manner?" He proposed to burn the paper. "No, you keep it," said Stalin.[21]

Confronted by this widening gap between his Wilsonian vision and the ignoble realities of power and interest, FDR "retreated into a protective ambivalence, waiting for something to turn up."[22] But it was becoming apparent that the absence of Big Three agreement on the shape of the postwar world might imperil American public support for the United Nations, the instrument by which FDR hoped to cushion and contain conflicting purposes and unruly forces. Like Wilson, who had bet everything on the League of Nations, FDR was in danger of having put the cart before the horse. Others saw this danger. Senator Arthur Vandenberg made a speech in January 1945 calling for an immediate "hard-and-fast treaty between the major allies" regarding postwar Germany, arguing that such a treaty would put an end to legitimate Russian concerns about the security of her European border and would thus invalidate Stalin's justifications for unilateral action in Eastern Europe.[23] Walter Lippmann hailed the speech because "Senator Vandenberg's proposal . . . would end the policy of postponement and thus restore American influence in the settlement of Europe."[24] *Life* magazine strongly supported the proposal in an editorial (January 23, 1945), as did John Foster Dulles, the leading Republican adviser on foreign policy. FDR asked for copies of the Vandenberg speech and carried them to Yalta, but there is no evidence he made any use of them. Similarly did he reject the key point in a State Department paper entitled "The Declaration on Liberated Europe" which called for the creation of a High Commission composed of Big Three representatives to "enforce" the principles of the Atlantic Charter in postwar Europe.[25]

YALTA

IN RAPIDLY failing health, FDR concentrated at Yalta on three points: Poland, Soviet participation in the Pacific War, and establishing the United Nations organization. But it was not only on the Polish question that Stalin now held the whip hand. On the question of Soviet intervention in the war against Japan, he was similarly in the catbird seat. U.S. military planners believed the Pacific War would last for eighteen months after Germany surrendered, even with large-scale Soviet participation. Without Soviet intervention to engage the 2 million Japanese troops in Manchuria, the war might last indefinitely, with unbearable losses. Because American development of the atomic bomb was not at this time sufficiently advanced to carry weight in U.S. military calculations, large-scale Soviet help was considered an imperative.[26]

Thus at Yalta the tables were turned. Stalin had his allies just where they had had him for three years. As had been the case with their planning for their reentry onto the Continent, he could arrange the timing and scale of his participation in the Pacific War to suit Soviet advantage.

On Poland, Stalin was willing to accommodate Anglo-American concerns about democracy and self-determination with words, but accepting verbal formulas did not alter his determination to achieve absolute control on Soviet terms. The final agreement, however, was even bleaker than the Americans had expected. Instead of a coalition government of London and Lublin Poles, Stalin agreed only to a "reorganization" of the Lublin government followed by "free elections," but with only the vaguest provisions for bringing these about. When Admiral Leahy saw the compromise formula, he said, "Mr. President, this is so elastic that the Russians can stretch it all the way from Yalta to Washington without technically breaking it." FDR replied, "I know, Bill—I know it. But it's the best I can do for Poland at this time."[27]

Roosevelt had reached the limits of his physical strength and his bargaining power. Forced to accept a spheres-of-influence arrangement in Eastern Europe by the inexorable fact of Soviet power, he continued to find it politically too dangerous to acknowledge the fact publicly—even as he strove to create a United Nations whose peacekeeping responsibilities would have to be based on the cooperation of those who possessed real power. The price of Soviet cooperation on the U.N. was Western accommodation to unpalatable aspects of the Soviet system, but without Soviet cooperation the new world organization could not be brought into being. Beset by the whir of contradictions and his own physical exhaustion, FDR sought to buy time with public opinion at home while he brought the German and Japanese wars to a successful close. Thereafter, as he planned it, he would "deal creatively" with the basic contradictions in his foreign policy.[28] But February 1945, he judged, was not a time to practice candor with the American people. In his report to Congress on the Yalta Conference, he thus chose to finesse the complicated truth. "The Crimea Conference," he said, "ought to spell the end of the system of unilateral action, the exclusive alliances, the spheres of influence, the balance of power, and all the other expedients that have been tried for centuries—and have always failed.''[29]

Reflecting after the war, Henry L. Stimson thought FDR's policy was ''often either unknown or not clear to those who had to execute it''; indeed major aspects of it ''seemed self-contradictory.'' He concluded that the President as a wartime leader ''proved himself as good as one man could be—but one man was not enough to keep track of so vast an undertaking.''[30]

CHAPTER 19

★ ★ ★

No Return to
Private Life

As the war came to an end, the bankers and lawyers and businessmen who had signed on for the duration began to leave government in droves. Their war experience, in Washington or elsewhere,
had enlarged their lives, infused them with a deeper appreciation for the
strength, skill, and patriotism of the American nation. All of this had left
an indelible impression. Now, however, they were anxious to return to
more normal pursuits and to financial opportunities beyond the strictures
of government salaries. The Wall Street group—Stimson, Lovett, McCloy,
Gates, Lewis Strauss, Hensel, et al.—men who were essentially nonpolitical, who had come to make their talented contribution in time of national
crisis—were now ready to depart, in the best tradition of the Eastern Establishment. The venerable Stimson retired at the end of September 1945,
and Forrestal's closest wartime collaborators, Lovett and McCloy, followed
soon afterward.

Forrestal talked continuously about his own plans to leave, took steps to
recover the Beekman Place house from a tenant, and warned his family
they would be back in New York by the end of 1945. At the persistent
urging of Cass Canfield, the editor of Harper and Brothers (who had been
after him since 1940), he reluctantly agreed to write a book about his public
service, at the same time expressing doubts that he had anything special to
say or was sufficiently articulate to make it interesting. Having signed the
contract, he reflected his continued ambivalence in a satirical note to Canfield, saying "I had thought I might gain greater distinction by being one
of the few who do not write one."[1] Forrestal directed Eugene Duffield to
draft an outline, but he did not pursue the matter further and the proposed
book was never written.[2]

PUBLISHING AND POLITICS

WHAT WOULD Forrestal do after he left? He was, he told friends, seriously interested in publishing a newspaper or founding an American magazine of political commentary based on the model of *The Economist* of London, which he greatly admired. Various friends in New York, including Clarence Dillon, Ferdinand Eberstadt, and Paul Shields, appeared willing, even eager, to raise the necessary money and install Forrestal as the directing head.

The first indication that his boyhood penchant for journalism—on the Beacon *Journal* and the *Daily Princetonian*—was still a lively interest had come in the late 1930s, when he persuaded his partners at Dillon, Read to buy a 51 percent interest in the Seattle *Times,* a daily then wholly owned by a well-known newspaper family named Ridder. As it turned out, the banking firm did very little to develop this investment, in large part because Forrestal's departure for Washington left its supervision in the hands of partners who lacked a feel for newspapering. But the Seattle property was still in the investment portfolio in late 1945 when Forrestal talked to Clarence Dillon about personally buying a controlling interest. His old partners were reportedly enthusiastic, the Ridders were agreeable, and a price satisfactory to all parties appeared to be negotiable. Then Forrestal lost interest. The specific reasons adduced were his realization, on reflection, that he had no desire to live in Seattle or to run a newspaper with only regional influence. But these seemed to mask a deep reluctance to leave government.[3]

The ambivalent search for a power base outside government nevertheless continued. Paul Nitze thought the *Wall Street Journal* a more suitable vehicle for Forrestal's talents and interests, and, with the Secretary's consent, offered to explore the possibility, but the *Journal* proved to be not for sale.[4] The Manchester *Union Leader,* then owned by the Frank Knox estate, was definitely on the block and came to the attention of Forrestal and his financial backers. They offered $7 million, but were outbid by William Loeb, an extremely conservative Republican who proceeded to turn it into a powerful instrument of right-wing politics in northern New England. One of Forrestal's purposes in the sporadic quest for a publishing property was apparently to find an appropriate place for his favorite editor, Palmer Hoyt, of the Denver *Post.* Hoyt's paper too came up for sale, but changed hands before Forrestal could make up his mind. In early 1947, again at Forrestal's request, John McCone (a California businessman who was later Under Secretary of the Air Force and Director of the CIA) negotiated a deal to purchase the San Francisco *Chronicle* and brought the final contract papers to Washington for him to sign. It was a done deal at an acceptable price, but once again Forrestal turned away at the point of decision.[5]

During this same general time period (1946 and early 1947) Henry Luce told Eliot Janeway that Joseph Kennedy was "dickering to buy Time Inc." and asked his advice. On several occasions Luce entertained the idea of selling his publishing empire, but, somewhat like Forrestal, he was ambivalent. Janeway, who wrote a column for *Fortune* magazine and was personally close to Luce, advised him strongly against selling to Kennedy, telling him Kennedy would almost certainly "destroy" everything distinctive that Luce had achieved in the building of *Time, Life*, and *Fortune*. He also told Luce that Forrestal "might" be an interested buyer, and they agreed he would be preferable to Kennedy. Janeway then went to Forrestal with the word that Luce seemed open to a bid, making the argument that the influential command post at Time Inc. would combine the best features of the Senate and the Cabinet. He added that Luce was anxious to drop his wife, Clare Boothe Luce (playwright, congresswoman, intellectual gadfly, and later ambassador to Italy), and as she was likely to be "avaricious," the publisher would welcome a healthy infusion of capital. Whether Forrestal gave the matter serious consideration or came close to making a bid is not known. Although Luce had not settled on a specific asking price for his company, it would have been many times larger than the sum required to buy any of the newspapers Forrestal had previously considered. What is known is that Forrestal never made a bid and Luce never sold to anyone, nor did he divorce his wife. According to Janeway, she was asking $14 million, including a large share of Time Inc. stock, and "at that price, Luce decided to stay married."[6]

Forrestal also flirted with elective office during this period, but, like his approach to publishing, it came to nothing, primarily because he could not make up his mind. Should he remain in the Executive Branch, or was a seat in the Senate a better place from which to shape public attitudes and official policies in support of what he saw as the need for a greatly expanded American role in world affairs? In the spring of 1946, frequent press stories, editorials, and columns by Arthur Krock argued that he would make an excellent governor or senator from New York.[7] Over dinner, Justice Douglas expressed confidence that Forrestal could win either nomination and urged him to take a definite stand.[8] His acknowledgment of these possibilities was carefully noncommittal, but friends were convinced he was genuinely interested, and they were ready to help. Clarence Dillon, intrigued by the role of political kingmaker, urged his former protégé to take the plunge and promised to raise the required campaign funds.[9]

On reflection, the Senate seemed the more appropriate place, as it offered greater scope for Forrestal's compelling interest in world affairs and also a better chance for electoral victory. Eliot Janeway pressed him to run, warning him that "the rule in politics is up or out . . . unless you have a fixed base for life, like a seat on the Supreme Court. A Cabinet position is not a power base . . . all you can be in the Cabinet is a voice without a vote . . . a second-class citizen with a chauffeured limousine existing at the President's pleasure."[10] This rationale was persuasive to a man keenly attuned to the realities of power, but Forrestal was characteristically pessimistic about his chances to win elective office. "I'm a lapsed Catholic," he told close friends in New York, "who also married a divorced woman. Politically, I'm dead." Janeway told him this judgment was just plain wrong. American life had moved into a new era, and Forrestal was a distinguished hero of the war: "Hell, you have made monumental contributions to the greatest military victory in American history. You are one of the commanding figures in the world today." No outdated religious prejudices could stand against such facts or the reputation for energy, integrity, and brilliance they supported, Janeway argued. Forrestal had become a public man. Elective office was the logical next step. It was within reach. "You're certainly not going back to the basement in Nassau Street, for Christ's sake."[11]

When Forrestal continued to worry about the attitude of the Catholic Church, Janeway advised him to discuss the matter directly with Francis Cardinal Spellman, the acknowledged arbiter of Democratic politics in New York. Forrestal did so. Spellman could not publicly endorse a lapsed Catholic, but he admired Forrestal's world views, including his staunch anti-Communism, and privately encouraged him to make the Senate race, giving assurances that there would be no public sniping from the Church. Spellman's promise of public neutrality removed what seemed the only major obstacle to a highly promising campaign, but once more Forrestal's innate caution or his inability to seize and exploit an inherently transient opportunity forfeited the chance, a consequence which vexed Janeway: "He couldn't stand up and he couldn't sit down. He couldn't leave the Navy Department and he couldn't see where he was going from it."[12]

In retrospect, it seems fairer to say that these excursions to find a new forum for his self-expression were essentially subconscious tests to determine where his compelling concerns and interests really lay. Each time he considered leaving, he seemed to conclude that his existing power base in the Executive Branch was the best available place from which to bring about changes in the structure and procedures of the U.S. government which he believed to be urgently necessary if the survival and success of the nation were to be assured in the postwar period. There was also the matter of institutional loyalty. Michael Forrestal thought the unexpected emergence of the "military unification" issue immediately after the war was a major factor in his father's decision to stay in government in 1945 and 1946. Truman's sudden push for a single defense department caught the navy off guard, and Forrestal, who thought the navy "politically dumb" and thus ill equipped to defend its independence, concluded that he must stay and help. In this, Michael believed, "he was a victim of his stupid Irish loyalty."[13]

CATALYST FOR GOVERNMENT REFORM

IT IS LIKELY, despite the appearance of continuing ambivalence through early 1947, that Forrestal's true convictions and intentions were revealed in a conversation with John J. McCloy in late 1945. McCloy, who was himself departing, spent a long evening with Forrestal, arguing that wartime officials ought to get out—for the sake of the nation as well as themselves. They were tired, in need of rest and change, and they were not indispensable. Able men were available to take their places. In the fullness of time, they might return for further service (McCloy returned twice, as president of the World Bank in 1947 and as High Commissioner for Germany in 1949). Forrestal listened intently and felt the weight of his friend's argument, but seemed intellectually and emotionally torn. Given the grave dangers and instabilities that loomed ahead in the world, how was the public to be educated to the need for America to shoulder major responsibility for rebuilding and then sustaining a shattered international system? Of even greater urgency, how was the U.S. government to be restructured to meet the unprecedented new demands on it? To Forrestal, it was "miraculous" that the "antique" system worked at all, so devoid was it of the means to assure continuity, coordination, and a permanent staff of high quality. McCloy agreed that vast problems remained to be tackled, but felt these were tasks—at least in the immediate future—for new and fresher men. His view seemed to reflect both a lesser interest than Forrestal's in questions of structure and process and a greater faith in the nation's natural ability to bring forth able and devoted men for government service. At the end of their talk, Forrestal briefly put his head in his hands and said with emotion: "Jack, I wish I could see it the way you do. But I can't, I just can't."[14]

Forrestal was acutely aware of the tremendous amount of wasted motion in the workings of the American government, the disordered verbosity of Cabinet discussions and the lack of any reliable mechanism for assuring the accurate and timely carrying through of presidential decisions where the coordination of several departments was required. He feared that even those effective, ad hoc instrumentalities, like the State-War-Navy Coordinating Committee (SWNCC) and the Joint Chiefs of Staff might well be allowed to lapse in the postwar period, for he vividly recalled how casually and inadvertently they had come into being—especially in the case of the JCS.

When Churchill arrived in Washington for critical consultations immediately after Pearl Harbor (for the first meeting between the two leaders
since America had come fully into the war) the British were flabbergasted
at the looseness of the American command arrangements, especially at
FDR's habit of dealing informally and often separately with his military
chiefs. "There are no regular meetings of their Chiefs of Staff," an astonished Field Marshal Sir John Dill wrote home to General Sir Alan Brooke,
"and if they do meet there is no secretariat to record their proceedings."
The President "just sees the Chiefs of Staff at odd times and again no
record. There is no such thing as a Cabinet meeting. The whole organization belongs to the days of George Washington." At Churchill's urging,
but without embarrassment, FDR created on the spot the U.S. Joint Chiefs
of Staff as a counterpart to the British triumvirate of military chiefs for
land, sea, and air. Not having an exact opposite number for the Chief of
the RAF, he merely added General Arnold, the senior army air forces
officer within the War Department. The word "joint" was devised to denote the coordination of military leaders within one country, while the
word "combined" was used to denote the British and American military
chiefs acting together. Thus the coming into existence of the wartime Joint
Chiefs of Staff and Combined Chiefs of Staff.[15] Forrestal was certain the
nation could no longer rely on such serendipity.

As a result of his war experience, he had developed a shining admiration
for the British system of government and for the quality of its permanent
civil servants. He especially envied the smooth way in which British Cabinet decisions were translated into thoroughly coordinated and timely executive actions. After reading the collected works of Walter Bagehot,
especially his comparative analysis of the British and American systems,
he ended up agreeing with Bagehot that the former was clearly superior in
providing institutional continuity, planning, and coordination. He absorbed
the slender volume *Government Control in War* by Lord Hankey, who had
served as Cabinet Secretary from 1912 until just before World War II.
Hankey devised and ran the coordinating mechanism that underpinned the
inner War Cabinet in World War I, which evolved into the Committee on
Imperial Defence (CID) in World War II. Forrestal concluded that the
urgent need in Washington was for a similar Cabinet Secretariat to "help
the President keep track of discussions and decisions" which were then
handed off to particular departments or agencies for implementation. He
began a campaign with President Truman and his Cabinet colleagues for
"an American Hankey."[16]

The idea encountered a good deal of inertial resistance and led to the
suspicion among several of Truman's cronies that this was a move designed
to enhance Forrestal's own power. However, according to Clinton Anderson, the Secretary of Agriculture, Truman saw the logic and merit of the

proposal and was moving toward appointment of Forrestal's candidate for the job, Averell Harriman, when he was faced with a crisis over Henry Wallace and the sudden need to replace him as Secretary of Commerce. He appointed Harriman. In the absence of a Harriman-Hankey, Forrestal suggested that the task of government-wide coordination be given to the Director of the Budget, who would "pedal his bike from department to department to make sure that what we decide is acted upon." In 1991, the U.S. government had not yet established a Cabinet secretariat, but the essential tasks of coordination were being performed by a combination of the Chief of Staff to the President and the Office of Management and Budget (successor to the Bureau of the Budget). While these arrangements represented a considerable advance in efficiency since 1945, they were far more politicized than the kind of secretariat, manned by the elite of a disinterested and permanent civil service, that Forrestal (and Hankey) had in mind.[17]

In June 1946, Forrestal sent Struve Hensel to London to study the British system firsthand, giving special attention to the Committee on Imperial Defense, which the Secretary perceived as the analogue to the National Security Council he and Eberstadt were putting forward as an alternative to the structural "unification" of the army and navy proposed by the War Department. Hensel's report confirmed the virtues of the CID and its able secretariat, but found that their success really depended on the whole elite tier of the British civil service (called the Administrative Class and numbering about 2,000). The high quality and homogeneity of this group, Hensel thought, was the real key to the success of the British system: "They think alike, dress alike . . . and regard themselves as a monastic group . . . definitely set apart and consecrated to the duty of seeing to it that the British Government runs smoothly." Their morale and sense of purpose were high because they occupied positions of genuine responsibility (like departmental Assistant Secretary) and could rise even higher (to Under Secretary or Permanent Secretary). They were well paid and "respected and honored in their communities."[18]

Forrestal agreed wholeheartedly with Hensel's conclusions and made them the basis for his own recommendation that the U.S. government create a similar group of high-level career managers, provided with sufficient incentives to attract first-rate college graduates who might otherwise choose business or law. About this same time, he wrote to William O. Douglas, "You and I share the belief that things have to be run, for good or ill, by men. They determine the fate of any organization."[19] In 1949, the Commission on Reorganization in the Executive Branch—generally known as the Hoover Commission, in whose creation Forrestal was a moving force—endorsed the idea, and Congress shortly thereafter translated it into law. This provided for three "supergrades" (GS-16, GS-17, GS-18) above the regular civil service ranks, and these remain a central feature of the government salary structure. Forrestal also pressed, unsuccessfully, for the appointment of a Permanent Under Secretary in each major department.

A recurring theme throughout Forrestal's public life was that the official in Washington was presented with the "impossible" dual task of "doing a good job and convincing Congress and the people that a good job was being done."[20] His proposed solution, also adapted from the British system, was to separate the two requirements: Cabinet members and other politically appointed department heads would deal with Congress and the press and provide political guidance to the career managers (would "tell the civil service what the public will not stand"); then the elite apolitical managers would administer the government.[21] One of Forrestal's principal purposes in proposing this kind of separation was to protect career managers from the "irrational gauntlet" of congressional pressures and also from direct exposure to the press. In his view, such protection was essential to sound and efficient administration. It was a basic feature of the British system, but Hensel thought it a "political question" for the American system. Administratively, the idea was entirely practical, "But whether the American people would accept a government group insulated against political reprisals at the polls is problematical."[22]

In another instance where his enthusiasm for British custom ran hard against the grain of the American system, Forrestal proposed in 1946 a scheme, in effect, to co-opt the American press. "The American press should be an instrument of our foreign policy, just as is the British press. And this doesn't involve government control or telling them what they should write, but rather giving them the opportunity to write on the basis of an informed understanding of our policies and problems."[23] To this end, he urged Secretary of State Byrnes to arrange regular and frequent briefings for selected "responsible journalists," including Henry Luce, Palmer Hoyt, Cyrus L. Sulzberger, Arthur Krock, Robert McLean (Associated Press), and Paul Smith (San Francisco *Chronicle*). This was an idea inimical to the constitutional guarantee of a free press aimed at making the Fourth Estate a member of the government team, and it was soon denounced as "the thin end of a totalitarian wedge." It would seem that this lapse of proportion and good judgment was a product of Forrestal's passion for orderliness and efficiency, and perhaps of a momentary hubris. It occurred at the highwater mark of his postwar self-confidence and physical vitality. Jonathan Daniels remembered him at this time as taut, contained, totally assured, prowling his office in little leaps—like a panther.[24]

What this evidence makes clear is that by the end of the war, Forrestal had become a serious, even impassioned student and preceptor of government. He felt that major reorganization of its structure and its processes were essential to the nation's long-term survival. Therefore, whatever his flirtations with publishing ventures or elective office, and whatever his protestations to the contrary, there seemed little likelihood that he would leave the Executive Branch of his own volition. It had become the place in which he would make his contribution to the nation and work out his own destiny. There would be no return to private life. At the end of 1946, he sold his Beekman Place town house to the songwriter Irving Berlin.

———————— ★ ★ ★ ————————

CHAPTER 20

The Emerging
Anti-Communist Consensus

O NE OF TRUMAN'S first acts as President was to appoint James F. Byrnes to replace Edward R. Stettinius as Secretary of State. According to Clinton P. Anderson, Truman took "an immediate dislike" to Stettinius for his "movie star face and wavy gray hair,"[1] but there were, of course, other considerations. An internationalist from South Carolina, Jimmy Byrnes had been congressman, senator, and Supreme Court justice. Then, after Pearl Harbor, FDR had pulled him off the Court to become wartime director of Economic Stabilization and then of War Mobilization, in which capacities he became indispensable in the untying of myriad political and economic knots and was widely acknowledged as "assistant president for the homefront." Seasoned, self-assured, patient, and persistent, Byrnes prided himself as a "conciliator in the most strained and tangled situations."[2]

He had been, with Roosevelt's encouragement, a leading candidate for Vice President in 1944 and was embittered (though not at Truman) by FDR's ultimate selection of the relatively unknown and lackluster senator from Missouri. (FDR's apparent calculation was that Byrnes's Southern views on race would adversely affect the Democratic vote in large urban centers north of the Mason-Dixon.) In part to assuage that disappointment, FDR began grooming Byrnes for Secretary of State. He took him to the Yalta Conference, where he gave him a prominent role as presidential adviser, though on a carefully selected range of issues. Byrnes kept a separate shorthand record of the discussions in which he participated, then flew back to Washington in advance of the main party to brief congressional leaders and the press on what had transpired. Although he carried out this final assignment with energy and fidelity, his bitterness toward FDR was unappeased, and shortly thereafter he resigned and returned to South Carolina.[3]

Two months later Roosevelt died, leaving his successor wholly unprepared to deal with one of the great turning points in modern history. The new President, nearly overwhelmed by anxiety, was desperate to find someone trustworthy who knew "something about foreign affairs." Forrestal, who admired Byrnes and had worked well with him on procurement matters during the war, proposed that Byrnes be brought back. Truman quickly accepted the suggestion, and Forrestal dispatched a navy plane to South Carolina to ferry him to Washington. To Truman this seemed the ideal solution, most immediately because he thought Byrnes was the only man who could tell him precisely what had happened at Yalta. More basically, Truman wanted him in the Cabinet because of his high standing in the Congress and the country and because, in the absence of a sitting Vice President, the Secretary of State was first in the line of succession to the presidency.[4]

During his first months in office, the new President made no attempt to conceal his ignorance of foreign affairs or his discomfort with the entire process of international diplomacy; he wanted to delegate that whole area to a man of trusted competence, and Byrnes quickly obliged him by becoming de facto "assistant president for foreign affairs." For a while this arrangement seemed to work well, but there were inherently discordant elements in the new relationship, and they surfaced within a few months. Byrnes could not forget that he had been Truman's mentor in the Senate and that, except for the magisterial manipulations of FDR, might himself be sitting in the Oval Office. He tended to dominate Cabinet discussions and to treat the new President with an easy familiarity bordering on condescension. For Truman, as he settled into the office and gained confidence, Byrnes's style began to grate. A major factor in the developing tension was Byrnes's ingrained habit of operating largely on his own while taking a casual approach to keeping the President informed, especially when, as Secretary of State, he was away at international conferences for several weeks at a time.[5]

It turned out that Byrnes was a major, unwitting cause of the profound confusion that enveloped the agreements reached at Yalta and thus of the subsequent bitterness in American public opinion at what appeared to be gross Soviet violations of the Yalta accords.[6] Unlike the previous wartime summit conferences, the meeting in the Crimea was conducted under a complete news blackout. Thus, political Washington and the press were in a state of pent-up expectation when Byrnes returned ahead of FDR and convened a press conference at the White House. The East Wing conference room was filled to overflowing—"every newspaper man who could crawl, walk or run was there"—and in a virtuoso performance, he established his own credentials as a top FDR adviser at Yalta. He then went on to say that concrete decisions ("not merely declarations") had been reached, all of them consistent with American principles and war aims. The decision of greatest importance, he asserted, was the Declaration on

Liberated Europe, which he represented as a strong expression of Big Three solidarity and therefore an assurance that future governments in Eastern Europe would come to power only through the prescribed means of "free and unfettered elections." As to Poland, the first test case, Byrnes said the Big Three would exercise joint control "to preserve order until the provisional government is established and elections held." FDR's own subsequent report to the Congress on March 28 tended to confirm this optimistic and misleading assessment of both Yalta and of prospects for a cooperative postwar world. Satisfaction with Big Three cooperation was immediately reflected in American opinion polls—a jump from 46 to 71 percent—and in bipartisan political support. Leading Republicans, from Senator Vandenberg to former President Hoover, agreed that the Yalta accords provided "a strong foundation on which to rebuild the world." The problem was that Byrnes had the facts wrong.[7]

There is now convincing evidence that Byrnes was not informed of several crucial decisions—those involving Poland and U.S.-British concessions to the Soviet Union in the Far East—which were taken after he had left Yalta; also that he did not grasp the full complexity—the duality—of FDR's strategy.[8] The evidence further suggests that FDR deliberately blocked Byrnes's access to the meetings at which these decisions were taken, while at the same time using him as a credible lobbyist in Washington. FDR ended up with few illusions about the decisive nature of Soviet leverage in Eastern Europe and consequently understood that the West could obtain no more than a few cosmetic concessions with regard to "democratic" and "representative" governments in Poland, Romania, and elsewhere in that region. But he needed those crumbs to maintain domestic political support for his larger goal of establishing a new system of international security through the United Nations.[9]

Uppermost in FDR's mind at Yalta was the military equation—especially the great need, based on unanimous military judgment, to bring the Soviets into the Pacific War in full force at the right time. Byrnes was not privy to the military discussions, and he left Yalta before FDR, Churchill, and Stalin signed a top-secret protocol on the Far East that granted major concessions to the Soviets, but was *not* published with the other Yalta results.[10]*

---

*In exchange for a Soviet declaration of war on Japan (three months after the surrender of Germany), this agreement "handed over" to the U.S.S.R. the Kurile Islands (a chain of fog-enshrouded crags off the east coast of Siberia dominating the northern approaches to Japan); the southern half of Sakhalin Island (an offshoot of the Siberian coast north of the Kuriles), which Japan had wrested from Czarist Russia in 1904–5; lease of a naval base at Port Arthur in China; "pre-eminent" Soviet interest in the port of Dairen in China; protection for the status quo in Outer Mongolia; and "joint operation" (de facto Soviet control) of the Chinese East Manchurian Railroad.

Byrnes's press conference was thus seriously misleading. It asserted solid agreement on Poland when nothing existed beyond Stalin's promise of a nominal reorganization of his chosen instrument, the Communist Lublin Poles. It omitted any mention of the existence of secret Far Eastern concessions to the Soviets as the price for their promise to enter the war against Japan. On both counts Byrnes's deception was unwitting, and on both counts he served FDR's short-term purposes. At the same time, his press conference fastened on American public opinion a myth about Yalta which aggravated the already grave misunderstandings between the two governments and led to bitter Republican charges of a "sellout" when the discrepancies between myth and fact could no longer be disguised.

THE GUN BEHIND THE DOOR

TRUMAN AND BYRNES were gradually made aware of the discrepancies between the facts of Yalta and their presentation to the American people, but they then found themselves in a terrible bind. The myth of the Yalta accords had become a political fact in the American system. It was the standard against which Soviet behavior was being and henceforward would be judged. An attempt to set the record straight looked like political suicide, not only for themselves, but also for FDR's reputation and the future of the Democratic Party. They were political survivors, not martyrs. Meanwhile, they were also convinced Wilsonians, deeply committed to carrying forward the central elements of FDR's legacy—especially a comprehensive system of collective security under the United Nations.[11]

After Potsdam, the Pacific War having been successfully ended by the atomic bomb, they thought they saw a way out of the dilemma. Both men (but especially Byrnes) believed they could continue to pursue FDR's double game—that is, press the Soviets to adopt policies of reasonable restraint and accommodation in Eastern Europe, thereby retaining the vision of a stable, cooperative postwar peace, which was, in turn, the precondition for domestic support of the United Nations. The key to success, in their reckoning, was the U.S. monopoly of the atomic bomb, an instrument not available to FDR. It would not be blatantly brandished, rather it would be, as Byrnes thought of it, "the gun behind the door."[12] This was a high-risk venture, for FDR's double strategy had been embodied almost entirely in his own person; it had no institutional base. Moreover, it rested on a moral sophistication—a readiness to have normal relations with a tyrannical system on a live-and-let-live basis, which the American people might not accept. But Byrnes thought it an acceptable risk, especially as he believed the U.S. atomic monopoly would last for ten or twenty years.

In this belief he relied on Forrestal, whose approach to problems he admired and whose judgment he trusted. Forrestal rejected the idea of sharing any atomic secrets with the Russians and accepted the optimistic assumption of U.S. military men that the American atomic monopoly would last a long time—a view not shared by most scientists. With Byrnes he tended to discount the practical wisdom of scientists as a group and to regard them as ill equipped to participate in the formulation of high policy.[13] On the broader question of whether it made sense to pursue FDR's double strategy, the evidence suggests that Forrestal would have preferred to expose the full evil of the Soviet system and confront it directly, without any attempt to pretend that meaningful Big Three cooperation was possible. Byrnes, however, approached the Russians initially as he might approach a difficult Republican senator or governor, believing that a genuine effort to understand their point of view, plus sufficient give-and-take on both sides, plus the American atomic bomb monopoly, would yield a compromise solution acceptable to both parties. Forrestal, while supporting Byrnes's belief in "the gun behind the door," was at the same time using his own influence to push U.S. policy toward an open break with the Russians. During the fall of 1945, he argued forcefully in Cabinet meetings and in testimony before the House Naval Affairs Committee that Soviet Communism was implacably dedicated to the destruction of the capitalist system.[14]*

The first effort at treaty making (the London Conference in September 1945) broke down in wrangling over procedure, which in fact reflected fundamental disagreements over the political character of the governments in Eastern Europe. When Byrnes and British Foreign Secretary Ernest Bevin proposed a normalization of relations with Italy, Molotov promptly linked this with normalization for Hungary, Bulgaria, and Romania. The Anglo-Americans balked at such linkage, citing the Yalta requirement for "democratic" and "representative" governments. Unimpressed by this argument, Molotov tabled draft treaties for the three Eastern European countries which merely confirmed the armistice arrangements, leaving Soviet authorities and the Red Army in full control.[15]

To Byrnes's surprise and disappointment, the tactic of treating the atomic bomb as a real but unmentioned presence had no measurable effect on the Soviet bargaining position, though Molotov used several social occasions to allude to the subject with sarcasm in an apparent effort to get the issue out on the table. At one point he asked Byrnes if he had an atomic bomb in his "side pocket," to which Byrnes replied that Americans carry their artillery in the "hip pocket." On another occasion, responding to a toast by the Secretary of State, Molotov said, "Of course we all have to pay great attention to what Mr. Byrnes says because the United States are the only people who are making the atomic bomb." On the question of trea-

*For a full account of Forrestal's views on atomic energy policy, see Chapter 22.

ties, Byrnes sought to persuade Molotov that governments in the East could be "representative" without being "unfriendly" to the U.S.S.R., but there was no meeting of minds. Indeed, Molotov accused the West of a double standard—seeking to open up Eastern Europe while insisting on a free hand for the British in Greece and de facto Anglo-American control in Italy. A day or so later, he added the American monopoly in the occupation of Japan. Byrnes admitted privately to a member of the U.S. delegation that Molotov had a point with respect to Japan.[16]

After two weeks of inconclusive debate, Byrnes, the accomplished fixer and horse trader, decided it was time to deal, to salvage at least the façade of Big Three unity. "We have pushed these babies as far as they will go, and I think we better start thinking about compromise," he told John Foster Dulles, the Republican foreign policy spokesman (and later Secretary of State) who was, in the interests of bipartisanship, an adviser to the delegation. But Dulles replied that to compromise the principle of free choice in Eastern Europe would be the first step toward appeasement, and he threatened a public attack on the administration if Byrnes fell away from the requirements of the Declaration on Liberated Europe. Byrnes retreated. The London Conference ended without issuing a communiqué, which was an open admission of failure.[17]

The British came away sobered and worried by the impasse, which clearly pointed toward an East-West polarization and, as they saw it, a drive to extend Soviet influence in southern Europe and to cut across British lines of communication in the Mediterranean. The Russians left the conference puzzled by the West's double standard on spheres of influence and with a growing sense of their own isolation. Byrnes came away discouraged and angry at Molotov, whom he looked upon as a dangerous distorter of Stalin's policy. Remembering Yalta (although not accurately), he now saw Stalin as the key to saving the peace, to reversing the ominous trend in U.S.-Soviet relations. It was a curious reliance, but Byrnes was not alone; Truman also shared this view, as did others in the State Department.[18] Forrestal, inherently more skeptical and increasingly convinced that a major confrontation between irreconcilable political systems was unavoidable, saw in the failed London Conference the urgent need for America and the West to gird for a long struggle for survival. He was pessimistic about the future.[19]

In November he received a firsthand report from McCloy, who was just back from a round-the-world inspection trip. The postwar conditions of unemployment, malnutrition, social unrest, and political anarchy were "global," McCloy said, as prevalent in Asia as in Europe, and all aggravated by a "universal fear of the Russian colossus" and the "locust-like effects" in every territory occupied by the Red Army. America was still "one beacon of hope" to millions of people, McCloy found, but U.S.

policy was beset by confusion and an unchecked demobilization that was draining away the stabilizing factor of America's military power, even casting doubt on the Pentagon's ability to retain enough troops for occupation duties in Germany and Japan.[20]

The immediate upshot of the failure at London was a rather sudden decision by Byrnes to convene the Big Three Foreign Ministers (excluding France and China) in Moscow in December and to arrange a direct meeting with Stalin. Acting with his usual independence, he did not obtain Truman's full approval in advance and also failed to consult the British, who were angered at the slight and also opposed to the meeting. The new Byrnes strategy (involving a 180-degree turn) was to get the atomic bomb out on the table and to offer the Soviets participation in the international control of atomic energy. Hastily arming himself with a U.S.-British-Canadian report which proposed a special U.N. commission on atomic policy to establish standards for the international exchange of atomic information, Byrnes called in Vandenberg and his colleagues on the Senate Foreign Relations Committee to explain his purpose and obtain "their last-minute backup."[21] Although the legislators did not challenge the Secretary of State directly, they came away shocked by his apparent intention to divulge information about the bomb. As soon as Byrnes had departed for Moscow, they descended on Truman to tell him that any exchange of data would be "sheer appeasement" because "Russia has nothing to exchange." Truman assured the senators he agreed with them and was certain they had misunderstood Byrnes, but when they insisted on seeing the Secretary's instructions (which he had no doubt prepared himself) their suspicions were confirmed.[22]

In truth, Byrnes (with Truman's tacit consent) was still trying to square FDR's circle—to assure Russia of America's peaceful intentions and respect for legitimate Russian security interests, and to obtain sufficient indications of "democracy" in Eastern Europe to convince the American people that Russia was a reasonably reliable partner in a worldwide peacekeeping system. But the obstacles were formidable, the Soviets were uncooperative, and domestic political support for a continuation of the quest was rapidly disappearing. Beginning to take serious heat from Congress and the press for what seemed—and was—an ambivalent policy, and handicapped by a lack of detailed information as to what Byrnes was actually saying and doing, Truman found himself more and more irritated at his Secretary of State for placing the administration in an increasingly untenable position at home. This was the beginning of the end for Byrnes, although he remained in office for another year, when he was succeeded by General Marshall.[23]

Within the framework of Byrnes's own objectives, the Moscow Conference was rather more productive than many had expected. The Soviets quickly agreed to the proposed U.N. Atomic Energy Commission; they agreed also to procedures which would provide some modest non-Communist representation in the governments of Romania and Bulgaria. Byrnes agreed to the establishment of a Far Eastern Advisory Commission which would give not only the Russians, but also the British, Australians, Chinese, and French, an innocuous advisory role in the occupation of Japan. Byrnes also proposed directly to Stalin a four-power guarantee against German resurgence for twenty-five years. Stalin expressed some interest in studying the proposal, but it was unfortunately an idea whose time had come and gone. Vandenberg had made the same proposal a year before, when the military and political situations were still fluid, and it had been widely endorsed (by Henry Luce and John Foster Dulles, among others), but FDR had chosen not to act on it at Yalta. Now, however, the war was over, Germany was conquered and divided into zones of occupation, and the demarcation lines of the emerging East-West conflict were rapidly congealing.[24]

THE COLD WAR ARRIVES

TRUMAN HAD CHUCKLED in October at the quip that "the State Department fiddles while Byrnes roams,"[25] but by December the President was irritated by the fact that the Secretary of State was not only out of town, but also out of touch. Byrnes's political antennae were sensitive, but his extended absences from Washington and his immersion in negotiating proposals and counterproposals had caused him to miss the dramatic shift in American attitudes since V-J Day. The new mood combined a strong Wilsonian idealism with an awareness of America's burgeoning postwar power, and it ushered in a feeling of responsibility for what happened all over the world. The country now grasped the truth that American aloofness from world affairs in the 1920s and 1930s had facilitated the rise of dictatorships that ultimately threatened American peace and security and forced the United States to go to war. At great cost in U.S. blood and treasure, these dictatorships had finally been confronted and destroyed. Now another threatening tyranny, perhaps more insidious than Hitler's Germany, was stamping out democratic freedoms wherever its power could be brought to bear. This was intolerable and must be strongly opposed—now. The only acceptable outcome of all the struggle and sacrifice of World War II was a world made safe for liberal democracy and liberal capitalism. America had the power to realize these great Wilsonian goals, and it must not fail to make the necessary effort.

At the end of 1945, therefore, Byrnes's strenuous diplomatic efforts to maintain a working relationship with the U.S.S.R. by acknowledging the legitimacy of Soviet security concerns were perceived at home as too soft, too concessionary. A powerful revival of the Wilsonian consensus (which had deep roots in the American psyche) demanded that the Soviets subscribe fully to a democratic "world system"—or else. But the chosen test cases—Poland and the rest of Eastern Europe—were not susceptible to a Soviet response acceptable to American opinion.[26] Moreover, Americans were unable to see that their own claims to exclusive spheres of influence in the entire Western Hemisphere, and more recently in the Pacific islands wrested from Japan, as well as in the Japanese home islands, were roughly analogous to the Soviet insistence on a "security belt" in Eastern Europe. Bevin told Byrnes at Moscow that the world seemed to be drifting into "Three Monroes"—American, British, and Soviet—but Byrnes rejected the notion because, he said, "spheres of influence" was not a term that could be used or implied in American political discourse.[27] What mattered to American public opinion, what aroused the messianic American spirit of support for democracy and human rights, were the daily stories of Soviet intransigence, brutality, and constant pressure to undermine established situations and arrangements. These dominated the headlines and shaped the gathering anti-Russian, anti-Communist consensus.

The new toughness in public opinion coincided perfectly with Forrestal's deepest convictions of what was right for American policy and necessary for American security in the postwar period. He was Wilsonian in a broad philosophical sense, but he was above all a believer in tangible power and was now determined that America must retain such power in its own hands. It was idle to talk of peace "unless it is based upon the maintenance of . . . naval and air strength" that is "swiftly and effectively usable against international brigands such as Hitler and Mussolini. . . . History should teach us that there will be such brigands. Geography should teach us that we have no immunity from their banditry."[28]

His speeches during and after the war dealt persistently with America's traditional failure to grasp the unbreakable connection between security and power, and he cited the many appalling acts of commission and omission in the period after Versailles and before Pearl Harbor which demonstrated the nation's almost suicidal indifference to the gathering of hostile military power on every side.[29] At the 1922 Disarmament Conference, he said, "We proceeded to sink 800,000 tons of combatant vessels which would have made our Navy supreme in the world." In addition, "we adhered meticulously" to these and other arms-limiting agreements while failing to insist that potential enemies like Japan also observe the limitations and refrain from territorial aggression. Such "paradoxical conduct" produced a policy of balanced impotence: "In the morning, the Secretary of State would write a sharp, truculent note to Japan about the Manchurian occupation, and in the afternoon, we would lop off several cruisers from our [naval ship] building program." Forrestal attributed these disastrous interwar lapses to "a false reading and teaching of history" for which "the intellectuals of our time must bear some responsibility." But his attack on liberals and isolationists was rendered curiously tentative by his admission that this might be "a prejudiced and biased point of view." It was both his strength and his weakness to see both sides of every question. On one point, however, he was categorically certain: "The only insurance of peace" was to keep "the means to wage war . . . in the hands of those nations that hate war."[30]

As 1946 opened, Forrestal thus had reason to be encouraged by the dramatic improvement in public understanding of the ominous trends in the world situation. Characteristically, however, he continued to worry that the new mood might prove to be superficial and subject to reversal. He was aware of the chronic gap between thought and action: Anti-Russian sentiment might be rising, but political pressures for rapid demobilization continued to erode U.S. military strength, and most Americans, especially the millions of returning war veterans, were occupied primarily with putting their personal lives back together. Furthermore, he was deeply troubled by the administration's inability to formulate a strategy capable of comprehending and coping with the Russian/Communist threat. He thought the development of an effective American stance in world affairs demanded far more intellectual vigor and clarity than anyone in Washington had as yet been able to muster.

In the early months of 1946, a series of mutually reinforcing events not only validated Forrestal's concerns, but also crystallized the American anti-Communist consensus and ushered in the cold war, a phenomenon that would dominate international relations for the next forty-five years. Stalin made a speech on February 9 announcing a new five-year plan for the U.S.S.R. which called for increased production to guarantee "against all kinds of eventualities" and also appeared to flaunt the power of the Red Army. In his broader analysis, he saw little possibility for a peaceful international order, owing to the fact that "capitalism, monopoly and imperialism" were in command outside the U.S.S.R.[31] The speech jolted Washington. *Time* described it as "the most warlike pronouncement uttered by any top-rank statesman since V-J Day."[32] Walter Lippmann concluded that Stalin had now decided to make military power his first priority, which meant that "we are forced to make a corresponding decision."[33] Justice William O. Douglas, an otherwise sensible man, told Forrestal the speech was tantamount to "the declaration of World War III."[34]

Concurrently, Soviet political and military activities gave indication that, far from being content merely to ensure their security zone in Eastern

Europe, Stalin and his cohorts were seeking to use their greater postwar leverage to improve the strategic position of the U.S.S.R. in geographical areas beyond Soviet borders, areas long the object of traditional Russian ambitions. Turkey was notified of Moscow's desire to amend the 1936 Montreux Convention so as to permit joint Soviet-Turkish control of the Black Sea Straits, including the Soviet right to fortify the waterway by stationing Russian troops on Turkish territory. Soviet pressure on Iran for annexation of the northern province of Azerbaijan soon confronted the U.N. Security Council with its first real East-West crisis, and a spy ring intent upon stealing atomic bomb data and operating out of the Soviet Embassy in Canada was exposed by the defection of one of its members. There seemed an ominous momentum to Soviet policy.[35]

Vandenberg made a tough speech on February 27 calling for a stiffer response to Soviet pressures and an end to the "miserable fiction" that frank exposure of U.S.-Soviet differences would jeopardize the peace. This was a clear shot at Byrnes's double strategy and a reinforcement of the more straightforward Forrestal view that the threat must be openly faced. Byrnes, by this time aware that he had fallen out of step, had by no means lost his ability to recognize and adjust to shifting political winds. The very day after Vandenberg's blast, he made a dramatic speech to the Overseas Press Club which brought him back into alignment with the new public mood.[36] "We will not and cannot stand aloof in the face of aggression," he said, whether this is "accomplished by coercion or pressure or by subterfuge such as political infiltration." Saying that "we cannot overlook a unilateral gnawing away at the status quo," he asserted the American right to interpret and regulate changes in the status quo anywhere in the world. If a particular change did not meet the American standard of legitimacy, then the United States would act in defense of the status quo.[37] The American press responded with enthusiasm and relief. One editorial called the speech "The Second Vandenberg Concerto"; the Washington *Post* proclaimed Byrnes's "fearless pledge" to assert America's "police power" on a global scale a "first-rate pronouncement" that would now give real meaning to the concept of collective security. The *New York Times* said editorially that the two speeches ushered in "a new orientation of America's international relations."[38]

On March 5, Winston Churchill put the capstone on the new structure with his definitive "Iron Curtain" speech at Westminster College in Fulton, Missouri: "From Stettin in the Baltic to Trieste in the Adriatic, an Iron Curtain has descended across the continent." The heart of the speech, however, and Churchill's first purpose, was a call for an Anglo-American military alliance based on the conviction that "our Russian friends" admire nothing so much as strength and disrespect nothing so much as weakness.[39] Byrnes received a "dress rehearsal" of the British leader's remarks and subsequently briefed the President.[40] A few weeks later, in an interview with *Pravda* (March 31), Stalin replied: "Mr. Churchill is now in the position of a firebrand of war. And Mr. Churchill is not alone here."[41] Forrestal told the Foreign Policy Association in Pittsburgh that the Soviet Union was "no longer an enigma," but a state dedicated to the conviction that "the capitalistic and communistic concepts cannot live together in the same world."[42]

The permanent division of Europe was now a stark image. The Truman administration had essentially ended its policy of seeking compromise on fundamental issues.

THE WALLACE DISSENT

THE COLD WAR consensus was now a palpable fact, but there remained dissenters inside the administration and outside it. The most notable of these was Henry Agard Wallace, Secretary of Commerce. "One of the oddest, yet best-intentioned public officials the United States ever produced,"[43] he was a Republican turned devout New Dealer whose father had served as Secretary of Agriculture under Presidents Harding and Coolidge. Wallace himself had been FDR's first Agriculture Secretary and then Vice President in 1940. Introverted, humanitarian, righteous, and naïve, he was an evangelical believer in the brotherhood of man. In 1946, he became the spokesman for the troubled component of American opinion that persisted in believing that the Russian Communist experiment represented a potential utopia for mankind and that every expression of anti-Communism reflected a Fascist, militaristic mind-set bent upon a new war. An extreme, but not atypical, expression of this view was contained in a memorandum to Wallace by a staff member of the War Production Board in November 1942, eleven months after the disaster at Pearl Harbor, when the issue of victory or defeat in the desperate war against the Axis powers still hung in the balance. "The governing military cliques in our Army and Navy are Fascist-minded," the memorandum said. "They have shown that they are willing to work with Darlan and Franco. They will be working next with Mussolini, Laval and Goering if we do not check them. Given free rein they will decide the war and the peace on lines that will make another war inevitable."[44]

In 1946, Wallace thought the deadlock in U.S.-Soviet relations was leading to World War III, and he put the blame primarily on American militarists, conservative Republicans in Congress, and Truman's appeasement of British imperialism. Beyond establishing blame, however, he was short on practical solutions and unable to see the evils of the Stalin dictatorship. Forrestal found it "very difficult" to discuss issues with Wallace "in practical language" or with any feeling "that he understood what I was talking about."[45] At a Cabinet meeting on April 19, 1946, he joined with Byrnes in protesting a recent Wallace speech which had called for the dismantling of American air bases in Iceland. Such "independent comments on foreign policy" by a Cabinet officer without any responsibility in that area were "most inappropriate," Forrestal asserted. These restrained words concealed a personal antipathy to Wallace and a strong desire, shared by Byrnes, to have Truman ask for Wallace's resignation.[46]

On September 12, 1946, Wallace made a speech in Madison Square Garden to a gathering of Democratic "progressives," an incident which demonstrated both the unresolved ideological divisions within the Democratic Party and the ineptitude of the Truman White House. On many points, Wallace's remarks were consistent with the Truman-Byrnes foreign policy, but the President, who personally cleared the speech, signally failed to grasp the import of certain key passages. "The tougher we get," the speech said, "the tougher the Russians will get . . . We must not let our Russian policy be guided or influenced by those . . . who want war with Russia." In addition, the speech casually dismissed the sacred Wilsonian insistence on a seamless democratic world by arguing that "whether we like it or not, the Russians will try to socialize their sphere of influence just as we try to democratize our sphere of influence."[47] Byrnes, at a foreign ministers' conference in Paris with Senators Vandenberg and Tom Connally (the visible embodiments of bipartisanship), was angered by what seemed an inexplicable undercutting of his policy.

There ensued a great uproar in Congress and the press, centered mainly on Truman's embarrassing efforts to explain his endorsement of the speech and then to distance himself from it. After an effort to temporize had created an even greater confusion, Byrnes declared that either he or Wallace must go; Truman decided it had to be Wallace.[48] In April 1947, the State Department warned Truman that Wallace, now a private citizen, was scheduled to make a speech in London criticizing the "bellicosity" of American policy toward the Soviet Union. When the matter came up at the next Cabinet meeting, Forrestal inquired as to why Wallace should not be denied a passport. After Truman dismissed the idea, saying such an action against a former Vice President and Cabinet officer would invite "severe public criticism," Forrestal replied he would rather take the criticism than permit Wallace to "interfere" with American policy[49]—a comment which revealed once more his qualified commitment to free speech when it came to Communism and "crackpots." A year later Wallace formed the Progressive Party and ran as a third-party candidate in the 1948 presidential election, a move which appeared to split the Democrats sufficiently to assure a victory for the Republican, Thomas E. Dewey.

But in fact, the Wallace dissent and breakaway served to strengthen the majority view that Russia and Communism were serious threats to national security and human freedom. This view now stood at the center of the national postwar consensus supported by policy-makers, congressmen, diplomats, military professionals, businessmen, labor leaders, bankers, and university presidents. Forrestal had played a significant, though not the primary, role in shaping this dramatic shift in public mood.

CHAPTER 21

━━━━━━━━━━━ ★ ★ ★ ━━━━━━━━━━━

The Godfather
of Containment

W ITH REGARD to the largest postwar issue—the challenge of
Soviet Communism—Forrestal, despite a flickering sympathy
for "socialistic" ideas at Princeton and in World War I, escaped
the insidious attraction of the experiment inspired by Marx and Lenin which
had infected so many thinkers of goodwill and liberal tendencies in America and Western Europe in the 1920s and 1930s. In the main, these people
chose to regard Communism as an inspired higher form of democracy
promising more dignity and equality than they perceived in their own class-
ridden capitalist societies. From his first awareness of the Communist phenomenon, Forrestal's skeptical mind seems to have seen clearly that it was
in basic conflict not only with free enterprise but with the human spirit,
that there was moral evil in the very nature of the system, and that this
defect made its promise to bring about the material and spiritual elevation
of mankind a gigantic falsehood and fraud. At a time when major figures
like Roosevelt, Hopkins, Stimson, Byrnes, Marshall, and Eisenhower were
acting on the belief that nothing basic about Stalin's Soviet Union precluded a friendly relationship with it, Forrestal perceived in its nature and
purposes a fundamental threat to the United States and to the idea of free
men. Beyond an inherent wariness, he was fortified by a natural patriotism,
first manifested during boyhood days in Beacon when he had scorned his
father's tenacious loyalty to Ireland and insisted that an American's allegiance must be to America. This feeling was strengthened during World
War II by his total dedication to the war effort, especially by the fierce
admiration he developed for the valor of the navy and the Marine Corps.
Reinforcing his faith in the capitalist system and his combative nature, these
factors made him a dedicated foe of Communism.

His first direct brush with Communists had come in his early period as
Navy Under Secretary when he confronted labor strikes (in plants with

navy contracts) fomented by American labor leaders who had ties to the American Communist Party or strong sympathies for Russia; he had duly noted that such politically inspired strikes ceased after Germany invaded Russia in the summer of 1941, although a wide range of management-labor disputes demanded his attention throughout the war.[1]

As the war gathered momentum he was importantly influenced by William Bullitt, who believed that Communism was at bottom "a religious movement" and that "world revolution was the core of the Communist religion."[2] Bullitt, voted "most brilliant" in the Yale class of 1912 (which also included Averell Harriman and Cole Porter), was FDR's first ambassador to the Soviet Union, in 1933. Initially an enthusiastic supporter of the Bolshevik experiment, he turned bitterly anti-Soviet. He was ambassador to France from 1936 until that nation's invasion and defeat in 1940. According to one account, FDR then offered him the Navy Secretaryship, but the post ultimately went to Knox. Insulted by FDR's 1942 offer to send him as U.S. minister to remote Australia, Bullitt finally found a place in the Navy Department as assistant to Knox, where his once shining career continued to spiral downward, accelerated by a growing reputation for meddling, erratic judgment, and a proclivity for disclosing military secrets at cocktail parties. He had become a loose cannon with the manner of an upper-class Philadelphian, a combination which many found insufferable. Nevertheless, his 1943 report to FDR on "civil administration in the occupied territories" was an almost clairvoyant warning that Stalin's postwar aim was to extend the Soviet system to adjacent areas as far as the traffic would bear and to retain control of foreign Communist parties. "When Germany collapses," he wrote, the Western Allies must be in a position "to prevent . . . the flow of the Red amoeba into Europe" and must set up democratic administrations in liberated countries which "will be strong enough to provide . . . defense against invasion by the Soviet Union." Foreshadowing the need for the NATO Alliance, he argued that Western Europe must not be allowed to remain "a military vacuum for the Soviet Union to flow into . . . An integrated democratic Europe, pacific but armed, is a vital element for the creation of world peace."[3]

Forrestal found himself in full agreement with Bullitt's dire assessment of Soviet ambitions, especially his view that Communism was fundamentally a religion, based on a faith transcending rational calculations. FDR was mainly perplexed. In an unsatisfactory exchange with Bullitt, the President said, "Bill, I don't dispute your facts [or] the logic of your reasoning. I just have a hunch Stalin is not that kind of man." FDR thought Lend-Lease would give Stalin a sense of security for Russia and that this would obviate his need to annex adjacent territories. Bullitt replied tartly that Stalin was not the Duke of Norfolk, but a Caucasian bandit "whose only thought when he got something for nothing was that the other fellow was an ass. . . .'' FDR, now angered, said brusquely, ''It's my responsibility, not yours, and I'm going to play my hunch.''[4]

In the summer of 1944, during his trip to observe the Allied landings in southern France, Forrestal had paid a visit to Charles de Gaulle at the general's headquarters in Algiers and had asked him whether Russia would replace Germany as a form of ''Red Fascism'' after Hitler was defeated. The general thought Soviet Communism had mellowed somewhat since Lenin's time and expressed confidence that France could hold its own in the postwar period, with American material and political support. Forrestal was more pessimistic, believing the outward thrust of Soviet ambitions exceeded Stalin's already unambiguous territorial claims in Eastern Europe, but he understood that this view was out of step with current American policy.[5] Shortly thereafter, in a letter to Palmer Hoyt of the Denver *Post,* he wrote that ''whenever any American suggests that we act in accordance with the needs of our security he is apt to be called a God-damned fascist or imperialist, while if Uncle Joe suggests that he needs the Baltic provinces, half of Poland, all of Bessarabia and access to the Mediterranean, all hands agree that he is a fine, frank, candid and generally delightful fellow who is easy to deal with because he is so explicit in what he wants.''[6] Publicly, however, Forrestal held to FDR's hopeful line that Russia was a valued ally with whom postwar collaboration was an important ingredient of world peace, but his innate skepticism always showed through. Speaking to the Investment Bankers Association in Chicago in 1944, he argued the need to recognize that Russia was making ''a great, although self-interested, contribution to the war against Germany'' and that America should conduct U.S.-Soviet relations ''with neither undue fear nor abject adulation.''[7]

With others in Washington he shared a brief moment of euphoria immediately after Yalta, but was quickly sobered by subsequent events in Eastern Europe and by reports from Averell Harriman, the U.S. ambassador in Moscow, who rushed back to Washington after FDR's death to establish his own position with the new administration and to warn Truman of the treacherous complexities awaiting him in U.S.-Soviet relations. Harriman, who also reflected the Wilsonian consensus for a ''world system,'' explained that the Soviets used the word ''democracy'' in ways quite unacceptable to the West, and he thought the professed Soviet need for ''a satellite security belt'' in Eastern Europe against a potentially resurgent Germany was ''a stalking horse'' for illegitimate territorial ambitions. He warned Forrestal and others of ''a barbarian invasion of Europe'' and said the West might well be facing ''ideological warfare'' every bit as intense and dangerous as it had encountered in the struggle against Nazism and Fascism.[8] Harriman too became a major influence in the development of Forrestal's thinking on Russia and Communism. He began inserting Harriman's cables in his "diaries" and staying up late at night to discuss the subject whenever the ambassador was in town.[9]

By V-E Day, Forrestal had concluded there was a real danger that most of Europe would "go Communist" unless the United States acted with great vigor to assist a recovery and a regeneration. He agreed with de Gaulle that "Germany cannot be destroyed" but had to be restored as an engine of European recovery (after an occupation stern enough and long enough to purge it of Nazism) and eventually integrated into a West European economic grouping. Predictably, de Gaulle had told him that such a grouping must be centered on France so that "the smaller powers will gather around France and not seek to gather around some other powerful nation, such as Russia."[10] Forrestal, while less precise about which nations should constitute the democratic-capitalist nucleus, was certain that a strong counterweight was imperative if Soviet Communism was to be prevented from penetrating and destroying the political system of Western Europe. He was not opposed to the United Nations, but thought it would be incapable of peacekeeping for a long time, owing to the lack of Soviet cooperation and the Soviet veto power in the Security Council, but also to the general inefficiency of large diverse coalitions. He soon reached the conclusion that American security, and world peace, must reside chiefly in U.S. military and economic power and that there were no available substitutes for these.

CAPITALISM UNDER SIEGE

FORRESTAL WAS also developing the sense that capitalism was everywhere coming under siege, and not only from Soviet Communism; he perceived indirect attacks within the Western system itself, pushed and promoted by myriad social theorists and "crackpots" who wanted to tamper with private property and free-market mechanisms—for example, Henry Wallace in the United States and Harold Laski in Britain.[11]

He thought Wallace a hopeless dreamer: "When Henry looks at me with that global stare, I really get frightened."[12] For his part, Wallace thought Forrestal "utterly hipped on Communism—maybe properly so [though] at the time I couldn't see it the way he did." Otherwise, he found the Navy Secretary "a very fair and decent kind of fellow . . . unless deeply touched emotionally."[13] Laski, a vocal professor at the London School of Economics, seemed to irritate Forrestal every time he expressed his leftist convictions. He was dedicated to reconstructing "The Socialist International" after the war and was waspishly anti-American ("England and France have undergone the common experience of foreign occupation, with the difference that England was occupied by the Americans").[14] In December 1945,

Forrestal wrote to a British M.P., Oliver Lyttleton, proposing that "you get me invited" to speak before an appropriate English audience so "I can make the case for a free and capitalistic society."[15]

In the early postwar period, Forrestal believed there was an intellectual continuum from the New Deal to Socialism to Communism, and he suspected that New Dealers welcomed the election of the British Labour government in 1945 because it represented what they wanted to see happen in America.[16] Shortly before the British elections in July of that year, during a dinner at the British Embassy, Harry Hopkins remarked that Europe as a whole "was definitely swinging toward the left" and that it would be unwise for U.S. policy to oppose the trend. Forrestal immediately challenged him, arguing that Britain could afford to "go Socialist" only if the experiment were underwritten by American tax dollars. Hopkins expressed mild skepticism about Forrestal's premise and passed on to another subject, but Forrestal felt he had smoked out an unspoken New Deal plot. "Harry obviously did not want to pursue this conversation too far," he confided to his diary, "because, I suspect, he did not want to be driven to the position that he was advocating either revolution or Communism for this country."[17] It is far more likely that the pragmatic Hopkins was merely saying that the undeniable leftward swing in world politics was occurring independently of Soviet efforts.

As this incident and others like it showed, Forrestal was becoming uncomfortable with the economic and social philosophy of the New Deal and suspicious that its advocates were seeking to extend it worldwide. These issues had been in abeyance during the fighting war, when American officials of widely different political persuasions were united in a common cause; now the divisive issues were resurfacing. "A lot of admittedly brainy men," he wrote in 1947, "believe that governments, history, science and business can be rationalized into a state of perfection. Their ideals all come out of the same hat whether it is worn by a German, a Russian, or a Stafford Cripps."[18] His perception here was flawed, for there existed, in fact, a bitter antagonism between left-center Social Democrats and Communists everywhere in Europe and between New Dealers and Communists in the United States. Forrestal gradually discovered this for himself during the concerted U.S. efforts to defeat the Communist general strike in France in 1947, and his notable personal exertions to assure a Social Democratic victory in the 1948 Italian elections. In both cases, the local Social Democrats proved to be the fiercest and most effective adversaries of the local Communists.*

---

*See Chapter 23 for a further discussion of the Italian elections.

DIALECTICAL MATERIALISM

W ITH THE END of hostilities and the expansion of his own policy concerns, Forrestal began a personal intellectual effort to come to grips with the "riddle" of Communism by studying the murky theory of dialectical materialism, the Marxist formula derived from Hegel which purported to explain the inevitable triumph of world Communism.* In part he was drawn to the exercise by a cast of mind which delighted in the discovery and analysis of secret intellectual conspiracies and complexities. "The Bolsheviks have the advantage over us," he wrote to Republican senator Homer Ferguson of Michigan three weeks after V-E Day, because they possess "a clear-cut line of economic philosophy amounting almost to a religion." This is, he explained, "the Marxian dialectic," which is "as incompatible with democracy as was Nazism or Fascism because it rests upon the willingness to apply force to gain the end. . . . There is no use fooling ourselves about the depth and extent of this problem. I have no answers—I have been concentrating on something else just as you have. But we had better try to get an answer."[19] His political antennae told him, however, that it was not yet time to assail Marxism publicly. Russia was still an ally fighting for the common cause, and the spirit of Russian-American friendship pervaded Washington, generated in part by the Red Army's tremendous victories over Hitler's armies and in part by the handouts on life in the Soviet Union from the liberal academics who staffed the Office of War Information. Unready as yet to swim against the tide, he asked Ferguson to hold his letter in confidence so that he, Forrestal, would not be called "a Fascist and various other forms of dangerous thought."[20]

In pursuit of further education, he asked his friend Archibald MacLeish, the new Librarian of Congress, to dig up a slender volume called *Aspects of Dialectical Materialism*, which he had discovered and perused in New York in the 1930s, but had subsequently lost track of.[21] MacLeish produced the book, and Forrestal was soon declaring at dinner parties that "the real question" was whether Stalin was guided by considerations of nation-state power or aimed to achieve "world revolution" by applying the "principles of dialectical materialism everywhere." In another formulation, he said "the fundamental question" was "whether we are dealing with a nation or a religion."[22] He was becoming deeply concerned that neither the U.S.

---

*Hegel argued that every idea ("thesis") is opposed by another idea ("antithesis") and that the clash of these opposites produces a new blend ("synthesis"). Marx appropriated this Hegelian dialectic and sought to apply it not to abstract ideas, but to social-economic classes. He predicted that a series of inexorable and bloody struggles between classes with conflicting interests would finally produce total victory for the working class—the proletariat. Thereafter, the human race would be organized as a single classless society of equality and brotherhood called Communism.

government nor American society had developed an adequate answer, nor indeed any informed understanding of Russian psychology and the modus operandi of the Stalinist regime. Yet these were, he sensed, absolute prerequisites to the formulation of an intelligent foreign policy. In December 1945, a column by Walter Lippmann provoked him to undertake the kind of rigorous research effort that would yield the answer. Lippmann had written that the current task of statesmanship is "not necessarily" to secure democracy for *all* the world, but "to discover the means by which democracy and communism . . . can find a way of living together."[23] Notifying Lippmann that he flatly disagreed, he launched his own study.[24]

To do the spadework, he called on Edward Willett, his general purpose researcher, to gather the facts and write a basic paper. Willett, like Forrestal, was a Princeton man. He had been brought into Dillon, Read by Ferdinand Eberstadt and had worked there for several years, but had only minimal contact with Forrestal. In 1939 he had a falling-out with the mercurial Eberstadt and left Wall Street to teach economics at Smith College. In 1945, when Forrestal asked his close friend whether Willett would be useful in Washington, Eberstadt thought him "too academic," but Forrestal took him on anyway, as a sort of "specialist for international affairs." Willett was soon gathering information and writing papers on an eclectic range of subjects that were of either fleeting or enduring interest to the Navy Secretary—from the British civil service to Jean-Paul Sartre and industrialist Henry J. Kaiser. Basically an economist, Willett usually started with little or no knowledge of the matter to be researched, but he was resourceful, clever, good-humored, and determined never to admit that an assignment was beyond his intellectual capacity.[25]

As he later admitted about his work for Forrestal, "I cribbed about 50 percent, as I rarely knew anything about the topic assigned me. Most of my papers were copied from the work of others—from whatever I could find to read." On one occasion, he wrote an essay on the new French constitution based entirely on a *New York Times* editorial. Forrestal, who presumably missed the editorial, was so impressed that he showed it to Arthur Krock, who promptly incorporated it into his own column on the editorial page of the *New York Times*! Willett declined to say who was most embarrassed by this episode.[26]

On the matter now uppermost in Forrestal's mind, Willett was indeed starting from scratch, for he had never before heard the term "dialectical materialism." He quickly got the impression, however, that Forrestal really wanted to know whether the Marxist theory was, like *Mein Kampf,* a program for Communist world conquest which the West could ignore only at its peril. This gave him an important clue, and, undaunted, he started reading available tracts, beginning with Forrestal's own copy of *Aspects of Dialectical Materialism* and a survey called *The Philosophy of Communism* by a Charles F. McFadden, a copy of which Monsignor Fulton J. Sheen had given to Forrestal. Then he started writing.[27]

The first effort, entitled "Random Thoughts on Dialectical Materialism and Russian Objectives," was sent to Forrestal on December 21, 1945, with a covering note which characterized it as "an extremely rough and still unorganized collection of ideas." This was an accurate summary. The paper was replete with unanswered questions about "the form of social order and economic organization they are trying to create" and "the geographical area—national or worldwide—which such a structure is intended to govern." It was, in fact, an amateurish, tendentious, and generally useless piece of work.[28] Forrestal found it abstruse and asked that it be rewritten with more emphasis on the implications of the dialectic for current U.S.-Soviet relations and future Soviet policy. He also posed several basic questions for Willett to ponder, e.g., do the Soviet leaders "still believe in the inevitable collapse of capitalism?" and do they have an "interest in the expediting of that process?" Presumably he imagined Willett knew the answers or could find them.[29]

Now quite out of his depth, Willett was fortuitously introduced, through another member of Forrestal's staff, to a Jesuit professor of political science at Catholic University in Washington. Whatever the quality of his credentials, Wilfred Parsons held strong views on the subject and imparted them to Willett at length. The creation of a security belt of satellite states on Russia's southern border was "in the first instance" a defensive measure, Parsons said, but it was equally "a springboard . . . [for] more effective offensive measures against capitalist nations." While this pronouncement did nothing to answer the "whether nation or religion" question, Parsons came down firmly on the assertion that major U.S.-Soviet conflicts would arise from their irreconcilable ideologies, rather than from normally fractious nation-state relations.[30]

Another cook soon stirring the soup was a young ensign, Tilghman Koons, who had studied Russian history at Princeton and the Russian language at the navy language school in Boulder, Colorado; indeed, he had been in the same class at Boulder with Michael Forrestal, who was now a young naval officer posted to Moscow. Although only nineteen years old, Koons had caught the attention of several people on Forrestal's staff as "a budding Russian specialist" and was brought into the "little State Department" group in the Navy Secretary's office. "It was a pretty heady experience," Koons recalled many years later. "I briefed Willett on the ins and outs of Marxism, and Forrestal on Russia generally."[31] Forrestal began including him in office luncheons to dispense his expertise for the enlightenment of senior naval officers. On one occasion Koons explained to Admiral Nimitz how the Soviets financed their military budget. Koons's views on Stalin and Soviet policy were definitely hard-line, and Forrestal seemed to find them entirely compatible with his own developing line of thought.[32]

Willett's second draft, "The Philosophy of Communism," dated January 7, 1946, predictably reflected the strong influence of Parsons and Koons. This made the paper harder and more pessimistic in tone and content, but also more coherent. The aim of Communism, it said, was to abolish the "twin evils" of private property and the capitalist state. Any "alleged abandonment" of this aim was only "a temporary movement" designed "to throw the opposition off its guard." Accordingly, no useful distinction could be drawn between an offensive and a defensive Soviet policy, for the "messianic goal" remained the same in either case. Therefore, unless basic changes occurred in either the capitalist or the Communist system, the situation appeared to "necessitate" an ultimately "violent conflict" between the United States and the U.S.S.R., in part because "to counter internal challenges the Kremlin leaders might deliberately provoke war with the U.S." The only safeguard available to the United States was to build an "invincible" defense and to refuse to send material aid to the U.S.S.R., which from now on must be regarded as the principal enemy.[33]

Forrestal asked for a few changes in the second draft and struck out a sentence that said "certain elements" of American labor "illustrated the Communist philosophy in action." But on the whole he was satisfied with the result. The final draft was ready on January 15, and he promptly dispatched copies to the President, the Cabinet, Senator David I. Walsh of the Naval Affairs Committee, Henry Luce, Walter Lippmann, and various others.[34] A copy was hand-delivered to the Pope by Myron Taylor, the President's special emissary to the Vatican.[35] In a covering letter to Luce, Forrestal made clear that the Hitler analogy was very much on his mind. "I realize it is easy to ridicule the need for such a study . . . but I think in the middle of that laughter we always should remember that we also laughed at Hitler."[36]

The responses to the Willett study were mixed, but the main thrust of informed comment was that it placed far too much emphasis on the "ideological" or "religious" as distinct from the "national" or "power" factor as an explanation of Soviet motivation. Professor Robert Strausz-Hupé of the University of Pennsylvania, a personal friend of Forrestal's, said, "I question the adequacy of an analysis of Russian policy based mainly on the deduction of dogma."[37] Philip Moseley, a noted Russian expert at Columbia University, could not agree that the Soviet government "operates blindly on the basis of philosophical assumptions"; that was "only one element" in the reaching of an "immediate and concrete decision."[38] Doubt was also expressed by the Office of Naval Intelligence that the ideological factor was paramount or would lead inevitably to war. Its director, Rear Admiral Thomas B. Inglis, portrayed the Soviet Union as basically a traditional power motivated by security concerns. Inglis wrote that the long-range Soviet purpose was not to bring about "world revolution as such," but rather to work at weakening the other major powers so that the Soviet Union emerged as "preeminent." He stressed the present fact that the Soviet Union was weak in every component of military power except ground forces, and was also economically bankrupt and plagued by domestic unrest.[39]

The Eastern European Division of the State Department, headed by Llewellyn Thompson (who later served with distinction as U.S. Ambassador to Vienna and Moscow), pointed out that "Marxist gospel" in the Soviet Union had been decisively modified and shaped by the pressures of Russian history and culture; moreover, that there was no affinity between "Social Democracy and Communist Totalitarianism"; on the contrary, there existed between the two a "basic antagonism," a point "apparently not understood" by the Willett study. Thompson further expressed the view that Soviet policy will seek "to avoid war with its most powerful opponents" while pursuing tactics of "infiltration and fifth-column activities" designed to pave the way for further accretions of Soviet power without resort to hostilities "on an international scale." Willett's conclusion that an "invincible" defense force was the only means by which the West could avoid defeat was, in Thompson's view, "a sorry contention." To meet the real Soviet challenge, he argued, "we must have faith and confidence in our own way of life and be prepared to convince the rest of the world of its advantages."[40] Years later, Michael Forrestal, whose law practice involved extensive commercial dealings with the Soviet Union, characterized the Willett-Koons study as "sophomoric" and thought it sad that his father 'had accepted such second- and third-rate stuff.'"[41]

Forrestal was sensitive to the weight of adverse comment on the Willett study, but it did not appear to weaken his conviction that a religious fanaticism was the main wellspring of Soviet behavior. On firmer ground, he remained in no doubt that the Soviet state was a single political-economic monopoly whose animating spirit and methods were totally repugnant to Western democracy. Total power was concentrated in the hands of the monopoly, the means of production were controlled by the monopoly, and the people were exploited by the monopoly. The only uncertainty was the proper weight to give the murky element of "Marxist ideology" or "religion" in Soviet psychology. Forrestal was inclined to give it great weight and to believe it could propel the Soviet Union to initiate all-out war against the West. He acknowledged, however, that the situation contained several variable, and perhaps unknowable, factors, and he was still pondering the conundrum when a soon-to-be famous document from Moscow arrived in Washington on February 22, 1946.

KENNAN AND THE LONG TELEGRAM

GEORGE KENNAN, a career foreign service officer, had been chargé d'affaires (deputy to Ambassador Harriman) in the American Embassy in Moscow since his posting there in July 1944. An expert on Soviet affairs of the "realist" school and a writer of rare expository power and eloquence, he believed that FDR's double-game strategy with the Soviets and his heavy reliance on personal diplomacy with Stalin were fatuous and doomed to failure because they rested on a fundamental ignorance of Soviet character and aims. A firm believer that world stability must be based on recognized spheres of influence reflecting real power, Kennan was not so much opposed to the idea of a United Nations as to the presumption that a world organization could in any way mitigate the coming communization of Eastern Europe. He believed that Stalin's agreement to join the U.N. rested entirely on his understanding with FDR that its foundation was Big Three unanimity, which meant to Stalin that the U.N. would serve as a means of assuring Anglo-American support for Soviet domination of Eastern Europe. Kennan was accordingly incensed at what he regarded as the naïve or dishonest American efforts at and after Yalta to hide the harsh reality of that dominance by recourse to meaningless agreements calling for governments founded on "a broader democratic basis" and "free and unfettered elections." These he thought to be "the shabbiest sort of equivocation" designed to "pull the wool over the eyes of the Western public."[42]

He had argued for a "showdown" with Moscow at the time of the Warsaw Uprising eight months before Yalta, when Stalin's refusal to aid the Polish underground against the German counterattack assured the destruction of the would-be leaders of a non-Communist postwar Poland. But there had been no showdown. Stalin had thrown down a gauntlet of defiance on Eastern Europe, but FDR and Churchill had not picked it up. They very much needed the support of Russian armies to complete the defeat of Germany and then to assist in the final assault on Japan. They could not afford at that point the moral indulgence available to an intellectual in the Moscow Embassy who did not have ultimate responsibility. Kennan's contempt for the Yalta decisions was further nurtured by Byrnes's effort at the subsequent Potsdam, London, and Moscow conferences to pursue FDR's double game—that is, to promote an all-embracing international security system based on democratic principles while simultaneously accepting de facto Soviet control in Eastern Europe, provided it could be gilded with a few superficial concessions to democratic procedure.[43]

Kennan was especially irritated by the hastily convened Moscow Conference in December 1945 and by Byrnes's belief that all problems could be solved if only he could talk directly to Stalin. He was also unfavorably impressed by Byrnes's wheeler-dealer approach to negotiations. Sitting directly behind the Secretary of State at the conference sessions, he observed: "He plays his negotiations by ear, going into them with no clear or fixed plan . . . He relies entirely on his own agility and presence of mind and hopes to take advantage of tactical openings . . . His main purpose is to achieve some sort of agreement, he doesn't much care what . . . He wants an agreement for its political effect at home."[44] It was, in large part, Kennan's disdain for Byrnes's performance at Moscow, he wrote, that caused "the pot of my patience to boil over." After two months of brooding gestation, he was moved by a routine inquiry from the Treasury Department to give Washington his own full explanation of the nature and purposes of the Soviet government. "Suddenly, my opinion was being asked . . . They had asked for it. Now, by God, they would have it."[45] The result was an 8,000-word telegram dispatched in five sections on Washington's Birthday, 1946.

Far more than the Willett study or any other official or semiofficial analysis then available to the policy elite in Washington, the Long Telegram provided a persuasive synthesis of the "Russian" and "Marxist," the "power" and "religious," elements in the psychology of the Soviet leaders. "At bottom of Kremlin's neurotic view of world affairs," Kennan wrote in telegramese, "is traditional and instinctive Russian sense of insecurity" caused primarily by countless foreign invasions across the defenseless plains separating Russia from Western Europe. But this insecurity had since 1917 been married to Marxist dogma, giving rise to a state of mind that was now beyond change by any agreement or arrangement with outside powers. The Kremlin leaders were now compelled by a combination of their fears and dreams to "work in patient but deadly struggle for total destruction of rival power." Normal coexistence, in the sense of live and let live, was impossible: "We have here a political force committed fanatically to the belief that with US there can be no permanent modus vivendi, that it is desirable and necessary that the internal harmony of our society be disrupted, our traditional way of life destroyed, the international power of our state be broken if Soviet power is to be secure." However, while "impervious to logic or reason" the Kremlin is "highly sensitive to logic of force . . . It can easily withdraw . . . and usually does—when strong resistance is encountered at any point."[46]

Nearly a half century later, the Long Telegram of 1946 looks like an exceedingly perceptive reading of the Kremlin's declaratory policy goals. But Kennan's presentation of Stalin as a fanatical revolutionary rather than a shrewd power calculator appears overdrawn, and his emphasis on Marxist ideology as a motivating force, as opposed to considerations of Russian security and national purpose, seems at odds with his later positions. Similarly, his assertion of the Kremlin's sensitivity to the "logic of force" implied the need for a Western response based heavily on military strength—an implication which he later sought to deny. But the Long Telegram should be read primarily as a reflection of Kennan's personal frustration at Washington's continued refusal (or inability) to define the Soviet threat in realistic terms and his determination to bring about an official repudiation of the FDR-Yalta-Byrnes double game, which he believed to involve very dangerous self-deception. In February 1946, his telegraphic essay hit Washington like a lightning flash that suddenly illuminates a darkened landscape for miles around. Like a powerful magnet it quickly attracted the various scattered pieces of evidence, opinion, theory, and emotion which at the time comprised the still confused and confusing elements of U.S. policy toward the Soviet Union. Washington was itself working on the puzzle, so the Long Telegram arrived at an especially propitious moment and drew most of the disparate pieces into a coherent mosaic. Policy planners promptly juxtaposed the Long Telegram to Stalin's bellicose speech of February 9.

To Forrestal, the Kennan essay was exactly the authoritative explanation he had been seeking through the amateurish efforts of Willett, Parsons, and Koons, and he immediately became the principal promoter of both document and author, responding, as Truman's biographer Robert Donovan put it, "like Paul Revere to the lanterns in the Old North Church."[47] Harriman thought Forrestal's reaction was a "decisive" catalyst in shaping American opinion on this issue.[48] Forrestal sent copies to the President and the Cabinet, to newspaper publishers and columnists throughout the country, to senators and congressmen, to bankers and businessmen. He made it required reading for thousands of officers in the navy. This wide dissemination was designed to push public opinion toward a state of alert by underlining the fundamental differences in assumptions and values between Russia and the West and the harsh reality of the East-West conflict. As Daniel Yergin later observed, "The postwar anti-communist consensus existed first in the center, in the policy elite, before it spread out to the nation."[49] Forrestal hardly achieved this single-handedly, but he was an exceptionally energetic and forceful figure in the vanguard.

Determined to exploit this newly discovered intellectual resource, he persuaded Byrnes to bring Kennan back from Moscow and arranged for his appointment as Deputy Head of the National War College, a newly created year-long resident seminar in political-military affairs for senior military officers and diplomats, in the establishment of which Forrestal had also played a leading role. The result of such sponsorship from a ranking Cabinet officer was to lift George Kennan out of bureaucratic anonymity to a high place in the policy-making elite, indeed as the leading guru on U.S.-Soviet relations.[50] As Kennan acknowledged in his memoirs, "My reputation was made. My voice now carried."[51] Forrestal had become his patron, a fact that was to have a significant bearing on the writing and publication a year later of the famous "X" article, the public statement which crystallized U.S. policy toward the Soviet Union into a one-word description—"containment."

THE "X" ARTICLE

FORRESTAL'S READING of the Long Telegram served to reinforce his own convictions about the nature and motivations of the Soviet government, but it left unnoticed important differences of emphasis between Kennan's view and his own. Citing Kennan but in fact pursuing his own line of argument, he spoke out with increasing vigor during the Iran and Trieste crises of 1946 and with respect to the urgent British request for a $5 billion loan. In a meeting of the State-War-Navy Coordinating Committee on March 6, he gave it as his opinion that the Kremlin aimed at world revolution and that Communist doctrine creates "a mystic support in its adherents" without regard to national boundaries and loyalties. As to Trieste, he said, "Tito is in fact Russia; therefore if any move is made [by Tito], it would be at Russian instigation." He did not argue that the loan request from a British Labour government was in any way inspired by the Kremlin, but he sought to prohibit the use of its proceeds to introduce "socialism" into the British zone of occupation in Germany. At the same time, he shared the determination of the American "free trade" advocates to drive a hard bargain in the negotiations, even against America's closest and most reliable ally, whose resources had been virtually wiped out in fighting a war of survival. Not only did the American negotiators reduce the loan principal to $3.75 billion, but also demanded the removal of all restrictions on the free exchange of sterling; this meant the end of "imperial preferences" within the British Commonwealth and opened the way for equal American access to those markets.[52]

On March 10, Forrestal saw Churchill for an hour on the latter's return to Washington from his Iron Curtain speech in Fulton, Missouri. He found the Englishman worried about Soviet pressures against Greece and Turkey, which Churchill interpreted as an effort to break the British lifeline in the Mediterranean. This, combined with a sense that France was being "inoculated" with Communism and that the virus was also beginning to "flow across Germany into Holland and Belgium," made the former Prime Minister "very gloomy" in the absence of a U.S.-British military alliance which made clear to the Russians that "they would be met with force if they continued their expansion."[53] Forrestal fully shared the view that more emphasis must be placed on a unified military response to the threat, but he seemed most pleased by Churchill's apparent agreement with his own analysis of the philosophical problem: that the West was facing not only

"Russia as a national entity," but also "the additional missionary force of a religion."[54]

As Kennan's leading patron in Washington, Forrestal sought the career officer's advice on current policy problems, as well as on more philosophical questions, but the relationship was strictly business and conducted mainly through Forrestal's personal counsel, John T. Connor. On the social side there was one evening cruise on the Navy Secretary's yacht which also included another notable Soviet expert, Charles E. "Chip" Bohlen, and one dinner at Forrestal's house. "I had only slight personal acquaintance with him," Kennan wrote some years later;[55] nevertheless, he formed firm impressions of the man: "He was plainly dedicated to his work in government . . . a man of burning, tireless energy . . . not so much himself a man of reflective and refined intelligence as he was a man who appreciated those qualities in others and was anxious to see them used . . . He had no fear of fresh and unusual opinion. On the contrary, he wanted it. I had the feeling he cared very little about me—or for that matter the rest of us—from the personal standpoint. He was interested in what we had to offer for the solution of government problems. He was prepared to back us if we were on the right track and brought results; otherwise, he simply wouldn't have had time for us."[56]

In more personal terms, Kennan found Forrestal "sharp, tense, inquisitive, potentially very much a hard-liner. He had, I thought, something of the ambitious tightness of the parvenu. He smacked a bit of F. Scott Fitzgerald. There was lacking, it seemed to me, the relaxation and languor of the securely well-born . . . He was surely one of the first senior figures in our government to realize that Stalin and the men around him were brutal and high-stepping gangsters with much blood on their hands who could not be appealed to by personal charm (as FDR fancied he could do)."[57] The superior-subordinate relationship between Cabinet officer and career civil servant is made clear by this passage: "I greatly appreciated his interest in my work, and his confidence . . . he was a man you could always go to to get an open-minded opinion and energetic assistance if you could prove to him you were right."[58]

In the summer of 1946, Forrestal asked Connor to obtain Kennan's views on the Willett study.* Kennan read the paper, but told Connor he would

---

*About this same time, Clark Clifford and George Elsey were developing a report on U.S.-Soviet relations based on the views of Kennan, Leahy, Byrnes, Acheson, Patterson, Forrestal, and others. It indicated a broad consensus within the government on the nature of the Soviet threat. President Truman found it "very valuable," but believed its publication would "blow the roof off the White House . . . and the Kremlin." He locked all twenty copies in his safe. Twenty years later, Clifford arranged for its publication as an appendix to Arthur Krock's *Memoirs.*

prefer not to comment, suggesting instead that the task be given to other Soviet experts like Philip Moseley and Llewellyn Thompson. Both of these men had already given Forrestal their views, but Connor nevertheless turned again to Thompson, whose second comment was dismissive: "Willett's paper in its present form and emphasis appears suitable only for use with religious groups."[59] Returning to Kennan, the persistent Connor finally persuaded him to offer a brief critique. The primary thrust of this was to challenge Willett's stress on the inevitability of war. Kennan thought the Soviets would resort to force against the West "only if the prospects for success are promising," but he believed there was little doubt the West could maintain "a preponderance of strength for the foreseeable future." Therefore, he concluded there was "little likelihood of Russia taking up arms against us. . . . I personally have no fear about our being able to contain the Russians for the foreseeable future." With regard to Eastern Europe, he was certain the Soviets would demand governments subservient to "Moscow's leadership," but he doubted whether the establishment of "Communism" there was more than "a secondary consideration."[60] Significantly, the Kennan comment avoided discussing (thereby implicitly discounting) the ideological/religious factor in Soviet motivation, although this was the central theme of the Willett study.

Forrestal's reaction to the Kennan critique of Willett was not explicit, but the faithful Connor, who thought his boss was sometimes "so introspective and complex" that he had difficulty "driving his thoughts from his mind into the outer world in any coherent form," sensed his dissatisfaction. He also sensed Forrestal's reluctance to expose his own slender credentials as an interpreter of Russian history and policy in a face-to-face debate with a man of Kennan's expertise and intellectual caliber. It became clear to Connor that what Forrestal wanted was for Kennan to undertake a basic reworking of the Willett paper, but without abandoning the Forrestal-Willett assumptions. Connor thereupon went back to Kennan, emphasizing Forrestal's "burning interest" in the project.[61]

Kennan was finally persuaded to undertake a thorough analysis, but refused simply to rework the Willett paper. "This," he wrote in his memoirs, "I found hard to do. It was a good paper. With parts of it I could agree; other parts were simply not put the way I would have put them."[62] In all probability, this was a diplomatic way of saying to Connor and Forrestal that the Willett paper was really too abstruse, too much based on dubious premises, to get a grip on. In the course of these exchanges, Connor got the increasing impression that Kennan was "uncomfortable" with Forrestal's persisting disposition to assert that Soviet "ideology" was the principal motivating factor in Kremlin policy.[63] In any event, Kennan sent the Willett study back to Connor with an offer to "address myself to the same subject in my own words."[64]

His first effort was "disappointing" to Forrestal, and Connor agreed: "It hadn't been thought through; the Secretary rejected it." Connor thereupon went back to Kennan with the request that he "take another crack at it." Somewhat to his surprise, he found that Kennan was also "displeased with his own effort" and now willing to undertake an evaluation more in line with Forrestal's views.[65] The result was the delivery to Forrestal "for his private and personal edification" of a paper entitled "Psychological Background of Soviet Foreign Policy." The date was January 31, 1947.[66] Two weeks later, Forrestal thanked him in a note saying, "I am most grateful for your final paper. It is extremely well done."[67] Shortly thereafter, Forrestal recommended to George Marshall (who had just become Secretary of State) that Kennan was the ideal man to head the new Policy Planning Staff in the State Department. He also wanted to give the paper wide circulation, especially in the press and on Capitol Hill, but accepted Kennan's reluctance to have his name publicly associated with it, given his status as a career foreign service officer.

In the same month of January, Kennan spoke informally, from notes, to the Council on Foreign Relations in New York on the same perplexing question of the nature and purposes of the Soviet Union and what line of policy the United States ought to pursue. Hamilton Fish Armstrong, the editor of *Foreign Affairs* (the quarterly magazine published by the council), asked him whether he had something in textual form along the lines of his talk that could be published in the magazine. According to Kennan, what came to mind was the paper he had prepared for Forrestal. He told Armstrong that his official position precluded a signed article, but asked the editor whether publication without attribution would suffice. Armstrong replied that the importance of the subject "more than outweighs . . . the disadvantage of anonymity."[68] There followed a request to Forrestal and Forrestal's agreement to have the paper published. Official clearance was obtained from the appropriate State Department committee, with the understanding that it be published anonymously. Six months later, in July 1947, the paper appeared under the title "The Sources of Soviet Conduct," by "Mr. X."[69]

Within a week Kennan's thin cover was blown in Arthur Krock's column in the *New York Times,* and it became apparent that Forrestal had given the story to his journalist friend, complete with an explanation that the authority and official position of its author meant the article was an accurate reflection of U.S. policy. The policy it argued for was a strategy of global confrontation involving the "long-term, patient but firm and vigilant containment of Russian expansive tendencies . . . by the adroit and vigilant application of counterforce at a series of constantly shifting geographical and political points corresponding to the shifts and maneuvers of Soviet policy . . ."[70]

The "X" article crystallized the U.S. "containment" policy in official Washington and in the public mind by providing a persuasive rationale for the kind of comprehensive approach to national security (integrating diplomacy, intelligence, economic resources, and military force) which Forrestal espoused. Kennan himself, however, soon recoiled from the general interpretation of his strategy as a primarily military response to a primarily military threat. He had meant to propound, he insisted, a strategy of predominantly political containment to meet a predominantly political threat. Kennan was a realist, and his strategy of "political" containment included a range of clandestine propaganda and paramilitary activities designed to give Stalin a severe pain in his own backyard.* But to accord too much emphasis to the military aspect of the Soviet threat involved, he argued, a dangerous oversimplification.

The problem was, and is, that the language of the "X" article did not provide convincing support for this post facto protest against a Western military buildup. Moreover, Kennan's anguished and continuing expressions of mea culpa—for the failure of the article to deal with the specific problem of Soviet power in Eastern Europe or to say that "containment" should be limited to certain key industrial areas of the world—did not remove the ambiguity or weaken the military implications of the published article.

Kennan's systematic efforts to dissociate himself from "Mr. X" raise not the question of its literal authorship, but the question of who possessed the dominant will in a collaboration between a senior Cabinet member and a civil servant. The question gains weight by a comparison of Kennan's talk to the Council on Foreign Relations and the paper that became the "X" article. Presumably he gave the paper to *Foreign Affairs* in the belief that its message accurately reflected the substance of his remarks to the council; in fact, there are striking differences of emphasis and tone. The talk was made from notes rather than a complete text, but a "Digest of Discussion" was prepared by the rapporteur, Edwin C. Hoyt, Jr. The talk paralleled the "X" article in explaining that Russia's historic xenophobia derived in part from endless foreign invasions and in part from the use of such foreign threats by always autocratic Russian governments to suppress internal opposition. For Russian governments the end always justified the means, and "these traditions and attitudes" were made to "dovetail conveniently" with Marxist ideology. In essence, Kennan said in his talk, the declared Marxist aim to liberate workingmen throughout the world had become merely the moral fig leaf for justifying a repressive regime at home and the expansionist aims of the Russian state. In short, considerations of

*See Chapter 23 for a fuller discussion of Forrestal, Kennan, and covert operations.

state security and ambition were primary; ideology was a tool to serve these primary purposes.[71]

In this assessment of the adversary, Kennan "found no cause for despair." He thought it "perfectly possible" for the United States and other countries "to contain Russian power, if it were done courteously and in a non-provocative way," and also to induce "internal changes in Russia, provided the effort was sustained over a sufficient time span." His basic optimism was based on his reading of Russian diplomacy as "enormously flexible." Soviet leaders always prepare an avenue of retreat and "are very cautious in a military sense, never allowing their commitments to exceed their capabilities." To be successful in these circumstances, U.S. policy had to be firm and self-assured, taking care to avoid "fatuous concessions without receiving a quid pro quo." But in the face of firm, proportioned containment, "the Russians will never challenge us to an open war."[72]

Between January and the publication of the "X" article in July, Kennan had taken positions in the momentous debates on Greek-Turkish aid (the Truman Doctrine) and on the comprehensive recovery program for Western Europe (the Marshall Plan) that were entirely consistent with his talk to the council study group. He protested, in vain, the sweeping language in the President's enunciation of the Truman Doctrine, for he feared it would launch a universal American crusade, committing the United States to provide aid to any country anywhere that could demonstrate the existence of a Communist threat. He also believed such an open-ended policy would intensify Soviet paranoia and intransigence. He argued that the President's declaration should be confined geographically to Greece and Turkey.[73] Here he was overruled by Dean Acheson, the Under Secretary of State, who was influenced by Senator Vandenberg's warning that congressional support for the aid program would be very difficult "unless you scared hell out of them."[74] With respect to the Marshall Plan, Kennan was more successful; his proportioned approach—which included the high risk of inviting the Soviets to participate, based on his shrewd calculation that the Kremlin would have to refuse—carried the day.

How then to explain the striking differences between the Kennan who spoke to the council advocating moderate, geographically limited responses to Soviet challenges during the spring of 1947 and the Kennan who authored the "X" article published in July. In his memoirs, Kennan edged crablike toward a kind of explanation by acknowledging that what became the "X" article was written to reflect "what I felt to be Mr. Forrestal's needs at the time when I prepared the original paper for him."[75] The official relationship of the two men must be kept in mind. Forrestal was a senior Cabinet officer of exceptional influence and reputation who had already done a great deal to advance Kennan's career. He wanted a statement of the Soviet problem which, like the Willett study, adhered closely to his own view that the Marxist dialectic was the paramount factor in the Kremlin's motivation, but he also desired a statement more erudite, more authoritative than Willett (or Forrestal himself) could produce. He asked Kennan to comment on the Willett study, and when the Soviet expert expressed a preference to write his own paper, Forrestal accepted this condition, read the resulting document critically, rejected the first draft, and asked for changes. Pressed for time, taking into account the sum total of the circumstances, and believing he was writing for Forrestal's "private and personal edification" Kennan in effect yielded, subtly and probably subconsciously, to the stronger will and the greater official authority. While the ideas in the "X" article were in large part a recapitulation of what Kennan had been expressing for several years, they were subjected to an odd, ambiguous skewing in this essay by the fact of being implicitly guided by the premises of the Willett study. In the end, the thrust of the paper was closer to Forrestal's view than to Kennan's, in the sense of inviting the interpretation that Western military strength must be the major component of a containment strategy.

This form of deferment to higher authority is an everyday occurrence in the bureaucracy; in a sense, it is necessary to the orderly operation of any hierarchical organization. The fair inference is that, in the light of his later intellectual eminence, Kennan could not bring himself to a full admission of what had happened here beyond the oblique reference to serving "Mr. Forrestal's needs at the time." Of course, neither he nor Forrestal realized at the time of writing that the paper would be published—and under circumstances that would quickly identify Kennan as the author. But though he was permanently anguished by the consequences for U.S. policy—which he accurately perceived as a steadily growing militarization of the containment doctrine—he chose to adhere to the position that the authorship was entirely his. By doing so, he ensnared himself in confessions of "egregious error" in efforts to dissociate himself from the logical implications of the paper's prescriptions and otherwise in endless explanations that did not explain.

Dean Acheson, who grew more caustic with the passing years, thought in 1967 that the explanation for the discrepancy lay in Kennan's "inherently literary and fuzzy mind." In Acheson's opinion, Kennan's paper for Forrestal said "exactly what he meant at the time," but he failed to perceive the military implications of his words. When the essay became the public "X" article, and critics—especially Walter Lippmann—reproached him as a militarist, he recoiled from the image.[76]

The differences in emphasis between Kennan and Forrestal were subtle and thus easily obscured, but they rested, in fact, on divergent assessments of the threat and of the level of military strength required for successful containment. Kennan was never called upon to define the level of military strength he considered adequate, but he consistently expressed the view that a rather modest level would suffice, given his conviction that Soviet leaders would not resort to war unless they foresaw an easy victory. Forrestal, on the other hand, saw the Red Army as the enforcing instrument of a group animated by a fanatical ideology and bent upon global conquest. He thought the Kremlin was ready to use force whenever the odds favored it even slightly, and in 1947–1948 he believed the balance of power was unfavorable to the West. He therefore held a firm view of the kind of analysis needed to form the intellectual basis of U.S. foreign policy. It must educate and arouse the citizenry to the danger. It must do so by stressing the global nature of the threat and the ideological wellsprings of Soviet behavior. It must point to the need for a U.S. response based primarily on military power. He succeeded in getting enough of these ideas into the "X" article to support his own position. Five months before its publication (when it was still titled "Psychological Background of Soviet Foreign Policy") he sent a copy to Clarence Dillon with a note which said, "Nothing about Russia can be understood without also understanding the implacable and unchanging direction of Lenin's religion-philosophy."[77]

The "X" article had a profound and cumulative effect on American policy thinking, but almost no immediate impact on the level of military preparedness. Truman's rigid insistence on balancing the budget, even in the face of global unrest and rising Soviet challenges to the status quo in both Europe and Asia, kept a tight lid on military spending until the attack on South Korea in June 1950. The President's budgetary stance was underpinned by threat assessments written by a Policy Planning Staff headed by Kennan. Substantial military buildup came only with the Korean War and other wrenching events—like the Communist victory in the Chinese civil war and Soviet development of the atomic bomb—that provoked intense American frustration, anger, and fear. On a rising tide of anti-Communism and a felt need to confront and defeat its every manifestation at every point on the globe, the Eisenhower administration proceeded to ring the Soviet Union and China with regional security pacts, a network of military bases, and military assistance programs in some forty-two countries. All or most of these developments were explained as actions within a strategy of containment, but this only proved the elasticity of the concept.

This American military response was ultimately excessive. It exaggerated the military threat and failed to meet the tests of reason and legitimate U.S. interest. It set the pace in the subsequent horrendous nuclear and conventional arms race which dominated the next four decades. It led to the Vietnam quagmire. Yet Forrestal was surely right in believing that some reasonable U.S. military buildup was prudent and necessary in 1947–1948, to provide a respectable base of power to deter Communist adventures and to underpin the rapidly accumulating American political and military commitments in a period of extreme tension and unrest throughout the world. Had Truman not been myopically focused on a balanced budget, he might have avoided the Korean War, for military stringency lay at the root of Secretary of State Dean Acheson's carefully considered policy speech on January 12, 1950, which tempted fate by defining the U.S. defense perimeter in Asia to exclude Korea and Formosa.

On the need for a U.S. military buildup in 1947–1948, Forrestal was more attuned to reality than both Truman and Kennan, but it was ironic that the otherwise pragmatic Wall Street banker and administrator—contemptuous of social planners and other theoretical meddlers—should have come to believe in the most abstract and theological explanation of Soviet motivation and behavior. The answer seemed to lie somewhere in his Catholic past, in his suspiciousness and insecurity, in his jesuitical fascination with intellectual complexity. The Forrestal who confronted the phenomenon of the Kremlin was Philip Barry's "Jimmy the Priest."

★ ★ ★

CHAPTER 22

Controlling the Bomb

THE ATOMIC BOMB lay at the core of the whole problem of postwar military policy. It had transformed the nature of warfare and thus of all previous strategy, but this was too stunning and too ramified a truth to be fully grasped by anyone in 1945 and 1946. Some thought the U.S. monopoly provided the leverage to obtain a postwar settlement largely on American terms. Others saw that this possibility clearly disturbed the Soviet Union, which, in the wake of its decisive victory over Hitler's Germany, had begun to feel secure again for the first time since 1917. Because the bomb seemed a weapon that could not be defeated by superior Soviet ground forces, the U.S. monopoly became, in fact, a new source of Soviet suspicion and fear. In addition, within a few weeks after Hiroshima and Nagasaki were obliterated, world opinion was demonstrating a deep anxiety about the bomb's implications for the survival of mankind and was beginning to make known its still groping, inchoate demands for international control.

AT A CABINET LUNCH on Tuesday, September 18, 1945, just a few weeks after his return from Potsdam, President Truman told his colleagues to prepare for a full-dress discussion of the whole question of atomic policy on Friday, the twenty-first. The ensuing debate was far more substantive than most Cabinet sessions, and it revealed sharp differences of approach. There was also some misunderstanding as to the question on which Truman was seeking advice. This was *not* whether to give away the atomic bomb, but whether to make available to other nations certain theoretical scientific data as a first step toward an international control system based on mutual confidence and trust. The President went around the table, turning first to the Secretary of War, who was resigning that afternoon on the occasion of his seventy-eighth birthday.[1]

Stimson had no illusions about the dictatorial and repressive character of the Soviet system, and he harbored fundamental doubts whether "permanently safe international relations" could be established between an open democracy and a closed police state.[2] Nevertheless, since Potsdam and the actual use of the bomb on Hiroshima and Nagasaki, he had concluded that the vital consideration for American policy would be the attitude of the Soviet Union at the time it acquired the capacity to produce its own atomic weapons—an acquisition which the scientific community regarded as inevitable within a few years. Moreover, the scientists believed that future atomic bombs would be infinitely more destructive, perhaps so powerful that their explosion might ignite the atmosphere and put an end to the world. Stimson therefore advocated a direct approach to the Soviets—a direct bilateral approach, with British knowledge and consent but not involving the lesser powers or the United Nations—in an effort "to control and limit the use of the atomic bomb as an instrument of war."[3] He had developed this position in an April 11 memorandum for Truman, and he now summarized the essence of his concerns. It would be a serious mistake, he thought, to try to use the bomb "as a direct lever" in an effort to force democratic reforms on the Soviet Union. In the first place, it wouldn't work. In the second place, it would only produce a further deterioration in U.S.-Soviet relations: "If we fail to approach them now, and merely continue to negotiate with them, having this weapon rather ostentatiously on our hip, their suspicions and their distrust of our purposes and motives will increase."[4]

Dean Acheson, sitting in for Byrnes, who was still at the London Conference, substantially supported Stimson. Recognizing the increasing distrust in the U.S.-Soviet relationship, Acheson nevertheless considered that "any semblance of long-term understanding would become impossible under a policy of Anglo-American exclusion of Russia from atomic development."[5]

Forrestal was in fierce and direct opposition to these views. He spoke from a memorandum which Henry Wallace later characterized as "prepared by his Admirals . . . a warlike big-Navy isolationist approach."[6] Both the atomic bomb and the scientific effort expended to achieve it were, Forrestal said, "the property of the American people," and no administration had the right to give away these assets until it was "very sure" the American people concurred. The Russians, like the Japanese, "are essentially Oriental in their thinking," and recent painful experience proved they could not be trusted. Therefore, in the absence of a much longer record of experience with the Russians, we should not try "to buy their understanding and sympathy. We tried that once with Hitler. There are no returns on appeasement." If, however, the U.S. government perceived an overriding need to reassure world opinion, "we could exercise a trusteeship over the atomic bomb on behalf of the United Nations."[7] Forrestal's convictions here reflected an innate nationalism intensified by his many trips to battle-fronts where American technology and bravery had clashed at the bloody divide between irreconcilable ideologies, and by his emotional response to the violent deaths of thousands of young Americans. This was now rein-forced by his total distrust of the Soviet government. He was loath to give away any advantage for U.S. security that he perceived as having been won by American sacrifice. To his mind, this would be a replay of the fatal retreat from reality after World War I.

As an exponent of realpolitik, he had persuaded Byrnes that the United States should be able to use the bomb as an effective, unspoken negotiating weapon ("the gun behind the door") to impose measurable restraints on the Soviet system and its international ambitions, for he accepted the op-timistic assumption of U.S. military men that the American monopoly would last a long time (General Leslie Groves, who had managed the building of the bomb, predicted "at least 20 years").[8] Broadly speaking, the scientific community held a quite different view. Vannevar Bush told Truman that the atomic "secret" resided essentially in "the details of construction of the bombs themselves and in the manufacturing process"; getting the bomb was thus largely a matter of organization and resources. Bush thought the Russians could produce one in five or six years, provided they applied a large part of their scientific and industrial capacity to the task.[9] As previously mentioned, Forrestal and Byrnes tended to discount the practical wisdom of scientists as a group and were not comfortable with their intrusion into the formulation of high policy.

Wallace also spoke out at the Cabinet meeting, in general support of the Stimson approach. He did not advocate giving the bomb to the Soviets or to anyone else, and he argued for retention of unique American engineering-manufacturing know-how, but he thought the United States should offer to share scientific data in exchange for access to Soviet research laboratories. In the course of his remarks, he cast doubt on Forrestal's assertion that the Russians were "essentially Oriental in their thinking." Having been an original member of the five-man group secretly designated by FDR to monitor the bomb project, Wallace reminded the Cabinet that the scientific data which made the bomb possible had come in 1939 from Jewish scien-tists in Europe who feared Hitler might build it first. Because "the whole approach had originated in Europe," Wallace argued, "it would be im-possible to bottle the thing up no matter how much we tried." There would be grave danger in adopting a "Maginot Line attitude of mind."[10] Forrestal was equally opposed to the Stimson and the Wallace views, but his diary notes focused exclusively on Wallace, whom he found "completely, ever-lastingly and wholeheartedly in favor of giving it [the atomic bomb] to the Russians."[11] Soon thereafter a story appeared in the *New York Times* which described the Stimson proposal, but attributed it to Wallace. Fingers were immediately and subsequently pointed at several possible perpetrators of the leak. Acheson thought it was Forrestal or a navy admiral to whom he had talked. President Truman thought it was Leo Crowley, the Foreign Economic Administrator, and banished him from all future Cabinet meetings. Wallace doubted that Forrestal was the culprit, although he "always felt" the Navy Secretary was "to some extent unbalanced." He finally decided it was probably Matt Connelly, Truman's Appointments Secretary, and he had no doubt the leak was a deliberate effort to reduce his political standing with middle-of-the-road Democrats.[12]

Forrestal's harder, stricter construction of the national interest on this point won the support of Attorney General Tom Clark, Treasury Secretary Fred Vinson, Agriculture Secretary Clinton Anderson, and John Snyder, the St. Louis banker who had succeeded Byrnes as head of War Mobilization. Furthermore, when Byrnes returned from London, he made clear his own opposition to sharing atomic data and thus repudiated the position Acheson had put forward on behalf of the State Department. Byrnes, however, was about to change his mind. Stimson's proposal was supported only by Wallace and Labor Secretary Lewis Schwellenbach, together with lesser lights from the Housing Administration and the War Manpower Commission. At the same time, there emerged from this Cabinet meeting a rough consensus on the need to develop definite proposals for some form of international control, including U.S. participation in an ongoing international organization dedicated to that task.[13]

Sensing a need to reconcile his own severely nationalist convictions with the political requirement for Truman to meet the developing pressure of world opinion, Forrestal returned to the Navy Department to wrestle with the dilemma. He drafted a proposal that would provide for the United States to hold a trusteeship from the United Nations over "all information regarding atomic power and its use as a weapon of war." To reassure the world that America would not abuse the role of primary guardian, it would pledge "to use this weapon only as directed by the Security Council itself in the maintenance of world peace and security."[14] Forrestal considered this formulation a compromise between "a flat refusal" to share control of the bomb and a "complete dissemination" of atomic data, which would result in loss of U.S. control. On reflection, however, he was dissatisfied with it—perhaps because it was, in fact, not much of a compromise, perhaps because it did not take into adequate account the Russian veto in the Security Council. In any event, he never sent the memorandum, but worked up a less muscular revision which was sent to the White House on October 1. This provided that if the United Nations objected to a U.S. trusteeship, the United States would "turn the entire issue over to that body" provided that "UN inspection teams could inspect atomic research in all countries and publish their findings."[15] The unsatisfactory vagueness of this alternative reflected the central dilemma confronting every effort by the U.S. government to find a solution to a problem that was without precedent.

FORMULAS FOR INTERNATIONAL CONTROL

THE COMPLEXITIES seemed infinite and Truman was resolved to move slowly, but a loose consensus was gradually gathering around the idea that the United States should offer to share basic theoretical data in return for comparable Soviet openness on a strict quid pro quo basis. Meanwhile, the new British Prime Minister, Labourite Clement Attlee, was calling for a review of the wartime atomic partnership of the United States, Britain, and Canada, and this led to a meeting of the three heads of state in Washington on November 10. Vannevar Bush, who was hastily called upon to develop an American plan for the meeting, wrote a memorandum which preserved the Stimson idea of a direct approach to the Soviets first, but the meeting itself turned into a piece of "helter skelter statecraft" caused and aggravated by the profound technical ignorance of the principal discussants—Truman, Attlee, and Canadian Prime Minister Mackenzie King.[16] Bush later wrote to Stimson that his experiences during that conference "would make a chapter in 'Alice in Wonderland.' " When the dust had settled, the three heads of state had in effect rejected the Stimson approach and proposed that international control of atomic energy be entrusted directly to a multinational United Nations Commission.[17]

At the same time, Byrnes, the deal maker, frustrated by his failure in London to move the Soviets toward U.S. positions by using the atomic monopoly as an implicit lever, now persuaded Truman the time had come to take the bomb out from behind the door and lay it on the table. Eager to negotiate on the basis of any plausible instrument, he offered the U.S.-British-Canadian proposal at the Moscow Conference a month later and, somewhat surprisingly, the Soviets gave their consent without much argument. They also agreed that the first meeting of the new United Nations Atomic Energy Commission should take place the following June 14.[18]

This gave the United States five months to develop a coherent policy, a task which was handed to Dean Acheson and a committee including Vannevar Bush, General Groves, John J. McCloy, and Dr. James Conant, a noted scientist who was president of Harvard. An advisory group, headed by David Lilienthal, Chairman of the Tennessee Valley Authority, and physicist J. Robert Oppenheimer, provided technical expertise. Forrestal and the navy were rather conspicuously excluded from this undertaking. The work of the group went forward in the winter and spring of 1946 against a background of events which included disclosure of the Soviet atomic spy ring in Canada and the crisis in Iran precipitated by a Soviet threat to annex the Iranian province of Azerbaijan. There was mounting hostility in Congress to any disclosure of atomic data—to the Soviets or any other foreign nation—and the gulf of mistrust between the United States and the U.S.S.R. widened daily.

The result of the work, known as the Acheson-Lilienthal Report, nevertheless reflected a serious effort to achieve genuine international control. It proposed an Atomic Development Authority under the United Nations which would acquire by purchase or lease all raw materials needed to produce atomic energy; the Authority would operate all plants that processed these materials to make weapons and would direct all research and license all national atomic activities. Intrusive U.N. inspection of all nationally owned raw materials and atomic research facilities, including those of the Soviet Union, would be required. As Acheson explained the proposal in a radio address, "In plain words, the Report sets up a plan under which no nation would make atomic bombs or the materials for them. All dangerous activities would be carried on . . . by a live, functioning international Authority . . ."[19] The coming into effect of these international controls would of necessity be gradual and accomplished in several defined "stages." Advance from one stage to another would require the consent of all parties. Meanwhile, the United States would retain its stockpile of bombs.

As a practical matter, the Acheson-Lilienthal Report was very unlikely to gain Soviet acceptance, but what happened next eliminated whatever small chance might have existed. Over Acheson's protest, Bernard Baruch was appointed as the U.S. delegate to the U.N. Atomic Energy Commission to present the U.S. plan and to debate the issues. The appointment was the work of Byrnes, whom Baruch had long befriended and financially supported, but it is quite possible that the idea came from Forrestal, for he and Byrnes were close collaborators on most issues and both were admirers of Baruch. This inference is strengthened by Baruch's subsequent turning to Ferdinand Eberstadt to be his chief deputy.

The seventy-five-year-old financier was a fellow South Carolinian who had often entertained Byrnes on his 13,000-acre estate in their home state. Many, including Forrestal and Eberstadt, thought him a statesman of rare common sense and patriotism, but many others, including Acheson and Lilienthal, considered him a shallow poseur. The original idea was for Baruch to add political palatability to the Acheson-Lilienthal Report among congressional conservatives, but this limited assignment affronted Baruch's vanity. Announcing that he was too old and seasoned to be "a messenger boy," he demanded the right to give distinctive shape to the presentation; Byrnes and Truman soothingly agreed.[20] Baruch then gathered a small staff, notable for its absence of scientists, and assigned Eberstadt the role of chief strategist and tactician. Eberstadt consulted at length with the Joint

Chiefs of Staff, who were categorically opposed to any steps that would "limit our capability to produce or use this weapon" or "further unbalance" the existing world power balance which, they argued, was already tipped against the United States. The military chiefs were obviously worried about the rapid deterioration of American conventional forces as a consequence of the swift and continuing postwar demobilization. In their calculations, the American atomic bomb monopoly was emerging as the essential counterweight, the equalizer, to the Soviet preponderance in ground forces, although it was not clear to them—or to anyone else— whether, and if so how, and under what circumstances, the United States could or would use atomic weapons. In the meantime, however, the JCS were opposed to any international constraints.[21]

As it finally emerged, the Baruch Plan was (in its essential elements) the Acheson-Lilienthal Report, but Baruch insisted on two melodramatic additions: One was to provide for "swift and sure punishment" for a violation; the other was to provide that in a case of violation by a permanent member of the Security Council, that member would not be permitted to veto punitive action voted by a majority of that body.[22] Acheson, Lilienthal, and others vainly protested that these were "very dangerous words" which added nothing to the proposed treaty, but were certain to convince the Soviets that the United States was seeking to turn the United Nations into an alliance to support a U.S. threat of war against the Soviet Union.[23] Truman, however, supported Baruch.

At what Truman's biographer, Robert Donovan, called "the high water mark of American dilettantism about the United Nations," Baruch unveiled his plan on June 14, 1946, at the temporary U.N. headquarters: "Fashionable women descended on Hunter College . . . as if it were opening night at the Metropolitan Opera, and heard in awe Mr. Baruch's introductory line (composed by [the journalist] Herbert Bayard Swope, then a member of the New York State Racing Commission): 'We are here to make a choice between the quick and the dead.' "[24]

The Baruch Plan appeared to the American press and public as a plausible, even noble formula for averting the catastrophe of nuclear war, and given the rising American distrust of everything relating to the Soviet Union, that was a logical American reaction. The *New York Times* applauded Baruch for having the courage to present a plan that would intrude upon the national sovereignty of the United States; "the mass of the American people . . . will agree with what Mr. Baruch has so movingly and solemnly said . . . Better foreign inspectors at Oak Ridge than foreign bombs over our cities."[25] Forrestal sent Baruch a one-word congratulatory telegram: "Bullseye."[26] Nevertheless, as political analysts soon noted, the plan, if accepted and carried into effect, would place the Soviet Union in a position of permanent inferiority—the Americans would remain in full possession of their atomic arsenal long after the Soviets had surrendered basic information about their uranium sources and had opened their research laboratories to international inspection.[27] James Reston, the *Times* diplomatic correspondent, wrote that the Executive Branch liked the plan because it "passed the ball" to the Congress and the Congress liked it because "it left the next tough moves to the Kremlin."[28]

Predictably, the Soviet delegate, Andrei Gromyko, soon presented a counterproposal totally at variance with Baruch's. This called for a U.N. resolution banning the production and use of atomic bombs, to be followed by the destruction of all existing weapons. It proposed no system of international inspection or control, while insisting the Big Power veto could not be removed from any U.N. decision relating to atomic energy.

The fundamental distrust between the two nations was now exposed on the most dramatic, life-and-death issue on the international stage. In all probability no conceivable plan would have been acceptable to both sides in 1946. The Americans would not give up what they were coming to see as the essential strategic equalizer in the emerging global confrontation with a treacherous and hostile system. The Soviets would not accept a position of permanent atomic inferiority. There ensued six months of futile debate on the Baruch and Gromyko plans, during which time a palpable impatience to settle the issue grew steadily in Washington. On the last day of the year, Baruch called for a vote. Ten nations approved the Baruch Plan. The Soviet Union chose not to exercise its veto, but to abstain, as did Poland. Without affirmative Soviet support, no implementation was possible. There was nothing more to say. Words had failed. The dangerous nuclear arms race was on in earnest, and no basis would exist for any agreement on controls and reductions until the Soviets had achieved something resembling parity.[29]

Forrestal strongly supported the decision to bring the Baruch Plan to a vote, for this cleared the air of lingering ambiguity. By showing the American people the Soviets were not amenable to reason (as embodied in the democratic belief in majority rule), the U.N. vote strengthened public support for measures Forrestal felt to be imperative—to halt demobilization, to devise an encompassing cold war strategy (which would involve the close meshing of diplomacy, intelligence collection, economic resources, and military capability), and to strengthen the armed forces. It was fundamental, in Forrestal's view, to rebuild and reassert American military power so the United States could contain Russian expansive tendencies and deal with the phenomenon of global Communism from what Dean Acheson later defined as "positions of strength."

CHAPTER 23

★ ★ ★

Waging Cold War

PACIFIC ISLAND BASES

ORRESTAL and the navy were disturbed by a memorandum from Under Secretary of State Stettinius on the subject of the "Mandated Islands" in the Pacific. The date was June 22, 1944, just two weeks after the Normandy landings and while the Pacific War was still gathering its violent momentum. The memorandum reflected the fact that Secretary of State Cordell Hull, being wholly removed from the conduct of the war, was occupying himself with large abstract plans for the coming peace. In preparing for the San Francisco Conference to establish the United Nations (scheduled for April 1945), the State Department was endeavoring to formulate a general policy toward those areas which had been "mandates" under the League of Nations—that is, areas in which peoples not considered ready for self-government were placed under the supervision of a designated League member who then became accountable to the League for its stewardship. Implicit in the mandate was the obligation to advance the backward peoples toward self-government.[1]

According to Stimson, it was FDR's hope that after World War II the mandate principle could be extended to all colonial territories, whether or not they had been held by an enemy before the war. His aim was to move toward the breakup of the European colonial system by placing all such areas in a transitional status. Because this approach confronted all of the pride, self-interest, and power of the remaining colonial nations—Britain, France, the Netherlands, Belgium, and Portugal—it was not a realistic idea. Nevertheless, Hull was pursuing it with FDR's approval, and he reasoned that the United States could hardly expect to sell the proposal to the world community unless it too was prepared to forgo annexation of territories gained in the war, but agreed instead to hold them under a U.N. trusteeship.[2]

Forrestal, somewhat incredulous at the substance of the State Department memorandum, asked Stettinius "if this was a serious document and if he understood that the President was committed to it." He added that "it seems to me a *sine qua non* of any postwar arrangements that there should be no debate as to who ran the Mandated Islands—that is, the islands formerly owned by Japan in the Central Pacific."[3] Stimson and the War Department took exactly the same position. Because the area in question was essentially uninhabited, Stimson argued, no purpose would be served by "classing such islands with colonial areas containing large populations and considerable economic resources. . . . They are not colonies; they are outposts of great strategic significance, restored to US control by an effort 'written in blood.' " Their acquisition "is appropriate under the general doctrine of self-defense by the power which guarantees the safety of that area of the world. . . . They must belong to the United States with absolute power to rule and fortify them."[4] The State Department understood and shared the desire for U.S. control of the islands, but felt the broader aim of achieving U.N. trusteeships elsewhere required a more generous bargaining position. Forrestal and the War Department adamantly disagreed and the matter dragged on for another year, with the U.S. retaining physical control of the islands.

In January 1946, Byrnes cabled from a conference in London asking President Truman to authorize him to make a statement that the United States would be prepared "to trustee" the Pacific islands under arrangements with the United Nations. Acheson, then Under Secretary of State, obtained Truman's approval without consulting the War or Navy departments. An angry Forrestal went to the White House on January 21 to protest and succeeded in obtaining assurances that Byrnes would "not commit this country to any definite position."[5] He also complained that Acheson's method of securing the President's approval was "a desertion of the general idea of cooperation" and he thought the incident reflected the "rapidly vanishing determination" in America to avoid the costly mistakes of 1918–1919, when those same strategic islands were secretly turned over to Japan. The next day he told Acheson "in very strong terms" that regular meetings of the State-War-Navy Coordinating Committee should not lapse simply because the war was over. Here he was emphasizing his basic conviction that a coherent foreign policy required continuous coordination between the State Department and the military services. "The tempo at which events are now moving," he told Acheson, "made it more important than ever to make sure that there were no slips between us."[6]

Throughout 1946, Forrestal continued to worry about the form in which the State Department would present the idea of trusteeships, feeling there was mounting pressure from domestic public opinion for further demobilization, reinforced by Republican complaints that U.S. military and economic commitments were too expensive and that the Joint Chiefs of Staff

Forrestal's navy team in early 1946.
Left to right: *Struve Hensel, Assistant Secretary; Artemus Gates,*
Assistant Secretary for Air; Forrestal; Ralph Bard, Under Secretary

were dictating foreign policy. Since V-J Day the armed forces had shrunk from about 12 million men to about 1.6 million. But even this reduction left the United States at a dramatically higher level than American forces had ever been maintained in a previous "peacetime" period, and it was too high for those who urged a return to "normalcy." In sharp contrast, Forrestal and others who were dealing every day with the severe dislocation, unrest, hunger, and revolutionary agitation in much of the world perceived a growing gap between America's unavoidable foreign commitments and its military power. He worried that "this drive [for demobilization] will be greatly intensified" with the "unwitting help" of leading Republicans "such as Taft, Taber, Knudsen, etc., whose services will be enlisted on the side of economy."[7]

To make sure the Pacific islands remained firmly in American hands, he lobbied Byrnes vigorously—and to good effect. As Byrnes later explained, "The Secretary of the Navy was very reasonable"; while not wishing to imply "lack of confidence in the United Nations," he wanted to make sure the arrangement "would permit the Navy to maintain adequate bases," for "he felt keenly the loss of life these islands had cost us."[8] In November

1946, Byrnes assured Forrestal that whatever the form of the final arrangements, they would give the navy "something that was tantamount to sovereignty,"[9] and that is how the matter was finally resolved. Thus, when Molotov told Byrnes in December that if the United States intended to fortify the islands, the Soviet Union must be a party to the decisions, Byrnes retorted that, in that event, the United States would require a voice in Soviet decisions regarding the Kuriles and Sakhalin. When Molotov said those Soviet holdings were not open to discussion, as the issues had been settled by previous agreement (at Yalta), Byrnes replied that he did not regard any subject as being closed to discussion by previous agreement.[10]

THE MEDITERRANEAN LIFELINE

AT POTSDAM, Stalin had sought U.S. and British support for a Soviet share in control of the Dardanelles, but they had rebuffed him. There followed heavy Soviet pressure on the Turks to negotiate a revision of the Montreux Convention looking to joint Soviet-Turkish defense of that sea passage. Concurrently the Soviets were in violation of a wartime agreement by refusing to withdraw their military forces from the province of Azerbaijan in northern Iran; and in nearby Greece a civil war was beginning between the supporters of the monarchy and a coalition of left-wing factions including the Greek Communists. The consensus in the foreign policy establishments of Washington and London was that in the tradition of the Czars, Stalin was probing for a breakthrough into the Mediterranean and that these probes must be resisted. Forrestal shared this assessment. He was also aware of Britain's impending financial exhaustion—the British had just asked for a $5 billion loan—and he seemed to grasp, more quickly than most, that this fact was undermining Britain's ability to play the role of primary stabilizing power in the Mediterranean.

The Turkish ambassador to the United States, Mehmed Ertegun, had died during the war, and his remains were temporarily interred at Arlington National Cemetery pending an opportunity to return them to his native land. In February 1946, Vice Admiral Forrest Sherman, perhaps the best strategic mind in the navy, proposed to Forrestal the idea of sending the body to Istanbul on a U.S. battleship, accompanied by an appropriate group of escorting warships.[11] It was a brilliant suggestion, offering an unprovocative opportunity to show the American flag in the Mediterranean and to demonstrate the presence of U.S. naval power in an area of pivotal strategic importance and waning British influence. Forrestal quickly accepted it. Byrnes agreed, and the two men conspired to make the scheme palatable to the White House by designating the U.S.S. *Missouri* as the principal capital ship. For reasons that remain unclear—some sources say the White

House accepted the idea of a single battleship, but thought a task force too provocative; other sources say the organization of a task force encountered operational problems within a rapidly demobilizing navy—the *Missouri* sailed alone on March 23 and arrived in Istanbul on April 5. Appropriate ceremonies accompanied delivery of the body to Turkish authorities, and there followed official courtesy calls, receptions, and shore leave for American sailors and marines, all of which proved immensely pleasing and reassuring to the Turks.[12]

Forrestal was disappointed not to have been able to send a task force, and his diary entry of March 10 recorded a conversation with Churchill (just returned to Washington from his Iron Curtain speech in Fulton, Missouri) in which the British lion complained that "a gesture of power not fully implemented was almost less effective than no gesture at all."[13] In fact, however, the *Missouri* ploy opened the door to a permanent and substantial U.S. naval presence in the Mediterranean. Just seven months after V-J Day, a prominent symbol of American might (which had been the platform for the Japanese surrender in Tokyo Bay) was riding at anchor in the port of Istanbul, conveying a message of U.S. support for Turkey and a readiness to take up the slack in British naval power in the Mediterranean. In the following year, Forrestal established a pattern of naval visits to all ports of consequence in the area, coupled with a gradual buildup of the force.

It was a timely action, for events in the Mediterranean moved swiftly in 1946 and 1947 against a background of deteriorating conditions at two key points. In Greece, covert aid to the insurgents from Albania, Yugoslavia, and Bulgaria intensified the civil war; in Turkey, there were increased Soviet pressures to obtain a Russian naval base on Turkish territory. On August 15, Acheson (acting for Byrnes, who was in Paris), Patterson, and Forrestal called on the President with a tough memorandum which advanced for the first time what later came to be known as the "domino theory." The primary Soviet objective, they said, was "to obtain control of Turkey," but if this happened, it would be "extremely difficult, if not impossible" to prevent Soviet control over "Greece and over the whole Near and Middle East." And if the Soviet Union gained "full mastery" of this vital territory with its oil and other resources, the Western position would be imperiled. To block such an outcome, they felt it imperative to leave the Soviets in no doubt that if the United Nations should prove unable to stop "Soviet aggression," then the United States "would not hesitate to join with other nations in meeting armed aggression by the force of American arms."[14] Truman quickly approved the proposed policy and said he was prepared to pursue it "to the end." On August 19, Acheson handed a note to the Soviet chargé d'affaires which said, "It is the firm opinion of this government that Turkey should continue to be primarily responsible for the defense of the Straits."[15]

At the same time, Forrestal won Truman's approval to send the new aircraft carrier, *Franklin D. Roosevelt,* to the Mediterranean with suitable escort vessels. Six months later, two carriers, seven cruisers, eighteen destroyers, and various auxiliary ships, in various groupings and rotations, had stopped at forty ports of call, where they and their crews were uniformly welcomed by Greeks, Italians, Sicilians, Cypriots, and North Africans.[16]

On September 30, 1946, Forrestal issued the first public acknowledgment of the new policy on Mediterranean deployments. Relating the U.S. naval presence in both the eastern Atlantic and the Mediterranean to "traditional American practice," he said the navy was "continuing" this in order to "support Allied occupation forces . . . [and] to protect US interests and to support US policy in the area." It was the intention, Forrestal said, to maintain naval ships in the Mediterranean "at a level consistent with the attainment of the foregoing purposes."[17] The New York *Herald Tribune* said editorially the next day that "the Forrestal statement formally linked naval operations with American foreign policy for the first time."[18] This action not only identified the Mediterranean area as a major U.S. strategic interest, but also established a military presence in being on the spot. It also proved a strong stabilizing factor in the enunciation and carrying through of the Truman Doctrine in 1947 and in the efforts to ensure a non-Communist victory in the Italian elections in 1948. Characteristically, Forrestal was applying relevant power unobtrusively.

AROUND THE WORLD IN THIRTY DAYS

IN THE EARLY SUMMER of 1946, Forrestal embarked on an unusually extended trip around the world. Its stated purpose was to observe the atomic bomb tests at Bikini atoll near Eniwetok in the Marshall Islands, but he also planned a global inspection of naval facilities from Pearl Harbor and Tokyo to the Mediterranean and the North Sea and talks with everyone from General Douglas MacArthur and Chiang Kai-shek to General Lucius Clay and King George VI of England. The timing of his departure seemed directly related to political controversies in Washington, for the heated debate over "military unification" had come to a delicate turning point.* Forrestal had fought vigorously to retain the navy's independence as an Executive department, but Truman had now endorsed a single Department of Defense within which the army, navy, and air force would be subordinate components. Forrestal had been a reluctant party to the final compromise, and there were rumors he would resign. A news story of May 26 suggested he might soon accept the presidency of the new International Bank for Reconstruction and Development (later known as the World Bank), but that

*For a detailed discussion of "military unification," see Chapters 24–27.

post went to John J. McCloy. Forrestal decided to use the scheduled Bikini tests as a convenient excuse to get out of town, thus avoiding difficult questions from the press and other manifestations of political fallout. He was away from Washington for nearly a month, which may have been the most important aspect of the trip. Otherwise, although the inspections and the talks were not without substance, the journey as a whole came close to being the kind of superficial junket for which senators and congressmen have become justly infamous. It was by turns bizarre, hilarious, and filled with peril.

He departed Washington on the evening of June 24 accompanied by his naval aide, Captain William Smedberg III, and two special assistants, Captains John A. Kennedy and Frank Nash. They were headed for Kwajalein with intermediate stops in San Francisco and Pearl Harbor. Stuart Symington, Assistant Secretary of War for Air, was proceeding independently as the top-ranking civilian observer for the War Department, accompanied by Major General Curtis E. LeMay, who was Deputy Chief of the Air Staff for Research and Development.[19]

Designated "Operation Crossroads" to connote the universal feeling that mankind now stood on the threshold of a wholly new era in warfare, the Bikini tests featured a cluster of obsolescent American and Japanese warships anchored in a shallow lagoon where they waited attack by one atomic bomb dropped from a B-29 and (four weeks later) by a second bomb detonated underwater. Forrestal witnessed only the first explosion and its consequences. Touring the lagoon afterward in a picket boat with Admiral William H. P. Blandy, the officer in charge of the tests, he noted the swift sinking of the Japanese light cruiser *Sakawa,* her superstructure flattened by the blast and her stern ripped open to the sea. The hull of an American submarine, *Skate,* was split open and engulfed in radioactivity so intense that the needle of the picket boat's monitoring Geiger counter "ran off the scale." On receiving this report, Blandy said laughingly, "Let's get the hell out of here," and ordered the craft to move on.[20]

From Blandy's flagship, Forrestal issued a vaguely reassuring statement saying, "There will be navies in the future"; meanwhile, he asserted, "the U.S. Navy will continue to be the most efficient, the most modern, the most powerful in the world."[21] But at the dawn of the nuclear age, everyone was groping in the dark. The week before, Hanson Baldwin of the *New York Times,* who thought the prospect "too new and too glittering to be analyzed and understood properly," had expressed a well-founded fear that the tests would be used for partisan purposes by "the fanatic and frenetic prophets of air power and sea power."[22]

From Bikini the party flew to Guam, en route to Tokyo, where General MacArthur was giving a large dinner in Forrestal's honor. But on the morning of scheduled departure out of Guam, Smedberg, who was up at

With Admiral H. P. Blandy at atomic bomb tests, Bikini Atoll, 1946

4:00 a.m. to check the weather, learned that a massive hurricane was moving across Japan; this would delay departure by four or five hours and would mean arrival in Tokyo much too late for dinner. To his later regret, Smedberg also asked for a weather report on Manila, the next stop after Tokyo, and "they told me Manila was clear. The storm had gone through a couple of days before." So he wakened Forrestal to tell him of the unavoidable change of plan. "How's the weather in Manila?" the Secretary asked, and when Smedberg told him it was clear, he said, "All right, we won't go to Tokyo now. We'll go later. Let's go to Manila."

"Sir," Smedberg replied, "we can't do that; they are not expecting us in Manila until next week."

"We'll go to Manila," Forrestal said, displaying his well-known aversion to prearranged commitments if he suddenly felt an urge to do something else. This arbitrary change of schedule assured that "everything was screwed up" from then on. To the political and military dignitaries in Manila who were planning elaborate receptions and inspections for Forrestal the following week, Smedberg was "a skunk" for changing the itinerary and forcing them into a frantic scramble.[23] Forrestal later wrote in his diary that the Philippine President, Manuel Roxas, "seems like an honest, decent, patriotic man."[24]

When they finally arrived in Tokyo, MacArthur was so put out that he flatly refused to entertain the Secretary of the Navy and was only, after much pressure from his own staff, persuaded to grant him a brief audience at his headquarters in the Dai Ichi Building. This lasted only twenty minutes, following which Smedberg asked Forrestal what he and the general had talked about. "I didn't talk at all," Forrestal replied. "I spent the entire time sitting in a chair watching MacArthur stride up and down, soliloquizing, trying to decide what religion he was going to permit the Japanese to pursue. He sounded like God."[25] MacArthur also told him it was imperative to revive the Japanese economy on a basis that would "produce sufficient export balances" to pay for needed imports of food and clothing, a comment which reads interestingly in the early 1990s. Forrestal later recorded in his diary that "MacArthur is doing splendid work in Japan."[26]

From Tokyo, Forrestal's party flew on to Chungking for talks with General Marshall, who was seeking to mediate the civil war between Chiang Kai-shek's Kuomintang and the Chinese Communists. On one day they had cocktails with Madame Chiang. When both Forrestal and Smedberg requested martinis, she clapped her hands and a servant entered with a large tray bearing the necessary ingredients. She poured two jiggers of gin in each glass and then, as Forrestal was saying "I like mine very dry," she added three jiggers of sweet vermouth. Forrestal later told Smedberg, "I thought she was a cosmopolite who knew everything, but she certainly didn't know anything about martinis."[27]

From China they flew to Bangkok, with a stop for dinner in Okinawa. There, in Smedberg's colorful account, "We discovered a great field . . . acres and acres of surplus liquor . . . [ready] to be sold by the War Surplus Administration. I remember each of us picked up four or five cases—$12 a case for Old Forester, Old Granddad and the best Scotch." All told they put "thirty or forty cases" aboard the plane. "We were flying in a C-54, a very comfortable, slow plane. It took us eight, ten, twelve, fifteen hours to go anyplace."

Also on Okinawa, Forrestal and Smedberg dined with the island commander, while the flight crew ate in the regular army mess. When they were an hour over the China Sea en route to Bangkok, the entire flight crew came down with ptomaine poisoning. "They were deathly sick. The copilot was so sick, I couldn't get him out of his bunk for twenty-four hours, even though I threatened him with court-martial." The pilot, however, managed to stay at the controls, and the redoubtable Smedberg slipped into the copilot seat and navigated across Indochina: "I find the Mekong River. It's a beautiful moonlight night. We're due to land at six o'clock the next morning at Bangkok, which we do." Meanwhile, the Secretary of the Navy, oblivious and unperturbed, was reading Edward Gibbon's classic on the decline and fall of Rome and sleeping in his bunk.

The Thai officials entertained Forrestal at an elaborate breakfast which turned the two-hour stopover into four hours. Then, owing to their late departure for India, they were promptly caught up in a fierce monsoon—"the damndest storm I've ever been in in my life"—that tossed the aircraft around like a toy, dropping and lifting it several thousand feet at a time. To make matters worse, the violence of the storm caused a leak in an outboard wing tank, so a steady stream of aviation gasoline was pouring out of the tank between the flaming exhaust pipes of the two starboard engines. "Once an hour the mechanic would flash his light out there to see if the stream was getting any bigger. Fortunately, it wasn't." Finally, the pilot found some quiet air at two hundred feet and they ran for quite some time over a large muddy delta area, skimming the sparse trees, in search of the Calcutta airport. But the British and Americans who had provided navigational aids during the war had now departed, with their equipment. "There were no beacons, no nothing. We were lost." Deciding to follow a major river, Smedberg finally found the Dum Dum airport, but the control tower flashed them a red light, which meant "You cannot land." A radio message then instructed them to proceed twenty-five miles to another airport, where the party of Indian officials was gathered. "We got to this other airport," Smedberg recalled, "and it's covered with cows strolling on the runway. We zoomed them a couple of times and finally landed"—with the gasoline gauges on empty.[28]

Throughout the ordeal Forrestal had remained stoical and calm, reading from the shelf of books he always carried with him on long trips. "He was a tremendous student," Smedberg recalled, "always learning, always studying, always reading, always asking questions of people in high places. I imagine he had a sort of speed-reading technique. He got the gist, but didn't take a long time about it. He read everything he could get his hands on about dialectical materialism." During the violent storm and when they were lost over the Indian jungles, Smedberg went frequently to Forrestal's compartment "to tell him we weren't quite sure where we were." When they finally put down, Forrestal said, "That was a pretty bad time, wasn't it?" and Smedberg replied, "Yes, sir, our pilot was magnificent and we're lucky to be alive." "That's what I figured," Forrestal said. That evening, he dined with the new governor general of India, a former leader in the London Transport Workers Union.

The odyssey continued on to Karachi, Cairo, and Rome, then over the Alps to Berlin. On that leg one of the C-54's engines went dead and the plane started to lose altitude. "I thought about those forty cases of liquor from Okinawa in the hold," Smedberg recalled. "We barely cleared the last peak, but finally got over the rim and down into Berlin."[29] At Tempelhof Airdrome the engine was replaced while Forrestal went to lunch with General Clay, who told him it was important to be "firm with the Russians but . . . very polite at the same time."[30] By this time, everyone in the party was exhausted from constant travel and official dinners and receptions, and Forrestal had a slight cold. The next item on the itinerary was Sweden.

"By the way," Forrestal asked Smedberg, "why are we going to Sweden?" Smedberg reminded him that Admiral Kent Hewitt would be there with a cruiser and two destroyers from the swiftly evaporating Atlantic Fleet and that the Swedish Minister of Defense had laid on a large official dinner. Also, Smedberg said, "my great-grandfather came from Stockholm and I've never been to Sweden." As they approached the Stockholm airport, the tired and elusive Forrestal told his aide, "Smeddy, I'm not going to that dinner. Send a message saying you want a navy doctor to meet the plane so he can certify that I am too sick to go." Smedberg protested strongly but in vain. On the tarmac, the navy doctor, having got "the word," examined the Secretary and recommended that he go directly to bed. Then, as Smedberg ushered him into his suite at the Grand Hotel and prepared to give the bad news to the Swedish officials, Forrestal looked at him with a grin and said, "Arrange a golf game for tomorrow."[31]

So the unflappable Smedberg went off to the Defense Minister's dinner with the "impossible task" of explaining to the Swedish hosts that his boss was too ill to dine, but might be up for a golf game in the morning. The Swedes were "pretty upset" about the guest of honor's empty chair, but Smedberg's astute diplomacy—and a little luck—made things come out all right. He was seated beside Prince Bertil, an Oxford-educated member of the Swedish royal family, who asked him if he liked to play golf. When Smedberg answered with an enthusiastic affirmative, the Prince invited him to play at his club the following day. "You know," Smedberg told him, "Secretary Forrestal also loves golf, and I think a round or two would be just the thing to get him out of bed." For the next three days, Smedberg and the Prince teamed up against Forrestal and the American chargé d'affaires, Christian Ravndal. The Prince and Ravndal were both scratch golfers, while Smedberg and Forrestal had handicaps of thirteen. "Perfectly wonderful matches," Smedberg recalled, all of them "decided on the eighteenth hole."[32] During a brief talk with Swedish parliamentarians, Forrestal learned that they were "uneasy about the proximity and power of Russia . . . but had no domestic communist problem."[33]

In London on July 19, Forrestal was joined by his wife for luncheon with the King and Queen. There followed a naval dinner hosted by the First Lord of the Admiralty at which the British military leaders expressed their concern over future relations with Russia, as well as their hope that American-British ties would "remain very close." Before returning to Washington, Forrestal received a firsthand report from the Director of Naval Intelligence, who had just completed his own inspection trip through Europe. He told the Navy Secretary that "his own intelligence officers were so burdened with official, social, and commercial duties that they were not of much use for intelligence.''[34]

Thus ended the only junket of Forrestal's career.

THREAT OF WORLD STAGNATION

B Y EARLY 1947, Soviet pressures on Iran and Turkey for strategic concessions, coupled with support of the Greek insurgency by Soviet proxies, brought the Western allies to the conclusion that the Kremlin was orchestrating a direct assault on every Western position within its reach. Some of the impulses for political change—for example, in Greece and Italy—were indigenous and genuine, but were being systematically magnified and distorted by the professional agitators and terrorists of Stalin's apparatus. Soviet policy now represented a frontal challenge to the status quo throughout Europe; Russian expansionism employing Marxist tactics was on the move, and its apparent aim was to bring about the breakdown of all existing organizations and institutions as a necessary prelude to revolutionary change. Soviet policy could no longer be explained merely in terms of its claim to need a buffer zone in the East.

A victory for the insurgency in Greece thus became an intolerable outcome for the West, for the insurgents were seen to be linked organically to the Soviet Union. Even an electoral victory for the left would be anathema, for it would mean a termination of the electoral process thereafter and the imposition of arbitrary one-party rule, as had already happened in Eastern Europe. We now know that while Stalin and his operatives worked to achieve total control over indigenous Communist parties outside Russia, their actual control was often tenuous. But in 1946–1947 the perception of an octopus power whose tentacles radiated outward from the Kremlin was a vivid and not inaccurate image in Western minds. Moreover, it was nearly impossible to know the true facts in each national case. The scale and tempo of the cold war were about to increase exponentially, and for the first time U.S. policy was about to move from rhetoric to operational response, involving substantial resources and risks.

On February 24, 1947, less than a year after receiving a loan of $3.75 billion from the United States, the British informed Washington they could no longer afford to provide financial and other vital support to the Greek government and economy. Marshall, now Secretary of State, showed Forrestal the British memorandum just before a Cabinet meeting, and Forrestal noted in his diary that this action ''dumped in our lap another most serious problem—that it was tantamount to British abdication from the Middle East, with obvious implications as to their successor.''[35] It was now apparent to Forrestal and others that the restrictive conditions put upon the

1946 loan had severely reduced its value to the British, but even without these restrictions a sharp curtailment of British strategic commitments was inevitable. The whole of Europe was sinking into economic stagnation and political turmoil. There was widespread unemployment, homelessness, hunger, and destitution; these were breeding grounds for the spread of extremist doctrines, and the Communists were those best organized to scavenge the situation.

It was at this point that Forrestal reached the conclusion that the challenge was total and could be adequately met only by a total response. "We shall have to harness all the talent and brains in this country," he told John Snyder at lunch on March 3, "just as we had to do during the war," and he saw that at bottom the problem was economic. People in Germany, Japan, England, France, Greece, and elsewhere had "to recapture the hope of being able to make a living." Salvation for free men lay in "a restoration of commerce, trade and business, and that would have to be done by businessmen."[36]

Although the immediate stimulus was the new challenge to American responsibility in Greece, Forrestal was thinking more broadly about the whole of Europe and Asia. Two days later, he met with Clark Clifford, now the President's counsel, who fully shared his views, and they agreed to prepare a memorandum for the President which "would endeavor to bring into sharper focus the central question"—namely, which of the two systems in mortal contention would survive.[37] At the Cabinet meeting on March 7, Truman told his colleagues he was facing a decision more serious than had ever confronted an American President: whether to assume primary responsibility for the future stability and well-being of much of the world or to let the matter go by default. He was aware, he said, that "the Greek government was not a satisfactory one to us; that it contained many elements that were reactionary" and that Soviet propaganda was effective because the Greek people were aware that official corruption and inefficiency were rampant in Athens.[38] But the wider threat was Communist domination, which would mean an end to free choice everywhere. Forrestal again spoke forcefully, saying it was necessary to recognize the "fundamental struggle" between two kinds of society and the need to organize "all of the talent and brains in the country . . . harnessed in a single team" with a prominent place for businessmen. Undergirding everything was the need for American strength, "for the Russians would not respond to anything except power."[39]

The product of Forrestal's meeting with Clifford was a memorandum drafted by Marx Leva, then counsel to the Navy Secretary. Presumably addressed to the immediate crisis in Greece, it reads today like a first draft of the Marshall Plan, although its scope was global rather than regionally European. It is a fighting document, a call to the full mobilization of

American resources based on a "grave threat to the continued existence of this country . . . at least as great as the danger" posed in the war against Germany and Japan. The domino theory was in evidence. In the cold war, "we have already lost Poland, Yugoslavia . . . and a number of others; Greece is in imminent peril; after Greece, France and Italy may follow," then "Great Britain, South America and ourselves." When we lost "strategic battlegrounds" during the war, we were concurrently planning offensives "to win the ultimate victory." We must do so again in new circumstances, for "the country cannot afford the deceptive luxury of waging defensive warfare.[40]

"Russia has a product . . . skillfully tailored to appeal to people who are in despair." America must supply "outstanding economic leadership" in order to create world conditions "under which a free society can live."[41]

Impounded Japanese assets of "some $137,000,000" should be set up as a revolving fund with which Japan could import raw materials for its industry, thereby permitting Japanese exports to reenter the channels of world trade and to give Japanese workers "something to eat." A similar fund should be set up for Germany. Financial support should be provided for "local enterprises" where a "helping hand" is needed, but such support should be handled "in every case" by "competent American personnel" in order to make sure "the money goes into *productive* enterprises of direct value to the country involved and to world trade." Whenever possible, "*private capital* should render the necessary assistance." A broad-based American task force should be organized immediately, consisting of the "best brains" from management, labor, and government, "for the issues . . . are crucial and we must attack if we are to survive."[42]

The memorandum was intended for the President over Forrestal's signature, but after he had made several revisions in the Leva draft he seemed to suffer a bout of indecision, centered this time on the question of protocol. On reflection, he thought it inappropriate for the Navy Secretary to send a memorandum of this scope directly to the President; it should properly go to the Secretary of State. Reticent about cutting across Marshall's bow, yet persuaded that the urgency of the situation required that the document go forward without delay, he instructed Leva to prepare the final draft with no signature and to send it to Clifford with a covering note signed by Leva. Whether this curious reticence, combined with his innate preference for indirection, made any difference is impossible to know. The memorandum seems not to have played any major part in the President's March 12 speech announcing the sweeping Truman Doctrine, but its arguments were very close to those used in the following months to formulate the Marshall Plan. In the President's mind, those two programs were really "two halves of the same walnut."[43]

THE CHINESE CIVIL WAR

THE DRAMATIC resignation (November 27, 1945) of Patrick Hurley, Truman's ambassador to China, who blamed the spreading Chinese civil war on the perfidy of American diplomats in Chungking, did more than throw a harsh spotlight on the impending revolutionary convulsion in that country; it proved also a harbinger of the poisonous phenomenon known as McCarthyism, which was characterized by savage, irresponsible attacks on Democrats for allegedly harboring Communists in the American bureaucracy and for pursuing a China policy which undercut Chiang Kai-shek and worked secretly for the victory of the Chinese Communists. Hurley was a strange man, quite possibly of less than sound mind, and he had resigned via the wire services without a word to Truman or Byrnes, indeed after having assured them both that he would return to his post. The stunning news reached Truman at a Cabinet meeting, where he brandished the White House press ticker and snapped, "See what a son-of-a-bitch just did to me."[44] Byrnes was especially embarrassed, for he had just told his Cabinet colleagues with smug confidence that he had, the previous day, talked Hurley out of resigning.[45]

Clinton Anderson suggested that the expected public firestorm could be quelled by the immediate appointment of General Marshall as Hurley's successor. Forrestal promptly seconded the idea. The President was reluctant to impose further burdens on Marshall, who had retired as Army Chief of Staff only the week before, but he had no doubt that the general's appointment would take the newspaper play away from Hurley; more important, there was need for a U.S. ambassador in Chungking who could talk sense to the warring factions in China.[46]

Marshall dutifully accepted the assignment, but his instructions were contradictory. He was to mediate the conflict, seeking to broaden the representative base of Chiang's government and to bring about a sharing of power with Mao Tse-tung; at the same time, however, the administration was determined that Chiang should remain the senior partner in a coalition, "the proper instrument" for developing a democratic nation and "the only legal government in China."[47] The statement announcing the Marshall mission also failed to disclose a basic decision that the United States would continue to support Chiang even if he failed to make reasonable concessions to the Communists.[48] Given the implacable hostility between the two factions, Marshall was undertaking an impossible task.

By January, however, he had arranged a general cease-fire, an agreement to convene a National Assembly in May, and a plan to integrate National and Communist troops into a single army. Washington was encouraged. Then, in April, the Soviets began withdrawing from their military positions in Manchuria and the Red Chinese troops quickly occupied them, with apparent Soviet cooperation. These actions immediately reopened large-scale hostilities between Nationalist and Communist forces and led Marshall to report to Washington that in the absence of a compromise agreement, he foresaw "utter chaos in North China."[49] In late May the Nationalists won a major victory by recapturing Changchun (the capital of Manchuria) and, now confident they could destroy the Communists by force, pushed on to Harbin and lost all interest in compromise. Marshall did succeed in bringing the two sides together for talks and conducted an intensive mediation effort, but Chiang's demands consistently exceeded the limits of Chou En-lai's willingness to make concessions. Marshall privately warned Chiang that his armies lacked the power to resolve the conflict by force, especially because they were dangerously overextended in North China, but the warning was ignored.[50]

FORRESTAL PLAYED only a peripheral role in the development and execution of U.S. policy in China, but his views on the subject reflected his deep-seated concern about the global spread of Communist ideology and power. They were, moreover, reinforced by the convictions of Admiral Arthur Radford, who argued that victory for Mao's forces would render Japan indefensible and make a U.S. war with China inevitable. Radford was prepared to consider a fifty-year war of attrition if that was necessary to eradicate Chinese Communism.[51] Forrestal's only handle on the problem was the presence of a Marine Corps contingent based in Tientsin and Tsing-tao which was guarding the rail lines of communication between Manchuria and Central China. The Marines had proved vital to the economy and thus the political stability of Central China in the winter of 1945–1946, for without their vigorous resistance to Red Chinese guerrilla attacks on the rail lines, very little coal would have been delivered to the main areas controlled by the Nationalists. During Forrestal's visit to China in July 1946, he was confirmed in his conviction that this Marine contingent (originally 50,000 men, but reduced by about half in mid-1946) was an indispensable element in the defense of non-Communist China. If it was withdrawn, senior American diplomats in China told him, "the Russians would surge in and flood Manchuria and North China." American withdrawal would mean "Communist domination . . . down to the Yangtse River."[52]

Forrestal thought Marshall was doing "a splendid job" and exerting himself "to the level of his capacity" in very difficult circumstances, but he felt the general was "a little overoptimistic" in thinking that any agreements reached would endure after "the architect of the agreement leaves China." The idea of a consolidated government in China "would have to travel a long road." At the same time, Forrestal was not ready to face the full implications of the unpalatable truth that the Chiang regime—to which Washington had committed so much political support, prestige, and material assistance—was corrupt and venal and that these defects might cause its defeat. In mid-1946, he seemed to fall back on a dictum that General MacArthur had propounded to him in Tokyo the week before: "We should support the Nationalists because they are on our side."[53] In a Cabinet debate on August 2, Secretary of Labor Lewis Schwellenbach said he saw no reason for the United States to interfere in Chinese affairs. If they wanted a civil war, let them have it. The Marines in China had carried out the orderly evacuation of a million Japanese troops; with that principal mission accomplished, they should be withdrawn. Forrestal fervently disagreed, saying "if we came out of China, Russian influence would flow in and over the country," creating a situation that "could not be permanently acceptable to the United States." Japan had dominated China in the 1930s. Forrestal was now concerned that "Russia will be substituted for Japan."[54] The political-military-economic situation continued to deteriorate through the remaining months of 1946, and in December, having failed to bring the warring parties together, Marshall ended his mission and returned home to assume his new duties as Secretary of State. In a significant statement on December 18, President Truman called the Chinese conflict "a threat to world stability and peace," but he also made clear that the United States would not throw its further weight upon the scales: "We are pledged not to interfere in the internal affairs of China."[55]

Frustration over the China problem was endemic in Washington, especially among a rabid cluster of conservative Republicans in the Congress who were either working with or captivated by the high-powered China lobby. Their common aim was all-out aid to Chiang Kai-shek and a policy of all-out anti-Communism everywhere. They accused the Truman administration of a do-nothing policy. In response to their heavy pressures, Marshall sent General Albert C. Wedemeyer, who had been the U.S. Commander in the China Theater from 1944 to 1946, to undertake a fact-finding mission. Wedemeyer was a close friend of Chiang's and shared Hurley's view that American foreign service offices in China harbored "a definite animus against the Nationalists." He recognized the dry rot of corruption in the Nationalist government, but was nevertheless convinced that Chiang must not be abandoned. In his report to Truman on September 19, 1947, he recommended not only increased military and economic aid, but also the assignment of U.S. military advisers to Nationalist combat units, training centers, and logistic agencies. In short, he sought to commit the United States unequivocally to Chiang, even to give professional American military officers a direct hand in commanding the Nationalist armies. For Manchuria, which he conceded was not militarily recoverable, he proposed a U.N. trusteeship.[56]

Truman and Marshall must have been surprised and displeased by the Wedemeyer Report, for it ran exactly counter to their own developing priorities and threatened, as they saw it, to enmesh the United States ever more deeply in a foreign civil war in support of a corrupt government that was bound to lose. Truman refused to make the report public and restricted copies to Marshall, Lovett, and Forrestal (who had just become Secretary of Defense). This action increased tensions between the administration and the congressional Republicans, and these were aggravated by press leaks in which Forrestal played a significant, if characteristically indirect, role.

Finding himself in substantial agreement with the Wedemeyer Report, he persuaded (or ordered) the general to give an off-the-record talk to the newly formed Overseas Writers Club. Presumably he acted at the request of Ernest K. Lindley, of *Newsweek,* the club's president, but it was evident that he wanted to expose leading journalists to Wedemeyer's views because they coincided with his own. Wedemeyer was reluctant to meet with the group, even under a seal of confidence, knowing that the Secretary of State would be furious if he learned of it, but he yielded to Forrestal's authority. In his talk, he laid emphasis on what he perceived as the dangers to the whole U.S. strategic position in Asia that would follow a victory for Mao's forces in China. No newspaper articles on the talk were ever published, but word did get around, and Wedemeyer was soon called on the carpet by Army Secretary Kenneth Royall, who had received an angry call from Marshall. "What the hell have you been up to?" Royall demanded. "I've been taking heavy flak from the Secretary of State about a talk you gave, criticizing him." Wedemeyer denied criticizing Marshall and explained that he had given the talk reluctantly, at the direct request of the Secretary of Defense, "who insisted that the education of the correspondents was important." After this painful dressing-down, he went to Forrestal to ask that he write or telephone Marshall to explain the circumstances. According to Wedemeyer, "He never did."[57]

It was becoming clear to Marshall and the State Department that the United States, notwithstanding its vast resources, could not deal simultaneously with open-ended crises of measureless implications in both Europe and Asia. Hard choices were unavoidable, and primary U.S. interests lay "in the vital industrial area of Western Europe with its traditions of free institutions."[58] It was accordingly necessary to adopt a Europe First policy and to acknowledge the corollary that the United States lacked the power to control events in Asia. On this fundamental question, however, there was a time lag in perception between State and the military departments. At a Cabinet meeting on February 12, 1948, Marshall argued that it was hopeless to give any further aid to the "reactionary clique" around Chiang. Forrestal's rejoinder was that such a cutoff would lead inexorably to greater Russian influence in China. He went on to recommend the sending of a financial and economic mission to help the government improve its management practices—a proposal rather like prescribing aspirin to combat cancer.[59] Probably he was aware of the transparent futility of such a proposal, but his mind was focused on the dire consequences of a Red Chinese victory, which he equated with a vast extension of Russian power, and he was unwilling to admit how little leverage Washington could exercise in the Chinese situation. He was frustrated by the desperate circumstances, as were the President and the Secretary of State, but unlike Marshall, Forrestal seemed incapable of a clinical analysis leading to a decision to cut U.S. losses and move on. In Marshall's famous phrase, he was "fighting the problem" rather than facing it.

Refusing to accept Marshall's position as final, Forrestal asked the National Security Council on February 26 and again on March 12 for a new statement on China policy. In response, the NSC staff issued a draft report on March 26 which recommended both economic and military aid "on a scale sufficient to retard economic and military deterioration" and to provide the Chiang government "an opportunity" to stabilize the political-military situation. Forrestal and the JCS supported this paper, but the State Department opposed any more military aid. However, before an NSC meeting could be called, the issue was preempted by the Congress.[60]

The congressional Republican majority on April 2 pushed through the China Aid Act of 1948, which provided $436 million in total aid, including $125 million for military weapons and other assistance. Forrestal and the Air and Navy secretaries (Stuart Symington and John Sullivan) endorsed this further military aid for Chiang, but Army Secretary Royall thought that anything less than $1 billion would be ineffective and thus wasted. At a meeting with Forrestal and the military secretaries on June 11, Marshall was primarily concerned with making sure that the aid relationship be handled in such a way as to guard against the United States "getting sucked in" to the further support of Chiang. Wedemeyer, who was present, surprisingly concurred, conceding that Chiang's lack of "moral courage" now guaranteed the regime's collapse and arguing that the United States must now take what steps were available to avoid being blamed for "the final debacle." Forrestal, tenacious and emotional, continued to resist the idea of an inevitable Chinese Communist victory and to seek ways to maintain an American military presence.[61]

The focus of the final phase of the Chinese denouement was the city of Tsingtao on the Shantung Peninsula in North China. This was the site of the largest remaining U.S. Marine garrison, as well as the training center for the Nationalist Chinese Navy. On May 3, 1948, the U.S. Naval Commander in the Western Pacific warned that its 3,600 officers, enlisted men, and dependents might be in danger; he recommended that the garrison be authorized to defend Tsingtao against Communist attack. The Joint Chiefs approved this recommendation pending discussion with the Secretary of

Defense and the State Department. Marshall's response was swift and clear: It would be "a terrible mistake" for U.S. troops to engage in open conflict with the Red Chinese. Once again Forrestal disagreed, but his position now was more equivocal. Rather than endorse the JCS position, he asked the NSC to make yet another study of the pros and cons. But while the study was in progress, the Soviets imposed their land and canal blockade of Berlin (June 24), which created the perception in Washington that withdrawal from Tsingtao would weaken the administration's effort to demonstrate steadfastness in Europe. To further complicate matters, the issue then got caught up in presidential politics. Stung by Republican criticism that he was pursuing a policy of "appeasement" in China, Truman "suggested" to the NSC that any withdrawal from Tsingtao be postponed until after the election.[62]

On November 3 (the day after the election), Forrestal was still doggedly arguing that evacuation of the Marines was unnecessary and was still trying to maximize American influence in North China, but his position was increasingly unreal, for the Nationalist forces were now in a state of galloping collapse. By early December all of Manchuria and the entire plain of North China were in Communist hands. Tsingtao was a doomed city, and Chiang soon decided to abandon the whole Shantung Peninsula and remove the naval facilities to Formosa. At an NSC meeting of December 16, the State Department pressed for prompt American withdrawal, but Forrestal once again refused to agree, insisting that they wait for an updated opinion from the JCS. This came four days later, and it endorsed withdrawal. Even then, Forrestal accepted the military advice only with great reluctance and did not personally endorse it.[63]

Forrestal's inability to face the hard facts of the China situation and his emotional reaction to the inevitable decision to withdraw the Marines must be counted as further evidence of the extreme fatigue and psychic deterioration that had overtaken him by late 1948. From Chiang's collapse and Mao's triumph, he drew the despairing conclusion that the virus of Communism was sweeping unchecked across the entire globe, destroying human freedom and capitalistic enterprise and "everything we care about," in William Bullitt's phrase. It was at this time a conclusion supported by vivid evidence on every side. For this desperate state of affairs, Forrestal assigned a large—and wholly disproportionate—share of the blame to himself.

COVERT OPERATIONS

As THE COMPLEXITY, scale, and malevolence of the Stalinist power drive to disrupt the status quo sank progressively into the consciousness of the foreign policy establishment in Washington, there was a realization that the West possessed little reliable information about the military and economic strengths and weaknesses of the Soviet Union; even the most elementary facts were unavailable—the location of railroads, roads, and bridges; the location of factories and the nature and volume of their production; the size and readiness of the Red Army, navy, and air force. The Soviet Union was a tightly closed society wrapped in ominous secrecy. The American Embassy in Moscow was isolated. American diplomats and a handful of journalists in the city lived on official handouts and personal speculation based on gossip. Additional information came from East European and Russian refugees, Red Army deserters, and German soldiers, but most of it was spotty, trivial, or out of date.

This general situation created an anxious uncertainty about the Kremlin's intentions. The top policy-makers in the government wanted answers, and there were few or none. Thus fed by the triple nature of the perceived threat—"the war scare, the spy scare, and the Red scare"[64]—Washington developed an urgent need to create an effective central intelligence organization. This had to provide a solid informational base for the development of policy toward the U.S.S.R., but that meant secret espionage behind the Iron Curtain, with emphasis on providing early warning of a Soviet military attack on the West. The organizational implications of this requirement gradually led to the further idea that the United States must develop a capability to wage secret guerrilla warfare inside the Soviet Union.

The wartime Office of Strategic Services possessed a capability for covert paramilitary operations, but Truman had abruptly dismantled it on September 20, 1945, reportedly because he distrusted General "Wild Bill" Donovan, the wily, freewheeling New York lawyer who ran it. Soon, however, the new President was frustrated by the often conflicting reports he was receiving from separate intelligence groups in the State, War, and Navy departments. He wanted a single "coordinated" report. To get this he turned to Sidney Souers, a mild-mannered businessman and insurance broker from St. Louis, a reserve rear admiral, and a Truman crony at the poker table. This led to the creation of a loose confederation known as the Central Intelligence Group, but Souers lacked both the knowledge and the personal force to achieve an integrated intelligence product, and the whole effort floundered until the Central Intelligence Agency was established in 1947 as part of the National Security Act. Forrestal was a vigorous advocate of a strong central intelligence effort, and provision for it was a major element of the original navy plan for national security coordination.

In mid-1947, after the United States was committed to resist Communist pressures on Greece and Turkey and to underwrite European economic recovery through the Marshall Plan, the State Department began preliminary planning for covert operations in a small unit with the deliberately innocuous title, "Office of Special Projects." The unit was headed by a New York lawyer named Frank Wisner ("balding and fleshy although he was not yet forty"),[65] who was a seasoned veteran of the wartime OSS "cloak and dagger" operations. Wisner worked under the direct supervision of George Kennan, Director of the Policy Planning Staff. As discussed in Chapter 21, Kennan later sought to distance himself from what he considered the "overmilitarization" of the containment strategy (with which his name was indelibly associated), but he was a resolute advocate of secret measures designed to weaken the Kremlin's control inside Russia and Eastern Europe.

A month after Forrestal became Secretary of Defense, Kennan wrote to him proposing the creation of a "guerrilla warfare corps" and an appropriate training school within the military establishment. It was necessary, Kennan argued, to "face the fact" that successful Soviet assaults on the status quo had been gained "in many areas" by "irregular and underground methods." While he felt the American public would not approve U.S. operations that "relied fundamentally" on similar methods, nevertheless there were cases where "it might be essential to our security that we fight fire with fire." Appended to the letter was a study prepared by two OSS veterans (Charles Thayer and Franklin Lindsay) which laid out in scholarly prose the human and organizational requirements for waging secret warfare against the Soviet Union.[66]

Forrestal thoroughly agreed with the concept and urged the President to adopt it, but recommended that the effort be established within the new CIA, feeling that the military establishment "couldn't" do it, and the State Department "shouldn't" do it.[67] The President expressed his agreement, and on December 13, 1947, the National Security Council approved a program of secret propaganda activities (NSC 4A) under CIA direction. Concurrently, Wisner's operation was shifted from State to CIA and redesignated "Office of Policy Coordination."[68]

Stalin's ruthless reprisal in early 1948 against a Czech government that had dared to accept an invitation to participate in the Marshall Plan was soon followed by the Soviet effort to cut off the Western position in Berlin. These events created a war scare that brought Washington, as one veteran intelligence officer observed, "to a point of near-hysteria."[69] The White House and the Pentagon were desperate to know the precise capabilities and intentions of the Soviet military forces facing Western Europe. At one conference with intelligence officers, an army colonel banged his fist on the table and shouted, "I want an agent with a radio on every goddam airfield between Berlin and the Urals." [70] But reliable information was very thin, which meant that the vacuum was quickly filled with exaggerated fears that gave rise to worst-case scenarios: The Red Army could march unimpeded to the English Channel, and it was all part of a "Grand Design," a "Blueprint for Global Conquest." This image of overwhelming Russian power was, in fact, remote from the reality of Russia's shattered economy and administrative confusion, civil unrest in several republics, and Stalin's inherent strategic caution. But the realities could not be clearly judged in Washington, and Stalin's menacing posture was designed to obscure them.

One important upshot of the winter crisis was Truman's approval in the following summer of two documents that became the basic charters for covert operations. The first (NSC 10/2) authorized (subject only to "plausible deniability") any and all covert activities related to "propaganda, economic warfare; preventive direct action, including sabotage, anti-sabotage, demolition and evacuation measures; subversion against hostile states, including assistance to underground resistance movements, guerrillas and refugee liberation groups, and support of indigenous anti-communist elements in threatened countries of the free world." [71] The only apparent exclusions here were conventional espionage (to be handled by another part of CIA) and large-scale military operations.

The second document (NSC 20) authorized the recruitment and training of Soviet émigré groups for the purpose of conducting guerrilla operations behind the Iron Curtain. The preface to NSC 20, written by Kennan, said that while "it is not our peacetime aim to overthrow the Soviet Government," the purpose was to create "circumstances and situations" that would make it difficult for the "present Soviet leaders . . . to retain their power in Russia." [72] Disaffected minorities and disillusioned refugees from Russia and Eastern Europe were the fertile recruiting grounds for the "guerrilla warfare corps," and the effort was soon under way, directed by Wisner's Office of Policy Coordination. Wisner was a dynamic, imaginative operator, but also something of a loose cannon whose anti-Communist zeal frequently outran his judgment. Until 1949, when General Walter Bedell Smith took charge of the CIA, Wisner eluded close supervision, owing in part to his personal relationships with high officials in the Truman administration, including Acheson and Forrestal. Wisner's recruits came mainly from the displaced persons camps in Germany, on the recommendation of a German general named Reinhard Gehlen, who had defected to the Americans with a large intelligence organization and voluminous Nazi files. Wisner placed great trust in the Gehlen operation.

A burning anti-Communism was considered an essential quality in candidates for the guerrilla warfare corps, but many of those selected were also notorious Nazi collaborators who had carried out mass executions of their fellow countrymen behind the German lines during the invasion of Russia.[73] "We knew what we were doing," a major figure in CIA secret operations said years later; "it was a visceral business of using any bastard so long as he was an anti-Communist. . . . You didn't look too closely at their credentials." Another senior covert operative, Franklin Lindsay, said, "You have to remember that in those days even men like George Kennan believed that there was a fifty-fifty chance of war with the Soviets within six months. . . . We were under tremendous pressure to do something, do anything" to blunt the Soviet military capability.[74]

One group that particularly attracted CIA attention and support was the Organization of Ukrainian Nationalists (OUN), a political-military underground movement that had long fought for Ukrainian independence—first against the Poles in the 1920s when Poland controlled the Ukraine and after 1939 against the Soviets. Though violently anti-Russian, the OUN was itself totalitarian and Fascist in character, as well as anti-Semitic. The Nazis poured money into the OUN after the German invasion of Russia and pretended to support the goal of Ukrainian national independence. In return, a large OUN militia, code-named Nachtigall, or Nightingale, provided local administrators, informers, and killers for the German invaders. Nazi-sponsored OUN police and militia formations were involved in "thousands of instances of mass murders of Jews and of families suspected of aiding Red Army partisans."[75] In his memoirs, Nikita Khrushchev, a Soviet official in the Ukraine during the war, wrote that the Carpathian Mountains were "literally out of bounds for us" because "from behind every tree, at every turn of the road," there lurked the danger of a terrorist attack.[76]

When the Germans were driven out of the Ukraine, many OUN members who had served the Nazis' police formations and execution squads fled with them, but several thousand retreated into the Carpathian Mountains to fight another day against the hated Soviet government. It was this remaining Nightingale group that fascinated the CIA and was recruited essentially en bloc. To bring its leaders to the United States for training and indoctrination required special bureaucratic exertions, as well as an immigration law permitting the admission of one hundred such immigrants per year, provided the Director of the CIA, the Attorney General, and the Commissioner of the Immigration and Naturalization Service all personally stated that the action was vital to national security.[77] As one army intelligence officer noted sardonically, one wing of the CIA was hunting Ukrainian Nazis to bring them to trial at Nuremberg, while another wing was recruiting them. By and large, however, Wisner and the OPC were successful in hiding their operations from the rest of the intelligence community.

After training in the United States, the Nightingale leaders were parachuted into the Ukraine to link up with their compatriots and to carry out measures of subversion, agitation, and sabotage, including assassination. But the OUN's wartime collaboration with the Nazis and their previous bloody history had "fatally severed" the movement from the great majority of the Ukrainian people and had thus cut off their grass-roots support. As a result, not many of the insurgents survived. Some groups and operations were infiltrated by Russian agents; others were betrayed by the British spy Kim Philby, who operated out of the British Embassy in Washington and was a professional colleague and social acquaintance of Frank Wisner's until his exposure and flight to the Soviet Union in 1963. Philby is credited with a chilling summary of one OUN mission whose failure he had assured: "I do not know what happened to the parties concerned. But I can make an informed guess."[78]

There are no records to indicate the degree of Forrestal's knowledge of specific covert operations, but he vigorously supported the program and presumably participated in the approval of the basic NSC charters as a member of the National Security Council. It is more than likely that he knew about Wisner's recruitment of Ukrainians who had committed atrocities as Nazi collaborators in German-occupied Russia. Whether this knowledge and its implications weighed on his conscience after his breakdown is speculative, but on the last night of his life, Forrestal was copying a Greek poem, "The Chorus from Ajax"; he stopped when he had written the first syllable of the word "nightingale."

THE 1948 ITALIAN ELECTIONS

THE ITALIAN elections of April 1948 confronted United States policy with another serious challenge, and coming hard on the heels of the Czech coup and the ominous overtures to the Berlin Blockade, they were perceived in Washington as another cold war battle which the West could not afford to lose. The effort to contain Soviet pressures against Turkey appeared to be succeeding; the struggle to avert a left-wing Communist victory in the Greek civil war was ongoing, and the issue was still in doubt. Italy appeared to offer Russia a singular opportunity to penetrate the Mediterranean by removing an important country from the democratic side of the ledger, for the Italian Communist Party was expected to score heavily at the polls, possibly even to win control of the government by democratic means.

Washington's apprehension was shared and reinforced by the Catholic Church, which greatly feared that a Communist electoral victory would put Italy behind the Iron Curtain and render the Vatican hostage to the

Kremlin. Coming on the heels of Communist takeovers in Poland, Yugoslavia, Hungary, and Czechoslovakia, the Italian prospect confronted the Catholic hierarchy with "the most profound crisis the church had seen in centuries."[79]

Forrestal placed himself in the vanguard of a response that was largely organized and coordinated by the CIA (but the effort was handled by the "intelligence" side of the house, not as a covert operation under Wisner). It comprised a crash program of persuasion, propaganda, overt and secret funding, sabotage, and strong-arm tactics involving very close coordination with the Catholic Church in Italy and America. On the public level, the United States provided $350 million in economic and military aid, while the CIA used at least $10 million from a large fund that had been captured and sequestered from Nazi sources. This "black currency" was part of the Economic Stabilization Fund controlled by U.S. Treasury Secretary John W. Snyder. Forrestal took the lead in persuading Snyder to tap this source, and Snyder then arranged for the Internal Revenue Service to help with laundering the money and transferring it into CIA-controlled accounts in Italy. Much of it was delivered to Italian Premier Alcide De Gasperi for use in funding the campaigns of Christian Democratic candidates. Some of it went to a "media blitz," which showered Italian newspapers with articles and photographs extolling American power and generosity and detailing the evils of Communist theory and practice. The archbishops of Milan and Palermo announced that anyone who voted Communist would be barred from receiving confession or absolution.[80]

While detailed evidence of Forrestal's activities is characteristically thin, Clinton Anderson is authority for the statement that the Secretary of Defense was "masterminding the American effort to keep Italy on our side." According to Anderson, Forrestal "conceived the idea of organizing the Italian community in the United States to influence voters in Italy, and he raised hundreds of thousands of dollars to send successful Italians back to the land of their origin to promote the American cause."[81] Some of the money raised by Forrestal was delivered directly to De Gasperi by Edmund Palmieri, a New York lawyer and former judge, on Forrestal's strict condition that the Italian Premier "never" collaborate with local Communists or admit any of their leaders to his government.[82] There is some indication that Forrestal, while participating at the policy level in officially approved actions, was also operating privately on his own in ways that might have invited White House censure. According to one source, he told Judge Palmieri that in sending him to De Gasperi with private money, he was acting without the knowledge of the State Department and was thus "risking his [Forrestal's] relations with Truman and his job."[83]

As Secretary of Agriculture, Anderson "got into the act because the undertaking also required food." Called one evening to Blair House (where

Truman was living during the White House renovation) he was told to do everything possible to "get more wheat to Italy." He promptly diverted several shiploads destined for Latin America, and they were received in Italian ports with much fanfare. The Christian Democratic politicians, "many of them in American pay," distributed the wheat in cars and trucks with American flags on the bumpers. Anderson credited the Secretary of Defense with this clever ploy. "It was all Forrestal's idea. His pragmatic position was: 'Damn it, don't be theoretical about this.' "[84] Forrestal also arranged for a shipload of American tanks, en route to Turkey, to be temporarily off-loaded in Naples and driven through the streets as further evidence of U.S. support for De Gasperi; similarly, he ordered carrier-based naval aircraft from the Mediterranean fleet to overfly major Italian cities during the campaign. In this undertaking, the jesuitical political operator was operating with maximum efficiency and zeal.[85]

The high-powered American effort was almost certainly the decisive ingredient in the elections. The Christian Democrats won by a substantial margin, sufficient to enable De Gasperi to avoid a coalition with the extreme left. The Italian Communists were defeated, despite heavy political and financial support, both overt and covert, from the Soviet Union.[86]

V

★ ★ ★

THE STRUGGLE
FOR MILITARY
UNIFICATION

CHAPTER 24

★ ★ ★

"A Task of Greatest Difficulty"

I N MARCH 1944, three months before the Allied cross-channel assault onto the Normandy beaches and eighteen months before the surrender of Japan, the House of Representatives created a Select Committee on Post-War Military Policy and held eleven days of hearings on a "Proposal to Establish a Single Department of Armed Forces." It was the opening gun in what soon became a wrenching, bitter struggle pitting army and air corps advocates of military "unification" or "consolidation" against navy defenders of the organizational status quo.

THE ESSENTIAL ELEMENTS of the proposal put before the Select Committee had been long and carefully nurtured by General George C. Marshall and Henry L. Stimson. They considered them imperative corrections to grave defects in existing arrangements whereunder the plans and actions of an independent army and an independent navy could be brought into alignment only by the personal intervention of the President. The particular 1944 proposal was presented by General Joseph T. McNarney, the Army Deputy Chief of Staff, and soon dubbed the McNarney Plan. It called for a single Department of Armed Forces under a Cabinet-level civilian Secretary who would administer land, sea, and air components through three civilian Under Secretaries for the Army, Navy, and Air Force. There would be a military chief for each service, but responsibility for strategic planning, for the military budget, and for actual command of the forces would reside in a single chief of staff. He would head a group comprising the military chiefs of each service and a director of "common supplies."[1]

The Navy Department was caught off guard and thrown on the defensive by this initiative, and this in itself was surprising, for both Marshall and Stimson had repeatedly expressed their belief that the war was demonstrating beyond doubt that unity of command over combined forces and unity of supply were the vital keys to military success. The pressures of real war provided evidence of the need for unified command in each major theater of operations. Eisenhower became Supreme Allied Commander in Europe, and a logical division was arranged between Nimitz and MacArthur in the Pacific; numerous arrangements of a similar nature were in place at lower levels along the chain of command. Yet, at best, they were all complicated ad hoc compromises painfully arrived at. In Washington, however, the army and navy remained separate entities, each making its own political and economic demands on the nation, despite the works of such coordinating mechanisms as the Joint Chiefs of Staff and the Munitions Board. Stimson and Marshall were convinced the nation could not survive another war with such a fragmented military organization. The navy, on the other hand, found positive virtue in its continued independence and separateness.[2]

Robert Lovett, the Assistant Secretary of War for Air, testifying in support of the McNarney Plan, argued that current interservice coordination depended on "temporary solutions and expedients" at all levels; he acknowledged that the successful prosecution of the war to date reflected well on "the personal qualities and abilities of our military leaders," but asserted that the organizational framework in which they were compelled to work was "not designed to translate the tremendous war effort . . . into maximum effectiveness." When Congressman Carl Vinson, an ardent navy defender, pointed out that unity of command had been established in all the major war theatres, Lovett replied, "I believe that is the trouble, Mr. Vinson; it is not just the theatre that needs unity of command, but the country as a whole needs it—at the top."[3]

In his appearance before the committee, Forrestal sought to address two separate questions: whether consolidation was desirable and whether, in any event, Congress should act while the war was still in progress. In a real sense, his testimony was an effort to buy time and forestall any hasty decision. The navy, he said, was "in complete accord" with the desirability of examining the "operations of our war machine," including "the procurement of material." He called the committee's attention to the different geopolitical situations of different nations, but argued that the American problem was unique: "The practices of other nations can be valuable and illuminating [but] the military problems of the United States are, and will continue to be, peculiarly our own."[4]

At the same time he expressed a basic doubt about the efficacy of ever-larger combinations. Drawing on his Wall Street experience, he said "any executive of a great corporation" formed by the consolidation of several companies "will tell you how difficult it is to preserve the vitality and initiative" of the formerly independent units. "Once swallowed in the amorphous mass of a vast and new organization, they are apt to be hamstrung by the very inertia of size." Moreover, could any one man comprehend and manage the consolidated armed forces? "You will recall that one architect of railroad consolidations, I believe it was James J. Hill, finally decided no one man could run more than 10,000 miles of railroad."[5]

When the committee chairman, Congressman Clifton A. Woodrum, expressed disappointment that the navy did not feel the experience of global war had "demonstrated the wisdom of one [military] department," Forrestal replied with graceful candor: "We are not hedging; there is no desire on our part to finesse or be subtle." But "if you ask the question, is it clear now . . . that there should be a consolidation . . . I will have to answer that it is not clear to me."

On the second question, whether Congress should act on this large matter in the middle of a war, he said succinctly, "The Navy is definitely in opposition."[6]

No further action was taken for several months, but a discernible political momentum in favor of the War Department proposals was gathering in the Congress. Sensitive to this development, Democratic senator David I. Walsh of Massachusetts, Chairman of the Senate Committee on Naval Affairs, urged Forrestal to develop a considered navy plan to rebut the army–air corps presumptions. Instead of entrusting the task to a select group of admirals, or to the Navy Under Secretary, Forrestal instinctively turned to Ferdinand Eberstadt, who had returned to private life in New York. Eberstadt gathered a staff of navy supporters (including Sidney Souers, Milton Katz of the Harvard Law School, and Douglas Dillon), worked through the summer of 1945, and rendered a report to Forrestal on September 25. He recommended against a single military department and a single chief of staff, but emphasized the need for new structures to coordinate military planning with both foreign policy and domestic economic policy. In the Eberstadt formulation, the War and Navy departments would remain intact, headed by civilians of Cabinet rank, and the same status would be accorded a new Department of the Air Force. The Joint Chiefs of Staff organization would be established in law but without change in structure. A National Security Council (comprising the President, the Secretary of State, and the Secretaries of the three military departments) would be created to coordinate foreign-military policy and to supervise a new Central Intelligence Agency. A National Security Resources Board would be established to coordinate economic planning for war mobilization. The principal coordinator of these wide-ranging, consequential efforts would be a Special Assistant to the President who would serve as staff director of both the NSC and the NSRB, supported by an appropriate secretariat.[7]

The basic elements of this proposal reflected Forrestal's great admiration for the British Cabinet system, especially for its wartime Committee on

Imperial Defence, and equally his categorical opposition to structural merger of the army and navy. The proposal in favor of a separate air force reflected Eberstadt's acceptance of what appeared to be a political inevitability, but it was not Forrestal's preferred position. He could support the idea, he wrote to his friend, "if I were sure we could confine a separate air arm to strategic operations," but he worried that once created, a separate air force would generate pressure to have all forms of air power "rolled together"; this would be "an easily saleable idea to the public," but "fatal" to the navy.[8]

There was never any doubt that the Eberstadt Report would reaffirm the navy's insistence on the organizational status quo; its first premise was that the navy must not be reduced to a mere component of a larger defense department and that naval plans and operations must not be subject to the orders of a single military chief of staff. Douglas Dillon, then a young naval reserve officer, learned this quickly. Assigned to analyze and make proposals on the Joint Chiefs of Staff organization, he applied a disinterested mind to the problem and recommended a JCS chairman with the power of decision. Eberstadt called him in and told him bluntly, "This won't do." And Forrestal said, "Thanks for the effort, but I can't buy that." It was then that Dillon realized "how deeply committed to the Navy" Forrestal had become.[9]

The broader proposals for systematic coordination of the political, military, economic, and intelligence aspects of national security were a dramatic, indeed revolutionary departure from past U.S. organization and practice. They were constructive, and they were pure Forrestal. He and Eberstadt conceived and presented them as a *substitute* for any basic change in the status of the War and Navy departments, but in reality they addressed problems far broader than army-navy cooperation and were not incompatible with various forms of military organization, including a single consolidated defense department. Indeed, as the debate progressed, advocates of the War Department position came to regard the Eberstadt Report as a clever attempt to obscure the basic question of military organization by shifting attention to the broader but different problem of government-wide coordination.

Surprisingly, the uniformed navy was slow to recognize the Eberstadt Report as a useful means of protecting the organizational status quo, or even as a necessary tactical counterpoint to the army plan. Admiral King, with his chronic resentment of all civilian authority, distrusted Eberstadt and his mainly civilian team, and his Scottish suspiciousness permeated the officer corps. Only when it became apparent that the uniformed navy was incapable of any more imaginative or persuasive response to the army challenge did the Eberstadt recommendations become the "Navy Plan for National Security," near the end of 1945.[10]

THE ISSUE IS JOINED

I N EACH HOUSE of Congress there was a "Military" and a "Naval" affairs committee, a fact which constituted a major structural obstacle to objective legislative thinking on the question of organizing the armed forces, for each committee was composed of congressmen or senators steeped in the lore and traditions and hard economic interests of one service or the other. Disinterestedness was hard to come by. Because the War Department had a more clearly defined position on the issue and was better organized to push it, the Senate Military Affairs Committee got the jump in the next round of the debate by scheduling hearings ahead of its naval counterpart. This meant that Forrestal had to present the navy's case initially before a group with a built-in army–air corps bias.

He began by saying, "I do not appear here simply in opposition to unification [but] to present a comprehensive and dynamic program to save and strengthen our national security." The steps urgently needed to assure that security were "the integration and meshing together of every agency of government whose activities touch upon that subject"; such steps were embodied in the Eberstadt Report, which "contemplates new organizational forms responsive to our new world position." On the question of reorganizing or realigning the army and the navy, however, Forrestal called for patient deliberation and careful planning, for the problem "cannot be solved by any hastily conceived formula." The war experience had proven the essential soundness of existing military arrangements, and it was therefore wiser to "cure" whatever its defects might be through "evolution." He seriously doubted whether the proposed consolidation "would provide guarantees of either efficiency or economy," for he believed "with conviction" that no single person—"no matter how brilliant or competent his training"—could administer a single consolidated military department "with any knowledge of how it is run."[11]

The committee's response was lukewarm at best. Even the wisdom of Forrestal's dramatic proposals for organizational integration of foreign, military, and economic policy were treated as interesting but unexceptionable and somewhat beside the point. Democratic Senator Lister Hill of Alabama said he understood, of course, the necessity for "a working relation" between the State Department and the armed forces, "but, after all, it is the armed forces that fight the war . . . [and] must fight as a team." Forrestal replied: "I do not agree with you. I think the State Department is a part of the team in peace and war."[12] His proposal for more extended study of the army-navy problem was perceived, accurately, as an attempt to buy time for the navy to organize and stage-manage an effective counteroffensive.

The committee found more persuasive the arguments of Robert Patterson, who had succeeded Stimson as Secretary of War. "I submit," Judge Patterson told the senators, "that the considerations which led us, under the spur of necessity, to set up unity of authority in the field point by every element of logic to the establishment of unity of authority at headquarters in Washington." In the years ahead, "we simply will not be able to afford two lines of supply, two hospital systems, two procurement agencies, two air transport systems, where one will do the job as effectively and for less money."[13]

Dwight D. Eisenhower, architect of victory over Nazi Germany, war hero, and the most popular military leader to come out of the war, testified on November 16, 1945, "as a soldier from the field." When the presiding chairman, Senator Olin Johnston, Democrat of South Carolina, graciously motioned him to be seated, Eisenhower said, "No, sir, I would rather stand up" and then proceeded to impress the committee with his easy air of command presence and his grasp of the subject at hand, as well as a singular sincerity and magnetism: "I come before you as a soldier to whom was entrusted the command of the greatest combined force ever brought to bear against an enemy . . . and as one who has experienced [with my thousands of comrades in arms] the successful conclusion of a great enterprise based on unity of command." Having thus established a position of invincible credibility, Eisenhower said he could "not perceive the logic behind the objections which are voiced against the proposal before you." If it was true that administering the combined armed forces was beyond the capacity of any one man, then it would follow that "no man has the capacity to assume the Presidency of the United States." Moreover, the voiced fears that a consolidated department would "subordinate one fighting service to another" are "groundless," for American military leaders are "big people . . . big enough not to place the requirements of their service or their prestige above their own country. . . . At one time I was an infantryman, but I have long since forgotten that fact under the responsibility of commanding combined arms."[14] It was by every measure a masterful performance.

Eberstadt, writing to Forrestal in late November, gave his view that the hearings had not gone well; the general public regarded the navy position as negative and defensive. Moreover, he thought it likely that the War Department would adopt the most attractive elements of the navy plan— like the coordinating mechanism of the proposed National Security Council—without giving up its push for a single integrated department of defense.[15] That is essentially what happened.

As the hearings progressed, Forrestal was made increasingly aware of a profound emotional resistance to integration within the navy officer corps, but also that this group seemed incapable of a persuasive defense against what it regarded as the dangerous simplicities of the War Department plan. Michael Forrestal said many years later that his father's decision to stay in government after 1945, when the family all expected him to leave, appeared to be the result of his conclusion that the navy was "politically dumb" and needed the kind of help which only he could provide.[16] Forrestal was convinced by the autumn of 1945 that some form of unification legislation was inevitable; at the same time, and pushed by Eberstadt, who thought the army plan presented an insidious challenge to the Constitution,[17] he was determined to do everything possible to prevent "a shotgun marriage."[18]

In early November he summoned Rear Admiral Arthur W. Radford from the West Coast to organize and lead a group of officers in Washington who could handle the navy's case in the intensifying unification debate.[19] Radford was a brilliant, audacious naval aviator who had commanded carrier forces in the Pacific and believed the navy's future rested primarily on its aviation. Confident and combative to the point of recklessness, he was a total navy partisan who "played hardball politics all day every day,"[20] and he soon gathered around him a group of like-minded hard-chargers (including Forrest P. Sherman and Arleigh "21-Knot" Burke, both of whom would later serve as Chief of Naval Operations). They were eager for a public relations battle for the honor and self-interest of their beloved navy, and over the next two months their attacks and counterattacks produced notable headlines in the press: "King Foresees Dictator Threat in Unification"; "Halsey Blasts Idea of Merging Forces"; "Leahy Assails Army-Navy Merger"; "Vandegrift Sees End of Marines in Unification"; "Forrestal Hits Doolittle Slur on Navy."[21]

THE PRESIDENT ENTERS THE FRAY

WHEN THE ISSUE of unification was first raised in 1944, President Roosevelt paid little or no attention, made no comment, and did not permit it to deflect his attention from the war. In the final months of 1945, however, it was evident that President Truman was more than an impartial observer. Based on his own exposure to the inner workings of the war effort as Chairman of the Senate Committee to Investigate the National Defense Program, he was a staunch proponent of the War Department point of view, including the conviction that basic changes had to be made quickly while memories of the difficulties encountered in the war were still vivid in the public mind. At the same time, he was keenly aware of the deep-seated resistance in the navy and among navy supporters in the Congress and throughout the country. He correctly diagnosed unification as a major political issue.[22]

In July at Potsdam he had told Forrestal he was planning to send a message to Congress which "wrapped the entire question into one package."[23] Now, on November 21, he invited Forrestal, Walsh, and Vinson to the White House for a discussion of the navy viewpoint. Both congressional leaders expressed the hope that the President would not sponsor a bill of his own, and Vinson predicted that no such bill would be passed "either this winter, next winter, or the winter after." Forrestal said he himself held no special brief for the status quo, but wanted "the best answer for the country." He felt, however, that the President had thus far lacked "an opportunity to consider the real merits of the [navy's] case.[24] Truman told them he proposed to send a message "which would not impair the Navy as an entity"; meanwhile, the navy was "entirely free" to continue the presentation of its arguments. The meeting was cordial, but it was clear to inside observers at the White House, like Clark Clifford, that "a titanic conflict of wills" was shaping up.[25] On several occasions during this period, Truman invited Forrestal to the White House for private chats in which, appealing to the Navy Secretary's loyalty and patriotism, he argued that navy support for military unification was an essential ingredient of national security and world peace. Forrestal expressed respect for the President's views, but remained unconvinced.[26] At lunch on December 14 with Arthur Hays Sulzberger of the *New York Times,* he was heartened by the publisher's comment that the navy was making "definite progress" with public opinion in its efforts to demonstrate that the unification problem was deeper than "simply the merger of two Cabinet offices."[27]

At the same time preparation of the President's message was going inexorably forward. In substance, it was the War Department plan for a single department and a single chief of staff. Forrestal, who received an advance copy with a request for comment on the text, replied to the President's speechwriter, Judge Samuel Rosenman; expressing his opposition to "the fundamental concept" of the message, he said it was therefore doubtful that he could make "any very helpful observation" on its language. He urged that "the President send no message and take no stand on this matter" until extended congressional hearings had run their course.[28]

At a Cabinet meeting on December 18, the Postmaster General, Robert Hannegan, expressed the view that the strength of congressional opposition to unification, especially in the House, made such a message a risky business; the President was inviting an unnecessary fight which he might lose with a damaging loss of prestige. Truman said he felt it was his duty to send the message because it represented his conviction. The navy, he said, had enjoyed "ample opportunity" to present its case, and no one had been muzzled. Forrestal replied that the navy case had not yet been "fully presented," for its only testimony had been before the Senate Military Affairs

Committee, which was "highly prejudiced" by its very composition. Truman said somewhat placatingly that he didn't intend to cut off discussion or muzzle anyone, but that the message would be sent.[29]

The Truman message of December 20, 1945, to Congress was eloquent, comprehensive, and proposed the most radical military reorganization in the nation's history. Pointing out the "necessity of making timely preparation for the nation's long-range security now—while we are still mindful of what it has cost us in this war to be unprepared," Truman argued that "there is enough evidence now at hand to demonstrate beyond question the need for a unified department." The primary lesson to be learned from "the costly and dangerous experience of the war" is that there must be "unified direction" of the armed forces in Washington as well as in the field. "We did not have that kind of direction when we were attacked four years ago—and we certainly paid a high price for not having it . . . we had two completely independent organizations with no well established habits of collaboration and cooperation. Only the President could make a decision effective on both."[30]

The "expedient" for meeting these defects in wartime was the creation of a Joint Chiefs of Staff. This was "better than no coordination at all," but JCS is "not a unified command." It is "a committee" dependent for success upon the "voluntary cooperation" of its members. The urgencies of war produced "a high degree of cooperation," but "it must not be taken for granted" that this situation will continue in a postwar period when "defense appropriations grow tighter" and "conflicting interests make themselves felt in major issues of policy and strategy." Because "the resources of this nation, in manpower and raw materials, are not unlimited," we must have "a unified military program and budget." The present situation of "two civilian secretaries" is defective because it gives each of them an unavoidably "restricted view" and casts them in the role of "partisans" for their respective services. Furthermore, "the President, as Commander-in-Chief, should not personally have to coordinate the Army and Navy and Air Force."[31]

Accordingly, there should be a single department, "with parity for air power," headed by a single Cabinet officer. There should be one chief of staff as well as a military head of each of the three component branches. Together these military leaders would constitute an advisory body to the Secretary of National Defense and the President. It would be wise to rotate the chief of staff post among the three services, but in any event nothing in law or regulation should prevent the President, the Secretary, or other civilian authorities from direct communication with the military heads of each service. "There is no basis for the fear that such an organization would lodge too much power in a single individual—that the concentration of so much military power would lead to militarism." Such a fear is groundless so long as "the traditional policy of the United States is followed that a civilian, subject to the President, the Congress and the will of the American people be placed at the head of this department." Safety for democracy lies in "the solid good sense and unshakable conviction" of the people.[32]

The navy should retain its ship-based, carrier-based, and water-based aviation, and the Marine Corps should remain an integral part of the navy. The message did not directly mention the Eberstadt-navy proposal for a National Security Council or a National Security Resources Board, but indicated that "once a unified [military] department has been established" the coordination of other elements of policy would be easier to achieve. It asserted the need for a foreign policy and a military policy that were "completely consistent." Truman ended by stressing that "unification of the services must be looked upon as a long-term job," and he said, "I make these recommendations in the full realization that we are undertaking a task of greatest difficulty."[33]

FORRESTAL RESISTS

DESPITE THE President's professed desire not to "muzzle" anyone, his message formally established the administration's position and thus made further public opposition from within the Executive Branch a breach of protocol. Constitutionally speaking, the President had a right, grounded in organizational logic and authority, to insist that all members of his administration now fall into line or resign. Forrestal was at first inclined to accept the fundamentals of the President's position, telling Ralph Bard that, while he didn't care "whether I stay in this place or not another day longer . . . I don't want to be fancy with the President." Eberstadt, however, reacted almost violently to the Truman message, because it finessed the wider proposals for foreign policy–military-intelligence-economic coordination. The President was a "fool" whose lack of vision would endanger national security; the fight must continue, especially because Forrestal "had the better case and couldn't lose."[34] Caught thus between powerful conflicting forces, Forrestal fell back on his strong personal convictions. A few days later, he told Clark Clifford that the proposals in the message were "completely unworkable" and that it would be impossible for him and senior naval officers to testify in support of them.[35] He made no mention of resigning, but the implication was unmistakable.

This blunt resistance created a serious dilemma for the White House, and the first staff reaction was to apply the motto of Brigadier General Harry Vaughan, the rumpled military aide: "Screw the Navy." Truman, however, understood that Forrestal represented a serious political problem.

He was a large, immensely respected public figure; he was the acknowledged navy spokesman, and the navy position had formidable support in the Congress and in the body politic. To fire Forrestal, or even to allow him to depart over the issue of the navy's independence, ran the serious risk of turning him into a martyr and thus dooming all hope for any form of military unification in the foreseeable future. Truman decided it would be better to treat him with patient tolerance while trying to move the whole enterprise toward a compromise acceptable to all parties. One major factor in this decision was Truman's genuine respect for Forrestal and his belief that the Navy Secretary's advocacy was the product of intellectual honesty and not driven by ambition for higher office.[36]

For his part, Forrestal was sensitive to the proprieties of the situation and, after further consultations with Rosenman and Clifford, he issued a directive within the navy. It stated that henceforward navy and Marine Corps officers were expected to refrain from opposition to the President's proposals in their "public utterances," except when called as witnesses before congressional committees; under those conditions "they will of course give frankly and freely their views and will respond to any questions asked."[37] As Forrestal foresaw, this language, while it met the requirements of protocol, also provided a large loophole for the continued presentation of the navy's case, especially before the sympathetic Naval Affairs committees of the Congress.

Tensions nevertheless mounted as the perception grew in Congress and the press that in the escalating public relations battle for public support, the navy was operating under a serious handicap. Deliberately or not, the President had established a double standard for freedom of speech on an issue that was loaded with emotion and political dynamite. The matter came to a boil in April 1946 when the Commandant of the Eighth Naval District in Dallas told a reporter sarcastically that in "the next war" the nation would need the "finest army and air force in the world" because the navy, "submerged under Army control," would be so weak that the fighting would be "on our own shores." Democratic Senator Willis Robertson of Virginia, a member of the Naval Affairs Committee, immediately asked the President to rescind his "gag" rule or, in fairness, apply it to all branches of the armed forces. But at a press conference the next day, a peppery Truman accused the navy of lobbying to block his unification proposals, while denying that he was "muzzling" individuals.[38]

On April 9, members of the Senate Military Affairs Committee introduced S.2044, a bill which closely followed the Truman proposals, but also attempted to accommodate the major coordinating mechanisms embodied in the Eberstadt Report. Hearings were held in April, and the committee approved the bill with only minor changes on May 13 by a vote of thirteen to two. Concurrent hearings in the Senate Naval Affairs Committee gave navy spokesmen and supporters their first full opportunity to present their case against merger in a sympathetic setting, and they made the most of it. Eight days of testimony, confined to pro-navy witnesses, produced a resoundingly negative reaction to S.2044, and the committee tabled the matter without any action.[39]

Forrestal, in his testimony, sought to ally himself and the navy with the President's "objective," which he defined as "an integrated military-diplomatic relations, industrial-economic organization which will meet the security needs of the nation." At the same time, he vigorously attacked the details of the Truman proposal. The bill, he argued, was based on "a false major premise" in that it failed to distinguish between the requirements for unified command in combat areas and the need for pluralistic deliberation in Washington. He objected to the removal of the service secretaries from the Cabinet and to the possibility that service functions could be altered by executive order, although he conceded that "these men" (an oblique reference to President Truman and General Marshall) were "much too sensible and patriotic" to harbor such an intent. Basically, he faulted the bill's assumption that "once you establish a single department and a single chief of staff, everything else will fall into place. . . . I do not believe that this extremely complex problem is susceptible of quite so easy a solution."[40]

The Commandant of the Marine Corps, General Alexander A. Vandegrift, did not grant any moral or patriotic restraint to the higher political powers, but told the senators that S.2044 "will in all probability spell extinction for the Marine Corps" because its "very existence" stood as "a continuing affront to the War Department General Staff." This opened up a highly emotional issue in almost inflammatory terms, one which was to complicate and distort the debate from that day forward.[41]

There were no immediate hearings in the House, but the navy's most powerful defender there, Carl Vinson, was not idle. On May 15, he joined with Senator Walsh in a long letter addressed, significantly, not to the President but to the Secretary of the Navy. Admitting that "some weaknesses" in defense organization were revealed by the war, they attacked the Truman proposals on both philosophical and emotional grounds. One secretary and one chief of staff in charge of all military forces "would concentrate too much power in the hands of too few men." It would establish controls "similar to those associated with dictatorships," and history shows that "one-man control" over a nation's armed forces has "always resulted in military defeat." They asserted that the bill would permit the transfer of "vital naval aviation functions to the Army Air Corps" and expressed similar fears that the Marine Corps would be absorbed into the army. The navy's removal from a place in the Cabinet "violates sound administrative procedure." The letter concluded by warning that Congress would not approve a single department, a single military commander, reduction or transfer of naval aviation or the Marine Corps, or removal of the Secretaries of War and the Navy from the Cabinet.[42]

THE LINES HARDEN

THE WALSH-VINSON LETTER, when added to the absence of any legislative action in either house, underscored the deepening political stalemate. Obviously frustrated by a lack of forward movement and by a highly emotional debate that seemed to be getting out of control, Truman called in the Secretaries of War and the Navy and their military chiefs on May 13, 1946, to make clear that he wanted the services to iron out their differences without more delay; if this proved impossible, they were to list their points of agreement and disagreement so he could make considered decisions on the remaining disagreements. Thereafter he would issue a directive with which he would expect all services to comply.[43]

The meeting was a large gathering that included the new air and navy chiefs, General Carl Spaatz and Admiral Chester Nimitz. Because General Eisenhower was in Japan, the army was represented by its Deputy Chief, General Thomas Handy. In the preceding weeks, the White House had been searching for a compromise formula to break the deadlock, and Clifford had persuaded Truman it was imperative to drop the army proposal for a single chief of staff in the hope of securing Forrestal's support for a single department headed by a single secretary. Quid pro quo. Thus by prior arrangement, Truman turned to Admiral Leahy (his liaison with the Joint Chiefs of Staff) and asked for his views. Leahy said he thought "something could be worked out" provided the single chief of staff idea was eliminated. Truman then said that after much reflection, he agreed that the idea carried with it some danger of "the man on horseback" and should be dropped. The President did not believe this, but he said it. The Secretary of War then stated (on cue) that while he believed strongly in the idea on the merits, he was not prepared to "jump into the ditch and die" for it. Regarding the scope of naval aviation, Leahy was hopeful that an equitable agreement could also be worked out; he added that he had been reassured by Eisenhower's statement on the Marine Corps the previous day.[44] Responding to a question at his Tokyo press conference evoked by General Vandegrift's testimony, Eisenhower had said that although he did not favor maintaining two land armies with the same mission, he would be "the last" to advocate "abolition" of the Marine Corps.[45]

The President and the War Department had thus made a major concession—on the single chief of staff—and had indicated a readiness to find compromise solutions to other points in an effort to obtain the navy's support for military reform. But these concessions were insufficient for Forrestal and the men in blue. Negotiations had, in fact, been going on between Patterson and Forrestal for several months, with Eberstadt acting as Forrestal's confidential intermediary, conducting numerous talks with Patterson and a few with Stuart Symington, who had replaced Robert Lovett as Assistant Secretary of War for Air. Patterson felt they faced a basic choice between two forms of organization: (1) a consolidated single department headed by a secretary who had authority to "administer" the whole department or (2) a three-department structure "capped" by a presiding secretary with authority to coordinate but not to "administer" (in the sense of issuing direct orders to the three services). Patterson definitely preferred alternative (1), for he felt that under (2) the secretary would find it difficult "to exercise the unifying and integrating control" he felt was necessary. He was all for preserving individual service pride and morale and would have the overall secretary "administer" the department through civilian heads of the three services, but he insisted on full authority at the top.[46]

The navy, on the other hand, remained dead set against placing anyone below the President who could give direct orders to the Secretary of the Navy.

Despite his perception that some further flexibility in the navy position was necessary, Forrestal seemed to be coming more and more under the influence of Radford and his band of hot-eyed true believers, who were issuing an endless stream of "position papers" couched in highly emotional prose. Eberstadt's powerful advocacy against compromise on the basic organizational issues was also a factor. Although Forrestal had told the military journalist Hanson Baldwin in March that he could see "great usefulness" for "a Minister of Defense with a small but highly competent staff" to provide "coordination and a source of decisions on unresolved issues,"[47] the official navy position continued to oppose a single civilian secretary. Patterson's position was more internally consistent and more firmly grounded in organizational logic. Forrestal seemed to be edging toward Patterson, but the uniformed navy refused to recognize organizational logic when this collided with its powerful desire to remain totally independent, and Forrestal seemed unable to choose between his instincts and his loyalty to the navy.

Shortly after the May 13 conference at the White House, Forrestal and Patterson agreed that "if" there were to be a single secretary, he would need the power to "establish unified military policy . . . integrate the budget . . . reconcile differences between the departments on budgetary matters . . . eliminate duplication and wasteful competition . . . and in general resolve conflicts between the services."[48] Thus, under the pressure of the Truman deadline, Forrestal was moving toward acceptance of a single secretary, while refusing to acknowledge that the broad responsibilities assigned to the new position could be effectively discharged only if it was endowed with full administrative authority. This would prove to be a fateful contradiction.

As May ran its course, moreover, Radford's group backed away from even a loosely coordinated federation of three departments (which Eberstadt and Forrestal accepted) and recommended that the navy revert to the existing situation—two independent departments, War and Navy, both represented in the Cabinet. A reply to the President listing agreements and disagreements was due on May 31, but Radford and his group were resistant to the idea of sending any letter at all. Eberstadt, finding their arrogant remoteness from political reality incredible and ominous, had to exert all of his persuasive powers to convince them that the President's request was an order from the Commander in Chief that had to be obeyed.[49]

As preparation of the letter to the President got under way, there were further disagreements as to whether the remaining army-navy conflicts— all of them fundamental—should be neutrally stated or subjectively argued. The army and the air corps objected to the argumentative style in the navy draft. The day before the letter was due at the White House, intra-navy negotiations continued in Forrestal's office until midnight, with Eberstadt again stressing the ridiculous, untenable situation that would arise "if the services couldn't even agree on a statement of their agreements and disagreements."[50] The letter was finally delivered, but when Clifford put it on Truman's desk, the President "almost snorted in a combination of annoyance and contempt," for there had been no movement on the four basic issues.[51]

The two departments reported agreement on eight points, including the creation of a National Security Council (which they called a Council of Common Defense), a Central Intelligence Agency, and a National Security Resources Board to plan for "maximum use" of the nation's resources in support of national security. They also agreed to formalize the existing organization of the Joint Chiefs of Staff (without a single chief or a chairman). They agreed to the creation of interservice bodies to "coordinate" military procurement, research, education, and training. Their disagreements remained on the fundamental issues of a single department, a single civilian secretary, the status of naval aviation, and the status of the Marine Corps.[52]

THE PRESIDENT DECIDES

WITHIN TWO WEEKS, the President announced his decisions on the points at issue. He endorsed a single department with a single secretary; he also supported the status quo for the Marine Corps and for naval aviation, except that land-based planes used for reconnaissance, antisubmarine warfare, and protection of shipping "can and should be manned by Air Force personnel."[53]

Forrestal was playing golf at Chevy Chase when the President's letter arrived in the early afternoon of June 15. By the time he returned to the Navy Department, Patterson had already released to the press a brief reply heartily supporting all of the Truman decisions. The Radford group, encamped in Forrestal's office, was full of gloom. After Forrestal read the President's letter, he gave no indication of his own reaction, but turned to Radford and said, "Raddy, I want you to draft a reply for my signature." Radford said, "Mr. Secretary, the only reply I can think of would be your resignation." Forrestal replied, "I don't think I can let the Navy down that way." He then asked Admiral D. C. Ramsey to undertake the navy response. There was no further discussion, and the grim, unhappy assemblage filed out of the Navy Secretary's office in a dark mood, their hope for salvation now wholly dependent on Carl Vinson's great clout on Capitol Hill and his repeated assertion that Congress would never accept the President's position.[54]

There ensued four days of loud silence out of the Navy Department during which the press reported the navy brass to be "irked" and "boiling" over the decisions, especially over a White House statement that the President expected all of the military services to "support" them.[55] Forrestal was unavailable for public comment of any kind, but his office indicated that he would attend the atomic bomb tests at Bikini atoll in late June and would go on from there to an extended inspection tour of naval installations throughout the world.* This announcement was taken by the press as an indication that his resignation was not imminent. "Despite his deep-rooted personal convictions," the New York Times reported on June 18, the Navy Secretary "intends neither to take issue with the Commander-in-Chief, nor resign his Cabinet post in protest."[56]

In fact, Forrestal had by no means given up the fight, or the threat of resignation. On the morning of June 19, he went to the White House. During a brief preliminary exchange with Clark Clifford, he spoke in "bitter and emotional terms" about army–air corps "steamroller tactics," but once inside the Oval Office he made a genuine effort to be conciliatory.[57] He told Truman that "all my civilian assistants" believe the President's decisions represented "a very sincere and earnest attempt to reconcile the different views"; moreover, the President's letter "showed how beneficial it had been to give this subject thorough study"; indeed, "the Navy was gratified that many of its ideas had found expression in his message."[58] After this cordial opening, however, he felt bound to say that the naval air people were "greatly disturbed" by the proposed assignment of land-based

*For details of this trip, see Chapter 23, pages 295–301.

naval air operations to the air force—indeed, they tended to be "fanatical" about it. According to his diary entry for that day, he persuaded Truman to modify this assignment so as to permit navy control over "some" land-based operations, but subsequent events did not bear this out.[59] Truman never changed his mind, but Congress did later return most land-based naval air activities to the navy.

Forrestal also told the President that the "essence of the matter" was whether a law could be written which would leave the Navy Secretary "free to run his own department without kibitzing from above" while at the same time giving the new single Secretary of National Defense "global authority . . . on broad issues." If these conditions could not be met, he would feel it was his obligation "to withdraw from the Cabinet."[60] Two weeks earlier, he had confided to his diary that the aim of his conduct in this matter was to obtain improvements in defense organization "without sacrificing the autonomy of the Navy." Yet in plain truth, these were contradictory goals. Any conceivable plan to improve military organization would have to involve some loss of navy autonomy, and Truman had now taken decisions that would explicitly subordinate the navy to the direction of an overall Secretary of Defense. The issues were clearly drawn. The conditions which Forrestal had set for his remaining in the Cabinet could not be met. Yet he did not go beyond a hint to the President that he might—under conditions of "sincere and major disagreement"—feel obliged to resign.[61]

His ambivalence and inner contradiction were evident: Convinced that some form of military unification was inevitable and even necessary, he was at the same time gripped by a fierce institutional loyalty to the navy—a loyalty which largely accepted (often against his better judgment) the narrow, rigid perspectives of its senior officers. He could not change the navy's institutional mind-set, but loath to leave government, engaged in consequential issues of national policy, passionately worried about the Soviet threat, ambitious for larger responsibility—perhaps as Secretary of State—he continued his efforts to square the circle on military unification.

At the same meeting of June 19, he also told the President that he wished to defer a formal navy reply to the decisions until the CNO, Admiral Nimitz, returned from an inspection trip in Texas. This was another time-buying device, for the navy was deeply divided on how to respond. Admiral Ramsey's draft as initially edited by Forrestal was considered "completely unsatisfactory" by the Radford group, and Radford urged Forrestal not to send it. While they waited for Nimitz, there was further pulling and hauling within the naval staff, conflicting advice, and repeated redrafting, but the letter was finally signed and sent on June 24. It was a model of tortured bureaucratic reasoning. Referring to the President's decisions as a "reorganization of the War and Navy Departments," the letter then paraphrased Truman's major objectives in heavily qualified language which reflected the navy's "understanding" of them. While there would be a single Secretary of National Defense, he would leave "full administration of their respective services to the Secretaries of War, Navy, and Air." The second objective attributed to Truman was preservation of the navy's "integrity and autonomy so as to insure the retention of those imponderables of spirit and morale so essential to a military service." The navy letter felt those objectives to be "attainable" and spoke of the "desire" of Forrestal and Nimitz to cooperate with the White House in the effort to achieve them, but nowhere did it use the word "support."[62]

Having (as he reckoned it) thus piloted his ship through another tricky channel with shrewdness and skill, avoiding both the "rocks" of a disagreement with Truman so sharp as to require his resignation and the "shoals" of circumstance that would cast doubt on his loyalty to the navy and his personal integrity, he promptly left to observe the atomic bomb tests at Bikini atoll in the far Pacific. He was gone for nearly a month, leaving Radford and others to deal with the political fallout. But the struggle for unification was far from finished.

IF FORRESTAL THOUGHT the navy's evasive reply to the President's June 15 decisions would pass muster at the White House, or at least put a poultice on the inflammation until he returned from his extended inspection trip, then he misjudged Truman. The President could be patient and conciliatory, but he was not immune to exasperation and was quite capable of playing political hardball. Forrestal's plane was sitting on the runway at the naval air station in San Francisco, refueled and ready to take off for Hawaii, when he was called to the telephone in the operations office. It was the President of the United States calling, and the room was promptly cleared so the conversation could be conducted in private. According to Captain Smedberg, the Navy Secretary returned to the plane "visibly disturbed"; after they were airborne and headed for Pearl Harbor, he called Smedberg to his compartment and told him what had happened. "That was the President," Forrestal said, "and he told me in no uncertain terms that, if I wouldn't go along with a single secretary and a single department of defense, he would transfer naval aviation to the Air Force and the Marine Corps to the Army."[63]

There is no reason to doubt the accuracy of Smedberg's recollection, but there is reason to doubt that the President really intended to carry out such a threat. For one thing, it would have created a gigantic political explosion in the Congress which would have demolished any chance of unification legislation for years to come. Harry S. Truman, the seasoned politician, knew this to be true, and it is doubtful that he was prepared to act against the grain of that truth; at the same time, he was prone to blow off steam from time to time when men and events seemed gathered in a conspiracy to frustrate his plans and programs. It is also possible that Forrestal gave Smedberg the impression that Truman's words were harsher than was actually the case. Still, it is clear that the President was putting Forrestal on notice that the navy's response to his June 15 decision was far from satisfactory.

Like the agile boxer and bureaucratic operator he was, Forrestal apparently gave Truman enough assurance of support to escape the full force of the punch. He would no longer speak out publicly against the President's position. "I had no alternative," he told his naval aide.[64] In fact, he (privately) and the Radford group (publicly) persisted in opposition to a single secretary for another six months and prevailed over the President on the single department issue until 1949, by which time Forrestal himself had become an advocate.

CHAPTER 25

★ ★ ★

The Weak Compromise

LEGISLATIVELY, the unification issue was on the back burner during the summer and early fall of 1946, and Forrestal sensed that the War Department was content to let the matter rest until Congress reconvened in January. The President's decisions on the four disputed points were on the table. In a letter of June 15 to Patterson and Forrestal, he had said how "gratifying" it was to have "both of you and General Eisenhower and Admiral Nimitz assure me that you would give your wholehearted support to a plan of unification no matter what the decision would be on those points upon which you did not fully agree."[1] While Forrestal's feelings fell far short of "wholehearted support," he had now pledged allegiance to the President's position and, left to his own devices, would probably have let the matter rest until it was taken up by Congress. It had been thoroughly debated, and the highest constitutional authority had now decided.

But Radford and his group continued to put pressure on him to go on resisting the President. Forrestal's press aide John Abbot (a reserve commander who had replaced Eugene Duffield in early 1946) now observed him "as a man who was getting terribly tired" and indecisive. He canceled several important speeches at the last moment without explanation, one of them after he was already airborne and headed for Pittsburgh. "He had no more than cleared the Anacostia Naval Air Station when the pilot radioed in to cancel the Secretary's speech," Abbot remembered. The admiral in charge of public relations, who had sent the speech "all over Washington," groaned when he got the word and then said half to himself in Abbot's presence, "What the hell is happening to Jim?" But the career naval officers knew "they had the best spokesman they would ever get in resisting the takeover, as they saw it" and they pushed him "tremendously" without letup to go on fighting a rearguard action.[2]

Radford and his group pressed him to take further initiatives in an effort to obtain additional concessions from the army and the air corps in order to move the White House closer to the navy position.[3] On August 27, Forrestal gave a small dinner aboard the *Sequoia* to sound out Patterson on the War Department's willingness to use the device of a presidential executive order to ratify the agreed-upon eight points, leaving only the remaining four controversies to be dealt with by Congress. This was an Eberstadt-Radford ploy, and its purpose was to "pocket" the army–air corps concession already made on the single chief of staff and thus confine legislative consideration to issues on which strong navy supporters in the Congress might defeat or modify other Truman proposals, e.g., a single department and a single secretary. Forrestal personally had doubts about the tactic, feeling it might weaken the navy position: The White House and the Congress would say "you have gone thus far, why not go the whole hog . . . and have a single man at the head."[4] It was unlike him to make a proposal to Patterson of which he was personally unpersuaded, and the episode seemed to Abbot another sign of serious fatigue.

At dinner on the *Sequoia,* Patterson seemed willing to consider the idea of an executive order, but felt it "was not a cure for the central problem." He also noted, as an example of the need for central direction, that the Joint Chiefs of Staff had been unable to agree on the composition of army and navy forces for 1947–1948, although they had been struggling with the problem for a full year. Forrestal responded by arguing that this matter could be resolved by the "active secretariat" he was recommending, but Patterson could not agree.[5] Forrestal could hardly have been surprised by Patterson's position, yet he fired off an angry memorandum to Clark Clifford asserting that "the Army is rigidly adhering to its conception of unification . . . is still wedded to the concept that a chart and 'straight-line of command' will solve all problems, as opposed to our belief that any plan, any chart, any system can only be as good as the men at the working level make them."[6] Whether this note reflected Forrestal personally or primarily Radford, it ignored the fact that the army's conception was also now the President's public position and that Forrestal was pledged to support the President.

At a large meeting of the principals on September 10, Truman quickly shot down the idea of embodying some elements of the new organization in an executive order, making clear that he felt the whole plan should be solidly embedded in law. All of the old disputes were rehearsed without any change of position, but Forrestal seemed not only defensive but also struggling to control strong emotions. Grim and intense, he proposed that, instead of a single department, there be created a Deputy to the President, whose functions would be strictly limited in scope. He was no longer concerned about the title—"Call him Secretary of Common Defense, or what you will''—but he wanted to be sure no real authority would be exercised over the services. He said that while he recognized the need for the President to have support from the Cabinet, he could not agree to testify before Congress in support of any bill ''which did violence to my principles''; if the President's bill took such form, he would have to resign. Truman took no offense at this unusual outburst, but replied calmly that he did not expect such a necessity to arise.[7]

When Eisenhower remarked that he could not conceive why the navy should fear that the proposed legislation would impair its ability to perform traditional naval missions, Forrestal replied that the navy ''did have deep apprehensions''; it feared the Marine Corps would be subject to ''great restrictions'' and that the navy would be denied the capacity to perform missions ''which only it fully comprehended.''[8] This last statement seemed to confirm what Stimson once called the navy's tendency, when logic failed, to retreat into ''a dim religious world in which Neptune was God, Mahan his prophet, and the United States Navy the only true Church.''[9]

Later in the meeting, Forrestal tabled a paper listing six ''fundamental areas'' where a Deputy to the President could be ''a source of decisions.'' They were:

1. Missions and Means
2. Cognizance of Weapons
3. Composition of Forces
4. Finances
5. Resolution of Command Disputes
6. Personnel (training, education, and recruiting).[10]

What was disquieting about this proposal was Forrestal's apparent conviction that decisions on such issues—all of them complicated by deeply held intellectual and emotional differences between the services—could be resolved by an official endowed with only broad coordinating powers and supported by only a small staff. Either he had become a mouthpiece for ''the admirals'' who wanted to make sure the new military overseer would lack the authority and the means to be an effective ''source of decisions,'' or else, wearied of the struggle, he was seeking to resolve an inner conflict (between his loyalty to the navy and his awareness of the inevitability of structural reform) by convincing himself that reasonableness, goodwill, and forbearance all around would prevail.

THE UTTERLY DETERMINED ANTAGONISTS

BUT IN THE atmosphere of Washington in mid-1946, it was surely unrealistic to believe the knotty problem of military organization could be resolved by primary reliance on goodwill and practical compromise. The combustible elements of a fierce interservice struggle for missions and weapons in the postwar period were everywhere to be seen. There was the youthful arrogance of the air corps, not merely determined to be independent, but also convinced that its preeminence as the dominant American military force in the era of "airpower supremacy" was inevitable; there was the navy, whose aircraft carriers had emerged from the war as the definitive expression of modern sea power and whose glamorous aviators, coming to major influence within the naval hierarchy, equated naval aviation with the future of the navy; there was the ongoing revolution in weapons technology—not only the atomic bomb, but also the prospect of guided missiles—which was blurring traditional distinctions between the functions of land, sea, and air forces, yet in a setting where each force was organized in a separate institution, tightly knit, empowered by history and tradition, and utterly determined not to be diminished by new circumstances. Finally, there was the impact of suddenly tight postwar budgets on military services that had grown accustomed to no limits on spending. All of these factors combined to add a new intensity, a jagged ferocity, to normal interservice rivalries.[11]

Relatively speaking, the prestige and mission of the army were not in doubt, and that service was fortunate in men like George Marshall, Dwight Eisenhower, Omar Bradley, and Lucius Clay, who possessed the broadest minds among the military leaders. The bitterest fight was between the air corps and the navy. This had become a mortal struggle between the destiny of the one and the survival of the other. Somehow, Forrestal failed to take the true measure of this visceral, corrosive factor in the equation; it was perhaps irrational beyond his comprehension.

Negotiations continued in an effort to narrow the differences. On November 7, Forrestal invited Symington and Lieutenant General Norstad to lunch at his house and arranged for Admirals Radford and Sherman to join the group for coffee and a thorough discussion of land-based naval aviation. Several commentators later described the meeting as a breakthrough, but it served mainly to show Forrestal how little "give" there was on either side. Radford and Sherman disclaimed any desire to exclude the air force from antisubmarine operations, but wanted the navy to develop the tactics and equipment and to train the air force squadrons. Symington and Norstad seemed able to live with that approach, but their response turned negative when Radford insisted that such squadrons must be "dedicated" solely to that one mission because "it was completely impractical to use a plane on one day for antisubmarine warfare and on the next for strategic bombing"; moreover, the navy would have to "control" those squadrons.[12]

As 1946 drew to a close, positions on both sides seemed to be hardening, and the navy was driven further into defensiveness and paranoia by what it considered the arrogance and presumption of several air force attitudes and actions. The naval staff reported to Forrestal that officers at the new Air University at Maxwell Field in Alabama were openly proclaiming the primary objective of the air force to be "complete domination of all military air activities in the United States."[13] At a dinner in Norfolk, Virginia, where local businessmen were entertaining army, navy, and air corps officers, an air corps brigadier told the guests in an "off-the-record" talk that his organization was tired of being "a subordinate outfit" and was now determined to dominate in peace and war: "Whether you like it or not," the new air force "is going to run the show." Air corps headquarters told inquiring reporters that the remarks "were intended to be entirely humorous," but the navy did not find them funny.[14] Fuel was added to the fire in the form of a bold tour de force by the senior air corps general, Carl Spaatz, who had commanded the massive air assaults on Germany. Spaatz invited Radford to lunch and bluntly invited him to transfer to the "new Air Force," intimating that naval aviation was in any event destined for incorporation in that emerging juggernaut. If Radford would come over, Spaatz said, it could even be arranged for him to succeed Spaatz as Air Force Chief of Staff. The admiral briskly declined the offer, remarking that most naval aviators were already embittered by the air corps' "tremendous propaganda campaign" to prove it had won the war single-handed, but despite Radford's refusal to transfer allegiance, air corps "recruiting raids" continued at lower levels, with up-and-coming young naval aviators being promised one- and two-rank promotions if they played their cards right.[15]

These indications of a relentless air force push for dominance revived the old fear of naval aviators that their fate would be the same as "what happened in England." There, between the wars, the air arm of the Royal Navy was absorbed into the Royal Air Force, and this reorganization, as Forrestal wrote in his diary after a conversation with the much-decorated American carrier admiral Marc Mitscher, "robbed British naval airmen of any chance for a career and of prestige within their own service."[16] Such parochial concerns perfectly demonstrated the fact that personal and institutional self-interest lay at the root of the interservice fight over reorganization. Few were the men, either military or civilian, who could rise to the level of disinterested concern for a solution that was best for the country.

Never one to avoid confrontation, Radford responded to these air corps presumptions by putting pressure on Forrestal to recede from the agreements so painfully reached with Patterson and Symington—that is, to reject a separate air force and insist on staying with a two-department setup with Cabinet representation for the navy. Forrestal recognized that such a position was now untenable and refused to accept it, but as deepening fatigue wore away his resilience, he seemed unable to moderate the increasingly strident, reckless stance of the navy professionals. At a further luncheon on December 4 with Symington, Norstad, Radford, and Sherman, the intrepid Radford once again expressed the "feeling" of naval aviators that the "granting of department status" to the air force was just the "first step" to its taking over "the whole business of national defense"; then, not content with merely angering Symington and Norstad, he drove the needle in deeper by expressing doubt that a future war held any role for a strategic air force. Big bombers, he said, would not be able to penetrate heavily defended targets without fighter cover, but the great overland distances to Russian targets precluded fighter cover. Aircraft carriers, on the other hand, could carry out effective attacks because they could launch their planes from various points closer to the targets.[17]

On January 3, 1947, Patterson rode back from a Cabinet meeting in Forrestal's car and remarked that he was much disturbed by "growing evidence of bitterness" between the services. Forrestal agreed, saying that he had recently discovered "a depth of feeling in naval aviation which had been very surprising to me," but he felt the disturbing emotionalism simply proved a point he had been trying to make for months: that unless "the two services" were "honestly and thoroughly" in support of a plan for reorganization, it was doomed to failure.[18] From this meeting came a mutual pledge to redouble their own efforts to restrain the controversy and to reach a final understanding before the matter was delivered to the congressional arena.

The final compromise owed much to General Norstad and Admiral Sherman, two officers of exceptional breadth and clarity of mind who established a working relationship of mutual trust. Norstad enjoyed Patterson's total confidence. Forrestal, aware that Radford was incapable of compromise, finally turned to Sherman, perhaps the only high-ranking naval officer genuinely in favor of a compromise solution. His broadmindedness did not go unpunished by his narrower peers, but Truman appointed him CNO after the unedifying "Admirals' Revolt" in 1949.

THE LAST ROUND

FINALLY, on January 16, 1947, the Secretaries of War and the Navy announced their agreement on the remaining points, thereby enabling President Truman to propose legislation that reflected at least formal harmony with his administration. In fact, agreement was made possible by a

Discussing the unification issue with Patterson, January 1947.
Behind them, left to right: *Major General Lauris Norstad, Admiral William*
D. Leahy, General of the Army Dwight D. Eisenhower,
Fleet Admiral Chester W. Nimitz, Vice Admiral Forrest P. Sherman

mutual willingness to finesse the crucial issue of service functions (roles and missions) by proposing that these be set forth in an executive order which the President would issue as soon as he approved the legislation passed by the Congress. This ploy postponed but did not settle the intractable questions of naval aviation and the Marine Corps, which would remain bitter bones of contention in the ensuing months and would contribute to Forrestal's frustration and sense of failure in the months after he became Secretary of Defense. Still, there was now formal agreement on an organizational framework: There would be a Secretary of National Defense with limited authority, and he would head an amalgam of three executive departments—for Army, Navy, and Air—each headed by a secretary. The Joint Chiefs of Staff would comprise the three military service chiefs, without benefit of a chairman or presiding officer. The War Department, with the President's approval, dropped the idea of a single executive department (in addition to having previously dropped the proposal for a single chief of prestaff). The air corps gave up, at least verbally, all claims to missions traditionally handled by land-based naval aviation. All concerned bowed to the extraordinary political clout of the Marine Corps by agreeing to leave it in status quo.[19]

So there was a formal package ready for legislative consideration, but it was held together by fragile strands of tenuous understandings, and it was vulnerable to the strong emotional winds blowing through Congress. The inner contradictions had, wittingly or not, been carefully preserved. The composition of the Joint Chiefs of Staff was the fatal flaw in the arrangement, for it remained a committee of equals representing large institutions unable to agree on a national military strategy in a period of sharp competition for missions, weapons, and public support and when tight money was turning the military budgeting process into a zero sum game. Truman had identified this weakness in his original message on the subject, but had then receded from the single chief of staff idea as the only means of coaxing Forrestal and the navy to accept some form of "unification."

Given the military implications in each complicated problem of foreign policy that confronted the United States in the immediate postwar period, the judgment of competent military authorities was an essential ingredient of U.S. policy. In addition, the victories over Germany and Japan had brought the prestige of U.S. military leaders to its highest point in American history; great weight was attached to their views, and there was in American society at that time no competing civilian competence such as was later embodied in a number of strategic think tanks in Washington and at leading universities. In the late 1940s, the Joint Chiefs of Staff were looked upon as the military equivalent of the Oracle of Delphi, and the 1947 act not only made them the principal source of advice and staff support on military matters, but also prohibited the Secretary of Defense from developing either a "military staff" of his own or of assembling a group of competent civilian analysts. This monopoly status, combined with their inherent incapacity to agree on strategy, missions, and budgets, soon created an impossible situation for the Secretary of Defense, the President, and the country.

THE WEARY unification warriors now girded themselves for the last round of the fight, which involved once more running the gauntlet of congressional committees whose members represented a wide spectrum of informed, semi-informed, ignorant, and unpredictable opinion. Senate hearings on the new bill (S.758), introduced on behalf of the administration, were held by the newly created Senate Armed Services Committee.* Forrestal, now a declared supporter of the White House position, con-

---

*A merger of the Military and Naval Affairs committees effected by a reorganization of Congress the previous year.

cluded his prepared statement by saying that while no bill "can legislate a spirit of unity," this one "provides an equitable and workable framework for the integration of all of the agencies of Government concerned with national defense."[20]

Congressional supporters of the navy and the Marine Corps remained suspicious of any military reorganization. Republican Senator Styles Bridges of New Hampshire wanted to know if the bill wasn't merely "making a bed of roses" for "this super deluxe secretary on top" to become an imperial Caesar who would strangle naval aviation and "put the Marine Corps out of business." Forrestal replied that from his own observations of how Washington works, "I think that kind of man would have an early grave politically." But, Bridges persisted, does the bill not provide "this super deluxe secretary" with "a blank check"? To which Forrestal replied, "The bill is written to prevent precisely that."[21]

General Eisenhower, asked why he had changed his mind on the single chief of staff, replied that the Secretary of Defense would be an effective substitute. "You will have directly superior to the Joint Chiefs of Staff a man who can put his whole time to these things . . . he can make the decision, you see." Still, he believed "time would show" a single chief of staff to be "a better system."[22] But in his later testimony before the House committee, he said that owing to "the terrible fears engendered" by the idea, "I would not do it now if I could." Pressed by the committee chairman, he conceded that he had made a pragmatic shift "in order to get this thing done."[23]

The Senate committee sent Bill S.758 to the floor on June 5 with only minor changes, and the full Senate approved it on July 9. It was, however, a different story in the House. These hearings were conducted by the Committee on Expenditures in the Executive Departments from April 2 through July 1. Major efforts were made by navy and Marine Corps partisans to weaken the authority of the proposed Secretary of Defense and to nail down absolute guarantees in law for navy autonomy in general, and/or naval aviation and the Marine Corps in particular. These efforts were largely successful.

Radford's testimony before the House committee was a remarkable piece of brass. Treating the White House as a sort of alien power which had nothing to do with the navy and showing no sensitivity to Forrestal's delicate position as a supporter of the painfully won compromise, he cavalierly opposed the idea of a Secretary of Defense. Because "the national security of this country really encompasses all of the executive departments," he said, it was really necessary for the coordination to be handled "directly from the President's office." He was concerned that a Secretary of Defense would "force decisions immediately that might be very unwise." When Republican New York congressman James W. Wadsworth retorted, "Well, somebody must make decisions,'' Radford replied, ''That is true. The question is when do you make them.'' From this exchange it was clear that, in Radford's view, a Secretary of Defense would be too close and too expert a monitor of the navy, whereas an Assistant to the President with broader duties and little staff, and physically separated from the naval staff, would be a more comfortable and manageable solution.[24]

Melvin J. Maas, a former congressman and current president of the Marine Reserve Officers Association, did not mince words. Ninety-five percent of his constituency, he said, hoped Congress would pass no military reorganization act of any kind, but if action was inevitable, then they insisted that guarantees for the unimpaired existence and mission of the Marine Corps be written into the new law. ''If you want a Marine Corps because you believe it is essential to the security of the country, we want you to say so, gentlemen, in legislative language. Then it can only be changed by you and not by some executive order.''[25] The Truman administration's plan to handle the touchy ''roles and missions'' issue by executive order was insufficient insurance for the Marines, Maas said, for an executive order could be altered by a President. The proposed Truman document provided ''Marine Forces . . . for the conduct of limited land operations'' in connection with naval campaigns involving ''the seizure or defense of advanced naval bases.'' This language had the formal approval of Forrestal, the Chief of Naval Operations, and the Commandant of the Marine Corps, but Maas airily told the committee, ''We want the word 'limited' stricken out. We see no purpose in saying 'limited operations.' ''[26] In subsequent testimony, the Marine Commandant, General Vandegrift, responded to leading and sympathetic questions by openly agreeing with Maas, thereby repudiating his previous endorsement of the President's language. Truman, who was not pleased by this fresh evidence of insubordination, sent Clark Clifford to tell Forrestal ''to rein in the Marines,'' but Forrestal responded ''testily,'' telling Clifford that Vandegrift was only reacting to ''provocative testimony'' by Eisenhower.[27]

In JCS debates the year before, General Eisenhower as Army Chief of Staff had expressed his convictions in strong terms. His view of land-sea-air battles (he had written in confidential memoranda) was that they required the cooperation of different forces, whereas the navy view was that ''without involving other services'' it should have ''all the tools'' to perform broad missions which it regarded as natural extensions of sea warfare. But ''the conduct of land warfare is a responsibility of the Army,'' he argued. ''Operationally, the navy does not belong on the land; it belongs on the sea.'' The ''emergency development'' of large Marine forces in World War II should not be viewed as ''assigning to the Navy a normal function of land warfare''; therefore, Marine units ''should not exceed the regiment in size.''[28]

Navy and Marine Corps partisans, seeing in Eisenhower's words a clear intention to "eliminate the Marine Corps as an effective combat element,"[29] made sure that sympathetic congressmen obtained copies of these JCS memoranda. Eisenhower was thus confronted by hard questioning at his appearance before the House committee. After a short span of bobbing and weaving, he said forthrightly, "Well, sir, it is very clear in the statement I made that I believe the Marines should not plan for and should not be allowed to build up great land armies to do exactly the same thing land armies do. If they consider this as a lessening of their functions, they would have to interpret it that way."[30]

On April 18, Forrestal invited Clark Clifford to lunch in his office with several key senators, including Leverett Saltonstall, a Republican patrician from Massachusetts; Millard Tydings, a senior Democrat from Maryland; and Willis Robertson, a conservative Virginian. The question on the table was whether to define the role of the Marine Corps in the new legislation or leave it in the proposed executive order. Clifford argued that legislative language was both unnecessary and unduly restrictive, but logic did not carry the day. Both Saltonstall and Tydings advised him gently not to "fool around" with the Marines, for they "occupy a unique and singular place in the hearts of the people." When Clifford protested that writing roles and missions into the law would be inconsistent with the Patterson-Forrestal agreement, which was now also the President's position, Forrestal supported the senators while "denying he had changed his position." Tydings told Clifford this was not a logical but an emotional issue: "These are the boys who took Mount Suribachi . . . Clark, you can't win this one." For Clifford the episode was "a short, sweet lesson in the political clout of the Marine Corps," and he moved pragmatically to assure that the concession was made, advising the President that otherwise "the whole bill could blow up in our face."[31]

Neither he nor Truman, nor many other serious military analysts over the ensuing years, believed there was any longer a valid military reason for the United States to maintain a separate Marine Corps—especially a large expensive combat force of three land divisions and three supporting air wings. Several years later, while still President, Truman blew off some steam in a letter to a congressman, saying the Marine Corps possessed "a propaganda machine that is almost equal to Stalin's." The high level of public outrage that greeted his remarks forced him to "clarify" them almost immediately. Many years later, Clifford wrote in his memoirs that "only politics keeps the Marines in being as an independent military force."[32]

The President's bill had been introduced on February 26, and the marathon hearings ran from early March to early May in the Senate and from early April to early July in the House. After the Senate approved its bill on July 9, the House voted favorably on its own measure on July 19. A Senate-House conference committee ironed out the differences, and the President was able to sign and proclaim the National Security Act of 1947 on July 26.[33]

The unrestrained representations by the navy and Marine Corps had a significant impact on the final legislation in ways that further diluted the authority of the Secretary of Defense and his ability to make organizational adjustments in response to changing conditions. In the final watered-down version he could establish only "general" policies and programs and exercise only "general" direction and control. Naval aviation was given statutory protection for all its functions, including all traditional land-based air activities; similar ironclad guarantees were provided for the Marine Corps. In one sense, the new law was a victory for paranoia and narrow, institutional self-interest, and a number of the broader minds, including Eisenhower and Patterson, expressed their disappointment. Neither did they make any effort to disguise their feeling that the navy's conduct during the last round of hearings had clearly breached the compromise agreement of January. Kenneth Royall, about to succeed Patterson and become the first Secretary of the Army, predicted that the awkward new arrangements would be not only inefficient but also unable to prevent further interservice conflict. Nevertheless, he recommended that the President sign the bill and make a start.[34]

Viewed broadly, and despite its glaring defects, the final measure was nevertheless a considerable political achievement—a triumph of patience, perseverance, and the capacity of the American system for compromise. Whether the compromise was workable was the question about to be tested.

Forrestal, who had often expressed his desire to leave government, now faced another logical juncture point when he could go gracefully with full honors and his high reputation intact. He had defended his beloved navy with brilliance and tenacity and could rightfully claim—indeed could not avoid the claim—that the final compromise on unification was largely the work of his hand. Not only had he preserved for the navy a large measure of freedom from unwanted interference, but he also had gained acceptance for his conception of wider governmental coordination—embodied in the National Security Council and the National Security Resources Board. The case for a triumphant departure from Washington was a strong one, but Forrestal showed no disposition to leave, nor did he show much interest in any of the alternatives that seemed available—to run for the Senate, publish a newspaper, or go back to the business of making money. The process of government and the exercise of governmental power had become the consuming passions of his life. He felt the perilous state of the world could be rendered less perilous only if the United States government was better organized, manned by a higher caliber of permanent official, and led by wise, far-seeing men. These were long-term challenges demanding dedication and continuity of effort; they could not be met and surmounted by a casual, intermittent approach to public service. Stimulated by the scope and complexity of the problems that were now his daily fare, he was too absorbed in the process to notice that its wear and tear over seven years had eroded his physical and mental resilience, leaving him more vulnerable than he realized to the continuing risks and pressures of high office.

Whether or not he reflected seriously on the question of leaving government at this time, developments soon confronted him with another

Marshall, Forrestal, and Patterson leaving a White House reception for Mexican president Miguel Aleman, April 1947

temptation to stay. Truman wanted to settle the appointment of the Secretary of Defense without delay, and Forrestal was widely touted in Congress and the press as a leading candidate. He was not Truman's first choice, but when Patterson was offered the post and declined it, the President turned to Forrestal. As an ardent defender of navy autonomy, he was in an awkward position to become overseer of all the armed forces, for his objectivity was a serious question mark to the other services. There was also a deeper problem, and it contained the seeds of tragedy. As Robert Lovett wrote many years later, no one realized in 1947 that Forrestal was "a burnt out case."[35]

★ ★ ★

CHAPTER 26

The First Secretary
of Defense

ORRESTAL WAS probably surprised to be named Secretary of Defense, even after it was known that Robert Patterson would not accept the job. Patterson was pressed financially by six years of government service and by an anxious wife who wanted him to return to the less stressful pace of private law practice. He was also aware of the severe weaknesses in the new law, especially those affecting the authority of the new Cabinet position. During the summer of 1947 the question of the appointment was much discussed at the White House and, according to Clark Clifford, Patterson's withdrawal had "left the choice wide open."[1]

On the surface it was surprising not only that Truman turned to Forrestal but also that Forrestal accepted, for he had fought the President's conception of military unification with a passion and zeal that several times edged close to insubordination. He was both architect and principal builder of the compromise structure, which placed severe limits on the authority of the new position, and he had originally opposed its construction in any form. Logic suggested the President would appoint someone who saw eye-to-eye with him on the needed solution. But who? There appeared to be a dearth of truly qualified candidates. In the end, Truman apparently reasoned that if Forrestal (whose ability he admired) remained Secretary of the Navy, he would probably make life miserable for the Secretary of Defense, whereas if he *was* the Secretary of Defense he would have to try to make the system work.[2] It was a shrewd political judgment.

The terms of the new law represented a victory for Forrestal's efforts as navy advocate, but it was evident they would make it very difficult for the Secretary of Defense to exercise any real control if the three services chose to resist his "coordination." In point of fact, success for the new regime depended on reasonableness and cooperation all around, on a cordial col-

Henry Stimson's 80th birthday party, September 1947

legial relationship among the four civilian Secretaries and especially among the three military commanders who comprised the Joint Chiefs of Staff. If the new system was to work, it was imperative that they demonstrate a preadiness to subordinate powerful institutional interests to a broad conception of the national interest. But there had been no evidence of such forbearance during the long, embittered debate to bring forth the new law; on the contrary, storm warnings were everywhere visible.

Forrestal accepted the post with characteristic determination to do his best, but showed little of the joy or excitement he had displayed on his appointment as Navy Secretary, and he wrote mordantly to his friend Robert Sherwood that "this office will probably be the greatest cemetery for dead cats in history."[3] To Dr. A. L. Barach, the psychiatrist who had treated Jo, he wrote with even more gallows humor: "Thanks for your note and your good wishes. I shall certainly need the latter—and probably the combined attention of Fulton Sheen and the entire psychiatric profession by the end of another year."[4] Six months before, he had publicly expressed the intention to resign during 1947: "The President knows that I want to get out this year . . . I'm no believer in the theory of the indispensability of any man."[5] Reminded of this statement at a press conference, he was asked why he had accepted the new post. Because "I have been asked to and I don't refuse." How long would he stay? Well, "There are a lot of imponderables, but a lot depends on how well I do the job . . . I had hoped it wouldn't be long." How long is "long"? the reporters persisted.

Forrestal laughed. Well, "When you are looking forward, a year looks long, but looking backward, seven years seems short." This came close to an admission that he had become addicted to the pace, the excitement, and the exercise of governmental power.[6]

He accepted the job without any of his usual soul-searching ambivalence, as an assignment fated by circumstance. The world was in crisis. The American people were only slowly awakening from the euphoria of victory and deliverance in World War II to the awareness that a new American effort on a vast scale—calling for vision, leadership, courage, money, and perseverance—was required to fend off yet another grave threat to Western civilization. The U.S. government was the decisive instrument in the struggle. In Forrestal's view, only a handful of people, in and out of government, fully grasped the lethal nature of the threat—even in 1947—and U.S. policy still did not constitute an adequate response. In May 1944, he had said to George Earle, U.S. Minister to Bulgaria and a former governor of Pennsylvania, "My God, George, you and I and Bill Bullitt are the only ones around the President who know the Russians for what they really are."[7]

For all of these reasons, acknowledged and subconscious, he did not linger over the personal benefits of a "time out" from the long, strenuous years of government service—a respite which had seemed sensible or compelling to Lovett, McCloy, Acheson, and many others—or over the risks of failure in the new defense position he had labored so skillfully to render ineffectual. Instead he told himself—against the evidence—that the 1947 act was a triumph for reasoned persuasion and honest compromise. The continuation of a gradualist approach, under his management, could strengthen the military services and thus the national security. While his notes to Sherwood and Barach revealed subconscious anxieties, he appeared to harbor no conscious doubts about his own physical or mental fitness.

UNCERTAIN BEGINNINGS

IN ORIGINALLY proposing the coordinating mechanism that became the National Security Council, Forrestal and Eberstadt had in mind a body that would operate, insofar as possible, along the lines of a high-level committee in the British Cabinet system. It would serve the President, but could act independently on many matters under the direction of a presidential assistant who enjoyed powers analogous to those of the British Cabinet Secretary. Under the law as finally passed, the Secretary of Defense was designated "the principal assistant to the President in all matters relating to the national security,"[8] and Forrestal chose to give this sentence

a literal interpretation. It was a presumption which led to a jolting disagreement with Truman at the very
outset of the new arrangements.
Forrestal expected to run the NSC,
control its staff, and house its operation at the Pentagon. But as the
implications of this arrangement
swam into focus, it became clear
that in one grand sweep the Secretary of Defense was planning to occupy a very considerable part of the
policy terrain traditionally reserved
to the State Department, and might
even dilute the day-to-day authority
of the President. Reaction was swift
in coming.[9]

Truman appointed his friend Sidney Souers to be the NSC Executive
Secretary and, with Clark Clifford's
guidance, Souers drafted a set of instructions to himself and his small
staff which made clear that the operation would be directly responsible

*The Secretary of Defense,
September 1947*

to the President. This led to a showdown on September 17 at a White House
meeting that included Eisenhower and Nimitz, but not Truman, who was
on his way home by ship from the Inter-American conference at Rio. As
expected, Forrestal angrily disputed the mandate Souers had prepared, insisting that the NSC staff should report to him and be under his direction.
The matter was debated for some minutes, following which Clifford spoke
on behalf of the President: The NSC system was not being created to
circumvent the State Department or diminish the President's role; the State
Department was central to the NSC decision-making process, and "the
President must control it."[10] Arrangements were made subsequently to
house the NSC operation next door to the White House in what is now the
Executive Office Building.

Forrestal was very unhappy about this development and recorded his
displeasure in his diary. Noting the "difference" between "some of the
White House staff and ourselves on the National Security Council—its
functions—its relationship to the President and myself," he added, "I regard it as an integral part of the national defense set-up and believe it was
so intended by the Congress."[11] Forrestal's interpretation here reflected
not the intention of Congress, but rather his own conviction of what was

necessary to achieve a true integration of American foreign-military policies and operations in the postwar period. His intellectual model was the
British Committee on Imperial Defence. But however meritorious the British arrangement might be, it could not be readily grafted onto the American political system. Keenly aware of the inefficiencies in that system,
admiring British administrative competence, and alarmed by the Russian
threat, Forrestal lapsed into a curious misreading of the policy-making
process in the Executive Branch and of the President's absolutely central
role. Along with other evidence, the episode seemed to reveal that Forrestal conceived of his new job primarily in terms of high-level policy-
making. On the assumption that the Secretaries of the Army, Navy, and
Air Force would "administer" their own departments, the "coordinating"
role of the Secretary of Defense would enable him to devote a major
portion of his time to grand strategy. This was a central and costly misjudgment.

AT HIS FIRST press conference, on September 23, 1947, Forrestal set
forth his gradualist approach to the problem of military unification. "The
process of integration," he told reporters, "will be a matter of many
months and maybe years." Asked whether he intended to create his own
central office for public statements and press relations, he replied that because it was the intent of the new law for "operations to continue within
the services . . . I look to the three departments to run their own public
relations." He added, "I hope to disappear, frankly, as quietly as possible,
from the public eye."

This statement astonished the reporters, who promptly asked, "Mr. Secretary, how can you disappear from the public eye when you are the only
Cabinet officer for the combined services?" Forrestal seemed taken aback
by the question. Well, perhaps he had indulged in a "rather careless use
of language." What he had meant to say was that he would devote his time
"to the work of integration" and let the Army, Navy, and Air Force secretaries speak for their own services. That was what the new law intended:
"preservation of the integrity of these services is most important." The
reporters persisted. "Mr. Secretary, when you speak, whom will you speak
for?" Again, his answer suggested he had not thought the matter through.
"Well, I guess I will be speaking for myself . . ."; he hesitated, then
added, "on behalf of the defense forces of the country." But what if a
statement or policy of one service is in conflict with your views or those
of the President? Would the Secretary of Defense have the power to override that service policy? "Well, I would want to consult my lawyer on that.
I hope I won't have to do any overriding . . . this is a team of people
working toward a common end. If you have to use authority, why you'd

better get out of your job." But what if the positions of the services were in conflict with each other? Well, he would cross that bridge when he came to it. "I don't expect any difficulty with any of my associates, and that is what I consider them as being."[12]

Whether this strangely euphoric approach to the momentous tasks ahead reflected unsuspected naïveté or the first signs of burnout, it was evident that Forrestal had not really grasped the full measure of the anomalies and basic contradictions in the new situation.

FORRESTAL DID NOT have a large voice in the selection of his principal civilian subordinates, the Secretaries of the Army, Navy, and Air Force; rather, he inherited people who were essentially in place, though now they would have different titles. Kenneth Royall, a North Carolina lawyer, was already Secretary of War, having succeeded Patterson a few months before. A graduate of Harvard Law School, Royall, then fifty-three, had been Under Secretary since 1945 and enjoyed the solid respect of both the army and the White House for his rational, even-tempered behavior during the unification debate. It was a foregone conclusion that he would become the first Secretary of the Army.[13]

Forrestal's last Under Secretary at the Navy Department was John L. Sullivan, a graduate of Dartmouth College and Harvard Law School and a New Hampshire lawyer who had served as counsel to Frank Knox's newspaper properties in that state. Long an activist in Democratic state politics, Sullivan had run unsuccessfully for governor in the 1930s. After a stint as Assistant Secretary of the Treasury (where his relations with Henry Morgenthau were strained), he was appointed Assistant Secretary of the Navy in 1945—over Forrestal's initial protests—and elevated to Under Secretary in June 1946. Sullivan was forty-eight, a good-natured political operator, adept at working with congressional committees and a team player. His heart was with the navy, but he was also loyal to Forrestal.[14]

Stuart Symington, forty-six, had succeeded Robert Lovett as Assistant Secretary of War for Air in February 1946, after breaking into government a year earlier as Surplus Property Administrator, a job for which he was recommended by Truman's friend John W. Snyder, who was now Secretary of the Treasury. Another staunch Symington supporter was Clark Clifford, the gifted trial lawyer from St. Louis who had come into the White House as Assistant Naval Aide, but was now the Special Counsel to the President. The two younger men had been friends since 1938, when Symington arrived in St. Louis to take over Emerson Electric, a failing company with a record of terrible labor relations. Symington had changed the atmosphere by establishing a profit-sharing plan for all employees and had turned the company into a profitable enterprise by obtaining war contracts to build power-driven gun turrets for British and American bombers. As described in Chapter 7, Forrestal played an important role, through his extensive banking and industry contacts, in securing the presidency of Emerson for Symington.[15]

A tall, rather dashing Yale man, Symington was also hypertensive and very competitive. No match for Lovett's intellect or intuitive wisdom, he possessed a sharp but shallow intelligence attuned to action and opportunity. Eugene Zuckert, who served under Symington as Air Force Assistant Secretary (and later was Air Force Secretary in the Kennedy administration) thought him a personality who moved primarily by intuition and impulse: "He was not a logical thinker."[16] There was about him a bold, damn-your-eyes defiance which found a natural outlet in taking long risks, in gambling against the odds. He could be charming, but also mean and small-minded. He played political hardball. Coming into the War Department shortly after the end of hostilities, he quickly and uncritically "imbibed" (in Clark Clifford's phrase) the heady visions of the air-power generals—Arnold, Spaatz, Vandenberg, Nathan F. Twining—and made their cause his own.[17] Between early 1946 and mid-1947, as the unification debate proceeded with increasing heat and bitterness, Symington and the army air forces watched with frustration and resentment as Forrestal conducted his skilled, resourceful rearguard action on behalf of the navy. The resulting law contained, in their view, far too many concessions to naval aviation and left the newly independent air force with far less than its rightful share of authority, money, and prestige. For Symington and the air force generals, passage of the 1947 act was not the end of a process, but an opportunity to wage further bureaucratic warfare from a stronger position. And, as Clifford put it, "Symington felt no loyalty to Forrestal."[18]

Forrestal had doubts about Symington's integrity and their ability to work together, but he must have recognized that this was a most difficult case to make at the Missouri White House, where Symington's support was very strong. In a meeting there on July 26, Truman consulted his Secretary of Defense-designate on "the posts for Air and for the Navy," having already decided to appoint Royall as Army Secretary. Forrestal replied that Sullivan "was the obvious man to succeed me." His assessment of Symington was lukewarm, but couched in diplomatic language that reflected his aversion to personal confrontation. As he later confided to his diary, "I felt he was an able man, [but wondered] whether two people who had known each other as long as he and I had could work successfully together. I said one's friends were frequently more difficult as partners than strangers."[19] Truman proceeded to appoint both Sullivan and Symington.

THE IMMEDIATE STAFF

T HE NEW LAW was at pains to limit the staff support available to the
Secretary of Defense. He had no general deputy and, indeed, no subordinates of any rank requiring presidential appointment and Senate confirmation. He was authorized to appoint three civilian Special Assistants
at salaries of $10,000, and could employ other civilian subordinates within
the framework of the civil service. In addition, military officers could be
"detailed to duty" as assistants or personal aides, but the law stipulated
that "he shall not establish a military staff."[20] These strictures were the
direct result of Forrestal's arguments before Congress, aimed at making
sure the Secretary of Defense could not "administer" the services; they
comported perfectly with his conviction that only a small staff was needed
to support the new office.

Even within these limits, however, the initial staffing of the Office of the
Secretary of Defense (OSD) seemed to suffer from a lack of imagination.
To fill two of the Special Assistant slots, Forrestal took the line of least
resistance by appointing his personal counsel and his budget director at the
Navy Department. Marx Leva, thirty-two, was a graduate of Harvard Law
School who had clerked for Supreme Court Justice Hugo Black and seen
combat action in the Mediterranean as a naval reserve officer before being
ordered to the Navy Secretary's office in early 1947. (Forrestal told him
during the initial interview: "Well, being a Jew will neither hurt you nor
help you in this office."[21]) Wilfred McNeil, forty-six, had been circulation
manager of the Washington *Post* from 1934 until 1941. As a naval reserve
officer during the war, he had proven to be an able and adept administrator
in a wide range of assignments involving procurement and budgetary matters. He rose to the rank of rear admiral and earned Forrestal's full confidence. Leva, who admired McNeil, felt, however, that he was "never able
to get rid of his pro-Navy bias"[22]; officials in the army and the air force
generally agreed with this judgment.

There was no immediate candidate for the third Special Assistant position, but Forrestal seemed to be considering still another person from the
navy. At that point Leva warned him that unless he appointed at least one
man from the War Department, he would be legitimately accused of trying
to put the navy in charge of the new military establishment.[23] This led to
the selection of John H. Ohly, thirty-six, who had been a research associate
and one of Leva's law instructors at Harvard, and had spent the war years
handling labor relations and plant takeovers for Robert Patterson in the
War Department. Ohly was an incisive and comprehensive analyst capable
of dealing with the broadest policy concepts and the smallest details, an
instinctive workaholic with a deceptively mild manner and a social shyness
not unlike Forrestal's.

All three Special Assistants were able men, dedicated to good government and disinterested public service; all three would go on to higher
responsibility, and each would make significant contributions to the country's defense policy. But in 1947 two of them were relatively young and all
three were essentially without reputation or personal influence of the kind
that would measurably strengthen Forrestal's position. Leva was charged
with legal and legislative affairs and McNeil with developing and managing
an integrated budget process—perhaps the single most important key to
centralized control of the sprawling military establishment. Somewhat as
an afterthought, Ohly was charged with "all the rest," which turned out
to involve the whole range of national and international policy matters
requiring Forrestal's attention. These included support for the Secretary's
participation on the National Security Council; liaison with the Joint Chiefs
of Staff, the Munitions Board, the Research and Development Board, and
the CIA; and also staff support for a broad miscellany of ad hoc study
groups ranging from joint military medical services to equal military pay.[24]

To assist them, the Special Assistants recruited a handful of equally
young men—like Theodore Tannenwald, a Harvard Law classmate of
Leva's who later became a federal judge; Felix Larkin, a lawyer who became president of W. R. Grace Company; Najeeb Halaby, who was Federal Aviation Administrator under President Kennedy and then president of
Pan American Airways; John Noble, a Boston lawyer who became president of the Trans-Arabian Pipeline Company; and Townsend Hoopes, who
was later Under Secretary of the Air Force. To these and other civilians
were added liaison officers from each military service together with supporting clerical staff. At the outset the OSD staff numbered about 45, but
had risen to 173 after six months and to 347 by the time Forrestal left
office. More than half of it, however, consisted of secretaries, clerks, mess
attendants, and chauffeurs. The substantive staff, both in numbers and in-
formality of organization, bore a general resemblance to a medium-sized
law firm.

All key members of the staff were infused with a sense of mission, based
in large part on their great respect for Forrestal's ability and integrity. Ohly
considered working in OSD "a great privilege,"[25] and Halaby wrote, "The
too brief time I spent working for him [Forrestal] was one of the most
exciting and stimulating periods of my life."[26] Initially, the nature and
scope of their work was far from clear. Ohly recalled that Forrestal's ideas
as to how OSD should function were rather "fuzzy" beyond his unreal
assumption that he would work quietly on "integration" while the service
Secretaries ran their own departments.

"My own concept of this office," Forrestal told reporters at his second
news conference, on November 12, 1947, "is that it will be a coordinating,
a planning, and an integrating rather than an operating office."[27] The basic
task, he told the assembled military brass and congressional leaders at a

buffet supper in the Pentagon eight days later, was "unifying the mentality of the men in the Army, Navy and Air Force—and I underline the word—of getting a common mental attitude toward a common problem, which is the security of this nation." At the same meeting, he stressed his view that the complexity of the security problems facing the United States offered no easy or simple solution. The only basis for security is "constant concern . . . and unceasing energy . . . I think worry is inherent if an individual is going to remain alive and solvent."[28] Was inclusion of the word "individual" in the last sentence a subconscious reference to his own personality? John J. McCloy had marked him during their wartime work together not only as a man of brooding introspection, but also as a "chronic worrier."[29]

WHATEVER Forrestal's preconceptions regarding the role of OSD, they were soon overtaken by the emergence of problems whose intractability and bitterness he had not foreseen. These were (1) a basic deadlock in the Joint Chiefs of Staff (on war plans, service roles and missions, assignment of weapons systems, and division of the budget), (2) the revival of the air force–naval aviation dispute in ever more virulent form, and (3) the pressures created by the congressional and public expectation that the Secretary of Defense would move swiftly "to eliminate unnecessary duplication or overlapping in the fields of procurement, supply, transportation, storage, health and research"[30] (in the comprehensive language of the statute). These problems fell upon OSD like an avalanche, both sudden and unending, and within a few weeks it was evident, as Ohly noted, that Forrestal had "vastly underestimated his need for staff support."[31] Without warning, the young staff was required to perform a wide range of technical, analytical, and administrative tasks which Forrestal had never imagined would be functions of the new office.

The able young men met these challenges with missionary zeal, and many became dedicated workaholics like their boss, but the weaknesses in their situation were intrinsic: They lacked adequate numbers, in many cases they lacked relevant experience, and they lacked adequate rank and standing to deal effectively with senior generals and admirals (Admiral Radford stated the problem from the standpoint of rank-conscious military officers: In dealing with the OSD civilians, he asked, "How could one determine who was most important?").[32] This last deficiency was compounded by the untested legal limits on the authority of the Secretary of Defense himself—whether he could make binding decisions on issues where one or more of the military services disagreed. His authority to set common policies for the three services had been at the core of the unification debate, but the outcome was ambiguous and contradictory. Moreover, Forrestal conceived of his role as a chairman of the board (*primus inter pares*—first among equals—in his own favorite phrase) and was not disposed to take hard decisions that would leave one party wounded and therefore resentful; he was philosophically committed to ruling by consensus. Nevertheless, as Ohly recalled, the practical day-to-day realities forced the Special Assistants to "operate as though we were undersecretaries, but there was just so much we could get away with,"[33] and the position of the more junior staff people was even more difficult. As a consequence, Forrestal was forced to deal personally with a myriad of purely administrative matters, to endure the tedium of endless efforts to mediate and arbitrate the fractionated army, navy, and air force positions in order that a common policy in a particular area could be adopted. Both he and his increasingly outgunned and beleaguered staff worked from early morning until late at night at the slogging task of reducing or resolving interservice feuds, great and small, but the days never seemed long enough to do all that had to be done. Forrestal had thought he could confine his energy and attention to the handful of fundamental security issues related to "grand strategy"; in the event, this was proving to be an illusion.

DIVIDED MILITARY JUDGMENT

BEYOND HIS immediate staff, he had expected to exercise effective guidance over the military establishment through three powerhouse agencies which had made decisive contributions to winning World War II. All three had now been given statutory basis in the new law and placed under the "general direction, authority and control" of the Secretary of Defense. They were the Munitions Board, the Research and Development Board, and the Joint Chiefs of Staff.

The first was charged with "joint logistical planning and joint procurement" with the aim of eliminating "needless duplication in purchasing"[34] and was now to be headed by a civilian chairman. Determined to obtain "the best man," Forrestal appointed Thomas Hargrave, president of Eastman Kodak (even though Hargrave agreed to serve only on a part-time basis and did not give up his corporate position) and gave him final authority to assign responsibility to one service (e.g., army) for purchasing one item (e.g., shoes) for all three services. But his directive to Hargrave was immediately resisted by the services, which claimed the Secretary of Defense had no authority to centralize "current" procurement operations, but only to coordinate plans for the mobilization of industry in the event of war. The army, navy, and air force members of the Munitions Board saw themselves as agents of their individual services, not as staff to the Secretary of Defense with responsibility to take a broad national view, and they based their position on the language of the 1947 act. In June 1948, Forrestal reluctantly accepted reality by rescinding his original directive to Hargrave.[35]

The same structural defect and parochial attitudes weakened Forrestal's efforts to establish a unified program of military research. A predecessor joint research board had operated during the war under Vannevar Bush, the strong-willed scientist and administrator who was also president of the Carnegie Institution in Washington; Forrestal persuaded him to carry on with the new board in the interests of continuity. Bush sought to compose his board exclusively of high-ranking military officers, but the service Secretaries found this idea inconsistent with their own ultimate responsibility for the use of public funds. Bush then made an agreement to sit in on the deliberations of the Joint Chiefs of Staff "on all appropriate occasions," but the JCS, wary of losing control over decisions on new weapons, never got around to inviting him to a meeting. When Bush stepped down in October 1948, the consensus in Forrestal's staff was that his "committee system" approach had failed to produce any movement toward the elimination of even the most obvious duplications in military research. Bush was succeeded by Karl T. Compton, president of M.I.T., who also proved unable to surmount the stubbornly tripartite character of the Research and Development Board.[36]

Despite these disappointments, Forrestal and his immediate staff— through reasoned argument, patience, and tenacity—gradually compiled a list of accomplishments in the direction of interservice integration. In this effort, Ohly was, according to one of his associates, "a real secret weapon" able "to turn out more good work under pressure than any man I've ever seen."[37] A few of these achievements, like a uniform code of military justice, a uniform military pay scale, and merger of the air force and navy air transport services, were conclusive. Others involved only tentative first steps forward, like a preliminary study of how to integrate existing army and navy medical and hospital facilities or the development of a catalogue of common spare parts to be used in joint procurement. These were important and hard-won, albeit mundane, advances, but they exacted a disproportionate toll of time and energy from the OSD staff and from Forrestal himself, which left them with limited reserves of both for dealing with the supreme issues—that is, the total size and composition of the military forces, the roles and missions to be assigned each service, war plans, and the division of the military budget.

The gravest defect in the 1947 act was to leave the Joint Chiefs of Staff as a tripartite committee of equal military service commanders, while at the same time formally establishing them as the "principal military advisers" to the President and the Secretary of Defense. This conceptual flaw (unerringly foreseen in Truman's message of December 19, 1945, proposing a single chief of staff) was both obscured and aggravated by the great prestige of the wartime JCS. Marshall, King, and Arnold had conceived the global strategies, planned the large and intricate operations and directed the powerful American forces which destroyed the Nazi and Fascist tyrannies in Europe, and pressed relentlessly across the Pacific reaches to force the surrender of Japan. Their brilliant success had been achieved, it was argued by navy partisans, through cooperation and compromise, through a synthesis of several minds, and without the dangers of a single dictatorial military chief. The facts were somewhat different. Relations within the wartime JCS were often strained, and all major conflicts had to be resolved by President Roosevelt, who performed in the fullest sense as Commander in Chief. Furthermore, military budgets were open-ended during the war, and duplication and waste were accepted as the price of victory.[38]

The situation in 1947 was dramatically different, but the Joint Chiefs of Staff were still surrounded by a special aura. There remained a definite mystery about the nature of military judgment and military advice, and civilian officials approached the subject with respect bordering on awe; especially did they acknowledge that senior military leaders were its only legitimate custodians. There were not as yet any competitive sources of competent analysis of strategy and weapons, like the several civilian think tanks which sprang up in universities and elsewhere over the following twenty years. In the circumstances, the Joint Chiefs of Staff were regarded as the only credible source of military advice in the American political system. If you needed it, you went to them.

By the time Forrestal assumed office as Secretary of Defense, the wartime chiefs had retired, but their successors were heroes of equal or greater stature—Eisenhower, Nimitz, and Spaatz. It was, moreover, a period of confused transition at home and of political upheaval across the globe. In the third postwar year America was still seeking to establish for itself a definitive role in a world that seemed to grow more chaotic and more dangerous with every passing day. The President and his principal Cabinet officers needed professional military advice on nearly every international question—from the Soviet threat in Europe and how the United States should meet it, to the civil war in China, to U.S. base requirements in the Pacific and the custody of atomic weapons inside the U.S. government.

Requests for JCS views were usually transmitted in writing from Forrestal's office and, as U.S.-Soviet relations visibly worsened and crises erupted from Turkey to Berlin, the number and complexity of the issues put to them soon overwhelmed the JCS organization. In part, this reflected the limited size of its support staff, confined by the 1947 law to one hundred officers. The root of the trouble, however, lay in the fact that the Joint Chiefs themselves were truly and entirely tripartite in structure and outlook. Lacking an independent head (a single superior officer or even a presiding chairman) who could look broadly at a given issue and move deliberations toward a coherent synthesis of military judgment that would be helpful to Forrestal and the President, the JCS were rarely able to reflect a unified view of the national interest. More often they responded—in "split papers"—as representatives of three different institutions, each with entrenched interests and subjective strategic perceptions they refused to compromise. There was, for example, no conceptual agreement on how the next war would be fought, what weapons would be most important, who would control their use, or how the current military budget should be divided among the competing interests. Nor was there any real prospect of resolving these issues short of a presidential decision, given the way the JCS was organized, the equivocal language of the statute, and Forrestal's determination to operate by consensus.[39]

The result was deadlock from the outset. Either Forrestal's urgent questions went unanswered for weeks or they came back as "split papers," with the army and the air force usually on one side and the navy on the other. A central component of JCS paralysis was the tight military budget ceilings imposed by President Truman and the fact that these could not accommodate the aspirations of both the air force and naval aviation. The bitter air force–navy dispute dominated Forrestal's tenure as Secretary of Defense and later exploded in an unedifying incident known as the Admirals' Revolt, when Forrestal's successor, Louis Johnson, canceled the "supercarrier" on which rested the navy's claim to participation in strategic atomic bombing.

CHAPTER 27

★ ★ ★

The Bitter Fight
over Air Power

FORRESTAL HAD directed the JCS to develop a "joint outline strategic war plan" by January 1, 1948, as a basis for budget planning,
but they asked for an extension to March 1. Meanwhile, President
Truman was reaching his own budgetary conclusions. In mid-January he
submitted to the Congress a budget request (called FY 1949) for the fiscal
year beginning the following July 1. This called for total government expenditures of $39.7 billion, including $4 billion for the first year of Marshall Plan assistance and substantial outlays for Greek-Turkish aid and other
foreign programs. He proposed $9.8 billion for total military expenditures,
which involved a 13 percent reduction in military manpower (down to 1.4
million men), but still provided for the largest standing force in American
history: eleven army divisions, a navy of 277 combatant ships (including
eleven heavy aircraft carriers), and an air force of fifty-five combat groups
(comprising a mix of bombers and fighters). Despite his New Deal politics,
Truman possessed the fiscal instincts of a small businessman and was determined to avoid deficit spending; his budget proposal earmarked $4.8
billion in anticipated revenues for reducing the national debt.[1]

The air force–naval aviation dispute emerged almost as soon as Forrestal
took office—in hearings held (September–November 1947) by the President's Air Power Commission, a blue-ribbon panel headed by a New York
lawyer, Thomas K. Finletter.* Truman had created the commission to study
and recommend a national policy on civil and military aviation. (Finletter
later served as Secretary of the Air Force.) The public hearings confirmed
the growing popular consensus that military aviation, combined with atomic

*Other members of the panel were George P. Baker, a Harvard economist; Palmer Hoyt, pub-
lisher of the Denver *Post;* John McCone, a California businessman; and Arthur Whiteside, Chairman of Dun and Bradstreet.

weapons, would probably determine the outcome of future wars, but the closed sessions were dominated by heated emotional disagreements between air force and navy spokesmen over how to develop the requisite military air power and who should control it. The air force called for a seventy-group force emphasizing the B-36 (a propeller-driven intercontinental bomber), but the navy argued that the sluggish B-36 could not penetrate Soviet defenses and insisted that carrier-based naval aircraft, able to attack the Russian heartland from several different points of the compass, were a far more reliable instrument.[2]

Dismayed by the vehemence of the contending arguments, Forrestal urged the Finletter Commission to avoid oversimplifying the issue. It was not at all clear how future wars would be fought, he told them: "conquering the Russians is one thing . . . [but] finding out what to do with them afterward is an entirely different problem." Moreover, the United States might not find itself confronted by "global war" but by the need to wage a protracted low-level "containing war" for which long-range bombers and carrier aircraft would both be unsuitable instruments (here he seemed to be reflecting Kennan). He expressed his agreement with President Truman that economic strength and political stability were the primary underpinnings of national security and that "huge sums" spent for defense might in the long run be more dangerous for the country than "a somewhat understaffed military establishment."[3] Unwilling, however, to accept this generalized strategic guidance from the civilian Secretary of Defense, the Finletter Commission insisted on obtaining a professional military judgment as to air force and naval air "requirements" without reference to cost. Forrestal, although reluctant to fuel the controversy, saw no legitimate way to block the inquiry. Unconstrained by cost factors, the JCS unanimously endorsed a general buildup of air-power capabilities, but also a parallel expansion of land and sea forces in order to provide a strong "balanced" military organization. In its public report, however, the Finletter group generally ignored the JCS emphasis on "balance" and asserted that U.S. "military security must be based on air power." It endorsed a seventy-group air force and a less specific strengthening of naval air and urged an acceleration of military aircraft procurement.[4]

The White House was displeased by the seventy-group recommendation, and Truman was personally irritated at Symington for not controlling the zealots in the new air force, not yet aware that Symington was one of them. He delayed release of the Finletter report until the day after his own budget proposals were submitted to Congress, but this tactic did not obscure the glaring disparity between the two proposals: Truman wanted fifty-five groups for the air force and all aircraft procurement funded within a $9.8 billion military budget. Finletter was urging a seventy-group air force plus accelerated aircraft procurement above and beyond the President's figure.

Testifying before the Finletter Commission.
Left to right: *Navy Secretary John L. Sullivan, Air Force Secretary*
Stuart Symington, and Secretary of Defense Forrestal

In early February, the Republican-controlled Eightieth Congress defied both the President and the worsening international situation by voting an across-the-board tax reduction which virtually assured a budget deficit unless there were further expenditure cuts. A battle was thus shaping up between a President determined to avoid deficit spending and a variety of congressional interests who seemed to want—simultaneously—lower taxes, reduced spending on "New Deal social programs," and increased support for the military forces.

THE FINLETTER REPORT's conclusion that U.S. military security must henceforward be based on air power and the favorable response to the report in the Congress gave Symington and the air force generals added confidence to press their case. Symington, no intellectual, leaned on generals with a similar cast of mind—like Spaatz and Hoyt Vandenberg, who were fine flying officers and great combat leaders but very much out of their depth in the broader realms of foreign affairs, economics, and history. They were essentially straight-line partisans for a stronger air force, and they in turn were influenced by their own protégés down the line—younger, important generals who had run large operations during the war and were accustomed to having things their own way. Several of these firebrands wanted a completely autonomous Department of Air Power, unencumbered by even nominal subordination to the Secretary of Defense or the Joint Chiefs of Staff.[5] Symington readily accepted and came to personify the callow views of those who were running the new air force. They were contemptuous of the assumption (embodied in the 1947 act) that Forrestal and three Special Assistants, who had only "coordinating" authority, could manage the vast military establishment, and they were certain such an arrangement could not last. Dominant influence and prestige would, they felt, inevitably gravitate to air power, but their tactic was to hasten the inevitable day by withholding cooperation and support from the new setup. Symington, moreover, embarked upon a kind of personal guerrilla warfare against the Secretary of Defense.

One tactic was to assign air force officers of indifferent quality, or without relevant experience, to the several joint boards and committees—especially to the Joint Staff, which provided underpinning for the JCS, while the army and the navy sent their best and brightest. The same approach was used in assigning liaison officers to Forrestal's office. In late 1947 this assignment was handed to an earnest young fighter pilot, Colonel Jerry Page, who had no previous experience in Washington and was wholly innocent of the frictions which had marked the unification debate. When Page sought advice on how to function, the air staff told him: "Keep your ears open and your mouth shut. Tell them nothing about the air force. Forrestal is still Navy. He hasn't changed." When Forrestal, in the normal course of business, asked Page to obtain the official air force position on particular questions, the young colonel found it was standard practice in the Air Staff to delay or stonewall a reply or to provide an arbitrary, uncooperative answer.[6]

The air force at this time had not gained authorization for its own academy and so was dependent on West Point and Annapolis as sources of regular officer material. It blatantly asked the army and navy to allocate 35 percent of each graduating class to the air force. The older services bristled at the size of the request, then offered 2 percent each, whereupon the air force reduced its request to 27 percent. Faced with another impasse on a peripheral issue, Forrestal asked Colonel Page for his opinion. Page suggested 3 percent for openers, combined with an agreement that an air force recruiting group could visit West Point and Annapolis each year to present the case to cadets and midshipmen for an air force career. Forrestal thought this a sensible solution and decided the question on that basis.

A week later Page suddenly received orders to Korea—the equivalent in 1948 of an assignment to Siberia. When he went to say good-bye to Forrestal, the Secretary of Defense was totally surprised. "What are you talking about?" he asked.

"Well, sir, I have orders to leave for Korea."

Forrestal immediately called Symington on the telephone and demanded an explanation. The Air Force Secretary told him, "Page is young. He needs experience in command." Forrestal said in icy tones, "If I had my choice between sending you or Page to Korea, I'd send you. Page belongs to me. He stays here." Later the same day, Page was summoned to Symington's office, where he found the lanky Air Force Secretary lounging in his chair, feet propped on the desk.

"Well, Colonel, I understand you are staying with us after all."

"Yes, sir."

"You made a serious mistake in not supporting the air force position on the academy graduates."

"Well, sir, I gave Secretary Forrestal my honest opinion."

"I have advice for you, son. Don't ever let your honesty interfere with your judgment."[7]

Not all senior air force officers approved of these tactics, and a few of them, including Lieutenant General Elwood Quesada and Major General Emmett O'Donnell, had "absolutely no use" for their civilian secretary, according to Hanson Baldwin, the military analyst for the *New York Times*. Baldwin's coverage of World War II had earned him a deserved reputation for authoritative, evenhanded reporting, but the fact that he was a Naval Academy graduate made him suspect in Symington's eyes. One evening Quesada was having cocktails with Baldwin at the Mayflower Hotel, when Symington walked into the bar and saw them together. The next day he called Quesada to his office and said, "You don't pick your drinking companions very carefully, do you?" Quesada, who had a fiery temper, managed to control his anger. "I pick my own friends," he told Symington, turned on his heel, and walked out.[8]

"Rosie" O'Donnell, who ran air force public relations and considered Symington's ceaseless conniving nasty and immoral, soon had a run-in which led to his reassignment. Symington then brought in a civilian PR man named Steve Leo, a propagandist who was responsive to the wild-blue-yonder elements in the air force. It was the opinion of the working press that Leo sharpened Symington's partisan views, but insiders like Zuckert felt that Leo in fact exerted a restraining influence on their impulsive, reflexive boss.[9] Another air force general who was coolly skeptical of Symington was Lauris Norstad, a West Pointer of exceptional ability. A rational air-power advocate, he took a much broader view than most of his fellow air force officers and strongly supported Eisenhower's vision of truly integrated forces. He went to Europe with Eisenhower in 1951, and succeeded him as NATO commander.[10]

One Symington tactic was to harass Forrestal on the office intercom, which was always open because Forrestal wished to be continuously available to his principal civilian associates. His own staff protested that this would confront him with endless interruptions during the busy workday, but he rejected their advice. Of the three service secretaries, Symington alone abused the privilege, and he did it, in the view of Forrestal intimates, with the deliberate intent of getting on Forrestal's nerves and wearing him down. Symington's own staff doubted whether he acted with malicious intent—they felt his addiction to the intercom was an expression of his intense and aggressive personality—but they did not deny that this practice cumulatively irritated Forrestal. Symington would ring him up several times a day to protest some alleged navy propaganda move or to question cost figures on aircraft carriers versus bombers: "Jim, I just got some new figures on the cost of the air wing aboard that carrier. You know, I think your figures are far too low. A realistic figure is nearly twice what the navy claims." As the weeks passed, this constant drumbeat had its effect on a Secretary of Defense already tired and tense, who was aware that his efforts to integrate the military services were not going well and that he had underestimated the depth and intensity of interservice rivalry. Symington was a relentless goad, and Forrestal took no measures to defend himself.[11]

The Navy Under Secretary, John Kenney, thought Symington was "in the front row of world-class double-dealers," a man who pretended to be Forrestal's friend but was "repeatedly disloyal."[12] Hanson Baldwin found Symington's methods "dirty pool, dirty politics."[13]

THE WAR SCARE

As 1948 OPENED, a series of dramatic events created an atmosphere of acute crisis in Washington which had the effect of sharpening all of the tensions surrounding the debate over foreign and defense policy. At the center of the controversy was the composition of U.S. forces and the size of the military budget. There had been a steady decline in enlistments and reenlistments following termination of the draft in the spring of 1947. The air force and the navy were losing many of their trained technicians, but the army was suffering wholesale losses. Army strength dropped by 165,000 men in six months, and Eisenhower, the outgoing Chief of Staff, warned that the army was "increasingly unable to mobilize the land power" he saw as indispensable "to support air and sea power in an emergency."[14] The Munitions Board found a few days later that the army was so short of basic equipment and spare parts that it could not outfit more than half its active and reserve divisions within the next eighteen months. Forrestal discussed these weaknesses with Truman in the context of U.S. commitments and possible emergencies in Germany, Greece, Palestine, Italy, and Korea. He emphasized Eisenhower's point that the air force, which needed forward bases to conduct offensive or retaliatory bombing operations, could not obtain and hold these without strong ground forces. The President was apparently unmoved until two precipitating events in Europe transformed the Washington scene.[15]

Both of these were part of the struggle between Russia and the West over the future of Germany. The Marshall Plan was now operative and aimed at bringing about the recovery of Western Europe; the economic and political rehabilitation of the three Western occupied zones of Germany (United States, Britain, and France) was regarded as a vital element of this plan. The Soviet Union, however, still rejected the idea of a self-supporting German economy, and was systematically stripping its own occupied zone of industrial plants, machinery, and equipment. In addition, it demanded the right to reparations from the other zones, but the Western powers had shut these off.

In January 1948, Stalin decided to "turn Eastern Germany into our own state"[16] and immediately organized troop movements and demonstrations of strength to create a deliberate war scare aimed at pressuring the Western powers out of Berlin, where Western access rested on fragile understandings reached in 1945 between Western and Soviet military commanders. On January 6, Soviet authorities in Berlin demanded inspection of a U.S. military freight train entering the eastern zone, and on January 24 they forced the removal of German passengers from a British train.[17] Stalin's next move was to put direct pressure on Czechoslovakia, the only East European country still free of explicit Soviet control. The Czechs had incurred his wrath by having the temerity to apply for participation in the Marshall Plan. After a sudden visit to Prague by the Soviet Deputy Foreign Minister, Czech President Edvard Beneš was forced to hand over all Cabinet posts to local Communists, except the Foreign Ministry, which remained under Jan Masaryk, the son of the Czech republic's founder.[18]

On March 5, the American commander in Germany, General Lucius Clay, sent to Washington a dramatic message which was immediately construed as a "war warning." Referring to his earlier view, "based on logical analysis," that "war was unlikely for at least ten years," Clay told his superiors at the Pentagon that "a subtle change in Soviet attitudes" gave him "a feeling" that war might now come "with dramatic suddenness."[19] It was later learned that Clay's message was prompted not by a perceived change in Soviet willingness to risk war, but by a discussion in Berlin with the visiting Director of Army Intelligence, Lieutenant General Stephen Chamberlin. The officer from Washington had drawn Clay's attention to the need to rally congressional opinion in support of higher military appropriations, given the perilous state of the world and the low state of U.S. military forces.

The Clay war warning hit Washington like a lightning bolt and set off a series of frantic responses. Forrestal briefed the President on March 6 and the Senate Armed Services Committee on March 8, and rumors of war spread through the city despite official efforts to maintain an outward calm. Tensions mounted to fever pitch on March 10, when Jan Masaryk's body was found in the stone courtyard beneath the window of his office at the Foreign Ministry in Prague. Czech authorities called the death a suicide, but Western reports, never fully verified, concluded it had been murder— a political assassination by the Communist secret police.[20]

THE JCS PARALYSIS on strategic war plans continued, owing primarily to the air force–navy conflict over the scope of naval aviation. Before the war scare, Forrestal had given the JCS until March 8 to promulgate an agreed-upon statement of roles and missions. When they failed to meet the deadline and asked that the matters in dispute be "resolved by higher authority," Forrestal summoned them to a closed-door conference at Key West, Florida, believing it was imperative in the new crisis situation to develop an agreed-upon emergency war plan. From March 11 through 14, Forrestal and his military advisers hammered out a statement of service functions presumably tighter and clearer than the executive order which had been issued concurrently with the 1947 act.

The new statement was based on a concept of "primary" and "collateral" missions ostensibly designed to assure the full use of forces and weapons against an enemy in wartime. Bureaucratically, it had the effect of prohibiting one service from claiming exclusive jurisdiction over a given function or the weapons and facilities needed to carry it out; it thus assured redundancy. On the most sensitive issue, "strategic air warfare," this was a victory for the navy. Thus, the air force was assigned primary responsibility, but the navy was given the collateral right "to participate in the overall air effort as directed by the Joint Chiefs of Staff." In addition, this "collateral" task was not to be interpreted "to prohibit the Navy from attacking any targets, inland or otherwise, necessary for the accomplishment of its mission." Finally, leaving nothing to chance, the navy succeeded in inserting into the official memorandum of record the statement that "if consideration of its purely naval function" did not justify a requirement for a "large carrier," nevertheless the "contribution which it [the carrier] could make to strategic air warfare might be enough to warrant its construction." The navy was absolutely determined not to be excluded from a role in delivering what was coming to be known as "the atomic counteroffensive," and its intended instrument was the proposed "supercarrier.'' The Key West Agreement gave the navy a large foot in that door, a development which angered Symington and the air force generals and deepened their conviction that Forrestal was still a navy partisan and an obstacle to the logical development of air force preeminence.[21]

The discussions at Key West also focused on the war scare in Europe. There was agreement on the need to revive the military draft and obtain a budget increase for all three services. Forrestal took the recommendations to the White House on March 15 and urged the President to act quickly. Recognizing the sudden gravity of the situation and the fears it was raising in the country and in Western Europe, the President appeared before a joint session of Congress two days later to condemn the ''ruthless course'' of Soviet policy. He asked for revival of the military draft, enactment of a Universal Military Training (UMT) program, and full funding for the Marshall Plan, but significantly he did not seek more money for U.S. military forces, except a modest increment for the army. The question of a military ''supplemental appropriation'' across the board was about to become another contentious case of differing perspectives and priorities in the White House and the Pentagon.[22]

Forrestal noted on his return from Key West that the newspapers were ''full of rumors and portents of war,'' whereas ''the fact is that this country and its government are desperately anxious to avoid war. It is simply a question of how best to do it.'' While he doubted that ''the gang who run Russia'' were ready for war, ''one always has to remember'' that Hitler's aggressions in 1939 also seemed unlikely. U.S. policy was now aimed at ''mak[ing] the Russians see the folly of continuing an aggression which will lead to war.'' One imperative step ''to restore them to sanity'' was to make a ''start'' on rearmament so that war would not catch the United States ''flat-footed,'' as it had done in 1941.[23] The Hitler and Pearl Harbor analogies dominated Forrestal's thinking in this critical period and led him to the conviction that war was probably coming whether or not the Soviets were precisely ''ready.''

This position put him increasingly at odds with Truman and Marshall, for while Forrestal stressed the Red Army's capability to overrun Western Europe and the fact that America had only two and a third army divisions in its strategic reserve, the President and the Secretary of State steadfastly held to the view that the Soviets were determined to avoid war, especially in the face of the American atomic bomb monopoly. Forrestal argued that more usable American military power was necessary to maintain the position in Berlin, but Truman chose to interpret this simple prudence as vacillation. On July 19, he recorded in his diary that he had ''made the decision ten days ago to stay in Berlin. [But] Jim wants to hedge—he always does.''[24] This comment was neither wholly accurate nor wholly fair. Truman's resolve to remain in Berlin fluctuated between January and July—

until the miraculous tour de force that came to be called the Berlin Airlift demonstrated that the city could be sustained without risking a frontal challenge to the Soviet land blockade. The pragmatic Forrestal was not "hedging" the ultimate Allied position in Berlin any more than was the President; he was merely underlining the fact of the West's extreme weakness in conventional military power.[25]

The need for some visible military buildup was widely acknowledged in Washington, especially as the Russians continued to tighten their slow squeeze on Berlin, e.g., demanding that military freight trains be cleared through Soviet checkpoints and that all cargo be inspected by Soviet authorities. The question was how to demonstrate strength and firmness without provoking a war in a situation where the Soviets possessed the positional leverage. General Clay advised Washington of his intention to resist the Russian demands by instructing his guards to open fire if Soviet soldiers attempted to enter American trains. Forrestal and the JCS firmly rejected this idea as provocative, following which Clay and his British counterpart started a small combined airlift to circumvent the interference with Allied trains. Soon thereafter a large-scale airlift was organized by General Curtis LeMay, the Air Force Commander in Europe, and Truman confirmed this on July 22 as the basic Allied strategy for remaining in Berlin. Also in July, Forrestal obtained British consent to receive two groups of B-29 bombers on bases in England; two more B-29 squadrons were sent to the American Zone in Germany. Washington wanted Moscow to draw the inference that the United States was prepared to use atomic weapons if the Red Army moved against any Allied position in Europe. In fact, at the time there was only one air group capable of delivering the large, cumbersome atomic bombs of that period, and none of the aircraft sent to England and Germany were so fitted out. Thus, the action was a kind of bluff, which underscored Forrestal's concern about American military weakness. In the ensuing months, however, a U.S. atomic capability in England was achieved, and atomic bombers remained on station there for the next forty years.[26]

THE SHORT-LIVED BUILDUP

MEANWHILE, U.S. intelligence agencies, after a careful study of all the factors, discounted Clay's war warning of March 5. Their report to the President in mid-March recognized "the ever present possibility" that "some miscalculation or incident" could trigger hostilities, but concluded that "no reliable evidence" existed to support the view that Russia "intends" to make war "within the next sixty days." A second report at the end of March extended this conclusion through 1948.[27]

This was the nerve-racking context in which the Truman administration and the Congress addressed the question of how much U.S. military power was enough. Truman's firmly established preference to avoid deficit spending was now reinforced by what the White House interpreted as reassuring intelligence reports, and he instructed Budget Director James Webb to hold a military "supplemental" to $1.5 billion. In a meeting with Webb on March 20, Forrestal said he thought it would be better to determine the "real" military requirements first, and then frame a supplemental budget. The logic of this approach was impeccable in the context of orderly planning, but it offered the JCS another opportunity to state the full measure of military "requirements," which were almost certain to be unacceptable to the White House. This is exactly what happened.

Forrestal finessed Webb's strong expression of the President's position, and the JCS asked for supplemental funds totaling $8.8 billion ($3 billion for immediate operational readiness and $5.8 billion in new contract authority for aircraft procurement). On March 23, Forrestal discussed these figures with the Secretary of State and sought his advice on the most effective strategy for presenting a supplemental request to Congress. The Forrestal-Marshall relationship had been correct if distant during the war, but had turned frosty in the ensuing unification debate when the two men advocated irreconcilable concepts of defense organization. Now the Secretary of Defense was concerned that the Secretary of State, despite his great military experience and prestige, did not fully grasp the lethal dimension of the Soviet threat and the serious risk of imminent war, while Marshall felt that Forrestal had lost his sense of proportion about both of these factors.[28] On this occasion, Marshall expressed his full agreement with the President that any new military funding should be held to a very modest level and that the administration should avoid "pessimistic or inflammatory" statements about Soviet capabilities or the risks of imminent war. Forrestal thought there was domestic political and international diplomatic danger in asking for too little. A compromise was reached with the President on a total supplemental figure of $3 billion, but $775 million of this was earmarked for aircraft procurement. Forrestal foresaw a "hell of a fight" over the allocation of the remainder if he hoped to preserve "any semblance of a balance of forces."[29]

On the eve of hearings in the Senate Armed Services Committee, Truman gathered Forrestal and the other top civilian and military leaders in the Oval Office to insist that they support the new spending limits. Looking around the room he said, "I want everybody to back this budget. If you have anything to say against it, say it now." He was looking straight at Symington, and he had in mind the limit of fifty-five air groups in the budget. The Air Force Secretary, who had recommended a seventy-group program to the Finletter Commission and in other forums, replied: "Mr.

President, are you asking me, in effect, to perjure myself if I am asked a question as to whether the Air Force can carry out its mission with this amount of money?'' Truman looked at him hard. ''Will you give me your word that you won't *originate* the question?'' Symington gave his word.[30]

At the hearings, Forrestal, Royall, and Sullivan all supported the agreed-upon position, but Symington jumped the traces, responding to leading questions from air-power supporters by making it clear that he advocated a seventy-group air force. He offered the opinion that the $3 billion supplemental would not suffice for air force requirements, but claimed that an additional $850 million would fund the full seventy-group program. Forrestal, caught off guard by this testimony, was recalled to the witness chair to confirm or deny Symington's claim. He told the committee that Symington's figure included only additional aircraft; to provide the additional ''balance'' of ground forces, naval forces, and logistical efforts necessary to support a seventy-group program would cost an additional $18 billion.[31]

This incident showed that Symington and the air force, encouraged by air-power advocates in the Congress, were willing to defy Forrestal and the President openly and publicly. They found political cover in the emergent fact that air power as the first line of defense possessed an irresistible political appeal in a period of tight military budgets. According to Eliot Janeway, Symington was privately encouraged by Congressman Lyndon Johnson, a rising star on the House Armed Services Committee, to make the bold case for air power in defiance of the President's budget limits, and also systematically to undercut Forrestal; in return Johnson would provide political protection and would use his influence to promote Symington for Secretary of Defense. In the 1950s, when both Symington and Johnson served in the Senate, their relationship was close.[32]

Truman was angered by Symington's testimony and said so at a press conference—a headline in the Washington *Times-Herald* said ''Truman Spanks Symington''—but he took no further public action. According to one source, however, he raised with Forrestal the question of replacing the Air Force Secretary, but Forrestal assured the President that he could handle the matter within the Pentagon without demanding Symington's resignation.[33] The incident deepened Forrestal's distrust of his former friend, but he seemed unaware that Symington had become an enemy.

The passivity of these responses emboldened Symington to greater assertiveness. Exuding confidence, he told Forrestal on March 31 that ''the press, the Congress, and the people are sold on this Air Force program''; in a period where ''there is not enough money,'' they will not support a ''balanced'' program of UMT, army and navy ''at the expense of the Air Force.''[34] At this critical juncture, Forrestal exhibited once again the aversion to confrontation which, aggravated by his fatigue, was making it difficult for him to make or stick with hard decisions. When he consulted his friend John J. McCloy, now president of the World Bank, McCloy came away from the meeting confirmed in his view that Forrestal was "a worrier . . . whose certainties rested on sand." Hands clasped behind his head, he had stared broodingly into space and asked McCloy, "What is the right thing to do? If only I had your wisdom, Jack."[35]

In the event, Forrestal made what appears in retrospect to have been the worst of several possible decisions. Instead of holding to the President's program and telling Symington to get on the team or get out, he privately conceded that Symington and the air-power zealots in Congress and the press might be right. He directed the JCS to estimate, first, the "size and cost" of a seventy-group air force within "a balanced military establishment." Then, further tempting fate, he asked the divided Oracles of Delphi whether they would support a seventy-group air force "regardless of whether the Army and Navy receive increases."[36] The answers were predictable and not at all helpful. On the first question, the army and navy now enthusiastically endorsed a parallel expansion of ground and sea forces to match a seventy-group air force, but declined to estimate the cost. On the second question, however, the two senior services argued that an isolated air force buildup would create a kind of fraudulent situation in which the air force could not effectively deploy its strategic aircraft against the enemy. Meanwhile, congressional leaders of all stripes were jumping on the air-power bandwagon, including Carl Vinson, the long-time champion of navy autonomy and supremacy.

Confronted by the unhelpful JCS responses, Forrestal on April 17 put additional questions to them. First, assuming an absolute supplemental limit of $3 billion, where would they scale down the desired buildup? Second, if $5 billion were available, what should be the size of each force and how should the money be divided? The larger figure came right out of Forrestal's hat and was clearly inconsistent with the President's position, but he was feeling pressure from all three military services, from Congress, and from the deteriorating situation in Europe. Reason and instinct told him that more U.S. military power was needed. After a long, hard meeting with the JCS on April 19, he obtained their agreement to a supplemental of $3.5 billion, and two days later Truman "tentatively" accepted this figure, pending review by the Budget Bureau. The result now appeared to represent a significant success for Forrestal's patient tenacity and even-handedness.[37]

But James Webb then put a stick in the spokes. He thought this supplemental figure excessive because it led inevitably to higher military budgets in future years—$17 or $18 billion—whereas he thought the tolerable limit, without imposing wage and price controls on the economy, was about $15 billion. He proposed to cut it to $2.5 billion and began telling friends that Forrestal was being "bulldozed" by the services and had "lost control" of the situation. Marshall, without addressing the military dollar figures, argued that Marshall Plan aid to Europe should have first priority and opposed "plunge[ing] into war preparations."[38] Truman, who found in Marshall's position reinforcement for his own determination to avoid deficit spending almost regardless of the world situation, was frustrated by the continuing impasse, and he divided the blame between Congress and Forrestal. "I want a balanced sensible defense for which the country can pay," he confided to his diary on May 7, but "the Congress can't bring itself to do the right thing. . . . The air boys are for glamour, and the Navy as always is the greatest propaganda machine. . . . Marshall is a tower of strength and common sense. So are Snyder and Webb. Forrestal can't take it. He wants to compromise with the opposition"—by "opposition" he meant not the Russians but American advocates of a larger military buildup.[39]

The final decision on the supplemental was $3.1 billion, a figure slightly larger than the compromise approved by the White House in late March. Nevertheless, it dismayed Forrestal because he saw it as marking the end of the short-lived impulse to strengthen the armed forces; it indicated that despite rising Soviet threats and pressures, military spending would fall to $15 billion for the coming year. His Special Assistant for budgetary matters, Wilfred McNeil, convinced him that the turbulence of interservice rivalries would now grow uncontrollable unless the President himself explained his position in a face-to-face meeting with the service secretaries and the military chiefs. Webb saw no reason why the President should have to explain his policy or the reasoning behind it to his military subordinates, and he took Forrestal's insistence on this point as further evidence that the Secretary of Defense was not in control at the Pentagon. Truman nonetheless agreed to hold the meeting, at which he read from a memorandum prepared by Forrestal and McNeil. At the same time, he left no one in doubt that even $3.1 billion in supplemental military funds were, in his view, excessive from the standpoint of their impact on the economy. His original budget request for FY 1949 (beginning July 1, 1948) had been $9.8 billion for all military purposes. The supplemental appropriations and certain other congressional actions brought the final total to $13.1 billion.[40]

CUSTODY OF THE ATOMIC STOCKPILE

ANOTHER SOURCE of frustration for Forrestal in mid-1948 was the fight over physical custody of the atomic bomb stockpile. Early in the previous year, all matters relating to the atomic energy program, including custody of the bombs, had been placed by law in a new Atomic Energy Commission (AEC), but the military services continued to argue that the weapons should be under military control on the grounds that availability "for instant use" was a "prerequisite for national security."[41] Forrestal supported this position both as Secretary of the Navy and as Secretary of Defense, but the AEC Chairman, David Lilienthal, and his fellow commissioners* were categorically opposed. The reference to "instant use" suggested to them that beyond simple physical custody, Forrestal and the military services were operating on the assumption that they could use nuclear weapons on their own authority under conditions deemed by them to be appropriate. Lilienthal recognized that, far from being merely a bureaucratic jurisdictional dispute, the issue of "use" involved considerations of the most fundamental national policy, indeed of the constitutional powers and prerogatives of the President.[42]

Forrestal was now very tired, more worn down physically and mentally than he or others realized, and this fact began to fray his judgment at the edges. He proved susceptible to a prevailing feeling in the Pentagon that there existed in the AEC "a pacifistic and unrealistic trend" which might lead, in a crisis, to dangerous delays in transferring the weapons into military hands.[43] He told several close advisers, including General Lauris Norstad, that on the bomb custody issue, he would put it to the President on a take-it-or-leave-it basis. If Truman's decision went against him, he would quit.[44]

The confrontation occurred at the White House on July 21. Forrestal argued that without military custody of atomic weapons "a surprise attack" could expose the nation to "unreasonable risk of mistake, confusion and failure to act with the necessary speed and precision"; with military custody, however, he felt these risks could be avoided, for it would then be possible to distribute bomb "components," in advance of a crisis, to the "most favorable strategic locations."[45] This was a reference to forward airfields beyond the boundaries of the continental United States which were the necessary launching pads for the air-atomic counteroffensive in the era of propeller-driven aircraft.

Lilienthal argued that all operational and technical questions were subordinate to the fundamental political issue of civilian control—and the *perception* of civilian control, not only by the American people but also by foreign countries, especially the Soviet Union.[46] Budget Director James Webb provided similar advice to Truman in a memorandum delivered the next day. "Public policy considerations" he said, argued strongly for retention of civilian control, for the atomic bomb had become a symbol of man's most elementary hopes and fears and thus "an instrument of inter-

---

*Lewis L. Strauss, an investment banker; W. W. Waymack, a newspaper editor from Des Moines, Iowa; Robert P. Bacher, a Los Alamos physicist; and Sumner T. Pike, a former member of the Securities and Exchange Commission.

national influence." Moreover, the tense confrontation in Berlin and other simmering crises along the East-West boundary line "could be made worse by a transfer of stockpile custody at this particular time." Finally, in a jab at Forrestal's failure to resolve interservice conflicts over roles and missions, Webb added that the raging air force–navy dispute over access to atomic weapons was another reason for the White House to doubt that handing the stockpile over to the Pentagon would be a safe or reliable solution.[47]

On July 23, Truman told Forrestal privately that "political considerations" ruled out any transfer now, but that he might take another look at the issue after the presidential election. He ruled formally in favor of the AEC on August 6. Forrestal took the decision as personal rebuff, and could not refrain, in his written response, from reiterating his "deep conviction" that custody transfer to the military services would "further the interests of national security." At the same time, he recognized the extra-military factors which "necessarily" influenced the President's decision and he promised full compliance with it.[48]

After the letter was sent, he talked emotionally about resigning for several days. Donald Carpenter, the new chairman of the Munitions Board, urged him not to do so, as did General Norstad. The wise and balanced Norstad thought the controversy had now passed the bounds of reason on both sides, but it was clear to him that public opinion overwhelmingly favored civilian control. The essential condition for military effectiveness, he told Forrestal, was not custody, but access. The military already had access under the law, and joint training programs with the AEC would steadily improve the efficiency of physical transfer in an emergency. Moreover, he argued, nothing could or should change the constitutional fact that only the President could authorize use of the bomb.[49]

SYMINGTON IS ALMOST FIRED

O N JULY 17, the Secretary of the Air Force delivered a speech to the Institute of Aeronautical Sciences in Los Angeles which came close to bringing about his dismissal. As reported two days later in the *New York Times,* "In a gloves-off talk . . . W. Stuart Symington roundly criticized the administration of the country's armed forces in several major respects." Assailing "axe-grinders dedicated to obsolete methods of warfare" who contended that more money for the air force might "unbalance" the three military services, Symington declared that "air power should be put in balance not with the Army or the Navy but with the power of potential enemies . . . the American people have put their money on air power." Referring sarcastically to "duplications and triplications" which "threatened to bankrupt the country,'' he asked, ''Why should the American taxpayer be forced to finance a plan unapproved by the Joint Chiefs of Staff?''[50]

He had been preceded at the rostrum by several senior naval officers who, as the *Times* story put it, ''did not go out of their way to extol'' the strategic bombardment theory of warfare expounded by the air force. It appeared that a hypercompetitive Symington had reacted emotionally to the navy presentations without fully realizing the effect of his hot words on the policy of the President and the Secretary of Defense.

On reading the *Times* dispatch, Forrestal acted swiftly and with uncharacteristic directness. In a message the same day, he told Symington: ''If the account of your speech . . . as reported by Gladwin Hill in today's *New York Times* is accurate, it was an act of official disobedience and personal disloyalty. I shall await your explanation.''[51] The same day he called the President to tell him he would have to ask for Symington's resignation ''unless he could provide a satisfactory explanation of his conduct in Los Angeles.'' He approached this decision ''with reluctance,'' but had concluded ''it was the only way.'' According to his diary entry, ''The President agreed and asked me to report on the conversation.''[52]

What happened next remains shrouded in ambiguity, but five days later, on July 23, Forrestal told the President he was no longer seeking Symington's dismissal: ''I told him [Truman], Mr. Symington had related extenuating circumstances in terms of arrival in nonusable form of the speech corrected in my office . . . plus the fact that he denied having made any impromptu remarks.''[53] Behind this dramatic reversal was a story whose outcome was determined not by the facts of the case, but by Forrestal's second thoughts about the political consequences of firing the Air Force Secretary.

On Symington's return to Washington, he was asked for an explanation. His first statement was that the *Times* dispatch was ''a pack of lies''; unfortunately for him, however, a navy lieutenant had taped all of the Los Angeles speeches from a position behind the rostrum. The tapes were produced, and they confirmed the *Times* story. A flustered Symington could only say it had been his understanding that his talk would be ''off the record.''[54] In later years, he reverted to the claim that he had never made the speech reported in the *Times*. That was, he said, a text prepared in the Air Force P.R. office and sent to him, but ''without the approval of my public relations man, Steve Leo. Some really dreadful person did this, because I had not seen the speech and did not approve it.'' The speech reported in the *Times* was, he claimed, so critical of Forrestal's policies that he rejected it out of hand, then wrote his own more moderate remarks, with the help of John McCone, with whom he was staying in California. He claimed McCone had confirmed to Forrestal the truth of this account, but no evidence of such confirmation was ever found.[55]

The established facts repudiated every point in Symington's explanation. There was indeed a text prepared in Washington, cleared through Forrestal's own public information office and sent to Symington. The *Times* story included these words: "It was learned that on Mr. Symington's arrival in Los Angeles last night, he was handed a prepared speech as approved by higher quarters of the Defense Department . . . [But] considering it as too inconsequential to deliver, it was stated, he summarily rejected it and spoke 'off the cuff' with frequent undisguised tinges of acerbity."[56]

Despite Symington's transparent fabrication, Forrestal decided not to demand his resignation. No reasons were ever stated, but the main considerations may be inferred from a knowledge of Forrestal and of the highly charged atmosphere in Washington at the time. To have fired Symington would have brought on the charge from powerful elements in Congress and industry that Forrestal retained a pro-navy bias. This in turn would have exacerbated the explosive air force–navy dispute and could have embarrassed the President, thus further reducing his already fading prospects for election in the fall. In addition, despite the diary reference to Truman's "agreement" that the incident warranted dismissal, Forrestal was not at all sure how the President would react to an actual firing. Symington was a Missourian with powerful friends on the White House staff. As John H. Ohly reflected on it years later: Forrestal "was up against an intractable personnel problem with Symington, as well as with some Navy people he knew as friends and former colleagues. And he hated to deal with, and was not good at dealing with, personnel problems."[57]

A bolder, more self-confident man would have acted on the facts and accepted the consequences; indeed, a man who understood the dynamics of power and authority would have seen the necessity to act in his own interest. Symington's insubordination in July was not an isolated incident, but merely the latest in an established pattern of behavior. To permit it to continue, unchallenged and unpunished, was to accept a further erosion of Forrestal's own authority. And that is what happened. A number of Forrestal's strong supporters in the Congress, the army, and the navy were "shaken" by his failure "to bring Symington to heel."[58] Others were deeply disappointed. John Kenney said some years later, "We would have thrown our hats in the air and gone on a three-day drunk if that [Symington's dismissal] had happened."[59] Kenney claimed that Truman later told him, "Forrestal made a mistake in not firing Symington. He would have been all right if he had done that."[60] And Forrestal later remarked opaquely to Admiral Robert Carney: "If the incident had occurred earlier, I wouldn't have rolled over for Symington."[61] But he did roll over, and was made weaker.

Some have suggested that Symington's conduct was due in part to the fact that he suffered from extremely high blood pressure, which produced a high-strung, at times frenetic pattern of behavior, aggravated by the relentless pace of normal working days at the Pentagon. When he left government in 1950, he underwent a dangerous operation to correct this condition. The procedure involved the cutting of the nerves on both sides of the spinal column. It was a painful ordeal involving a long convalescence, and it left him with a persistent sensitivity to cold, owing to the removal of the body's natural "thermostat," but the operation was successful.[62] According to Clark Clifford, it "greatly calmed" Symington's nervous system and made him "more stable, more emotionally consistent, with good results" during his long subsequent service in the Senate.[63]

VI

★ ★ ★

EXHAUSTION AND TRAGEDY

CHAPTER 28

★ ★ ★

The Palestine Imbroglio

THE QUESTION OF a Jewish state in Palestine was one of the most vexing and explosive issues confronting the American government in the immediate postwar period. It created a conflict between the rational claims of U.S. national interest and the humanitarian claims of an organized religious group 6 million of whose members had been systematically exterminated by Adolf Hitler. It posed an international diplomatic and a domestic political problem.

The goal of a Jewish state had long antedated the Holocaust. The World Zionist Organization had fixed on Palestine before the end of World War I, and with single-minded determination had exacted from the British government the Balfour Declaration of 1917, which promised ''favorable consideration'' of a Jewish homeland in that ancient, barren land; at the same time, however, the British promised self-government to the Palestinian Arabs. After World War I, Britain held a mandate from the League of Nations to administer Palestine, to mediate relations between Arabs and Jews, and to control immigration.[1]

During the 1930s and throughout World War II, FDR expressed vague sympathies for the Zionist cause, but carefully avoided any commitment; aware of the critical wartime need to support Britain's strategic dominance in the Middle East, he assured the Arabs there would be no decisions to alter the existing situation in Palestine without ''full consultation with both Arabs and Jews.'' He understood the growing European dependence on Middle East oil and held the considered view that a Jewish state in Palestine ''could be established and maintained only by military force.''[2]

During World War II, the Zionists duly noted that British and French power was inevitably on the wane in the Middle East, indeed, that colonialism was finished, and they saw in this development a new opportunity to establish an independent Jewish state. The key to success was support from the rising world power, the United States. Thus, in May 1942, the World Zionist Organization, at a historic conference in the Biltmore Hotel in New York, drew up a platform calling for a Jewish Commonwealth in Palestine, unlimited immigration, unrestricted sale of land, and a Jewish army to safeguard the new sovereign state. The argument used to advance this goal was a passionate humanitarian concern for the Jewish victims of Hitler. It was an argument with compelling resonance, but behind it lay the drive to impose an exclusionary theocratic state against the will of the Arab majority in Palestine. The effective Zionist propaganda machine had gained a wide measure of support in state legislatures and at the federal level in Washington by the end of the war. Aided by a general American ignorance of the geography and history of the Middle East, the Zionist effort thrust the Palestine issue onto the center of the political stage.[3]

By the time of FDR's death, the question of how and where to settle European Jews, uprooted and demoralized by the terrible depravities of the Nazi regime, was creating heavy pressures on the American political system. With Jewish voting blocs in New York, Pennsylvania, Illinois, New Jersey, Ohio, and California, the 1944 platforms of both major political parties called for unrestricted immigration into Palestine. American Jewish leaders began pressing Truman for support almost as soon as he became President, and their entreaties found him sympathetic, and also sensitive to the political fact that both parties were now competing for the Jewish vote. His professional instinct being to avoid partisan disadvantage, he chose to support larger immigration while leaving the longer-term consequences to some vague action by the United Nations. By the end of 1945, however, after seven months in office, he was convinced by the British and his own State Department that unrestricted Jewish immigration would lead straight to a Middle East war. Writing to Senator Joseph Ball of Minnesota, he defined the situation as "very explosive" and said that unless the Jews can "furnish me with five hundred thousand men to carry on a war with the Arabs," the only practical course was to continue efforts to reach a peaceful compromise.[4]

OIL AND THE AMERICAN INTEREST

FORRESTAL'S initial focus of concern was the long-term importance of Arab oil to the U.S. and European economies. It was a fact that the role of oil was central to all plans for peace and war. The enormous energy demands generated by World War II had been met almost entirely out of American reserves—6 billion barrels out of a total of 7 billion used by the Allied war effort. During the war, the United States produced 75 percent of the world's oil and the Middle East a tiny 5 percent. By 1947, it was known that the Middle East oil fields were the largest in the world, but they remained relatively undeveloped. The United States still accounted for 60 percent of the world's production, but only 31 percent of its known reserves, and American production was running well ahead of new domestic discoveries, creating a net depletion.[5]

Forrestal and other policy-makers recognized that American reserves were insufficient for the United States to continue to be the world's main supplier, let alone "to oil another war" in Harold Ickes's phrase. Forrestal accordingly wanted to encourage foreign oil production, especially in the Middle East, and to curtail the export of American oil. "If we ever got into another World War it is quite possible that we would not have access to reserves held in the Middle East," he told James Byrnes in 1946, "but in the meantime the use of those reserves would prevent a depletion of our own."[6] Under his direction, the navy had begun buying oil from Saudi Arabia during the war, an arrangement which had the double advantage of a lower price and a shorter haul for supplying the Pacific Fleet. In 1946, the four American companies operating in Saudi Arabia* formed the ARAMCO consortium and, with strong political support from the United States government, became a foundation stone of the postwar international economic system. By 1947, 17 percent (60,000 barrels out of 343,000 barrels per day) of the oil consumed by all three American armed forces was coming from the Middle East, and large quantities were also going to Western Europe to fuel the Marshall Plan.[7]

In the middle of the war, Secretary of Interior Ickes, who was also Petroleum Coordinator, had proposed that the United States adopt the British pattern of governmental control over the Anglo-Iranian Oil Company by creating an equivalent American instrument in Saudi Arabia. Several private American companies were operating there, and Ickes proposed to have the U.S. government form a consortium and purchase the controlling interest. His purpose was to assure a major U.S. role in the development of Middle East oil, and his assumption was that government capital investment was necessary to move the project forward on a large enough scale. However, the private companies strenuously objected to the idea of government ownership, wanting Washington as a protector but not a partner, and their opposition was sufficient to kill the idea.[8] Forrestal and the navy were neutral on the question of ownership, but anxious to achieve a program of aggressive exploitation. "I am not an advocate of public ownership," he wrote in March 1944, "but if some modified version is the only way to assure ourselves of our share in the Near East output, then I would want to take another look . . . I have no preconceptions, except that I believe we should plant our feet firmly wherever American interests have

*Texaco, Standard of California, Standard of New Jersey, and Standard of New York.

valuable oil concessions.''[9] After encountering the ''violent objection'' from the American companies, Forrestal later made clear that his pragmatic purpose had been ''to get the oil—and that was all.''[10]

In negotiations with Texaco in 1944 and 1945, the navy sought an option on one billion barrels of Saudi oil at a fixed price in lieu of buying the concession itself. The State and War departments also declared themselves interested parties and were soon full participants in the negotiations. To sweeten the talks, FDR declared Saudi Arabia eligible for Lend-Lease, and Ickes proposed to build a pipeline across the Arabian peninsula to Lebanon with an outlet on the Mediterranean, to be funded by the Reconstruction Finance Corporation. The navy deal was concluded in July 1945 at a price of $1.05 per barrel, of which 42 cents went to the Saudis.[11]

As Secretary of the Navy, Forrestal was responsible not only for assuring the effective operation of the fleet but also for safeguarding the nation's oil reserves. These responsibilities, when he became Secretary of Defense, were extended to the effectiveness of all the armed forces. He took them seriously. Aware that a serious breach between the United States and the Arabs was in the making over Palestine, he wanted to be sure the outcome did not put the oil supply in jeopardy. As Lovett later said, he and Forrestal, and indeed the whole State Department, ''saw the issue through the same lens.''[12]

Forrestal was not in any sense motivated by anti-Semitism. He had worked in harmony with many Jewish bankers and friends, both on Wall Street and in government. In 1951, two years after Forrestal's death, Herbert Elliston, the editor of the Washington *Post,* wrote that the Zionist charge of anti-Semitism was ''absurd . . . no man had less race or class consciousness.''[13] Robert Lovett wrote, ''He was accused of being anti-Semitic. The charge is false. Here I can speak with sureness.''[14] Forrestal's Jewish assistant, Marx Leva, thought him ''patriotic, sensitive, intelligent and just,'' entirely sympathetic to the plight of the European Jews and their desire for a homeland, but unable to agree that that desire should be allowed to override every other national consideration. ''He was not anti-Semitic,'' Leva said flatly.[15] Anyone, however, who expressed doubts about the primacy of a Jewish homeland became a Zionist target. Middle East experts in the State Department, who were mainly pro-Arab, were denounced as ''anti-Semites.'' The *New York Times* and its publisher, Arthur Hays Sulzberger, were openly attacked when the newspaper in 1943 criticized Zionism as a ''dangerously chauvinist movement'' not representative of mainstream Jewish opinion.[16] The trouble was, as Dean Acheson later observed, that the Zionist position was propelled by a passionate emotionalism which virtually precluded rational discussion. Acheson had come ''to understand, but not to share, the mystical emotion of the Jews to return to Palestine and end the Diaspora,'' for he saw that a realization of the Zionist goal would "imperil not only American but all Western interests in the Near East." By pressing the U.S. government to support a state of Israel, American Zionists were, in his view, ignoring "the totality of American interests."[17]

Jewish pressure on the President and the whole American political system continued relentlessly, as did the stream of illegal Jewish immigration into Palestine, which was met by rising Arab violence. Jewish leaders in every walk of life—from Chaim Weizmann (president of the World Zionist Organization) and Rabbis Stephen S. Wise and Abba Hillel Silver (co-chairmen of the American Zionist Emergency Council), to Bernard Baruch, Justice Felix Frankfurter, Congressman Emanuel Celler, and Eddie Jacobson (Truman's former business partner in Kansas City)—formed a phalanx which carried on an impassioned lobbying operation, aided importantly by the pivotal position and aggressive action of David K. Niles, the son of a Russian Jewish immigrant who was a holdover assistant in the White House. Meanwhile, the Jewish community in Palestine was creating a state within a state, complete with schools, public services, and a tough illegal army which—in alliance with two Jewish terrorist groups, the Stern Gang and Irgun Zvai Leumi—was engaged in both defense against Arab terrorism and a steady escalation of violent attacks against British facilities and personnel. On July 22, 1946, the Irgun bombed British military headquarters in the King David Hotel in Jerusalem, killing ninety-one persons.[18]

Truman was sympathetic to the Jewish cause, but also increasingly exasperated by the relentlessness of the political bombardment from its spokesmen and vexed by the crossfire coming from the British and other advocates of an evenhanded approach. To ease the pressure, he endorsed a Zionist proposal (in April 1946) to admit 100,000 additional Jews into Palestine immediately. Then, in an effort to calm the British, who were angered by this announcement, he appointed a sub-Cabinet committee to work out a common position with their British counterparts. From this exercise came the Grady-Morrison plan for a Palestine federation divided into four areas: (1) an Arab province, (2) a Jewish province, (3) a district of Jerusalem, and (4) a district of the Negev desert. Each area was to be responsible for managing its local affairs, but all would be subject to a central British administration which would, among other things, regulate immigration. Truman thought the plan a fair compromise, but the American Jewish community was outraged, which in turn angered the President.[19] Receiving the two New York senators (James Mead and Robert Wagner), who were escorting James G. MacDonald, a former high commissioner for refugees from Germany in the 1930s and a strong advocate for a Jewish state, the President refused to let MacDonald read a one-page memorandum. "I am not a New Yorker," he snapped, "I am an American. All these people are pleading for a special interest." To Henry Wallace he said privately, "Jesus Christ couldn't please them when he was here on earth . . . I can't do it now."[20]

But the partisan political competition continued to heat up, and proved inescapable. Rabbi Silver, who had drafted the pro-Zionist plank in the 1944 Republican platform and whom Truman despised as a reckless firebrand, persuaded Republican senator Robert Taft of Ohio to attack the Grady-Morrison plan. Soon thereafter, the Republican governor of New York, Thomas E. Dewey, told a Jewish dinner audience that "it must be an immigration of not one hundred thousand, but of several hundreds of thousands."[21] With the approach of the 1946 congressional elections and with the next presidential race only two years away, these statements by the two leading GOP candidates for President set off alarm bells in Democratic Party councils and forced Truman to take notice. At the end of the summer, when the State Department arranged for him to meet with four American ambassadors to Arab countries, including Saudi Arabia, to hear their argument that "the natural rights of the Arabs" in Palestine "go back thousands of years," he listened patiently. Then he said, "I am sorry, gentlemen, but I have to answer to hundreds of thousands who are anxious for the success of Zionism. I do not have hundreds of thousands of Arabs among my constituents."[22]

On the eve of Yom Kippur (October 4, 1946), just a month before Election Day, the White House issued a statement citing the Jewish Agency's proposal for partition of Palestine and saying, "To such a solution our government could give its support."[23] The hand of David K. Niles was evident. King Ibn Saud of Saudi Arabia reacted with "astonishment" to "the latest announcements issued in your name" which would "alter the basic situation in Palestine in contradiction to previous promises."[24] Ernest Bevin, the British Foreign Secretary, had pleaded with Byrnes to persuade the President to withhold the statement, but Byrnes told him that if Truman did not speak out, Dewey would. In the event, the action did not help the Democrats, for, the Yom Kippur statement notwithstanding, the Republicans won a landslide victory in the 1946 congressional elections. Public irritation with the confusion of postwar adjustment, including a beef shortage and a rash of railroad, automobile, and coal strikes, gave the GOP a winning slogan—"Had Enough? Vote Republican."[25]

As 1947 began, all signs pointed to "increasing violence and grave danger to our interests in that area," as Dean Acheson wrote in a memorandum to Loy Henderson, who headed the Near East division of the State Department.[26] Determined to get rid of the British, Jewish terrorist bombings and machine-gun assassinations steadily escalated, and the London government in February 1947 referred the whole problem to the United Nations, which in turn established a U.N. Special Committee on Palestine

(UNSCOP). On August 31, a majority of this group voted to terminate the British mandate and to partition Palestine into an Arab state and a Jewish state within an economic union, with the City of Jerusalem to be held under a U.N. trusteeship. The stage was now set for a full vote in the General Assembly, which was certain to usher in even more intense and confused maneuvering for advantage among the contending parties.

"TO LIFT PALESTINE OUT OF POLITICS"

FORRESTAL WAS deeply concerned by the extreme emotionalism surrounding the Palestine debate and the "squalid" pressures being put upon the President and the whole political system, which, in his view, served only to obscure serious consideration of basic U.S. security interests in the Middle East. Seeing the injection of the Palestine issue into domestic American politics as cynical and dangerous, he decided upon a major personal effort to lift the issue above partisanship and hysteria. It was a decision he pursued with passionate sincerity; given the coarse realities of the American political system, it was also doomed to failure.

At a Cabinet lunch on September 29, 1947, Forrestal, who had just become Secretary of Defense, asked the President whether he thought it possible to "lift the Jewish-Palestine question out of politics." Truman replied it was "worth trying," but "he obviously was skeptical." Clinton Anderson asked Forrestal what he would do if he were a member of the Republican Party. Forrestal replied that he would "listen patiently to the impact of this question on the security of the United States," and if it appeared "dangerous" to let the Zionist claims continue to be "a matter of barter between the two parties" he would try to address the issue on "a national and bipartisan basis."[27] Two months later, he buttonholed Rhode Island Democratic Senator J. Howard McGrath, the National Chairman of the Democratic Party, arguing that Palestine was "similar to the Eire-Irish question" and should not be allowed to have a "substantial influence" on national policy. McGrath, a gritty professional pol, reminded him that Jewish contributions represented a "substantial part" of the Democratic Party funding and that the donors "expected to have their views seriously considered on . . . the Palestine question." Some of them indeed felt the administration was not doing enough to solicit U.N. votes for partition. To this Forrestal objected, telling McGrath that such "proselytizing" was precisely what the State Department wanted to avoid, as it would "add to the already serious alienation of Arab goodwill."[28] There was clearly no meeting of minds.

Lovett told him on December 1 that he had "never in his life been subject to as much pressure" as had been applied in the past three days—

from people like Baruch, Herbert Bayard Swope (a noted journalist and former editor of the New York *World*), and Robert Nathan (a prominent New Deal economist). Two days later Forrestal inquired of Byrnes (who was no longer in office) whether he thought it possible for the two parties to place the Palestine question on "a nonpolitical basis." Byrnes was "not particularly optimistic," in part because Rabbi Silver had become a close adviser to Senator Taft. Forrestal told him it was "disastrous" to have U.S. foreign policy determined by the financial contributions of "a particular bloc." A week later he approached Senator Arthur Vandenberg, a recent convert to responsible internationalism and a key Republican supporter of a bipartisan foreign policy. Vandenberg was also sympathetic, but thought the difficulty lay in a Republican feeling that the Democrats were already using the Palestine issue for partisan purposes—a statement which Forrestal could not deny.[29]

At the Gridiron Dinner on December 13, he put his question to Dewey, who had lost the presidential election to FDR in 1944. Dewey agreed "in principle," but felt "it was a difficult matter to get results" owing to "the intemperate attitude of the Jewish people," who had seized on Palestine as an "emotional symbol." Moreover, he had become rather cynical about "gentlemen's agreements" since FDR "double-crossed" him in 1944 on what he thought was an understanding not to mention the possible use of force by the United Nations.[30]

Completely rebuffed in his earnest efforts to put aside political passions and bring about a clear-eyed debate that would focus on the "national interest," Forrestal nevertheless doggedly persisted in speaking his mind on the Palestine issue. Baruch warned him to be less active in the matter, as he was tending to injure his own position in the administration and with public opinion, but he did not heed the warning. Nor did the debate become more rational.[31]

AS THE FINAL VOTE on partition approached in the General Assembly, the maneuvering was characterized by an orgy of political pressure tactics, vote bartering, and even cash bribes. New York Democratic congressman Sol Bloom, Chairman of the House Committee on Foreign Affairs, lobbied delegates from Haiti and Liberia. Clark Clifford bluntly warned the Philippine ambassador that a vote opposing partition would impair U.S.-Philippine relations. Justice Frankfurter lent his own weight to the pressure on the Philippines. The president of the Firestone Tire and Rubber Company, who had a large plant in Liberia and feared a Jewish boycott of his products, pressed the Liberian government to support partition. Baruch told William Bullitt to warn the Chinese ambassador that failure to support partition would lead to a cutoff of military aid. To the French U.N. delegate, Baruch contented himself with putting a question: "How can France expect full support under the Marshall Plan if she fails to vote the right way on Palestine partition?"[32] A few of the efforts were further tainted by cash bribes. The final vote (on November 29, 1947) was thirty-three to thirteen in favor of partition, with ten abstentions. Beyond chicanery and vote buying, the result turned perhaps decisively on the fact that the Soviets had also supported partition, for this deprived the Arabs of their threat to play the Soviet card.[33]

Two months later, Forrestal had a startling, though instructive, conversation with Bloom, as they shared a train ride to Washington from New York. Bloom told him he was in "violent disagreement" with the Zionists, who were a "political-emotional movement largely reflecting the ambitions of Rabbi Silver and the emotional zeal of what he called a lot of reform Jews who live on Park Avenue and would not think of going to Palestine." The partition scheme was "completely unworkable" because it could not be implemented without military force, but neither the President nor the Congress would "give consideration to sending [American] troops . . . anywhere in the world, but last of all to Palestine." An Orthodox Jew, Bloom thought his coreligionists should "not extend religion into politics." A surprised Secretary of Defense asked him why, then, had he brought such heavy pressure to bear on Liberia, Haiti, and the Philippines to vote for partition. Because, the congressman replied, the stated U.S. policy was in favor of partition and therefore "its prestige had to be sustained before the world."[34]

At a Cabinet luncheon two days after the U.N. vote, the President, obviously pleased by the outcome, seemed to minimize the potential consequences for the United States, citing certain elements of the resolution that made further U.S. involvement unlikely. A skeptical Forrestal told him it was difficult to see how partition could in fact be implemented without the presence of an outside peacekeeping force, as the Arabs were determined to resist the decision with organized violence. He expected that the United Nations would ask for a U.S. contribution to such a force and he was concerned that its efforts to enforce partition could lead to American soldiers shooting Arabs. Even if the worst did not occur, U.S. participation would provoke Arab hostility, with serious consequences for U.S. access to oil, base rights, and trade. There was the further possibility that the Arabs would turn to the Soviets for political and military support. In sum, Forrestal felt the new Middle East situation was "fraught with great danger for the future security of this country."[35]

The U.N. vote for partition, in fact, did nothing to ameliorate the situation in Palestine, for the Arabs were in violent opposition to the idea, and were organizing their armies for all-out war against the Jewish community. The British made clear they would not take part in any effort to enforce partition and announced their intention to withdraw in May 1948. The Arab League, a loose grouping of Arab states formed in 1945 to oppose Jewish ambitions, said it would suspend oil rights to American companies until Washington changed its policy and declared that the armies of Egypt, Lebanon, Iraq, Saudi Arabia, Syria, Transjordan, and Yemen would occupy all of Palestine when the British departed. The Jewish Agency stated that either the U.N. must create an international force to impose partition or the Jews must be allowed to import arms and organize an army of their own.[36]

The State Department soon concluded that partition was unworkable and that some alternative approach must be found to an "almost unsolvable problem." Meanwhile, it recommended that the United States should take no further initiatives and should "endeavor as far as possible to spread responsibility for the future handling of this question."[37] The idea of a U.N. trusteeship soon emerged as the alternative in State Department thinking, but it was hardly a panacea. While it would please the Arabs by undoing the U.N. decision on partition, it would inflame the Jews. Moreover, it would require a U.N. force, almost certainly involving a U.S. and a Soviet military contingent. Truman was worried by the argument that U.S. troops would be needed, and Forrestal added to the President's concern by telling him, in effect, there were not enough troops to go around. The Joint Chiefs of Staff believed a U.S. force of 100,000 men (predominantly ground troops) would be required and would have to be increased— "perhaps doubled or tripled"—if a completely effective truce could not be secured. Given the existing troop requirements for occupation duty in Germany and Japan and the unrepaired effects of demobilization, the military leaders believed a troop commitment to Palestine would require partial mobilization.[38]

FORRESTAL AS ZIONIST TARGET

FORRESTAL CONTINUED to rely heavily for information and advice on senior executives of the major oil companies associated with the ARAMCO consortium, and they became more and more convinced that the turmoil in Palestine and U.S. support for partition would jeopardize the oil concessions in Saudi Arabia and throughout the region. One such executive, Brewster Jennings, told Forrestal at breakfast on January 6, 1948, that ARAMCO had decided to suspend work on the trans-Arabian pipeline owing to "disturbed conditions in Palestine."[39] A week later Forrestal told a Cabinet meeting that without access to Middle East oil, the Marshall Plan could not succeed; more basically, the United States could not fight a war without such access or even sustain the current tempo of its peacetime economy. In a subsidiary argument which tended to trivialize an otherwise strong case, he said that without Middle East oil, American automobile manufacturers would have to convert to four-cylinder cars "within ten years."[40]

On January 19, he appeared before the House Armed Services Committee, which was studying the impact on national defense of several shortages related to the production and distribution of oil—including tanker ships, railroad tank cars, pipe, and certain drilling equipment. Forrestal was the first witness: "Oil," he said, "is the lifeblood of a modern war machine" and by far the largest component of a military logistical effort. Petroleum products amounted to 60 percent of the dead-weight tonnage of overseas military shipments, sixteen times heavier than food. The JCS estimated, Forrestal said, that in the event of another war, the combined military and civilian petroleum requirements would exceed available domestic supplies by 2 million barrels a day. He emphasized the critical importance of future access to Middle East oil. Republican congressman Dewey Short of Missouri then led the Secretary of Defense into an answer which irritated the White House, angered the Zionists and their supporters, and made Forrestal a principal target of their hostility and frustration. The exchange went like this:

> SHORT: "Hasn't the UN decision regarding Palestine [the vote for partition on November 29] rendered our situation more insecure, considering the 350 million people of the Moslem world—are we in jeopardy of having those [proposed] pipelines cut?"
> FORRESTAL: "The answer is yes."
> SHORT: "There is no question about that?"
> FORRESTAL: "None."[41]

The following day, *New York Times* correspondent William S. White wrote that Forrestal's testimony was being taken as "oblique criticism of the UN action which was led by representatives of the United States."[42] On February 17, Forrestal denied the implication of the *Times* story and said he was not opposed to the administration's policy of supporting Palestine partition. "I have enough to do without interfering with the State Department," he told reporters.[43] Nevertheless, in public and private utterances he stuck to his thesis that access to Middle East oil was an economic and military necessity, a fundamental fact that could not be wished away, and he directly linked access to Arab goodwill. The Zionist attack on him was not long in coming.

The first shots came from Drew Pearson and Walter Winchell, syndicated columnists and ardent pro-Zionists who were later to embark upon a savage campaign of distortion and vilification designed to "get" Forrestal and drive him from office. On February 29, Pearson wrote that "Secretary of Defense Forrestal, bitter opponent of Palestine partition, invited top Washington newsmen to a hush-hush dinner the other night to assure them he isn't going to resign as a result of Palestine."[44]

The definitive attack came on March 10 in a long, carefully prepared speech by a California lawyer, Catholic and Zionist, who edited a left-wing newspaper, named Bartley Crum. The speech was emotional and demagogic, seeking to portray Forrestal as the central figure in a powerful conspiracy of vested interests who were opposed not only to a Jewish state in Palestine, but also to the United Nations, peace, and democracy. His arguments and phraseology were soon picked up and used by others, including Henry Wallace, who was now a presidential candidate on the Progressive Party ticket. It was not the President or the State Department who was responsible for the deadlock in U.S. policy that continued to frustrate Jewish hopes, Crum argued. No, it was Forrestal: "There is one man in Washington who has the power to decide the Palestine question, without reference to the honor or integrity of our nation, without reference to the peace or destruction of our world. That man is the Secretary of Defense, Mr. James Forrestal."[45]

If it is asked, "Upon what meat does this our Caesar feed, that he has grown so great?" the answer is "a new diet which even a Caesar might envy. It is oil, Arabian oil." Forrestal's partiality to oil, Crum continued, was directly traceable to Wall Street, Dillon, Read, and his civilian colleagues in the Pentagon—"all three [military] branches . . . include men who have had close private interests in the oil business." In the circumstances, "does not justice require" that Forrestal remove himself "instantly and unhesitatingly" from the Palestine issue in which the oil companies have "an unconcealed interest"? He next dilated on a theme that Drew Pearson was to hammer home in the waning months of 1948— that Forrestal was by far the most powerful and most dangerous man in the Cabinet: He controls "one-third of the national budget . . . has access to secret intelligence services . . . is so powerful that he could, if he desired, raise a rumor to the status of an indubitable and frightening fact . . . Congressmen bow to him." Crum charged that Forrestal, as a public official, had no right "to spearhead the oil lobby," which he was doing from "the most important single office in our government outside of the President's."[46]

The speech was a thing of gross distortions and falsehoods, readily recognized as such by participants and observers on the Washington scene, but far more plausible to the partisan audience in the Cleveland auditorium where it was delivered and to the readers of *The Jewish Outlook* in which it was later printed. The truth was that Forrestal did not exercise half the real power Crum ascribed to him, and on the Palestine issue he had neither Truman's full confidence nor access to the inner circle of advisers who were framing U.S. policy. Nor was he in any sense a "spearhead" for the oil lobby. Both at the Navy Department and as Secretary of Defense, he had endorsed policies strongly opposed by both wings of the American oil industry, whose interests were quite divergent. He had offended "Big Oil" by countenancing partial government ownership of an American Middle East consortium. He had equally offended the smaller "independent" domestic companies, who feared that imported Middle East oil would ruin their domestic markets (the "independents" were unrealistically optimistic about the size of domestic oil reserves in relation to growing domestic demand).

Forrestal was motivated by a felt need to uphold the national interest, including the need to be certain that U.S. armed forces, for which he was specifically responsible, would have the wherewithal to fight effectively if the nation decided that fighting was necessary. In his analysis, this required assured access to Middle East oil. His dogged insistence that undeniable facts, as well as reason and proportion, should not be expunged from the debate made him, however, the convenient whipping boy for nearly every shade of pro-Zionist opinion.

Using Crum's arguments, others made follow-up attacks. Idaho Democratic senator Glen H. Taylor, who ran as vice-presidential candidate on Henry Wallace's surreal third-party ticket, wrote to Truman ten days after Crum's speech, asserting that Forrestal's removal from office was necessary "if our national policy is to be free from the taint of oil imperialism." The same day, Rabbi Silver accused "oil interests" of working to defeat the partition plan and asserted that this effort had won "the enthusiastic support of Secretary of Defense James Forrestal, who has been identified with oil interests for years."[47] Later in the year Henry Wallace, campaigning for the presidency, charged that not only were Forrestal's hands "stained with oil" but "also stained with blood." He was responsible, Wallace asserted, for all of the Jews killed in the ongoing fighting "against the oppression of Arab oil kings supported by Mr. Forrestal and men like him."[48]

MOUNTING CONFUSION

THE WHOLE QUESTION continued to be handled with mounting confusion and misunderstanding in an atmosphere of vicious political crosscurrents. The State Department now formally recommended a U.N. trusteeship. Truman appeared to approve this approach on February 22 and the specific move to a trusteeship on March 5. But he seems to have understood, incorrectly, that such a move was only temporary and transitional and would not affect prospects for partition. At the same time he declared himself so exasperated with the Zionists that he refused to receive any more of them. Only after the most urgent personal entreaty by his old Kansas City crony, Eddie Jacobson, did he agree to hold a secret meeting with Chaim Weizmann on March 18, during which he appeared to promise continued U.S. support for partition.[49]

Twenty-four hours later, the U.S. Ambassador to the United Nations, Warren Austin, made a speech in the Security Council recommending a U.N. trusteeship for Palestine in lieu of partition. When this created a firestorm of Jewish protest, Truman angrily charged that the State Department had "pulled the rug from under me" and caused Weizmann to think him "a plain liar," but he cooled down after Secretary Marshall said at a press conference that the President "approved my recommendation" for trusteeship. It has been argued that the State Department should have informed the White House as to the precise timing of Austin's U.N. speech. That is a reasonable point, but the department believed it had full authority for the policy shift and had not been informed of the President's secret meeting with Weizmann. The heart of the trouble appeared to be Truman's failure to grasp the fact that partition and trusteeship were incompatible alternatives. Amid this further evidence of confusion and ineptitude, the President publicly endorsed the trusteeship alternative as official U.S. policy.[50]

On April 12, the General Zionist Council in Tel Aviv took matters into its own hands, declaring that the Jewish state would "come into being" simultaneously with termination of the British mandate on May 14. This declaration was quickly perceived as a new opportunity for Democratic Party strategists to recover lost ground with Jewish voters and thus to brighten their dim prospects in the impending presidential election. At the same time, the President recognized the moral case for a Jewish homeland. Meanwhile, the fighting in Palestine grew more intense, with both sides ignoring repeated U.N. calls for a cease-fire. To the general surprise of world opinion, the Jewish military forces were more than holding their own, and it began to appear that the self-proclaimed Jewish state would be able to defend its own territory.[51]

Two days before the British mandate was to expire, Truman called a strategy conference to consider how the United States should respond to the new circumstances. Marshall and Lovett represented the State Department, and Clifford and George Elsey the White House staff. Forrestal was not present. Marshall opened the meeting by describing his warning of May 8 to a representative of the Jewish Agency. Believing it premature to create a Jewish state, he had told the agency official, Moshe Shertok, that it was "extremely dangerous" to base long-term policy on "temporary military success," and had warned him not to expect military help from the United States if the tide of battle should turn against the Jewish forces.[52]

When Truman then asked Clifford to make the case for recognition of the Jewish state, Marshall said coldly, "Mr. President, I am at a loss to understand why Mr. Clifford is present at this meeting," to which Truman replied, "General, he is here because I asked him to be here." He had, in fact, instructed Clifford on May 7 to "make the case for recognition just as though you were making an argument before the Supreme Court of the United States."[53] The ensuing presentation infuriated the usually cool and magisterial Secretary of State, for Clifford emphasized the domestic political considerations involved in an issue that Marshall regarded as primarily an international matter within his own jurisdiction. The sixty-seven-year-old general "bristled" at the mere presence of the forty-one-year-old Special Counsel and "glared" at him throughout the presentation.[54]

Clifford discounted the possibility of a military truce, to which the State Department clung, and urged Truman to move quickly to recognize the Jewish state as a means of reaffirming his support for partition and thus of restoring the administration's standing with Jewish voters; there was a need, he argued, to undo the effects of the firestorm caused by Ambassador Austin's U.N. speech. Furthermore, the President should beat the Soviets to the punch by proclaiming recognition of Israel the next day, May 13, twenty-four hours before the expiration of the British mandate. Lovett's rebuttal on behalf of postponing recognition was cogent but technical, centering on the fact that the United States was still actively seeking broad international support for a U.N. trusteeship. Marshall, however, brought the meeting to an emotional climax by an uncharacteristic burst of indignation. He thought Clifford's strategy would demean the dignity of the presidency by showing itself as a transparent grab for votes; he thought it would boomerang on the Democrats. As he recorded it, "I said bluntly that if the President were to follow Mr. Clifford's advice and if in the elections I were to vote, I would vote against the President."[55]

Truman, who revered Marshall, must have gritted his teeth through this encounter, but he now regarded recognition as inevitable at some point and was accordingly disposed to arrange the timing for maximum political advantage. At the same time, he did not want and could not afford an open break with a man whose national prestige and reputation for integrity were far higher than his own. After the meeting, Truman and Clifford were uncertain as to how they should proceed. Then in the late afternoon, Clifford received a telephone call from Lovett, inviting him to stop by Lovett's house for a drink at the end of the day. Over a Scotch and soda, the following exchange occurred:

"Was the position that you presented also the President's position?" Lovett asked.

"Yes."

"So we are on a collision course?"

"It would appear so."

"Under the circumstances, General Marshall may feel obliged to resign."

"The President would regret that."[56]

Faced with a difficult decision, Marshall chose, on further reflection, to reaffirm his fundamental loyalty to the Constitution and the presidency (if not personally to Truman) and did not resign. Lovett and Clifford lunched the next day at the F Street Club. Clifford said the President was under "unbearable pressure" to recognize the Jewish state "promptly." Lovett again urged a more deliberate pace lest "many years of hard work" to gain Arab goodwill be sacrificed at one stroke, but he recognized that further protests were futile. Later that afternoon, after a series of feverish telephone exchanges between the two men, Clifford told him that Truman would announce recognition a few minutes after six o'clock.[57]

The decision caused intense heartburn in the State Department and pandemonium in the General Assembly, where the U.S. delegates, still working hard to line up votes for trusteeship, were suddenly and totally undercut. The Soviet delegate, Andrei Gromyko, accused the United States of "unprincipled conduct," and Charles Malik of Lebanon cried, "We were dupes and the whole thing was a show and a game" manipulated by Washington. Marshall and Lovett were forced to take swift damage-limiting action to prevent the wholesale resignation of the U.S. delegation. But, tacitly assured of Marshall's loyalty and silence, Truman "lunged at the political opportunity" and ignored the short-term bedlam.[58]

THE COST TO FORRESTAL

FORRESTAL, Marshall, Lovett, the State Department, and the Joint Chiefs of Staff were all agreed that a war in the Middle East into which American troops might be drawn, loss of Arab friendship, and long-range turbulence in the whole region were too high a price to pay for a Jewish state. They underestimated, however, the elemental force of the Zionist movement and the need of a politically weak administration for the support of Jewish votes. Ironically, although he was not, in fact, a central figure in developing and carrying out U.S. policy on Palestine, Forrestal took a disproportionate share of the heat and suffered heavier damage to his reputation from hostile press attacks than any of the others. In part, this seemed the consequence of his outspoken insistence on reasoned argument and orderly process, an inability to conceal his dismay at the sorry, fantastically disordered performance of government officials and special interest lobbyists and their feckless indifference to the consequences of their actions. It was a spectacle entailing everything Forrestal considered inimical to good government.

Events proved him wrong on two short-term calculations: (1) the U.S. recognition of Israel did not cause the Arabs to cut off the oil supply to the West, and (2) the Jews were not driven into the sea by the combined Arab armies. As to the first, it was astonishing that Forrestal—and especially the oil company executives on whose judgment he heavily relied— did not see that a cutoff was unlikely, as it would deprive the Arabs of their markets and thus of their principal revenues; their only means of selling their product was through a marketing apparatus controlled by American and European oil companies. As to the second, Forrestal's miscalculation was shared by everyone in Washington—the White House, the State Department, the Joint Chiefs of Staff, and the Congress. The fighting qualities of the fledgling Israeli army astonished the world. In a real sense, this was the factor that made recognition an acceptable, indeed nearly a painless risk for the Truman administration. If the Jews in Palestine had been in severe danger of being overrun and destroyed, U.S. recognition would have carried with it far heavier consequences, including a moral obligation to send American troops to fight alongside the Israeli army. Such an extreme situation might well have led to a cutoff of Arab oil in the context of a "holy war" against the Western Infidel, and the Arabs might well have turned to the Soviet Union for arms and political support. Either consequence would have produced corrosive divisions in the American body politic. The Truman administration was extremely lucky that the Israeli army was able to hold its own.

In the longer perspective, it is hard to fault those who in 1948 argued that sponsoring a state of Israel was not in the U.S. national interest. The United States has paid, and continues to pay, an extremely high political and economic price for its indulgent support of that nation. Instability in the Middle East over the past forty years would have existed had there been no Israel, but the unending Arab-Israeli antagonism has inexorably bifurcated the U.S. approach to the Middle East, making it impossible for Washington to define and pursue U.S. interests there without ambivalence and contradiction, or to promote the economic development of the region as a whole. A series of bloody Arab-Israeli wars has not perceptibly mitigated the hostility or the vicious complications, and these conditions continue to fuel a relentless arms buildup on both sides (including nuclear, chemical, and biological weapons) that makes the Middle East the most overarmed and explosive region in the world. "The melancholy outcome," Robert Lovett said in 1985, "is in the day's headline."[59] His statement applies with equal force in 1991, even after the U.S.-led Persian Gulf War against Iraq. The Palestinians remain a permanently dispossessed people.

Forrestal, Lovett added, "warned that unless the American support of the Zionist demands guaranteed that the rights of the Palestinians would be justly upheld and the boundaries of the new state explicitly drawn, the

United States would alienate not alone the Arabs of the Middle East, but of the whole Moslem world . . . and the eventual harvest would be not a peaceful homeland for a race exhausted by persecution and massacre, but a reaping of a whirlwind of hate for all of us.''[60]

The immediate consequence for Forrestal, however, was to become the target of ''an outpouring of slander and calumny that must surely be judged one of the most shameful intervals in American journalism.''[61]

★ ★ ★

CHAPTER 29

Strategy Deadlock

WORK ON the military budget for the period beginning July 1, 1949, would normally have begun in January 1948—a full eighteen months before it went into effect—but the European crisis in the winter and spring of that year and the ensuing struggle over the size of the military "supplemental" so preoccupied Pentagon planners that it was May before they could turn to it. The new budget cycle was of special significance to Forrestal, for it was the first whose preparation could be fully guided and "integrated" by the Secretary of Defense. As he perceived it, the process should start with a considered paper from the National Security Council setting forth the basic policies of the United States in its relations with the rest of the world. This would provide the political guidance needed by the Joint Chiefs of Staff to develop a "strategic concept" or "annual operating plan" covering the size and composition of the armed forces, their level of readiness, and how they would be deployed in the event of war.[1]

As of May 1948, however, the NSC had developed no broad foreign policy guidance, and military planning efforts were still hobbled by basic interservice differences over how and by what means a war—in which Russia was the assumed enemy—should be fought. Admiral Leahy, still serving as Chief of Staff to the President (in the postwar period an anomalous role of little substance) complained that in the absence of a clear NSC statement, the JCS were forced to "work in the dark."[2] In late May they did produce an emergency war plan (called HALFMOON) which assumed war would start with a Soviet invasion of Western Europe. Their recommended U.S. response was to secure vital air bases in England, the Cairo-Suez area, and Okinawa as staging points for a strategic air offensive against Russia, employing atomic bombs, while the United States mobilized for a massive reinvasion of the European continent. Such a mobilization was estimated to require a full year.[3]

The requirement for massive ground operations in Europe seemed to reflect a disagreement as to whether the strategic air offensive would be decisive. A more basic disagreement concerned the extent of navy participation in that air offensive, and this in turn focused the debate on the navy's plan to build a 65,000-ton flush-deck "supercarrier" capable of handling longer-range aircraft. Forrestal had approved the new "super" while still Secretary of the Navy, but in the tight budget context of 1948, it appeared to be a weapon of unwarranted cost and dubious need. The navy sought to justify it in the usual vague terms—as vital for maintaining freedom of the seas—but in truth it represented that service's determination not to be excluded from a major role in a nuclear-age war. As the Army Chief of Staff, General Omar Bradley, noted, "It was the Navy's only hope of getting its hands on atomic bombs," and it would clearly "duplicate the primary mission of the air force."[4] The issue of the supercarrier had not been debated directly at the Key West Conference, though the navy had inserted a statement about it in the official memorandum of record; now it became the central bone of contention in the JCS effort to write an agreed war plan. Unable to agree, the JCS informed Forrestal that any further refinement of HALFMOON would require further "clarification" of the "collateral" missions assigned at the Key West Conference just six weeks before. They made no attempt to estimate the cost of executing the emergency plan or even the cost of readying the armed forces to carry out the first stages.[5]

While the central planning agencies were thus floundering around, the President (on June 3) sent Forrestal very specific instructions on the size and cost of the armed forces for the coming budget year and made clear that he expected the Secretary of Defense "to provide the necessary direction." He imposed manpower ceilings of 1,539,000 (assuming congressional reenactment of the draft), put limits on the number of active aircraft in the air force and navy, and expressed his desire to improve the national defense posture "at a steady rate" while avoiding "an immediate very large increase."[6] Truman's purpose, according to his Budget Director, was to develop a federal budget for "postwar recovery, to revive the economy and provide jobs, to send a signal to our wartime partners that we could and would work with them to avoid chaos" and also to warn the Soviets, through revival of the draft and a measurable increase in military spending, that "we were deliberately bending the curve" of military preparedness "to an upward slant."[7] A week later, the President gave Forrestal the further instruction that he was "basing his military policy on the assumption that there would not be war."[8]

This was clear authoritative guidance from the Commander in Chief, but Forrestal resisted it intellectually and maneuvered in his own indirect ways to evade it. He shared Truman's concern about the economic danger of "runaway inflation," but was more concerned that the United States was drifting into that "most dangerous" condition where "our policy outstrips our power."[9] In a meeting with the JCS on June 11, he showed himself skeptical of Truman's premise that there would be no war. He was not convinced war would come, but his doubts were such that he wanted to hedge the bets somewhere between the economic and military dangers. He wanted, he said, the President and the Secretary of State to "reflect on that a little bit, to see whether that is the policy they wish us to hold to," for a clear-cut "no war" assumption would dictate budgetary decisions. In serious disagreement with the President's estimate of what was necessary militarily, he shared in broad terms the President's estimate of what was supportable economically. His ambivalence on this central issue left him vulnerable to being crushed between colliding objectives.[10]

His efforts to obtain a clear statement of U.S. foreign policy continued to encounter frustration. At his urging, the National Security Council staff had produced a general guideline at the time of the war scare in March. Called NSC-7, it recommended a military buildup but of unspecified size, together with a "worldwide counteroffensive" of political and economic measures to arrest the momentum of Communist advance.[11] This paper was unexceptionable, but much too general to serve as a basis for budget decisions. At Forrestal's further urging, George Kennan developed a Policy Planning Staff paper known as PPS-33, but this too failed to meet the needs of the Secretary of Defense. Kennan emphasized the massive destruction suffered by the Soviet Union in the war against Hitler and the slow pace of recovery and reached the conclusion that "intentional" Soviet military aggression was doubtful. At the same time, his paper regarded war as a "possibility" serious enough "to be taken account of fully in our military and political planning." But it did not support a military buildup or recommend a military budget figure. It recommended a steady level of U.S. military preparedness over an indefinite period. Like the many-faceted situation it tried to assess, Kennan's paper was tantalizingly ambivalent and far less specific than Forrestal had hoped for.[12]

ABSTRACTION VS. REALITY

IN ALL OF THIS there was a lot of shadow boxing, an excessive reliance on organizational abstractions, and a denial of constitutional realities. The President—the ultimate and only constitutional authority in the Executive Branch—had established clear guidelines for the military budget, but Forrestal refused to take him at his word. Instead he turned to the National Security Council—the other presumed Oracle of Delphi—to provide wiser political guidance on the composition and readiness level of the armed forces. But the NSC was a committee composed of the President, the Secretary of State, the Secretary of Defense, and the three military service secretaries. It was supported by a skeletal staff not competent to perform substantive analysis, but only to refer tough policy questions to one or more of the member agencies. In reality, Forrestal's repeated requests for NSC guidance and the NSC responses were an indirect dialogue between Forrestal and Kennan. But Kennan's view of the Soviet threat was not fully congruent with Forrestal's. It reflected a more complex assessment, one which basically rejected the Hitler analogy and doubted whether the Soviets, despite the manifest evil of their system, had a blueprint for world conquest that included deliberate resort to war. Moreover, Kennan's view was fully supported by Marshall, for whose judgment the President had almost unqualified respect.

In any event, the NSC existed only to advise the President. The power of decision was his alone, and Truman had now made this quite clear to all concerned. Forrestal, the godfather of the NSC and passionate advocate of a broad-based integration of policy planning in foreign and military affairs, was up against the difficulty of trying to apply a set of procedures well suited to the collective Cabinet responsibility of a parliamentary system to a very different American presidential system, where all executive power is concentrated in one person.

Forrestal's thinking, however, was tightly wrapped in these rational abstractions, and he was passionately determined that national policy must be orderly and comprehensive. The Berlin situation was now ominous: On June 24, 1948, in response to the U.S., British, and French decision to introduce a new currency into the Western Zones of Berlin, the Soviets closed down all surface traffic from the west; the city was now wholly cut off, an isolated island in the Soviet-controlled East Zone. On July 10, Forrestal asked the NSC, as a matter of "the highest priority," to assess the "degree and character of military preparedness required by the world situation" and to tell him what kinds of armament should be developed and to list all U.S. international commitments where the use of force might have to be contemplated.[13] At the same time he gave the President his view that this study was an "indispensable" prerequisite to "determining the level and character of forces" the United States should maintain.[14] Truman's reply was quick and tart. He was agreeable to the study, but rejected the contention that it was a necessary basis for the military budget. "It seems to me," Truman wrote on July 13, "that the proper thing for you to do is to get the Army, Navy and Air Force together and establish a program within the budget limits which have been allowed. It seems to me that is your responsibility."[15] If this signal was not sufficiently explicit, the President notified Forrestal two days later that "for immediate planning purposes" the new military budget (for FY 1950) should not exceed $15 billion, and the next day Webb indicated that $525 million of this would be set aside for stockpiling critical and strategic materials, leaving $14.475 billion for military operations.[16]

Worried about what he saw as the looming danger of war (which he believed might be started by an overt Russian attack), and frustrated by the refusal of the White House to share his view of the necessary military response, Forrestal continued to evade clear-cut presidential directives. On July 17 he ordered the JCS to provide him, within a month, with specific force recommendations "based on military considerations alone." He added that if these exceeded budget limits, they must, of course, be modified downward, but he wanted, first, an expression of pure military judgment. A week later the JCS informed him that owing to their inability to agree on the specific scope of certain "collateral" mission assignments, it was not possible for them to present an integrated plan. The heart of the difficulty remained the navy's relentless insistence—spurred by the dashing Arthur Radford, now Vice Chief of Naval Operations—on a major role in the "strategic counteroffensive" employing atomic weapons. The army and the air force were increasingly embittered by this undisguised navy power grab. (One senior army officer remarked sardonically that the navy wants "a five-ocean Navy to fight a no-ocean enemy," but this missed the real point: What the navy wanted was a strategic bombing capability to attack Russia.) With the navy thus insisting on the broadest possible interpretation of its collateral role in strategic bombing under terms of the Key West Agreement, the Joint Chiefs in effect threw up their hands by sending to Forrestal not even the semblance of an integrated plan, but merely a catalogue of the force "requirements" recommended by each separate service. The manpower figure came to more than 2 million men and the cost to $29 billion.[17]

By this time Forrestal and the OSD staff were convinced that key elements of the 1947 act—especially the organizational structure of the JCS—were fundamentally defective. Military planning efforts in that body were not only embittered, but also chaotic, yet the Secretary of Defense had no other source of military expertise to help him sort out the endless, useless "split" papers that arrived on his desk from the appointed oracles of military wisdom. During the summer several possible remedies were explored: One was to appoint a committee of JCS deputies ("Little Chiefs") to handle the great bulk of mundane issues and operational questions, leaving to the Chiefs of Staff only questions of supreme national importance; another was similarly to empower the Director of the Joint Staff, Army Major General Alfred Gruenther. The first proposal would reduce the JCS work load, but would do nothing to resolve interservice differences; the second would, in Gruenther's opinion, be unacceptable to the JCS because a "mundane" issue to one service would turn out to be a "critical" issue to another.[18]

A more promising idea was to create a presiding JCS chairman who would also function, de facto, as principal military adviser to the Secretary of Defense. Forrestal, who had come to have great respect for the solid soldierly qualities of Omar Bradley, especially his practical common sense and objectivity, decided that Bradley was the man for the job. But Bradley declined when the offer was made to him through Army Secretary Royall. He had been Army Chief of Staff for only three months; moreover, he was mindful that 1948 was an election year in which President Truman's defeat seemed highly probable. If Truman lost, Forrestal would be replaced, and the new post of JCS chairman, having no legal status, might well be abolished. This was the "career risk." In addition, Bradley told Royall, he could "scarcely conceal" his view that the navy budget was too big and that the supercarrier should be canceled. But if he was successful in persuading Forrestal on these points, "there was little doubt that the Navy would launch a vicious attack on me and probably on the Army."[19] Royall reported to Forrestal that Bradley could not be "spared" at this critical point in the army's postwar redevelopment, and there the matter rested for several months.[20]

In addition, Forrestal now accepted the view of his staff that he needed an Under Secretary of Defense to serve as his general deputy, and possibly several Assistant Secretaries of Defense as well, but no action was taken in 1948.[21]

THE NEWPORT CONFERENCE

THE GLARING structural defects of the JCS and the bitterness of interservice feuding continued to dominate all considerations at the Pentagon, and they had now produced military budget proposals twice as large as the President's ceiling. Obviously frustrated and vexed, Forrestal perceived that the continuing dispute over roles and missions was still the root of the problem, and he was determined to resolve it. So he took the Joint Chiefs of Staff off for another concentrated meeting away from Washington—this time to the Naval War College in Newport, Rhode Island, from August 20 to 22.[22]

It seems reasonably clear that he could have resolved the basic points at issue by his own decisions, and made them stick by demanding that the President support him, including support for the removal of any military chief or civilian secretary who did not fall into line. Failing to obtain such presidential support, he could have resigned. Truman was indeed irritated by the unedifying air force–navy propaganda war being fought in the public press, and he blamed Forrestal for allowing it to continue. In May, the navy had leaked to Drew Pearson an outrageous internal memorandum which argued that the air force was incapable of carrying out the strategic bombing mission and should accordingly confine itself to continental air defense while leaving "massive retaliation" to carrier-based aircraft.[23] At the same time, the White House had suffered a defeat when the House and Senate voted overwhelmingly to increase air force strength from Truman's fifty-five groups to sixty-six groups. Without question, the President was growing impatient about the unruly situation at the Pentagon, and he wanted it resolved.

But sharp, straightforward action ran against the grain of Forrestal's whole philosophical approach and foundered on his temperamental incapacity for confrontation, aggravated now by his fatigue. He saw both sides of the question and could not decide between them. And resigning had become the thing furthest from his mind, for his job had become his life. Outwardly at least, he still chose to regard the parochial zealots in the services as men of integrity and goodwill who were merely advancing their honest convictions of what was best for the national security, but this required a suppression of the full truth. What drove them was the need to secure the power and prestige of their own particular service, and they were oblivious or hostile to broader concerns.

The Newport Conference might nevertheless have forced Forrestal to take some very tough decisions regarding the supercarrier and the naval role in strategic bombing if it had not been for an unexpected switch of position by General Spaatz, the recently retired Air Force Chief. Forrestal had asked him and Admiral John Towers, the commander of the Pacific fleet, to study the problem. At Newport, to Bradley's "utter astonishment," Spaatz reversed his previous position and now argued that "the Navy should be equipped with carrier-launched atomic bombers that could be utilized to attack strategic targets."[24] On examination, the Spaatz reversal was devoid of interservice altruism, but was based on a technological breakthrough. The assumed scarcity of fissionable material necessary for the manufacture of atomic bombs had limited the number of bombs in the stockpile and had made their allocation to one service or another a matter of jealous competition. But recent tests had shown that far more powerful bombs (twice the destructive power of those dropped on Hiroshima and Nagasaki) could now be made with far less fissionable material. The indications were that by 1950 the United States could have as many as four hundred atomic bombs. Given such prospective abundance, Spaatz concluded that the navy could share in the strategic bombing mission without encroaching on air force primacy. The navy, of course, hastened to agree, and Bradley and the new Air Force Chief, General Hoyt Vandenberg, were carried along on the argument that "all available resources must be used to the maximum overall effectiveness" against Russia. Forrestal could only concur.[25]

This decision seemed to provide a solution to the most acute bureaucratic problem, but it was in fact a shortsighted fix that created a bad precedent, for it sidestepped serious questions of the supercarrier's high cost and vulnerability and whether there was any objective military need for duplicating the strategic bombing function. It was perhaps the first major example of the political logrolling which later became the principal means of doing business in the Joint Chiefs of Staff. What the decision said in essence was: If there is an abundance of resources (in this case atomic bombs), then duplication or overlapping missions don't really matter; the power and the glory of existing institutions are more important than the achievement of an integrated, economically efficient military establishment. This principle was to be applied repeatedly over the next forty years.

THE NAVY REBELLION

FORRESTAL WAS cautiously optimistic after the Newport Conference, feeling he had lanced the sorest boil, but further JCS efforts to refine the HALFMOON war plan did not bring its cost within reach of the President's ceiling. Cuts were made in all three service programs, but the remaining cost was $23.6 billion. Reminded by Forrestal that this was not a sufficient reduction, the JCS looked for further cuts by altering the concept of the plan. In the course of this examination, the army and the air force jointly challenged the navy "requirement" for twelve heavy aircraft carriers and proposed to reduce it by deleting all planned land, sea, and air operations in the Eastern Mediterranean. Bradley and Vandenberg believed this would save $6.5 billion, and Forrestal agreed that some reductions in navy carriers were necessary in the circumstances. But the navy refused to compromise, and its stiff-necked resistance to any cuts distressed him.[26] After one particularly frustrating session with the JCS and their usual retinue, he invited Radford to stop by his office. "Raddy," he asked him, "as one of my old Navy friends, why can't you help me more by agreeing to some of the cuts proposed by the Army or the Air Force?" He needed some evidence of accommodation to budget realities, he said, especially on essentially technical military questions. Radford, still the navy's dominant personality and driving force, although he was not CNO, gave him a stiff bureaucratic answer: The navy could not be expected to change its views about "its own requirements," he said, but would, of course, "accept" decisions made by the Secretary of Defense. In effect, he offered no comfort or assistance, but simply hit the ball back into Forrestal's court.[27]

The official navy response to the Bradley-Vandenberg proposal was not only uncompromising; it was a bitter, provocative attack on the competence of the air force, employing in official debate the same assertions made in the memorandum secretly leaked to Drew Pearson in May. In a meeting with Forrestal and the JCS on October 4, the Navy Chief, Admiral Louis Denfeld, speaking from a long prepared statement, said, "The Navy has honest and sincere misgivings as to the ability of the Air Force successfully to deliver the [atomic] weapon by means of unescorted missions flown by present-day bombers, deep into enemy territory in the face of strong Soviet air defenses, and to drop it on targets whose locations are not accurately known." Navy aircraft carriers, Denfeld asserted, could do the job.[28]

The gloves were off, and there followed several harsh and bitter exchanges between the divided military chiefs. Exhausted and exasperated, Forrestal was also angered by the thinly disguised hostility directed at him by the senior navy people present, especially Vice Admiral Robert Carney, the Deputy CNO for Logistics. When the group adjourned for lunch in the Secretary's dining room, Carney suddenly found himself politely but firmly barred from entering the room by one of Forrestal's aides—the only member of the group not admitted. In a cold fury, he sought out the Navy Under Secretary, John Kenney, and told him that what Forrestal had done was "an insult to myself and to the Navy." Kenney told him to calm down. "There has obviously been a misunderstanding. The Secretary is exhausted, a victim of combat fatigue. You should know the signs." While Carney simmered, Kenney phoned Forrestal in the dining room and urged him to mend the slight. A few moments later he turned to Carney and said, "The Secretary wants you to return and join him for coffee." Carney replied, "No. I'm damned if I will," but Kenney persisted, saying that Forrestal "needs help from all of us . . . he can't seem to make decisions any more."[29]

Carney went back to the dining room to find that Forrestal was alone, the luncheon guests having departed. Forrestal looked grim and pensive. "Why are you so hostile to me?" he asked. "Why are so many in the Navy now opposing whatever I try to do?"

"We are not hostile to you," Carney replied. "You misjudge us, sir."

"But you do not support me."

Carney drew himself up and stood ramrod stiff before Forrestal's chair. "Mr. Secretary, the Navy has lost confidence in the durability of your decisions." Although Carney refused thereafter to reveal precisely what he meant by this statement, it is reasonable to infer that it reflected concern that Forrestal was edging toward support for the army–air force proposal to eliminate several aircraft carriers, which seemed to the navy a backsliding from the Newport Agreement.[30]

As the fractious, wearing bureaucratic warfare continued in the crucible of interservice strife, the hard-pressed Secretary of Defense came more and more to value and respect the integrity, breadth, and common sense of senior army officers and to grow more disenchanted with the self-righteous arrogance of senior navy officers and their rigid peddling of the party line. A month before he left office he confided to Eisenhower that "in the Army there are many that I trust—Bradley, [J. Lawton] Collins, Gruenther, Wedemeyer, [Lyman L.] Lemnitzer and [Leroy] Lutes . . . In the Navy, I think of only Sherman and [William H. P.] Blandy among the higher ones. Possibly [Richard L.] Connolly also." Eisenhower further confided to his diary: "It must have cost him a lot to come to such a conclusion."[31]

In late August, Hanson Baldwin had written a long appraisal of Forrestal's first year as Secretary of Defense, calling him "a philosopher at heart, a pragmatist by conviction, and a Cabinet officer by circumstance . . . His ability and his active, inquiring mind have made him 'a power behind the throne.' " Yet he is "really very shy—the antithesis of a back-slapper," a man who has "built around himself an armor of energy and a moat of intellectual activity; the man is obscured by the mind." Baldwin's assessment was candid: "He entered upon his new duties with high reputation. Today his public stature is somewhat diminished. His efforts to saddle the wild mare of divergent service viewpoints and ancient jealousies and to harness a new governmental organization have not met with full success; the frictions and controversies—notably the Air Force–Navy disputes and the differences with Secretary of the Air Force Symington—have been conspicuous."[32]

Newsweek noted in mid-September, in an article entitled "Divided They Stand," that many in Congress and the country now doubted that "unification" could ever work under the present law. Forrestal "might have bitten off more than he could chew," for interservice feelings were in some areas "even more bitter than before unification" and there seemed no real desire to pull together. The navy was now in full rebellion against even the modest strictures on its autonomy proposed by a Secretary of Defense whose inherent sympathies for that service were well known. An equally conspicuous example of "psychological disunity" at the Pentagon was the air force celebration of September 18, not as the first anniversary of unification, but as Air Force Day—year one of air force existence as an independent service.[33]

★ ★ ★

CHAPTER 30

The Final
Budget Fight

D ESPITE HIS now advanced disenchantment and exhaustion, Forrestal assured the President on October 5 that he would obtain from
the JCS a statement of forces that could be supported by a budget
of $14.4 billion. At the same time, he warned Truman that such a ceiling,
in the event of war, would essentially confine the U.S. response to reprisal
air strikes against the Soviet Union. He thought $18.5 billion would be
needed to add defensive operations in Greece, Turkey, and other parts of
the Mediterranean area. Truman, in the thick of a presidential campaign
against Thomas E. Dewey which everyone expected him to lose, agreed
that the larger sum might be needed if the international situation deterio-
rated further, but he doubted there would be a recurrence of the acute
crisis they had faced in the spring.[1]

In September, what had appeared to be hopeful negotiations to end the
Berlin Blockade collapsed amid signs of a deepening East-West confrontation, but these developments did not alter the White House position on
military spending. The Truman campaign themes stressed a sound economy at home and the administration's efforts to revive Europe through the
$17 billion European Recovery Program, known as the Marshall Plan.
There was a conscious effort to downplay the U.S.-Soviet confrontation
and to avoid the appearance of a crisis.[2]

On October 6, Forrestal firmly instructed the JCS to agree to a distribution of $14.4 billion, telling them, "I want it clearly established in your
minds that I am expecting a definitive recommendation from you, as an
entity, as to the division of funds"; this meant "specific allocations to the
respective services."[3] But once again, the JCS returned a split response.
The army agreed to $4.9 billion and the air force to $5.1 billion, but
Admiral Denfeld reserved final approval of $4.4 billion for the navy until
further study could ascertain the detailed impact on naval operations. The

JCS did agree that the proposed budget as a whole was "insufficient" to meet "any probable war situation."[4] With a sense of despair, Forrestal remarked to the military leaders, "Our efforts have degenerated into a competition for dollars."[5]

The following day he sought counsel and assistance from General Eisenhower, who was now president of Columbia University, asking him in a short letter to set aside some time for a talk about "fundamentals: policy, budget, and our whole military-diplomatic position." After an initial chat, Eisenhower agreed with some reluctance to return to the Pentagon in late January on a part-time basis, primarily to sit with the JCS and guide them to a genuine agreement on a war plan.[6] As Eisenhower confided to his diary, "Except for my liking, admiration and respect for his [Forrestal's] great qualities, I'd not go near Washington," but he was greatly disturbed by the nasty interservice cat-and-dog fights being waged in the press, and he judged accurately that they were eroding public respect for the nation's military leaders and institutions. He was genuinely shocked at their brazen resistance to constituted civilian authority: "Some of our [military] seniors are forgetting that they have a commander-in-chief. They must be reminded of this in direct, unequivocal language. If this is not soon done, some day we're going to have a blowup." He was accordingly sympathetic to Forrestal's situation—to his "terrific, almost tragic disappointment" at the failure of the military leaders to "get together," but he feared that this distress had led Forrestal into "certain errors," the worst of which was "the way he treats himself. He gives his mind no recess, and he works hours that would kill a horse."[7]

But Eisenhower's great prestige and persuasive powers would not be available for another three months. Meanwhile, Forrestal could not bring himself to force a clear-cut decision on the military budget—in effect, to force the navy to live within the President's ceiling. As John Kenney had noted, he now seemed incapable of doing so. James Webb offered to sit in with Forrestal while the military chiefs continued their debate, and he ended up spending five days at the Pentagon. After the last military advocate had left the room, Webb went to the door, closed it, returned to the table, and asked Forrestal directly, "Well, what do you think, Mr. Secretary?" Forrestal looked at him nervously. "What do you think?" he asked Webb. He then went on to complain that not enough was being done to cope with the rising Soviet threat. This was a view shared by thoughtful members of the press and, privately, by a number of senior people in the administration, but Webb thought Forrestal "possessed no clear idea of a strategy capable of meeting that threat." Because Forrestal remained "fuzzy" on the allocation of roles and missions, Webb thought it was impossible to calculate "with any degree of accuracy" the size or character of the forces needed and the cost of providing them. Webb was reflecting

Truman's own rising frustration with Forrestal's handling of the military budget when he said, "There was nothing for us at the White House to get a grip on."[8]

On the same day that he sent his despairing comment on "dollar competition" to the JCS, Forrestal left the matter open by asking them to supply force recommendations "in the general area" of the Truman ceiling; simultaneously he sought Budget Director Webb's agreement to delay final submission of the military budget until after the presidential election. Offered this new encouragement, the JCS propounded new force plans that could be supported at $16.9 billion, and Forrestal, in a fateful October 15 meeting with Bradley and Denfeld, agreed to present this figure to the President as an "intermediate budget," between the JCS preference for $23.6 billion and the Truman ceiling of $14.4 billion.[9]

Aware that he would need strong allies in his quest to change Truman's mind, he consulted the Secretary of State, but Marshall, who had just returned from Paris, was far less concerned about U.S. military capabilities than about the desperate need to strengthen European confidence and morale. The Europeans, he told Forrestal, "are sitting on their nerves" and what they needed fast was a flow of munitions and equipment via the recently enacted foreign military assistance program. In Paris, General Alphonse Juin had told him, "I could arm a million young Frenchmen if only I had the equipment." In Marshall's view, that problem should have a higher priority than a buildup of U.S. forces. Rebuffed, Forrestal nevertheless again sought Marshall's guidance and support two weeks later, characterizing the President's $14.4 billion ceiling as "tentative" and indicating that he might urge the White House, "as my own recommendation," to accept the "intermediate" figure. What did Marshall think? But Marshall, who had now returned to Paris for a meeting of the United Nations, was not disposed to reopen the question. In a cable to his deputy, Lovett, he declined to address the specifics of the military budget, but advised that his earlier view of priorities "still holds."[10]

On November 2, to the complete surprise of almost all informed observers in America and Europe—including especially the seasoned politicians and the pundits in the media—Truman beat Dewey and was thus elected President of the United States in his own right. Forrestal wired his "congratulations on a gallant fight and a splendid victory" and went down to Union Station with other Cabinet members and well-wishers to meet the President's train on his triumphant return from Kansas City.[11] Truman left Washington almost immediately thereafter for a vacation in Key West, but found time before departure to remind Forrestal of his previous instruction not to plan for a military establishment the economy could not sustain.[12] The voters' support for his policies had reinforced his self-confidence.

By this time, Forrestal had clearly lost his sense of political reality, for he refused either to accept the President's position or to resign. On November 9, in a now desperate search for allies, he flew off to Paris, Frankfurt, Berlin, and London for four frantic days of talks with American and European officials, but came back empty-handed. In Berlin, the U.S. Ambassador to Moscow, Walter Bedell Smith, agreed that maintenance of an effective U.S. deterrent capability justified some deficit spending, but General Clay, the U.S. Military Governor for Germany, disagreed. Clay thought budget deficits in America would stir up European fears that the same "inflationary processes" which had proven so "disastrous" for Europe were now at work in the country they counted on to support their survival and recovery.[13]

In Paris, the French Premier, Paul Ramadier, emphasized the same points that Juin had conveyed to Marshall, namely, France could raise thirty divisions and build a defense east of the Rhine, provided only that America would provide the weapons and heavy equipment. In London, there were glimmerings that the British were already beginning to see the virtue (born of economic necessity) of basing their future defense on the deterrent effect of the atomic bomb, although the term "nuclear deterrence" would not be coined for several years. Churchill warned Forrestal that the United States must not "write down" the value of the atomic bomb as both a deterrent to Russian aggression and a bulwark of West European morale. In short, the British already perceived that air-atomic power was probably destined to become the main reliance of Western defense. At the same time, they regarded full American participation in the developing North Atlantic Treaty as the keystone in the arch; anything less would be "totally inadequate."[14]

The trip could not possibly have raised Forrestal's hopes of bringing effective pressure to bear on Truman to increase U.S. defense spending, yet he now seemed blindly committed to continuing a hopeless fight. On November 17, he sent to the NSC a long catalogue of U.S. defense commitments, actual and potential, around the globe, including occupation duties in Germany and Japan, support of U.N. peacekeeping, foreign military aid, and prospective force allocations to Europe under the developing North Atlantic Treaty. In an accompanying statement, the JCS pointed to the evident gap between these commitments and existing U.S. capabilities and warned that this condition presented serious dangers in an international situation that contained "the distinct possibility of global warfare." The document left no doubt that Forrestal and the JCS regarded the existing U.S. military posture as dangerously inadequate, but for all the impact it had on the White House and the State Department they might have dropped it down a well.[15]

The final blow fell on November 23, when the long-awaited basic statement of national policy objectives, which Forrestal had requested five months earlier, was discussed and formally adopted by the National Security Council. Developed primarily by Kennan's Policy Planning Staff, NSC 20/4 was a restrained and cautious assessment of the world situation which gave no comfort to advocates of more U.S. military spending. It made no mention of a need for increased military preparedness and indeed warned against "excessive" armaments as a danger to the nation's economic health and stability. It called for a steady-state level of readiness that would provide a base for rapid mobilization and also be sustainable over an indefinite period of years. It acknowledged the Soviet ability to overrun Western Europe, the Middle East, and parts of Asia, but expressed doubt that the Soviets would resort to war.[16]

Now beleaguered and defeated, yet too committed to his military constituency to pull back, and psychologically incapable of resigning, Forrestal submitted the $14.4 billion budget on December 1, but on the same day sent a letter to the President outlining three different budgets—for $23.6 billion, $16.9 billion, and $14.4 billion. In his judgment, he told Truman, the first was too high, but he felt compelled to recommend against the third because the JCS could not in good conscience guarantee that U.S. security would be "adequately safeguarded" at that low level of expenditure. He advised the President to accept the intermediate figure. After a last-minute appeal to Lovett, he was able to include a final paragraph which carried Marshall's endorsement of the intermediate figure "as better calculated . . . to instill the necessary confidence in democratic nations."[17]

Truman gave the alternatives no consideration whatsoever, his mind having been made up long before. Briskly forwarding Forrestal's letter to his Budget Director, he instructed him to adopt the $14.4 billion figure and expressed surprise that Forrestal had submitted a range of budget options. A further flogging of the dead horse was nevertheless carried out on December 9 when Forrestal and the JCS went to the White House to explain their recommendations, complete with charts, graphs, and pointers. The President listened politely, but nothing said at the meeting had the slightest effect on his decision. Forrestal left the White House despondent and shaken, but also in some awe of Truman's extraordinary confidence and self-assertion.[18]

Forrestal's defeat was now complete, his influence rapidly draining away. He had tried to steer a middle course between a concern for the economy and the need to take measures to close what he perceived as an ominous gap between American commitments and military capabilities. As the crises of 1948 deepened he had leaned more and more to the judgment of military professionals that a general buildup of U.S. forces was necessary to guard against the likelihood of general war. This put him increasingly at odds with the President and the Secretary of State, and he repeatedly tempted fate by seeking to evade or ignore increasingly explicit presidential expressions on the limits of military spending. Resisting these guidelines in part because he doubted Truman's competence and judgment in foreign affairs, he was also moved by a passionate need for an orderly, comprehensive process of planning and decision making, which he believed was seriously lacking in the President's approach. A number of other discerning minds in Washington, in both government and the press, shared Forrestal's assessment of Truman's shortcomings—that he was shallow in comprehension and simplistic in reasoning. One White House insider later expressed the view that the President "failed to grasp the full dimensions of the world crisis in 1948, and therefore failed to see that it was a mistake to impose a rigid ceiling on military spending."[19] Forrestal sought to modify or circumvent these presidential weaknesses by bringing to bear the higher order of expertise and wisdom he believed to reside in the National Security Council and the Joint Chiefs of Staff. But his problem here was twofold: First, he confronted a President who, whatever his inadequacies, knew his own mind and would not permit his power of decision to be hemmed in by advisory groups, however expert or prestigious; second, these institutions were not the lofty and comprehending oracles of Forrestal's hopes and intellectual vision.

The NSC was no more than a Cabinet committee with the President in the chair, and the primary source of its staff work on global assessments was the Policy Planning Staff in the State Department, dominated by George Kennan. The JCS was not a fount of harmonious military formulations for the integrated strategies and forces required to preserve the peace or to wage a winning war. It was a committee of three powerful, self-interested military services caught simultaneously in a technological revolution and a budget squeeze, each member prepared to fight tooth and claw to achieve or preserve desired positions of power and prestige which it insisted could only be defined by itself. Each service naturally claimed that its "requirements" were designed solely to strengthen national security, but its capacity for self-serving rationalization was almost unlimited. This last statement applied least to the army, whose leaders consistently demonstrated a broader view of national security and a more informed concern for the political and economic aspects of the problem. All of Forrestal's tragic misconceptions regarding the ability of the Secretary of Defense (armed with only "general" and "coordinating" powers) to harmonize the actions of the army, navy, and air force through appeals to reason and compromise came a cropper in the Joint Chiefs of Staff. Both he and his benign conception of the office were overwhelmed by these institutional forces and their allies in Congress whose determined pursuit of narrow self-interest he had grossly failed to measure.

There was, finally, a sad irony in the passion and energy which Forrestal had expended in fighting for the "intermediate" budget, for that modest increase over the Truman ceiling would not have made much difference in any realistic accounting of the gap between potential commitments and capabilities. Truman's insistent stringency rested on a judgment that the Soviets would not precipitate war. It carried a serious risk of military unreadiness if war should nevertheless occur, but in that event—as the initial U.S. response to the 1950 attack on South Korea demonstrated—an extra $2.5 billion would not have been nearly enough. For his part, Marshall chose to accept Truman's budget decision and thus the risk; he took the position that if any incremental military spending was contemplated, first priority should go to rebuilding the military forces in Western Europe. Forrestal chose to stake his reputation and his standing with the President on the difference between two expenditure ceilings, both of which were inadequate to support a foreign policy that now assumed primary U.S. responsibility for the security and stability of the ''Free World.''

Driven by his habit of intense, almost endless analysis, and increasingly gripped by an apocalyptic view of the Soviet threat, Forrestal convinced himself that whereas the Truman budget ceiling spelled disaster for the country, a modest addition could provide the essential elements of basic security. It was further evidence that physical exhaustion, unremitting pressures, hostile attacks, and a gnawing sense of failure had combined to erode his sense of proportion and his judgment. It would have been more consistent with his assessment of the threat to put forward the preferred JCS budget of $23.6 billion and then to resign if the President refused to support it. But he was caught by sympathy for Truman's concern about the economy and by a compelling personal need to remain in government. This combination reduced his role to one of ineffectual mediation between the President and the military chiefs.

CHAPTER 31

★ ★ ★

Things Fall Apart

THE PRESIDENTIAL ELECTION and its stunning result now confronted Forrestal with a deeper anxiety about his standing at the White House and about his own future. He had expected Dewey to win, but also appears to have told Dewey privately that he would be available to serve in a Republican administration, as Secretary of Defense or Secretary of State.[1] In the interests of bipartisanship, and with Truman's knowledge and approval, he had sent Struve Hensel, who had gone to law school with Dewey, to brief the GOP candidate on the military situation.[2] Responding to press allegations that he had conspired with the Republicans, Forrestal denied he had personally been "in communication with Governor Dewey during the campaign,"[3] but eleven years later Dewey disclosed that Forrestal "came to see me at least two or three times in the latter half of 1948. He was disturbed about the condition of our defense and we discussed it at considerable length." Having been nominated but not elected, Dewey thought it would have been "presumptuous" for him to have raised the question of a Cabinet post for Forrestal, "but I confess I had given it some consideration."[4]

Forrestal had also given it some consideration. Basically, he wanted to stay in government as a major player in the development and execution of U.S. foreign policy and concurrently in the reshaping of governmental structures and processes to enable the nation to meet the severe tests of the cold war. He believed such tasks did, or should, transcend partisan politics; as the year unfolded it is also reasonable to infer that he came to believe not only that Dewey was going to win, but also that he was more likely to share Forrestal's sense of need for a stronger military establishment. Although Forrestal was concerned about the capacity of the American economy to carry greater burdens, he was clearly exasperated with what he saw as Truman's myopic penny-pinching on military spending.

His apparent confidence that his own fate was not tied exclusively to the Democrats was reinforced by evidence that a number of influential Republicans admired him and hoped to see him in the Dewey Cabinet. Typical of these sentiments was a speech by Republican congresswoman Margaret Chase Smith of Maine, a member of the Armed Services Committee: "There is one man in the Truman Cabinet who richly deserves to be retained. That is James Forrestal . . . He has won the confidence of the country for his alert, vigorous administration of this new and exceedingly important office . . . Mr. Forrestal has had to work under difficulties . . . coordinating the presumably coequal branches of defense . . . which have tried hard to go their own way, and have not scrupled to go over the Secretary's head . . . His selection as Secretary of Defense in the Dewey Cabinet—if he could be prevailed upon to continue—would meet with hearty approval in Congress and out."[5]

On the conscious level, Forrestal's strongest reason for wanting to continue in office was to resolve the frustrations and repair the undeniable mistakes of his first fourteen months in the Pentagon, thereby to achieve success for a "unification" process that was now widely labeled an unworkable mess. By midsummer of 1948 he had finally accepted the truth that his original conception of the task was founded on a basic contradiction, on the wishful notion that the military services could at once retain their autonomy and be made to operate as a unified whole. He now acknowledged that the loose confederation of feuding baronies over which he presided was a weird anomaly largely of his own devising and one that created an impossible task for even the most energetic and determined administrator.

Just a month before the 1948 elections, on October 5, he had acknowledged to the President that the 1947 act was inadequate, that he couldn't make it work, that strengthening amendments were therefore necessary. He had begun expressing private doubts to Clark Clifford as early as July, and Clifford had encouraged him to take the matter to Truman "whenever you feel like it," as the President was vitally interested and "is always ready to see you" about practical improvements in military organization.[6] Instead, Forrestal used the summer to conduct a series of meetings with high-level military officers in an attempt to develop an in-house consensus for change. That effort produced encouraging support from the army and the air force for movement toward more central authority in the hands of the Secretary of Defense; the navy, however, was not only opposed to further integration, but reacted with open bitterness to Forrestal's apparent change of heart. It was his urging of amendments to strengthen the hand of the Secretary of Defense that cost him the remaining support and loyalty of many of his former friends and colleagues in the navy, and the loss was a heavy emotional blow to him.[7]

Nevertheless, he saw the necessity for change and took his case to the President with the forthright admission that his original conception had been flawed. Truman accepted Forrestal's conclusion in a similarly straight-forward way, with no "I-told-you-so" attempt to demonstrate his own prior wisdom on the subject, and the two men agreed to the creation of a drafting team headed by Frank Pace, the Deputy Budget Director, and including Clark Clifford from the White House and Marx Leva from Forrestal's staff. Although it was recognized that pressures of the electoral campaign would preclude any definitive results until the end of the year, it was agreed that work should begin immediately. Forrestal now believed five changes were needed: (1) to convert the anomalous "National Military Establishment" into a single executive department, (2) to provide the Secretary of Defense with unequivocal power to exercise authority and control over all the armed forces, (3) to create the position of Deputy Secretary of Defense to serve as alter ego to the Secretary, (4) to make provisions for a larger and stronger OSD staff, and (5) to create the position of Chairman of the Joint Chiefs of Staff, at a minimum to preside over the JCS and to focus their deliberations.[8]

Due in some large part to Forrestal's vigorous lobbying efforts, Congress had the year before created a commission to study the organization of the Executive Branch, and Truman had appointed former President Herbert Hoover to head it. Forrestal was appointed as a member. The Hoover Commission in turn created separate task forces for each of several exec-utive departments and agencies, and not entirely by coincidence Ferdinand Eberstadt became chairman of the task force on National Security Orga-nization. This group comprised a judicious mix of businessmen and college presidents, but the weight of its military expertise resided in Eberstadt, Robert Patterson (now returned to private law practice), John J. McCloy (now president of the World Bank), and Hanson Baldwin of the *New York Times*. Their recommendations proved to be very similar to those finally made by Forrestal and the White House, but their critical analysis of the 1947 act amounted to a devastating indictment of Forrestal's original con-ception. The task force found that the authority of the Secretary of Defense, "and hence the control of the President," was "weak and heavily quali-fied" by the "rigid structure of federation" imposed by the original law. So much statutory authority was left to the three military services that the Secretary of Defense was unable to "enforce consistent policies." In the circumstances, "centralized civilian control scarcely exists [and] . . . the Joint Chiefs of Staff are virtually a law unto themselves."[9]

Forrestal now privately concluded that the JCS must be transformed into a planning body and its members removed from the operational command of their respective services. In this way the most senior military officers would be divorced from parochial allegiances and be able to think in terms of the national interest as a whole. He wanted a JCS Chairman who would also be "principal military adviser" to the Secretary of Defense and the President. However, when congressional and military opposition to this bolder reform proved to be formidable, Forrestal ended by recommending only a presiding Chairman for a JCS whose other members continued in command of their individual services. This modest change was echoed by the Eberstadt task force and by the full Hoover Commission itself; both were unwilling to buck the self-interested preference of the Congress for a certain looseness of military authority. [10]

But three members of the commission, led by its vice chairman, Dean Acheson, argued for a less temporizing solution in a statement that amounted to a pungent minority dissent. As presently organized, Acheson asserted, the Joint Chiefs of Staff were "too remote" from civilian control and unavoidably immersed in the parochial views of their particular services: "Effective civilian leadership depends on military staff advice that is responsive directly to the needs of the Secretary of Defense and the President, and not to particular service interests." If these high political authorities were to decide intelligently and if Congress were to legislate and appropriate wisely, both must have advice "from an overall strategic point of view," not on the basis of "a compromise of the desires of three separate services." The Acheson group recommended a single chief of staff. [11]

THE NEED TO REMAIN IN OFFICE

FORRESTAL SEEMED to be operating on two related assumptions during October and November: One was that the amendments to strengthen the authority of his office were essential to retrieve a situation of serious confusion at the Pentagon; the other was that he was the logical man to wield that greater authority, whether under Truman or Dewey. Privately, he perceived his remaining in office as essential to making "unification" work. This was the conscious rationale for his determination to stay in government. At the deeper level of the subconscious, however, he had reached a point where he was psychologically incapable of leaving office; the self-assessment that told him he was indispensable to the enterprise was a subjective imperative, for his job had become his life support system. Despite its relentless pressures and punishing frictions, its bone-wearying demands on his time and energy, and its problems with contentious or disloyal subordinates, he was now dependent upon it for holding himself together. Meshed with its consuming routines, supported by his staff, his military aide, his limousine, his private airplane, he could function rationally and retain the outward appearance of competence and control; inside he was a man being eroded by cumulative fatigue and a mounting sense of personal failure—failure to bring order and harmony to military unification, failure to persuade the President to support an adequate military budget, failure to arouse the American people or even his governmental colleagues to what he saw as a mortal threat to the survival of the nation and of human freedom. Exhaustion bred anxiety, and anxiety distorted his sense of proportion.

He was also cruelly disillusioned by the attitude, behavior, and tactics of many senior military officers who had proven incapable of perceiving, on any issue, a distinction between what was good for their particular service and what was good for their country.[12] Steeped in the doctrinaire conviction that loyalty to the first was automatically loyalty to the second, they were essentially deaf and blind to suggestions that they should rise above narrow service interests in order to serve the nation better. In this sense, Forrestal was not worn down by "villains" deliberately intent upon his defeat and destruction, but rather by an impersonal clash of forces represented by men who were serving specific interests they had been taught to equate with the national interest.

By the late summer of 1948, Forrestal was slipping into a deep sense of disillusionment, impelled by some penchant for dark tragedy in his Irish soul; at the same time his every instinct rejected the idea of resigning. An obsessive sense of urgency about the state of the world and the state of the nation made it impossible for him even to consider a vacation. Given the extent and pace of his decline, it is astonishing that colleagues at the Pentagon, including members of his inner staff, failed to recognize it. In retrospect they attribute their failure to Forrestal's formidable self-control, his brusque, impersonal method of dealing with staff, and the simple fact that they saw him too frequently to note much change in his condition or demeanor.[13]

Certain friends caught revealing glimpses of his inner state, but only in the privacy of small dinners at his home. As if in a conscious effort to break the bonds of total immersion in his job and his worries, especially during the summer of 1948, Forrestal would have his military aide round up a few friends on very short notice for dinner at Prospect House. In such a mood he seemed to reach for people he had known socially in New York who were entirely remote from his current preoccupations, and he was willing to make do with whoever in that category could be summoned on three hours' notice during Washington's desultory hot season that extended itself well into September. Somewhat to her surprise, a young Georgetown woman named Janet Barnes, whose mother-in-law had been a good friend of the Forrestals on Long Island, found herself frequently on the guest list, often without her husband, who traveled extensively for the State Department. She remembered that John Fell (an old friend from New York) was "always" there and the Arthur Krocks "a few times." Josephine was there about "half the time," and when she was, the Filipino butler spent a good deal of his energy "keeping her away from the booze, for when she drank she was coarse and abusive." Janet Barnes remembered that Forrestal was notably irritated by his wife's presence and behavior and made a sustained effort to ignore both.[14]

But if he had designed these evenings to give himself respite from the burdens of the Pentagon and the world, he was incapable of taking it. Janet Barnes, who as a young girl had admired Forrestal for his "great charm and wit" and "his aura of famousness," remembered him during these dinners as tense and nervous, gray with fatigue, and obsessed with what the Russians "might be planning to do." He seemed to start every conversation with the half-jocular, half-cynical observation, "Well, I suppose you think the Russians are nice fellows."[15]

What was remarkable was his continued outward self-control. During the alarming war scare in the spring and early summer that had coincided with his emotionally intense clash with Stuart Symington, first over the air force budget and then over the disloyal speech in Los Angeles, he developed the nervous habit of dipping his fingers into his water glass and compulsively wetting his lips, completely unconscious of these movements as he talked with others at the table.[16] By late summer, however, he seemed calm once more, and members of his staff and other government colleagues who saw him frequently failed to notice any unfavorable change in his behavior. "I never thought of him as a happy man," John McCone recalled. "He seldom smiled, his laugh was fleeting, I never heard him tell a joke, but he was always in control of himself and the situation."[17] His armor against the world, long and assiduously developed, concealed the vulnerable and wounded man who wore it.

Returning now from Europe on November 16, where he had gone in search of supporters for a larger military budget, and while the governments of the world still pondered the implications of Truman's startling electoral victory, Forrestal was preoccupied with the subjectively central question of his own standing at the White House; the uncertainties in the new situation filled him with anxiety. Truman was still vacationing in Florida, resting from the arduous campaign, but was due back in Washington in a few days. The sensible course would have been to seek a private talk soon after the President's return, but, nervous and edgy, Forrestal telephoned Key West on November 17 to ask for an immediate appointment and was invited to fly down for lunch the following day. Before departing he held a press conference, ostensibly to give a public account of his European inspection trip, but the reporters were interested chiefly in the question of whether he would remain in the Cabinet. He told them he was "at the service of the President," adding that "the Cabinet is singularly his business." He then flew off to Florida, accompanied by Major General Alfred Gruenther and Marx Leva, and returned to Washington in the late evening of the same day.[18]

The purpose of the trip was to settle the question of his tenure, but when he arrived at the Key West naval base, where the President's party was staying, he quickly perceived that the atmosphere and timing were all wrong. Truman and the closest members of his Missouri entourage—Clark Clifford, Charles Ross, Harry Vaughan, Matthew Connelly—were in a festive mood, decked out in floral Hawaiian shirts and bantering happily with a covey of Florida politicians, including Senator Claude Pepper, Representative George Smathers, and Governor Fuller Warren. The atmosphere combined political courthouse gossip with a night out with the boys, all lubricated by a steady flow of bourbon and branch water. The President was cordial, but took no initiative to see Forrestal alone, and this added to the Secretary's sense of estrangement.[19] In the circumstances, Forrestal chose not to raise the central question he had come to discuss, but offered Truman a report on his European trip. Even here, however, the President showed no more than a polite interest, and after five minutes or so the Secretary of Defense, feeling both weary and demeaned, turned the briefing over to Gruenther.[20]

After Forrestal had departed, the reporters asked the White House press secretary whether he would remain in the Cabinet, to which Ross replied ambiguously: "I don't know what is in Mr. Forrestal's mind."[21] This statement fell far short of a ringing endorsement of a valued Cabinet member whose advice and counsel the President wished to have close at hand in the future. So once again Forrestal returned empty-handed, without a clear indication of where he stood or even an expression of presidential appreciation for past service.

ENEMIES IN THE WHITE HOUSE

GIVEN THE TIMING and the circumstances, it seems likely that Truman had not yet seriously addressed the question of his Cabinet for the new term (a month before, even his staunchest supporters would have considered this a frivolous exercise, a waste of precious time and energy in a desperately uphill campaign). Nevertheless, he had developed questions and doubts about Forrestal and was beginning to consider whether it was time for a fresh man at the Pentagon. In this consideration he was strongly pushed by members of the White House staff—especially Vaughan, Connelly, and David Niles—who disliked Forrestal intensely. The main points against him were resistance (as Navy Secretary) to Truman's proposals for military unification, resistance to the Truman budget ceiling on military spending, resistance to the partition of Palestine, and his attempt to assert personal control of the National Security Council and its staff. There were more minor irritations, such as Forrestal's proposals to create a Cabinet secretariat and an elite corps of government managers and executives. Those and other initiatives seemed to small-minded White House loyalists like efforts to enhance Forrestal's own power and prestige, especially to give the impression that he was a kind of philosopher-king whose broad and varied talents outshone those of Harry S. Truman.

There was special resentment among partisans that Forrestal had not participated actively in the campaign, and their feeling was inflamed by the persisting rumor that he had conspired with Dewey with a view to arranging for the Republican victors to retain him at the Pentagon.[22] On the first question, the evidence is reasonably clear. According to Army Secretary Royall, someone in the White House purporting to speak for the President asked Forrestal to "take charge of raising money for his campaign." Forrestal thought it inappropriate for the Secretary of Defense or any of the service Secretaries to do this and, after conferring with Royall, who fully agreed, he gave the White House a negative answer together with his reasons. Shortly thereafter, the President made clear to Marshall, Lovett, Forrestal, and the Secretaries of the Army, Navy, and Air Force that they should stand aloof from active political campaigning in the interests of preserving bipartisan support for U.S. foreign policy.[23]

On the "conspiracy" charge, it is now clear that Forrestal talked privately to Dewey, and it is a fair inference that the two men reached an understanding—no doubt with mutual disclaimers of any commitment—that Forrestal might be available for further service. Truman loyalists also alleged that he gave money to the Dewey campaign. No evidence of this has been found, but the handling of his contributions to the Democrats suggests something less than total enthusiasm for the cause. In August he instructed a lawyer, Walter Dunnington, to send $2,500 to the Truman-Barkley* Committee. But because this was drawn on an account established years before to permit anonymous donations, the contribution was credited to Dunnington, not Forrestal. The lawyer wrote to Truman explaining that this was really Forrestal's money, but three weeks before the election a Democratic stalwart, George Allen, wrote to Forrestal asking for a contribution, unaware of the previous $2,500. Without enlightening Allen, Forrestal sent a marine sergeant to the Democratic campaign headquarters with $100 in cash. One day before the election, Allen again solicited him, this time by telephone, and Forrestal agreed to contribute to the Democrats' congressional campaign fund. Not, however, until November 9,

---

*Alben Barkley, Majority Leader of the Senate and a former governor of Kentucky, was Truman's running mate in 1948.

a week after the election, did he send a check for $250. The date of the check was noted in a story in the Washington *Times-Herald* of January 12, 1949.[24]

Of greater consequence was the fact that he had taken positions which placed him in a posture of sustained opposition to several presidential policies. In differences between Presidents and their senior subordinates, there comes a moment when the prudent subordinate gives way in recognition of superior authority or else resigns. But on critical issues Forrestal had not given way and had indeed used the implied threat of resignation as a lever to move the President's positions closer to his own. In the eyes of his detractors, he was thus a man of doubtful loyalty to the boss, a maverick, a nuisance who generated a cumulative impatience among them—and they continuously imparted this feeling to their chief. And though Truman respected Forrestal's ability and integrity, he was to some degree influenced by the philosophical differences between them. Despite his small-business fiscal instincts, Truman was a New Dealer, a strong supporter of the Rooseveltian programs created to help the "little man" in America. Forrestal, on the other hand, was an intrinsic free enterpriser, a man of the professional managerial class who instinctively turned to successful businessmen, bankers, and lawyers to help him with problems of policy, organization, and management, and his consultations of this kind were without regard to either political or philosophical sensitivities. He continued, for example, to consult with Bernard Baruch and James Byrnes long after they had become anathema to Truman, and he brought to the Pentagon, for seminars on management problems, businessmen and industrialists (like Crawford Greenwalt of the DuPont Company) who were openly disparaging of Truman.[25]

If Forrestal (like Stimson, Lovett, and McCloy) had consistently played the role of apolitical public servant and management expert, the friction with the White House would almost certainly have been milder. But with his penchant for political maneuver, for finding and using the key power source in every situation, for savoring the pleasures of subtle conspiracies, he was impelled to act in both camps. To his detriment, he tended to equate his own political instincts, which he had inherited from his father, with genuine professional political expertise. He kept in touch with New York pols like James Farley, William O'Dwyer, and Ed Flynn and presumed at times to interpret the New York political situation to Truman, which caused the President to remark privately to a friend that "Forrestal was making a fool of himself."[26] Even his perceptive friend Lovett sensed something "phony" about Forrestal's simultaneous effort to demonstrate concern and expertise about politics and his often expressed aversion to the process of partisan grubbing that politics unavoidably entailed. This seemed another manifestation of an inherent identity problem, an innate ambivalence that showed itself here as a strained effort to ingratiate himself with the President—to prove he was one of the pols.[27]

LOUIS JOHNSON

F INALLY, there was for Truman the unavoidable consideration of Louis Johnson, the hulking West Virginia lawyer and American Legion panjandrum who had volunteered to be the principal Democratic fund-raiser for Truman's campaign, after several more prominent money men had politely refused the honor in a year when a Republican sweep was considered inevitable. Johnson delivered the goods, and Truman won the election. It was later widely held that Johnson's condition for taking on the fund-raising task was that he be appointed Secretary of Defense in the event of a Democratic victory.[28] Clark Clifford and others close to the President regard such a prior commitment as unlikely, for in their view it would have been uncharacteristic of Truman. At the same time, it must be assumed that Truman knew of Johnson's ambition and that Johnson's claim to preferment would be nearly irresistible in the event of Truman's election. With victory now a fact, Vaughan and Connelly began a steady drumbeat for the replacement of Forrestal by their fellow legionnaire.[29] The Pentagon post, they and Johnson believed, was a stepping-stone to the presidency. Johnson was not an attractive figure physically, intellectually, or socially. As Assistant Secretary of War in the late 1930s, he quarreled with his superior, Harry Woodring, and was soon marked as a nakedly ambitious troublemaker. FDR fired him without tears. John Kenney thought him "a miserable creature, driven to live in an atmosphere of strife and discord of his own making." Forrestal regarded him with contempt and found degrading the idea that he might be displaced by such a man. "He is incompetent," he told Kenney.[30]

According to Colonel Robert Wood, his military aide, Forrestal got the first intimations as early as September—probably from Arthur Krock or another of his journalist friends—that Johnson was definitely in line to be Secretary of Defense in the event of a Truman victory. In a private huddle at Prospect House, Eberstadt urged his friend to resign immediately, while he could still depart with dignity and flags flying, but Forrestal was determined to temporize. He pointed to the uncertainties of the political campaign and the heavy odds against Truman's election and thus against the appointment of Johnson. He told Eberstadt, "Let's wait and see."[31]

The Ross statement at Key West could be interpreted to mean that Truman was waiting for Forrestal to resign gracefully, but if such was its intent it failed to register on a Cabinet officer whose inner stability now depended on his work and who was thus compelled to rationalize that psychological necessity. The day after he returned from Florida, Forrestal wrote to Ralph Bard, conceding that the Pentagon job had become a "strain," but concluding that "if my continued presence for a while longer will contribute to cementing the foundations which are pretty far along, I will probably have to yield [to those who want me to stay]."[32] A few friends were indeed expressing the hope that he would stay on, but the closest ones, particularly Eberstadt, were urging him to step down and take a long rest. The President had given him no indication, one way or the other.

Despite the generally cheerful tone of the letter to Bard and a similar one to Senator Willis Robertson, Forrestal was slipping ever deeper into a state of anxiety and despondency from which he never recovered. According to Colonel Wood, he grew listless and indecisive following the presidential election, and his unspoken unhappiness permeated the office. Though nothing had been announced officially, Forrestal seemed to know that Louis Johnson had been promised his job. He lost interest in his work. Papers brought to him by Wood from McNeil, Leva, and Ohly—seeking his comment or decision or proposing a particular meeting—remained on his desk for days on end. He would not be rushed. If Wood brought a paper requiring immediate signature, he would say, "Put it down. I will deal with it later. Just leave it there." He became loath to leave his desk, clinging to it as though it were a life raft. Well past the dinner hour, he would remain in his office fussing over papers. "Hadn't you better go home, Mr. Secretary?" Wood suggested one evening when the hands of the clock stood at nine-thirty. Forrestal looked up bleakly. "Go home? Home to what?" It was a rare, unguarded reply, the first time in Wood's experience that Forrestal had ever dropped the silent guardrail he had erected around the ruin of his family life.[33]

He invited Hanson Baldwin to breakfast in late November, but Baldwin was reluctant to accept, feeling it was a "terrible thing" for "this poor man" to be seeing people so early in the morning. "He never had any peace." On this occasion, Baldwin noted that his host was "nervous and tense, skipping from one subject to another," worried about the unresolved conflicts of military unification and the fact that "the Russians were building up power." But the matter uppermost in his mind was "the feeling that he didn't have the support of the President," although the name of Louis Johnson was not mentioned. In December Baldwin was invited again, this time to a small cocktail party at Prospect House. Forrestal had stressed the point that this would be another opportunity for a private chat, but he was repeatedly interrupted by telephone calls, and about six-thirty Baldwin stood up to leave. "Oh no, don't go," Forrestal told him. "Stay and we'll have dinner with Josie." Josephine, whom Baldwin knew to be "an alcoholic," was in bed with a cold, "so we went up to her bedroom and had dinner on our knees, and she talked. She made a little sense, not too much."[34]

On December 7, the President told a press conference that Marshall and Forrestal had been asked to stay on, but this seemed essentially a stopgap statement to quell rumors and satisfy public curiosity while more definitive planning for the new term continued.

Forrestal had still not talked privately with Truman, but he sought and found encouragement in the President's remarks, for he told his son Michael at Christmas, "I am going to stay on."[35] Beneath a thin surface confidence, however, he was beset by anxiety and depression—aggravated now by hostile attacks in the press. Through his strenuous personal efforts to deny the Communists an electoral victory in the 1948 Italian elections, he had incurred the hostility not only of European Communists and their Soviet mentors, but also of elements on the radical left in the United States, including the followers of Henry Wallace, who insisted the cold war was essentially a Wall Street–imperialist plot. Nor was this the worst. His candid warnings that access to Middle East oil was a vital requirement for national security and that American support for Israel seriously risked Arab hostility and a cutoff had earned him the undying enmity of the Zionists. Owing to these several grievances, Forrestal became the target of increasingly reckless attacks.

Typical of these was an assertion, on a radio program, by the economist Ira Hirschmann that the I. G. Farben works in Frankfurt had not been bombed during the war because Forrestal owned stock in that company. The assertion was a blatant untruth with monstrous implications. Forrestal telephoned the radio station, WNBC in New York, to deny the charge categorically, and that same evening the station issued a formal retraction. But the attacks continued from certain sectors of the press and radio—especially from Drew Pearson.[36]

THE DREW PEARSON EFFECT

DREW PEARSON was a muckraking journalist of demonic dimensions whom *Time* described in the early 1940s as "the most intensely feared and hated man in Washington." Endowed through a perversion of his Quaker origins with an invincible self-righteousness, he was the self-appointed Grand Inquisitor of Washington officialdom, ferreting out and exposing everyone and everything he saw as a subverter of the American political system. Regarding himself as the leading defender of "the humanitarian cause," he was, in fact, moved by his own ingrained prejudices, and he found in Forrestal a man who had flagrantly sinned against nearly all of them. Pearson loathed Wall Street, Big Oil, The Military, everything German, and all opposition to a homeland for the Jews. Because Forrestal had opposed swift demobilization, pushed for a substantial defense budget and a centralized intelligence effort, warned against the threat of Soviet Communism, and disputed the U.S. national interest in supporting a Jewish state—all with persuasive vigor and relative success—he became for Pearson "the most dangerous man in America." In Pearson's eyes, Forrestal was a primary causal factor in bringing on the cold war, the Cabinet member most responsible for pushing Truman into a tough anti-Russian stance that greatly increased the risks of a shooting war.[37]

Pearson was not scrupulous about facts. They existed to be turned and twisted to reinforce his attacks on the symbols of his loathing. His technique was to personalize abstract symbols, to identify a particular person with particular iniquities defined by himself, then to pound relentlessly on these themes until "the great rancid mass of the American people" could not think of the person without immediately seeing him as the symbol of the iniquities. "He gathers slime, mud and slander from all parts of the earth," as one senator put it, "and lets them ooze out through his radio broadcasts and . . . [the] few newspapers which have not yet found him out." Carried along by his self-righteousness, Pearson had an almost inexhaustible zest for the ugly, protracted vendetta.[38]

From Pearson's perspective, Forrestal was a "Trojan Horse of the Right," lodged inside the highest counsels of a presumably liberal Democratic administration. From 1947, when Forrestal became Secretary of Defense, the "one objective that stood above all others" for Pearson, as his associate Jack Anderson later revealed, was "to expose Forrestal, his financial ties and his militaristic inclinations."[39]

The bitter competition among the three military services, which continued unabated after passage of the 1947 National Security Act, created opportunities for Pearson and his staff to elicit slanted disclosures of antagonisms and administrative fiascoes inside the Pentagon. As the legman, Anderson, later wrote, "I was soon in unseemly alliance with generals, admirals, assistant secretaries, yes, even secretaries (whose names I cannot in honor divulge even after the passage of three decades). Thanks to their whisperings, I began to bring Drew one scoop after another." This led to "a calibrated assault" on Forrestal, designed to destroy official and public confidence in his performance. It was conducted "on an average of once a week . . . in print and on the air," mixing in a few convenient facts, but striking "over and over" the various "anti-Forrestal chords."[40] Two typical examples follow:

November 13, 1947—Pearson wrote that loans to Germany by Forrestal's "Wall Street" banking firm had rebuilt steel plants "which Hitler later turned into the most efficient war machine in Europe." The "chief moneyraiser for Germany being the same man who now heads our National Defense Department—James Forrestal."

May 4, 1948—"The same gang that overcharged the U.S. Navy for Arabian oil, finagled lush loans for King Ibn Saud," and "lobbied to kill the partition of Palestine" is still at work. "It is significant that the Wall Street firm of J. V. Forrestal, now the most potent man in the Cabinet, once handled the finances of the Arab-American oil interests."[41]

Because ceaseless rivalry is the distinguishing trait of political Washington, with everyone trying to put something over on someone else, Pearson's sources and confidants included some very high government officials who found the journalist a useful instrument to advance their own agendas or settle their own scores. But dealing with him was inherently dangerous, for, serving only his own interests, he could turn on his sources like a snake.

The remarkable thing about this relentless cannonade was that it rumbled on for a full year without perceptible impact on Forrestal personally or his reputation. The observant Anderson, covering the Pentagon for Pearson, felt that Forrestal "gave off discordant vibes . . . a detached intellect seemed at odds with a wariness of eye." Anderson was aware of "tenseness" and "sometimes a sense of beleaguerment," but the overall impression remained one of "calm mastery" over "an awesome array of strategic concept and tactical detail."[42] It was only in the late fall of 1948, during and after the presidential election, that Forrestal began to be visibly unsettled by Pearson's attacks. By then he was weakened by fatigue and anxiety over his standing with the President. By then also Pearson had made a personal resolve to force Forrestal from office whatever the outcome of the election. He set about this by stirring up the key power blocs in the Democratic Party—labor, liberals, blacks, Jews—so that they would be "putting the screws" on Truman to dump his Secretary of Defense. In this endeavor he quickly formed a bond with Louis Johnson.[43]

The first attack in the new phase, which came on September 3, 1948, was nasty but not inaccurate. It charged that Forrestal had met secretly with Dewey and that his desire to hold his job regardless of who won the election was "an open secret." In subsequent columns, Forrestal became the "Cabinet Judas" and "Dewey's friend." He was linked with Bernard Baruch, John Sullivan, and Kenneth Royall as men who had "deserted the ship" during the presidential campaign, who had "basked in the October sunshine on the golf course . . . lifting no finger to help Truman," confident that "Dewey was going to win." After the election Pearson wrote that Forrestal was "now frantically contacting friends to help him keep his job . . . frantically painting himself as a true and loyal Democrat."[44]

Forrestal conferred many times during this period with his close friend Supreme Court Justice William O. Douglas. "Louis Johnson's friends in the press were laying down a barrage on Jim and he could not stand that kind of pressure," Douglas wrote in his memoirs. In "a long, long talk of several hours'' at the Pentagon, "I laid out a program of counterattack. . . . I said 'this is war, Jim; it's like Iwo Jima, but it's newsprint not bullets that's being used against you.' " Douglas recommended a public relations man who could mount a hardball counterattack, a man who had served Douglas in the bitter fights between the SEC and the Wall Street establishment in the 1930s. Forrestal "almost agreed, then rejected the idea."[45]

With the election won, however, and despite continuous sniping from Pearson, Truman did not take any action to replace Forrestal. Pearson was rattled by this evidence of the President's "unpredictable streak of magnanimity," and Louis Johnson was reduced to incredulous consternation.[46] November became December and then January without any definitive movement by the White House.

It was now clear that Forrestal's enemies within the government were leaking information which had some semblance of fact and which then became grist for Pearson's malicious distortions. There is also evidence that these emotion-laden misrepresentations incited others outside the government—Zionists, Communist agents, or anarchist crazies—not merely to indignation and anger, but also to threats of violence. When John McCone arrived one day for lunch at Prospect House, Forrestal quietly pulled down two of the shades in the dining room and took a seat away from the window, explaining to McCone without a trace of humor that he wanted to avoid giving a sniper a good target.[47] That the passions aroused by the Palestine issue did indeed produce death threats was confirmed in the course of a 1982 interview with Lovett, who, with Marshall, had been in the vanguard of State Department opposition to the partition of Palestine and the creation of Israel. Lovett reported to Truman that he had received several threatening telephone calls, whereupon Truman promptly offered special Secret Service protection. But the Under Secretary of State, a balanced man and cavalier about the risks, declined the offer on pragmatic grounds. His study was on the first floor of a house on Kalorama Road, he told the President, which made it easy for any determined terrorist "to ride by on a bicycle any evening, and lob a grenade through the front window." He doubted whether a Secret Service detail could be effective.[48]

THE SHOCK OF DISMISSAL

ON JANUARY 7, Truman announced the resignations of Marshall and Lovett from the two top State Department positions, and the appointment of their successors, Dean Acheson and James Webb—all to be effective the day after Inauguration. This was clear indication that a number of important Cabinet changes would be made, with the aim of bringing new men and fresh ideas into the administration. The moves further weakened and isolated Forrestal's position, for in Lovett he would be losing his closest friend and most valued collaborator, and in Acheson and Webb he would be gaining two colleagues who, in varying degree, disdained and distrusted him. His relationship with Marshall had always been correct, though formal, but adversely affected by their quite opposite philosophies on the matter of military organization.[49]

Why Truman did not at the same time announce Forrestal's departure and his replacement by Louis Johnson is unknown. Johnson was pressing his claim both personally and through his White House surrogates, as well as working hand in glove with Drew Pearson to discredit Forrestal, but Truman continued to put him off. Later the President told one of his assistants that he had begged Johnson to accept several other positions, but that Johnson had refused. Only one job would satisfy his deep need for vindication for his dismissal from the War Department by FDR and provide the platform for his now undisguised ambition to be President of the United States.[50] The clear inference is that Truman was caught in a dilemma. He respected Forrestal, was aware of his high public standing, and wished to avoid a sudden callous act; at the same time he was persuaded that a change at the Pentagon was necessary. Johnson had a strong claim to the job, but his crude vigor and known ambition put Truman on his guard. The result was that he kept postponing a decision, which had the effect of leaving a vulnerable Forrestal, anxious and uncertain, exposed to the pressures of office for another two months, even as the President was noting his growing indecisiveness and diminished powers of concentration. Forrestal's discourse was now often broken by unexplained silences during which he stared blankly and withdrew into some distant inner recess.[51] The result of postponement was an unintended cruelty to a sick man. Truman kept his own counsel on the matter and did not inform even his closest colleagues of his intention until he was ready to announce the changeover. What seems finally to have decided him was undeniable evidence of Forrestal's progressive disintegration.

"Do you know who the Secretary of Defense is?" Truman asked Captain Dennison, his naval aide, one day in January.

"Yes, sir," Dennison replied, playing along with what he considered a genial presidential effort to be humorous. "It's James Forrestal."

"You're wrong," Truman told him. "I'm the Secretary of Defense. Jim calls me ten times a day to ask me to make decisions that are completely within his competence, and it's getting more burdensome all the time."[52] He related the same story to Navy Under Secretary Kenney, adding, "I can't be the Secretary of Defense."[53]

On January 9, two days after the State Department changes were announced, Walter Winchell, an ardent Zionist, attacked Forrestal on his nationwide radio program for seeking "dangerous new powers" via the proposed amendments to the National Security Act. In addition, he assailed Forrestal's character by reviving the story of the Canadian company by means of which he had escaped certain taxes in 1929. Winchell also predicted that Truman would call for Forrestal's resignation within a week. Next day White House press secretary Charles Ross, confronted by the Winchell prediction, told reporters it had no basis in fact; at the same time, he said it was customary for all Cabinet members to submit their resignations on the eve of a new administration.[54]

Two days later, on January 11, Forrestal finally had a private talk with the President. While documentary evidence is wholly lacking, it seems certain that this was the meeting at which Truman told him that he was going to appoint Louis Johnson and that he hoped Forrestal would work closely with Johnson during an interim period pending public announcement. Forrestal could not really have been surprised by this development, for rumors of the Johnson appointment were all over town, planted and nurtured by Johnson himself and his supporters. Nevertheless, when rumor was converted to cold fact, it came as a double shock—first, because he could not face the reality of dismissal after eight years of continuous service; second, because he regarded Johnson as totally unqualified for the job. The President's action was a reality he was not prepared to confront, and a part of his mind continued to reject it.[55]

Emerging from the White House after his talk with Truman, he ran the gantlet of waiting reporters grim-faced and taut, looking suddenly not only very tired, but also very old. What was the verdict, they asked. Did the President ask for his resignation? He told them he had not, in fact, submitted a "routine resignation," but would do so before Inauguration on January 20. The reporters persisted: If the letter of resignation was merely "routine," did that mean he was going to stay? Apparently bound to silence during the agreed transition period, until Truman announced the Johnson appointment, Forrestal's answer was both ambiguous and bitter; in the light of subsequent events, it seemed a fleeting exposure of the despair that lay tightly coiled in the depths of a tormented soul. "Yes," he said, "I am a victim of the Washington scene."[56] Two days later, when asked whether Forrestal's remarks meant he would be staying in the Cabinet, Truman replied with equal ambiguity that "they meant exactly what they said."[57]

In this same time frame, Forrestal's former naval aide, the redoubtable Smedberg, just returned from sea duty and en route to Annapolis to become Superintendent of the Naval Academy, paid a courtesy call on the Secretary of Defense. He was dismayed at his old boss's physical appearance. Forrestal's face was ashen gray, his shoulders slumped, his eyes listless. He looked gaunt. Refusing to talk about himself and his possible future plans, he questioned Smedberg about his coming assignment to the Academy, but could not refrain from expressing his "bitter disappointment" at the pending elevation of Louis Johnson. "Smeddy, this is a bad day for the Navy [*sic*]. The man knows nothing. He is incompetent and a braggart."[58]

As if unable to admit even to himself that the end of his long and distinguished public service was at hand, Forrestal made no mention in his diaries of his watershed talk with the President, nor do subsequent entries make any mention of Louis Johnson or any account of the terms of the transition apparently worked out with Truman. Moreover, he did not tell even the closest members of his staff (Leva was not aware of the Johnson appointment until the White House asked for Forrestal's resignation on March 1). In a letter to a friend, he stretched the truth to the limit without quite breaking it, saying, "I will stay on for an additional period." His pro forma letter of resignation, promptly written and dispatched to the White House, was more elaborately casual than seemed necessary to hide the new situation until Truman was ready to announce Johnson's appointment; it seemed to reflect a felt need to hide the unwelcome facts from himself. He wrote: "I send you at this time my formal resignation as Secretary of Defense. I believe there is such a document now in your files, but in order to be sure there is one in your possession I am forwarding this so that you may have it available in the consideration of plans for your Cabinet at inauguration time."[59]

On the evening of January 16, Drew Pearson renewed his running radio attack, asserting that Forrestal would already be gone from office had not Winchell's prediction angered President Truman, who refused to have it appear that he was subject to the dictates of radio journalists. In the same broadcast, Pearson repeated the story of tax avoidance in 1929. Not content with these charges, however, he then (as Jack Anderson later wrote) "descended into poison gas"[60] by presenting a malicious distortion of the 1937 incident in New York when Josephine Forrestal was robbed of her jewels in front of the house on Beekman Place—a totally false version that depicted Forrestal as a personal coward. Always emotionally affected by attacks on his personal integrity, as distinct from criticism of his public positions, Forrestal was now, in his advanced state of anxiety and exhaustion, profoundly vulnerable. Angry and upset, he summoned his lawyer, John Cahill, from New York and pondered the pros and cons of a libel suit against Pearson. Cahill thought it a "no-win" situation and urged Forrestal to resign from government and then, if he wished, "go and break Pearson's face."[61]

This particular Pearson attack, going far beyond legitimate reporting or even the limits of ideological advocacy, was vicious propaganda designed to destroy not only the reputation but also the man. Pearson had heard stories of Forrestal's erratic behavior and was angered by the silence of the "elite press" and by Truman's failure to act, both of which he took as signs that the "establishment" was conspiring to protect a man whose mental instability made him too dangerous to remain in public office.[62]

Stung by criticism from other segments of the press, Pearson later disclaimed responsibility for the wild inaccuracies in his telling of the robbery story, saying he had written it exactly as it had come from his "source." The only person in Washington who had firsthand knowledge of that remote, little-remarked incident in Manhattan was Stuart Symington. No direct evidence links him to this particular item, but it was well known that Symington was a confidant who regularly fed Pearson with air force propaganda detrimental to the navy and to Forrestal.[63] In a 1989 interview, Pearson's widow said with emphasis that her husband and Symington were "very close friends."[64]

Forrestal did not take his lawyer's advice to resign. Instead, he turned to Tom Clark, the Attorney General, for a second opinion, unaware that Clark was also a Pearson confidant and informer. Clark advised him not to sue for libel and immediately reported the conversation to Pearson, telling the journalist that Forrestal seemed "as nervous as a whore in church." Unaware of Clark's treachery, but sensing he was increasingly alone, beset by enemies seen and unseen and by perilous circumstances with which his tired mind and body could no longer fully cope, he descended into a sort of controlled frenzy. In the following days, Clark told Pearson that Forrestal was telephoning him at odd hours of the night to complain that he was "being followed by Jews or Zionist agents." A few days later he accused Clark of having him shadowed by the FBI. "You've got your men over here . . . They've been all over the house . . . They've tapped my wires. They're trying to get something on me." Clark denied the accusations, but Forrestal now insisted Clark was trying to "crucify" him.[65] In this disturbing tale, one cannot ignore the real possibility that Truman had ordered the FBI to watch Forrestal in view of the cumulative reports of his erratic behavior.

In the few short weeks that remained of his public life, he conferred repeatedly with Douglas, who later wrote that he was with Forrestal "night after night, pacing the floor, trying to help him untangle the imaginary [sic] skein of troubles and woes that seemed to encompass him." This man of "unflinching physical courage, who landed with the Marines at Iwo Jima, was not at home in the world of psychological warfare." He left white tie dinners to walk with Douglas in the dark, "unburdening himself, transferring his problems to me . . . He would say 'Bill, something awful is about to happen to me.' "[66]

THE LAST MILE

O N J A N U A R Y 2 8 , Forrestal met secretly with Louis Johnson at the White House, following a regular Cabinet meeting. Forrestal's appointment calendar shows he went to the White House about ten o'clock in the morning, but nothing in his diaries or in any other of his papers indicates the fact or the substance of the talk with his designated successor. The only surviving account is Louis Johnson's: "Then it was that Mr. Forrestal asked me, with the approval of the President, to take over his job as Secretary of Defense. . . . I told Mr. Forrestal that a story had been printed saying I had been undercutting him—seeking his job. Mr. Forrestal replied that he had double-checked the story and was satisfied that there was not, and had never been, a word of truth in it . . . Mr. Forrestal and I [then] visited with the President, who insisted I accept his offer . . ."[67]

Johnson disclosed these meetings in the course of remarks five days before Forrestal's death. It is unlikely that Forrestal "asked" Johnson to replace him or that he dismissed as untrue the newspaper story that Johnson was "undercutting" him. Johnson's reputation for veracity was not high, and Forrestal knew he was working with Pearson to destroy his reputation and hasten his departure from office. There is, however, no reason to doubt that the meeting took place. In the course of the same speech, Johnson said the agreement with Truman and Forrestal was that he would become head man at the Pentagon on May 1, which defined a transitional period of roughly three months, during which there would be no public announcement. The length of the transition and the requirement for secrecy are both unexplained mysteries and in sharp contrast to the way in which Truman handled the changeovers at the State Department.[68]

In keeping with the President's desire for a secret transition period, Johnson did not go to the Pentagon for orientation briefings; instead, Forrestal paid a two-hour visit to Johnson's law offices in the Shoreham Building. Shortly thereafter, on February 7, Johnson departed for Key West laden with "a lot of secret papers" to study the issues that would soon be his to deal with and decide. More data were forwarded to him in Florida through his law office.[69] Later on in March, after the changeover was announced, Johnson came to the Pentagon for further briefings, and Forrestal was confirmed in his first impression that the man was worse than incompetent— a blunderbuss, a classic bull in a china shop.[70]

One incident remained indelible in the mind of General Lyman Lemnitzer, then Forrestal's representative to the confidential talks in Western Europe aimed at creating what became the North Atlantic Treaty Organization (NATO). Lemnitzer (who was later Army Chief of Staff and NATO Commander) was called suddenly from his post at the National War College to brief "Colonel" Johnson on the NATO talks. Forrestal opened the meeting simply by saying, "Colonel Johnson is taking over from me. Please tell him what we are doing about setting up the NATO organization."

Lemnitzer began: "Colonel Johnson, the State Department and the military services are discussing with European governments the important question of how we can form a military alliance." Johnson's large face suddenly darkened, and he held up his hand. "General, what is this talk about an alliance?" Lemnitzer said nothing. Johnson went on, his voice rising. "General, don't you realize that a fortnight ago I gave a speech to the Daughters of the American Revolution at Constitution Hall? I told them it was important for Americans to remember George Washington who warned us to avoid entangling alliances." Lemnitzer looked at Forrestal, whose face was ashen. Before the Secretary of Defense could speak, Lemnitzer said, "Colonel Johnson, you would be well advised to remember that, as the second witness before the Senate Foreign Relations Committee next week, following Secretary Acheson, you will be called upon to urge the ratification of the alliance treaty." Johnson got to his feet and glared at the general. The meeting was over.[71]

Forrestal's negative assessment of Johnson led him to some free-lance maneuvering that would not have pleased the President had he been fully aware of it. On December 3, he had proposed that Truman ask Congress to create the post of Under Secretary of Defense "immediately"—ahead of the several other amendments still under study—and the President had done this. Then, on February 4, as soon as he left Johnson's law offices, he telephoned Senator Millard Tydings, Chairman of the Senate Armed Services Committee, to urge that the separate Under Secretary bill be given priority treatment. He told Tydings that Carl Vinson had already introduced such a bill in the House and was confident it would pass "very quickly."[72] A day or so later, Forrestal revealed to Marx Leva the scheme that was running through his mind: to bring Johnson in as Under Secretary for an unspecified period, following which the West Virginia lawyer might "fleet up" (in navy jargon) to the Secretaryship. That he seemed to assume such an arrangement would be acceptable to President Truman—or to Johnson— is a further reflection on his loss of political judgment and his desperate need to stay in office. But even this kind of dubious delaying tactic did not wholly define the limits of his fanciful planning. A few days later, he expressed to Leva the view that someone other than Johnson might succeed him when he finally stepped down.[73]

When Charles S. Thomas, an old friend (and future Navy Secretary), came to pay a visit, Forrestal asked him abruptly, "Should I quit this job?" failing to tell his guest the die was already cast. When Thomas, unaware of Forrestal's true condition, expressed the hope that he would stay in public life for the good of the country, Forrestal replied bitterly that he hated it, everything about it, especially the publicity that went with it. He seemed to be venting impotent rage at the venomous press attacks that were falling on him like poisoned arrows. At the end of the visit, he told Thomas he had informed the President of his firm intention to leave by the first of June. A few days later, Thomas learned from a member of the White House staff that May 1 was the date agreed on with Truman.[74] It may have been about this time that Forrestal received an offer, or the intimation of an offer, to take a major ambassadorial post, but if it was proffered, he declined. Clark Clifford, who in 1989 had never heard of this, felt it would have been uncharacteristic of Truman, although, assuming the offer was made, he was not surprised that Forrestal declined. On February 28, Forrestal made his last major decision as Secretary of Defense by authorizing jet engines for the propeller-driven B-36 bomber. These would increase its speed and range and thus improve its ability to penetrate Soviet air defenses without fighter escort.[75]

In late February, Pearson breakfasted with David K. Niles, who told him Forrestal was "definitely out" as of April 1. A jubilant Louis Johnson conveyed the same information to Pearson after a talk with Truman.[76] On March 1, Forrestal was summoned to the White House for a private meeting with the President at twelve-thirty. He returned to the Pentagon about two hours later, where he saw four visitors between two-thirty and four-fifteen, then remained alone in his office until six-forty-five, when he went home.[77] He spoke to no one about his meeting with Truman, but by evening, when he telephoned Leva and Eberstadt, it became apparent that the President now wanted his resignation "at once" and that this action had hit him like a brick wall. Leva, at home with two young children while his wife was taking a medical school exam, could not make himself available. So, alone in his large house overlooking the Potomac River and the Francis Scott Key Bridge in upper Georgetown, Forrestal began drafting the letter at fever pitch, speaking several times to Eberstadt in New York.[78]

The next morning at the Pentagon, with Leva now participating, the letter went through several revisions, but with Leva finding it difficult to pin down the effective date of resignation desired by the White House. The President had requested the letter "at once," which implied a desire to make it effective immediately. But as the drafting continued, Forrestal kept inserting later dates—March 3, then March 15, and finally March 31. Leva, who was growing disturbed by these apparently arbitrary extensions, felt it necessary to ask directly what the White House expected. Did the President say that March 31 was an acceptable date for the changeover? Forrestal replied that Truman wanted him to stay until June 1, but that he wanted to leave sooner.[79] It was an answer that squared neither with the facts nor with the circumstances surrounding his summons to the White House the previous day. It was the answer of a man who, psychologically unable to bear departure from office, was intent upon extending his fragile tenure as far as he thought it would be acceptable to an impatient superior. It was the pathetic pleading of a distinguished public servant whose energy and intellect were now spent, who clung desperately to office because otherwise he would fly apart.

Again, the reason for Truman's sudden cutting short of the transition period is not documented; therefore, explanations are speculative. According to one account, Louis Johnson, becoming not only impatient but also fearful that Truman, like Roosevelt, had betrayed him and that he wouldn't get the job, pressed his case with greater insistence, both personally and through his White House supporters and, more indirectly, through Pearson's attacks.[80] This is a plausible explanation, but equal weight must be given to the cumulative reports of Forrestal's unstable and eccentric behavior reaching Truman; these brought the President at last to the conclusion that in Forrestal's personal interest and in the nation's it was imperative to make the changeover without more delay. The tragedy was that he had not acted sooner, either immediately following the election or at least simultaneously with the changes at the State Department. Why he delayed informing Forrestal that a change would be made, and then devised a three-month transition, may never be fully known. It is a fair inference that he was reluctant to lose Forrestal and to appoint Johnson.

Michael Forrestal later blamed Truman for only one thing regarding his father: letting him hang in limbo—twisting in the wind of uncertainty— during a period of nearly five months.[81] This is a telling criticism. But in fairness to the President there was probably no compelling evidence of Forrestal's disintegration until late January or early February, and much of it was subject to varied interpretation. In retrospect, his associates remembered telltale signs of deterioration and disorientation, but these went mainly unheeded at the time: a loss of physical stamina, an uneven capacity to concentrate; at times a confident assertiveness; at other times a nervous uncertainty. Donald Carpenter recalled that "this was a man who a year before had been keen, quick and decisive, who had given me twelve answers in as many minutes or less. Now in twenty minutes he couldn't answer one question."[82] Mrs. Arthur Krock, who saw a good deal of Forrestal socially, warned her husband in February that "Jim is cracking up," but Krock told her not to be silly. Their friend was too strong and durable to lose command of himself. Everything would be all right once he left government and got some rest.[83] No one seemed to understand that government had become his indispensable life support system, that every additional day he remained—after Johnson's appointment was announced on March 4—deepened the obsessive need to stay and made departure ever more emotionally unbearable.

On March 28, with farewell ceremonies at the Pentagon scheduled for noon, the President received a telephone call in the Oval Office while his naval aide, Captain Robert Dennison, stood nearby. Truman listened to the caller for a few moments, then said, "Yes, Jim, that's the way I want it." After he hung up, he turned to Dennison and said, "That was Forrestal. He wanted me to tell him whether I really wanted him to be relieved by Louis Johnson today."[84]

CHAPTER 32

★ ★ ★

Breakdown

ORRESTAL WAS present at Louis Johnson's swearing-in ceremony at the Pentagon on the morning of March 28. Shortly thereafter, in accordance with custom, he drove to the White House for a final good-bye to the President. To his surprise, Truman had assembled the entire Cabinet, the Joint Chiefs of Staff, and other government dignitaries, and there followed a second ceremony, this one honoring the retiring Secretary of Defense for "meritorious and distinguished service." The President, beaming and ebullient, added his personal congratulations in effusive terms, and the audience warmly applauded the honored man. Forrestal was visibly flustered and so choked with emotion that he was totally unable to respond, but the audience did not appear to regard this as any cause for alarm, or even unexpected, given the inherently emotional nature of the occasion and the general recognition of Forrestal's physical exhaustion.[1]

The next day, accompanied by Marx Leva, he went to Capitol Hill to be further honored at a special meeting of the House Armed Services Committee. There waiting for him, in addition to Carl Vinson and the entire panel of congressmen, were Louis Johnson and the three service secretaries, Kenneth Royall, John Sullivan, and Stuart Symington. Vinson paid tribute to Forrestal's "long and brilliant career," noting that while much of it had been devoted to finance and business, it was "as a high official of our Government that you have most singularly distinguished yourself among your fellow citizens."[2] He then entered upon a rather lengthy review of Forrestal's record: "It was your responsibility and high historic privilege to guide the destiny of the largest Navy in all the history of man—probably the largest Navy ever again to be seen. . . . Then on September 17 [1947] you become the country's first Secretary of Defense," charged with the task of "welding our armed forces into an effective team. Assuredly, this has not been and is not today an easy task," but "your efforts have been highly successful.'' The members of the Armed Services Committee, Vinson continued, ''want it long remembered and permanently recorded here that your outstanding talents and accomplishments on the highest levels of our Government have been appreciated and valued highly.'' He then presented Forrestal with a silver bowl engraved with the names of the committee members ''in testimony of our regard. That regard is also indelibly inscribed in our hearts.''

Similar sentiments were expressed by the ranking Republican member, the eloquent and bibulous congressman Dewey Short. Louis Johnson subscribed ''to everything that has been said'' and added his own admiration of Forrestal's ''keen, incisive mind''; then he mawkishly promised that ''never knowingly'' would ''a word come out of the Pentagon against the great record of Jim Forrestal.'' On this occasion, Forrestal was not taken by surprise and was thus better prepared to sift the honest accolades from the inflated congressional blubber and the thinly disguised hypocrisy of his successor. Addressing Vinson's remarks, he said he was ''too much overcome by what I consider to be a very gracious and very moving testimonial of your friendship and of these deeper feelings that come from the heart.'' Then with characteristic modesty and grace, he turned the spotlight on Vinson and the committee. It was their ''high intelligence and their continuing zest for work which really built the American Navy and which will build the defense forces under the unification which I know will be ably guided by Colonel Johnson, my successor.'' He also paid tribute to the three service Secretaries, but subtly distinguished between Royall's ''loyal service'' and Symington's ''zeal and high devotion to his beliefs.''[3]

Apparently buoyed by a wave of warm feeling, he left the Old House Office Building and prepared to drive back to the Pentagon with Leva, to an office that had been set aside for him to respond to the many letters of praise and tribute that were pouring in from all over the country. Symington expressed a desire to accompany Forrestal on the ride back, saying, ''There is something I want to talk to you about,'' so Leva got into another car and Symington drove off with Forrestal.[4] What Symington said to Forrestal on this short trip remains a mystery. Symington later denied the trip had occurred or that he was alone with Forrestal, but Leva and Ohly are insistent on that point. They imply Symington said something that shattered Forrestal's last remaining defenses, for when Leva entered Forrestal's office a short time later he was sitting in an extremely rigid position, still wearing his hat and staring blankly at a bare wall. The silver bowl from the Vinson committee was on the desk. A troubled Leva inquired if everything was all right. Forrestal did not reply and seemed unaware of everything around him. Leva persisted. Forrestal finally responded, saying, ''You are a loyal fellow,'' a phrase he repeated several times.

''Is there anything I can do for you?''

Louis Johnson just after being sworn in as Secretary of Defense, March 28, 1949.
Left to right: *Johnson, Forrestal, and Chief Justice Fred M. Vinson*

"Yes. Call for my car. I want to go home."[5]

This request presented a minor problem, for Forrestal no longer commanded an official car; it had passed to Louis Johnson. Now quite alarmed, Leva returned to his own office and telephoned Eberstadt, who was on Capitol Hill testifying on the Hoover Commission recommendations for strengthening the authority of the Secretary of Defense. Then he commandeered Vannevar Bush's chauffeured limousine and accompanied Forrestal to Prospect House.

Eberstadt phoned Forrestal from downtown, but was informed by the Filipino houseboy, Remy, that Forrestal would not come to the phone. "You tell James," Eberstadt said, "that he can get away with that with some people, but not with me." When Forrestal finally came on the line, the following brief exchange took place:

"I'll be right out."

"For your own sake, I advise you not to."

"I'm on my way."[6]

When Eberstadt arrived at Prospect House in midafternoon, the house was dark and all the blinds were drawn. The houseboy, visibly upset, told Eberstadt that his boss seemed to be very sick and that Mrs. Forrestal was

President Truman honors Forrestal at the White House, March 28, 1949

in Hobe Sound. In a few minutes Forrestal shuffled down the stairs, no-
ticeably thinner and more haggard than Eberstadt had previously seen him,
his collar hanging loosely from his wrinkled neck. Forrestal told his close
friend that a number of people—an unidentified "they," whom Eberstadt
gradually discerned as Communists, Zionists, and persons in the White
House—had formed a conspiracy to "get" him and had finally succeeded.
He cautioned Eberstadt not to speak above a whisper, for "they" had wired
the house. He parted a blind and pointed to two disreputable-looking men
on the corner who he insisted were shadowing him. Suddenly the doorbell
rang and the houseboy opened the door on an odd-looking man who proceeded to tell Eberstadt he had been an alternate delegate from North
Carolina to the 1948 Democratic National Convention and was seeking
Forrestal's support for appointment to postmaster in his hometown. Surprised by this strange coincidence, Eberstadt nevertheless quickly dispatched the man by telling him to write a letter. When he left, Forrestal
watched warily as he made his way to the corner, where he stopped to talk
to the other two men. "You see, he is one of them," Forrestal said excit-
edly. To Eberstadt, however, it was soon apparent that the third man was

merely asking directions. A trolley car came along, the others pointed to it, and he got aboard.[7]

Over the next hour of disjointed talk, Eberstadt learned that Forrestal had been suffering from severe insomnia for a long time—''he hadn't had a full night's sleep in months''—and that his teeth ached, his intestines were disordered, and many other normal bodily functions were breaking down. He told Eberstadt his life was a wreck, his career a total failure, and he was considering suicide.[8] Shocked by his friend's disintegration, Eberstadt concluded that he must immediately get him out of the morbid atmosphere of Prospect House—and out of Washington. Forrestal initially rejected any idea of leaving the house, but was overborne by Eberstadt's insistence that he go to Florida for a long rest. Remy hastily packed a suitcase with sports clothes and brought Forrestal's golf clubs to the front door. Eberstadt then telephoned Louis Johnson to report that Forrestal was a sick man in need of immediate medical attention and to ask for an aircraft to fly him to Hobe Sound, where he could rest in the sunshine and the company of close friends. Johnson agreed, and an air force Constellation was immediately made ready for the trip to Florida. Eberstadt next telephoned Lovett in Hobe Sound, gave him a brief report on Forrestal's condition, and asked him to meet the plane. Leva was summoned and drove Forrestal and Eberstadt to the airport in his Chevrolet, Forrestal subdued and unresisting, but repeating several times that Leva was ''a loyal fellow.''[9]

Forrestal boarded the aircraft, unaccompanied except for the air force crew, and flew off to Hobe Sound, putting down at a private airfield near the Jupiter Island Club in the early evening of the same day he had been honored by the House Armed Services Committee.

Meanwhile, Eberstadt flew to New York to consult with Dr. Howard Rusk, medical editor of the *New York Times,* to find out who was the most eminent psychiatrist in the country. Rusk recommended Dr. William Menninger of the Menninger Clinic in Topeka, Kansas. By coincidence, the psychiatrist was in New York City, quickly agreed to see Forrestal, and flew to Hobe Sound the next day, March 30, accompanied by Eberstadt and Forrestal's lawyer, John Cahill. By another ironic twist, Menninger had been called to the Pentagon just three months earlier to help set in motion a study of the phenomenon known as combat fatigue. John Ohly, the Forrestal assistant in charge of the study, was canvassing the field of psychiatry to find the most suitable experts to serve on the study group, and he had arranged for Menninger to come to Washington. The psychiatrist had spent half a morning with Forrestal discussing various aspects of combat fatigue, but so far as is known he did not notice any trace of this condition, or any other mental or emotional abnormality, in the behavior of the Secretary of Defense.[10]

Forrestal was met at the airfield by his wife, Robert and Adele Lovett, and a small circle of friends that included Douglas Dillon and Philip and Ellen Barry. Lovett later recalled that his friend was so altered in appearance that he hardly recognized him; he was "a wizened, shrunken man, uncertain of movement"; his thin mouth was so tightly drawn that his lips were all but hidden; his eyes searched suspiciously the faces of the people who were gathered to greet him, and he almost fell off the narrow ladder while descending from the plane. When Lovett reached up to steady him, it seemed to him that Forrestal's body was a bag of loose bones. "I'm glad you brought your golf clubs," he said in an effort to be jocular, "because I'm going to take every dollar you've got," but Forrestal only stared at him with a haunted look and said, "Bob, they're after me."[11]

Finding proper accommodations for Forrestal took some doing. Jo had not rented a house, but was staying at the Jupiter Island Club. The Barrys had a guest in their small cottage, and the Lovetts also had house guests. However, as soon as the seriousness of Forrestal's condition was recognized, Mr. and Mrs. Wilson G. Wing turned over their house to him and to the group of guardians (including Eberstadt, Cahill, Dr. Menninger, and Forrestal's former naval aide, Rear Admiral John E. Gingrich) who assembled to comfort him and thwart any suicide attempts.[12] All implements usable in suicides were removed or hidden, and Forrestal was never left alone. With the aid of a sedative he slept soundly the first night, but the entire household was awakened at 6:00 a.m. by a screaming fire siren in the nearby town, and all ran out of the house to see what was happening.[13] Satisfied that the trouble was elsewhere, they went back to bed. His friends stayed with him everywhere—when he was shaving or taking a shower, strolling on the beach, or swimming in the surf. At times he seemed more relaxed and was able to joke about the fact that his friends would not allow him to be alone even on the toilet. But his depression and despondency did not depart, nor did his conviction that "they" were lurking everywhere and determined to get him. Walking on the beach with Lovett, he pointed to a row of metal sockets fixed in the sand to hold beach umbrellas. "We had better not discuss anything here. Those things are wired, and everything we say is being recorded." He expressed anxiety about the presence of Communists or Communist influence in the White House, which he said had driven him from office. He thought he had been marked for liquidation for his efforts to alert America to the menace, indeed, that the Kremlin planned to assassinate the whole top leadership in Washington. He was convinced the Communists were planning an invasion of the United States, and at certain moments he talked as if this had already begun.[14]

To Lovett, he also revealed a deep but unidentified guilt. "I've done a bad thing," he said, or, "I've done something bad." But he was never specific, and Lovett and others were never sure what he meant. Some years later, Lovett thought the problem was that "somewhere he had played a double game in politics"—an allusion to his private discussions with Dewey during the 1948 campaign—but stronger evidence indicates that the main cause of Forrestal's guilt was his rupture with the Catholic Church when he left Princeton in 1915.[15]

Dr. Menninger had several lengthy talks with him on March 30 and 31 and concluded that Forrestal was suffering from severe "reactive depression"—essentially the condition of combat fatigue seen with such frequency during World War II—which results from an accumulation of intense external pressures that overwhelm the mind and the nervous system. In Forrestal's case the principal symptoms were anxiety, paranoia, and a sense of total failure that produced impulses to suicide. Menninger thought immediate treatment was indicated and offered the facilities of his clinic in Kansas. When Lovett asked him how collapse could have come so swiftly to a man who had been so careful about maintaining his physical fitness, Menninger replied that Forrestal had expended tremendous energy to suppress his mounting anxieties over a long period of time—especially through the intense strain of his last year in office. The effort to keep everything locked up had consumed him physically and spiritually. His collapse had been swift because he was used up.[16]

At this point, the matter was complicated by the arrival of Captain George N. Raines, the chief psychiatrist at the naval hospital in Bethesda, just outside Washington. Eberstadt's telephone call to Louis Johnson had alerted the administration to the probability that Forrestal's undeniable exhaustion had now developed into serious neurosis, and the White House wanted to be certain it had all the facts and was in a position to influence the way in which the matter was presented to the press and the public. Allegations that decisions relating to national security in a period of extreme international tension had been in the hands of a "crazy" could seriously damage the administration domestically and might even affect the question of peace or war. Dr. Raines was not, however, a political agent for the White House, and his appearance at Hobe Sound was in large part the result of the navy's natural human concern for a man it admired and regarded as one of its own. Noting on his arrival that Forrestal was already in the hands of the eminent Dr. Menninger, Raines felt it was improper "on ethical grounds" for him to inject himself into the case, and he did not interview Forrestal until several days later at the Bethesda Naval Hospital.[17]

FATEFUL DECISION ON WHERE

THERE ENSUED, however, a fateful debate about whether Forrestal should go to the Menninger Clinic or to Bethesda. Those principally involved seem to have been Jo Forrestal, Eberstadt, Menninger, and Raines. In his press statement two days after Forrestal's suicide on May 22, Raines said, ''I had no voice in the selection of a hospital except to assure the men concerned of our [the navy's] utmost cooperation.''[18] It seems a reasonable inference that while technically accurate, this statement omits the virtual certainty that Raines presented the advantages of a general hospital like Bethesda in response to questions from the others. The decision was not an easy one. Menninger and Eberstadt were for publicly acknowledging Forrestal's condition of ''combat fatigue'' and sending him to Topeka for treatment that had proved successful in hundreds of similar cases. But there were countervailing considerations. The national and international repercussions of admitting ''mental illness'' were acknowledged as carrying some weight, and it was argued that the specific nature of the illness could be more easily kept from the public if Forrestal was treated at Bethesda, not only because it was a general hospital but also because the whole naval organization was better equipped to screen visitors and isolate the patient from inquiring newspapermen. Furthermore, in a general hospital Forrestal might feel less stigmatized by his condition and thus more optimistic about his chances for recovery. Finally, treatment in a suburb of Washington would give him the comfort of easy access to friends and associates.[19]

As the debate went back and forth, it turned more and more on the question of whether the primary consideration should be to assure Forrestal's recovery or to protect his reputation and avoid embarrassment to the administration. Yet even here the facts did not facilitate a clear-cut decision, for no one doubted the high quality of treatment he would receive at Bethesda. It appears that Jo Forrestal was determined to protect her husband's reputation by avoiding the stigma that she felt would result from public revelation of his condition; if he was sent to a famous psychiatric clinic, the nature of his illness would become immediately apparent. At some point in the process she telephoned President Truman (or he called her) to discuss the pros and cons, and apparently he reinforced her inclination to favor the naval hospital. In the end, everyone involved seemed to accept this solution by a kind of tacit consensus. A week after Forrestal's death, Menninger wrote to Eberstadt. Taking note of the recent tragedy, he continued: ''I appreciated your thoughtfulness in sending me a copy of your letter that you wrote to Dr. Raines and it is of course quite true that the decision was reached by a joint agreement among many people and not merely at your instigation or direction.''[20]

The decision having thus been taken, Forrestal was flown to Washington on April 2, accompanied by Menninger, Eberstadt, and Gingrich, and he was formally admitted to the naval hospital that evening. The aircraft taxied to a remote corner of the field before off-loading in order to escape the attention of the press. Although heavily sedated, Forrestal was in a state of extreme agitation during the flight, convinced that his enemies were omnipresent and determined to get him. He now wondered aloud whether the root cause of his troubles had been his break with the Catholic Church forty years before, whether he was being "punished" for being "a bad Catholic." The stern indoctrination by the Church and his rigid mother had left him with a guilt which, though suppressed for forty years, had never been eradicated. Efforts by his companions to assure him that no one wished him ill or wanted to destroy him were unavailing, and during the limousine ride to the hospital he made at least one attempt to throw himself out of the car. Arriving at Bethesda, he declared that he did not expect to leave the place alive.[21]

Dr. Menninger talked to Forrestal on April 3 and again on April 6, but did not see him thereafter. Responsibility had passed to Dr. Raines and the navy, but recent evidence suggests that the White House was beginning to exert its influence on physical arrangements and public relations. In 1984, Dr. Robert P. Nenno, a young assistant to Dr. Raines from 1952 to 1959, disclosed that Raines had been instructed by "the people downtown" to put Forrestal in the VIP suite on the sixteenth floor of the hospital. Dr. Nenno emphasized that Raines's disclosure to him was entirely ethical, but that "he did speak to me because we were close friends." The decision to put Forrestal in the tower suite was regarded by the psychiatric staff as "extraordinary" for a patient who was "seriously depressed and potentially suicidal," especially when the hospital possessed two one-story buildings directly adjacent to the main structure that were specifically organized and staffed to handle mentally disturbed patients. Nenno added, "I have always guessed that the order came from the White House."[22]

Apparently determined to make the best of a decision he could not effectively resist, Raines had special security screens installed on the windows of Forrestal's room and established a system of around-the-clock surveillance by doctors, nurses, and enlisted medical corpsmen. He said in his postmortem report that Dr. Menninger inspected and approved these arrangements, as well as the general course of treatment Raines proposed to pursue.[23]

After he had conducted his own interviews with Forrestal, Raines confirmed Menninger's diagnosis of reactive depression. Some other members of the psychiatric staff at Bethesda thought the condition was closer to "involutional melancholia," a variant of manic-depression and a form of schizophrenia. This was not inconsistent with the Menninger-Raines diagnosis, but somewhat broader and more serious. As explained in one textbook, involutional melancholia is a depression most prevalent in persons of middle age. There is a tendency to "bewail the past and to feel the future has nothing in store. The patient is preoccupied with what might have been, and the inevitable regrets bring on self-doubt, indecision, anxiety, and fear. The glands of internal secretion begin to fail in their functioning and the bodily health is lowered." Persons who develop this illness are often "sensitive, meticulous, over-conscientious, over-scrupulous, busy, active people" with a "narrow range of interests . . . a proclivity to reticence . . . [and] a poor facility for readjustment." In addition, "suicide is always a great risk."[24]

Rumors that Forrestal had returned suddenly from Florida and had been admitted to the naval hospital were filtering through official and social Washington, and some reputable reporters, columnists, and other news-gathering agencies had uncovered the basic facts. But in the absence of any official announcement, they chose not to publish what they knew; whether it was to avoid giving the Russians an embarrassing propaganda opportunity or to protect the reputation of a man they generally admired was not entirely clear. Finally, on April 8, the *New York Times* reported that "doctors" at Bethesda had disclosed that the former Secretary of Defense was under treatment for "nervous and physical exhaustion."[25]

One journalistic dissenter from this tacit consensus was Drew Pearson, who grew frustrated "to the point of explosion" by the reticence of what he called the "Forrestal Cabal" within the "prestige press."[26] His own sleuths had developed certain facts about Forrestal's behavior at Hobe Sound, but either they or Pearson himself had enlarged and distorted them. Not content with driving Forrestal from office, Pearson now conceived it his "moral duty" to expose him as a "madman" who had had access to atomic bombs and to raise questions as to how long he had been impaired and how gravely his impairment had jeopardized the U.S. national security. Pearson, who contended that Forrestal and like-minded others in the government were wholly responsible for the cold war, perceived Forrestal's sudden incapacity as a new lever with which to force a critical review of what he termed "Forrestal's policies"; he defined these as "having atomic bombs as the centerpiece." Though he was said by his staff to feel a "restrained sympathy" for those who were acting to protect Forrestal's future from "the stigma of mental instability," Pearson had, in fact, decided to fire his heaviest ammunition in a radio broadcast on April 9. He charged that Forrestal, awakened by the sound of a fire siren (on the night of April 1 at Hobe Sound), had rushed out of his cottage screaming, "The Russians are attacking." He defined Forrestal's condition as "temporary insanity." In subsequent newspaper columns he asserted that Forrestal had made three suicide attempts while in Florida—by drug overdose, by hanging, and by slashing his wrists.[27] According to a later statement by Raines, all of these assertions were lies. Although Forrestal *talked* of suicide in Florida, Raines said, he made no attempt to kill himself.[28] According to Eliot Janeway, however, Eberstadt told him privately that Forrestal had made one suicide attempt at Hobe Sound.[29]

Forrestal's friends and well-wishers were deeply troubled by the Pearson disclosures, but in the absence of any official statement from the hospital or the administration, it was awkward for private individuals to attempt a public rebuttal. A letter from Menninger to Eberstadt on April 16 made clear that both men had urged the White House to make a prompt disclosure of the relevant facts but that this advice had been rejected.

Referring to the Pearson broadcast, Menninger wrote, "I thought the very unfortunate report over the radio last Sunday night was pretty bad . . . I can't help but feel, however, that if the White House had taken our advice we might have avoided that particular thing."[30] Immediately after Pearson's broadcast, the Washington *Post* said editorially what "had long been known," namely, that the former Secretary of Defense was "worn out" by "the onerousness of the burden that is imposed upon . . . public servants in these harassing days," a burden requiring them to live and work "under the white glare of criticism."[31]

On April 11, the administration finally made a statement. Rear Admiral N. L. Pugh, the Deputy Chief of the Bureau of Medicine and Surgery, informed the press that Forrestal was suffering from "occupational fatigue." This condition affected a person "physically and mentally," Pugh said, but the patient was "progressing satisfactorily" and could be expected to leave the hospital "in a short time." In response to a question, he cited a recent conversation with Forrestal in which the former official "talked very rationally."[32] The following day the *New York Times* explained editorially that "occupational" or "operational" fatigue was the civilian analogue to the condition so prevalent in World War II known as "combat fatigue." This was the "physical and emotional reaction that came from fighting too long without respite." Stamina and resistance varied from man to man, but "every man has a breaking point, and when this point comes he must rest." Forrestal, the editorial continued, had fought "in the front lines" seven days a week for eight years, and these "untiring efforts and self-sacrifice have earned for him the gratitude and respect of his fellow citizens, and the rest he so richly deserves."[33]

In a related story on April 14, the *Post* discussed the serious problem of "decompression" that confronts high-level officials when they are suddenly released from high-pressure jobs, and it quoted Winston Churchill's reaction to his own forced resignation from the British Admiralty in 1915: "Like a sea beast flushed up from the depths, or a diver suddenly hoisted, my veins threatened to burst from the fall in pressure. I had great anxiety and no means of relieving it; I had vehement convictions and no power to give effect to them.''[34]

IN THE PERIOD from Forrestal's resignation on March 2 until his death, a number of people were moved to reflect on his contributions to the nation, his value as a public servant, and his intrinsic human worth, and they set down their feelings in literally hundreds of personal letters to him. Because these were written to the living man, they escape the taint of eulogy. They were written by friends and strangers, by rich and poor, by the famous and the unknown. Most of them—and some of the most eloquent—were from people who knew Forrestal only by the impressions they had gained of him through photographs and newspaper accounts. They demonstrate beyond doubt that this shy and secretive man who dreaded demonstrations of affection had, in roughly nine years of public life, gained the genuine respect and gratitude of his countrymen to a remarkable degree. The specifics of what he accomplished were mentioned so seldom as to suggest they were hardly known to the writers, but without exception they seemed to understand that he was a rare public servant—a meld of high ability, deep dedication, and selfless labor—who had served his country honorably and honestly to the limits of his talent and his strength.

Ordinary citizens who knew Forrestal only as a public figure wrote spontaneously, mostly by hand. The fact of their initiative was extraordinary in itself, and each letter seemed to carry an unspoken message of affection within its expressions of respect and gratitude.

''My husband and I wish to thank you for your long service to our country,'' Cicely Easley wrote from San Francisco. ''We appreciate everything you did. . . . Please know we *are* aware and more than appreciate your heavy task you so ably performed. There are millions who feel as we do—but you know how human nature is—people do not write and tell you—even though in their hearts they are grateful.''

Arthur O. Newell, of Northport, New York, wrote: ''As a plain, ordinary citizen, who feels that our appreciation of the services that you have performed for our country has not been sufficiently expressed, let me wish you a speedy recovery and continued good health. I cannot help but feel that your efforts as Defense Secretary have lessened the likelihood that my son may ever have to go to war.''

Leslie F. Biebl of Red Bank, New Jersey, wrote: ''I am grateful to you, sir, not only for the immense job you have done for our country, but also for that individual share of protection that I have received through your efforts. Thank you—very much!''

Many citizens reacted to the printed and broadcast barbarities of Pearson and Winchell. John A. Logan of San Francisco wrote that he wanted ''just to convey a few words to show my indignation and how I know millions out here feel at the conduct of that radio madman, Drew Pearson. . . .'' A patient at the United States Naval Hospital in San Diego told him that he and his fellow patients ''deplore the unfair and nauseating below the belt attacks, which surely could only emanate from one proficient in un-loosing skunk spray.'' Also noting the skunk spray was Mrs. Herbert Clark of Dallas, who sought to convince Forrestal that ''completely unknown to you, I and others alike have watched with respect and appreciation your skillful endeavor to make the utmost success of the difficult tasks assigned to you. This note simply carries sincerest wishes for a complete recovery to health and happiness.''

A New York reporter recorded his thanks for the remembered courtesies shown him ''around 1923,'' when Forrestal was on the way up in Wall Street. A friend in the Washington press corps, Jerry Greene of the New York *Daily News,* wrote that ''I'd like you to know that in the 20 years I have been kicking around in my racket I have never known a man in public life, bar none, who carried out his duties so ably and so faithfully.''

There were many letters from navy enlisted men, who do not often think of their civilian Secretaries with affection. Seaman Barney Weinstein of Brooklyn scrawled across a commercial get-well card, ''To the greatest!'' Another, Russell Cable of Portland, Oregon, wrote: ''You will always be admired and have the respect of us Navy men.'' Despite the strains generated by Forrestal's efforts to mediate interservice rivalries, admirals and captains expressed their warm feelings about him: ''You have the utmost respect and admiration of all those in the Navy with whom I have come in contact,'' said Rear Admiral Thomas H. Robbins, Jr. ''Your ideals and your singleness of purpose . . . have left their mark, and all of us are better men as a result.'' A line with the ring of an epitaph—''You were the true public servant''—occurred in a letter from Captain E. E. Yeomans.

One navy letter, evidently typed by the man who signed it, bore five blue stars in a tiny circle on the letterhead and the date of April 15, 1949:

Dear Mr. Forrestal,

I noted in the newspapers a couple of days ago that you were able to send word to Senator Tydings about your condition which is good news.

Indeed, I have been very sorry that you were taken ill some ten days ago. Naturally, I hope and expect that your improvement is already underway and that you will be able to go to work and be your old self in a very short time.

Sincerely yours,
Ernest J. King

There were numerous notes from personal friends and from colleagues in government:

Robert Patterson's wife, Margaret, noting that "Bob" had returned to private life in a "jolly state of mind" and was enjoying the life of "unburdened private citizen," urged Forrestal to go and do likewise.

Mrs. du Val R. Goldwaithe urged him to follow the Chinese proverb "Enjoy yourself, it is later than you think." She added, "But I'm not sanguine, because you are such a high strung race horse."

Charles Thomas, a close friend, suggested a weekend of recreation, adding, "I'm not smart enough to stimulate your mind, so you would get a complete mental rest."

From Cardinal Spellman in New York came a card with a handwritten message: "Dear Jim—my prayers, my good wishes, and always my admiration and affection."

Hugh D. Auchincloss, a Washington stockbroker, offered Forrestal a diagnosis and a prescription: "I guess it is just a case of having worked too damn hard, too damn long, under too damn much of a strain; and then having too quick and complete a letup. That, as you know, is enough to kill a horse so you have nothing to be ashamed of. . . . Here's hoping they at least give you a good looking nurse. But I am sure you won't be there long."

A summons to his favorite golf course on Long Island came from Mrs. John R. Fell: "Meadowbrook is looking green and lovely. Lots of love, dear Jim. Fifi Fell."

A note on a small card, signed only with a diminutive of a woman's first name, echoed her anguish: "Dear Jim: I am so distressed about you and upset that I bothered you. Forget it, and get well soon and completely rested. You can't shoulder the world's cares entirely—tho it seems you have. Let evolution do it too. What you have done has been widely and deeply appreciated. And you have the affection and loyalty and respect of everyone. And I humbly add mine."[35]

A sad fact was that Forrestal neither saw nor wanted to see most of these letters. They were in any event too numerous for an exhausted man to cope with, and his doctors passed on to him only a select few.

On the whole, then (with the notable exception of Drew Pearson), the response from the press and the general public was one of shock, sympathetic concern, and gratitude, accompanied by a disinclination to probe for the full facts. Pearson's charges were not credible, and no one was prepared to repeat them, but many were troubled that the paucity of official information made public opinion vulnerable to sensational distortions. On May 5, Marquis Childs, a syndicated columnist who admired Forrestal, attacked both Pearson and the administration. Pearson's "sensationalism and exaggeration" gave "what Forrestal's friends and family say was a false picture of his illness," but the administration's failure to rebut Pearson was providing a base for a "widespread Communist propaganda campaign." Behind the Iron Curtain, millions of people were being led to believe that Forrestal's "insanity" was an explanation for the Marshall Plan and the NATO Pact. In fairness to Forrestal and to protect the credibility of sound American policy, the true facts of the case should be revealed. Childs was making a compelling point, but the exact nature of Forrestal's illness was not disclosed until after his death. Meanwhile, rumor and Drew Pearson strove to fill the information vacuum.[36]

PSYCHIATRIC TREATMENT

AT THE HOSPITAL, Raines was prescribing treatment in accordance with his diagnosis of reactive depression and was talking to his patient on the average of three hours a day. "I was given complete control," he later told a reporter, "and I possessed the complete confidence of the Forrestal family." Narcosis* was employed during the first week of treatment, and Forrestal's response was encouraging; this was followed by four weeks of subshock insulin therapy. Here the results were less successful than Raines had hoped for, but he decided not to use the more controversial electric shock treatment, at least until it was shown that more moderate measures had failed to produce improvement. As the days passed, Forrestal showed incremental gains in stability, though not a steady upward advance; he moved more in a "wavelike" pattern that flowed, then ebbed, then flowed again, but Raines was encouraged and electric shock was never used.[37]

In their daily psychoanalytic conversations, the talk became increasingly candid. When Forrestal asked Raines why the heavy screens were affixed to the windows of his room, Raines told him, "That's to keep you from jumping out the window." Forrestal replied that he never could bring himself to jump out of a window, nor could he even slash his wrists. He thought it possible that he could hang himself or take an overdose of sleeping pills. He told Raines he had failed in his job at the Pentagon because he had gambled that the military services could be unified on the basis of reasoned cooperation instead of "banging heads together"; the gamble had failed and Forrestal berated himself for naïve misjudgment. Raines later told a reporter he had come to regard Forrestal as "the most honest and idealistic man I ever met" and one of the most intelligent. On one occasion, when Forrestal read several newspaper editorials praising him for his record of

*The use of sedatives and tranquilizers to reduce tension in the body and the mind and to induce a passive condition.

public service, he threw them to one side, exclaiming: "The fools. Don't they know that I betrayed my country?"[38] During the first weeks at Bethesda, he never left his room and kept the blinds drawn out of a sense he was being spied on. One day he sent for Rear Admiral Sidney Souers, the executive secretary of the National Security Council, telling him to bring an instrument for detecting listening devices because the hospital room was "wired." Souers examined the room with the device and told Forrestal he could find nothing. Forrestal replied, "They knew you were coming and took them out. Now they'll put them back again."[39]

Raines noted that Forrestal's depression was moderate and stable on Mondays and showed regular improvement through the week until Thursday night. Then it began to worsen until he descended into a state of nervous agitation and anxiety on Saturday and Sunday. Raines asked what Forrestal thought were the causes of this predictable mood change, but for a week he evaded the question; then he told the psychiatrist that the answer was Pearson and Winchell, whose broadcasts aired on Sunday evening. As their talk brought this matter into the open, Forrestal acknowledged that he had never been able to overcome his acute sensitivity to attacks on his personal integrity. Rational, even irrational, criticisms of his public positions he could handle with poise and equanimity, but personal assaults on his motives or his manliness shook him to the core. According to Raines, Forrestal simply could not comprehend the "fanatical viciousness" of someone like Pearson, who in effect had pursued him into the sickroom and continued to hound him every Sunday evening.[40]

Forrestal was not allowed to listen to the radio, but according to Raines, he "made" Raines give him an oral summary of Pearson's Sunday-night broadcast when they met the following morning. In his postmortem interview with Robert Sherrod of *Time,* Raines said, "Drew Pearson and Walter Winchell killed Forrestal." Sherrod thought this a sensational statement, which it was, but before *Time* could go to press, Raines had second thoughts and retracted the statement. Also, according to Sherrod, "he ran out on half of what he told me and refused to be quoted on any of it." In addition, Raines insisted that Sherrod's memorandum of the interview be reviewed by the chief public information officer at the Pentagon. That review apparently sanitized the interview beyond any news value, for *"Time* used very little, if any, of the remainder."[41]

Initially no visitors were allowed except members of the immediate family. Josephine appears to have stayed in Washington during the first few weeks of her husband's hospitalization; Michael was there for a similar period before he returned to Paris, where he was working for Averell Harriman, now roving ambassador for the Marshall Plan; Peter was a student at Princeton with the prospect of a summer job as copyboy at the Washington *Post.* Jo's visits were not frequent. President Truman called on

April 23, bearing a bottle of bourbon, and after leaving Forrestal he went into another part of the hospital to visit with Admiral Leahy, who was recovering from a minor operation.[42] Louis Johnson, the Secretary of Defense, spent thirty minutes with his predecessor on April 27 and told reporters afterward that the patient "looked fine" and was "making good progress." He also let it be known that President Truman had offered Forrestal a plane in which to take "a restful trip around the world" following his recovery.[43] According to one source, Truman also wrote to Forrestal telling him that "several" interesting government posts awaited him whenever he was ready to make a decision. Congressman Lyndon Johnson managed to gain entrance to the suite "against Forrestal's wishes."[44]

The brief, infrequent bulletins out of Bethesda Naval Hospital were all upbeat. On April 17, the hospital executive officer, Captain Hogan, said that recovery was "only a matter of time" and that no "turns for the worse" were expected.[45] On May 18, the hospital announced that Forrestal had regained twelve of the fifteen pounds he had lost during his last months in office.[46]

Henry Forrestal visited his brother four times. His first impression was that Forrestal "looked much better than I expected; his eyes seemed clear; he was sharp and decisive," and the patient assured him, "I'll be all right, we'll pull out of this."[47] After his first visit, Henry told Raines that "what my brother needs is not to be cooped up there on the 16th floor. He needs to be on an estate somewhere, among friends, where he can walk around in the sun. He has been an exceedingly active man."[48] A young lawyer, David Ginsburg, summoned by Forrestal for a further discussion of Israel and the Middle East, came away with a similar impression: "The sterile atmosphere of the hospital room was depressing . . . The poor man needed sunshine and someone to cuddle him."[49] Raines did not release his patient, but he did tell Henry that his brother was "fundamentally okay."[50] Henry also pressed Raines to allow Father Maurice S. Sheehy, a Catholic priest, to visit Forrestal, but Raines was opposed. According to Michael Forrestal, his father had met Sheehy, "a short, dark man of the shadows," sometime during his last months in office when "he was groping for a way back to his boyhood faith." Forrestal had asked to see Sheehy "to help him return to the Catholic Church, almost from the first day he entered the hospital," and concurrently he was reading Monsignor Fulton J. Sheen's *Peace of Soul*.[51] For reasons never adequately explained, Raines turned down these requests while providing assurances that everything would be possible at the proper time. Henry Forrestal, who was Father Sheehy's ally in this undertaking, asked, "How long do you want to wait, Doctor? Delays in such cases can be dangerous. Have you ever heard of a case where being visited by a clergyman has hurt a man?" But Raines, for his own reasons, perhaps because he thought the reopening of the Catholic issue would be disquieting to the patient, or possibly because a Catholic confessional might risk disclosing sensitive national security information, continued to put him off. On May 18, Henry Forrestal and Sheehy took their exasperation to the Navy Secretary, John L. Sullivan. He telephoned Raines, who seemed to promise an early visit by Sheehy, but three days later Forrestal was dead.[52]

MISCALCULATED RISKS

IN RESPONSE to signs which Raines took to mean that Forrestal was recovering, close watch over his movements was relaxed somewhat in the early part of May. An enlisted corpsman remained on duty in the corridor just outside Forrestal's door, but the patient was encouraged to leave his room occasionally, to visit with nurses and other patients on the same floor, and to use a small pantry across the hall where he could pour himself a cup of coffee or prepare a snack. Fatefully, the pantry window was not equipped with the heavy tamper-proof screen that had been affixed to the windows of his bedroom; it had only a light screen fastened by small hooks.

This relaxation of restrictions was later described by Raines as "one of the calculated risks of therapy,"[53] and he hoped Forrestal would see his greater freedom of movement as reinforcement of the medical judgment that he was recovering—as objective evidence that he was now trusted not to take his own life. Raines was now so confident of his patient's progress that he advised Jo Forrestal she could return to Europe on May 12, as planned, and that Michael could resume his work for the Marshall Plan in Paris. Peter Forrestal would remain in Washington for the summer. Raines discontinued his daily psychotherapy sessions with Forrestal on May 14 and saw him for the last time on May 18. He felt, as he later reported, "that barring any unforeseen incident" Forrestal would be able to "carry along" during Raines's planned weeklong absence for a combination of vacation and attendance at a meeting of the American Psychiatric Association in Montreal. What he said next, however, raised the most serious question as to whether he should have left the hospital and Forrestal at that particular time: "I further recognized the well-known psychiatric fact that the next thirty days would constitute the most dangerous period of the illness as far as suicide was concerned, inasmuch as suicidal preoccupations had to be present, and at the same time privileges had to be extended to the patient to allow his full recovery."[54]

Apparently, Forrestal was now finding it possible to take the onset of Drew Pearson's Sunday-night broadcasts in stride, for on Friday, May 20, two days after Raines's departure, there was no visible sign of the anxiety that had shaken him on the approach of previous weekends. On the contrary, he seemed in high spirits. On Saturday, Rear Admiral Morton D. Willcutts, the commanding officer at Bethesda, watched him consume a large steak lunch and found him ebullient, meticulously shaven, and eager to greet a few scheduled visitors, among them Peter. Nothing untoward occurred during the afternoon and early evening. Then, late in the evening, he informed the corpsman on duty that he did not want a sedative or a sleeping pill because he was planning to stay up quite late and read. The corpsman was Edward Prise, the most sensitive (and the one Forrestal liked best) of the three who rotated round-the-clock eight-hour shifts outside his door. One of the other corpsmen had chosen Friday to go absent without leave and get drunk, which meant that Prise was to be relieved at midnight by a substitute for the fellow who had gone AWOL; the new man was a stranger to Forrestal and to the subtleties and dangers of the situation. Prise had observed that Forrestal, though more energetic than usual, was also more restless, and this worried him. He tried to alert the young doctor who had night duty and slept in a room next to Forrestal's. But the doctor was accustomed to restless patients and not readily open to advice on the subject from an enlisted corpsman. Midnight arrived and with it the substitute corpsman, but Prise nevertheless lingered on for perhaps half an hour, held by some nameless, instinctive anxiety. But he could not stay forever. Regulations, custom, and his own ingrained discipline forbade it.[55]

At one-forty-five on Sunday morning, May 22, the new corpsman looked in on Forrestal, who was busy copying onto several sheets of paper the brooding classical poem "The Chorus from Ajax" by Sophocles, in which Ajax, forlorn and far from home, contemplates suicide.* The book was bound in red leather and decorated with gold.

> Fair Salamis, the billows' roar
>   Wander around thee yet,
> And sailors gaze upon thy shore
>   Firm in the Ocean set.
> Thy son is in a foreign clime
>   Where Ida feeds her countless flocks,
>   Far from thy dear, remembered rocks,
> Worn by the waste of time—
> Comfortless, nameless, hopeless save
> In the dark prospect of the yawning grave. . . .
>
> Woe to the mother in her close of day,
> Woe to her desolate heart and temples gray,
>   When she shall hear

*As translated by William Mackworth Praed in Mark Van Doren's *Anthology of World Poetry*.

> Her loved one's story whispered in her ear!
> "Woe, woe!" will be the cry—
> No quiet murmur like the tremulous wail
> Of the lone bird, the querulous nightingale—

When Forrestal had written the syllable "night" of the word "nightingale," he stopped his copying. It remains a speculation whether the word "nightingale" triggered what Dr. Raines later called Forrestal's "sudden fit of despondence,"[56] but a coincidence should not go unremarked. As discussed in Chapter 23, "Nightingale" was the name of an anti-Communist guerrilla army made up of Ukrainian refugees, recruited and trained by the CIA to carry on a secret war against the Soviet Union from behind the Iron Curtain. Many of the recruits were Nazi collaborators who had carried out mass executions of their fellow countrymen, including thousands of Jews, behind the German lines during the war. As a member of NSC, Forrestal had authorized the operation.[57]

In most accounts of what happened next, it is said that the inexperienced corpsman "went on a brief errand."[58] However, Dr. Robert Nenno, the young psychiatrist who later worked for Dr. Raines, quotes Raines as telling him that Forrestal "pulled rank" and ordered the nervous young corpsman to go on some errand that was designed to remove him from the premises.[59]

After writing the syllable "night" of the word "nightingale," Forrestal inserted his sheets of paper in the book between the last page and the back cover and placed the book on the bed table, open to the poem. Then he quickly walked across the corridor into the diet kitchen. Tying one end of his dressing-gown sash to the radiator just below the window, and the other around his neck, he removed the simple screen and climbed out the window. No one knows whether he then jumped or hung until the silk sash gave way, but scratches found on the cement work just below the window suggest that he may have hung for at least one terrible moment, then changed his mind—too late—before the sash gave way and he plunged thirteen stories to his death. Only seconds after he entered the diet kitchen, a nurse on the seventh floor heard a loud crash. His broken body had landed on the roof of a third-floor passageway, the dressing-gown sash still tied around his neck and his watch still running. The Montgomery County coroner concluded that death was instantaneous.[60]

The corpsman Prise had returned to his barracks room, but could not sleep. After tossing restlessly for an hour, he got dressed and was walking across the hospital yard for a cup of coffee at the canteen when he was suddenly aware of a great commotion all around him. Instantly, instinctively, he knew what had happened. Racing to the hospital lobby, he arrived just as the young doctor whom he had tried unsuccessfully to warn emerged from an elevator. The doctor's face was a mask of anguish and agony. As Prise watched, he grasped the left sleeve of his white jacket with his right hand and, in a moment of blind madness, tore it from his arm. Prise was doubly crushed by Forrestal's death; in frequent friendly exchanges over several weeks, he had come to regard Forrestal as "the most interesting man I ever met." But more than that, Forrestal had asked Prise to work for him after he left the hospital—as chauffeur, valet, man Friday. The details had not been filled in, but Prise felt there was a genuine bond between them, and a job with a great and famous man meant a once-in-a-lifetime opportunity. "It was my one big chance," he said later.[61]

In Paris, Michael Forrestal telephoned Oatsie Lighter, who was in France for a few days. He was excited, his voice taut with apprehension. "I've just heard the most incredible rumor. On the radio. Something about my father having jumped out of the hospital window. I've tried to call the Embassy, but no one knows anything." Mrs. Lighter told him to get hold of the Embassy duty officer. Half an hour later he called back and said simply, "It's true." They agreed they should both get over to the Ritz, where Jo was staying, as soon as possible. When Oatsie Lighter arrived in the suite, Jo had evidently heard the news and was already putting clothes in a suitcase for the trip back to Washington. "Oh, I'm so glad you came over," she said. "Have a drink." They both had a drink. Jo seemed subdued, but composed and unemotional. She made no mention of her husband and, so, neither did her friend. For some reason, Michael did not arrive. When one suitcase was packed, but before Jo could start on a second, Oatsie said, "Let's get out of this room." So "we went down to the garden of the Ritz, and at that moment the Duchess of Argyll came along and I introduced her to Jo. It was a beautiful day in May. The conversation went on as if absolutely nothing had happened."[62]

President Truman learned of the suicide on a 7:00 a.m. radio broadcast and promptly issued a statement saying he was "inexpressibly shocked and grieved." He added, "This able and devoted public servant was as truly a casualty of the war as if he had died on the firing line." He declared a period of national mourning to last for three days (until after Forrestal's funeral on May 25), during which all government flags at home, abroad, and at sea were to be flown at half-mast. He sent his personal aircraft, the *Independence,* to Paris to bring back Jo Forrestal and Michael. Acting Army Secretary Gordon Gray called Forrestal a "pioneer of unification" who suffered "all the hardships" which come to "true pioneers in a great cause." Navy Secretary John J. Sullivan mourned "the passing of this distinguished public servant" whose accomplishments had "earned him the admiration of all Americans." Air Force Secretary Stuart Symington called attention to his own "many years of personal and official association" with Forrestal which added, he said, to his "great shock" at Forrestal's death.[63]

Bernard Baruch said Forrestal "died from duty in war and public service" and that duty is "the most ennobling spirit that drives us." Louis Johnson said, "The shock of Mr. Forrestal's death touches me deeply." Dwight D. Eisenhower said America has "lost a citizen of heroic mold" who "dedicated all his strengths and all his talents to our country."

Statements of sadness, condolence, and affection poured in from all over the world. Newspaper editorials expressed high praise, including the London *Times,* which called Forrestal "one of the most able statesmen" of his country and "a firm friend of Britain."[64]

The navy was gravely embarrassed by the suicide. Raines returned immediately from the psychiatric conference in Montreal and accepted full responsibility for the tragedy, but his public explanation was unavoidably defensive and less than persuasive: "Psychiatrically, it is my opinion that Mr. Forrestal was seized with a sudden fit of despondence in the evening and early morning of May 22." Such a seizure is "extremely common" in severe depressions and is an inherent risk. The navy believes that "calculated risks must be accepted for the practice of modern psychiatry" and "does not subscribe to the view that psychiatric patients should be thrown in a dungeon."[65] This was presumably an effort to explain why the navy had taken elaborate precautions to make the windows of Forrestal's room tamper-proof while leaving totally unguarded the window of the diet kitchen which he was encouraged to use. There was a certain logic in the view that granting the patient increasing latitude and trust was essential to his recovery, but there was no logic in housing a suicidal patient in a tower room sixteen floors above the ground. An unbarred window in a pantry on the first floor would have been a reasonable risk to take; on the sixteenth floor it represented a tragic possibility whose damage could not be limited.

Raines was not responsible for putting Forrestal in the tower room, and he had recognized the dangers and taken certain measures to reduce them. But the unguarded pantry window was an astonishing oversight. Even then, however, it might not have proved a fatal flaw if Forrestal had been dealing with a navy corpsman who knew him, understood the risks of leaving him unattended, and was firmly determined to carry out his orders. One might say that the chance events which brought a new corpsman to duty at midnight were an intervention of fate which, when added to Raines's terrible mistake of not barring the pantry window, produced a tragedy that would otherwise have been averted. But this scenario leaves out the intentions— sudden or premeditated—of a highly intelligent, shrewd, and secretive patient. At one point after the event, Raines told Robert Sherrod of *Time,* "He could have killed himself many different ways. He was a very smart man."[66] It was, however, the navy's first duty to make sure that did not happen.

The first error was the political decision, taken by Josephine with White House reinforcement, to send Forrestal to Bethesda rather than to the Menninger Clinic. The second error was to put him in the VIP suite on the sixteenth floor instead of the one-story psychiatric building that was staffed and equipped to deal with mental patients. The third error was not to secure the exit from the pantry window as the windows of his bedroom had been secured. The last and in many ways the culminating error was for Raines to leave town for a week at the beginning of a period which he later described as "the most dangerous period of the illness as far as sui-cide was concerned" for "suicidal preoccupations had to be present, and at the same time privileges had to be extended" to promote recovery.[67]

The editor of the Washington *Post,* Herbert Elliston, wrote that the numbing shock of the suicide was a matter for which "the doctors and their bulletins are in great part to blame." There was "something wicked" about the disingenuous way in which the illness was handled. "The med-ical men certainly owe an explanation for their false reporting or for their carelessness in looking after their distinguished patient."[68]

A more direct attack on the navy came from the American Psychiatric Association. Reflecting an apparent consensus of its members, Albert Deutsch wrote that "the most serious aspect" of the suicide "lies in the fact that the Brass Hats not only told the public that Forrestal had no psychosis, but that they really believed what they said." It is "no secret," Deutsch argued, that "Navy medicine is hostile to psychiatry," believes mental illness is a "disgrace" and that it is unpatriotic to admit the pos-sibility, especially in any case involving "a Very Important Person." The navy's frequent references to "battle fatigue" and "nervous exhaustion" and its placement of the patient in the VIP suite on the sixteenth floor underline the navy's adherence to "these pernicious myths."[69]

Forrestal's death fostered several enduring suppositions that the end was not suicide, but murder. Henry Forrestal, for one, believed "they" mur-dered his brother, a position based in large part on his conviction that no man of Forrestal's courage and stamina could kill himself. The murderous "they" were variously identified as "the Communists" or "the Jews," and their nefarious work had the necessary connivance of the highest au-thorities in the United States government. But the facts of the case, begin-ning well before Forrestal entered the hospital and including the Menninger and Raines diagnoses of his illness, effectively refute the murder theory.[70]

CHAPTER 33

★ ★ ★

Final Honors
and Assessment

O N THE MORNING of May 25, a bright clear day in spring, Forrestal was buried with full military honors in Arlington National
Cemetery, at a ceremony attended by the President and his Cabinet, the leaders of Congress, the diplomatic corps, and about 2,500 friends
and associates. An additional 4,000 onlookers stood beyond a velvet rope
at the end of the large white marble amphitheater. Howitzers boomed each
gun of a nineteen-gun salute at three-minute intervals, as the caisson bearing the flag-draped casket, led by troops of all the military services, wound
slowly up the sloping road to a deliberate beat of muffled drums. In the
background, the Naval Academy Band played Beethoven's "March of the
Hero," Chopin's "Funeral March," and Handel's "March from *Saul*."
President Truman and Vice President Alben Barkley met the casket on the
stage of the chapel, together with the honorary pallbearers chosen from
among Forrestal's closest friends.* The Right Reverend Wallace Bishop of
the Protestant Episcopal Diocese of Chicago read from the forty-sixth and
one hundred thirtieth psalms and from First Corinthians 15:20-58 in *The
Episcopal Book of Common Prayer.*[1] Senator Arthur Vandenberg confided
his impressions to his diary that evening: "It was a full military funeral.
Of course Jimmy wasn't very big, but the casket looked so *small*! . . .
There was something about it all which was infinitely tragic and yet so
spiritually exalted."[2]

Following the official ceremony, the casket was returned to the caisson
and wheeled a few hundred yards to the gravesite, where the burial was
witnessed by the immediate family, relatives, and a few close associates.
Josephine did not attend the larger official ceremony, but was at the grave-

---

*The honorary pallbearers were Herbert Hoover, Fred Vinson, James Byrnes, George Marshall,
Dwight Eisenhower, Bernard Baruch, Ferdinand Eberstadt, Dean Mathey, and Paul Shields.

site with her two sons. Forrestal's brother, Henry, was present, together with his wife and their two children (a daughter, Mary, and a son, James, named for the former Secretary of Defense). Michael Forrestal said later this was the first time he had ever met any member of his father's family.[3]

The inscription finally engraved on the tombstone reads:

James Forrestal
Lt., U.S.N.R.F.
World War I
Under Secretary of the Navy
Secretary of the Navy
First Secretary of Defense
World War II
Born 1892—Died 1949

In The Great Cause of Good Government

Expressions of sympathy and praise continued to pour in, and all of them showed an awareness that Forrestal's exertions on behalf of his country had been exceptional. Senator Millard Tydings called him "part poet and part warrior," and Illinois Democratic Senator Scott Lucas, the Senate Majority Leader, said Forrestal had given "every ounce of his energy, every thought of his brilliant mind to the service of his country." Congressman Paul Shafer, a member of the House Armed Services Committee, said, "J. V. Forrestal hated the Communists . . . hated the thoughts of their undermining this land of ours, in which he had been able to work himself up from a poor man to one of wealth and high position . . . Let us pray that all of us fight as good and as long a fight as did Jim Forrestal."[4]

Democratic congressman Hale Boggs (from Louisiana) was one of the first to link the "tragic manner" of Forrestal's death with "a campaign of abuse and vilification the like of which I have never heard." Without naming Drew Pearson or Walter Winchell, he castigated "irresponsible elements" of the press for "attacking men of character and honor" with "the cruel weapons of distorted words," which are "more devastating than machine-guns or mortars."[5]

The lead editorial in *Newsday* for May 24 accused the American public of having a large hand in the tragedy—for its tradition of ingratitude to able public servants. Under monarchies "they were awarded homage and honors in accordance with their worth," but under the American political system "they are excoriated by panderers of unfounded and false tales of their personal lives. . . . Unfortunately, there is a public appetite for the poisonous fare of these gossips."[6] Hanson Baldwin thought the attacks imposed a "burden of shame" on the whole American press and "seared deeply a very sensitive man"; he expressed regret that Forrestal had not resigned as Secretary of Defense six months after he had launched the new enterprise: "His contribution had been made and it was a great one; he had worn himself out for the nation; he deserved a rest."[7]

On May 23, the American Psychiatric Association issued a statement from Montreal which seemed to support Dr. Raines's private comment to *Time* correspondent Robert Sherrod that "Pearson and Winchell killed Forrestal." Noting that for every person there is a breaking point in the face of ceaseless pressures, the association said that while Forrestal was "being given the finest kind of medical care he was subjected to the destructive influence of unenlightened attacks." The suicide was "a familiar reaction to excessive stresses and strains."[8]

Arthur Krock, calling the death "a very great tragedy of our time," drew a parallel between Forrestal and Castlereagh, the British Foreign Secretary who masterminded the Congress of Vienna in 1815 which gave Europe what was later somewhat inaccurately proclaimed "a hundred years of peace" following the Napoleonic Wars. Exhausted from his labors to maintain the fragile three-power unity of England, France, and Russia that undergirded the arrangement, Castlereagh was beset by a "flood of calumny" from enemies in Parliament and the press and thereby reduced to the point of nervous collapse. Suspecting spies everywhere and threats upon his life, he stabbed himself with a small penknife which his friends had failed to notice when they had taken away his pistols and razors several days before. On the morning of August 12, 1822, he summoned his doctor to come at once to his bedroom. When the doctor arrived, Castlereagh was standing by the window looking out, his hands above his head and his throat cut. "Bankhead," he gasped, "let me fall on your arm; I have opened my throat; it is all over."[9]

Drew Pearson tried to shift criticism away from himself to the "little coterie" of friends and newspapermen who had urged Forrestal to stay in office long after he was "not a well man." He confided to his diary, which was published in 1974, that Forrestal had died because "he had no spiritual reserves [and] . . . no calluses. . . . He had traveled not on the hard political path of the politician, but on the protected, cloistered avenue of the Wall Street bankers. . . . He did not know what the lash of criticism meant."[10] This further demagoguery proved an unconvincing defense. Several years later, Pearson's right-hand man, Jack Anderson, wrote a remarkable indictment of Pearson's behavior in the Forrestal case and of Anderson's own part in the deliberate, carefully calibrated character assassination.

Anderson acknowledged that "our hand was surely in this tragedy" and that Pearson's methods flagrantly exceeded the norms of legitimate reporting and even the furthest limits of advocacy: the use of symbols depicting Forrestal as a "Wall Streeter" (after eight years of continuous public service) and thus automatically as an accomplice of oil barons and Arab sheiks; the "repeated draping of Hitler around Forrestal's neck" because he had belonged to a firm that sold German bonds in the 1920s; the insistent theme that Forrestal's support for a policy of economic recovery in Germany was sowing the seeds of another German-instigated world war.[11] These demagogic themes, played and replayed in prescheduled weekly assaults, were techniques freely used by Nazi and Communist propagandists, but rarely seen in the American press, or at least in those segments of any reputation for integrity. Moreover, the attacks were not pegged to any fresh information that might conceivably be considered "news," but were simply an endless repetition of stale falsehoods calculated, like the Chinese water torture, to drive the victim to distraction, to destroy a high reputation, to hound a dedicated patriot from office.

The breakdown and suicide were "a searing experience" for Robert Lovett and others who "loved Jim Forrestal." Aware of his friend's strengths and vulnerabilities, Lovett's memory was haunted for a long time thereafter by "the shocking state of a mind unhinged . . . the dismal spectacle of a man we cherished and admired—at bay, alone, persecuted and on the defensive, without cause, without reason."[12]

ASSESSMENT

JAMES FORRESTAL was an exceedingly complex personality whose central characteristic may have been its elusiveness. Ernest Havemann of *Life*, interviewing him for an article in 1947, concluded that only a novel could encompass the subtle shadings and contradictions of his character, and indeed John O'Hara, John Dos Passos, and George Backer all wrote novels whose central figures were modeled on Forrestal. There is in the Forrestal story a good deal of the stuff of ancient legend: the young man from the provinces whose origins are obscure, even mysterious, and which he is at pains not to clarify; equipped with intelligence, ambition, pride, and poverty, he determines upon a campaign to know and conquer the Great World, initially to gain a share of the power and pleasure that are to be found there in abundance, but ultimately to formulate and pursue a transcendent ideal. To reach these goals he takes real risks with his life. At the same time, his swift progress leaves him uncertain of his true identity, and to mask this vulnerability he builds around himself a protective wall of reserve and mystery, a barrier that subtly armors him against intrusion or precise definition. Forrestal was "the Dane, the divided man," his friend John J. McCloy said of him,[13] and numerous people over the years thought he gave the curious impression of a man everybody and nobody knew, combining a gregarious disposition with a solitary soul.

These complexities and contradictions were traceable to his roots in the economically and socially humble part of Dutchess County and to the prevailing American ethos at the beginning of the twentieth century. A boy of sensitive intelligence, he quickly perceived it was better to be rich than poor, white than black, Protestant than Catholic. He was naturally ambitious in a period dominated by the Horatio Alger work ethic. Distinction, not equality, was the goal, and there was in the precariousness of Forrestal's family situation a natural incentive to break out and achieve "success." Early circumstance thus imbued him with a consuming desire to get on, to keep moving, onward and upward, in a restless drive for the prizes acclaimed by society. That he was a driven man no one doubted. His boyhood friends could not remember a time when he was without ambition or stubborn resolve to succeed, and no one in their circle worked harder or longer or with more single-minded determination to master the matter immediately at hand. But the sources of his drive were complex: The combination of a stern, religious mother and a pliable, permissive father produced in the son a personality that was more introspective and uncertain than intrinsically self-confident, and this insecurity led to extraordinary efforts to prove himself—to develop a fighting physique, to become learned, to get rich, to exercise power, to impress others in his later years as the very model of a modern philosopher-king, even as some objective inner sentinel deflated the importance or consequence of his achievements (and found expression in the wry self-derogation that characterizes much of his correspondence).

He seemed to work throughout his life, not merely for success, but in search of some majestic solitude, some emotionally unassailable status which he seemed to regard as the means to a transcendent ideal of mastery; to reach this state, it was necessary steadfastly to evade and reject emotional commitments of a personal nature. Most men try to build and nurture emotional refuges against the world's adversity. Forrestal did not. When adversity arrived in great strength, he was utterly alone, yet fatally unequipped to sustain the psychological isolation he had long cultivated and finally achieved.

His insecurities were revealed in various ways at critical junctures in his life—his abrupt departure from Princeton owing to his lack of one credit confronted him with the humiliation of not graduating with his class; his cautious refusal to go beyond covert support for Wall Street reforms; his unreadiness to risk a break with Clarence Dillon and start a new firm with Ferdinand Eberstadt; his inability to deal rationally with Josephine's illness or with the tattered ruins of their marriage; the apparent emotional emptiness of his love affairs; and his acute vulnerability to press attacks on his personal integrity and his manhood.

Like a character in a Theodore Dreiser tragedy, or the hero of F. Scott

Fitzgerald's *The Great Gatsby,* he seemed permanently uncertain of place: the Wall Street conservative who was uncomfortable with liberals in Washington, but who was more liberal than his Wall Street associates; the Irish mick who had thought that Princeton and Wall Street spelled the ultimate in grace, charm, success, and strength, but who came to a later awareness of the shallower aspects of the American Dream while continuing to seek diversion (as one friend said) in "the company of men who never ceased to see the Racquet Club as a social nirvana."[14]

He was extremely intelligent, but rarely gave himself time for reflection and assimilation. Throughout the Wall Street period, he was a driven striver, always on the go, and the urgent circumstances of the war and its aftermath did not facilitate long-range thinking. But even by the contemporary standards of the time, Forrestal was a conspicuous workaholic driven by the immediate practical problems. In Washington, seeking background on broad policy issues, he tried to digest large, intricate subjects from terse memoranda written at his direction by staffers whose own comprehension was at best questionable. An exceedingly quick study, he could parade his new knowledge persuasively in Cabinet meetings or across dinner tables, but his views often lacked the depth and conviction that come from mature consideration. The Washington *Post*'s Herbert Elliston wrote that Forrestal read voraciously, but "whether he digested what he read is another matter."[15] At the same time, he was a man of genuine intellectual humility and eagerness for new knowledge. Aware that solutions to large problems involve continuous adjustment and refinement, he was unafraid of new ideas and approaches and disposed to doubt that any existing situation was fully satisfactory. This posture proved a strength and a weakness. It enlarged his understanding of major issues—he "grew but never swelled," as one admirer wrote—but a greater appreciation of their complexities also reinforced an innate caution, a natural ambivalence, and rendered it ever more difficult for him to make decisions with confidence or conviction. He was in a sense "cursed" by the ability to see both sides of every hard question.

After mid-1947, these tendencies were aggravated by a severe and progressive fatigue. It was his tragedy, and the nation's, that he could not leave government at any one of several logical juncture points and give himself an interval for rest and reflection, but could respond to mounting difficulties only by working even harder and longer. Propelled by a growing obsession with the Communist threat and a sense that the whole American system was failing to meet the mortal challenge, he placed ever greater demands on his extraordinary physical stamina and disciplined drive which, more than his intellect, had formed the basis of the conspicuous success he had achieved through most of his life. He had geared his life to this driven style and could not live otherwise. In his tired mind, he was led to the conclusion that he must personally remain in permanent vigil on the watchtower. The nation's danger became his danger; the nation's failure, his failure. The result was a reckless abuse of his physical and mental powers which, aggravated by hostile press attacks and growing self-doubt, led predictably to exhaustion and despair, and to a wholly disproportionate sense of personal failure; these in turn snapped his vaunted control and made him victim to inner demons he had long suppressed.

Forrestal's tragic end does not in any way obscure the fact that, throughout most of his life, he was a man of singular attractiveness, an ebullient man who savored life's challenges and pleasures and the rewards of success, and who performed his work with conspicuous ability and distinction. He was, until his last few months in office, a public servant of great talent, influence, and accomplishment. The single most impressive and least ambiguous achievement of his career was the building of the magnificent navy that crushed its Japanese counterpart in the Pacific and supported massive amphibious invasions and landings along the road to victory in Europe, Asia, and Africa. That extraordinary feat was, of course, the work of many thousands of dedicated people, civilian and military, in the navy and in industry. But it was Forrestal primarily who analyzed, organized, rationalized, energized, and accelerated the whole vast, intricate process. As Congressman Vinson put it at the farewell ceremony, it was Forrestal's "high historic privilege to guide the destiny of the largest Navy in all the history of man—probably the largest Navy ever again to be seen."[16]

Late in the war and throughout the early postwar period, Forrestal made major contributions to national policy; yet his dominant concern, growing as experience confirmed his instinctive appreciation of the need, was often less for the content of policy than for the means of devising and applying it. In his period of Cabinet rank he understood, better than anyone else at the top of government, that the United States urgently needed, and dangerously lacked, the men and the methods to identify and define its own critical security problems and to meet these with reasoned policies backed by coordinated effort and resources. He grasped the necessity to deal with the components of international problems—their political, military, economic, informational, and scientific elements—as parts of a related whole. And he succeeded in bringing this concept to organizational reality at a time when most of his colleagues in government, including the Presidents he served, regarded this as "a novel and rather annoying doctrine."[17] In a real sense, he was the godfather of the national security state.

When he addressed the question of postwar organization of the military services per se, his judgment failed him, in largest part because he had become too much a navy partisan who could not separate his emotional loyalty to that service from his instinctive awareness that some form of "unification" was both a practical necessity and a political inevitability.

Allowing himself to become the principal spokesman for a navy officer corps that was bitterly opposed to any organizational change, he succeeded in achieving a weak and unworkable compromise, an outcome that deprived the new overseer, the Secretary of Defense, of both the authority and the staff required to tame the fierce interservice rivalries and to channel their energies into an integrated military strategy. Then, fatefully, he accepted the new job and discovered he had succeeded only too well.

The emerging realization that his concept of military organization was seriously flawed delivered a severe shock to his self-confidence and presented him with the prospect of a major personal failure—perhaps for the first time in his life. Already tired from eight years of unremitting labor for the nation, his response to the new difficulty was to apply himself with redoubled effort to make the flawed system work. But he compounded the legal limitations on his authority by an unwillingness to "crack down and make heads roll" in the face of the persistent refusal of the military services to agree on common strategies.[18] Lacking the hard convictions of simpler men, temperamentally and philosophically unready to dismiss uncooperative or disloyal subordinates, he was unable to impose his will on the sprawling hybrid then called the National Military Establishment.

He discerned in Soviet purposes a clear threat to American security sooner than did many of his peers in government, and his firm convictions here contributed importantly to bringing forth a coherent policy of containment out of the welter of confusion in the immediate aftermath of war. Following the recklessly swift demobilization of America's wartime armed forces, he advocated a moderate rebuilding of military strength to balance off Russian power and impose caution on its Communist leaders, but he was never an advocate of preventive war. Near the end of his tenure, he developed an obsession about Communism, to the point of frenzy, convinced that the cold war was merely the prelude to shooting war, but this was only one of many symptoms of the physical and psychological disintegration triggered by his physical exhaustion.

His stance on the size of U.S. military forces was reasonable and moderate, but it was frustrated by President Truman's categorical insistence on a balanced budget, even in the face of increasingly ominous world developments. Forrestal shared Truman's concern that excessive military spending could endanger the economy, but felt that to tempt the Soviet Union with military weakness was a greater danger. In retrospect, it is clear that both he and Truman seriously underestimated the strength and productive capacity of the American economy. He sought to hold a reasonable balance between the nation's commitments and its capabilities, but his effort to find a middle ground between the President and the military services cost him Truman's confidence without satisfying the Joint Chiefs of Staff.

The need for greater military readiness was painfully realized in 1950 when the attack on South Korea found the United States woefully unprepared to respond. At the same time, it must be noted that the Joint Chiefs had no plans to defend Korea in wartime and that Forrestal's slightly larger military budget would not have significantly strengthened the ability of American forces to deter or repel the initial attack. Nevertheless, Truman's rejection of his estimate of military requirements was a depressing experience for Forrestal; it led him to believe that the White House, like the country, was oblivious to what he saw as the mounting danger that the Soviets would at some point resort to military attack. Truman was proved right in relying on the judgment of Soviet experts who advised that Stalin would not initiate *general* war, but both he and they misjudged the Kremlin's readiness to effect changes in the world power balance by proxy wars and other limited military means. Also, Truman was lucky that the success of the Berlin Airlift obviated the need for the Western allies to assert their right of access to the German capital by more direct and more dangerous military means.

In the Palestine affair, Forrestal was, along with the entire leadership of the State Department and the military services, concerned with the protection of U.S. interests in the Middle East, which they felt would be seriously jeopardized by American sponsorship of a Jewish state. His innate patriotism led him to believe American Jews would, or should, be U.S. citizens first and thus ready to recognize and support evident national interests. He had always despised his immigrant father's pro-Irish stance and had severed his own residual ties of sentiment to the Old World. This seemed to him the clear civic duty of every American, but he paid dearly for his lack of sophistication on that point. Beyond the substantive issue, he was troubled and alarmed by the messy, sordid, fantastically disordered way in which American policy on Palestine was determined, for he was passionately devoted to orderly process.

Indeed, Walter Lippmann thought Forrestal's deepest anguish was the "almost unmanageable" character of the American government in the postwar period and what he saw as the general failure to modify its organization and its methods to meet the new requirements of global responsibility, including the creation of incentives to attract and hold the most competent and wisest men. This preoccupation became Forrestal's "own insoluble and unendurable personal problem," and he blamed himself for an inordinate share of the institutional failure.[19] The appointment of Louis Johnson must have been a crushing blow to his conviction that survival of the nation depended on bringing forth the best men to lead the government. It may well have been the final disillusion to his whole idea of disinterested excellence in the public service.

In his passionate labors "In The Great Cause of Good Government" (the inscription on his tombstone), which more and more came to resemble the legendary hero's quest for the transcendent ideal, Forrestal tended to minimize the central place of politics in the American system and thus to believe the process of government could be more rational than was actually the case. He liked to dabble on the political fringes and was effective in working with elected officials, but he shrank from what seemed to him the squalor of full participation. Franklin Roosevelt liked and valued him; Harry Truman respected him; neither was wholly at ease with him, nor he with them, for his inability to come fully to terms with the less attractive aspects of politics made it impossible for him to come fully to terms with those two thoroughly professional politicians.[20]

In sum, Forrestal was a meld of great ability, noble ambition, innate patriotism, deep dedication, and selfless labor, and his contributions to government rank with those of his distinguished contemporaries, including Henry Stimson, George Marshall, Dwight Eisenhower, Ernest J. King, Chester Nimitz, Robert Patterson, Robert Lovett, John McCloy, Dean Acheson, and Averell Harriman, who fashioned the great victory of World War II and then laid the solid foundations of the postwar era. He cared deeply about government, and he brought to public service a rare, instinctive appetite for its work. He believed the United States must have the very best attainable government, best in terms of both organization and men. His tragedy was that his standards were higher and nobler than contemporary circumstances could sustain, and he was thus consumed by his quest for a transcendent ideal.

It is plausible to see James Forrestal as a figure of fate in the classic sense, doomed by his genes, by the times, by his inner nature—a man so driven by habit, by the compulsion to master and resolve, by the fear of failure, by the fear of love—that confrontation with intractable obstacles never led him to detached reflection and reconsideration of his premises, but always to a frenzied redoubling of personal effort. It is plausible to conclude that his inability ever to pause, look back, disengage himself even temporarily from the swift onrush of impersonal events led inexorably to the window in the hospital tower at Bethesda. Michael Forrestal once remarked that had his father been more balanced he would have been less interesting.

FORRESTAL'S COUNTRYMEN showed their respect for his impressive and enduring contributions to the nation by establishing several public monuments in his honor and to his memory. The navy's newest and largest cant-deck aircraft carrier was christened the U.S.S. *Forrestal* in 1954; an imposing new office building in downtown Washington, part of a quadrangle known as L'Enfant Plaza, was named the James Forrestal Building; and in 1975, Princeton University named its new corporate research park, adjacent to the campus, the Princeton Forrestal Center, and it soon attracted over fifty corporate tenants, including IBM, Exxon, and RCA.

Josephine Forrestal spent a number of years after her husband's death traveling restlessly, living in France, Ireland, and Jamaica, before eventually settling in Newport, Rhode Island. The house on Prospect Street in Washington was sold in 1951 to a North Carolina congressman for $187,000. According to friends, Jo was "in and out of clinics" for a number of years, but there was no significant change in her condition. She kept an apartment at 399 Park Avenue in New York and for a time rented this to Robert Sherrod, the war correspondent who had become editor of *The Saturday Evening Post*. According to Sherrod, she would appear infrequently on a trip from France or Ireland and drop in for a drink: "By this time she had devised a sort of reverse martini—four parts vermouth to one part gin; unfortunately, this conscious dilution of content did not significantly alter the result." On another occasion she telephoned her old friends the William Lords, who were now living in Easthampton, Long Island. Jo was in the adjacent town of Southampton and wanted to visit them for two or three days. Her Southampton hostess chauffeured her to the Lords', afraid to trust her alone on the highway. Jo put on ostrich feathers for dinner, but could not manage to match her stockings, and her behavior was so bizarre that even the usually relaxed and tolerant Lords found it impossible to cope with it. Jo departed the next day.

Living in Newport, she developed a close relationship with a great-niece, Millicent Ogden McKinley Cox, and dabbled in the performing arts. She backed several local theatrical productions, including *Double Dublin* and Leonard Bernstein's *Theatre Sons,* and made sporadic efforts to write seriously. She finished a play called *Democracy,* set in Washington in 1889

Peter, Josephine, and Michael Forrestal at the launching of the U.S.S. Forrestal
(CVA-59), Newport News, Virginia, December 1954

and bearing a resemblance to Henry Adams's famous novel of the same name and setting. In a comment on the transient nature of prestige and social standing in democratic America, one of her characters says that every "kindly mannered, pleasant voiced" woman and every "brave, unassuming" man is given "a free pass in every city and village," but it is marked "Good for This Generation Only." The play was never produced. The journalist John McLain asked her to collaborate with him on a biography of Forrestal, but the project "ultimately failed to excite her." McLain started work on the book, but died before its completion; some of his research appears to have been used in Arnold Rogow's 1963 biography. Josephine Ogden Forrestal died on January 5, 1976, twenty-seven years after her husband's death. She was seventy-six.

After his work with the Marshall Plan in Paris and graduation from the Harvard Law School in 1953, Michael Forrestal joined the New York firm of Shearman and Sterling. In 1962, he went to Washington as a member of the small, elite National Security Council staff under McGeorge Bundy in the Kennedy White House. In Washington, he lived with the Averell Harrimans, who, since his father's death, had taken him under their sheltering and affectionate wing almost like an adopted son. After President

Kennedy's assassination in 1963, he was back in his New York law practice, where he remained for the next twenty-five years as a partner and later a senior partner of the firm. He worked quietly and effectively to promote trade and better understanding between the United States and the Soviet Union. He was president of the US-USSR Trade Council (1978–1980) and later a founder of the American Trade Consortium, which sought to arrange joint ventures with Soviet commercial interests. He served as president of the trustees of Phillips Exeter Academy and was a long-time patron of the Metropolitan Opera in New York, as well as an avid deepwater sailor who voyaged extensively in the Caribbean and other seas of the world. He never married. He died instantly on January 11, 1989, of an aneurysm, while chairing a committee of the governing board of Lincoln Center. He was sixty-one.

After Princeton, Peter Forrestal went to work for Dillon, Read, then moved over to F. Eberstadt and Company and later to Train and Cabot, an investment advisory firm. Like his mother, he loved horses and was an expert, dashing rider. And like his mother, he had difficulty handling alcoholic drink. His last job was with Bankers Trust in London, and he had a place in Ireland where he kept his horses. He died alone there in 1983 of a massive abdominal hemorrhage caused by years of heavy drinking. He was fifty-two. Twelve months before, he had married a young woman from New Jersey, Katherine ''Kit'' Callahan, and she was pregnant with their child when he died. She gave birth to a daughter named Francesca. As a friend later noted with sadness, ''Kit was a bride, a widow and a mother all within the space of a single year.''

NOTES

ACRONYMS AND ABBREVIATIONS

FDRL   Franklin D. Roosevelt Library, Hyde Park, New York,

JVF   James V. Forrestal

FRUS   U.S. Department of State. Foreign Relations of the United States. Washington, D.C.: Council on Foreign Relations

JFP   The Papers of James V. Forrestal, Seeley Mudd Library, Princeton University, Princeton, New Jersey

OSD   Office of the Secretary of Defense Historical Office, Pentagon, Arlington, Virginia

PPF   President's Personal File, Franklin D. Roosevelt Library, Hyde Park, New York

The 1951 edition of *The Forrestal Diaries* (Viking Press, New York), edited by Walter Millis, was a valuable source in the preparation of this book. Prior to its publication, a number of the diary entries were deleted by government censors on the grounds of national security. In recent years, however, all of these unpublished entries have been available to scholars at the Seeley G. Mudd Library at Princeton University, at the Office of the Defense Historian at the Pentagon, and at the Naval Historical Center, Washington, D.C. Citations from the complete unedited materials are identified in these notes as Unpublished Forrestal Diaries.

CHAPTER 1   FOREBEARS, PARENTS, AND SIBLINGS

1. *Peekskill, Matteawan, and Cold Spring* (Newark, N.J., 1892), pp. 44–65. Published the year of Forrestal's birth, the book includes a chapter, "Fishkill-on-Hudson," that offers a detailed description of 1890s Matteawan as well as a historical overview of Fishkill Township.

2. Ibid. See also James H. Smith, *History of Dutchess County* (Syracuse, 1882), p. 529.

3. Morgan H. Hoyt, "Turning Back the Clock," Beacon *News,* March 1, 1949. Hoyt owned the Matteawan *Journal* for over twenty-five years. After Hoyt retired from the publishing business in 1946 he became a columnist with the Beacon *News.* His column, "Turning Back the Clock," reminisced about the early years of the century. Much of the material in this chapter about Matteawan and the young James Forrestal comes from Hoyt's columns in the late 1940s and early 1950s.

4. American Guide Series, *Dutchess County* (Federal Writers' Project, 1937), pp. 62–78.

5. Ibid.

6. James V. Forrestal speech, New York Rubber Corporation, Beacon, N.Y., Oc-

tober 18, 1943, The Papers of Forrestal, Box 5, Seeley G. Mudd Library, Princeton University (hereafter cited as JFP).

7. JVF to Ernest Havemann, August 26, 1947, Princeton University, JFP. See also Quentin Reynolds, "He Built Our Navy," *Collier's,* July 15, 1944, p. 71.

8. "Forrestal's Father Came Alone from Ireland at the Age of 9," Boston *Globe,* May 13, 1944. For overviews of the Irish migration to America, see Kerby Miller, *Emigrants and Exiles: Ireland and the Irish Exodus to North America* (Baltimore, 1985), and Carl Witkee, *The Irish in America* (Baton Rouge, 1956).

9. For a brief overview of Forrestal's childhood, see Arnold A. Rogow, *James Forrestal: A Study of Personality, Politics, and Policy* (New York, 1963), pp. 49–57. See also Brinkley interview with Michael Forrestal, April 27, 1988.

10. Ibid. See also JVF to Michael Forrestal, December 5, 1945, Princeton University, JFP.

11. Morgan H. Hoyt and P. H. Vosburgh, *Beacon circa 1900,* a souvenir program printed at the time of the annual firemen's parade.

12. For information on Mary Forrestal, see Rogow, *James Forrestal,* pp. 52–54; James V. Forrestal speech, Newburgh, N.Y., Chamber of Commerce, March 7, 1947, Princeton University, JFP; and Brinkley interview with Michael Forrestal, April 27, 1988.

13. Brinkley interview with Michael Forrestal, May 18, 1988. For a Sullivan biography that includes an early social history of boxing in America, see Michael T. Isenberg, *John L. Sullivan and His America* (Urbana, Ill., 1988). For Beacon boxing lore see Morgan H. Hoyt, "Recollections of Old Dutchess" (unpublished manuscript), Chapter 7, "Pastimes of Past Times" (in authors' possession).

14. Ernest Havemann, "Forrestal," *Life,* October 6, 1948, pp. 67–77.

15. James V. Forrestal speech, Friendly Sons of St. Patrick, NYC, March 17, 1949, Princeton University, JFP.

16. Rogow, *James Forrestal,* p. 51; Brinkley interview with Michael Forrestal, April 27, 1988.

17. For information on Henry and Will Forrestal, see Rogow, *James Forrestal,* pp. 54–55; Leon Prochnik, *Endings* (New York, 1980), p. 124; and Brinkley interview with Michael Forrestal, April 27, 1988.

18. Edythe Holbrook interview with Mary Pennybacker, October 5, 1982.

19. Brinkley interview with Michael Forrestal, April 27, 1988; Rogow, *James Forrestal,* pp. 49–56; and Forrestal speech, Newburgh, N.Y., Chamber of Commerce, March 7, 1947, Princeton University, JFP.

20. Havemann, "Forrestal," *Life,* October 6, 1948, p. 68. See also Prochnik, *Endings,* p. 124.

21. JVF to Sarah W. Snowden, March 15, 1947, Princeton University, JFP.

22. See Hoyt and Vosburgh, *Beacon circa 1900,* and Hoyt's columns, "Turning Back the Clock," which often mention James Forrestal, Sr. See also Brinkley interview with Michael Forrestal, April 27, 1988. Michael Forrestal spent an afternoon with Farley discussing his father and grandfather.

23. For Hoyt-Forrestal conversation regarding the 1910 election and young FDR, see Hoyt, "The Dutchess County Roosevelt," Chapter 1, "Roosevelt Enters Politics." See also Ted Morgan, *FDR: A Biography* (New York, 1985), p. 114.

24. Quoted in Hoyt, "The Dutchess County Roosevelt," Chapter 1, "Roosevelt Enters Politics," p. 3.

25. Hoyt, "The Dutchess County Roosevelt," Chapter 5, "And Now He Is President." Hoyt describes all of FDR's presidential campaigns in Dutchess County.

26. Photo inscription published in Rogow, *James Forrestal,* p. 51. For Henry Forrestal's recollection of FDR staying in the Forrestal home in Beacon, see, "Forrestal's Father Came Alone from Ireland at the Age of 9," Boston *Globe,* May 13, 1944. See also Franklin D. Roosevelt to James Forrestal, Sr., November 12, 1912, FDR Memorial Library, Hyde Park, N.Y., and Arthur M. Schlesinger, Jr., *The Age of Roosevelt: The Crisis of the Old Order, 1919–1933* (Boston, 1957), pp. 333–334.

27. For James V. Forrestal's recollections of his father, see Forrestal speech, Commission on Army and Navy Chaplains, Washington, D.C., October 29, 1947, Princeton University, JFP.

CHAPTER 2 GROWING UP IRISH

1. Hoyt is quoted in "Morg Hoyt Recalls Forrestal's 'Scoop' of Henry Thaw Escape," Beacon *News,* June 1944.

2. Hoopes interview with Mrs. Ellen Barry, May 14, 1988.

3. For a discussion of the domineering Irish mother, see Hasia Diner, *Erin's Daughters in America* (Baltimore, 1985).

4. Morgan H. Hoyt, "Turning Back the Clock," *Evening News,* Beacon, N.Y., February 15, 1951, and another Hoyt clipping, date unreadable. See also Brinkley interview with Michael Forrestal, April 27, 1988.

5. For Beacon boxing lore, see Morgan H. Hoyt, "Recollections of Old Dutchess" (unpublished manuscript), Chapter 7, "Pastimes of Past Times" (in authors' possession).

6. Brinkley interview with Michael Forrestal, May 18, 1988.

7. Forrestal's grades are given in Arnold A. Rogow, *James Forrestal: A Study of Personality, Politics, and Policy* (New York, 1963), p. 56.

8. JVF to Judge Flannery, February 12, 1947, Princeton University, JFP.

9. JVF to Miss Eunice Sherwood, February 12, 1947, Princeton University, JFP.

10. Edythe Holbrook interview with Mary Pennybacker, October 5, 1982; Brinkley interview with Michael Forrestal, April 27, 1988.

11. JVF to Robert Matter, October 6, 1947, Princeton University, JFP. For Forrestal's frustration with carpentry, see JVF to William J. O'Dwyer, May 30, 1947, Princeton University, JFP.

12. Holbrook interview with Mary Pennybacker, October 5, 1982.

13. "Morgan H. Hoyt Dies; Dean of Newspapermen," Beacon *News,* February 23, 1953.

14. For Hoyt's recollections of young Vincent working for his newspaper, see Morgan H. Hoyt, "Printer's Ink and High Finance" (unpublished essay in authors' possession; parts of the twenty-one-page manuscript appeared in Hoyt's "Turning Back the Clock" column). See also Morgan H. Hoyt to JVF, November 30, 1948, Princeton University, JFP, and "Morg Hoyt Recalls Forrestal's 'Scoop' of Henry Thaw Escape," Beacon *News,* June 1944.

15. For a discussion of Hoyt's "boys," see Hoyt, "Printer's Ink and High Finance." See also Brinkley interview with Michael Forrestal, May 18, 1988.

16. Holbrook interview with Mary Pennybacker, October 5, 1982.

17. Ibid.

18. JVF to Frances Fiske (society editor, *Daily Argus*), August 9, 1947, Princeton University, JFP.

19. Morgan H. Hoyt, "The Dutchess County Roosevelt," Chapter 5, "And Now

He Is President," p. 4, President's Personal File (PPF 990), FDR Library, Hyde Park, N.Y. Henry Forrestal would claim that his brother's association with FDR was "extremely intimate." See "Forrestal's Father Came Alone from Ireland at the Age of 9," Boston *Globe,* May 13, 1944.

20. Hoyt, "The Dutchess County Roosevelt," Chapter 5, "And Now He Is President," pp. 6–7.

21. Forrestal's first ground-breaking news story is recounted in Morgan H. Hoyt, "Turning Back the Clock," *Evening News,* Beacon, N.Y., March 7, 1951; "Secretary Is Recalled Here as Able Youthful Reporter," Beacon *News,* May 1944; and JVF to Morgan H. Hoyt, November 3, 1945, Princeton University, JFP.

22. James V. Forrestal speech, New York Rubber Corporation, Beacon, N.Y., October 18, 1943, Box 5, Princeton University, JFP.

CHAPTER 3   THE PRINCETON YEARS

1. Brinkley interview with Eliot Janeway, May 30, 1990.

2. Dean Charles F. Emerson to Professor C. W. McAlpin, October 7, 1912, Confidential Files, Alumni Records, Princeton University. Also quoted in Arnold A. Rogow, *James Forrestal: A Study of Personality, Politics, and Policy* (New York, 1963), p. 57.

3. Rogow, *James Forrestal,* p. 53.

4. *Fifty Year Record: Class of 1915 Princeton University* (Princeton, 1965), p. 194.

5. Rogow, *James Forrestal,* p. 58.

6. *Princeton Directory,* 1912–1913.

7. Brinkley interview with Michael Forrestal, April 27, 1988.

8. F. Scott Fitzgerald, "Princeton," in *Afternoon of an Author* (New York, 1987), p. 73. The essay was first published in the December 1927 issue of *College Humor.*

9. Quoted in *Fifty Year Record: Class of 1915,* p. 14.

10. Daniel Carruthers (Princeton class of 1915) to JVF, May 21, 1944, Princeton University, JFP; Harold Dodds Oral History interview 1966, Columbia University (Dodds was a Princeton graduate student at the time). For Wilson's tenure as Princeton University president, see John M. Mulder, *Woodrow Wilson: The Years of Preparation* (Princeton, 1978), pp. 159–182.

11. [James V. Forrestal], "Editorial," *Daily Princetonian,* May 6, 1914.

12. G. Frederick Riegel, "History of the Class of 1915," *Nassau Herald, 1915,* pp. 9–40.

13. JVF to Dean Andres Flemings West, May 16, 1943, Princeton University, JFP.

14. Forrestal Princeton Academic Transcript, Princeton University, JFP.

15. Holbrook interview with William Long, October 2, 1982.

16. Holbrook interview with Henry C. Merritt, December 13, 1986.

17. See Forrestal profile in *Fifty Year Record: Class of 1915,* pp. 194–198.

18. Quoted in F. Scott Fitzgerald, *This Side of Paradise* (1920; reprinted New York, 1986), p. 44.

19. Holbrook interview with William Long, October 2, 1982; Brinkley interview with Michael Forrestal, April 27, 1988; and Harold Dodds Oral History interview

1966, Columbia University. For biographical profiles of Riegel, Rentschler, and Christie, see *Fifty Year Record: Class of 1915.*

20. Fitzgerald, *This Side of Paradise,* p. 45.

21. Ferdinand Eberstadt to George Fielding Eliot, August 7, 1947, Ferdinand Eberstadt Papers, Forrestal Files, Seeley G. Mudd Library, Princeton University.

22. Brinkley interview with Ferdinand Eberstadt, Jr., May 4, 1989.

23. For biographical information on Eberstadt's early life, see Robert C. Perez and Edward F. Willett, *The Will to Win: A Biography of Ferdinand Eberstadt* (Westport, Conn., 1989), pp. 15–28; "Ferdinand Eberstadt," *Fortune,* April 1939, pp. 72–75; and Calvin Lee Christman, "Ferdinand Eberstadt and Economic Mobilization for War, 1941–1943," Ph.D. dissertation, Ohio State University, 1971, pp. 1–10. See also Calvin Lee Christman interview with Ferdinand Eberstadt, July 17, 1969, transcript, Ferdinand Eberstadt Papers, Seeley G. Mudd Library, Princeton University.

24. Virginia K. Creesy, "The Princetonian's First Century," *Princeton Alumni Weekly,* January 31, 1977.

25. See James Bruce and J. Vincent Forrestal, *College Journalism* (Princeton, 1914).

26. [James V. Forrestal], "Editorial," *Daily Princetonian,* May 24, 1914.

27. Rogow, *James Forrestal,* pp. 64–65; Brinkley interview with Michael Forrestal, April 27, 1988.

28. [James V. Forrestal], "Editorial," *Daily Princetonian,* May 28, 1914.

29. G. Frederick Riegel, "History of the Class of 1915," *Nassau Herald,* 1915, pp. 9–40; Charles J. V. Murphy Notes.

30. [James V. Forrestal], "Editorial," *Daily Princetonian,* May 1914.

31. John Brooks, *Once in Golconda—A True Drama of Wall Street, 1920–1938* (New York, 1969), p. 57.

32. Rogow, *James Forrestal,* pp. 65–66; Holbrook interview with Henry C. Merritt, December 13, 1986; and Brinkley interview with Michael Forrestal, April 27, 1988.

33. Rogow, *James Forrestal,* pp. 63–65.

34. Although Forrestal never graduated he stayed extremely active in Princeton alumni matters. See Forrestal and Princeton alumni affairs, Box 10, Princeton University, JFP, and Confidential Files, Alumni Records, Princeton University.

35. Rogow, *James Forrestal,* pp. 65–66; Brinkley interview with Michael Forrestal, April 27, 1988.

36. Dean Mathey, *Fifty Years of Wall Street* (Privately printed, Princeton, N.J., 1966), pp. 9–10.

37. JVF to Edward J. Noble, June 12, 1944, Princeton University, JFP.

CHAPTER 4   LOVE AND MARRIAGE IN THE JAZZ AGE

1. JVF to Ledyard Cogswell, September 22, 1947, Princeton University, JFP. For a discussion of Forrestal during WWI, see also Arnold A. Rogow, *James Forrestal: A Study of Personality, Politics, and Policy* (New York, 1963), pp. 67–68, and Forrestal remarks to Team Unification Meeting, November 20, 1947, Princeton University, JFP. American life during WWI is best captured in David M. Kennedy, *Over Here: The First World War and American Society* (New York, 1980).

2. Ernest Havemann, "Forrestal," *Life,* October 6, 1948, p. 74.

3. Quentin Reynolds, "He Built Our Navy," *Collier's,* July 15, 1944.

4. Rogow, *James Forrestal,* pp. 69–70. See also Robert A. Lovett Oral History interview, May 13, 1974, OSD Historical Office, Pentagon, Arlington, Va.

5. Brinkley interview with Michael Forrestal, May 18, 1988.

6. Lyttleton B. P. Gould to Arthur Krock, July 27, 1947, Arthur M. Krock Papers, Seeley G. Mudd Library, Princeton University, JFP.

7. Allen report quoted in Rogow, *James Forrestal,* pp. 67–68. See also Biography of Forrestal, Biographical File, Operational Archives, Washington Navy Yard, Washington, D.C., and Lyttleton B. P. Gould to Arthur Krock, July 27, 1947, Krock Papers, Princeton University.

8. Paolo E. Coletta, *Patrick N. L. Bellinger and U.S. Naval Aviation* (Lanham, Md, 1987), p. 210.

9. Charles L. Eidlitz to JVF, January 28, 1947; JVF to Eidlitz, January 29, 1947, Princeton University, JFP.

10. JVF to Professor Collins, January 15, 1918, Confidential File, Alumni Records, Princeton University. For a discussion of Dewey, Flexner, and progressive education, see Lawrence A. Cremin, *The Transformation of the School* (New York, 1981).

11. Malcolm Cowley, *A Second Flowering: Works and Days of the Lost Generation* (New York, 1973), pp. 19–47.

12. John Osborne, "Forrestal," unpublished manuscript outline.

13. Brinkley interview with Michael Forrestal, May 18, 1988.

14. John O'Hara, *The Collected Stories of John O'Hara* (New York, 1984).

15. Ibid. See also Osborne, "Forrestal," unpublished manuscript outline.

16. Joseph Wood Krutch, *The Modern Temper* (New York, 1929).

17. Malcolm Cowley, *Exile's Return* (New York, 1934), p. 237.

18. F. Scott Fitzgerald, *The Great Gatsby* (New York, 1925).

19. Osborne, "Forrestal," unpublished manuscript outline.

20. Hoopes interview with Fitzhugh Green, June 14, 1989.

21. Dean Mathey, *Fifty Years on Wall Street with Anecdotania* (Princeton, N.J.: privately printed, 1966), pp. 65–67. See also "Wall Street Firm Announces Changes: J. V. Forrestal Promoted," *New York Times,* January 2, 1923, 23:2.

22. See Rogow, *James Forrestal,* pp. 66–71; Edythe Holbrook interview with Adele Lovett, October 2, 1982; Brinkley interviews with Michael Forrestal, April 27, 1988, and Eliot Janeway, October 16, 1990. For information on Vincent, see *Yale University 1916 Senior Class Book;* on Shea, see Edward Shea File, Alumni Files and Clippings, Princeton University. See also Faris Russell to Ferdinand Eberstadt, May 24, 1949, Ferdinand Eberstadt Papers, Forrestal Files, Seeley G. Mudd Library, Princeton University.

23. Joseph Clark Baldwin, Oral History, 1950, Oral History Research Office, Columbia University.

24. Brinkley interview with Michael Forrestal, April 27, 1988; Rogow, *James Forrestal,* pp. 66–71.

25. Charles J. V. Murphy interview with Robert A. Lovett, May 11, 1982; Osborne, "Forrestal."

26. Rogow, *James Forrestal,* pp. 66–71; Brinkley interview with Michael Forrestal, April 27, 1988.

27. John Osborne, "Forrestal," unpublished manuscript outline.

28. Alfred Goldberg and Harry B. Yoshpe interview with Robert A. Lovett, May 13, 1974, Department of Defense Historical Office, Pentagon, Arlington, Va.

29. Elting E. Morison, *Turmoil and Tradition: A Study of the Life and Times of Henry L. Stimson* (Boston, 1960), pp. 492–493.

30. Ibid.

31. For biographical information on Lovett's early life, see Jonathan Foster Fanton, "Robert A. Lovett, The War Years," Ph.D. dissertation, Yale University, 1978, pp. 1–27; Ralph O. Paine, *The First Yale Unit* (New York, 1925); and Walter Isaacson and Evan Thomas, *The Wise Men* (New York, 1986), pp. 60–209.

32. Holbrook interview with Adele Lovett, October 2, 1982; see also Frank P. Leslie, *James Forrestal* (Wayzata, Minn., 1951), pp. 3–4.

33. Hoopes interview with Mrs. Burroughs Hoffman, May 11, 1989.

34. Brinkley interview with Michael Forrestal, April 27, 1988; Rogow, *James Forrestal*, pp. 70–71; JVF to Michael Forrestal, December 5, 1945, Box 39, Princeton University, and JVF to Beardsley Ruml, April 20, 1943, Princeton University, JFP. See also Isaacson and Thomas, *The Wise Men*, p. 483.

35. *New York Times,* October 14, 1926, 21:2.

36. Mathey, *Fifty Years on Wall Street*, pp. 56–62. Also quoted in Rogow, *James Forrestal*, p. 71, and Isaacson and Thomas, *The Wise Men*, p. 483. See also Hoopes interview with Paul H. Nitze, June 23, 1989.

37. For Ogden ancestral information, see Eleanor M. Hartman (cousin of Josephine), "Reminiscence," pamphlet privately written in February 1983, and an unidentifiable newspaper clipping given to authors by Michael Forrestal.

38. Ibid.

39. Hartman, "Reminiscence"; Rogow, *James Forrestal*, p. 70.

40. Holbrook interview with Diana Vreeland, November 17, 1982.

41. Holbrook interview with Adele Lovett, October 2, 1982.

42. John Dos Passos, *The Great Days* (New York, 1958). One of the leading characters in the novel—Roger Thurloe—is drawn directly from the governmental career of Forrestal. For a brief discussion of why Dos Passos used Forrestal as a model for a character in his novel, see Townsend Ludington, *John Dos Passos: A Twentieth Century Odyssey* (New York, 1980), pp. 454, 473, 487, and Donald Pizer, ed., *John Dos Passos: The Major Nonfiction Prose* (Detroit, 1988), pp. 245–246.

43. Holbrook interview with Jeanne Ballot Winham (secretary to Frank Crowninshield), January 10, 1983.

44. For histories of *Vogue* in the 1920s see Edna Woolman Chase and Ilka Chase, *Always in Vogue* (Garden City, N.Y., 1954); Caroline Seebohm, *The Man Who Was Vogue: The Life and Times of Condé Nast* (New York, 1982); and Lynn Darling, "The Vreeland Legend," *Newsday,* August 24, 1989, Part II, p. 4.

45. For examples of Josephine Ogden's column, see "Seen in the Shops," *Vogue,* Anniversary Issue, January 1923. See also *Vogue,* February 15, 1925.

46. Holbrook interview with Adele Lovett, October 2, 1982; Brinkley interview with Michael Forrestal, April 27, 1988; and Seebohm, *The Man Who Was Vogue,* pp. 124–128.

47. Holbrook interview with Adele Lovett, October 2, 1982; Brinkley interview with Michael Forrestal, April 27, 1988.

48. Brinkley interview with Michael Forrestal, April 27, 1988; Holbrook interview with Millicent Cox (Josephine's great-niece), January 12, 1983.

49. Osborne, "Forrestal," unpublished manuscript outline.

50. Rogow, *James Forrestal,* p. 65.

51. *New York Times,* October 14, 1926, 21:2.

52. Holbrook interview with Adele Lovett, October 2, 1982.

53. Osborne, "Forrestal," unpublished manuscript outline.

54. Brinkley interview with Michael Forrestal, April 27, 1988; Holbrook interview with Millicent Cox, January 12, 1983; Osborne, "Forrestal," unpublished manuscript outline.

55. Holbrook interview with Diana Vreeland, November 17, 1982.

56. Holbrook interview with Michael Forrestal, October 3, 1984.

57. Murphy interview with Robert A. Lovett, April 28, 1983; Holbrook interview with Adele Lovett, October 2, 1982.

58. Hoopes interview with Ellen Barry, May 14, 1988. See also Barbara Gamarekian, "Ellen Barry: Reliving the Unforgettable Years of the 20's and 30's," *New York Times,* April 21, 1980, B15.

CHAPTER 5   GETTING RICH ON WALL STREET

1. JVF memorandum to Ernest Havemann, August 26, 1947, Princeton University, JFP.

2. Ibid.

3. Robert Sobel, *The Great Bull Market: Wall Street in the 1920s* (New York, 1968), pp. 36–48, and John Brooks, *Once in Golconda: A True Drama of Wall Street, 1920–1938* (New York, 1969).

4. Sobel, *The Great Bull Market,* Chapters 4, 6, 9, and Henry Morton Robinson, *Fantastic Interim: A Hindsight History of American Manners, Morals, and Mistakes Between Versailles and Pearl Harbor* (Freeport, N.Y., 1971), Chapters 1 and 2.

5. Sobel, *The Great Bull Market,* p. 51.

6. Sobel, *The Great Bull Market,* p. 52.

7. John K. Winkler, "A Billion Dollar Banker," *The New Yorker,* October 20, 1928.

8. Ibid. See also Brinkley interviews with Douglas Dillon, June 16, 1989, and Eliot Janeway, September 28, 1990. For Dillon's discreet Jewishness, see Stephen Birmingham, *Our Crowd: The Great Jewish Families of New York* (New York, 1967), p. 374.

9. "Clarence Dillon: Portrait," *Newsweek,* October 24, 1933.

10. Winkler, "A Billion Dollar Banker," *The New Yorker.*

11. Ibid.

12. Bernard M. Baruch, *Baruch: The Public Years* (New York, 1960), p. 80. See also James Grant, *Bernard Baruch: The Adventures of a Wall Street Legend* (New York, 1983), p. 172, and Jordan A. Schwarz, *The Speculator: Bernard M. Baruch in Washington, 1917–1965* (Chapel Hill, N.C., 1981), pp. 367, 525.

13. Ibid. See also Winkler, "A Billion Dollar Banker," *The New Yorker.*

14. Winkler, "A Billion Dollar Banker," *The New Yorker.* See also James C. Young, "Clarence Dillon Become Banker Through Chance," *New York Times,* January 10, 1926, VIII, p. 6.

15. Hoopes interview with Paul H. Nitze, June 23, 1989.

16. Brinkley interview with Eliot Janeway, September 28, 1990.

17. Robert Sobel, *The Life and Times of Dillon Read* (New York, 1991), p. 194.

18. Ibid, pp. 134–135. See also Brinkley interview with Robert Sobel, October 7, 1990.

19. "Wall Street Firms Announce Changes: J. V. Forrestal Promoted," *New York Times*, January 2, 1923, 23:2. For the influence of William Phillips on Forrestal, see Dean Mathey, *Fifty Years of Wall Street with Anecdotiana* (Privately printed, Princeton, N.J., 1966), pp. 9–10.

20. *New York Times*, July 27, 1947. See also Herbert Elliston, "Jim Forrestal: A Portrait in Politics," *Atlantic Monthly* (November 1951), pp. 73–80. For Arthur Krock's impressions of Forrestal, see Arthur Krock, *Memoirs: Sixty Years on the Firing Line* (New York, 1968), pp. 249–252.

21. Brinkley interview with Frederick Eberstadt, Jr., September 28, 1990.

22. Hoopes interview with Paul H. Nitze, June 23, 1989.

23. Ibid.

24. Frank J. Williams, "Rise of New York's Great Investment Houses: No. 3—Dillon, Read & Company," New York *Evening Post*, October 14, 1926 (clipping from Dillon, Read and Company firm history file), and Frank J. Williams, "A New Leader in Finance: Clarence Dillon," *American Review of Reviews* (February 1926), pp. 147–148.

25. Brooks, *Once in Golconda*, p. 46. For a history of Morgan banking, see Ron Chernow, *The House of Morgan* (New York, 1990).

26. Brooks, *Once in Golconda*, pp. 50–52. For a history of Kuhn, Loeb, see Mary Jane Matz, *The Many Lives of Otto Kahn* (New York, 1963).

27. Norman Beasley, *Men Working: A Story of Goodyear Tire and Rubber Company* (New York, 1931), pp. 86–96.

28. Ibid. See also Hugh Allen, *The House of Goodyear* (Privately printed, Cleveland, 1943), pp. 47–54.

29. Laura Jereski, "Clarence Dillon: Using Other People's Money," *Forbes*, July 13, 1987, p. 270. See also "Goodyear Tire Plan Put into Operation," *New York Times*, May 17, 1921, p. 25, and "Announcement of Settlement of Goodyear Litigation," May 25, 1927 (signed document), Ferdinand Eberstadt Papers, Forrestal Files, Seeley G. Mudd Library, Princeton University.

30. Williams, "A New Leader in Finance," *American Review of Reviews*, pp. 146–147. See also Beasley, *Men Working*, pp. 86–96, and Sobel, *The Life and Times of Dillon Read*, pp. 59–72.

31. Charles J. V. Murphy interview with Edward F. Willett, June 10, 1982. See also Sobel, *The Life and Times of Dillon Read*, pp. 59–72, and "Sues to Oust Board of Goodyear Tire: Prosecutor in Ohio Attacks Reorganization of Company in 1921 as Illegal," *New York Times*, August 24, 1926, 24:4.

32. Beasley, *Men Working*, pp. 86–96. For excerpts of Forrestal testimony, see *New York Times*, February 3, 1927, and March 11, 1927.

33. *New York Times*, March 11, 1927.

34. "Dillon Didn't Know He Had Offices," *New York Times*, February 3, 1927, 23:1.

35. "Goodyear Fight Is Ended," Akron *Times-Press*, May 12, 1927, p. 1 (found in Eberstadt Papers, Princeton University). See also "Goodyear Suit Ends Outside of Court; Charges Dropped," *New York Times*, May 16, 1927, p. 1; Allen, *The House of Goodyear*, p. 54, and "Announcement of Settlement of Goodyear Litigation," May 15, 1927, Eberstadt Papers, Princeton University.

36. For a brief history of Dodge Motors, see Caroline Latham and David Agresta,

The Dodge Dynasty (New York, 1989). For the death of the Dodge brothers, see Robert C. Perez and Edward F. Willett, *The Will to Win: A Biography of Ferdinand Eberstadt* (Westport, Conn., 1989), p. 39.

37. Perez and Willett, *The Will to Win*, p. 40. See also Mathey, *Fifty Years of Wall Street*, pp. 12-14.

38. Perez and Willett, *The Will to Win*, p. 40. See also "The Dodge Deal," *Literary Digest*, April 25, 1925, p. 80.

39. Arnold A. Rogow, *James Forrestal: A Study of Personality, Politics, and Policy* (New York, 1963), p. 82; Perez and Willett, *The Will to Win*, p. 41; and "The Dodge Deal," *Literary Digest*, pp. 80-82.

40. Winkler, "A Billion Dollar Banker," *The New Yorker*.

41. Ibid.

42. Ibid.

43. Ibid. See also Charles J. V. Murphy Notes and "Charles Schwartz Is Dead; Vice Chairman of Bache & Co.," *New York Times*, June 25, 1990.

44. Hoopes interview with Michael Forrestal, October 12, 1988.

45. Perez and Willett, *The Will to Win*, p. 40.

46. "Chrysler," *Fortune*, August 1935, pp. 68-69. See also Perez and Willett, *The Will to Win*, p. 40.

47. "Chrysler," *Fortune*, pp. 68-69. See also Perez and Willett, *The Will to Win*, p. 41, and "A Third Motor Car Colossus: The Chrysler-Dodge Merger," *Literary Digest*, June 16, 1928, p. 12.

48. "Dodge Stock Buying Caps Chrysler Deal," *New York Times*, July 31, 1928, p. 1. See also Perez and Willett, *The Will to Win*, p. 41, and Rogow, *James Forrestal*, pp. 82-83.

49. Hoopes interview with Eliot Janeway, July 5, 1990.

50. Brinkley interviews with Frederick Eberstadt, Jr., September 28, 1990, and Eliot Janeway, September 28, 1990.

51. Peter Walker interview with Frederick Eberstadt, Jr., March 18, 1987.

52. Joseph W. Alsop and Adam Platt, *The Memoirs of Joseph W. Alsop*, prepublication manuscript, pp. 2-3 (courtesy of Mr. Platt).

53. Murphy interview with Edward F. Willett, June 10, 1982.

54. Hoopes interview with Eliot Janeway, September 28, 1990.

55. Robinson, *Fantastic Interim*, pp. 144-145. See also "Ferdinand Eberstadt," *Fortune*, April 1939, pp. 72-75.

56. Robinson, *Fantastic Interim*, pp. 144-151.

57. Walker interview with Frederick Eberstadt, Jr., March 18, 1987.

58. Perez and Willett, *The Will to Win*, pp. 35-39. See also "Eberstadt," *Fortune*, pp. 72-75, and "Dillon Read Opens Paris Office," *New York Times*, March 12, 1928, p. 35. For an idea of the Eberstadt view of European markets, see Edward F. Willett, "Coal, Iron and Steel in Europe," a booklet published in Paris by Dillon, Read and Company (Paris, 1928), and Eberstadt Paris Diary excerpts, July 7-10, 1926, Eberstadt Papers, Princeton University.

59. Perez and Willett, *The Will to Win*, pp. 35-39. For information regarding the Eberstadt-Stresemann relationship and Eberstadt's European contacts, see Eric Sulton, ed. and trans., *Gustav Stresemann: His Diaries, Letters and Papers*, Vols. 1-3 (London, 1935-1940), pp. 415-417, and Eberstadt to Clarence Dillon, October 31, 1926, November 4, 1926, and November 20, 1926, Eberstadt Papers, Princeton University.

60. Perez and Willett, *The Will to Win*, p. 101.

61. Perez and Willett, *The Will to Win*, p. 107.

62. Walker interview with Frederick Eberstadt, Jr., March 18, 1987.

63. Brinkley interview with Eliot Janeway, September 28, 1990.

64. Perez and Willett, *The Will to Win*, p. 42.

65. Ibid.

66. Brinkley interview with Eliot Janeway, September 28, 1990.

67. Perez and Willett, *The Will to Win*, p. 43.

68. Ibid.

69. Ibid.

70. Mathey, *Fifty Years of Wall Street*, pp. 9–12.

71. Walker interview with Frederick Eberstadt, Jr., March 18, 1987.

72. Brinkley interview with Douglas Dillon, June 16, 1989.

73. Calvin Lee Christman, "Ferdinand Eberstadt and Economic Mobilization for War, 1941–1943," Ph.D. dissertation, Ohio State University, 1971.

74. Ibid.

75. Hoopes interview with Paul H. Nitze, June 23, 1989.

76. Brinkley interview with Eliot Janeway, September 28, 1990.

77. "Eberstadt," *Fortune*, pp. 72–75.

78. Perez and Willett, *The Will to Win*, p. 71; and Brinkley interview with Paul H. Nitze, September 26, 1987.

79. Perez and Willett, *The Will to Win*, p. 132.

CHAPTER 6 SURVIVING THE CRASH OF 1929

1. Robert Sobel, *The Great Bull Market: Wall Street in the* 1920*s* (New York, 1968), p. 12. See also John Kenneth Galbraith, *The Great Crash* (Boston, 1955), and Giulio Pontecorvo, "Investment Banking and Security Speculation in the Late 1920's," *Business History Review* 32 (Summer 1958), pp. 166–191.

2. Sobel, *The Great Bull Market*, p. 74.

3. John Brooks, *Once in Golconda: A True Drama of Wall Street, 1920–1938* (New York, 1969), p. 99.

4. Sobel, *The Great Bull Market*, p. 115.

5. Ibid.

6. Sobel, *The Great Bull Market*, p. 118.

7. Ibid.

8. Sobel, *The Great Bull Market*, p. 117.

9. Hoopes interview with Paul H. Nitze, June 23, 1989. For information regarding Nitze's early years on Wall Street, see Paul H. Nitze, with Ann M. Smith and Steve L. Rearden, *From Hiroshima to Wall Street: At the Center of Decision—A Memoir* (New York, 1989), pp. xvii–xxii, and David Callahan, *Dangerous Capabilities: Paul Nitze and the Cold War* (New York, 1990), pp. 11–32.

10. Callahan, *Dangerous Capabilities*, pp. 20–21.

11. Sobel, *The Great Bull Market*, p. 126.

12. Hoopes interview with Paul H. Nitze, June 23, 1989.

13. Ibid. See also Callahan, *Dangerous Capabilities*, pp. 20–21, and Nitze, *From Hiroshima to Wall Street*, pp. xvii–xviii.

14. Sobel, *The Great Bull Market*, p. 134.

15. Henry Morton Robinson, *Fantastic Interim: A Hindsight History of American*

Manners, Morals, and Mistakes Between Versailles and Pearl Harbor (Freeport, N.Y., 1971), pp. 80–81.

16. Sobel, *The Great Bull Market,* pp. 136–137.

17. Robinson, *Fantastic Interim,* p. 181.

18. Sobel, *The Great Bull Market,* p. 151. See also Galbraith, *The Great Crash.*

19. "Dillon, Read and Company," Committee on Banking and Currency, U.S. Congress, Senate, 73rd Cong., 2nd Session, October 3–13, 1933, pp. 2053–2076; "Dillon Loan List Names H. C. Couch," *New York Times,* October 14, 1933, p. 1; and Arnold A. Rogow, *James Forrestal: A Study of Personality, Politics, and Policy* (New York, 1963), pp. 82–88.

20. Sobel, *The Great Bull Market,* p.151, and Galbraith, *The Great Crash.*

21. Robinson, *Fantastic Interim,* pp. 182–183.

22. George H. Nash, *The Life of Herbert Hoover* (New York, 1983).

CHAPTER 7   FAMILY LIFE

1. Peggy and Roger Gerry, *Old Roslyn,* published by the Bryant Library, 1954, p. 27. See also "Nassau County Deals," *New York Times,* February 2, 1929, 32:3.

2. Monica Randall, *Mansions of the Gold Coast* (New York, 1979).

3. F. Scott Fitzgerald, *The Great Gatsby* (New York, 1925). Discussions with Professor Natalie Naylor, director of the Long Island Study Center, Hofstra University, enhanced our understanding of the Gold Coast in the 1920s.

4. Jonathan Foster Fanton, "Robert A. Lovett: The War Years," Ph.D. dissertation, Yale University, 1978, pp. 6–7, and Charles J. V. Murphy interview with Robert Lovett, May 1982.

5. Brinkley interview with Stuart Symington, November 17, 1987. For Symington's early life and business career, see Paul I. Wellman, *Stuart Symington: Portrait of a Man with a Mission* (New York, 1960), pp. 53–109.

6. Brinkley interview with Michael Forrestal, April 27, 1988.

7. Edythe Holbrook interview with Adele Lovett, October 2, 1982.

8. Brinkley interview with Michael Forrestal, April 27, 1988. See also Arnold A. Rogow, *James Forrestal: A Study of Personality, Politics, and Policy* (New York, 1963), pp. 75–76.

9. Brinkley interview with Stuart Symington, November 17, 1987.

10. Holbrook interview with Adele Lovett, October 2, 1982.

11. Hoopes interview with Mrs. William Lord, July 20, 1988.

12. Charles J. V. Murphy interview with Robert Lovett, April 28, 1983.

13. Hoopes interview with Mrs. William Lord, July 20, 1988.

14. Murphy interview with Anne Cannell (Eberstadt's daughter), May 7, 1983. For information pertaining to Eberstadt's social life on Long Island, see Calvin Lee Christman, "Ferdinand Eberstadt and Economic Mobilization for War, 1940–1943," Ph.D. dissertation, Ohio State University, 1971, pp. 16–17, and Robert C. Perez and Edward F. Willett, *The Will to Win: A Biography of Ferdinand Eberstadt* (Westport, Conn., 1989), pp. 15–26.

15. Hoopes interview with Ellen Barry, May 14, 1988.

16. Murphy interview with Daniel Caulkins, May 10, 1982.

17. Brinkley interview with Eliot Janeway, September 28, 1990.

18. Hoopes interview with Ellen Barry, May 14, 1988. See also Fanton, "Robert A. Lovett: The War Years," pp. 12–13.

19. Hoopes interview with Ellen Barry, May 14, 1988. For biographical information and critical assessments of Barry's twenty-one full-length plays that were produced on Broadway, along with his other literary efforts, see John Patrick Roppolo, *Philip Barry* (New York, 1965), and Gerald Hamm, "The Drama of Philip Barry," Ph.D. dissertation, University of Pennsylvania, 1948 (contains material obtained through interviews with Barry).

20. Matthew J. Bruccoli, *The O'Hara Concern: A Biography of John O'Hara* (New York, 1975), pp. 170–171. See also John O'Hara, *From the Terrace* (New York, 1958).

21. Hoopes interview with Mrs. William Lord, July 20, 1988.

22. John O'Hara to Josephine Forrestal, October 24, 1947, Michael Forrestal papers (in the authors' possession).

23. Hoopes interview with Ellen Barry, May 14, 1988.

24. Peter Walker interview with Joseph Alsop, April 17, 1987.

25. Holbrook interview with Adele Lovett, October 2, 1982.

26. Hoopes interview with Ellen Barry, May 14, 1988.

27. Holbrook interview with Adele Lovett, October 2, 1982. See also Rogow, *James Forrestal,* pp. 71–75.

28. Brinkley interview with Michael Forrestal, April 27, 1988.

29. Ibid.

30. Holbrook interview with Mrs. William McKinley (Josephine's great-niece), January 12, 1983.

31. Brinkley interview with Michael Forrestal, April 27, 1988. See also Cholly Knickerbocker, " 'Jim' Forrestals Give Party for Coopers," New York *Post,* 1933 (clipping, n.d.).

32. Brinkley interview with Michael Forrestal, September 11, 1988.

33. Hoopes interview with Ellen Barry, May 14, 1988.

34. See Christine M. Miles, *Harold Sterner: Architect and Artist* (New York: Catalogue of Sterner's work, 1978).

35. Holbrook interview with Adele Lovett, October 2, 1982, and Brinkley interview with Eliot Janeway, September 28, 1990.

36. Ibid.

37. Babette Rosmond, *Robert Benchley: His Life and Good Times* (Garden City, N.Y., 1970), p. 185.

38. Rosmond, *Robert Benchley,* p. 188.

39. Cholly Knickerbocker, " 'Jim' Forrestals Give Party for Coopers," New York *Post,* 1933.

40. "Woman Is Held Up in Beekman Place," *New York Times,* July 2, 1937, 44:3; "$48,000 Gems Taken in Forrestal Raid," *New York Times,* July 3, 1937, 32:1; "Reward for Stolen Jewelry," *New York Times,* July 16, 1937, 23:7; and "Thugs Rob Broker's Wife of $100,000 in Jewels," New York *Daily News,* July 2, 1937, p. 2.

41. For the Pearson and Winchell attacks, see Rogow, *James Forrestal,* pp. 28–33; Jack Anderson, with James Boyd, *Confessions of a Muckraker* (New York, 1979), pp. 139–168; Tyler Abell, ed., *Drew Pearson Diaries, 1949–1969* (New York, 1974); and Walter Winchell, *Winchell Exclusive* (Englewood Cliffs, N.J., 1975), pp. 212–219. Drew Pearson collected dozens of robbery clippings and reports for his personal

Forrestal File, including a detailed map of Forrestal's street and an architectural blueprint of his home. See Forrestal—Jewel Robbery File, Drew Pearson Papers, Lyndon B. Johnson Library (LBJL), Austin, Texas.

42. Hoopes interview with Ellen Barry, May 14, 1988.

43. Alice-Leone Moats, "Married Men in Season," *Town & Country,* January 1936. Taken from Adele Lovett's 1936 clipping album.

44. Alex Karmer, *History of the Jupiter Island Club* (Hobe Sound, Fl.: privately printed).

45. Holbrook interview with Adele Lovett, October 2, 1982.

46. Hoopes interview with Michael Forrestal, October 12, 1988.

47. Murphy interview with Arthur Krock, April 10, 1982. See also the Josephine Forrestal–Arthur Krock correspondence, Arthur Krock·Papers, Seeley G. Mudd Library, Princeton University.

48. Brinkley interview with Michael Forrestal, September 11, 1988.

49. Hoopes interview with Ellen Barry, May 14, 1988.

50. Brinkley interview with Michael Forrestal, April 27, 1988.

51. Hoopes interview with Ellen Barry, May 14, 1988.

52. Brinkley interview with Michael Forrestal, April 27, 1988.

53. Hoopes interview with Michael Forrestal, October 12, 1988.

54. Brinkley interview with Michael Forrestal, April 27, 1988.

55. Ibid.

56. Ibid.

57. Tom Driberg, *The Mystery of Moral Rearmament: A Study of Frank Buchman* (New York, 1965), and Peter Howard, "Frank Buchman," in *The World Rebuilt* (London, 1951), pp. 124–135.

58. Brinkley interview with Michael Forrestal, April 27, 1988.

59. Ibid.

60. Ibid.

61. Ibid. See also Rogow, *James Forrestal,* pp. 77–78.

62. Ibid. See also Rogow, *James Forrestal,* pp. 79–80.

63. Hoopes interview with James Symington, April 16, 1989.

64. Brinkley interview with Michael Forrestal, April 27, 1988.

65. Peter Forrestal to Josephine Forrestal, undated; Michael Forrestal papers (in authors' possession).

66. JVF to Thomas Lamont, November 12, 1945, Princeton University, JFP.

67. Brinkley interview with Michael Forrestal, April 27, 1988.

68. Rogow, *James Forrestal,* p. 80.

69. Hoopes interview with Michael Forrestal, October 12, 1988. From 1945 to 1948 Forrestal frequently wrote his son. See JVF letters to Michael Forrestal (scattered), Princeton University, JFP. Michael's letters to his father from Moscow can be found in Boxes 11 and 41, Princeton University, JFP.

70. Ibid.

71. JVF to Dr. Claude M. Fuess, August 30, 1944, Princeton University, JFP.

72. JVF to Peter Forrestal, March 18, 1948, Princeton University, JFP.

73. JVF to Robert Matter (former Princeton classmate), September 26, 1947, Princeton University, JFP.

74. JVF to Peter Forrestal, February 1, 1947, Princeton University, JFP.

75. JVF to Peter Forrestal, March 18, 1948, Princeton University, JFP.

76. Hoopes interview with Michael Forrestal, October 12, 1988.

77. Excerpts from Kamut Chandruang, *My Boyhood in Siam* (New York, 1940).

Also quoted in Rogow, *James Forrestal*, p. 261. Forrestal's Black Notebook can be found in Box 13, Princeton University, JFP.

CHAPTER 8   THE STRUGGLE FOR WALL STREET REFORM

1. William O. Douglas, *Go East, Young Man, The Early Years: The Autobiography of William O. Douglas* (New York, 1974), pp. 271–272. See also Robert Sobel, *The Great Bull Market: Wall Street in the 1920s* (New York, 1968), p. 159, and Thomas Ferguson, "Industrial Conflict and the Coming of the New Deal," in Steve Fraser and Garry Gestle, eds., *The Rise and Fall of the New Deal Order, 1930–1980* (Princeton, 1989), pp. 3–31.

2. Douglas, *Go East, Young Man*, pp. 257–315.

3. Vincent P. Carosso, *Investment Banking in America* (Cambridge, 1970), pp. 326–327.

4. "The Pecora Hearings," *Newsweek*, June 10, 1933, p. 16.

5. Ferdinand Pecora, *Wall Street Under Oath: The Story of Our Modern Money Changers* (New York, 1939), p. 3.

6. John Brooks, *Once in Golconda: A True Drama of Wall Street, 1920–1938* (New York, 1969), p. 191.

7. Brooks, *Once in Golconda*, pp. 180–183.

8. Ibid.

9. Douglas, *Go East, Young Man*, p. 290.

10. *Newsweek*, October 14, 1933, p. 21.

11. Ibid.

12. Carosso, *Investment Banking in America*, pp. 275–287.

13. "Dillon, Read and Company," Committee on Banking and Currency, U.S. Congress, Senate, 73rd Cong., 2nd Session, October 3–13, 1933 (hereafter referred to as *Pecora Hearings*), pp. 2053–2076.

14. Ibid. See also *New York Times*, October 4, 1933.

15. *Pecora Hearings*, pp. 1555–1606.

16. Ibid.

17. Ibid. See also *New York Times*, October 4, 1933.

18. *Pecora Hearings*, pp. 1555–1606.

19. Quoted in Carosso, *Investment Banking in America*, p. 346.

20. *Pecora Hearings*, pp. 1555–1606. See also Arnold A. Rogow, *James Forrestal: A Study of Personality, Politics, and Policy* (New York, 1963), pp. 81–88, and "Dillon Loan List Names H. C. Couch," *New York Times*, October 14, 1933. For information on Forrestal's Dillon, Read dealings, see JVF memorandum to Marx Leva, January 28, 1948; JVF to Douglas Dillon, January 17, 1946; and memorandum from Marx Leva to JVF, January 25, 1949, Princeton University, JFP.

21. Rogow, *James Forrestal*, pp. 81–88. See also Robert Sobel, *The Life and Times of Dillon Read* (New York, 1991), pp. 172–189.

22. *Pecora Hearings*, pp. 2058–2059. See also "Dillon Didn't Know He Had Ohio Offices," *New York Times*, February 3, 1927, and Eberstadt-Strieffler confidential memorandum on the Beekman Corporation, May 4, 1933, Ferdinand Eberstadt Papers, Forrestal Files, Seeley G. Mudd Library, Princeton University.

23. Ibid.

24. Brinkley interview with Douglas Dillon, June 16, 1989.

25. Ibid.

26. Brinkley interview with Eliot Janeway, September 28, 1990.

27. Brinkley interview with Douglas Dillon, June 16, 1989.

28. Ibid.

29. Ibid.

30. Robert Sobel, *The Life and Times of Dillon Read*, pp. 190–219.

31. Ibid. See also Brooks, *Once in Golconda*, pp. 100–104, and Carosso, *Investment Banking in America*, pp. 322–351.

32. Douglas, *Go East, Young Man*, p. 289.

33. Robert Sobel, *The Life and Times of Dillon Read*, pp. 197–199. See also Marx Leva memorandum to JVF, January 25, 1949 (includes JVF's 1948 testimony on his Wall Street dealings), and Marx Leva memorandum to JVF, January 28, 1948, Princeton University, JFP.

34. Hoopes interview with Paul H. Nitze, June 23, 1989. See also Daniel Yergin, *The Prize: The Epic Quest for Oil, Money and Power* (New York, 1991), pp. 299–300. De Golyer is also mentioned in David Painter, *Oil and the American Century: The Political Economy of U.S. Foreign Oil Policy, 1941–1954* (Baltimore, 1986), pp. 97, 101. See also Irvine H. Anderson, *Aramco, The United States and Saudi Arabia* (Princeton, 1981).

35. Lloyd C. Gardner, *Architects of Illusion: Men and Ideas in American Foreign Policy, 1941–1949* (Chicago, 1970), p. 15.

36. Henry Morton Robinson, *Fantastic Interim: A Hindsight History of American Manners, Morals, and Mistakes Between Versailles and Pearl Harbor* (Freeport, N.Y., 1971), pp. 252–254. See also Alan Brinkley, *Voices of Protest: Huey Long, Father Coughlin and the Great Depression* (New York, 1982).

37. Gardner, *Architects of Illusion*, p. 12.

38. Brooks, *Once in Golconda*, pp. 197–202.

39. Brooks, *Once in Golconda*, pp. 242–245. See also Brinkley interview with Eliot Janeway, September 28, 1990, and Forrestal-Shields telephone conversation (transcript), March 20, 1947, Princeton University, JFP.

40. Brooks, *Once in Golconda*, p. 212.

41. Douglas, *Go East, Young Man*, pp. 290–291.

42. Brinkley interview with Eliot Janeway, September 28, 1990. See also James F. Simon, *Independent Journey: The Life of William O. Douglas* (New York, 1980), pp. 257–275.

43. Douglas, *Go East, Young Man*, p. 289.

44. Ibid.

45. Brinkley interview with Eliot Janeway, September 28, 1990. See also Arthur M. Schlesinger, Jr., *The Age of Roosevelt*, Vol III: *The Politics of Upheaval* (Boston, 1960), p. 362.

46. Douglas, *Go East, Young Man*, pp. 290–293.

47. Douglas, *Go East, Young Man*, p. 287.

48. Douglas, *Go East, Young Man*, p. 286.

CHAPTER 9 WASHINGTON 1940

1. See Forrestal-Corcoran correspondence, T. G. Corcoran Papers, FDR Library, Hyde Park, N.Y., and Princeton University, JFP, and Eliot Janeway, *The Economics of Chaos* (New York, 1989), pp. 208–212. For Douglas's promoting Forrestal to FDR, see William O. Douglas to Robert Albion, January 14, 1954, William O. Douglas

Papers, General Correspondence, Forrestal File, Library of Congress, Washington, D.C.

2. Arthur Krock, *Memoirs: Sixty Years on the Firing Line* (New York, 1968), p. 184.

3. Charles J. V. Murphy interview with Paul Shields, October 17, 1982.

4. For a discussion on the destroyer-base deal, see Philip Goodhart, *Fifty Ships That Saved the World* (Garden City, N.Y., 1965), and James MacGregor Burns, *Roosevelt: Soldier of Freedom, 1940–1945* (New York, 1970), pp. 11–12.

5. Winston Churchill speech on Dunkirk, House of Commons, June 4, 1940,

6. Undated note from JVF to T. G. Corcoran, quoted in Robert Greenhalgh Albion and Robert Howe Connery, *Forrestal and the Navy* (New York, 1962), p. 4.

7. Hoopes interview with Paul H. Nitze, June 23, 1989. See also Paul H. Nitze, with Ann M. Smith and Steve L. Rearden, *From Hiroshima to Glasnost: At the Center of Decision—A Memoir* (New York, 1989), pp. 6–7.

8. Albion and Connery, *Forrestal and the Navy*, pp. 4–7. Also John L. Sullivan Oral History, 1974, Harry S. Truman Library, Independence, Mo.

9. Undated note, T. G. Corcoran to Franklin D. Roosevelt, spring 1940, quoted in Albion and Connery, *Forrestal and the Navy*, p. 3.

10. Hoopes interview with Michael Forrestal, October 12, 1988.

11. Edythe Holbrook interview with Adele Lovett, October 2, 1982.

12. Hoopes interview with Michael Forrestal, October 12, 1988.

13. Peter Walker interview with Emilio G. Collado (former director of the World Bank), April 3, 1987.

14. Hoopes interview with Michael Forrestal, October 12, 1988, and Holbrooke interview with Adele Lovett, October 2, 1982.

15. Franklin D. Roosevelt to JVF, April 11, 1940, President's Personal File (PPF), FDRL, Hyde Park, N.Y.

16. JVF to Franklin D. Roosevelt, April 1940 (handwritten note, n.d.), PPF, FDRL, Hyde Park, N.Y.

17. See Forrestal-Roosevelt correspondence, PPF, Box 6567, FDRL.

18. *Newsweek,* July 8, 1940.

19. *Time,* July 1, 1940, 36:62. See also James MacGregor Burns, *Roosevelt: The Soldier of Freedom, 1940–1945*, pp. 36–40.

20. David Brinkley, *Washington Goes to War* (New York, 1988), p. 9.

21. Ibid.

22. Brinkley, *Washington Goes to War,* p. 12.

23. William F. Leuchtenberg, *Franklin D. Roosevelt and the New Deal* (New York, 1963), and Arthur M. Schlesinger, Jr., *The Age of Roosevelt,* Vol. III: *The Politics of Upheaval* (Boston, 1960).

24. Jonathan Daniels, *Frontier on the Potomac* (New York, 1946), p. 6.

25. Louis J. Halle, *Spring in Washington* (New York, 1947), p. 6.

26. Daniels, *Frontier on the Potomac,* p. 1.

27. JVF memorandum, enclosed with a letter to Bernard Baruch, July 26, 1940, Baruch Papers, v. 47, Princeton University, and JVF memorandum to the President, March 24, 1941, Princeton University, JFP.

28. Cordell Hull, *The Memoirs of Cordell Hull,* Vol. I (New York, 1948), pp. 813–830.

29. Edward L. and Frederick H. Schapsmeir, *Prophet in Politics: Henry A. Wallace and the War Years, 1940–1945* (Ames, Iowa, 1970), pp. 38–49.

30. Franklin D. Roosevelt to JVF, September 27, 1940, Princeton University, JFP.

31. Charles J. V. Murphy interview with James Rowe, September 3, 1981. See also Nitze, *From Hiroshima to Glasnost,* pp. 7–11.

32. Murphy interview with James Rowe, September 3, 1981. Also, Osborne, "Forrestal," unpublished manuscript outline.

33. Hoopes interview with Paul H. Nitze, June 23, 1989. See also Strobe Talbott, *The Master of the Game* (New York, 1988), pp. 30–31.

34. Nitze, *From Hiroshima to Glasnost,* pp. 7–11.

35. Osborne, "Forrestal," unpublished manuscript outline. Hoopes interview with Paul H. Nitze, June 23, 1989. See also Brinkley interview with Eliot Janeway, September 28, 1990.

CHAPTER 10   NEW BURDENS

1. Robert Greenhalgh Albion and Robert Howe Connery, *Forrestal and the Navy* (New York, 1962), pp. 5–6. The creation of the Under Secretary post was made official by the Naval Reorganization Act, 54 Stat. 394 (July 20, 1940).

2. Ibid. For naval armament information, see also Fleet Admiral Ernest J. King, *U.S. Navy at War, 1941–1945: Official Reports to the Secretary of the Navy* (Washington, D.C., 1946), pp. 4–20.

3. George Lobdell, "Frank Knox," in Paolo F. Coletta, ed., *American Secretaries of the Navy* (Annapolis, Md., 1980).

4. Elting E. Morison, *Turmoil and Tradition: A Study of the Life of Henry L. Stimson* (Boston, 1960), pp. 477–500. For Stimson's governmental career and working relationship with FDR, see Henry L. Stimson and McGeorge Bundy, *On Active Service in Peace and War* (New York, 1948); and Godfrey Hodgson, *The Colonel: The Life and Wars of Henry Stimson, 1867–1950* (New York, 1990).

5. Albion and Connery, *Forrestal and the Navy,* p. 7. See also Richard Dunlop, *Donovan: America's Master Spy* (Chicago, 1982), p. 202.

6. Harold L. Ickes, *The Secret Diary of Harold L. Ickes,* Vol. III: *The Lowering Clouds* (New York, 1954), p. 391. For the Forrestal-Ickes relationship, see Harold L. Ickes, "The Forrestal Tragedy," *The New Republic,* June 13, 1949, pp. 15–16.

7. Frank Knox to Annie R. Knox, July 14, 1940, in Albion and Connery, *Forrestal and the Navy,* p. 8.

8. Ibid. See also "Forrestal Is Sworn In," *New York Times,* August 23, 1940, 10:4, and the John H. Towers diary entry, August 22, 1940 (courtesy of Professor Clark G. Reynolds).

9. JVF to Douglas Dillon, January 8, 1946, Princeton University, JFP. See also Albion and Connery, *Forrestal and the Navy,* p. 10.

10. Charles J. V. Murphy interview with Robert Lovett, October 6, 1982. See also Jonathan Foster Fanton, "Robert Lovett: The War Years," Ph.D. dissertation, Yale University, 1978, pp. 20–102, and conversation with Robert A. Lovett, November 16, 1976, Henry Arnold Project 12, Oral History Research Office, Columbia University.

11. Robert Lovett to Robert Patterson, November 22, 1940, Lovett Papers, RG 107-39, National Archives, Washington, D.C.

12. Ibid.

13. Morison, *Turmoil and Tradition,* p. 504.

14. Brinkley and Hoopes interviews with Michael Forrestal, April 27, 1988, and October 7, 1988.

15. John Osborne, "Forrestal," unpublished manuscript outline.

16. Ibid.

17. Hoopes interview with Ellen Barry, May 14, 1988.

18. Brinkley interview with Michael Forrestal, April 27, 1988.

19. Hoopes interview with Michael Forrestal, October 7, 1988.

20. Hoopes interview with Ellen Barry, May 14, 1988.

21. Edythe Holbrook interview with Adele Lovett, October 2, 1982.

22. Murphy interview with Daniel Caulkins, May 10, 1982.

23. Peter Walker interview with Oatsie Lighter (Mrs. Robert Charles), May 2, 1987.

24. Arnold A. Rogow, *James Forrestal: A Study of Personality, Politics, and Policy* (New York, 1963), p. 113; Josephine Forrestal and Mainbocher, Forrestal File, Drew Pearson Papers, Lyndon B. Johnson Library (LBJL), Austin, Texas; and Brinkley interview with H. Struve Hensel, June 6, 1988.

25. Josephine Forrestal to Franklin D. Roosevelt, July 28, 1943, President's Personal File (PPF), FDRL, Hyde Park, N.Y.

26. Franklin D. Roosevelt to Josephine Forrestal, PPF, FDRL.

27. Walker interview with Oatsie Lighter (Mrs. Robert Charles), May 2, 1987.

28. Hoopes interview with Gertrude Legendre, May 14, 1988.

29. Walker interview with Oatsie Lighter (Mrs. Robert Charles), May 2, 1987.

30. Joseph W. Alsop and Adam Platt, *The Memoirs of Joseph W. Alsop,* prepublication manuscript (courtesy of Mr. Platt). Also Brinkley interview with Joseph W. Alsop, March 12, 1988.

31. Hoopes interview with George Elsey, February 16, 1989.

32. Walker interview with Ellie Reich, April 22, 1987.

33. Brinkley interview with Eliot Janeway, October 16, 1990.

34. Hoopes interview with Ellen Barry, May 14, 1988.

35. John Osborne, "Forrestal," unpublished manuscript outline.

CHAPTER 11   ENCOUNTERING THE NAVY

1. Robert Greenhalgh Albion and Robert Howe Connery, *Forrestal and the Navy* (New York, 1962), p. 39.

2. Elihu Root, *Annual Report of the Secretary of War, 1903*, p. 6. See also Albion and Connery, *Forrestal and the Navy,* pp. 230–231. Shortly before entering government Forrestal read Philip Jessup, *Elihu Root* (New York, 1938).

3. "Reminiscences of Hanson Weightman Baldwin," Vol. II, U.S. Naval Institute Oral History, Annapolis, Md., 1975.

4. B. Mitchell Simpson III, "Harold Raynsford Stark," in Robert William Love, Jr., ed., *The Chiefs of Naval Operations* (Annapolis, Md., 1980), pp. 119–135. See also B. Mitchell Simpson III, *Admiral Harold R. Stark: Architect of Victory, 1939–1945* (Columbia, S.C., 1989).

5. "Reminiscences of Vice Admiral William R. Smedberg III," U.S. Naval Institute Oral History, Annapolis, Md., 1976.

6. Hoopes interview with W. John Kenney, May 29, 1989.

7. Albion and Connery, *Forrestal and the Navy,* p. 46.

8. Albion and Connery, *Forrestal and the Navy,* p. 229.

9. Albion and Connery, *Forrestal and the Navy,* pp. 50–51. See also Husband E. Kimmel, *Admiral Kimmel's Story* (Chicago, 1955).

10. Albion and Connery, *Forrestal and the Navy,* pp. 50–51. See also Robert J. Quinlan, "The United States Fleet: Diplomacy, Strategy and the Allocation of Ships

(1940–1941)," in Harold Stein, ed., *American Civil Military Decisions* (Birmingham, Ala., 1963); and Waldo Heinrichs, *Threshold of War: Franklin D. Roosevelt and American Entry Into World War II* (New York, 1988).

11. Charles J. V. Murphy interview with Charles Detmar, January 11, 1983.

12. Ibid.

13. Albion and Connery, *Forrestal and the Navy*, p. 34.

14. JVF to President Truman, April 14, 1945, Princeton University, JFP.

15. Robert H. Connery, *The Navy and the Industrial Mobilization in World War II* (Princeton, 1951), p. 57. See also Julius A. Furer, *Administration by the Navy Department in World War II* (Washington, D.C., 1959).

16. Albion and Connery, *Forrestal and the Navy*, pp. 34–37. See also Brinkley interview with H. Struve Hensel, June 6, 1988, and Walter Millis, ed., with E. S. Duffield, *The Forrestal Diaries* (New York, 1951), p. xi.

17. Hoopes interview with H. Struve Hensel, January 20, 1989. See also the Personal Papers of H. Struve Hensel, 1940–1941, Files (given to the authors by Mr. Hensel).

18. Ibid.

19. Ibid.

20. Murphy interview with James Rowe, September 3, 1981.

21. Albion and Connery, *Forrestal and the Navy*, pp. 14–37.

22. Albion and Connery, *Forrestal and the Navy*, p. 20. See also Rogow, *Forrestal*, pp. 89–121; Hoopes interview with Paul H. Nitze, June 23, 1989; and Robert Cutler, *No Time for Rest* (Boston, 1965), pp. 242–259.

23. Hoopes interview with H. Struve Hensel, January 20, 1989.

24. Hoopes interview with Clark Clifford, January 26, 1989.

25. Albion and Connery, *Forrestal and the Navy*, p. 19.

26. Albion and Connery, *Forrestal and the Navy*, pp. 16–17. See also Forrestal, "Christmas list," Box 37, Princeton University, JFP.

27. Albion and Connery, *Forrestal and the Navy*, p. 17.

28. JVF to Arthur Krock, October 17, 1945, Princeton University, JFP.

29. Forrestal speech to the New York *Herald Tribune* Forum, November 16, 1943, Princeton University, JFP.

30. JVF to Arthur Krock, October 17, 1945, Princeton University, JFP.

31. Albion and Connery, *Forrestal and the Navy*, pp. 27–28.

32. Albion and Connery, *Forrestal and the Navy*, p. 18. The Op-Nav officer was Vice Admiral George L. Russell.

33. Charles J. V. Murphy interview with Chester T. Lane, February 16, 1983.

34. James MacGregor Burns, *Roosevelt: The Soldier of Freedom, 1940–1945* (New York, 1970), p. 13.

35. Burns, *Roosevelt: The Soldier of Freedom*, p. 26.

36. Burns, *Roosevelt: The Soldier of Freedom*, pp. 28–29. See also Winston Churchill, *The Second World War*, Vol. II: *Their Finest Hour* (Boston, 1959), p. 566.

37. Hoopes interview with H. Struve Hensel, January 20, 1989. See also Albion and Connery, *Forrestal and the Navy*, pp. 74–75.

38. Eric Larrabee, *Commander in Chief: Franklin Delano Roosevelt, His Lieutenants and Their War* (New York, 1987), p. 46.

39. Frank L. Kluckhohn, "Aid Steps Mapped," *New York Times,* February 27, 1941, 1:8.

40. Murphy interview with Duncan Read, March 7, 1982.

CHAPTER 12 ASSERTING CIVILIAN CONTROL

1. Robert E. Sherwood, *Roosevelt and Hopkins: An Intimate History* (New York, 1948), pp. 131–132. See also Wayne S. Cole, *Charles A. Lindbergh and the Battle Against Intervention in World War II* (New York, 1974).

2. Robert Dallek, *Franklin D. Roosevelt and American Foreign Policy, 1932–1945* (New York, 1979).

3. Sherwood, *Roosevelt and Hopkins*, p. 132.

4. Robert Greenhalgh Albion and Robert Howe Connery, *Forrestal and the Navy* (New York, 1962), pp. 70–71. For an excellent detailed discussion of FDR's war planning in the late 1930s, See Edward Miller, *War Plan Orange* (Annapolis, Md., 1991).

5. Robert Connery, *The Navy and the Industrial Mobilization in World War II* (Princeton, 1951), pp. 48–49.

6. Hugh Johnson to Edward Stettinius, August 28, 1939, quoted in Connery, *The Navy and the Industrial Mobilization in World War II*, p. 50.

7. Albion and Connery, *Forrestal and the Navy*, p. 71.

8. Ibid.

9. Ibid.

10. Albion and Connery, *Forrestal and the Navy*, pp. 71–75. For the navy's relationship with business during WWII, see Donald M. Nelson, *Arsenal of Democracy* (New York, 1946); John Morton Blum, *V Was for Victory: Politics and American Culture During World War II* (New York, 1976), pp. 117–146; and Bruce Catton, *The War Lords of Washington* (New York, 1948).

11. Henry L. Stimson and McGeorge Bundy, *On Active Service in Peace and War* (New York, 1948), p. 354. See also Turner Catledge, "Knudsen Key Man," *New York Times*, December 19, 1940, 1:8; Hoopes interview with H. Struve Hensel, January 20, 1989; and John H. Towers, diary entries, December 16, 17, 18, 19 (courtesy of Professor Clark G. Reynolds).

12. David Brinkley, *Washington Goes to War* (New York, 1988), p. 63.

13. John Osborne, "Forrestal," unpublished manuscript outline. See also Richard M. Ketchum, *The Borrowed Years: 1938–1941* (New York, 1989), pp. 620–621.

14. Albion and Connery, *Forrestal and the Navy*, pp. 79–80. See also Eric Larrabee, *Commander in Chief: Franklin Delano Roosevelt, His Lieutenants and Their War* (New York, 1987), pp. 153–205, and JVF to Senator Harvey Kilgore, April 19, 1943, Princeton University, JFP.

15. Albion and Connery, *Forrestal and the Navy*, pp. 80–81. See also Connery, *The Navy and the Industrial Mobilization in World War II*, pp. 100–101.

16. Albion and Connery, *Forrestal and the Navy*, p. 73. See also James Fesler, *Industrial Mobilization for War, 1940–1945* (Washington, D.C., 1947).

17. Connery, *The Navy and the Industrial Mobilization in World War II*, pp. 59–60.

18. Hoopes interview with H. Struve Hensel, January 20, 1989. See also Connery, *The Navy and Industrial Mobilization in World War II*, pp. 59–60.

19. Connery, *The Navy and Industrial Mobilization in World War II*, pp. 91–92.

20. Brinkley interview with H. Struve Hensel, June 6, 1988. For biographical information on Hensel, see Connery, *Industrial Mobilization in World War II*, pp. 60–61.

21. H. Struve Hensel, memorandum of record, April 7, 1943, Personal Papers of H. Struve Hensel, 1940–1941, Files (given to the authors by Mr. Hensel).

22. Ibid. See also Brinkley interview with H. Struve Hensel, June 11, 1988.

23. Brinkley interview with H. Struve Hensel, June 6, 1988.

24. Hoopes interview with H. Struve Hensel, January 20, 1989. See also Connery, *Industrial Mobilization in World War II,* p. 61.

25. Brinkley interview with H. Struve Hensel, June 6, 1988.

26. Hoopes interview with H. Struve Hensel, January 20, 1989. See also Connery, *The Navy and Industrial Mobilization in World War II,* pp. 60–62.

27. H. Struve Hensel memorandum to James Forrestal, "Preparation and Signing of the Navy Department Contracts," March 25, 1941 (known as the Hensel-Kenny Report), Personal Papers of H. Struve Hensel. See also Connery, *The Navy and Industrial Mobilization in World War II,* pp. 62–70.

28. Connery, *The Navy and the Industrial Mobilization in World War II,* p. 70. See also Albion and Connery, *Forrestal and the Navy,* pp. 63–64, and H. Struve Hensel, "Explanation of Navy Contract Procedure and Personnel Engaged in Navy Contracting," April 9, 1943, Personal Papers of H. Struve Hensel (committee print).

29. Brinkley interview with H. Struve Hensel, June 6, 1988.

30. H. Struve Hensel memorandum to James Forrestal, April 28, 1941, Personal Papers of H. Struve Hensel. See also U.S. Congress, Committee on Naval Affairs, Hearings, "The Reorganization of Procurement Procedures and Coordination of Legal Services in the Navy Department," 78th Cong., 1st Session, 1943.

31. Ibid. See also Connery, *Industrial Mobilization in World War II,* p. 71.

32. Connery, *Industrial Mobilization in World War II,* pp. 70–71. See also Hoopes interviews with H. Struve Hensel, January 20, 1989, and W. John Kenney, May 29, 1989.

33. U.S. Congress, House Naval Affairs Committee, Hearings on "Sundry Legislation Affecting the Naval Establishment," 77th Cong., 1st Session, 1941. See also Albion and Connery, *Forrestal and the Navy,* pp. 66–67. For a discussion of Congressman Vinson's impact on naval affairs, see Calvin Enders, "The Vinson Navy," Ph.D. dissertation, Michigan State University, 1970.

34. Hoopes interview with H. Struve Hensel, January 20, 1989.

35. Judge Advocate General (Woodson) memorandum to Secretary of the Navy, July 2, 1941, in Albion and Connery, *Forrestal and the Navy,* p. 66.

36. Hoopes interview with H. Struve Hensel, January 20, 1989.

37. H. Struve Hensel, "Explanation of Navy Contract Procedure and Personnel Engaged in Navy Contracting," April 9, 1943, and Hensel memorandum, "How the December 13 Directive Came to be Issued," (n.d.), Personal Papers of H. Struve Hensel (committee print). See also Albion and Connery, *Forrestal and the Navy,* pp. 110–111, and JVF to Senator Harvey Kilgore, April 19, 1943, Princeton University, JFP.

38. Brinkley interview with H. Struve Hensel, June 6, 1988.

39. Ibid.

40. Ibid.

CHAPTER 13 GATHERING MOMENTUM

1. Robert H. Connery, *The Navy and the Industrial Mobilization in World War II* (Princeton, 1951), pp. 131–134.

2. Ibid. Also Brinkley interview with Robert Nathan, June 12, 1990.

3. Connery, *The Navy and the Industrial Mobilization in World War II,* pp. 145–146.

4. Hoopes interview with H. Struve Hensel, January 20, 1989.

5. Donald Nelson, *Arsenal of Democracy* (New York, 1946), p. 43.

6. JVF to Eliot Janeway, July 4, 1944, Princeton University, JFP. See also Connery, *The Navy and the Industrial Mobilization in World War II*, p. 146.

7. JVF memorandum to Secretary Frank Knox, December 24, 1942, Princeton University, JFP, and Connery, *The Navy and the Industrial Mobilization in WWII*, pp. 147–153.

8. H. Struve Hensel speech to meeting of former Navy General counsels, April 21, 1951, Personal Papers of H. Struve Hensel (given to authors by Mr. Hensel). See also Albion and Connery, *Forrestal and the Navy* (New York, 1962), pp. 94–95.

9. Godfrey Hodgson, *The Colonel: The Life and Wars of Henry L. Stimson, 1867–1950* (New York, 1990), pp. 246–247.

10. Charles Hurd, "No. 2 Men with No. 1 Jobs," *The New York Times Magazine*, December 7, 1941, pp. 9, 26. See also Robert E. Sherwood, *Roosevelt and Hopkins: An Intimate History* (New York, 1948), pp. 163–164.

11. Arthur Krock, "A Logical Promotion: Truman's Nomination of Patterson to War Post Follows Roosevelt Policy," *New York Times*, September 19, 1945, 17:5.

12. Ernest K. Lindley, *Newsweek*, July 23, 1947.

13. Albion and Connery, *Forrestal and the Navy*, pp. 76–77.

14. JVF to Herbert Bayard Swope, July 23, 1947, Princeton University, JFP.

15. Ferdinand Eberstadt, Report to Under Secretaries Patterson and Forrestal in Regard to the Army and Navy Munitions Board, November 26, 1941, Ferdinand Eberstadt Papers, Forrestal Files, Seeley G. Mudd Library, Princeton University.

16. Ibid.

17. Hoopes interview with H. Struve Hensel, January 20, 1989.

18. Albion and Connery, *Forrestal and the Navy*, pp. 103–108. See also Nelson, *Arsenal of Democracy*, pp. 304–308.

19. Connery, *Industrial Mobilization in World War II*, pp. 164–165. See also Albion and Connery, *Forrestal and the Navy*, pp. 103–108.

20. Robert C. Perez and Edward F. Willett, *The Will to Win: A Biography of Ferdinand Eberstadt* (Westport, Conn., 1989), pp. 5–9.

21. U.S. Congress, Special Committee Investigations, Hearings, "The National Defense Program," October 22, 1947, from the Charles J. V. Murphy Papers (in authors' possession).

22. Jonathan Daniels, *Frontier on the Potomac* (New York, 1946), pp. 2–3.

23. Forrestal speech at Princeton, June 21, 1944, Princeton University, JFP.

24. Albion and Connery, *Forrestal and the Navy*, pp. 30–31.

25. Forrestal speech to Harvard Business School alumni, June 12, 1943, Princeton University, JFP.

CHAPTER 14   TROUBLES WITH ADMIRAL KING

1. For information on King's early life and U.S. Naval Academy experiences, see Ernest J. King and Walter Muir Whitehill, *Fleet Admiral King: A Naval Record* (New York, 1952), pp. 9–34.

2. Elting E. Morison, *Turmoil and Tradition: A Study of the Life and Times of Henry L. Stimson* (Boston, 1960), p. 567.

3. Elmo R. Zumwalt, Jr., "King of the U.S. Navy," Washington *Post*, May 4, 1980 (a book review of *Master of Sea Power*, Thomas Buell's biography of King).

King's daughter is quoted in Eric Larrabee, *Commander in Chief: Franklin Roosevelt, His Lieutenants and Their War* (New York, 1987), p. 155.

4. "Reminiscences of Vice Admiral William R. Smedberg III," June 9, 1976, U.S. Naval Institute Oral History, Annapolis, Md., 1979.

5. Robert H. Ferrell, ed., *The Eisenhower Diaries,* February 23 and March 10, 1942 (New York, 1981), pp. 49–50.

6. Larrabee, *Commander in Chief,* pp. 192–193. See also Robert William Love, Jr., "Ernest Joseph King," in Robert William Love, Jr., ed., *The Chiefs of Naval Operations* (Annapolis, Md., 1980), pp. 137–139.

7. Henry L. Stimson and McGeorge Bundy, *On Active Service in Peace and War* (New York, 1948), p. 506.

8. Love, "Ernest Joseph King," *The Chiefs of Naval Operations,* pp. 162–163; and Larrabee, *Commander in Chief,* pp. 143–199. See also Forrest C. Pogue, *George C. Marshall,* Vol. II: *Ordeal and Hope, 1939–1942* (New York, 1966).

9. Thomas B. Buell, *Master of Sea Power: A Biography of Fleet Admiral Ernest J. King* (Boston, 1980), pp. 171–172; Elliott Roosevelt, *As He Saw It* (New York, 1946), p. 82; and Larrabee, *Commander in Chief,* pp. 153–154.

10. Robert William Love, Jr., "Fighting a Global War, 1941–1945," in Kenneth J. Hagan, ed., *In Peace and War: Interpretations of American Naval History, 1775–1978* (Westport, Conn., 1978), p. 264; Buell, *Master of Sea Power,* p. 89; and Larrabee, *Commander in Chief,* pp. 155–156.

11. B. Mitchell Simpson III, *Admiral Harold R. Stark: Architect of Victory, 1939–1945* (Columbia, S.C., 1989), pp. 61–96.

12. Patrick Abbazia, *Mr. Roosevelt's Navy: The Private War of the U.S. Atlantic Fleet* (Annapolis, Md., 1975), pp. 277–280, and Larrabee, *Commander in Chief,* pp. 160–163.

13. Larrabee, *Commander in Chief,* p. 169.

14. Robert Greenhalgh Albion and Robert Howe Connery, *Forrestal and the Navy* (New York, 1962), pp. 84–85.

15. Albion and Connery, *Forrestal and the Navy,* p. 40. For Forrestal's contention of August 13, 1945, that Stark should never again "hold any position in the United States Navy which requires the exercise of superior judgment," See Gordon W. Prange with Donald M. Goldstein, *Pearl Harbor: The Verdict of History* (New York, 1986), pp. 229–230.

16. JVF to Frank White Harned, May 7, 1945, Princeton University, JFP.

17. Buell, *Master of Sea Power,* pp. 151–154.

18. Buell, *Master of Sea Power,* pp. 162–178.

19. Buell, *Master of Sea Power,* p. 179. The March 12, 1942, Executive Order is reprinted as Appendix IV.

20. Albion and Connery, *Forrestal and the Navy,* p. 124.

21. Buell, *Master of Sea Power,* pp. 236–237.

22. JVF to Frank Knox, May 27, 1942, Princeton University, JFP.

23. Buell, *Master of Sea Power,* pp. 236–237. See also Larrabee, *Commander in Chief,* pp. 194–195.

24. Buell, *Master of Sea Power,* p. 236.

25. Quoted in Buell, *Master of Sea Power,* p. 237; and Larrabee, *Commander in Chief,* pp. 194–195.

26. Brinkley interview with H. Struve Hensel, June 11, 1990.

27. Buell, *Master of Sea Power,* p. 237.

28. Albion and Connery, *Forrestal and the Navy*, pp. 124–125; Buell, *Master of Sea Power*, p. 237; and King and Whitehill, *Fleet Admiral King: A Naval Record*, p. 629.

29. George Lobdell, "Frank Knox," in Paolo E. Coletta, ed., *American Secretaries of the Navy* (Annapolis, Md., 1980).

30. Felix Frankfurter to Frank Knox, July 2, 1941, Knox Papers. Library of Congress, Washington, D.C.

31. Admiral Ernest King to Frank Knox, October 2, 1943, Knox Papers, Library of Congress, Washington, D.C.

32. Frank Knox to Admiral King, October 12, 1943. Knox Papers, Library of Congress, Washington, D.C.

33. Buell, *Master of Sea Power*, pp. 237–239, and Albion and Connery, *Forrestal and the Navy*, pp. 124–127.

34. William D. Leahy, *I Was There* (New York, 1950), p. 222.

35. Albion and Connery, *Forrestal and the Navy*, p. 125. See also King and Whitehill, *Fleet Admiral King*, pp. 629–637.

36. Frank Knox to Admiral Ernest King, January 23, 1944, quoted in Albion and Connery, *Forrestal and the Navy*, pp. 126–127.

37. Leahy, *I Was There*, p. 222.

38. Buell, *Master of Sea Power*, p. 379; Larrabee, *Commander in Chief*, p. 199; and Hoopes interview with H. Struve Hensel, January 20, 1989.

39. Buell, *Master of Sea Power*, p. 238.

40. Buell, *Master of Sea Power*, p. 239.

41. Hoopes interview with H. Struve Hensel, January 20, 1989, and W. John Kenney. May 29, 1989.

42. Albion and Connery, *Forrestal and the Navy*, p. 92.

43. King quote from Walter M. Whitehill, "[comments on] Secretaries Knox and Forrestal," Whitehill-Buehl mss., Naval War College, Newport, Rhode Island. For further explanations of the frosty Forrestal-King relationship, see Albion and Connery, *Forrestal and the Navy*, pp. 92–93; and Buell, *Master of Sea Power*, pp. 449–453.

44. Morris J. MacGregor, Jr., *Integration of the Armed Forces, 1940–1965* (Washington, D.C., 1981), p. 60.

45. MacGregor, *Integration of the Armed Forces*, pp. 61–75.

46. MacGregor, *Integration of the Armed Forces*, pp. 63–84. See also "The Navy Makes a Gesture," *Crisis* 49 (May 1942), p. 51, and Ralph W. Donnelly, *Blacks in the Marine Corps* (Washington, D.C., 1975).

47. MacGregor, *Integration of the Armed Forces*, pp. 88–89; Buell, *Master of Sea Power*, p. 343, and Donald R. McCoy and Richard T. Ruetten, *Quest and Response: Minority Rights and the Truman Administration* (Lawrence, Kan., 1973), pp. 35–36.

48. Dennis D. Nelson, *The Integration of the Negro into the U.S. Navy* (New York, 1951), p. 46.

49. MacGregor, *Integration of the Armed Forces*, p. 77.

50. MacGregor, *Integration of the Armed Forces*, pp. 97–98.

51. Oral History interview, Mildred McAfee Horton, August 25, 1969, Center of Naval History, Washington, D.C.

52. Larrabee, *Commander in Chief*, p. 198.

53. John Osborne, "Forrestal," unpublished manuscript outline.

CHAPTER 15 SECRETARY OF THE NAVY

1. "Forrestal Looms to Succeed Knox," *New York Times,* April 28, 1944, 21:1.

2. Congressman Carl Vinson to JVF, May 18, 1944, Princeton University, JFP.

3. *Time,* May 15, 1944; Arthur Krock, "Mr. Forrestal's Promotion and the Campaign," *New York Times,* May 12, 1944, 18:5; and *Business Week,* May 6, 1944.

4. Ferdinand Eberstadt to Paul Shields, April 28, 1944, Ferdinand Eberstadt Papers, Seeley G. Mudd Library, Princeton University.

5. JVF to Edward Bermingham, May 16, 1944, Princeton University, JFP.

6. *Time,* May 22, 1944.

7. Robert Greenhalgh Albion and Robert Howe Connery, *Forrestal and the Navy* (New York, 1962), p. 13.

8. Jonathan Daniels, *Frontier on the Potomac* (New York, 1946), p. 223.

9. JVF to Henry Luce, May 11, 1944, Princeton University, JFP.

10. Henry Luce to JVF, May 15, 1944, Princeton University, JFP, and *Time,* October 29, 1945.

11. JVF to Congressman Carl Vinson, August 30, 1944, Princeton University, JFP.

12. Quentin Reynolds, "He Built Our Navy," *Collier's,* July 15, 1944.

13. Daniels, *Frontier on the Potomac,* p. 224.

14. Hoopes interview with Arthur Hadley, July 25, 1990.

15. James M. Barnes memorandum to the President, July 4, 1944, and Grace Tully memorandum to the President, July 13, 1944, PSF Navy, Forrestal File, FDRL, Hyde Park, N.Y.

16. Franklin D. Roosevelt memorandum to the Secretary of the Navy, July 13, 1944, PSF Navy, Forrestal File, FDRL, Hyde Park, N.Y.

17. Grace Tully memorandum to the President, July 13, 1944, PSF Navy, Forrestal File, FDRL, Hyde Park, N.Y.

18. Walter Millis, ed., *The Forrestal Diaries,* July 4, 1944 (New York, 1951), p. 5.

19. Millis, ed., *The Forrestal Diaries,* November 4, 1944, p. 13.

20. Sidney Shalett, "Forrestal Finds Japanese Sagging," *New York Times,* May 18, 1944, 8:2.

21. "Navy in Pacific Lists 2,005 Sorties in Week," *New York Times,* May 25, 1944, 10:4.

22. "Landing Craft Goal Topped 70%; Navy Reports Invasion Needs Met," *New York Times,* June 1, 1944, 3:2.

23. "Forrestal Warns of 'Bitter Fighting,' " *New York Times,* June 6, 1944, 11:6.

24. Shalett, "Forrestal Finds Japanese Sagging," *New York Times,* May 18, 1944, 8:2.

25. "Reminiscences of Vice Admiral William R. Smedberg III," June 9, 1976, U.S. Naval Institute Oral History, Annapolis, Md., July 1979.

26. Ibid. For a concise Forrestal explanation on why the navy needed to wage a public relations campaign, see JVF to Admiral Chester W. Nimitz, September 6, 1944, Princeton University, JFP, and Vincent Davis, *Postwar Defense and the U.S. Navy, 1943–1946* (Chapel Hill, N.C., 1966), pp. 82–88.

27. Charles J. V. Murphy interview with Harold Miller, October 16, 1983.

28. Ibid.

29. E. P. Potter, *Nimitz* (Annapolis, Md., 1976), pp. 363–364.

30. Potter, *Nimitz,* pp. 401–411. See also Steven T. Ross, "Chester William Nimitz," in Robert William Love, Jr., *The Chiefs of Naval Operations* (Annapolis, Md., 1980), pp. 181–191; and Forrestal memorandum to Admiral King, May 25, 1943, Princeton University, JFP.

31. JVF to Franklin D. Roosevelt, September 27, 1944, Princeton University, JFP.

32. Matthew J. Bruccoli, *The O'Hara Concern: A Biography of John O'Hara* (New York, 1975), p. 171.

33. Ibid.

34. JVF to John McLain, April 19, 1944, Princeton University, JFP. See also Ronald H. Spector, *Eagle Against the Sun: The American War with Japan* (New York, 1984), pp. 252–323.

35. Brinkley interview with Admiral Robert B. Carney, April 6, 1988.

36. "Eisenhower Sees War Won by Arms," *New York Times,* August 25, 1944, 3:1.

37. James Forrestal, Trip Report, "Diary of Mediterranean Trip," August 4–23, 1944 (unpublished), Box 38, Princeton University, JFP. See also "Forrestal Also in Italy," *New York Times,* August 15, 1944, 8:4.

38. Forrestal, Trip Report, "Diary of Mediterranean Trip."

39. Hoopes interview with Ellen Barry, May 14, 1988.

40. Kent R. Greenfield, *American Strategy in World War II: A Reconsideration* (Baltimore, 1963), p. 1. See also Bill D. Ross, *Iwo Jima: Legacy of Valor* (New York, 1985).

41. Robert Sherrod, *On to the Westward* (New York, 1945), p. 160.

42. Sherrod, *On to the Westward,* pp. 160–161. See also Potter, *Nimitz,* pp. 359–360.

43. Potter, *Nimitz,* pp. 158–159. See also Norman V. Cooper, "The Military Career of Lieutenant General Holland M. Smith," Ph.D. dissertation, University of Alabama, 1971.

44. Ross, *Iwo Jima: Legacy of Valor* (official U.S. Marine Corps figures provided by Major General Fred Haynes, USMC [Ret.]).

45. Courtney Whitney, *MacArthur: His Rendezvous with History* (New York, 1956), pp. 269–302.

46. Potter, *Nimitz,* p. 363.

47. Ibid.

48. "Forrestal Pays Tribute to Marines; He Hit Iwo Beach Behind Them," *New York Times,* February 26, 1945, 1:6.

49. The radio address was published in the *Congressional Record,* March 7, 1945, p. A1039.

50. Arthur Krock, "An Observer at the Battle of Iwo Jima," *New York Times,* February 27, 1945, 18:5.

51. Whitney, *MacArthur: His Rendezvous with History,* pp. 302–313. See also Millis, ed., *The Forrestal Diaries,* February 28, 1945, p. 31.

52. Herbert Hoover to Douglas MacArthur, September 3, 17, 1953; MacArthur to Hoover, September 9, 1953; Douglas MacArthur Papers, MacArthur Memorial Library Bureau of Archives, Norfolk, Va.

53. Franklin D. Roosevelt to JVF, March 2, 1945, President's Personal File (PPF), FDRL, Hyde Park, N.Y.

54. Rear Admiral Ellis M. Zacharias, "The Forrestal Enigma," *United Nations World,* November 1945.

55. Ibid.

56. Ibid.

57. Brinkley interview with Eliot Janeway, September 28, 1990.

58. Millis, ed., *The Forrestal Diaries,* March 10, 1945, pp. 32–33.

CHAPTER 16   ENDING THE WAR

1. Walter Millis, ed., *The Forrestal Diaries* March 13, 1945 (New York, 1951), p. 35. See also JVF to Edward R. Stettinius, March 4, 1945, Princeton University, JFP, and Unpublished Forrestal Diaries, March 13, 1945, p. 227 (housed with JVF's personal papers at Princeton and at the OSD Historical Office in the Pentagon).

2. Millis, ed., *The Forrestal Diaries,* April 2, 1945, pp. 38–39.

3. Ibid, p. 39.

4. Ibid., April 12, 1945, pp. 42–43.

5. John Osborne, "Forrestal," unpublished manuscript outline.

6. Harry S. Truman, *Memoirs: 1945, Year of Decisions* (Garden City, N.Y. 1955), p. 19.

7. Robert J. Donovan, *Conflict and Crisis: The Presidency of Harry S. Truman, 1945–1948* (New York, 1977), pp. 13–14.

8. Donovan, *Conflict and Crisis,* p. 73.

9. Millis, ed., *The Forrestal Diaries,* April 23, 1945, pp. 48–49. See also Thomas M. Campbell and George C. Herring, eds., *The Diaries of Edward R. Stettinius, Jr., 1943–1946* (New York, 1975), pp. 328–329. In addition to the President, Forrestal, Stettinius, Stimson, Admiral King, General Marshall, Admiral Leahy, Ambassador Harriman, Major General John R. Deane, Chip Bohlen, and James Dunn were all present.

10. Millis, ed., *The Forrestal Diaries,* April 23, 1945, pp. 48–51.

11. Ibid.

12. Daniel Yergin, *Shattered Peace: The Origins of the Cold War and the National Security State* (Boston, 1977), pp. 80–86; Donovan, *Conflict and Crisis,* pp. 39–42; Harry S. Truman, *Memoirs, 1945, Year of Decisions* (Garden City, N.Y., 1955), pp. 75–82; and *FRUS,* 1945, 5:235–255.

13. Winston Churchill, *Triumph and Tragedy* (Boston, 1953), pp. 511–512. See also Donovan, *Conflict and Crisis,* pp. 52–53.

14. *FRUS,* Conference of Berlin (Potsdam), 1945, 1:3–4.

15. Donovan, *Conflict and Crisis,* p. 51., For the full text of the broadcast, see *Public Papers of the Presidents of the U.S.: Harry S. Truman: 1945* (Washington, D.C.), p. 50.

16. Unpublished Forrestal Diaries, May 8, 1945, Princeton University, JFP, and OSO Historical Office, Pentagon, p. 326, and minutes of the Committee of Three, May 8, 1945, National Archives, 59, General Records of the State Department, Washington, D.C.

17. Millis, ed., *The Forrestal Diaries,* April 25, 1947, p. 265. See also JVF to Joseph E. Ridder, December 16, 1944, Princeton University, JFP.

18, Millis, ed., *The Forrestal Diaries,* May 1, 1945, p. 53.

19. Millis, ed., *The Forrestal Diaries,* "To Homer Ferguson, May 14, 1945," p. 57. See also JVF to Homer Ferguson, May 14, 1945, Princeton University, JFP.

20. Millis, ed., *The Forrestal Diaries,* May 12, 1945, p. 56.

21. Ibid.

22. Millis, ed., *The Forrestal Diaries,* State-War-Navy Meetings, May 29, 1945, June 12, 1945, and June 19, 1945, pp. 66–70.

23. Donovan, *Conflict and Crisis,* p. 91.

24. Cordell Hull, *Memoirs of Cordell Hull,* Vol. II (New York, 1948), pp. 1593–1594. See also Donovan, *Conflict and Crisis,* p. 91.

25. Eric Larrabee, *Commander in Chief: Franklin Roosevelt, His Lieutenants and Their War* (New York, 1987), p. 3.

26. Millis, ed., *The Forrestal Diaries,* April 22, 1947, pp. 256–266.

27. Donovan, *Conflict and Crisis,* p. 46. See also Henry L. Stimson, "Memorandum Discussed with the President, April 25, 1945," in Henry L. Stimson and McGeorge Bundy, *On Active Service in Peace and War* (New York, 1948), pp. 635ff.

28. Donovan, *Conflict and Crisis,* pp. 48–50; Joseph L. Lieberman, *The Scorpion and the Tarantula: The Struggle to Control Atomic Weapons, 1945–49* (Boston, 1970), pp. 85–96; Elting E. Morison, *Turmoil and Tradition: A Study of the Life and Times of Henry L. Stimson* (Boston, 1960), pp. 623–630; and Michael S. Sherry, *Preparing for the Next War: American Plans for Postwar Defense, 1941–45* (New Haven, 1977).

29. Donovan, *Conflict and Crisis,* pp. 48–50; Lieberman, *The Scorpion and the Tarantula,* pp. 85–96; Morison, *Turmoil and Tradition,* pp. 623–630.

30. Donovan, *Conflict and Crisis,* pp. 48–50; Lieberman, *The Scorpion and the Tarantula,* pp. 85–96; and Morison, *Turmoil and Tradition,* pp. 623–630.

31. Ernest J. King and Walter Muir Whitehall, *Fleet Admiral King: A Naval Record* (New York, 1952), p. 604. See also minutes, JCS meeting with President, June 18, 1945, National Archives, RG 165.

32. *FRUS,* Conference of Berlin (Potsdam), 1945, 1:903–10. See also Sherry, *Preparing for the Next War,* pp. 187–188.

33. James H. and William M. Belote, *Typhoon of Steel: The Battle of Okinawa* (New York, 1970), and Ronald H. Spector, *Eagle Against the Sun: The American War with Japan* (New York, 1985), pp. 532–555.

34. Millis, ed., *The Forrestal Diaries,* July 15, 1945, pp. 75–76.

35. Ibid., July 24, 1945, pp. 76–77.

36. Donovan, *Conflict and Crisis,* p. 66, and Stimson and Bundy, *On Active Service in Peace and War,* p. 117.

37. Lieberman, *The Scorpion and the Tarantula,* pp. 91–92.

38. Ibid.

39. Barton J. Bernstein, ed., *The Atomic Bomb: The Critical Issues* (Boston, 1976), and Martin Sherwin, *A World Destroyed: The Atomic Bomb and the Grand Alliance* (New York, 1975).

40. Robert Greenhalgh Albion and Robert Howe Connery, *Forrestal and the Navy* (New York, 1962), pp. 174–176.

41. "General Curtis LeMay," *New York Times,* October 2, 1990.

42. *FRUS,* Conference of Berlin (Potsdam), 1945, 2:1284. See also Donovan, *Conflict and Crisis,* pp. 80–104; Charles L. Mee, Jr., *Meeting at Potsdam* (New York, 1975), pp. 15–16; and Barton J. Bernstein, "Truman at Potsdam," *Foreign Service Journal* (July/August 1983), pp. 29–35.

43. Donovan, *Conflict and Crisis,* p. 93.

44. Ibid., p. 94.

45. Richard F. Haynes, *The Awesome Power: Harry S. Truman as Commander in Chief* (Baton Rouge, 1973), p. 51. See also Stimson and Bundy, *On Active Service in Peace and War,* pp. 626–627; Truman, *Memoirs: 1945, Year of Decisions,* pp. 427–

428; James F. Byrnes, *Speaking Frankly* (New York, 1947), p. 209; and Millis, ed., *The Forrestal Diaries,* August 10, 1945, pp. 84-85.

46. Byrnes, *Speaking Frankly,* p. 212.

47. Donovan, *Conflict and Crisis,* p. 97.

CHAPTER 17 PRIVATE LIFE IN THE NATION'S CAPITAL

1. Charles J. V. Murphy interview with John McLain, April 6, 1982.

2. Joseph W. Alsop and Adam Platt, *The Memoirs of Joseph W. Alsop,* prepublication manuscript, p. 423 (courtesy of Mr. Platt).

3. Murphy interview with John J. McCloy, October 11, 1982.

4. Hoopes interview with Ellen Barry, May 14, 1988.

5. Hoopes interview with Nina Auchincloss Straight, December 20, 1989.

6. Hoopes interview with Phyllis Wright, June 22, 1989.

7. William D. Hassett, *Off the Record with FDR, 1942-1945* (New Brunswick, N.J., 1958), p. 323.

8. Hoopes interview with Lucius Battle, November 28, 1988.

9. Hoopes interview with Mrs. Burroughs Hoffman, May 11, 1989.

10. Hoopes interview with W. John Kenney, May 29, 1989.

11. Hoopes interview with H. Struve Hensel, January 20, 1989.

12. Hoopes interview with Paul H. Nitze, June 23, 1989.

13. Murphy interview with Daniel Caulkins, October 7, 1983.

14. Hoopes interviews with Peter Walker and Benjamin Reid, February 14, 1989.

15. Hoopes interview with Phyllis Wright, June 22, 1989.

16. Murphy interview with Robert A. Lovett, September 22, 1983.

17. Hoopes interview with Marian Christie, June 21, 1989. For biographical information on Mrs. Dwight Davis see "Mrs. Davis Dead; GOP Ex-Aide, 68," *New York Times,* December 29, 1952, and Estelle Jackson, "Repeal Was Worth the Fight," Washington *Post* Newspaper Archive, Davis File (5 profiles).

18. Alsop and Platt, *The Memoirs of Joseph W. Alsop,* p. 109. For biographical information on Dwight Davis, see *New York Times,* "Dwight Davis Dies; War Ex-Secretary," November 29, 1945, and Washington *Post* Newspaper Archive, Davis File.

19. Dudley Harmon, "About the Town," Washington *Post,* 1942 (clipping, n.d.).

20. Hoopes interview with Marian Christie, June 21, 1989.

21. Pauline Davis to JVF, April 1949, Princeton University, JFP.

22. Edythe Holbrook interview with Adele Lovett, October 2, 1982.

23. Hoopes interview with Clark Clifford, January 26, 1989.

24. Roy Jenkins, *Truman* (New York, 1986), p. 69.

25. "Reminiscences of Vice Admiral William R. Smedberg III," June 9, 1976, U.S. Naval Institute Oral History, Annapolis, July 1979, pp. 330-333.

26. Ibid.

27. Ibid.

28. Ibid.

29. Ibid., p. 324.

30. John T. Connor, "Impressions of the Secretary," October 23, 1961, memorandum, pp. 3-5, Arthur M. Krock Papers, Seeley G. Mudd Library, Princeton University.

31. Ibid.

CHAPTER 18   THE FDR LEGACY

1. JVF to Joseph Ridder, December 16, 1944, Princeton University, JFP.

2. Henry L. Stimson and McGeorge Bundy, *On Active Service in Peace and War* (New York, 1947), pp. 561–562.

3. Quoted in Lloyd C. Gardner, *Architects of Illusion: Men and Ideas in American Foreign Policy, 1941–1949* (Chicago, 1970), p. 4.

4. The Atlantic Charter Press Release (for delivery to press and radio at 0900 EST on Thursday, August 14, 1941), FDRL, Hyde Park, N.Y.

5. Gardner, *Architects of Illusion,* pp. 26–54. See also Theodore A. Wilson, *The First Summit: Roosevelt and Churchill at Placentia Bay, 1941* (Boston, 1969), and James MacGregor Burns, *Roosevelt: The Soldier of Freedom, 1940–1945* (New York, 1970), pp. 130–131.

6. Burns, *Roosevelt: The Soldier of Freedom,* pp. 231–243, and Gardner, *Architects of Illusion,* pp. 26–54.

7. Roosevelt-Molotov conversation, *FRUS,* May 1942, 3:575–583.

8. Forrest C. Pogue, *George C. Marshall,* Vol. II: *Ordeal and Hope, 1939–1942* (New York, 1966), pp. 325–328.

9. Burns, *Roosevelt: The Soldier of Freedom,* p. 235.

10. Robert E. Sherwood, *Roosevelt and Hopkins: An Intimate History* (New York, 1948), pp. 557–576. See also Burns, *Roosevelt: The Soldier of Freedom,* pp. 228–243.

11. Burns, *Roosevelt: The Soldier of Freedom,* p. 237. See also Ernest J. King and Walter Muir Whitehall, *Fleet Admiral King: A Naval Record* (New York, 1952), pp. 416–417; Maurice Matloff, *Strategic Planning for Coalition Warfare, 1943–1944* (Washington, D.C., 1953), pp. 19–36.

12. Burns, *Roosevelt: The Soldier of Freedom,* pp. 305–330.

13. Anne Armstrong, *Unconditional Surrender: The Impact of the Casablanca Policy Upon World War II* (New Brunswick, N.J., 1961); Sherwood, *Roosevelt and Hopkins,* pp. 674–694; and Roosevelt-Molotov conversation, *FRUS,* May 1942, 3:575.

14. John Lewis Gaddis, *The United States and the Origins of the Cold War, 1941–1947* (New York, 1972), p. 74, and Burns, *Roosevelt: The Soldier of Freedom,* pp. 282–284.

15. Roosevelt-Eden discussions, *FRUS,* 1943, 3:13–39, and Anthony Eden, *The Eden Memoirs: The Reckoning* (London, 1965), pp. 373–374.

16. Cairo-Teheran, *FRUS,* November 1943, 56–58. See also Keith Eubank, *Summit at Teheran* (New York, 1985), and W. Averell Harriman and Ellie Abel, *Special Envoy to Churchill and Stalin: 1941–1946* (New York, 1975), pp. 256–283.

17. Gaddis, *The United States and the Origins of the Cold War,* pp. 161–163, and Burns, *Roosevelt: The Soldier of Freedom,* pp. 534–539.

18. Burns, *Roosevelt: The Soldier of Freedom,* p. 535.

19. Burns, *Roosevelt: The Soldier of Freedom,* p. 534.

20. Burns, *Roosevelt: The Soldier of Freedom,* pp. 536–539.

21. Winston Churchill, *The Second World War: Triumph and Tragedy* (Boston, 1953), pp. 226–228.

22. Gardner, *Architects of Illusion,* p. 51.

23. Arthur H. Vandenberg, Jr., ed., *The Private Papers of Senator Vandenberg* (Boston, 1952), pp. 126–145.

24. Vandenberg, *The Private Papers of Senator Vandenberg,* p. 141.

25. Editorial, *Life,* January 23, 1945, p. 26, and Gardner, *Architects of Illusion,* p. 50.

26. Malta-Yalta, *FRUS,* 1945; Diane Shaver Clemens, *Yalta* (New York, 1970); Robert L. Messer; *The End of an Alliance: James F. Byrnes, Roosevelt, Truman, and the Origins of the Cold War* (Chapel Hill, N.C., 1982), pp. 31–70; and Harriman and Abel, *Special Envoy to Churchill and Stalin,* pp. 388–446.

27. William D. Leahy, *I Was There* (New York, 1950), pp. 315–316.

28. Daniel Yergin, *Shattered Peace: The Origins of the Cold War and the National Security State* (Boston, 1977), pp. 58–68.

29. FDR's Address to Congress (Yalta), March 1, 1945, in Samuel I. Rosenman, ed., *The Public Papers and Addresses of Franklin D. Roosevelt,* Vol. II, *1944–45* (New York, 1950), pp. 570–586.

30. Stimson and Bundy, *On Active Service in Peace and War,* pp. 563–564.

CHAPTER 19   NO RETURN TO PRIVATE LIFE

1. JVF to Cass Canfield, March 16, 1946, Princeton University, JFP.

2. For chapter drafts of JVF's proposed book, see Box 36, Princeton University, JFP. See also Arnold A. Rogow, *James Forrestal: A Study of Personality, Politics, and Policy* (New York, 1963), pp. 251–252.

3. Brinkley interview with Eliot Janeway, September 18, 1990. See also "Seattle Paper–Palmer Hoyt" File, Princeton University, Box 42, JFP.

4. Hoopes interview with Paul H. Nitze, June 23, 1989.

5. Brinkley interview with Eliot Janeway, September 18, 1990.

6. Hoopes interview with Eliot Janeway, July 5, 1990.

7. Lewis L. Strauss, *Men and Decisions* (Garden City, N.Y., 1962), pp. 156–157. See also Rogow, *James Forrestal,* pp. 239–249.

8. Walter Millis, ed., *The Forrestal Diaries,* January 21, 1946 (New York, 1951), p. 130.

9. Hoopes interview with Eliot Janeway, July 5, 1990. See also Cecilia Stiles Cornell, "James V. Forrestal and the American National Security Policy, 1940–1949," Ph.D. dissertation, Vanderbilt University, 1987, pp. 33–34.

10. Brinkley interview with Eliot Janeway, September 18, 1990.

11. Ibid.

12. Ibid. See also Rogow, *James Forrestal,* p. 130.

13. Hoopes interview with Michael Forrestal, October 12, 1988.

14. Charles J. V. Murphy interview with John J. McCloy, October 16, 1983.

15. Arthur Bryant, *A History of the War Years Based on the Diaries of Field-Marshal Lord Alanbrooke, Chief of the Imperial General Staff,* Vol. I: *The Turn of the Tide* (Garden City, N.Y., 1957), p. 234. See also Eric Larrabee, *Commander in Chief: Franklin Delano Roosevelt, His Lieutenants and Their War* (New York, 1987), pp. 16–19.

16. Herbert Elliston, "Jim Forrestal: A Portrait in Politics," *Atlantic Monthly* (November 1951), pp. 73–80. See also Rogow, *James Forrestal,* pp. 255–262. The Hankey book that impressed JVF the most was *Government Control in War* (London, 1945). JVF read the complete works of Bagehot; "The Defect of America: Presidential and Ministerial Governments Compared," *The Economist,* Vol. 20, December 6, 1862, pp. 1346–1347, and "The Special Danger of Men of Business as Administrators," *The Economist,* Vol. 29, March 18, 1872, pp. 309–310, being particular favorites.

17. Elliston, "Jim Forrestal: A Portrait of Politics," *Atlantic Monthly,* pp. 73–80.

18. Hensel Report to Secretary Forrestal, "British Civil Service and Government Coordination," June 10, 1946, Personal Papers of H. Struve Hensel, 1940, 1941, Files (given to the authors by Mr. Hensel).

19. JVF to William O. Douglas, August 21, 1947, Princeton University, JFP.

20. Forrestal speech to Princeton University Bicentennial Symposium, "The University and Public Service," November 14, 1946, Princeton University, JFP.

21. Ibid.

22. Hensel Report to Secretary Forrestal, "British Civil Service and Government Coordination," June 10, 1946.

23. JVF to James Byrnes, December 1946, Princeton University, JFP.

24. Jonathan Daniels, *Frontier on the Potomac* (New York, 1946).

CHAPTER 20   THE EMERGING ANTI-COMMUNIST CONSENSUS

1. Clinton P. Anderson, with Milton Viorst, *Outsider in the Senate: Senator Clinton Anderson's Memoirs* (New York, 1970), p. 74.

2. Robert L. Messer, *The End of an Alliance: James F. Byrnes, Roosevelt, Truman, and the Origins of the Cold War* (Chapel Hill, N.C., 1982), p. 6. See also James F. Byrnes, *All in One Lifetime* (New York, 1958), and *Speaking Frankly* (New York, 1947).

3. Lloyd C. Gardner, *Architects of Illusion: Men and Ideas in American Foreign Policy, 1941–1949* (Chicago, 1970), pp. 84–112.

4. Messer, *The End of an Alliance,* pp. 66–67.

5. Robert J. Donovan, *Conflict and Crisis: The Presidency of Harry S. Truman, 1945–1948* (New York, 1977), pp. 155–162. See also Anderson, *Outsider in the Senate,* p. 78.

6. Messer, *The End of an Alliance,* pp. 50–70. See also James F. Byrnes, White House Press Conference, February 13, 1945, Office of War Mobilization and Reconversion, Press and Radio Conference #9, James F. Byrnes Papers, Clemson University, Clemson, South Carolina.

7. Messer, *The End of an Alliance,* pp. 54–70. See also *New York Times,* February 13, 1945, pp. 1–2, and Byrnes White House Press Conference, February 13, 1945.

8. Messer, *The End of an Alliance,* pp. 50–70.

9. Ibid.

10. Ibid.

11. Ibid., pp. 71–88.

12. Ibid., p. 89.

13. Daniel Yergin, *Shattered Peace: The Origins of the Cold War and the National Security State* (Boston, 1977), pp. 136–137.

14. U.S. Congress, House Naval Affairs Committee, "Composition of the Postwar Navy," Hearings pursuant to H. Con. Res. 80, September 19–28, 1945, pp. 1159–1497; Vincent Davis, *Postwar Defense Policy and the U.S. Navy, 1943–1946* (Chapel Hill, N.C., 1966), pp. 182–194; Michael S. Sherry, *Preparing for the Next War: American Plans for Postwar Defense, 1941–45* (New Haven, 1977), pp. 208–212; Richard G. Hewlet and Francis Duncan, *Nuclear Navy, 1946–1952* (Chicago, 1944), pp. 24–27; Robert Greenhalgh Albion and Robert Howe Connery, *Forrestal and the*

Navy (New York, 1962), pp. 181–182; Walter Millis, ed., *The Forrestal Diaries, September 7, 1945* (New York, 1951), pp. 93–96; Cecilia Stiles Cornell, "James V. Forrestal and American National Security Policy, 1940–1944," Ph.D. dissertation, Vanderbilt University, 1987, pp. 186–187; and JVF to Harry S. Truman, October 1, 1945, Princeton University, JFP.

15. Messer, *The End of an Alliance*, pp. 115–136. See also Patricia Dawson Ward, *Threat of Peace: James F. Byrnes and the Council of Foreign Ministers, 1945–46* (Kent, O., 1979), and Greg Herken, *The Winning Weapon: The Atomic Bomb in the Cold War, 1945–1950* (New York, 1980), pp. 43–59.

16. Messer, *The End of an Alliance*, pp. 128–129. See also Yergin, *Shattered Peace*, pp. 131–133.

17. Messer, *The End of an Alliance*, pp. 132–133.

18. Ibid., pp. 133–156. See also James L. Gormly, "The Washington Declaration and the 'Poor Relation': Anglo-American Atomic Diplomacy, 1945–46": *Diplomatic History* 8 (Spring 1984): 125–134.

19. Millis, ed., *The Forrestal Diaries*, October 16, 1945, pp. 101–102; October 26, 1945, pp. 103–106; and December 16, 1945, pp. 233–234. See also Byrnes, *Speaking Frankly*, pp. 152–155.

20. Millis, ed., *The Forrestal Diaries*, November 5, 1945, pp. 105–108. See also Unpublished Forrestal Diaries, Princeton University, JFP, and OSD Historical Office, Pentagon, pp. 590–592.

21. Messer, *The End of an Alliance*, pp. 143–144, and Arthur H. Vandenberg, Jr., ed., *The Private Papers of Senator Vandenberg* (Boston, 1952), pp. 227–228.

22. Vandenberg, ed., *The Private Papers of Senator Vandenberg*, pp. 229–230.

23. Donovan, *Conflict and Crisis*, pp. 155–162.

24. Messer, *The End of an Alliance*, pp. 148–155.

25. Donovan, *Conflict and Crisis*, p. 185.

26. Yergin, *Shattered Peace*, pp. 84–85.

27. Yergin, *Shattered Peace*, p. 148.

28. Forrestal speech to Wednesday Law Club, Baltimore, May 26, 1943, Princeton University, JFP.

29. Transcripts of all Forrestal speeches from 1941 to 1949 are located in Boxes 5 and 6, Princeton University, JFP.

30. Forrestal speech to Wednesday Law Club, Baltimore, May 26, 1943, Princeton University, JFP. See also Forrestal speech, Jackson Day Dinner, New Orleans, March 23, 1946; Forrestal speech, National Geographic Society, Washington, D.C., March 31, 1944; and Forrestal speech, Navy League, Los Angeles, October 27, 1943, Princeton University, JFP. Many of his concerns about unilateral disarmament are pulled together in James Forrestal, "Will We Choose Naval Suicide Again?," *The Saturday Evening Post*, June 24, 1944, p. 9, and "Keep the Navy to Keep the Peace," *Sea Power*, July 1945, pp. 21–22.

31. Donovan, *Conflict and Crisis*, p. 187, and Joseph Stalin address, February 9, 1946, *Vital Speeches* 12 (March 1, 1946), pp. 300–304. See also *New York Times*, February 10, 1946, p. 30.

32. *Time*, February 18, 1946, pp. 29–30. See also John Lewis Gaddis, *The United States and the Origins of the Cold War 1941–1947*, (New York, 1972) p. 300.

33. Quoted in Donovan, *Conflict and Crisis*, p. 187.

34. Millis, ed., *The Forrestal Diaries*, February 17, 1946, p. 134.

35. Messer, *The End of an Alliance*, pp. 181–194.

36. Messer, *The End of an Alliance*, pp. 188–189. See also James F. Byrnes speech,

Overseas Press Club, February 28, 1946 (Byrnes's reading copy with Truman notations in the margins), Speeches, 1946, Byrnes Papers, Clemson University, and *New York Times,* March 1, 1946, p. 1 (full text, p. 10).

37. James F. Byrnes speech, Overseas Press Club, February 28, 1946.

38. *New York Times,* March 1, 1946, pp. 1, 20; March 2, p. 1; Washington *Post,* March 2, 1946, p. 7; and Messer, *The End of an Alliance,* p. 189.

39. Winston Churchill address, Fulton, Missouri, March 5, 1946, *Vital Speeches* 12 (March 15, 1946), pp. 329–332.

40. Byrnes, *All in One Lifetime,* p. 349. See also Gaddis, *The United States and the Origins of the Cold War,* p. 308.

41. Donovan, *Conflict and Crisis,* p. 192.

42. Forrestal speech to Pittsburgh Foreign Policy Association, April 29, 1946, Princeton University, JFP.

43. Donovan, *Conflict and Crisis,* p. 220.

44. Mordecai Ezekiell to Henry Wallace, November 23, 1942, Henry Wallace Papers, University of Iowa, Ames, Iowa.

45. Millis, ed., *The Forrestal Diaries,* February 17, 1946, p. 134, and Arnold A. Rogow, *James Forrestal: A Study of Personality, Politics, and Policy* (New York, 1963), pp. 132–144.

46. Millis, ed., *The Forrestal Diaries,* April 19, 1946, pp. 154–155, and Rogow, *James Forrestal,* pp. 137–144.

47. Donovan, *Conflict and Crisis,* pp. 222–228. See also John Morton Blum, ed., *The Price of Vision: The Diary of Henry A. Wallace, 1942–1946* (Boston, 1973), pp. 582–629, and Richard J. Walton, *Henry Wallace, Harry Truman, and the Cold War* (New York, 1976), pp. 97–101.

48. Donovan, *Conflict and Crisis,* pp. 223–228. For JVF's criticism of the Wallace speech, see Forrestal speech to the Navy Industrial Association, Waldorf-Astoria, New York, September 17, 1945, Princeton University, JFP.

49. Millis, ed., *The Forrestal Diaries,* April 14, 1947, pp. 260–262.

CHAPTER 21   THE GODFATHER OF CONTAINMENT

1. Hoopes interview with John H. Ohly, August 20, 1989.

2. Beatrice Farnsworth, *William C. Bullitt and the Soviet Union* (Bloomington, Ind., 1967), p. 151.

3. Will Brownell and Richard N. Billings, *So Close to Greatness: A Biography of William C. Bullitt* (New York, 1987), p. 290.

4. Brownell and Billings, *So Close to Greatness,* p. 293.

5. Forrestal–De Gaulle, conference meeting memorandum (by Lt. Commander John Davis Lodge, USNR, JVF's aide and translator), August 18, 1944, Princeton University, JFP.

6. JVF to Palmer "Ep" Hoyt, September 2, 1944, Princeton University, JFP.

7. Forrestal speech to the Investment Bankers Association, Chicago, November 28, 1944, Princeton University, JFP.

8. Walter Millis, ed., *The Forrestal Diaries,* April 20, 1945 (New York, 1951), pp. 47–48. See also Unpublished Forrestal Diaries, April 20, 1945, Princeton University, JFP, and OSD Historical Office, Pentagon, p. 307, and Daniel Yergin, *Shattered Peace: The Origins of the Cold War and the National Security State* (Boston, 1977), pp. 74–77.

9. The folder marked "Russia," Box 24, Princeton University, JFP, contains copies of six Harriman telegrams to Secretary of State Byrnes, all composed in April 1945 and dealing with the Soviet threat. See also Millis, ed., *The Forrestal Diaries*, pp. 47–48, 55–58, 79–81, and Brinkley interview with Michael Forrestal, April 27, 1988.

10. Forrestal–De Gaulle meeting memorandum (by Lt. Commander John Davis Lodge), August 18, 1944, Princeton University, JFP.

11. Millis, ed., *The Forrestal Diaries*, July 29, 1945, pp. 79–80, and Arnold A. Rogow, *James Forrestal: A Study of Personality, Politics, and Policy* (New York, 1963), pp. 132–149.

12. Brinkley interview with Eliot Janeway, September 28, 1990.

13. Henry A. Wallace Oral History interview, 1953, Oral History Research Office, Columbia University, p. 1191.

14. Rogow, *James Forrestal*, pp. 145–148; Harold Laski, *The Secret Battalion: An Examination of the Communist Attitude to the Labour Party* (The Labour [Party] Publications Department, April 1966), and Kingsley Martin, *Harold Laski: A Biographical Memoir* (London, 1953), pp. 40–45.

15. JVF to Oliver Lyttleton, M.P. (Conservative), December 4, 1945, Princeton University, JFP. See also Rogow, *James Forrestal*, p. 146.

16. Lloyd C. Gardner, *Architects of Illusion: Men and Ideas in American Foreign Policy, 1941–1949* (Chicago, 1970), pp. 271–273.

17. Millis, ed., *The Forrestal Diaries*, June 30, 1945, pp. 72–73, and Unpublished Forrestal Diaries, Princeton University, JFP, and OSD Historical Office, Pentagon, p. 378. See also Gardner, *Architects of Illusion*, pp. 271–273.

18. JVF to William C. Patten, September 2, 1947, Princeton University, JFP.

19. JVF to Senator Homer Ferguson, May 14, 1945, Princeton University, JFP. An edited portion of the letter appears in Millis, ed., *The Forrestal Diaries*, May 14, 1945, pp. 57–58.

20. Ibid.

21. The book *Aspects of Dialectical Materialism* (London, 1935) was based on a British Scholars lecture series at the Society of Cultural Revolution, with contributing essays by H. Levy, John MacMurray, Ralph Fox, R. Page Arnot, J. O. Bernal, and E. F. Carritt.

22. Millis, ed., *The Forrestal Diaries*, July 30, 1945, pp. 72–73, and January 2, 1946, pp. 126–127, and Brinkley interview with Michael Forrestal, April 27, 1988.

23. Millis, ed., *The Forrestal Diaries*, January 2, 1946, pp. 126–127. JVF was responding to a Walter Lippmann "Today and Tomorrow" column in the New York *Herald Tribune*.

24. JVF to Walter Lippmann, January 7, 1946, Princeton University, JFP. See also edited version in Millis, ed., *The Forrestal Diaries*, p. 128.

25. Edythe Holbrook interview with Edward F. Willett, September 16, 1985. See also Rogow, *James Forrestal*, pp. 151–154.

26. Holbrook interview with Edward F. Willett, September 16, 1985.

27. Monsignor Fulton J. Sheen to JVF, September 5, 1945, Princeton University, JFP, and Charles J. McFadden, *The Philosophy of Communism* (New York, 1939).

28. Edward F. Willett, "Random Thoughts on Dialectical Materialism and Russian Objectives," December 21, 1945, National Archives, RG 80, S.C. Subject Files, 1942–1948. See also Cecilia Stiles Cornell, "James V. Forrestal and American National Security Policy, 1940–1949," Ph.D. dissertation, Vanderbilt University, 1987, pp. 196–198.

29. JVF to Edward F. Willett (late December 1945), Princeton University, JFP.

30. Edward F. Willett to JVF, December 28, 1945, Princeton University, JFP. See also Cornell, "James V. Forrestal and American National Security Policy, 1940-1949," pp. 199-200.

31. Holbrook interview with Tilghman Koons, April 3, 1985.

32. Brinkley interview with Tilghman Koons, November 18, 1990. For example, Forrestal had Koons draft a 23-page analysis of Stalin's speeches. See Tilghman Koons, "Stalin: Greatest Interpreter of Marxism-Leninism," December 1946, Tilghman Koons Personal Papers, New York, N.Y.

33. Edward F. Willett, "The Philosophy of Communism," January 7, 1946, National Archives, RG 80, S.C. Subject Files, 1942-1948.

34. Edward F. Willett, "Random Thoughts on Dialectical Materialism and Russian Objectives," January 14, 1946, National Archives, RG 80, S.C. Subject Files, 1942-1948.

35. Robert Greenhalgh Albion and Robert Howe Connery, *Forrestal and the Navy* (New York, 1962), p. 185.

36. JVF to Henry Luce, January 6, 1946, Princeton University, JFP. See also Millis, ed., *The Forrestal Diaries,* January 7, 1946, p. 128.

37. Robert Strausz-Hupé to JVF, March 14, 1946, Princeton University, JFP.

38. Philip Moseley to JVF, October 14, 1947, Princeton University, JFP.

39. Thomas B. Inglis, "Soviet Capabilities and Possible Intentions—Résumé of," January 21, 1946, National Archives, RG 80, S.C. Subject Files, 1942-1948, Secretary of the Navy, Black Notebook, and Cornell, "James V. Forrestal and American National Security Policy, 1940-1949," pp. 204-205.

40. Llewellyn Thompson to JVF, National Archives, RG 80, S.C. Subject Files, 1942-1948, Secretary of the Navy, Black Notebook.

41. Hoopes interview with Michael Forrestal, October 12, 1988.

42. George F. Kennan, *Memoirs, 1925-1950* (Boston, 1967), pp. 211-212. See also Walter L. Hixson, *George F. Kennan: Cold War Iconoclast* (New York, 1989); David Mayers, *George Kennan and the Dilemmas of U.S. Foreign Policy* (New York, 1988); and Anders Stephanson, *Kennan and the Art of Foreign Policy* (Cambridge, Mass., 1989).

43. Kennan, *Memoirs,* pp. 284-290.

44. Kennan, *Memoirs,* pp. 286-288.

45. Kennan, *Memoirs,* pp. 293.

46. George F. Kennan to State Department (the Long Telegram), February 22, 1946, National Archives, RG 80, General Correspondence, and Millis, ed., *The Forrestal Diaries,* pp. 135-140. See also Kennan, *Memoirs,* pp. 292-297.

47. Robert J. Donovan, *Conflict and Crisis: The Presidency of Harry S. Truman, 1945-1948* (New York, 1977), p. 188.

48. W. Averell Harriman and Elie Abel, *Special Envoy to Churchill and Stalin: 1941-1946* (New York, 1975), p. 548.

49. Yergin, *Shattered Peace,* p. 171.

50. Mayers, *George Kennan and the Dilemmas of U.S. Foreign Policy,* pp. 107-108.

51. Kennan, *Memoirs,* p. 295.

52. Minutes of the Meeting of the Committee of Three, March 6, 1956, National Archives, RG 59, General Records of the Department of State.

53. Millis, ed., *The Forrestal Diaries,* March 10, 1946, pp. 144-145.

54. Ibid.

55. George F. Kennan to Edythe Holbrook, February 22, 1982 (copy of letter given

to authors by Ms. Holbrook). An unpublished article draft by Ms. Holbrook helped us better understand the Forrestal-Kennan relationship.

56. George F. Kennan to John Osborne, July 31, 1962, George F. Kennan Papers, Seeley G. Mudd Library, Princeton University, Princeton, N.J. (the authors would like to thank Professor Kennan for permission to quote from his papers).

57. Kennan to Holbrook, February 22, 1982 (copy of letter given to authors by Ms. Holbrook).

58. Kennan to Osborne, July 31, 1962, George F. Kennan Papers, Princeton University.

59. Llewellyn Thompson to John T. Connor, October 9, 1946, Princeton University, JFP.

60. George F. Kennan's memorandum to Admiral Hill, October 7, 1946, File "K," Princeton University, JFP. See also Mayers, *George Kennan and the Dilemmas of U.S. Foreign Policy,* pp. 108–109.

61. John T. Connor, "Impressions of the Secretary," October 23, 1962, Arthur M. Krock Papers, Seeley G. Mudd Library, Princeton University.

62. Kennan, *Memoirs,* p. 354.

63. Connor, "Impressions of the Secretary," October 23, 1961, Arthur M. Krock Papers, Seeley G. Mudd Library, Princeton University.

64. Kennan, *Memoirs,* p. 354.

65. Connor, "Impressions of the Secretary," October 23, 1962, Arthur M. Krock Papers, Princeton University. See also Hixson, *George F. Kennan: Cold War Iconoclast,* p. 41.

66. George F. Kennan, "Psychological Background of Soviet Foreign Policy," January 31, 1947, Box 18, Princeton University, JFP.

67. Hixson, *George F. Kennan: Cold War Iconoclast,* p. 41.

68. George F. Kennan to John T. Connor, March 10, 1947, Kennan Papers, Princeton University.

69. Mayers, *George Kennan and the Dilemmas of U.S. Foreign Policy,* p. 113.

70. George F. Kennan [Mr. X], "The Sources of Soviet Conduct," *Foreign Affairs* 25 (July 1947), pp. 566–582.

71. Edwin C. Hoyt, Jr., "Digest of Discussion: Soviet Foreign Policy," Council on Foreign Relations, January 7, 1947 (Subject: The Soviet Way of Thought and Its Effect on Soviet Foreign Policy).

72. Ibid.

73. Kennan, *Memoirs,* pp. 314–324; Hixson, *George F. Kennan: Cold War Iconoclast,* pp. 59–61; and Mayers, *George Kennan and the Dilemmas of U.S. Foreign Policy,* pp. 135–138.

74. Dean Acheson, *Present at the Creation: My Years in the State Department* (New York, 1969), pp. 220–225. Hoopes interview with Dean Acheson, October 11, 1967. Also see Dean Acheson, *Sketches from Life of Men I Have Known* (New York, 1961), p. 108.

75. Kennan, *Memoirs,* p. 358.

76. Douglas Brinkley, "Kennan-Acheson: The Disengagement Debate," *The Atlantic Community Quarterly* (Winter 1987–1988), pp. 423–424.

77. JVF to Clarence Dillon, February 11, 1947, Princeton University, JFP. See also Gardner, *Architects of Illusion,* p. 282.

CHAPTER 22 CONTROLLING THE BOMB

1. Walter Millis, ed., *The Forrestal Diaries,* September 21, 1945 (New York, 1951), pp. 94–95. See also Henry L. Stimson and McGeorge Bundy, *On Active Service in Peace and War* (New York, 1947), p. 657.

2. Stimson and Bundy, *On Active Service in Peace and War,* p. 639.

3. Stimson and Bundy, *On Active Service in Peace and War,* p. 645.

4. Stimson and Bundy, *On Active Service in Peace and War,* pp. 643–645. See also Elting E. Morison, *Turmoil and Tradition: A Study of the Life and Times of Henry L. Stimson* (Boston, 1960), pp. 640–643; Godfrey Hodgson, *The Colonel: The Life and Wars of Henry L. Stimson, 1867–1950* (New York, 1990), pp. 362–363; and Henry L. Stimson Diary, August 12–September 3, 1945, September 4, 12, 17, 21, 1945, Sterling Memorial Library, Yale University.

5. Dean Acheson, *Present at the Creation: My Years in the State Department* (New York, 1969), p. 123.

6. Henry A. Wallace Oral History interview, 1953, Oral History Research Office, Columbia University. See also John Morton Blum, ed., *The Price of Vision: The Diary of Henry A. Wallace, 1942–1946* (Boston, 1973), pp. 482–484, and Norman D. Markowitz, *The Rise and Fall of the People's Century: Henry A. Wallace and American Liberalism* (New York, 1973), pp. 174–176.

7. Millis, ed., *The Forrestal Diaries,* September 7, 1945, pp. 94–96.

8. Quoted in Daniel Yergin, *Shattered Peace: The Origins of the Cold War and the National Security State* (Boston, 1977), p. 135.

9. Ibid. See also Vannevar Bush, *Pieces of Action* (New York, 1970), pp. 294–295.

10. Blum, ed., *The Price of Vision,* p. 483.

11. Millis, ed., *The Forrestal Diaries,* September 7, 1945, p. 95. See also Edward L. and Fredrick H. Schapsmier, *Prophet in Politics: Henry A. Wallace and the War Years, 1940–1965* (Ames, Ia., 1970), pp. 138–139.

12. Henry A. Wallace Oral History interview, 1953, Columbia University, "September 21, 1945, Cabinet Meeting: Atomic Energy," p. 4096. See also E. L. and F. H. Schapsmier, *Prophet in Politics,* p. 139.

13. Yergin, *Shattered Peace,* pp. 132–136; Robert Donovan, *Conflict and Crisis: The Presidency of Harry S. Truman, 1945–1948* (New York, 1977), p. 131; Henry Wallace Oral History interview, Columbia University, pp. 4100–4110; and Herbert Feis, *From Trust to Terror: The Onset of the Cold War, 1945–50* (New York, 1970), pp. 95–97.

14. Forrestal memorandum to President Truman, September 29, 1945 (unsent), Princeton University, JFP.

15. Forrestal memorandum to President Truman, October 1, 1945, Princeton University, JFP. See also Cecilia Stiles Cornell, "James V. Forrestal and American National Security Policy, 1940–1949," Ph.D. dissertation, Vanderbilt University, pp. 185–186.

16. Donovan, *Conflict and Crisis,* pp. 135–136.

17. Ibid. See also John Lewis Gaddis, *The United States and the Origins of the Cold War, 1941–1947* (New York, 1972), p. 272.

18. Robert L. Messer, *The End of an Alliance: James F. Byrnes, Roosevelt, Truman,*

and the Origins of the Cold War (Chapel Hill, N.C., 1982), pp. 138–139, 150–152. See also Donovan, *Conflict and Crisis*, pp. 198–207.

19. Acheson, *Present at the Creation*, p. 153. See also Robert L. Messer, "Acheson, the Bomb, and the Cold War," in Douglas Brinkley, ed., *Dean Acheson and the Making of U.S. Foreign Policy* (New York, 1992), pp. 55–72, and Greg Herken, *The Winning Weapon: The Atomic Bomb in the Cold War, 1945–1950* (New York, 1980), pp. 158–161.

20. Margaret L. Coit, *Mr. Baruch* (Boston, 1957), pp. 567–576; Bernard M. Baruch, *Baruch: The Public Years* (New York, 1960), p. 367; David Lilienthal, *Journals: The Atomic Energy Years, 1945–50* (New York, 1964), pp. 30–59; and Yergin, *Shattered Peace*, pp. 237–238.

21. Lilienthal, *Journals*, p. 123; Yergin, *Shattered Peace*, p. 238; and Joseph Lieberman, *The Scorpion and the Tarantula: The Struggle to Control Atomic Weapons, 1945–1949* (Boston, 1970), p. 274.

22. James Byrnes, *Speaking Frankly* (New York, 1947), p. 269, and Acheson, *Present at the Creation*, p. 155.

23. Acheson, *Present at the Creation*, p. 155.

24. Donovan, *Conflict and Crisis*, p. 206, and Baruch, *Baruch: The Public Years*, p. 369.

25. Lieberman, *The Scorpion and the Tarantula*, p. 303, and *New York Times*, June 15, 1946.

26. Lieberman, *The Scorpion and the Tarantula*, p. 305.

27. Yergin, *Shattered Peace*, pp. 238–241.

28. Lieberman, *The Scorpion and the Tarantula*, p. 304, and *New York Times*, June 16, 1946.

29. Yergin, *Shattered Peace*, pp. 238–241; Messer, "Acheson, the Bomb, and the Cold War," in Brinkley, ed., *Dean Acheson and the Making of U.S. Foreign Policy*, pp. 55–72; Lieberman, *The Scorpion and the Tarantula*, pp. 305–386; and Herken, *The Winning Weapon*, pp. 264–265.

CHAPTER 23 WAGING COLD WAR

1. Robert Greenhalgh Albion and Robert Howe Connery, *Forrestal and the Navy* (New York, 1962), pp. 169–170.

2. Henry L. Stimson and McGeorge Bundy, *On Active Service in Peace and War* (New York, 1947), pp. 599–605.

3. Walter Millis, ed., *The Forrestal Diaries*, July 4, 1944 (New York, 1951), p. 8.

4. Stimson and Bundy, *On Active Service in Peace and War*, pp. 600–601.

5. Millis, ed., *The Forrestal Diaries*, January 21, 1946, pp. 130–131.

6. Millis, ed., *The Forrestal Diaries*, January 21 and 22, 1946, pp. 130–132.

7. Millis, ed., *The Forrestal Diaries*, October 22, 1946, pp. 213–214.

8. James F. Byrnes, *Speaking Frankly* (New York, 1947), p. 220.

9. Millis, ed., *The Forrestal Diaries*, November 26, 1946, p. 216.

10. Millis, ed., *The Forrestal Diaries*, December 16, 1946, pp. 233–234.

11. Marx Leva memorandum, "The Events of February and March 1946, with Some

of the Related Background Events of 1944 and 1945,'' in *The View Back,* July 14, 1962, Personal Papers of Marx Leva (given to authors by Mr. Leva).

12. Ibid.

13. Millis, ed., *The Forrestal Diaries,* March 10, 1946, pp. 144-147.

14. *FRUS,* 1946, 7:840-842; Dean Acheson, *Present at the Creation: My Years in the State Department* (New York, 1969), pp. 194-197; Robert J. Donovan, *Conflict and Crisis: The Presidency of Harry S. Truman, 1945-1948* (New York, 1977), pp. 250-252; and Bruce R. Kuniholm, *The Origins of the Cold War in the Near East: Great Power Conflict and Diplomacy in Iran, Turkey and Greece* (Princeton, 1980).

15. *FRUS,* 1946, 7:847-848; Donovan, *Conflict and Crisis,* p. 251; and James Marion Jones, *Fifteen Weeks, February 21-June 5, 1947* (New York, 1955), pp. 63-64.

16. Albion and Connery, *Forrestal and the Navy,* p. 138; Harry S. Truman, *Memoirs,* Vol. II: *Years of Trial and Hope* (Garden City, N.Y., 1956); and Francis Williams, *Twilight of Empire: Memoirs of Prime Minister Clement Attlee* (Westport, Conn., 1978, reprint), p. 163.

17. U.S. Navy press release, September 30, 1946, in Millis, ed., *The Forrestal Diaries,* pp. 211-212.

18. New York *Herald Tribune,* October 1, 1946. See also Millis, ed., *The Forrestal Diaries,* September 30, 1946, p. 211.

19. "Reminiscences of Vice Admiral William R. Smedberg III," June 9, 1976, U.S. Naval Institute Oral History, Annapolis, Md., July 1979.

20. *New York Times,* July 1, 1946.

21. Ibid.

22. Ibid., June 26, 1946.

23. Ibid. See also John A. Kennedy Oral History interview, April 13, 1974, Harry S. Truman Library (HSTL), July 1978, pp. 38-42.

24. Millis, ed., *The Forrestal Diaries,* July 16, 1946, p. 180.

25. "Reminiscences of Vice Admiral William R. Smedberg III," June 9, 1976.

26. Millis, ed., *The Forrestal Diaries,* July 16, 1946, p. 179, and JVF to Douglas MacArthur, April 20, 1946, Princeton University, JFP.

27. "Reminiscences of Vice Admiral William R. Smedberg III," June 9, 1976. See also Unpublished Forrestal Diaries, July 14, 1946, Princeton University, JFP, pp. 1151-1156.

28. "Reminiscences of Vice Admiral William R. Smedberg III," June 9, 1976.

29. Ibid.

30. Millis, ed., *The Forrestal Diaries,* July 16, 1946, p. 182.

31. "Reminiscences of Vice Admiral William R. Smedberg III," June 9, 1976.

32. Ibid. See also John A. Kennedy Oral History interview, April 13, 1974, pp. 40-42.

33. Millis, ed., *The Forrestal Diaries,* July 16, 1946, p. 183.

34. Ibid.

35. Millis, ed., *The Forrestal Diaries,* February 24, 1947, pp. 245-246. See also Yergin, *Shattered Peace: The Origins of the Cold War and the National Security State* (Boston, 1977), pp. 288-296, and Lawrence S. Wittner, *American Intervention in Greece, 1943-1949* (New York, 1982).

36. Millis, ed., *The Forrestal Diaries,* March 3, 1947, pp. 247-248. See also Richard M. Freeland, *The Truman Doctrine and the Origins of McCarthyism: Foreign*

Policy, Domestic Politics, and International Security, 1946–1948 (New York, 1972), pp. 70–75.

37. Millis, ed., *The Forrestal Diaries*, March 5, 1947, pp. 248–249.

38. Millis, ed., *The Forrestal Diaries*, March 7, 1947, pp. 250–252. See also Hoopes interviews with Clark Clifford, January 26, 1989, and Marx Leva, January 15, 1989, and *FRUS*, 1947, 5:54–58.

39. Millis, ed., *The Forrestal Diaries*, March 7, 1947, pp. 250–252.

40. Forrestal-Clifford memorandum to the President, March 5, 1947 (drafted by Marx Leva) (authors' possession, courtesy of Mr. Leva). See also Hoopes interviews with Clark Clifford, January 26, 1989, and Marx Leva, January 15, 1989. The memorandum can also be found in Carl W. Borklund, *Men of the Pentagon: Forrestal to McNamara* (New York, 1966), pp. 23–25.

41. Ibid.

42. Ibid. See also Marx Leva to JVF, March 8, 1947, National Archives, RG 80, General Correspondence, Sec. Nav.

43. Steven L. Rearden, *History of the Office of the Secretary of Defense: The Formative Years, 1947–1950* (Washington, D.C., 1984), pp. 8–11.

44. Donovan, *Conflict and Crisis*, p. 149.

45. Clinton P. Anderson, with Milton Viorst, *Outsider in the Senate: Senator Clinton Anderson's Memoirs* (New York, 1970), pp. 76–80.

46. Ibid. See also John Morton Blum, ed., *The Price of Vision: The Diary of Henry A. Wallace, 1942–1946* (Boston, 1973), p. 522.

47. Donovan, *Conflict and Crisis*, pp. 149–154.

48. Ibid.

49. Ibid.

50. Ibid.

51. William V. Shannon, New York *Post*, May 17, 1953.

52. Millis, ed., *The Forrestal Diaries*, July 8, 1946, pp. 174–175.

53. Millis, ed., *The Forrestal Diaries*, July 14, 1946, pp. 179–178.

54. Millis, ed., *The Forrestal Diaries*, August 2, 1946, pp. 189–191.

55. *Public Papers of the Presidents of the United States: Harry S. Truman: 1946* (Washington, D.C., 1962), pp. 499ff.

56. Lt. General Albert C. Wedemeyer Report to the President on China-Korea, September 19, 1947, National Archives, RG 330. See also William W. Stueck, Jr., *The Road to Confrontation: American Policy Toward China and Korea, 1947–50* (Chapel Hill, N.C., 1981), pp. 38–45, and Albert C. Wedemeyer, *Wedemeyer Reports!* (New York, 1958), pp. 368–388.

57. Charles J. V. Murphy interview with Albert C. Wedemeyer, April 2, 1982.

58. Unpublished Forrestal Diaries, February 12, 1948, Princeton University, JFP, and OSD Historical Office, Pentagon, p. 2070. See also Department of State, "United States Relations with China with Special Reference to the Period 1944–1949," Department of State Publication No. 3573 (Washington, D.C., 1949), pp. 380–384 (China White Paper).

59. Ibid. See also Rearden, *History of the Office of the Secretary of Defense*, pp. 215–216.

60. Forrestal memorandum for Executive Secretary/NSC, February 26, 1948, and March 12, 1948, National Archives, RG 330. See also Rearden, *History of the Office of the Secretary of Defense*, pp. 216–217.

61. John H. Feaver, "The China Aid Bill of 1948: Limited Assistance as a Cold

War Strategy," *Diplomatic History* 5 (Spring 1981), pp. 107–120, and Rearden, *History of the Office of the Secretary of Defense*, pp. 217–220.

62. *FRUS*, 1948, 8:181 and 8:331–332; Kenneth W. Condit, *The History of the Joint Chiefs of Staff*, Vol. II: *The Joint Chiefs of Staff and National Policy, 1947–1949* (Washington, D.C., 1976), pp. 459–461; and Rearden, *History of the Office of the Secretary of Defense*, pp. 221–224.

63. Unpublished Forrestal Diaries, November 3, 1948, Princeton University, JFP, and OSD Historical Office, Pentagon, p. 2820; *FRUS*, 1948, 8:334–335; and Rearden, *History of the Office of the Secretary of Defense*, pp. 221–224.

64. Henry Rositske, *CIA's Secret Operations* (New York, 1977), p. 11.

65. John Loftus, *The Belarus Secret* (New York, 1982), p. 1.

66. George Kennan to JVF, September 29, 1947, National Archives, RG 330.

67. Hoopes interview with Laurence Houston (former CIA general counsel), January 3, 1991.

68. John Prados, *Presidents' Secret Wars* (New York, 1986), p. 33. See also Hoopes interview with Houston, January 3, 1991.

69. Rositske, *CIA's Secret Operations*, p. 21.

70. Ibid.

71. National Security Council Paper NSC 10/2, approved June 18, 1948.

72. National Security Council Paper NSC 20, approved August 1948.

73. See Christopher Simpson, *Blowback* (New York, 1988); Prados, *Presidents' Secret Wars*, p. 33; John Loftus, *The Belarus Secret*, p. 1.

74. Simpson, *Blowback*, pp. 157–160.

75. Simpson, *Blowback*, p. 161–162.

76. Rositske, *CIA's Secret Operations*, p. 19.

77. Simpson, *Blowback*, p. 168.

78. Loftus, *The Belarus Secret*, p. 110.

79. Simpson, *Blowback*, pp. 89–90.

80. G.J.A. O'Toole, *Honorable Treachery: A History of U.S. Intelligence, Espionage, and Covert Action from the American Revolution to the CIA* (New York, 1991), pp. 436–437. Also see Simpson, *Blowback*, pp. 90–95.

81. Anderson, *Outsider in the Senate*, pp. 70–71.

82. Edmund L. Palmieri, "Fight for Italy," *Reader's Digest*, November 1948, 53:–11.

83. Anderson, *Outsider in the Senate*, pp. 70–71.

84. Ibid.

85. Hoopes interview with Michael Forrestal, October 12, 1988.

86. O'Toole, *Honorable Treachery*, p. 437.

CHAPTER 24 "A TASK OF GREATEST DIFFICULTY"

1. Alice C. Cole, Alfred Goldberg, Samuel A. Tucker, and Rudolph A. Winnacker, eds., *The Department of Defense: Documents on Establishment and Organization, 1944–1978* (Washington, D.C., 1978), p. 4, and Demetrios Caraley, *The Politics of Military Unification* (New York, 1966), pp. 27–29.

2. Dean Allard, "Interservice Differences in the United States, 1945–1950: A Naval Perspective," *Airpower Journal* (Winter 1989), pp. 72–74.

3. U.S. Congress, House of Representatives, Select Committee on Post-War Mil-

itary Policy, *Proposal to Establish a Single Department of Armed Forces,* Hearings before the Select Committee on Post-war Military Policy, 78th Cong., 2nd Session, "Robert Lovett Testimony, April 26, 1944" (Washington, D.C., 1944), pp. 48–68.

4. Ibid., "James V. Forrestal Testimony, April 28, 1944" (Hearings 1944), pp. 121–125.

5. Ibid.

6. Ibid.

7. Eberstadt Report, U.S. Congress, Senate Committee on Naval Affairs, *Unification of the War and Navy Departments and Postwar Organization for National Security, Report to Hon. James Forrestal, Secretary of the Navy,* Committee Print, 79th Cong., 1st Session (Washington, D.C., 1945).

8. JVF to Ferdinand Eberstadt, October 6, 1945, Eberstadt Papers, Seeley G. Mudd Library, Princeton University.

9. Brinkley interview with Douglas Dillon, June 16, 1989.

10. Jeffrey M. Dorwart, *Eberstadt and Forrestal* (Texas A&M Press, 1991), p. 115.

11. U.S. Congress, Senate Committee on Military Affairs, Hearings on S.84 and S.1492, Department of Armed Forces, Department of Military Security, 79th Cong., 1st Session, "Forrestal Testimony, October 22, 1945" (Washington, D.C., 1945), pp. 97–108.

12. Ibid., p. 108.

13. Ibid., "Robert P. Patterson Statement," October 17, 1945, pp. 9–18.

14. Ibid., "Eisenhower Statement," November 16, 1945, pp. 359–366.

15. Eberstadt to JVF, November 15, 1945, Eberstadt Papers, Princeton University.

16. Hoopes interview with Michael Forrestal, October 7, 1988.

17. Dorwart, *Eberstadt and Forrestal,* p. 116.

18. JVF to Paul C. Smith (San Francisco *Chronicle*), December 4, 1945, Princeton University, JFP.

19. Stephen Jurika, Jr., ed., *From Pearl Harbor to Vietnam: The Memoirs of Admiral Arthur W. Radford* (Stanford, Calif., 1980), pp. 101–115.

20. Charles J. V. Murphy interview with John McCone, February 11, 1984.

21. Robert Greenhalgh Albion and Robert Howe Connery, *Forrestal and the Navy* (New York, 1962), p. 266. See also Clark G. Reynolds, "Forrest Percival Sherman," pp. 209–232, and David Alan Rosenberg, "Arleigh Albert Burke," pp. 263–319, in Robert William Love, Jr., ed., *The Chiefs of Naval Operations* (Annapolis, Md., 1980).

22. Caraley, *The Politics of Military Unification,* pp. 14–56.

23. Walter Millis, ed., *The Forrestal Diaries,* November 14, 1945 (New York, 1951), p. 115.

24. Ibid., November 21, 1945, pp. 115–116.

25. Hoopes interview with Clark Clifford, January 26, 1989.

26. Dorwart, *Eberstadt and Forrestal,* p. 127.

27. Millis, ed., *The Forrestal Diaries,* December 14, 1945, pp. 117–118.

28. Jurika, ed., *From Pearl Harbor to Vietnam,* pp. 83–84.

29. Millis, ed., *The Forrestal Diaries,* December 18, 1945, pp. 118–119.

30. *Public Papers of the Presidents of the United States: Harry S. Truman: 1945* (Washington, D.C., 1961), pp. 546–560. See also Cole et al., eds., *The Department of Defense,* pp. 7–17.

31. Ibid.

32. Ibid.

33. Ibid.

34. Dorwart, *Eberstadt and Forrestal,* p. 126.

35. Clark Clifford, *Counsel to the President* (New York, 1991), p. 149; also Hoopes interview with Clifford, January 26, 1989. See also JVF to William M. Chadbourne, December 22, 1945, Princeton University, JFP.

36. Ibid.

37. Jurika, ed., *From Pearl Harbor to Vietnam,* p. 84. See also JVF to Clark Clifford, December 22, 1945, Princeton University, JFP.

38. Albion and Connery, *Forrestal and the Navy,* pp. 269–271.

39. Ibid.

40. U.S. Congress, Senate Committee on Naval Affairs, *Hearings on S. 2044: Unification of the Armed Forces,* 79th Cong., 2nd Session, "James Forrestal Statement, May 1, 1946" (Washington, D.C., 1946), pp. 31–32.

41. Ibid., "Gen. Alexander A. Vandegrift Statement, May 6, 1946," pp. 105–106.

42. David I. Walsh and Carl Vinson to Secretary Forrestal, May 15, 1946, in Cole et al., eds., *The Department of Defense,* pp. 18–21.

43. Jurika, ed., *From Pearl Harbor to Vietnam,* pp. 89–90.

44. Millis, ed., *The Forrestal Diaries,* May 13, 1946, pp. 160–162. See also Caraley, *The Politics of Military Unification,* pp. 135–136.

45. *New York Times,* May 12, 1946.

46. Eberstadt memorandum of discussion, May 14, 1946, Eberstadt Papers, Princeton University.

47. JVF to Hanson Baldwin, March 14, 1946, Princeton University, JFP.

48. Eberstadt memorandum of discussion, May 14, 1946, Eberstadt Papers, Princeton University.

49. Eberstadt memorandum of record, May 31, 1946, Eberstadt Papers, Princeton University.

50. Ibid.

51. Clifford, *Counsel to the President,* p. 150.

52. Forrestal-Patterson letter to President Truman, May 31, 1946, in U.S. Congress, *Congressional Record,* Vol. 92, Part 6 (Washington, D.C., 1946), pp. 7424–7426. See also Cole et al., eds., *The Department of Defense,* pp. 22–26.

53. Ibid.

54. Jurika, ed., *From Pearl Harbor to Vietnam,* p. 93.

55. *New York Times,* June 18, 1946.

56. Ibid.

57. Clifford, *Counsel to the President,* p. 151.

58. Millis, ed., *The Forrestal Diaries,* June 16, 1946, pp. 168–170.

59. Ibid.

60. Ibid.

61. Ibid.

62. JVF to President Truman, June 24, 1946, Princeton University, JFP. Text reprinted in *New York Times,* June 25, 1946. See also Unpublished Forrestal Diaries, June 24, 1946, Princeton University, JFP, OSD Historical Office, Pentagon, and JVF to Congressman Vinson, June 24, 1946, National Archives, RG 80, General Correspondence.

63. "Reminiscences of Vice Admiral William R. Smedberg III," June 9, 1976, U.S. Naval Institute Oral History, Annapolis, Md., July 1979.

64. Ibid.

CHAPTER 25   THE WEAK COMPROMISE

1. President Truman to Secretaries Patterson and Forrestal, June 15, 1946, Princeton University, JFP. See also Demetrios Caraley, *The Politics of Military Unification* (New York, 1966), pp. 137–139.

2. John Abbot Oral History interview, December 1970, Harry S. Truman Library (HSTL), December 1970.

3. Stephen Jurika, Jr., ed., *From Pearl Harbor to Vietnam: The Memoirs of Admiral Arthur W. Radford* (Stanford, Calif., 1980), pp. 96–98.

4. Walter Millis, ed., *The Forrestal Diaries* (New York, 1951), August 27, 1946, pp. 201–202.

5. Ibid.

6. JVF to Clark Clifford, September 7, 1946, Princeton University, JFP.

7. Clark Clifford, *Counsel to the President*, p. 154. See also Millis, ed., *The Forrestal Diaries*, September 10, 1946, pp. 203–205.

8. Millis, ed., *The Forrestal Diaries*, p. 205.

9. Henry L. Stimson and McGeorge Bundy, *On Active Service in Peace and War* (New York, 1947), p. 506.

10. Millis, ed., *The Forrestal Diaries*, September 10, 1946, p. 204.

11. Michael S. Sherry, *Preparing for the Next War: American Plans for Postwar Defense, 1941–45* (New Haven, 1977), and Vincent Davis, *Postwar Defense Policy and the U.S. Navy, 1943–1946* (Chapel Hill, N.C., 1966).

12. Jurika, ed., *From Pearl Harbor to Vietnam*, pp. 97–98.

13. Millis, ed., *The Forrestal Diaries*, December 5, 1946, p. 226.

14. Robert Greenhalgh Albion and Robert Howe Connery, *Forrestal and the Navy* (New York, 1962), pp. 269–270.

15. Jurika, ed., *From Pearl Harbor to Vietnam*, p. 226.

16. Millis, ed., *The Forrestal Diaries*, December 5, 1946, pp. 226–227.

17. Ibid., December 4, 1946, p. 225.

18. Ibid., January 3, 1947, pp. 228–229.

19. Ibid., January 16, 1947, pp. 229–230. See also Alice C. Cole, Alfred Goldberg, Samuel A. Tucker, and Rudolph A. Winnacker, eds., *The Department of Defense: Documents on Establishment and Organization, 1944–1978* (Washington, D.C., 1978), pp. 31–33.

20. U.S. Congress Senate Committee on Armed Services, *National Security Act of 1947,* S. Rpt. 80th Cong., 1st Session, "James Forrestal Statement, March 18, 1947" (Washington, D.C., 1947), pp. 21–32.

21. Ibid.

22. Ibid., "Dwight D. Eisenhower Statement, March 25, 1947," pp. 98–113.

23. U.S. Congress, House of Representatives, Committee on Expenditures in the Executive Departments, *Hearings on H.R. 2319: National Security Act of 1947,* 80th Cong., 1st Session, "Dwight D. Eisenhower Statement, May 7, 1947" (Washington, D.C., 1947), pp. 288–321.

24. Ibid. "Arthur W. Radford Testimony, June 26, 1947," pp. 571–637.

25. U.S. Congress Senate Committee on Armed Services, National Security Act of 1947, S. Rpt. 80th Cong., 1st Session, "Melvin J. Maas Statement" (Washington, D.C., 1947), pp. 447–448.

26. Ibid.

27. Clifford, *Counsel to the President,* p. 155, and Hoopes interview with Clark Clifford, April 18, 1989. See also Gordon W. Keiser, *The U.S. Marine Corps and Defense Unification, 1944-1947* (Washington, D.C., 1982).

28. Eisenhower memorandum to JCS, March 16, 1946, printed in U.S. Congress, Committee on Armed Services, *National Security Act of 1947,* S. Rpt. 80th Cong., 1st Session (Washington, D.C., 1947), pp. 637-640.

29. Nimitz memorandum to JCS, March 30, 1946, printed in U.S. Congress, Committee on Armed Services, *National Security Act of 1947,* S. Rpt. 80th Cong., 1st Session (Washington, D.C., 1947), p. 640.

30. U.S. Congress, House of Representatives, Committee on Expenditures in the Executive Departments, *Hearings on H.R. 2319: National Security Act of 1947,* 80th Cong., 1st Session, "Dwight D. Eisenhower Statement, May 7, 1947," p. 321.

31. Clifford, *Counsel to the President,* p. 155, and Hoopes interview with Clark Clifford, April 18, 1989.

32. Ibid.

33. *National Security Act of 1947, Public Law 253,* Chapter 343, S.758, 80th Cong., 1st Session, July 26, 1947, printed in Cole et al., eds., *The Department of Defense,* pp. 35-50.

34. JVF to Kenneth Royall, July 28, 1947, Princeton University, JFP.

35. Robert Lovett, "Reflections on Jim Forrestal," March 12, 1985 (unpublished essay in authors' possession).

CHAPTER 26   THE FIRST SECRETARY OF DEFENSE

1. Clark Clifford, *Counsel to the President,* p. 158, and Hoopes interview with Clark Clifford, April 18, 1989.

2. Ibid.

3. JVF to Robert Sherwood, August 27, 1947, Princeton University, JFP. See also Walter Millis, ed., *The Forrestal Diaries* (New York, 1951), pp. 299-300.

4. JVF to Dr. A. L. Barach, 1947, Princeton University, JFP.

5. *New York Times,* January 3, 1947.

6. Navy Department Transcript of Forrestal press conference, July 28, 1947, OSD Historical Office, Pentagon, Arlington, Va.

7. Will Brownell and Richard N. Billings, *So Close to Greatness: A Biography of William C. Bullitt* (New York, 1987), p. 301.

8. *National Security Act of 1947, Public Law 253,* Chapter 343, S.758, 80th Cong., 1st Session, July 26, 1947, Sec. 202(a), printed in Alice C. Cole, Alfred Goldberg, Samuel A. Tucker, and Rudolph A. Winnacker, eds., *The Department of Defense: Documents on Establishment and Organization, 1944-1978* (Washington, D.C., 1978), p. 40.

9. Anna Kasten Nelson, "President Truman and the Evolution of the National Security Council," *Journal of American History* 72 (September 1985), pp. 360-378, and Ralph Gordon Hoxie, *Command Decision and the Presidency: A Study in National Security Policy and Organization* (New York, 1977), pp. 129-152. Also Osborne, "Forrestal," unpublished manuscript outline.

10. Clifford, *Counsel to the President,* p. 163, and Hoopes interview with Clark Clifford, April 18, 1989.

11. Millis, ed., *The Forrestal Diaries*, September 17, 1947, pp. 316–317, and Meeting of the Advisory Group to the Secretary of Defense, September 17, 1947, National Archives, RG 330.

12. Joseph A. Loftus, "Forrestal Begins Duties in Pentagon," *New York Times*, September 24, 1947, 2:6. See also Navy Department Transcript of Forrestal press conference, September 23, 1947, OSD Historical Office, Pentagon, Arlington, Va.

13. "America's New Defense Team," *New York Times*, September 21, 1947, VI, p. 10.

14. Paolo E. Coletta, "John Lawrence Sullivan," in Paolo E. Coletta, ed., *American Secretaries of the Navy*, Vol. II (Annapolis, Md., 1980), pp. 747–780.

15. Murray Green, "Stuart Symington and the B-36," Ph.D. dissertation, American University, 1960, and Paul I. Wellman, *Stuart Symington: Portrait of a Man with a Mission* (Garden City, N.Y., 1960).

16. Hoopes interview with Eugene Zuckert, April 10, 1991.

17. Hoopes interview with Clark Clifford, January 26, 1989.

18. Ibid.

19. Millis, ed., *The Forrestal Diaries*, July 26, 1947, pp. 295–297.

20. *National Security Act of 1947, Public Law 253*, Chapter 343, S.758, 80th Cong., 1st Session, July 26, 1947, Sec. 203, 204, printed in Cole et al., *The Department of Defense*, p. 41.

21. Hoopes interview with Marx Leva, January 15, 1989.

22. Steven L. Rearden, *History of the Office of the Secretary of Defense: The Formative Years, 1947–1950* (Washington, D.C., 1984), pp. 66–67.

23. Hoopes interview with Marx Leva, January 15, 1989.

24. Hoopes interview with John H. Ohly, August 20, 1989.

25. Rearden, *History of the Office of the Secretary of Defense*, p. 61.

26. Najeeb E. Halaby, *Cross-Winds: An Airman's Memoir* (Garden City, N.Y., 1978), p. 43. See also Hoopes interview with Najeeb Halaby, April 11, 1990.

27. "Forrestal Pushes Air Warning Plan," *New York Times*, November 13, 1947, 32:3. See also Navy Department Transcript of Forrestal press conference, November 12, 1947, OSD Historical Office, Pentagon, Arlington, Va.

28. Forrestal remarks at the Team Unification Meeting, November 20, 1947, National Defense Building, Washington, D.C., Princeton University, JFP.

29. Charles J. V. Murphy interview with John J. McCloy, October 8, 1982.

30. *National Security Act of 1947, Public Law 253*, Chapter 343, S.758, 80th Cong., 1st Session, July 26, 1947, Sec. 203, 204, printed in Cole et al., *The Department of Defense*: pp. 40–41.

31. Rearden, *History of the Office of the Secretary of Defense*, p. 61.

32. Stephen Jurika, Jr., ed., *From Pearl Harbor to Vietnam: The Memoirs of Admiral Arthur W. Radford* (Stanford, Calif., 1980), p. 112.

33. Rearden, *History of the Office of the Secretary of Defense*, p. 61.

34. [Elliott Cassidy], "Munitions Board Organizational History: An Analysis as of November 1, 1949," Office of the Secretary of Defense History, OSD Historical Office, Pentagon, Arlington, Va, pp. 1–10.

35. Rearden, *History of the Office of the Secretary of Defense*, pp. 91–92.

36. Rearden, *History of the Office of the Secretary of Defense*, pp. 96–105; Vannevar Bush, *Modern Arms and Free Men: A Discussion of the Role of Science in Preserving Democracy* (New York, 1949), pp. 3–6; and Allen G. Greb, "Military Research and Development: A Postwar History," *Bulletin of the Atomic Scientists* 33 (January 1977), pp. 13–26.

37. Carl W. Borklund, *Men of the Pentagon: From Forrestal to McNamara* (New York, 1966), p. 40. See also Rearden, *History of the Office of the Secretary of Defense,* p. 65.

38. Eric Larrabee, *Commander in Chief: Franklin Delano Roosevelt, His Lieutenants and Their War* (New York, 1987), and Michael S. Sherry, *Preparing for the Next War: American Plans for Postwar Defense, 1941–45* (New Haven, 1977).

39. Kenneth W. Condit, *The History of the Joint Chiefs of Staff,* Vol. II: *The Joint Chiefs of Staff and National Policy, 1947–1949* (Washington, D.C., 1978).

CHAPTER 27   THE BITTER FIGHT OVER AIR POWER

1. Steven L. Rearden, *History of the Office of the Secretary of Defense: The Formative Years, 1947–1950* (Washington, D.C., 1984), pp. 309–314.

2. Kenneth Condit, *The Joint Chiefs of Staff and National Policy, 1947–1949* (Washington, D.C., pp. 333–337, and Perry McCoy Smith, *The Air Force Plans for Peace, 1943–1945* (Baltimore, 1970). See also President's Air Policy Commission, *Survival in the Air Age* (Washington, D.C., 1948).

3. Rearden, *History of the Office of the Secretary of Defense,* p. 315.

4. Forrestal statement for the Finletter Commission, November 3, 1947, Princeton University, JFP. See also Smith, *The Air Force Plans for Peace,* and Forrestal statement for Truman's Air Policy Commission, December 3, 1947, Princeton University, JFP.

5. Charles J. V. Murphy interview with Major General Jerry Page, USAF (Ret.), October 11, 1983.

6. Ibid.

7. Ibid.

8. "Reminiscences of Hanson Weightman Baldwin," July 28, 1975, U.S. Naval Institute Oral History, Vol. II, Annapolis, Md., 1976.

9. Hoopes interview with Eugene Zuckert, April 10, 1991.

10. Hoopes interviews with Marx Leva, January 15, 1989, and John Ohly, August 15, 1989. See also Brinkley interview with Lauris Norstad, March 6, 1988.

11. Hoopes interview with Marx Leva, January 15, 1989.

12. Hoopes interview with W. John Kenney, May 29, 1989.

13. "Reminiscences of Hanson Weightman Baldwin," July 28, 1975.

14. Unpublished Forrestal Diaries, Princeton University, JFP, and OSD Historical Office, Pentagon, pp. 2086–2088. See also Walter Millis, ed., *The Forrestal Diaries,* February 18, 1948 (New York, 1951), pp. 374–377, and Rearden, *History of the Office of the Secretary of Defense,* p. 317.

15. Rearden, *History of the Office of the Secretary of Defense,* p. 317.

16. Milovan Djilas, *Conversations with Stalin,* trans. Michael B. Petrovich (New York, 1962), p. 153.

17. Jean Edward Smith, *The Defense of Berlin* (Baltimore, 1963), pp. 100–102; Avi Shlaim, *The United States and the Berlin Blockade: A Study in Crisis Decision Making* (Berkeley, 1983), pp. 27–39; and Jean Edward Smith, *Lucius D. Clay: An American Life* (New York, 1990).

18. *FRUS,* 1948, 4:747–754, and Jiri Pelikan, ed., *The Czechoslovak Political Trials, 1950–1954* (London: Macdonald, 1971), and Melvyn P. Leffler, "The American Conception of National Security and the Beginnings of the Cold War, 1945–1948," *American Historical Review* 89 (April 1984), pp. 369–378.

19. General Lucius Clay cable to Lt. General Stephen J. Chamberlin (Army Director of Intelligence), March 5, 1948, in Jean Edward Smith, ed., *The Papers of General Lucius D. Clay,* Vol. II, pp. 568–569. See also Rearden, *History of the Office of the Secretary of Defense,* p. 281.

20. *FRUS,* 1948, 4:747–754, and Daniel Yergin, *Shattered Peace: The Origins of the Cold War and the National Security State* (Boston, 1977), pp. 343–356.

21. "Functions of the Armed Forces and the Joint Chiefs of Staff," April 21, 1948, in Alice C. Cole, Alfred Goldberg, Samuel A. Tucker, and Rudolph A. Winnacker, eds., *The Department of Defense: Documents on Establishment and Organization, 1944–1978* (Washington, D.C., 1978), pp. 276–289. In particular see the JCS Key West Conference memorandum for the record, March 26, 1948, pp. 286–289.

22. Millis, ed., *The Forrestal Diaries,* March 11–15, 1948, pp. 391–395. See also Unpublished Forrestal Diaries, March 11–15, 1948, Princeton University, JFP.

23. Millis, ed., *The Forrestal Diaries,* March 16, 1948, pp. 394–395.

24. Robert H. Ferrell, ed., *Off the Record: The Private Papers of Harry S. Truman* (New York, 1980), p. 145.

25. Rearden, *History of the Office of the Secretary of Defense,* pp. 281–308.

26. Rearden, *History of the Office of the Secretary of Defense,* pp. 281–308. See also Lucius D. Clay, *Decision in Germany* (Garden City, N.Y., 1950), and Philips Davison, *The Berlin Blockade: A Study in Cold War Politics* (Princeton, 1958).

27. Rearden, *History of the Office of the Secretary of Defense,* pp. 318–320.

28. Brinkley and Hoopes interview with Forrest Pogue, March 5, 1989.

29. Robert Cutler, *No Time for Rest* (Boston, 1965), p. 246.

30. Brinkley interview with Stuart Symington, November 17, 1987.

31. Millis, ed., *The Forrestal Diaries,* pp. 400–402. See also Rearden, *History of the Office of the Secretary of Defense,* pp. 320–322.

32. Brinkley interview with Eliot Janeway, September 18, 1990.

33. Stuart Symington Oral History interview, May 27, 1981, OSD Historical Office, Pentagon, Arlington, Va. See also Frank L. Kluckhohn and Jay Franklin, *The Drew Pearson Story* (Chicago, 1967), pp. 49–62.

34. Symington memorandum to Forrestal, March 31, 1948, Carl Spaatz Papers, MSS., Library of Congress, Washington, D.C. See also Rearden, *History of the Office of the Secretary of Defense,* p. 321.

35. Murphy interview with John J. McCloy, September 28, 1982.

36. Forrestal memorandum to JCS, April 8, 1948, National Archives, Modern Military Branch, RG330. See also Rearden, *History of the Office of the Secretary of Defense,* p. 322.

37. Forrestal memorandum to JCS, April 17, 1948, National Archives, Modern Military Branch, RG330 and Millis, ed., *The Forrestal Diaries,* April 19, 1948, pp. 418–421.

38. Rearden, *History of the Office of the Secretary of Defense,* pp. 326–330.

39. Ferrell, *Off the Record,* p. 134.

40. Peter Walker interview with James E. Webb, April 22, 1987. See also Rearden, *History of the Office of the Secretary of Defense,* pp. 227–330.

41. Rearden, *History of the Office of the Secretary of Defense,* pp. 423–426.

42. Rearden, *History of the Office of the Secretary of Defense,* p. 427.

43. Millis, ed., *The Forrestal Diaries,* January 22, 1947, pp. 240–241. See also Richard G. Hewlett and Francis Duncan, *Atomic Shield, 1947–1952,* Vol. II in *A History of the United States Atomic Energy Commission* (University Park, Pa., 1969), pp. 48–53.

44. Rearden, *History of the Office of the Secretary of Defense,* pp. 425–428; Donald Carpenter, "Confidential Recollections," Carpenter Papers, Box 32, HSTL, pp. 54–93; and Murphy interview with Lauris Norstad, April 17, 1982.

45. JVF to President Truman, July 21, 1948, National Archives, RG 330. See also Rearden, *History of the Office of the Secretary of Defense,* p. 430.

46. Lilienthal, *Journals: The Atomic Energy Years 1945–50,* pp. 388–392.

47. James Webb memorandum to President Truman, July 22, 1948, President's Secretary's File (PSF), Truman Papers, HSTL.

48. Millis, ed., *The Forrestal Diaries,* July 21, 1948, pp. 460–461 and President Truman to JVF, August 6, 1948, National Archives, RG 330. See also Carpenter, "Confidential Recollections," pp. 54–93; and Rearden, *History of the Office of the Secretary of Defense,* pp. 431–432.

49. Carpenter, "Confidential Recollections"; and Murphy interview with Lauris Norstad, April 17, 1982.

50. Gladwin Hill, "Symington Assails Defense Quarrels," *New York Times,* July 18, 1948.

51. Unpublished Forrestal Diaries, Princeton University, JFP, and OSD Historical Office, Pentagon, p. 2367.

52. Ibid.

53. Unpublished Forrestal Diaries, p. 2382.

54. Vice Admiral Fitzhugh Lee, Oral History interview, August 9, 1970, U.S. Naval Institute, Annapolis, Md.

55. Stuart Symington Oral History interview, May 27, 1981.

56. Hill, "Symington Assails Defense Quarrels."

57. John H. Ohly letter to Hoopes, January 3, 1989.

58. Vice Admiral Fitzhugh Lee Oral History interview, August 9, 1970.

59. Hoopes interview with W. John Kenney, May 29, 1989.

60. Brinkley interview with W. John Kenney, January 12, 1990.

61. Brinkley interview with Admiral Robert B. Carney, April 6, 1988.

62. Hoopes interview with James Symington, April 16, 1989.

63. Hoopes interview with Clark Clifford, January 26, 1989.

CHAPTER 28   THE PALESTINE IMBROGLIO

1. Walter Laqueur, *A History of Zionism* (New York, 1976), and Herbert Feis, *The Birth of Israel: The Tousled Diplomatic Bed* (New York, 1969).

2. Robert J. Donovan, *Conflict and Crisis: The Presidency of Harry S. Truman, 1945–1948* (New York, 1977), pp. 312–313. For an influential report which Forrestal read regarding possible post–WW II American attitudes toward a Jewish homeland in Palestine, see Isaiah Bowman (rapporteur), "The New Zionism and a Policy for the United States," October 19, 1943, Council on Foreign Relations Study in the "Territorial Series" (strictly confidential).

3. Evan M. Wilson, *Decision on Palestine* (Stanford, Calif., 1979), pp. 23–26; J. C. Hurewitz, *The Struggle for Palestine* (New York, 1950), pp. 156–159; and Laqueur, *A History of Zionism,* pp. 545–558. For the article which revived the idea of a Jewish State, see Chaim Weizmann, "Palestine's Role in the Solution of the Jewish Problem," *Foreign Affairs* 20, no. 2 (January 1942), pp. 324–338. For a documented discussion about the importance of U.S. public opinion regarding the Palestine question, see Bruce J. Evensen, "The Truman Administration's Struggle to Shape Conven-

tional Wisdom on Palestine," *Diplomatic History,* vol. 15, no. 3 (Summer 1991), pp. 339–359.

4. Donovan, *Conflict and Crisis,* p. 315. See also *FRUS,* 1944, 5:655–657; *FRUS* 1945, 8:678–704; and Wilson, *Decision on Palestine,* pp. 40–67.

5. Michael B. Stoff, *Oil, War, and American Security: The Search for a National Policy on Foreign Oil, 1941–1947* (New Haven, 1980), pp. 209–215.

6. JVF to James F. Byrnes, April 5, 1946, Princeton University, JFP. For the influence of DeGoyler and Ickes on Forrestal's oil concerns, see Daniel Yergin, *The Prize: The Epic Quest for Oil, Money and Power* (New York, 1991), pp. 406–408.

7. Irvine H. Anderson, *Aramco, The United States and Saudi Arabia: A Study of the Dynamics of Foreign Oil Policy, 1933–1950* (Princeton, 1981), and David Painter, *Oil and the American Century: The Political Economy of U.S. Foreign Oil Policy* (Baltimore, 1986).

8. T. H. Watkins, *Righteous Pilgrim: The Life and Times of Harold L. Ickes, 1874–1952* (New York, 1990), pp. 749–752, and Painter, *Oil and the American Century,* pp. 32–73.

9. JVF to Jake Jacobsen, March 22, 1944, Princeton University, JFP.

10. JVF to Admiral A. F. Carter, November 3, 1947, Princeton University, JFP.

11. U.S. Congress, Senate, Special Committee Investigating the National Defense Program, *Investigation of the National Defense Program, Part 41: Petroleum Arrangements with Saudi Arabia,* 80th Cong., 1st Session, 1948, p. 25281. See also *New York Times,* January 20, 1948, and Forrestal memorandum to Secretary James F. Byrnes, September 3, 1945, Princeton University, JFP.

12. Charles J. V. Murphy interview with Robert A. Lovett, April 3, 1984.

13. Herbert Elliston, "Jim Forrestal: A Portrait in Politics," *Atlantic Monthly* (November 1951), pp. 73–74.

14. Robert A. Lovett, "Reflections on Jim Forrestal," unpublished book preface, March 12, 1985.

15. Hoopes interview with Marx Leva, January 15, 1989.

16. H. G. Nicholas, *Washington Dispatches, 1941–1945* (Chicago, 1981), pp. 239–240. (Isaiah Berlin dispatch to the British Foreign Office, August 28, 1943).

17. Dean Acheson, *Present at the Creation: My Years in the State Department* (New York, 1969), p. 169.

18. Michael J. Cohen, *Palestine and the Great Powers, 1945–1948* (Princeton, N.J., 1982), Chap. 4, and Michael J. Cohen, *Truman and Israel* (Berkeley, 1990), pp. 122–139.

19. Cohen, *Truman and Israel,* pp. 109–121.

20. John Morton Blum, ed., *The Price of Vision: The Diary of Henry A. Wallace, 1942–1946* (Boston, 1973), pp. 606–607. See also Donovan, *Conflict and Crisis,* p. 319.

21. Donovan, *Conflict and Crisis,* p. 320. For more on the Truman-Silver relationship, see Cohen, *Truman and Israel,* pp. 63–70.

22. Cohen, *Truman and Israel,* p. 322.

23. *Public Papers of the Presidents of the United States: Harry S. Truman; 1946* (Washington, D.C., 1962), pp. 442–444. See also Acheson, *Present at the Creation,* pp. 176–180.

24. Donovan, *Conflict and Crisis,* p. 321. See also Cohen, *Truman and Israel,* pp. 137–146.

25. Donovan, *Conflict and Crisis,* p. 320. See also Cohen, *Truman and Israel,* pp. 137–146.

26. *FRUS*, 1947, 5:1048–49.

27. Walter Millis, ed., *The Forrestal Diaries* (New York, 1951), pp. 321–322.

28. Millis, ed., *The Forrestal Diaries*, November 26, 1947, pp. 344–345.

29. Millis, ed., *The Forrestal Diaries*, December 3, 1947, pp. 346–348.

30. Millis, ed., *The Forrestal Diaries*, December 13, 1947, pp. 348–349.

31. Arnold A. Rogow, *James Forrestal: A Study in Personality, Politics, and Policy* (New York, 1963), p. 185, and Cohen, *Truman and Israel*, p. 177. See also Forrestal speech to Machinery and Allied Products Institute, Washington, D.C., December 12, 1947, Princeton University, JFP.

32. Unpublished Forrestal Diaries, January 9, 1948, p. 2019, Princeton University, JFP, and OSD Historical Office, Pentagon, p. 2019.

33. Donovan, *Conflict and Crisis*, p. 331.

34. Unpublished Forrestal Diaries, February 22, 1948, pp. 2094–2095, Princeton University, JFP, and OSD Historical Office, Pentagon, pp. 2094–2095.

35. Millis, ed., *The Forrestal Diaries*, December 1, 1947, p. 346.

36. Cohen, *Truman and Israel*, pp. 173–198.

37. *FRUS*, 1948, 2:546–54, and Steven L. Rearden, *History of the Office of the Secretary of Defense: The Formative Years, 1947–1950* (Washington, D.C., 1984), p. 184.

38. Unpublished Forrestal Diaries, April 4, 1948, pp. 2183–2186, Princeton University, JFP, and OSD Historical Office, Pentagon, pp. 2183–2186.

39. Millis, ed., *The Forrestal Diaries*, January 6, 1948, pp. 356–357.

40. Millis, ed., *The Forrestal Diaries*, January 9, 1948, p. 358.

41. U.S. Congress, Committee on Armed Services, Special Subcommittee on Petroleum, *Petroleum for National Defense*, 80th Cong., 2nd Session, 1948 (January 20, 1948).

42. William S. White, "Shortage of Oil Threatens Our Defense, Forrestal Says," *New York Times*, January 20, 1948, 1:2.

43. *New York Times*, February 17, 1948.

44. Jack Anderson, with James Boyd, *Confessions of a Muckraker* (New York, 1979), p. 150.

45. "Bartley C. Crum Assails Palestine Position of United States," Public Auditorium Music Hall, Cleveland, O., Wednesday, March 10, 1984, printed in *The Jewish Outlook*, April 1, 1948, pp. 3–5.

46. Ibid. For Forrestal's oil dealings with Dillon, Read prior to 1940, see Forrestal's (first draft) statement on Middle East oil, May 2, 1947, Princeton University, JFP.

47. "Glen Taylor Asks Forrestal Ouster," *New York Times*, March 22, 1948, 15:4. See also the follow-up story, "Taylor Sees Move to Ban His Talks," *New York Times*, March 25, 1948, 32:2. The Silver quote comes from a different article on the same day.

48. *New York Times*, September 30, 1948.

49. Cohen, *Truman and Israel*, pp. 182–187.

50. Donovan, *Conflict and Crisis*, pp. 376–377; Clark Clifford, "Factors Influencing President Truman's Decision to Support Partition and Recognize the State of Israel," address to the annual meeting of the American Historical Association in Washington, D.C., December 28, 1976; and Margaret Truman, *Harry S. Truman* (New York, 1973), p. 388.

51. Donovan, *Conflict and Crisis*, p. 380, and Cohen, *Truman and Israel*, pp. 207–222.

52. Donovan, *Conflict and Crisis*, pp. 380–381. See also Clark Clifford, *Counsel to the President*, p. 10.

53. Hoopes interview with Clark Clifford, January 26, 1989.

54. Clifford, *Counsel to the President*, p. 12; Donovan, *Conflict and Crisis*, p. 381; and Hoopes interview with Clark Clifford, January 26, 1989.

55. Donovan, *Conflict and Crisis*, pp. 382–384.

56. Hoopes interview with Clark Clifford, January 26, 1989.

57. Donovan, *Conflict and Crisis*, pp. 383–384.

58. Donovan, *Conflict and Crisis*, pp. 383–386.

59. Robert A. Lovett, "Reflections on Jim Forrestal," unpublished book preface, March 12, 1985.

60. Ibid.

61. Ibid.

CHAPTER 29 STRATEGY DEADLOCK

1. Warner R. Schilling, "The Politics of National Defense Fiscal 1950," in Warner R. Schilling, Paul Y. Hammond, and Glen H. Snyder, *Strategy, Politics and Defense Budgets* (New York, 1962), pp. 1–266, and Lawrence J. Korb, "The Secretary of Defense and the Joint Chiefs of Staff: Conflict in the Budgetary Process, 1947–1971," *Naval War College Review* 24 (December 1971), pp. 21–42.

2. Steven L. Rearden, *History of the Office of the Secretary of Defense: The Formative Years, 1947–1950* (Washington, D.C., 1984), p. 339.

3. Rearden, *History of the Office of the Secretary of Defense*, pp. 337–339. See also Greg Herken, *The Winning Weapon* (New York, 1980), pp. 195–304.

4. Omar Bradley and Clay Blair, *A General's Life: An Autobiography* (New York, 1983), p. 492.

5. David A. Rosenberg, "American Postwar Air Doctrine and Organization: The Navy Experience," in Alfred F. Hurley and Robert C. Ehrhart, eds., *Air Power and Warfare* (Washington, D.C., 1979), pp. 245–290. For naval carrier developments, see Clark G. Reynolds, *The Fast Carriers: The Forging of an Air Navy* (New York, 1968), and Norman Friedman, *Carrier Air Power* (Annapolis, Md., 1981).

6. President Truman to JVF, June 3, 1948, National Archives, Modern Military Archives, RG330.

7. Peter Walker interview with James Webb, April 22, 1987.

8. Forrestal conference with JCS, June 11, 1948, Princeton University, JFP. See also Rearden, *History of the Office of the Secretary of Defense*, pp. 338–339.

9. Forrestal remarks at the Team Unification Meeting, National Defense Building, November 20, 1947, Princeton University, JFP.

10. Forrestal conference with JCS, June 11, 1948.

11. NSC-7, March 30, 1948, in *FRUS*, 1948 (Part 2):545–550.

12. PPS-33, June 23, 1948 (published as NSC 20/2, August 25, 1948), in *FRUS*, 1948, 615–624.

13. Rearden, *History of the Office of the Secretary of Defense*, pp. 340–341.

14. JVF memorandum to President Truman, July 10, 1948, National Archives, Modern Military Branch, RG330. See also *FRUS*, 1948 (Part 2):592–593.

15. President Truman memorandum to JVF, July 13, 1948, President's Secretary's File (PSF), Truman Papers, Harry S. Truman Library. See also Rearden, *History of the Office of the Secretary of Defense*, pp. 340–341.

16. President Truman to JVF, July 15, 1948, National Archives, Modern Military Branch, RG330. See also Rearden, *History of the Office of the Secretary of Defense*, p. 341.

17. Rearden, *History of the Office of the Secretary of Defense*, pp. 341–342.

18. John H. Ohly memorandum for the record, August 23, 1948, in Alice C. Cole, Alfred Goldberg, Samuel A. Tucker, and Rudolph A. Winnacker, *The Department of Defense: Documents on Establishment and Organization, 1944–1978* (Washington, D.C., 1978), pp. 290–293.

19. Bradley and Blair, *A General's Life,* p. 494.

20. Ibid.

21. John H. Ohly memorandum for the record, August 23, 1948, in Cole et al., *The Department of Defense,* pp. 290–293.

22. Forrestal to JCS, July 23, 1948, National Archives, Modern Military Branch, RG330. See also Rearden, *History of the Office of the Secretary of Defense,* pp. 397–402.

23. Bradley and Blair, *A General's Life,* p. 493.

24. Ibid.

25. John H. Ohly memorandum for the record, August 23, 1948, in Cole et al., *The Department of Defense,* pp. 29–93. Ohly produced two separate memos—"Newport Conference—Decisions with Respect to Command" and "Newport Conference—Summary of Conclusions Reached and Decisions Made." See also Unpublished Forrestal Diaries, Princeton University, JFP, and OSD Historical Office, Pentagon, pp. 2436–2443; and "Agreed Final Version of Minutes of Newport Meetings 20–22 August 1948," National Archives, Modern Military Branch, RG330.

26. Rearden, *History of the Office of the Secretary of Defense,* p. 344, and Phillip S. Meilinger, *Hoyt S. Vandenberg: The Life of a General* (Bloomington, Ind., 1989), pp. 128–131.

27. Stephen Jurika, Jr., ed., *From Pearl Harbor to Vietnam: The Memoirs of Admiral Arthur W. Radford* (Stanford, Calif., 1980), p. 126.

28. Rearden, *History of the Office of the Secretary of Defense,* p. 344. See also Admiral William D. Leahy Diary, October 4, 1948, Leahy Papers, Manuscript Division, Library of Congress, Washington, D.C.

29. Hoopes interview with W. John Kenney, May 29, 1989.

30. Brinkley interview with Admiral Robert B. Carney, April 6, 1988.

31. Robert H. Ferrell, ed., *The Eisenhower Diaries* (New York, 1981), p. 156.

32. Hanson Baldwin, "Big Boss of the Pentagon," *New York Times Magazine,* August 29, 1948, pp. 9ff.

33. "Divided They Stand," *Newsweek,* September 20, 1948.

CHAPTER 30   THE FINAL BUDGET FIGHT

1. Unpublished Forrestal Diaries, Princeton University, JFP, and OSD Historical Office, Pentagon, pp. 2543–2544. See also Steven L. Rearden, *History of the Office of the Secretary of Defense: The Formative Years, 1947–1950* (Washington, D.C., 1984), p. 345.

2. Michael Hogan, *The Marshall Plan: America, Britain, and the Reconstruction of Europe* (Cambridge, Eng., 1987).

3. Forrestal memorandum for JCS, October 6, 1948, National Archives, Modern Military Branch, RG330.

4. Ibid.

5. Forrestal letter to JCS, October 8, 1948, National Archives, Modern Military Branch, RG330.

6. Walter Millis, ed., *The Forrestal Diaries* (New York, 1951), pp. 499–500, 547.

7. Robert H. Ferrell, ed., *The Eisenhower Diaries* (New York, 1981), pp. 152–153.

8. Charles J. V. Murphy interview with James Webb, October 11, 1982.

9. Unpublished Forrestal Diaries, Princeton University, JFP, and OSD Historical Office, Pentagon, pp. 2571–2581. See also Rearden, *History of the Office of the Secretary of Defense,* p. 346.

10. Millis, ed., *The Forrestal Diaries,* pp. 500–506; Rearden, *History of the Office of the Secretary of Defense,* pp. 347–348; *FRUS,* 1948, I (Part 2):644–646; and JVF to George Marshall, October 31, 1948 (attached memorandum), National Archives, Modern Military Branch, RG330.

11. Millis, ed., *The Forrestal Diaries,* p. 519.

12. President Truman to JVF, November 3, 1948, quoted in Rearden, *The History of the Office of the Secretary of Defense,* p. 348.

13. Millis, ed., *The Forrestal Diaries,* pp. 520–530. See also JVF to President Truman, November 9, 1948, National Archives, Modern Military Branch, RG330.

14. Ibid.

15. *FRUS,* 1948, I (Part 2):656–662.

16. NSC 20/4, November 23, 1948, National Archives, Modern Military Branch, RG330. See also *FRUS,* 1948, I (Part 2):663–669.

17. JVF to President Truman, December 1, 1948, National Archives, Modern Military Branch, RG330. See also *FRUS,* 1948, I (Part 2):663–669.

18. Rearden, *The History of the Office of the Secretary of Defense,* p. 351. See also Forrestal speech to the National Press Club, February 1, 1949, and his interview with ABC Radio, December 30, 1948, Princeton University, JFP.

19. Hoopes interview with George Elsey, February 16, 1989.

CHAPTER 31 THINGS FALL APART

1. Arnold A. Rogow, *James Forrestal: A Study of Personality, Politics, and Policy* (New York, 1963), pp. 276–281. For the impact of Truman's foreign policy on the election outcome, see Robert A. Divine, "The Cold War and the Election of 1948," *Journal of American History* 59 (June 1972), pp. 90–110.

2. Hoopes interview with H. Struve Hensel, January 20, 1989.

3. Forrestal address to the National Press Club, February 1, 1949, Princeton University, JFP.

4. Thomas Dewey to Arnold A. Rogow, June 25, 1959, quoted in Rogow, *James Forrestal,* p. 276.

5. Remarks of Congresswoman Margaret Chase Smith, July 16, 1948, in *Congressional Record,* Appendix, July 26, 1948, p. A4864.

6. Clark Clifford, *Counsel to the President,* p. 160. Also Hoopes interview with Clark Clifford, April 18, 1989.

7. Steven L. Rearden, *History of the Office of the Secretary of Defense: The Formative Years, 1947–1950,* p. 45, and Hoopes interview with Marx Leva, January 15, 1989.

8. Clark Clifford, *Counsel to the President,* p. 161; and Hoopes interviews with Clark Clifford, January 26, 1989, and Marx Leva, January 15, 1989. See also John H. Ohly memorandum to Forrestal, August 17, 1948, September 7, 1948, and September 17, 1948, Ohly Papers (given to authors by Mr. Ohly).

9. U.S. Commission on Organization of the Executive Branch of the Government (The Hoover Commission), Committee on the National Security Organization, *Task*

Force Report on National Security Organization (known as the Eberstadt Task Force Study, May 15–November 15, 1948), Appendix (Washington, D.C., 1948), pp. 11–22. See also Symington's serious concerns about the task force, Ferdinand Eberstadt Diary entry, May 22, 1948, Eberstadt to Herbert Hoover, May 21, 1948; and Stuart Symington memorandum to JVF, May 21, 1948. For Forrestal's views on the various organizational and bureaucratic nuances of the Hoover Commission, see JVF to service Secretaries, August 4, 1940; JVF to John A. McCone, December 3, 1948, Princeton University, JFP; and JVF telephone conversation with Marx Leva, September 16, 1948, National Archives, Modern Military Branch, RG330.

10. U.S. Commission on Organization of the Executive Branch of the Government (The Hoover Commission), *The National Security Organization. A Report to the Congress* (Washington, D.C., 1949), pp. 12–13, 16–21. Having had the benefit of the Eberstadt Task Force Study, the Hoover Commission submitted its report on the National Security Organization to Congress on February 15, 1949.

11. Statement "What Is Wrong with the Present Organization" by Commissioners Acheson, Mead, Pollack, and Rowe, appended to the Hoover Commission Report, February 15, 1949, pp. 5–30.

12. Hoopes interviews with John H. Ohly, August 15, 1989, and Marx Leva, January 15, 1989. See also Marx Leva, "The Most Unforgettable Character I Have Ever Met," April 18, 1962, Ferdinand Eberstadt Papers, Forrestal Files, Seeley G. Mudd Library, Princeton University, JFP.

13. Hoopes interviews with W. John Kenney, May 29, 1989; Marx Leva, January 15, 1989; and John H. Ohly, August 15, 1989. See also Marx Leva, "The Most Unforgettable Character I Have Ever Met."

14. Hoopes interview with Janet Barnes, January 3, 1990.

15. Ibid.

16. Leon Prochnik, *Endings* (New York, 1980), p. 133.

17. Charles J. V. Murphy interview with John McCone, February 11, 1984. See also McCone to Murphy, July 1, 1981 (authors' possession).

18. Walter Millis, ed., *The Forrestal Diaries* (New York, 1951), pp. 528–529. See also *New York Times,* November 18, 1948.

19. Clifford, *Counsel to the President,* p. 161. See also Hoopes interview with Clark Clifford, January 26, 1989.

20. Hoopes interviews with Marx Leva, January 15, 1989, and H. Struve Hensel, January 20, 1989.

21. Millis, ed., *The Forrestal Diaries,* p. 529. See also New York *Herald Tribune,* November 19, 1948.

22. Rogow, *James Forrestal,* pp. 276–278.

23. Kenneth Royall, Oral History Interview, 1963, Oral History Research Office, Columbia University.

24. Rogow, *James Forrestal,* pp. 278–280.

25. Eugene E. Wilson (wartime president of United Aircraft Corporation), "James Forrestal's Martyrdom," address prepared for delivery to the Men's Club of the First Presbyterian Church, Lake Worth, Florida, February 8, 1962 (authors' possession); Robert Greenhalgh Albion and Robert Howe Connery, *Forrestal and the Navy* (New York, 1962), p. 221; and Donald Carpenter, "Confidential Recollections of Washington, 1947–1949," Carpenter Papers, Harry S. Truman Library,

26. Hoopes interview with W. John Kenney, August 15, 1989. See also Rogow, *James Forrestal,* pp. 243–244.

27. John Osborne, "Forrestal," unpublished manuscript outline, and Robert Lovett,

"Reflections on Jim Forrestal," unpublished manuscript, March 12, 1989. See also "Good Man Lists" in Appendix to Dorwart, "Eberstadt and Forrestal," p. 181.

28. Jack Alexander, "Stormy New Boss of the Pentagon," *The Saturday Evening Post,* July 30, 1949, pp. 26ff; Carl M. Borklund, *Men of the Pentagon: From Forrestal to McNamara* (New York, 1966), pp. 65–88; and Boyd B. Stutler, "Louis A. Johnson—A Prominent West Virginian," *West Virginia Review* (May 1931) pp. 1–3.

29. Hoopes interview with Clark Clifford, April 18, 1989.

30. Hoopes interview with W. John Kenney, May 29, 1989. See also Alexander, "Stormy New Boss of the Pentagon."

31. Murphy interview with Colonel Robert Wood, October 25, 1983.

32. JVF to Ralph Bard, November 20, 1948, Princeton University, JFP.

33. Murphy interview with Colonel Robert Wood, October 25, 1983.

34. "Reminiscences of Hanson Weightman Baldwin," Vol. II, July 28, 1975, U.S. Naval Institute Oral History, Annapolis, Md., 1976.

35. Brinkley interview with Michael Forrestal, October 2, 1988. See also Rogow, *James Forrestal,* p. 308.

36. Rogow, *James Forrestal,* pp. 28–29.

37. Jack Anderson, with James Boyd, *Confessions of a Muckraker* (New York, 1979), pp. 8, 144. For biographical information on Pearson, see Oliver Pilat, *Drew Pearson: An Unauthorized Biography* (New York, 1973); Tyler Abell, ed., *Drew Pearson Diaries, 1949–1959* (New York, 1974); and Frank Kluckhohn and Jay Franklin, *The Drew Pearson Story* (Chicago, 1967).

38. Anderson, with Boyd, *Confessions of a Muckraker,* pp. 9, 13.

39. Anderson, with Boyd, *Confessions of a Muckraker,* p. 139.

40. Anderson, with Boyd, *Confessions of a Muckraker,* pp. 139–168.

41. Drew Pearson's columns in the Washington *Times-Herald,* Drew Pearson Papers, Forrestal File, Lyndon B. Johnson Library (LBJL), Austin, Texas.

42. Anderson, with Boyd, *Confessions of a Muckraker,* p. 143.

43. Anderson, with Boyd, *Confessions of a Muckraker,* p. 147.

44. Anderson, with Boyd, *Confessions of a Muckraker,* pp. 139–168.

45. William O. Douglas, *Go East, Young Man, The Early Years: The Autobiography of William O. Douglas* (New York, 1974), p. 288.

46. Anderson, with Boyd, *Confessions of a Muckraker,* pp. 139–168.

47. Murphy interview with John McCone, February 11, 1984.

48. Robert A. Lovett Oral History interview, May 13, 1974, OSD Historical Office, Pentagon, Arlington, Va.

49. *New York Times,* January 8, 1949; and Brinkley interview with Forrest Pogue, March 14, 1989.

50. Rogow, *James Forrestal,* p. 309. See also Hoopes interview with Marx Leva, January 15, 1989.

51. Prochnik, *Endings,* p. 134; John Osborne "Forrestal," unpublished manuscript outline; and Robert H. Ferrell, *Off the Record: The Private Papers of Harry S. Truman* (New York, 1980), p. 174.

52. "Reminiscences of Admiral Robert Lee Dennison," January 17, 1973, U.S. Naval Institute, Annapolis, Md., 1975.

53. Hoopes interview with W. John Kenney, May 29, 1989.

54. Millis, ed., *The Forrestal Diaries,* p. 544. See also *New York Times,* January 11, 1949; Rogow, *James Forrestal,* pp. 27–28; and Westbrook Pegler, "As Pegler Sees It: Reviews Radio Reporting in Career of Forrestal," New York *Journal-American,*

May 23, 1949. For Winchell's story of Forrestal's demise, see Walter Winchell, *Winchell Exclusive* (Englewood Cliffs, N.J., 1975), pp. 213-219.

55. Millis, ed., *The Forrestal Diaries*, p. 544.

56. *New York Times*, January 12, 1949.

57. *New York Times*, January 14, 1949.

58. "Reminiscences of Vice Admiral William R. Smedberg III," June 9, 1976, U.S. Naval Institute Oral History, Annapolis, Md., July 1979.

59. Millis, ed., *The Forrestal Diaries*, p. 545. See also Hoopes interview with Marx Leva, January 15, 1989.

60. Anderson, with Boyd, *Confessions of a Muckraker*, p. 155.

61. Hoopes interview with Marx Leva, January 15, 1989, and Rogow, *James Forrestal*, pp. 28-34.

62. Anderson, with Boyd, *Confessions of a Muckraker*, pp. 139-168, and Drew Pearson surveillance notes, Pearson Papers, Forrestal File, LBJL.

63. Hoopes interview with Marx Leva, January 15, 1989.

64. Brinkley interview with Mrs. Drew Pearson, April 7, 1990.

65. Anderson, with Boyd, *Confessions of a Muckraker*, pp. 140-141.

66. Douglas, *Go East, Young Man*, p. 287.

67. Louis Johnson remarks to the Post Mortem Club, Washington, D.C., May 17, 1949, H. Struve Hensel Papers, 1940-1941, Files (given to authors by Mr. Hensel).

68. Ibid.

69. Millis, ed., *The Forrestal Diaries*, p. 550. See also John H. Ohly memorandum to Louis Johnson, "List of Major Problems" (requested by Forrestal), February 1949, National Archives, Modern Military Branch, RG330.

70. Hoopes interviews with W. John Kenney, June 6, 1989, and Marx Leva, January 15, 1989.

71. Murphy interview with Major General Lyman Lemnitzer, June 6, 1983.

72. Millis, ed., *The Forrestal Diaries*, p. 550.

73. Hoopes interview with Marx Leva, January 15, 1989.

74. Millis, ed., *The Forrestal Diaries*, pp. 550-551.

75. Ibid. See Harry Truman to JVF, March 2, 1949, Princeton University, JFP.

76. Anderson, with Boyd, *Confessions of a Muckraker*, p. 156.

77. Millis, ed., *The Forrestal Diaries*, p. 552.

78. Hoopes interview with Marx Leva, January 15, 1989.

79. Ibid.

80. William Bradford Huie, "Untold Facts in the Forrestal Case," *The New American Mercury* 71, no. 324 (December 1950), pp. 643-652.

81. Brinkley interview with Michael Forrestal, April 27, 1988.

82. Carpenter, "Confidential Recollections of Washington, 1947-1949."

83. John Osborne, "Forrestal," unpublished manuscript outline.

84. "Reminiscences of Admiral Robert Lee Dennison."

CHAPTER 32 BREAKDOWN

1. Arnold Rogow, *James Forrestal: A Study of Personality, Politics, and Policy* (New York, 1963), p. 1.

2. *Congressional Record*, House of Representatives, March 30, 1949.

3. Ibid. See also Rogow, *James Forrestal*, pp. 2-3.

4. Rogow, *James Forrestal*, p. 3, and Hoopes interview with Marx Leva, January 15, 1989.

5. Marx Leva interview, December 9, 1969, and June 12, 1970, Oral History Collection, Harry S. Truman Library (HSTL).

6. Arthur Krock memorandum of talk with Ferdinand Eberstadt, May 6, 1949, Arthur M. Krock Papers, Seeley G. Mudd Library, Princeton University, JFP. For a slightly different version, see Arthur Krock, *Memoirs: Sixty Years on the Firing Line* (New York, 1968), pp. 254–255.

7. Ibid.

8. Rogow, *James Forrestal*, p. 4.

9. Arthur Krock memorandum of talk with Ferdinand Eberstadt, May 6, 1949; Rogow, *James Forrestal*, p. 5; and Robert Lovett, OSD Oral History interview, May 13, 1974, Historical Office, Pentagon, Arlington, Va.

10. Arthur Krock memorandum of talk with Ferdinand Eberstadt, May 6, 1949, and Hoopes interview with John H. Ohly, August 20, 1989.

11. Robert Lovett OSD Oral History interview, May 13, 1974. See also Charles J. V. Murphy interview with Robert Lovett, April 28, 1983.

12. Hoopes interview with Mrs. Ellen Barry, May 14, 1988.

13. Arthur Krock memorandum of talk with Ferdinand Eberstadt, May 6, 1949, Krock Papers.

14. Rogow, *James Forrestal*, pp. 5–8. See also Brinkley and Hoopes interviews with Michael Forrestal, April 27, 1988, and October 12, 1988.

15. Robert Lovett, OSD Oral History interview, May 13, 1974. See also Murphy interview with Robert Lovett, April 28, 1983.

16. Ibid. For an overview of Menninger's career and methods, see Lawrence J. Freidman, *Menninger* (New York, 1990).

17. Rogow, *James Forrestal*, pp. 5–8.

18. *New York Times*, May 24, 1949.

19. Rogow, *James Forrestal*, pp. 8–11.

20. D. William C. Menninger to Ferdinand Eberstadt, May 31, 1949, Eberstadt Papers, Forrestal File, Seeley G. Mudd Library, Princeton University. See also Brinkley interview with Michael Forrestal, April 27, 1989.

21. Rogow, *James Forrestal*, pp. 8–9.

22. Dr. Robert P. Nenno to Charles J. V. Murphy, July 9, 1984, Murphy Papers (in authors' possession).

23. *New York Times*, May 24, 1949.

24. Sir David Henderson and R. D. Gillespie, *A Text Book of Psychiatry*, 7th ed. (New York, 1950), p. 272, quoted in Rogow, *James Forrestal*; Milton Greenblatt, M.D., "Power and Impairment of Great Leaders," *American Journal of Social Psychiatry* 4, no. 2 (Spring 1984), pp. 11–18; and William C. Bullitt and Sigmund Freud, *Thomas Woodrow Wilson—A Psychological Study* (Boston, 1967).

25. *New York Times*, April 8, 1949.

26. Jack Anderson, with James Boyd, *Confessions of a Muckraker* (New York, 1979), p. 159.

27. Anderson, with Boyd, *Confessions of a Muckraker*, p. 160, and Drew Pearson columns, notes, and transcriptions, Pearson Papers, Forrestal File, Lyndon B. Johnson Library (LBJL), Austin, Texas.

28. Robert Sherrod, "James Forrestal Suicide," memorandum for John Osborne, March 2, 1962, Robert Sherrod Personal Papers, Washington, D.C.

29. Brinkley interview with Eliot Janeway, September 27, 1990.

30. Dr. William C. Menninger to Ferdinand Eberstadt, April 16, 1949, Eberstadt Papers.

31. Washington *Post,* April 10, 1949.

32. "Bulletin on Mr. Forrestal," April 11, 1949, U.S. Naval Hospital, Bethesda, Maryland, Drew Pearson Papers, Lyndon B. Johnson Library (LBJL), Austin, Texas. Also *New York Times,* April 12, 1949.

33. *New York Times,* April 12, 1949.

34. Washington *Post,* April 14, 1949.

35. All letters of sympathy and gratitude received by Forrestal during his early hospitalization are among the Forrestal papers at Princeton University. Several of the letters quoted in the text also appear in John Osborne's unpublished book outline "Forrestal."

36. Quoted in Rogow, *James Forrestal,* p. 13.

37. Sherrod, "James Forrestal Suicide."

38. Robert Sherrod, rough draft of story for *Time* magazine, May 27, 1949, Sherrod Personal Papers.

39. Ibid. See also Arthur Krock private memorandum, May 30, 1949, Krock Papers.

40. Sherrod, "James Forrestal Suicide."

41. Ibid.

42. *New York Times,* April 24, 1949.

43. *New York Times,* April 28, 1949.

44. Hoopes interview with Marx Leva, January 15, 1989.

45. *New York Times,* April 17, 1949.

46. *New York Times,* May 18, 1949. According to Arthur Krock, Forrestal regained only five pounds, all of it in the last weeks of his life. See Arthur Krock Private Memorandum, May 30, 1949.

47. William Bradford Huie, "Untold Facts in the Forrestal Case," *The New American Mercury* 71, no. 324 (December 1950), pp. 643–652.

48. Rogow, *James Forrestal,* p. 45.

49. Hoopes interview with David Ginsburg, January 22, 1991.

50. Rogow, *James Forrestal,* pp. 45–46.

51. Hoopes interview with Michael Forrestal, October 12, 1988.

52. Huie, "Untold Facts in the Forrestal Case," pp. 643–652, and Sherrod, "James Forrestal Suicide."

53. *New York Times,* May 24, 1949.

54. New York *Herald Tribune* and *New York Times,* May 24, 1949.

55. Osborne, "Forrestal," unpublished manuscript outline; Rogow, *James Forrestal,* pp. 16–17; and Lyle Stuart, *Why: The Magazine of Popular Psychology* 1, no. 1 (November 1950), pp. 3–9, 20–27.

56. Rogow, *James Forrestal,* pp. 17–18, and *New York Times,* May 24, 1949.

57. John Loftus to Edythe Holbrook, January 25, 1983 (in authors' possession); John Loftus, *The Belarus Secret* (New York, 1982); and Henry Rositzke, *CIA's Secret Operations* (New York, 1977).

58. Rogow, *James Forrestal,* p. 15.

59. Dr. Robert P. Nenno to Charles J. V. Murphy, July 9, 1984, Murphy Papers (in authors' possession).

60. Rogow, *James Forrestal,* pp. 18–19.

61. Osborne, "Forrestal," unpublished manuscript outline.

62. Peter Walker interview with Oatsie Lighter, May 2, 1987.

63. *New York Times,* May 23, 1949.

64. Ibid.

65. New York *Herald Tribune,* May 24, 1949. See also Rogow, *James Forrestal,* p. 19.

66. Sherrod, "James Forrestal Suicide."

67. New York *Herald Tribune,* May 24, 1949.

68. Herbert Elliston, "Jim Forrestal: A Portrait in Politics," *Atlantic Monthly,* November 1951, pp. 73–80, and Washington *Post,* May 23, 1949.

69. Albert Deutsch, "Forrestal's Death," *Daily Compass,* May 23 and 29, 1949, quoted in Rogow, *James Forrestal,* p. 44.

70. For Henry Forrestal's concerns and the "murder-conspiracy" theory, see Cornell Simpson, *The Death of James Forrestal* (Belmont, Mass., 1966), and Huie, "Untold Facts in the Forrestal Case," pp. 643–652.

CHAPTER 33   FINAL HONORS AND ASSESSMENT

1. *New York Times,* May 26, 1989, and Arnold A. Rogow, *James Forrestal: A Study of Personality, Politics, and Policy* (New York, 1963), pp. 19–20.

2. Arthur H. Vandenberg, Jr., *The Private Papers of Senator Vandenberg* (Boston, 1952), pp. 486–487.

3. Hoopes interview with Michael Forrestal, October 12, 1988.

4. Rogow, *James Forrestal,* pp. 24–25.

5. Rogow, *James Forrestal,* pp. 25–26. See also Robert Sherrod, "James Forrestal Suicide," memorandum for John Osborne, March 2, 1962, Sherrod Personal Papers.

6. *New York Times,* May 24, 1949.

7. *Newsday,* May 24, 1949.

8. Rogow, *James Forrestal,* p. 30.

9. *New York Times,* May 24, 1949, quoted in Harold Nicolson, *The Congress of Vienna* (New York, 1946).

10. Jack Anderson, with James Boyd, *Confessions of a Muckraker* (New York, 1979), p. 164.

11. Anderson, with James Boyd, *Confessions of a Muckraker,* p. 166.

12. Robert Lovett, "Reflections on Jim Forrestal," unpublished book preface, March 12, 1985.

13. Murphy interview with John J. McCloy, October 16, 1983.

14. John Osborne, "Forrestal," unpublished manuscript outline.

15. Washington *Post,* May 23, 1949.

16. Remarks by Congressman Carl Vinson at ceremony for Forrestal, March 29, 1949 *(Congressional Record,* March 30, 1949).

17. Osborne, "Forrestal," unpublished manuscript outline.

18. Hanson Baldwin, *New York Times,* May 24, 1949.

19. Walter Lippmann, New York *Herald Tribune,* May 24, 1949.

20. Osborne, "Forrestal," unpublished manuscript outline.

BIBLIOGRAPHY

ARCHIVES AND MANUSCRIPT COLLECTIONS

Alumni Records. Confidential Records. Princeton University, Princeton, New Jersey.

Baruch, Bernard M. Papers. Seeley G. Mudd Library, Princeton University, Princeton, New Jersey.

Carpenter, Donald. Papers. Harry S. Truman Library, Independence, Missouri.

Corcoran, T. G. Papers. Franklin D. Roosevelt Memorial Library, Hyde Park, New York.

Douglas, William O. Papers. Manuscript Divison, Library of Congress, Washington D.C.

Eberstadt, Ferdinand. Papers. Seeley G. Mudd Library, Princeton University, Princeton, New Jersey.

Forrestal, James V. Papers. Seeley G. Mudd Library, Princeton University, Princeton, New Jersey.

Forrestal, James V. Unpublished Diaries. Seeley G. Mudd Library, Princeton University, Princeton, New Jersey, and Office of the Secretary of Defense Historical Office, Pentagon, Arlington, Virginia.

Kennan, George F. Papers. Seeley G. Mudd Library, Princeton University, Princeton, New Jersey.

W. John Kenney Papers. Harry S. Truman Library, Independence, Missouri.

Ernest J. King Papers. Library of Congress, Washington, D.C.

Knox, Frank. Papers. Library of Congress, Washington, D.C.

Krock, Arthur M. Papers. Seeley G. Mudd Library, Princeton University, Princeton, New Jersey.

Leahy, William D. Papers. Manuscript Division, Library of Congress, Washington, D.C.

Lovett, Robert A. Papers. National Archives, Washington, D.C.

MacArthur, Douglas. Papers. MacArthur Memorial Library, Bureau of Archives, Norfolk, Virginia.

National Archives, Washington, D.C.
  Navy/Old Army Branch
    Record Group 80, General Records of the Department of the Navy
  Modern Military Branch
    Record Group 330, Records of the Office of the Secretary of Defense
    Record Group 107, Records of the Office of the Secretary of War
    Record Group 165, Records of the War Department General and Special Staffs Plans and Operations Division
    Record Group 319, Records of the Army Staff Plans and Operations Division
  Diplomatic Branch
    Record Group 59, General Records of the Department of State

Operational Archives, Washington Navy Yard, Washington, D.C.
  Biographical Files
  Diaries of James V. Forrestal
  Papers Relating to Secretary of the Navy James V. Forrestal
  Ernest J. King Papers
  William D. Leahy Papers
  Chester W. Nimitz Papers
Oral Histories. Center of Naval History, Washington, D.C.
  Mildred McAfee Horton 1969
Oral Histories. Oral History Research Office, Columbia University. New York City.
  Joseph Clark Baldwin, 1950
  Harold Dodds, 1966
  Robert A. Lovett, 1959, 1971, 1976
  Kenneth Royall, 1963
  Henry Wallace, 1953, 1961
Oral Histories. Harry S. Truman Library, Independence, Missouri.
  John Abbot, 1970
  Robert L. Dennison, 1972
  George M. Elsey, 1974
  John A. Kennedy, 1978
  Mark Leva, 1972
  John L. Sullivan, 1974
Oral Histories. U.S. Naval Institute Oral History Project, Annapolis, Maryland.
  William R. Smedberg III, 1976
  Hanson W. Baldwin, 1975
  Robert Lee Dennison, 1973
Oral Histories. Office of the Secretary of Defense Historical Office, Pentagon, Arlington, Virginia.
  Robert A. Lovett, 1974
  Stuart Symington, 1981
Patterson, Robert P. Letters. Library of Congress, Washington, D.C.
Pearson, Drew. Papers. Lyndon B. Johnson Library, Austin, Texas.
Roosevelt, Franklin D. Papers. Franklin D. Roosevelt Memorial Library, Hyde Park, New York.
  President's Official File
  President's Secretary's File
Sherrod, Robert. Papers. George Arents Research Library, Syracuse University, Syracuse, New York.
Smith, Harold D. Papers, Franklin D. Roosevelt Library, Hyde Park, N.Y.
Spaatz, Carl. Papers. Library of Congress, Washington, D.C.
Stimson, Henry L. Diaries. Sterling Memorial Library, Yale University, New Haven, Connecticut.
Sullivan, John L. Harry S. Truman Library, Independence, Missouri.
Symington, Stuart. Papers. Harry S. Truman Library, Independence, Missouri.
Truman, Harry S. Papers. Harry S. Truman Library, Independence, Missouri.
  President's Official File
  President's Secretary's File
Wallace, Henry A. Papers. University of Iowa, Ames, Iowa.
Washington Post. Newspaper Archive, Washington, D.C.
Whitehill, Walter M. Whitehill-Buehl Mss.

PRIVATE PAPERS

Michael Forrestal Papers; in author's possesion.
H. Struve Hensel Papers; in author's possession.
Tilghman Koons Personal Papers, New York, N.Y.
Marx Leva Papers; in author's possession.
Charles J.V. Murphy Papers; in author's possession.
John H. Ohly Papers; in author's possession.
Robert Sherrod Personal Papers, Washington D.C.
John H. Towers Diaries, Charleston, South Carolina (in the custudy of Professor Clark
    Reynolds).

BOOKS

Abbazia, Patrick. *Mr. Roosevelt's Navy: The Private War of the U.S. Atlantic Fleet.*
    Annapolis, Md.: Naval Institute Press, 1975.
Abel, Tyler. *Drew Pearson Diaries, 1949–1969.* New York: Holt, Rinehart and Win-
    ston, 1974.
Acheson, Dean. *Present at the Creation: My Years in the State Department.* New York:
    W.W. Norton and Co., 1969.
Acheson, Dean. *Sketches from Life of Men I Have Known.* New York: Harper &
    Brothers, 1961.
Albion, Robert Greenhalgh, and Robert Howe Connery. *Forrestal and the Navy.* New
    York: Columbia University Press, 1962.
Allen, Hugh. *The House of Goodyear.* Cleveland: privately published, 1948.
American Guide Series. *Dutchess County.* New York: Federal Writers Project, 1937.
Anderson, Clinton P., with Milton Viorst. *Outsider in the Senate: Senator Clinton
    Anderson's Memoirs.* New York: The World Publishing Co., 1970.
Anderson, Irvine H. *Aramco, the United States and Saudi Arabia.* Princeton, N.J.:
    Princeton University Press, 1981.
Anderson, Jack, with James Boyd. *Confessions of a Muckraker.* New York: Ballantine
    Books, 1979.
Armstrong, Anne. *Unconditional Surrender: The Impact of the Casablanca Policy upon
    World War II.* New Brunswick, N.J.: Rutgers University Press, 1961.
Attlee, Clement. *Twilight of Empire: Memoirs of Prime Minister Clement Attlee,* ed.
    Francis Williams. Westport, Conn.: Greenwood Press, 1978. Reprint.
Baruch, Bernard M. *Baruch: The Public Years.* New York: Holt, Rinehart and Win-
    ston, 1960.
Beasley, Norman. *Men Working: A Story of Goodyear Tire and Rubber Company.* New
    York: Harper and Brothers, 1931.
Belote, William M., and James H. Belote. *Typhoon of Steel: The Battle of Okinawa.*
    New York: Harper and Row, 1970.
Bernstein, Barton J., ed. *The Atomic Bomb: The Critical Issues.* Boston: Little, Brown, 1976.
Birmingham, Stephen. *Our Crowd: The Great Jewish Families of New York.* New
    York: Harper and Row, 1967.
Blum, John Morton. *V Was for Victory: Politics and American Culture During World
    War II.* New York: Harcourt Brace Jovanovich, 1976.
Borklund, Carl W. *Men of the Pentagon: From Forrestal to McNamara.* New York:
    Frederick A. Praeger, 1966.

Bradley, Omar N., and Clay Blair. *A General's Life: An Autobiography.* New York: Simon and Schuster, 1983.

Brinkley, Alan. *Voices of Protest: Huey Long, Father Coughlin and the Great Depression.* New York: Alfred A. Knopf, 1982.

Brinkley, David. *Washington Goes to War.* New York: Alfred A. Knopf, 1988.

Brinkley, Douglas, ed. *Dean Acheson and the Making of U.S. Foreign Policy.* New York: St. Martin's Press, 1992.

Brooks, John. *Once in Golconda—A True Drama of Wall Street, 1920–1938.* New York: Harper and Row, 1969.

Brownell, Will, and Richard N. Billings. *So Close to Greatness: A Biography of William C. Bullitt.* New York: Macmillan, 1987.

Bruccoli, Matthew J. *The O'Hara Concern: A Biography of John O'Hara.* New York: Random House, 1975.

Bruce, James, and J. Vincent Forrestal. *College Journalism.* Princeton, N.J., Princeton University Press, 1914.

Bryant, Arthur. *A History of the War Years Based on the Diaries of Field Marshal Lord Alanbrooke, Chief of the Imperial General Staff.* Vol I: *The Turn of the Tide.* Garden City, N.Y.: Doubleday, 1957.

Buell, Thomas B. *Master of Sea Power: A Biography of Fleet Admiral Ernest J. King.* Boston: Little, Brown, 1980.

Bullitt, William C., and Sigmund Freud. *Thomas Woodrow Wilson—A Psychological Study.* Boston: Houghton Mifflin, 1967.

Burns, James MacGregor. *Roosevelt: Soldier of Freedom.* New York: Harcourt Brace Jovanovich, 1970.

Bush, Vannevar. *Modern Arms and Free Men: A Discussion of the Role of the Sciences in Preserving Democracy.* New York: Simon and Schuster, 1949.

——. *Pieces of Action.* New York: William Morrow, 1970.

Byrnes, James F. *Speaking Frankly.* New York: Harper and Brothers, 1947.

——. *All in One Lifetime.* New York: Harper and Brothers, 1958.

Callahan, David. *Dangerous Capabilities: Paul Nitze and the Cold War.* New York: Harper and Collins, 1990.

Caraley, Demetrios. *The Politics of Military Unification.* New York: Columbia University Press, 1966.

Carosso, Vincent P. *Investment Banking in America.* Cambridge Eng.: Cambridge University Press, 1970.

Catton, Bruce. *The War Lords of Washington.* New York: Harcourt Brace and Co., 1948.

Chandruang, Kamut. *My Boyhood in Siam.* New York: John Day and Company, 1940.

Chase, Edna Wollman, and Ilka Chase. *Always in Vogue.* Garden City, N.Y.: Doubleday, 1954.

Chernow, Ron. *The House of Morgan.* Boston: Atlantic Monthly, 1990.

Churchill, Winston. *Triumph and Tragedy.* Boston: Houghton Mifflin, 1953.

——. *Their Finest Hour.* Boston: Houghton Mifflin, 1959.

Clay, Lucius D. *Decision in Germany.* Garden City: Doubleday, 1950.

Clemens, Diane Shaver. *Yalta.* New York: Oxford University Press, 1970.

Clifford, Clark, with Richard Holbrooke. *Counsel to the President: A Memoir.* New York: Random House, 1991.

Cohen, Michael. *Palestine and the Great Powers, 1945–1948.* Princeton: Princeton University Press, 1982.

——. *Truman and Israel.* Berkeley: University of California Press, 1990.

Coit, Margaret L. *Mr. Baruch.* Boston: Houghton Mifflin, 1957.

Cole, Alice C., Alfred Goldberg, Samuel A. Tucker, and Rudolph A. Winnacker, eds. *The Documents on Establishment and Organization, 1944–1978.* Washington, D.C.: Office of the Secretary of Defense, Historical Office, 1978.

Cole, Wayne S. *Charles A. Lindbergh and the Battle Against Intervention in World War II.* New York: Harcourt, Brace, 1947.

Coletta, Paolo F. *Patrick N. L. Bellinger and U.S. Naval Aviation.* Lanham, Md.: University Press of America, 1987.

——, ed. *American Secretaries of the Navy.* Vol. II. Annapolis, Md.: Naval Institute Press, 1980.

Condit, Kenneth W. *The Joint Chiefs of Staff and National Policy, 1947–1949.* Washington, D.C.: Joint Chiefs of Staff, 1978.

Connery, Robert H. *The Navy and the Industrial Mobilization in World War II.* Princeton: Princeton University Press, 1951.

Cowley, Malcolm. *Exile's Return.* New York: Viking Press, 1934.

——. *A Second Flowering: Works and Days of the Lost Generation.* New York: Viking Press, 1956.

Cremin, Lawrence. *The Transformation of the School.* New York: Alfred A. Knopf, 1981.

Cutler, Robert. *No Time for Rest.* Boston: Little, Brown, 1965.

Dallek, Robert. *Franklin D. Roosevelt and American Foreign Policy, 1932–1945.* New York: Oxford University Press, 1979.

Daniels, Jonathan. *Frontier on the Potomac.* New York: Macmillan, 1946.

Davis, Vincent. *Postwar Defense and the U.S. Navy, 1943–1946.* Chapel Hill: University of North Carolina Press, 1966.

Davison, Philips. *The Berlin Blockade: A Study in Cold War Politics.* Princeton: Princeton University Press, 1958.

Diner, Hasia. *Erin's Daughters in America.* Baltimore: The Johns Hopkins University Press, 1985.

Djilas, Milovan. *Conversations with Stalin.* New York: Harcourt, Brace and World, 1962.

Donovan, Robert J. *Conflict and Crisis: The Presidency of Harry S. Truman, 1945–1948.* New York: W. W. Norton and Co., 1977.

Dos Passos, John. *The Great Days.* New York: Sagamore Press, 1958.

——. *John Dos Passos: The Major Nonfiction Prose,* ed. Donald Pizer. Detroit: Wayne State University Press, 1988.

Douglas, William O. *Go East, Young Man: The Early Years. The Autobiography of William O. Douglas.* New York: Random House, 1974.

Dowart, Jeffrey M. *Eberstadt and Forrestal: A National Security Partnership, 1909–1949.* College Station: Texas A&M University Press, 1991.

Driberg, Tom. *The Mystery of Moral Rearmament: A Study of Buchman.* New York: Alfred A. Knopf, 1965.

Dunlop, Richard. *Donovan: America's Master Spy.* Chicago: Rand McNally & Co., 1982.

Eden, Anthony. *The Eden Memoirs: The Reckoning.* London: Cassell & Co., 1965.

Eisenhower, Dwight D. *The Eisenhower Diaries,* ed. Robert H. Ferrell. New York: W. W. Norton and Co., 1981.

Eubank, Keith. *Summit at Tehran.* New York: William Morrow, 1985.

Farnsworth, Beatrice. *William C. Bullitt and the Soviet Union.* Bloomington, Ind.: Indiana University Press, 1967.

Feis, Herbert. *The Birth of Israel: The Tousled Diplomatic Bed.* New York: W.W. Norton and Co., 1969.

———. *From Trust to Terror: The Onset of the Cold War, 1945–50.* New York: W. W. Norton and Co., 1970.

Fesler, James. *Industrial Mobilization for War, 1940–1945.* Washington, D.C.: Government Printing Office for Civilian Production Administration, 1947.

Fifty Year Record: Class of 1915. Princeton, N.J.: Princeton University Press, 1965.

Fitzgerald, F. Scott. *The Great Gatsby.* New York: Charles Scribner's Sons, 1925.

———. *This Side of Paradise.* New York: 1920 reprint, First Scribner Classic/Collier Edition, 1986.

———. *Afternoon of an Author.* New York: First Scribner Classic/Collier Edition, 1987.

Forrestal, James. *The Navy: A Study in Administration.* Chicago: Public Administration Service, 1946.

———. *The Forrestal Diaries,* ed. Walter Millis, with Eugene S. Duffield. New York: Viking Press, 1951.

Fraser, Steve, and Garry Gestle, eds. *The Rise and Fall of the New Deal Order, 1930–1980.* Princeton, N.J.: Princeton University Press, 1989.

Freeland, Richard M. *The Truman Doctrine and the Origins of McCarthyism: Foreign Policy, Domestic Politics and International Security, 1946–1948.* New York: Alfred A. Knopf, 1972.

Friedman, Lawrence J. *Menninger.* New York: Alfred A. Knopf, 1990.

Friedman, Norman. *Carrier Air Power.* Annapolis, Md.: Naval Institute Press, 1981.

Furer, Julius. *Administration by the Navy Department in World War II.* Washington, D.C.: Government Printing Office, 1959.

Gaddis, John Lewis. *The United States and the Origins of the Cold War, 1941–1947.* New York: Columbia University Press, 1972.

Galbraith, John Kenneth. *The Great Crash.* Boston: Houghton Mifflin, 1955.

Gardner, Lloyd C. *Architects of Illusion: Men and Ideas in American Foreign Policy, 1941–1949.* Chicago: Quadrangle Books, 1970.

Gerry, Peggy and Roger. *Old Roslyn.* Roslyn, N.Y.: Bryant Library, 1954.

Goodhart, Philip. *Fifty Ships That Saved the World.* Garden City, N.Y.: Doubleday, 1965.

Grant, James. *Bernard Baruch: The Adventures of a Wall Street Legend.* New York: Simon and Schuster, 1983.

Greenfield, Kent R. *American Strategy in World War II: A Reconsideration.* Baltimore: The Johns Hopkins University Press, 1963.

Hagan, Kenneth J., ed. *In Peace and War: Interpretations of American Naval History, 1775–1978.* Westport, Conn.: Greenwood Press, 1978.

Halaby, Najeeb E. *Crosswinds: An Airman's Memoir.* Garden City, N.Y.: Doubleday, 1978.

Halle, Louis J. *Spring in Washington.* New York: Harper and Row, 1947.

Hankey, Maurice. *Government Control in War.* London: Cambridge University Press, 1945.

Harriman, W. Averell, and Elie Abel. *Special Envoy to Churchill and Stalin, 1941–1946.* New York: Random House, 1975.

Hassett, William D. *Off the Record with FDR, 1942–1945.* New Brunswick, N.J.: Rutgers University Press, 1958.

Haynes, Richard F. *The Awesome Power: Harry S. Truman as Commander in Chief.* Baton Rouge: Louisiana State University Press, 1973.

Henderson, Sir David, and R. D. Gillespie. *A Text Book of Psychiatry,* 7th ed. New York: Oxford University Press, 1950.

Herken, Gregg. *The Winning Weapon: The Atomic Bomb in the Cold War, 1945–1950.* New York: Alfred A. Knopf, 1980.

Hewlett, Richard G., and Oscar Edward Anderson. *A History of the United States Atomic Energy Commission,* Vol. II. University Park, Penn.: Pennsylvania State University Press, 1969.

Hewlett, Richard G., and Francis Duncan. *The Nuclear Navy, 1946–1952.* Chicago: University of Chicago Press, 1955.

Hixson, Walter L. *George F. Kennan: Cold War Iconoclast.* New York: Columbia University Press, 1989.

Hodgson, Godfrey. *The Colonel: The Life and Wars of Henry Stimson, 1867–1950.* New York: Alfred A. Knopf, 1990.

Hogan, Michael. *The Marshall Plan: America, Britain, and the Reconstruction of Europe.* Cambridge: Cambridge University Press, 1987.

Howard, Peter. *The World Rebuilt.* London: Stanford Press, 1951.

Hoxie, Ralph Gordon. *Command Decision and the Presidency: A Study in National Security Policy and Organization.* New York: Reader's Digest, 1977.

Hull, Cordell. *Memoirs,* Vols. I & II. New York: Macmillan, 1948.

Hurewitz, J. C. *The Struggle for Palestine.* New York: W. W. Norton and Co., 1950.

Hurley, Alfred F., and Robert C. Ehrhart, eds. *Airpower and Warfare.* Washington, D.C.: Office of the Air Force, 1979.

Ickes, Harold L. *The Secret Diary of Harold L. Ickes: The Lowering Clouds,* Vol. III. New York: Simon & Schuster, 1954.

Isaacson, Walter, and Evan Thomas. *The Wise Men: Architects of the American Century.* New York: Simon and Schuster, 1986.

Isenberg, Michael T. *John L. Sullivan and His America.* Urbana: University of Illinois Press, 1988.

Janeway, Eliot. *The Economics of Chaos.* New York: E. P. Dutton, 1989.

Jenkins, Roy. *Truman.* New York: Harper and Row, 1986.

Jessup, Philip. *Elihu Root.* New York: Dodd Mead, 1938.

Jones, James Marion. *Fifteen Weeks, February 21–June 5, 1947.* New York: Viking Press, 1955.

Keiser, Gordon W. *The United States Marine Corps and Defense Unification, 1944–1947.* Washington, D.C.: National Defense University Press, 1982.

Kennan, George F. *Memoirs, 1925–1950.* Boston: Little, Brown, 1967.

Kennedy, David M. *Over Here: The First World War and American Society.* New York: Oxford University Press, 1980.

Ketchum, Richard M. *The Borrowed Years, 1938–1941.* New York: Random House, 1989.

Kimmel, Husband E. *Admiral Kimmel's Story.* Chicago: Henry Regnery Co., 1955.

King, Ernest J. *U.S. Navy at War, 1941–1945: Official Reports to the Secretary of the Navy.* Washington, D.C.: U.S. Navy Department, 1946.

——, and Walter Muir Whitehall. *Fleet Admiral King: A Naval Record.* New York: W. W. Norton & Co., 1952.

Kluckhohn, Frank, and Jay Franklin. *The Drew Pearson Story.* Chicago: Chas. Hallberg & Co., 1967.

Krock, Arthur. *Memoirs: Sixty Years on the Firing Line.* New York: Funk and Wagnalls, 1968.

Krutch, Joseph Wood. *The Modern Temper.* New York: Harcourt, Brace & Co., 1929.

Kuniholm, Bruce R. *The Origins of the Cold War in the Near East: Great Power Conflict and Diplomacy in Iran, Turkey and Greece.* Princeton: Princeton University Press, 1980.

Laqueur, Walter. *A History of Zionism.* New York: Holt, Rinehart and Winston, 1976.

Larrabee, Eric. *Commander in Chief: Franklin Delano Roosevelt, His Lieutenants and Their War.* New York: Harper and Row, 1987.

Laski, Harold. *The Secret Battalion: An Examination of the Communist Attitude to the Labour Party.* London: Labor Publications Department, 1966.

Latham, Caroline, and David Agresta. *The Dodge Dynasty.* San Diego: Harcourt Brace Jovanovich, 1989.

Leahy, William D. *I Was There.* New York: McGraw-Hill, 1950.

Leslie, Frank P. *James Forrestal.* Wayzata, Minn.: Maplewoods, 1951.

Leuchtenberg, William F. *Franklin D. Roosevelt and the New Deal.* New York: Harper and Row, 1963.

Lieberman, Joseph L. *The Scorpion and the Tarantula: The Struggle to Control Atomic Weapons, 1945–49.* Boston: Houghton Mifflin, 1970.

Lilienthal, David E. *Journals: The Atomic Energy Years, 1945–1950.* New York: Harper and Row, 1964.

Loftus, John. *The Belarus Secret.* New York: Alfred A. Knopf, 1982.

Love, Robert William, Jr., ed. *The Chiefs of Naval Operations.* Annapolis, Md.: U.S. Naval Institute Press, 1980.

Ludington, Townsend. *John Dos Passos: A Twentieth Century Odyssey.* New York: E. P. Dutton, 1980.

McCoy, Donald R., and Richard T. Ruetten. *Quest and Response: Minority Rights and the Truman Administration.* Lawrence: The University of Kansas Press, 1973.

McFadden, Charles J. *The Philosophy of Communism.* New York: Benzinger Brothers, Inc., 1939.

MacGregor, Morris J., Jr. *Integration of the Armed Forces, 1940–1965.* Washington, D.C.: Center of Military History, United States Army, 1981.

Markowitz, Norman D. *The Rise and Fall of the People's Century: Henry A. Wallace and American Liberalism.* New York: The Free Press, 1973.

Marling, Karal Ann, and Wetenhall, John. *Iwo Jima: Monuments, Memories and the American Hero.* Cambridge, Mass.: Harvard University Press, 1991.

Martin, Kingsley. *Harold Laski: A Biographical Memoir.* London: Victor Gollancz, Ltd., 1953.

Mathey, Dean. *Fifty Years of Wall Street with Anecdotiana.* Princeton: privately published, 1966.

Matloff, Maurice. *Strategic Planning for Coalition Warfare, 1943–1944.* Washington, D.C.: Office of the Chief of Military History, Department of the Army, 1953.

Matz, Mary Jane. *The Many Lives of Otto Kahn.* New York: Macmillan, 1963.

Mayers, David. *George Kennan and the Dilemmas of U.S. Foreign Policy.* New York: Oxford University Press, 1988.

Mee, Charles L., Jr. *Meeting at Potsdam.* New York: Evans, 1975.

Meilinger, Phillip S. *Hoyt S. Vandenberg: The Life of a General.* Bloomington: Indiana University Press, 1989.

Messer, Robert L. *The End of an Alliance: James F. Byrnes, Roosevelt, Truman and the Origins of the Cold War.* Chapel Hill: University of North Carolina Press, 1982.

Miles, Christine M. *Harold Sterner: Architect and Artist.* New York: catalogue of Sterner's work, 1978.

Miller, Edward. *War Plan Orange.* Annapolis, Md.: U.S. Naval Institute Press, 1991.

Miller, Kerby. *Emigrants and Exiles: Ireland and the Irish Exodus to North America.* Baltimore: The Johns Hopkins University Press, 1985.

Morgan, Ted. *FDR: A Biography.* New York: Simon and Schuster, 1985.

Morison, Elting E. *Turmoil and Tradition: A Study of the Life and Times of Henry L. Stimson.* Boston: Houghton Mifflin, 1960.

Mulder, John M. *Woodrow Wilson: The Years of Preparation.* Princeton: Princeton University Press, 1978.

Nash, George H. *The Life of Herbert Hoover.* New York: W. W. Norton and Co, 1983.

Nelson, Dennis M. *The Integration of the Negro into the U.S. Navy.* New York: Farrar, Straus and Young, 1951.

Nelson, Donald M. *Arsenal of Democracy.* New York: Harcourt, Brace & Co., 1946.

Nicholas, H. G. *Washington Dispatches, 1941–1945.* Chicago: University of Chicago Press, 1981.

Nitze, Paul H.; with Ann M. Smith and Steve L. Rearden. *From Hiroshima to Glasnost: At the Center of Decision—A Memoir.* New York: Grove Weidenfeld, 1989.

O'Hara, John. *From the Terrace.* New York: Random House, 1958.

——. *The Collected Stories of John O'Hara.* New York: Random House, 1984.

O'Toole, G. J. A. *Honorable Treachery: A History of U.S. Intelligence, Espionage, and Covert Action from the American Revolution to the CIA.* New York: The Atlantic Monthly Press, 1991.

Paine, Ralph D. *The First Yale Unit.* Cambridge: Riverside Press, 1925.

Painter, David. *Oil and the American Century: The Political Economy of U.S. Foreign Oil Policy, 1941–1954.* Baltimore: The Johns Hopkins University Press, 1986.

Pecora, Ferdinand. *Wall Street Under Oath: The Story of Our Modern Money Changers.* New York: Simon and Schuster, 1939.

Peekskill, Matteawan and Cold Spring. Newark, N.J.: Mercantile Publishing, 1892.

Pelikan, Jiri, ed. *The Czechoslovak Political Trials, 1950–1954.* London: Macdonald, 1971.

Perez, Robert C., and Edward F. Willett. *The Will to Win: A Biography of Ferdinand Eberstadt.* Westport, Conn.: Greenwood Press, 1989.

Pogue, Forrest C. *George C. Marshall,* Vol. II: *Ordeal and Hope, 1939–1942.* New York: Viking Press, 1966.

Potter, E. P. *Nimitz.* Annapolis, Md.: Naval Institute Press, 1976.

Prados, John. *Presidents' Secret Wars.* New York: William Morrow and Co., 1986.

Prange, Gordon W., with Donald M. Goldstein. *Pearl Harbor: The Verdict of History.* New York: McGraw-Hill, 1986.

The Princeton Catalogue, 1914–1915. Privately printed.

Princeton Directory, 1912–1913. Privately printed.

Prochnik, Leon. *Endings.* New York: Crown, 1980.

Radford, Arthur W. *From Pearl Harbor to Vietnam: The Memoirs of Admiral Arthur W. Radford,* ed. Stephen Jurika, Jr. Stanford, Calif.: Hoover Institution Press, 1980.

Randall, Monica. *Mansions of Long Island's Gold Coast.* New York: Hastings House, 1979.

Rearden, Stephen L. *History of the Office of the Secretary of Defense: The Formative Years, 1947–1950.* Washington, D.C.: Office of the Secretary of Defense, 1984.

Reynolds, Clark G. *The Fast Carriers: The Forging of an Air Navy.* New York: McGraw-Hill, 1968.

Robinson, Henry Morton. *Fantastic Interim: A Hindsight History of American Manners, Morals and Mistakes Between Versailles and Pearl Harbor.* Freeport, N.Y.: Books for Libraries, 1971.

Rogow, Arnold A. *James Forrestal: A Study of Personality, Politics and Policy.* New York: Macmillan, 1963.

Roosevelt, Elliott. *As He Saw It.* New York: Duell, Sloan and Pierce, 1946.

Roosevelt, Franklin D. *The Public Papers and Addresses of Franklin D. Roosevelt,* ed. Samuel I. Rosenman. *Vol. II, 1944–45.* New York: Harper & Brothers, 1950.

Root, Elihu. *Annual Report of the Secretary of War, 1903.* Washington, D.C.: Government Printing Office.

Roppulo, Patrick. *Philip Barry.* New York: Twayne Publishers, 1965.

Rositzke, Henry. *The CIA's Secret Operations.* New York: Reader's Digest, 1977.

Rosmond, Babette. *Robert Benchley: His Life and Good Times.* Garden City, N.Y.: Doubleday, 1970.

Ross, Bill D. *Iwo Jima: Legacy of Valor.* New York: Vanguard, 1985.

Schapsmier, Edward L., and Frederick Schapsmier. *Prophet in Politics: Henry A. Wallace in the War Years, 1940–1965.* Ames: Iowa State University Press, 1970.

Schilling, Warner R., Paul Y. Hammond, and Glen H. Snyder. *Strategy, Politics and Defense Budgets.* New York: Columbia University Press, 1962.

Schlaim, Avi. *The United States and the Berlin Blockade: A Study in Crisis Decision-making.* Berkeley: University of California Press, 1983.

Schlesinger, Arthur M., Jr. *The Crisis of the Old Order.* Boston: Houghton Mifflin, 1957.

———. *The Politics of Upheaval.* Boston: Houghton Mifflin, 1960.

Schwartz, Jordan A. *The Speculator: Bernard M. Baruch in Washington, 1917–1965.* Chapel Hill: University of North Carolina, 1981.

Seebohm, Caroline. *The Man Who Was Vogue: The Life and Times of Condé Nast.* New York: Viking Press, 1982.

Sherrod, Robert. *On to the Westward.* New York: Duell, Sloan & Pierce, 1945.

Sherry, Michael S. *Preparing for the Next War: American Plans for Postwar Defense, 1941–45.* New Haven, Conn.: Yale University Press, 1977.

Sherwin, Martin J. *A World Destroyed: The Atomic Bomb and the Grand Alliance.* New York: Alfred A. Knopf, 1975.

Sherwood, Robert E. *Roosevelt and Hopkins.: An Intimate History.* New York: Harper and Brothers, 1948.

Simon, James F. *Independent Journey: The Life of William O. Douglas.* New York: Harper and Row, 1980.

Simpson, Cornell. *The Death of James Forrestal.* Belmont, Mass.: Western Islands, 1966.

Simpson, Mitchell B. III. *Admiral Harold R. Stark: Architect of Victory, 1939–1945.* Columbia: University of South Carolina Press, 1989.

Smith, Edward Jean. *The Defense of Berlin.* Baltimore: The Johns Hopkins University Press, 1963.

———. *Lucius D. Clay: An American Life.* New York: Henry Holt & Co., 1990.

Smith, James. *History of Dutchess County.* Syracuse, N.Y.: D. Mason & Co., 1882.

Smith, Perry McCoy. *The Air Force Plans for Peace, 1943–1945.* Baltimore: The Johns Hopkins University Press, 1970.

Sobel, Robert. *The Great Bull Market: Wall Street in the 1920's.* New York: W. W. Norton and Co., 1968.

———. *The Life and Times of Dillon Read.* New York: Truman Talley Books/Dutton, 1991.

Spector, Ronald. *Eagle Against the Sun: The American War with Japan.* New York: The Free Press, 1984.

Stein, Harold, ed. *American Civil Military Decisions.* Birmingham: University of Alabama Press, 1963.

Stephanson, Anders. *Kennan and the Art of Foreign Policy.* Cambridge, Mass.: Harvard University Press, 1989.

Stettinius, Edward R. *The Diaries of Edward R. Stettinius, 1943–1946,* eds. Thomas M. Campbell and George C. Herring. New York: New Viewpoints, 1975.

Stimson, Henry L., and McGeorge Bundy. *On Active Service in Peace and War.* New York: Harper & Brothers, 1948.

Stoff, Michael B. *Oil War and American Security: The Search for a National Policy on Foreign Oil, 1941–1947.* New Haven, Conn.: Yale University Press, 1980.

Strauss, Lewis L. *Men and Decisions.* Garden City, N.Y.: Doubleday, 1962.

Stresemann, Gustav. *Gustav Stresemann: His Diaries, Letters and Papers,* Vols. 1–3, ed. and trans. Eric Sulton. London: Macmillan & Company, 1935–1940.

Stueck, William W., Jr. *The Road to Confrontation: American Policy Toward China and Korea, 1947–50.* Chapel Hill: University of North Carolina Press, 1981.

Talbott, Strobe. *The Master of the Game.* New York: Alfred A. Knopf, 1988.

Truman, Harry S. *Memoirs: 1945, Year of Decisions.* Garden City, N.Y.: Doubleday, 1955.

———. *Memoirs: Years of Trial and Hope, 1946–1952.* Garden City, N.Y.: Doubleday, 1956.

———. *Off the Record: The Private Papers of Harry S. Truman,* ed. Robert H. Ferrell. New York: Harper and Row, 1980.

Truman, Margaret. *Harry S. Truman.* New York: William Morrow, 1973.

Vandenberg, Arthur H. *The Private Papers of Senator Vandenberg,* ed. Arthur H. Vandenberg, Jr. Boston: Houghton Mifflin, 1952.

Wallace, Henry A. *The Price of Vision: The Diary of Henry A. Wallace, 1942–1946,* ed. John Morton Blum. Boston: Houghton Mifflin, 1973.

Walton, Richard J. *Henry Wallace, Harry Truman and the Cold War.* New York: Viking, 1976.

Ward, Patricia Dawson. *Threat of Peace: James F. Byrnes and the Council of Foreign Ministers, 1945–46.* Kent, Ohio: Kent State University Press, 1979.

Watkins, T. H. *Righteous Pilgrim: The Life and Times of Harold L. Ickes, 1879–1952.* New York: Henry Holt & Co., 1990.

Wedemeyer, Albert C. *Wedemeyer Reports.* New York: Henry Holt & Co., 1958.

Welles, Sumner. *The Time for Decision.* New York: Harper and Brothers, 1944.

Wellman, Paul I. *Stuart Symington: Portrait of a Man with a Mission.* New York: Doubleday, 1960.

Whitney, Courtney. *MacArthur: His Rendezvous with History.* New York: Alfred A. Knopf, 1956.

Wilson, Evan M. *Decision on Palestine.* Stanford, Calif.: Hoover Institution Press, 1979.

Wilson, Theodore A. *The First Summit: Roosevelt and Churchill at Placentia Bay, 1941.* Boston: Houghton Mifflin, 1969.

Winchell, Walter. *Winchell Exclusive.* Englewood Cliffs, N.J.: Prentice Hall, Inc., 1975.

Witkee, Carl. *The Irish in America.* Baton Rouge: Louisiana State University Press, 1956.

Wittner, Lawrence S. *American Intervention in Greece, 1943–1969.* New York: Columbia University Press, 1982.

Yale University 1916 Senior Class Book. Privately printed.

Yergin, Daniel. *Shattered Peace: The Origins of the Cold War and the National Security State.* Boston: Houghton Mifflin, 1977.

——. *The Prize: The Epic Quest for Oil, Money and Power.* New York: Simon and Schuster, 1991.

ARTICLES

Alexander, Jack. "Stormy New Boss of the Pentagon," *The Saturday Evening Post,* July 30, 1949, pp. 26ff.

Allard, Dean. "Interservice Differences in the United States, 1945–1950: A Naval Perspective," *Airpower Journal,* Winter 1989, pp. 72–74.

"A Third Motor Car Colossus: The Chrysler-Dodge Merger," *Literary Digest,* June 16, 1928.

Bagehot, Walter. "The Defect of America: Presidential and Ministerial Governments Compared," *The Economist,* December 16, 1862, Vol. XX, pp. 1346–47.

——. "The Special Danger of Men of Business as Administrators," *The Economist,* March 18, 1872, Vol. XXIX, pp. 309–310.

Bernstein, Barton J. "Truman at Potsdam," *Foreign Service Journal,* July/August 1983, pp. 29–35.

Brinkley, Douglas. "Kennan-Acheson: The Disengagement Debate," *The Atlantic Community Quarterly,* Winter 1987–1988, pp. 423–424.

"Chrysler," *Fortune,* August 1935, pp. 68–69.

"Clarence Dillon: Portrait," *Newsweek,* October 24, 1933.

Creesy, Virginia K. "The Princetonian's First Century," *Princeton Alumni Weekly,* January 31, 1977.

"Divided They Stand," *Newsweek,* September 20, 1948.

Divine, Robert A. "The Cold War and the Election of 1948," *Journal of American History,* 59 (June 1972), pp. 90–110.

"The Dodge Deal," *Literary Digest,* April 25, 1925.

"Editorial," *Life,* XXII, January 23, 1945, p. 26.

Elliston, Herbert. "Jim Forrestal: A Portrait in Politics," *Atlantic Monthly*, 188 (November 1951), pp. 73-74.

Evensen, Bruce J. "The Truman Administration's Struggle to Shape Conventional Wisdom on Palestine," *Diplomatic History*, vol. 15, no. 3 (Summer 1991), pp. 339-359.

Feaver, John H. "The China Aid Bill of 1948: Limited Assistance as a Cold War Strategy," *Diplomatic History*, 5 (Spring 1981), pp. 107-120.

"Ferdinand Eberstadt," *Fortune*, April 1939, pp. 72-75.

Forrestal, James V. "Editorial," *Daily Princetonian*, May 6, 1914.

——. "Will We Choose Naval Suicide Again?," *The Saturday Evening Post*, June 24, 1944, p. 9.

——. "Keep the Navy to Keep Peace," *Sea Power*, July 1945, pp. 21-22.

Gormly, James L. "The Washington Declaration and the 'Poor Relation': Anglo-American Diplomacy, 1945-46," *Diplomatic History*, 8 (Spring 1984).

Greb, Allen G. "Military Research and Development: A Postwar History," *Bulletin of the Atomic Scientists*, 33 (January 1977), pp. 13-26.

Greenblatt, Milton, M.D. "Power and Impairment of Great Leaders," *American Journal of Social Psychiatry*, IV (Spring 1984), pp. 11-18.

Havemann, Ernest. "Forrestal," *Life*, October 6, 1948, pp. 67-77.

Huie, William Bradford. "Untold Facts in the Forrestal Case," *The American Mercury*, Vol. LXXI, No. 324 (December 1950), pp. 643-652.

Hurd, Charles. "No. 2 Men with No. 1 Jobs," *The New York Times Magazine*, December 7, 1941, pp. 9, 26.

Ickes, Harold L. "The Forrestal Tragedy," *The New Republic*, June 13, 1949, 120, pp. 15-16.

Jereski, Laura. "Clarence Dillon: Using Other People's Money," *Forbes*, July 13, 1987.

Kennan, George F. "Sources of Soviet Conduct," *Foreign Affairs*, 25 (July 1947), pp. 566-582.

Korb, Lawrence J. "The Secretary of Defense and the Joint Chiefs of Staff: Conflict in the Budgetary Process, 1947-1971," *Naval War College Review*, 24 (December 1971), pp. 21-42.

Leffler, Melvyn P. "The American Conception of Naval Security and the Beginnings of the Cold War, 1945-1948," *American Historical Review*, 89 (April 1984).

Moats, Alice-Leone. "Married Men in Season," *Town and Country*, January 1936.

"The Navy Makes a Gesture," *Crisis*, 49 (May 1942), p. 51.

Nelson, Anna Kasten. "President Truman and the Evolution of the National Security Council," *Journal of American History*, 72 (September 1985), pp. 360-378.

Ogden, Josephine. "Seen in the Shops," *Vogue*, Anniversary Issue, January 1923.

"The Pecora Hearings," *Newsweek*, June 10, 1933, p. 16.

Palmieri, Edmund L. "Fight for Italy," *Reader's Digest*, November 1948, 53:1-11.

Pontecorvo, Giulio. "Investment Banking and Security Speculation in the Late 1920's," *Business History Review*, XXXII (Summer 1958), pp. 166-191.

Reynolds, Quentin. "He Built Our Navy," *Collier's*, July 15, 1944, p. 71.

Steinberg, Alfred. "Mr. Truman's Mystery Man," *Saturday Evening Post*, December 24, 1949, pp. 24, 69-70.

Stuart, Lyle. *Why: The Magazine of Popular Psychology*, Vol. 1, No. 1 (November 1950), pp. 3-9, 20-27.

Stutler, Boyd B. "Louis A. Johnson—A Prominent West Virginian," *West Virginia Review*, May 1931, pp. 1-3.

Weizmann, Chaim. "Palestine's Role in the Solution of the Jewish Problem," *Foreign Affairs*, Vol. 20, no. 2 (January 1942), pp. 324-338.

Williams, Frank J. "A New Leader in Finance: Clarence Dillon," *American Review of Reviews,* February 1926.
Winkler, John K. "A Billion Dollar Banker," *The New Yorker,* October 20, 1928.
Zacharias, Ellis M. "The Forrestal Enigma," *United Nations World,* November 1945.

UNPUBLISHED MATERIAL

Alsop, Joseph W., and Adam Platt. "The Memoirs of Joseph W. Alsop." Prepublication manuscript.
Bowman, Isaiah. "The New Zionism and a Policy for the U.S.," October 19, 1943. Council on Foreign Relations Study in Territorial Series (strictly confidential).
Christman, Calvin Lee. "Ferdinand Eberstadt and Economic Mobilization for War, 1941–1943." Ph.D. dissertation, Ohio State University, 1971.
Clifford, Clark. "Factors Influencing President Truman's Decision to Support Partition and Recognize the State of Israel." Address to the Annual Meeting of the American Historical Association in Washington, D.C., December 28, 1976.
Cooper, Norman V. "The Military Career of Lieutenant General Holland M. Smith." Ph.D. dissertation, University of Alabama, 1971.
Cornell, Cecilia Stiles. "James V. Forrestal and the American National Security Policy, 1940–1949." Ph.D. dissertation, Vanderbilt University, 1987.
Enders, Calvin. "The Vinson Navy." Ph.D. dissertation, Michigan State University, 1970.
Fanton, Jonathan Foster. "Robert A. Lovett, The War Years." Ph.D. dissertation, Yale University, 1978.
Green, Murray. "Stuart Symington and the B-36." Ph.D. dissertation, American University, 1960.
Hamm, Gerald. "The Drama of Philip Barry." Ph.D. dissertation, University of Pennsylvania, 1948.
Hartman, Eleanor M. "Reminiscence." Pamphlet privately written, February 1983.
Hoyt, Edwin C. "Digest of Discussion: Soviet Foreign Policy." Council on Foreign Relations, January 7, 1947.
Hoyt, Morgan H. "The Dutchess County Roosevelt." Unpublished manuscript.
———. "Recollections of Old Dutchess." Unpublished manuscript.
Lovett, Robert A. "Reflections on Jim Forrestal." Unpublished book preface, March 12, 1985.
Osborne, John. "Forrestal." Unpublished manuscript outline.
Towers, John H. Diary. Unpublished manuscript in the possession of Clark Reynolds.

PUBLIC DOCUMENTS

Public Papers of the Presidents: Harry S. Truman, 1945–1953. Washington, D.C.: Government Printing Office, 1961–1966.
U.S. The Commission on Organization of the Executive Branch of the Government. The Committee on the National Security Organization. *Task Force Report on National Security Organization.* 1949.

U.S. Congress. *Congressional Record: Proceedings and Debates of the 79th–81st Congress,* Vols. 91–96.

———. House of Representatives. Committee on Expenditures in the Executive Departments. *National Security Act of 1947.* 80th Cong., 1st sess., 1947.

———. ———. Naval Affairs Committee. *Composition of the Postwar Navy.* 79th Cong., 1st sess., 1945.

———. ———. ———. *Sundry Legislation Affecting the Naval Establishment.* 77th Cong., 1st sess., 1941.

———. ———. ———. *The Reorganization of Procurement Procedures and Coordination of Legal Services in the Navy Department.* 78th Cong., 1st sess., 1943.

———. ———. Select Committee on Post-War Military Policy. *Proposal to Establish a Single Department of Defense.* 78th Cong., 2nd sess., 1944.

———. ———. Special Subcommittee on Petroleum of the Committee on Armed Services. *Petroleum for National Defense.* 80th Cong., 2nd sess., 1948.

———. Senate. Armed Services Committee. *National Defense Establishment (Unification of the Armed Services).* 80th Cong., 1st sess., 1947.

———. ———. ———. *National Security Act of 1947,* S. Rpt. 239. 80th Cong., 1st sess., 1947.

———. ———. Committee on Banking and Currency. *Dillon, Read, and Company.* 73rd Cong., 2nd sess., 1933.

———. ———. Committee on Military Affairs. *Hearings on S. 84 and S. 1482.* 79th Cong., 1st sess., 1945.

———. ———. Committee on Naval Affairs. *Hearings on S. 2044. Unification of the Armed Forces.* 79th Cong., 2nd sess., 1946.

———. ———. ———. *Unification of the War and Navy Departments and Postwar Organization for National Security, Report to Hon. James Forrestal, Secretary of the Navy (Eberstadt Report).* 79th Cong., 1st sess., 1945.

———. ———. Special Committee Investigating the National Defense Program. *Investigation of the National Defense Program, Part 41: Petroleum Arrangements with Saudi Arabia.* 80th Cong., 1st sess., 1947.

———. ———. Special Committee on Atomic Energy. *Hearings on Atomic Energy Commission.* January 23, 1946.

U.S. Department of State. *Foreign Relations of the United States (FRUS),* 1943–1948.

Vital Speeches of the Day

NEWSPAPERS

Akron-Times Press

The Beacon News

The Boston Globe

Daily News

Daily Princetonian

Evening News

Nassau Herald

New York *Evening Post*

New York *Herald Tribune*

New York Post

New York Times

Newsday

The Saturday Evening Post

Washington Post

INTERVIEWS BY TOWNSEND HOOPES

Dean Acheson
  October 11, 1967
Janet Barnes
  January 3, 1990
Ellen Barry
  May 14, 1988
Lucius Battle
  November 28, 1988
Marian Christie
  June 21, 1989
Clark Clifford
  January 26, 1989
  April 18, 1989
Arthur Macy Cox
  June 15, 1990
George Elsey
  February 16, 1989
Katherine Callahan Forrestal
  April 11, 1989
Michael Forrestal
  October 12, 1988
David Ginsberg
  January 22, 1991
Fitzhugh Green
  June 14, 1989
Arthur Hadley
  July 25, 1990
Najeeb Halaby
  April 11, 1990
Maj. Gen. Fred Hayes, USMC (Ret.)
  date unknown
H. Struve Hensel
  January 20, 1989

Mrs. Burroughs Hoffman
  May 11, 1989
Lawrence Houston
  January 3, 1991
Eliot Janeway
  July 5, 1990
W. John Kenney
  May 29, 1989
  August 15, 1989
Gertrude Legendre
  May 14, 1988
Marx Leva
  January 15, 1989
Mrs. William Lord
  July 20, 1988
Paul H. Nitze
  June 23, 1989
John H. Ohly
  August 15, 1989
  August 20, 1989
Benjamin Reid
  February 14, 1989
Nina Auchincloss Straight
  December 20, 1989
James Symington
  April 16, 1989
Peter Walker
  February 14, 1989
Alexandra Whitney
  September 20, 1989
Jerauld Wright
  June 22, 1989
Eugene Zuckert
  April 10, 1991

INTERVIEWS BY DOUGLAS BRINKLEY

Joseph W. Alsop
    March 12, 1988
Adm. Robert B. Carney
    April 6, 1988
C. Douglas Dillon
    June 16, 1989
Frederick Eberstadt, Jr.
    May 4, 1989
    September 28, 1990
Michael Forrestal
    April 27, 1988
    May 18, 1988
    September 11, 1988
H. Struve Hensel
    June 6, 1988
    June 11, 1990
Eliot Janeway
    May 30, 1990
    September 18, 1990
    September 28, 1990
    October 16, 1990

W. John Kenney
    January 12, 1990
Tilghman Koons
    January 12, 1990
Robert Nathan
    June 12, 1990
Paul H. Nitze
    September 26, 1987
Mrs. Drew Pearson
    April 7, 1990
Forrest Pogue
    March 14, 1989
Robert Sobel
    October 7, 1990
Stuart Symington
    November 17, 1987

INTERVIEWS BY CHARLES J. V. MURPHY

Daniel Caulkins
    May 10, 1982
Charles Detmar
    January 11, 1983
Arthur Krock
    April 10, 1982
Chester T. Lane
    February 16, 1983
Robert Lovett
    May 11, 1982
    October 6, 1982
    April 28, 1983
    September 22, 1983
    April 3, 1984
John J. McCloy
    September 28, 1982
    October 8, 1982
    October 16, 1983
John McCone
    February 11, 1984

John McLain
    April 6, 1982
Harold Miller
    October 16, 1983
Lauris Norstad
    April 17, 1982
Maj. Gen. Jerry Page, USAF (Ret.)
    October 11, 1983
Duncan Read
    March 7, 1982
James T. Rowe
    September 3, 1981
Paul Shields
    October 17, 1982
James Webb
    October 11, 1982
Albert Wedemeyer
    April 12, 1982

INTERVIEWS BY EDYTHE HOLBROOK

Anne Cannell
  May 7, 1983
Millicent Cox
  January 12, 1983
Michael Forrestal
  October 3, 1984
Tilghman Koons
  April 3, 1985
William Long
  October 2, 1982
Adele Lovett
  October 2, 1982

Mrs. William McKinley
  January 12, 1983
Henry C. Merritt
  December 13, 1982
Mary Pennybacker
  October 5, 1982
Diana Vreeland
  November 17, 1982
Edward F. Willett
  September 16, 1985
Jeanne Ballot Winham
  January 10, 1983

INTERVIEWS BY PETER WALKER

Joseph Alsop
  April 17, 1987
Emilio G. Collado
  April 3, 1987
Frederick Eberstadt, Jr.
  March 18, 1987

Oatsie Lighter
  May 2, 1987
Ellie Reich
  April 22, 1987
James E. Webb
  April 22, 1987

INDEX

Numerals in *italics* indicate illustrations.

TOWNSEND HOOPES has pursued careers in several fields: government service, business management, and writing. Educated at Andover and Yale, he was a Marine officer in World War II. After the war, he served successively as assistant to the Chairman of the House Armed Services Committee, as a member of Secretary of Defense Forrestal's staff, as Principal Deputy Assistant Secretary for International Security Affairs at the Pentagon, and as Under Secretary of the Air Force. He was president of the Association of American Publishers from 1973 to 1986. His first book, *The Limits of Intervention*—an assessment of the Vietnam War—won the Overseas Writers Award for Best Book on Foreign Policy, and his biography *The Devil and John Foster Dulles* received a Bancroft Prize in History from Columbia University. He is currently a Distinguished International Executive at the University of Maryland.

DOUGLAS BRINKLEY is Assistant Professor of History and Teaching Fellow at New College, Hofstra University, where he is also codirector of the Center for American-Netherlands Studies. After graduating from Ohio State University, he earned his doctorate in U.S. diplomatic history from Georgetown University and has taught at the U.S. Naval Academy and Princeton University. He is a director of the Jean Monnet Council, the Franklin and Eleanor Roosevelt Institute, and the Theodore Roosevelt Association. He is author of *Dean Acheson: The Cold War Years 1953–1971*, and editor of two other books on international affairs.